Quest for Hope in the Slum Community

For Hannah, Philip and Laura
And the generation inheriting our cities

Quest for Hope in the Slum Community

A Global Urban Reader

Scott Bessenecker
Editor

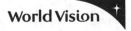

Published in partnership with World Vision Resources

Authentic
We welcome your comments and questions.
129 Mobilization Drive, Waynesboro, GA 30830 USA authentic@stl.org
and 9 Holdom Avenue, Bletchley, Milton Keynes, Bucks, MK1 1QR, UK
www.authenticbooks.com

If you would like a copy of our current catalog, contact us at:
1-8MORE-BOOKS
ordersusa@stl.org

Quest for Hope in the Slum Community
ISBN: 1-932805-19-2

09 08 07 06 05 / 6 5 4 3 2 1

Published in partnership with World Vision
34834 Weyerhaeuser Way South, P.O. Box 9716, Federal Way, WA 98063 USA
www.worldvision.org

Scripture references for section introductions and conclusion:
All scripture quotations, unless otherwise indicated, are taken from the HOLY BIBLE,
NEW INTERNATIONAL VERSION®. NIV®. Copyright ©1973, 1978, 1984 by
International Bible Society. Used by permission of Zondervan. All rights reserved.

Scripture quotations marked NRSV are taken from the New Revised Standard Version Bible,
copyright 1989, Division of Christian Education of the National Council of the Churches of
Christ in the United States of America. Used by permission. All rights reserved.

Scripture references for chapters:
Scripture references vary and are appropriately noted in the copyright sections of the works
from they they have been excerpted.

Cover design: Paul Lewis
Interior design: Angela Duerksen
Editorial team: Tom Richards, Megan Kassebaum, Carolyn Ziegler

Cover image (top): Stephen Punton

Printed in the United States of America

CONTENTS

Part IV: Social Hope

Part V: Environmental Hope

ACKNOWLEDGEMENTS

Janine, my wife, played a huge role in bringing this work into reality. First thanks must go to her. The anthology you now hold grew out of a Masters degree[1] that Janine encouraged me to take. This was a costly program in many ways. I suppose most graduate work is. I worked full time during all but the last few months of the program which took five years to complete. While I tried to keep myself faithful to my first calling as father and husband, Janine and the kids no doubt paid for my diminished availability—Janine especially. In fact, Janine took up a newspaper route to help pay for the program on top of having added responsibilities in caring for our family due to my study schedule. What's more, they each enthusiastically took on the many challenges of leading students into a garbage community in Cairo, Egypt where we lived for a summer and out of which many of the examples in my section introductions come. Outside of that monumental summer for our family, my work on this anthology has been of very little benefit to them personally. Yet they were glad to support me in this process and somehow they have shared in my joy in producing it. If it benefits anybody "out there" you have my family to thank.

Since 2000, when the first collection of readings was assembled, there have been numerous revisions. In particular I want to thank Grace Eng, Mark Kramer, Paul Grant, Randy White, and Heidi Williams for suggesting articles or books to consider. Jill Feldkamp and Heidi Williams poured over my introductions and helped me to say more clearly what I was trying to say in my muddy first drafts. I am so glad to be yoked together with them in the work of releasing college students as servants to the poor, the lost and the broken.

Besides Heidi and Jill, my friends and colleagues at the National Service Center of InterVarsity Christian Fellowship have been huge supporters. When I began to take seriously the need to see a fresh infusion of servants into slum communities, they stood with me as I developed a series of short-term projects known as the Global Urban Trek. Roy and Becky Stephen, Grace Eng, Mack Stiles, Bill McConnell, Rich Henderson, John Criswell, Randy White and Jack and Mary Anne Voelkel have urged me on in this work when I was ready to give up. Many others have as well—too many to mention. The men and women who have directed these projects and the participants now living among the urban poor have gone far beyond simply reading this stuff and have begun to put into practice lifestyles of transformation. Their zeal is inspiring.

With gratitude,
Scott Bessenecker

Notes

1. William Carey International University offers a very innovative Masters in International Development. With the conviction that people in ministry ought to stay engaged in ministry, they have tried to design a Masters degree that allows one to continue working while pursuing this integrated studies program.

FOREWORD

I have just been preaching in a slum church planted some 25 years ago, when I was a young graduate enthusiastically pioneering a new kind of urban mission. It reminded me of an email five years ago from a then-unknown brother with a dream to get thousands of American students into the slums of the world's megacities each summer. This email caused something to stir in me, and I laughed tears of joy in my quiet study.

This man, Scott Bessenecker, made his dream into the Global Urban Trek, a group of summer projects sending U.S. university students to seek Jesus in the slums. Each year since 2001 I have watched amazed as the number of enthusiastic participants has grown, and then as many of them have committed themselves to migrating from affluence to longer term involvement with the oppressed.

Underneath all this is a disciplined leadership of the Global Urban Trek that has not only sought exposure to poverty and injustice, but also encouraged healthy reflection on the struggles of these communities. In the collection of papers in this book, Scott has over some years gathered a refined and balanced basis of information for such analysis.

For in the struggles of those of us who choose to go into the slums, along with the physical pain, emotional pain, and social rejection, there is also an ear-splitting pain that goes on in our minds. We face a thousand complex social and political and spiritual problems and often have few tools to process them. Thus month after month we battle on, not fully understanding, and our minds suffer. And if the mind suffers, the spirit suffers, for God is the integrator of mind and spirit. To survive well, we must be people of both action and reflection.

Our task in the slums is to bring the hope of Christ into places of despair, the joy of Christ into communities of catastrophe, the healing of Christ into people of pain, the life-giving economics of Christ into material dispossession, the servanthood of Christ into oppression. These readings, dealing with topics of such gravity, still indicate the positive dynamics of transformative hope, for they emphasize our Lord Christ as the answer. Not the answer to nonsense issues, but the answer to some of the most complex issues on the globe, as the one who by his Spirit transforms individuals, communities and the very structures of the nations, who integrates all in all.

A few weeks ago I listened to 40 slum movement leaders from Asia, Latin

America, Oceania and the US agree to ask God for 50,000 new cross-cultural workers to establish movements of churches in the slums of the 1700 least evangelized cities. We have some little ideas of how God will do this, but we know he wills it. May this set of readings become a significant stepping stone for thousands to come to terms with the process of walking with Jesus among the poor and proclaiming Jesus by word and deed among the poor.

I have watched over the past generation as individuals—some hardworking, some gifted, some damaged, all idealists—became molded into teams of effective workers among the poor, learning disciplines for the sake of their great hearts of love and for their passion to know the God who dwells among the poor and the needy. They have been the forerunners, and now God is raising up a mighty international array of such men and women.

But for some years another prayer has been brought before the Lord asking for thousands from the educated Western elite who will speak as advocates for justice for the oppressed poor, until we see not only the poor touched by God but poverty itself abolished in city after city because the godly have risen up to defend the poor. Such advocacy requires much learning, much study, and much thinking, for the issues are complex, the debates are furious, the battle against corruption and oppression is dangerous, and engagement in these matters requires great wisdom. My prayer is that these articles and any accompanying exposure the reader might have in the slums would be the first step to lead graduates into fields where they become change agents in such arenas, bringing truth and the values of the Kingdom to bear in such a way that global transformation of the slums begins to gain momentum.

Out of incarnation comes proclamation. Out of proclamation comes personal and then community transformation. Out of new communities of the King come transformation of the structures that cause poverty. May these readings lead many into transformative processes.

Viv Grigg, Director
Urban Leadership Foundation
Auckland, New Zealand

INTRODUCTION
Scott Bessenecker

Where on Earth are We Headed?

Urbanization is a fairly recent human development. The fact that one million people live in a ditch outside of Nairobi, huddled under corrugated-tin sheets, is something new to the human experience. Humanity has existed on earth for thousands of years, yet we are just now beginning to experience a kind of community that has never before existed—the slum community. Most slum communities are less than 50 years old. They collectively hold one billion of the earth's people. They are marked by crowded conditions, makeshift housing, questionable sanitation, unbelievable unemployment rates, desperate poverty and, too often, despair. Despair is the most destructive force in slum communities and is essentially a spiritual issue. When slum dwellers lose all sense of hope, they stop caring about what happens to themselves, their families and the people around them. Despair rules the slum. What's scary is that corrugated communities of despair are on the rise at an alarming rate. The UN expects our planet to go from 1 billion slum dwellers in 2003 to two billion in 2020[1]. Here's the question I keep asking myself, "Has industrialization and urbanization made the majority of life on our planet better? Has modernization really improved the *quality* of my life? Is the world better off than it was 200 years ago?" Perhaps the agrarian life isn't all that bad.

Maybe the Amish are on to something. Maybe human beings were designed to coexist in communities of less than 100 families, living off the land, never moving far from home, and looking out for the welfare of our neighbors. Every time someone undertakes a measurement of the gap between rich and poor, they find it larger than when it was last measured. If you are an American who has had the privilege of attending college you are on the rich side of the gap. It will be almost impossible for you to imagine a place where the rule of law has dissolved, where children work ten-hour days, and where seven family members compete for sleeping space in a scrap metal lean-to. I believe beyond a doubt that God's plan for humanity does not include certain aspects of slum communities. Things like child prostitution, 30 percent unemployment rates, or collapsing corrugated-tin homes. God's original design did not include a world where a few of earth's residents live in luxury struggling to decide how many cars they should own while so many millions live in abject poverty struggling to decide whether or not to sell their daughter into the sex industry in order for the rest of the family to survive. But just how exactly do we change the course of the speeding freight train of global urban poverty?

Transformation is Tricky

Slum communities are very complex social structures. If you pull what seems to be a loose thread at one end, things begin to unravel at the other end. Take, for example, the garbage community in Cairo, Egypt with whom my family and a group of students lived for a summer. First of all, imagine a city growing by hundreds of thousands of people a year. How do you find housing and jobs and provide sanitation for such a yearly influx? The simple answer is that you don't. Infrastructure essentially collapses. Industrious poor people take advantage of the infrastructure vacuum and begin to gather trash. Soon there is a thriving garbage village right inside the city limits (there are at least five in Cairo). Within that community there is a steady source of compostable waste with which to raise animals, so a farming community also grows up within the garbage village.

The sights and smells of living among rubbish and animals and people was quite shocking to us at first. Our immediate thought was how can we work to get rid of this place? But after living there a while we began to see how thorny the solutions become. The sanitation system is actually pretty efficient. Eighty percent of the trash in Cairo is recycled or re-used because of this hands-on method of dealing with waste. In the West we bury 80 percent of our garbage. To hire a multinational waste management organization who would bring in heavy equipment and create massive landfills is not only worse for the environment, but the livelihoods of so many that depend on the trash are placed in jeopardy. To be sure, the living conditions of a garbage village are unacceptable. Humans should not suffer the kind of sicknesses and hardships that exist in that place. But urban transformation is a tricky business. If you "rescue" a child from working in a sweat shop, you plunge his family into even more desperate poverty. You might deliver a 15 year old girl from the horrors of living in a brothel, but unless you deal with the physical, emotional, familial and spiritual consequences of child prostitution she will return to the community that can relate best to her situation—the brothel from which she came. After all, she can hardly go home to the family that sold her into that life in the first place.

So can we really facilitate the kind of global change necessary to eradicate the nasty aspects of slum communities? As Christians, is it even Scriptural to focus on changing socio-political systems and addressing systemic evil? Why not simply focus on spiritual things like church-planting and evangelism? And finally, can spoiled, rich Americans in their 20's and 30's make any difference at all in poverty alleviation?

Jesus and the Poor

When Jesus was anointed at Bethany with "expensive perfume made of pure nard," he chided those who were concerned about using that money for the poor with the words, "The poor you will always have with you" (Mark 14:7). Some may take this to suggest that Christians should not be obsessed with lifting the poor out of their poverty. Wasn't the Spirit of the Sovereign Lord upon Jesus not to feed or clothe or house the poor but to "preach good news" to them (Luke 4:18)? His "Great Commission" to his followers was to go and *make disciples* of all nations (Matthew 28:19), not to go and *feed* all nations. Why, then, should we as Christians care about the poor?

1. Jesus identified himself most closely with the poor and marginalized. It is true that Jesus does not want us to venerate the poor any more than he wants us to worship the rich. However, Jesus was united with the poor in an extraordinary way. He walked and taught among them as one of them. When he sent out his disciples, he stripped them of their material possessions and made them poor (Mark 6:8-13). Even more disturbing than Jesus' personal association with the social underbelly of first century Palestine, was his clear statement that our treatment of the poor was identical to our treatment of him. To those who disregard people with no food, unsafe drinking water, who are sick or foreigners (or any discriminated underclass), those who are poorly clothed, homeless or serving hard time, he said something quite startling. He said in the parable of the sheep and the goats, "Whatever you did not do for one of the least of these, you did not do for me" (Matthew 25:31-46). More frightening still, Jesus connects salvation in this parable with our response to the destitute. Ron Sider understands this to suggest that our response to the marginalized is a window on our faith, " . . . the reality of saving faith is exhibited in serving love"[2].

2. God will bring judgment to his children when they ignore the poor.

"Why exactly did God destroy Sodom?" asks Ray Bakke in his book *A Theology as Big as the City*[3]. According to Ezekiel, it was because they did not help the poor and needy (Ezek. 16:49-50). Throughout the Old Testament and particularly in the minor prophets, God brings judgment on his people for two prominent sins: idolatry and callousness toward four kinds of people: the poor, the alien, the fatherless and the widow. Idolatry is related to hard-heartedness. It is self-serving. A person obsessed with self will be deaf to the cry of the poor. The book of Proverbs states it axiomatically, "If a man shuts his ears to the cry of the poor, he too will cry out and not be answered" (Prov. 21:13). Judgment begins with the house of God, and God judges his people for hardheartedness toward the poor.

3. The ministry of Christ and his followers is a ministry of compassionate deliverance. When Jesus sent out the disciples, he gave them the following instructions, "As you go, preach this message: 'The kingdom of heaven is near.' Heal the sick, raise the dead, cleanse those who have leprosy, drive out demons. Freely you have received, freely give" (Matt. 10:6-8). Evangelicals have been pretty good at preaching the message. But much of Jesus and the disciples' activity was focused on a ministry of deliverance. People who are poor, particularly the urban poor, face numerous places of oppression and subsequent need for deliverance. Beyond the oppressive nature of drugs, alcohol and prostitution, the urban poor often face systemic oppression such as unsympathetic bureaucracies, various forces keeping economic underclasses alive in order to serve upper classes, and ethnic discrimination. What's more, the urban poor are often both victims and victimizers of all kinds of crime. If the church is to follow in her Master's footsteps, she will be given over to the task of seeing Jesus rescue people from oppression, thereby ushering in the "kingdom of heaven" about which she preaches.

So why should Christians care about the poor? Because, as Mother Teresa put it, "in the poor, we find Jesus in distressing disguise."[4] We care about the poor because God commands it and has promised judgment for those who disregard the cry of the poor. We care about the poor because Jesus cares about the poor and because we were commissioned by him to preach, heal and deliver those in distress.

Spoiled Rich Kids

What about American college students for whom this anthology is designed? Can spoiled rich kids muster what it will take to enter the reality of the slum community as agents of transformation?

History is rife with children of aristocracy who abandoned the opportunity, privilege and wealth of their social status to tie themselves with the poor. Many of those who joined the medieval monastic orders were of this breed. But long before St. Francis left his life as a wealthy playboy, there was Brigid of Kildare[5]. Brigid was a 5th century convert of St. Patrick, and her father did not think much of his daughter's new faith. It seems that Brigid had embraced a love for the poor that reflected her Savior's own passion for the neglected. Since Brigid had no wealth of her own to give away to beggars, she took to giving away her father's, provoking him to fits of rage. Since he was a man of some means (quickly diminishing due to his daughter's charity), he purposed to get rid of the girl and cut his losses by selling her to the King of Leinster. Tossing her in the back of a carriage, he zipped off to the king to see what kind of price might be negotiated. While her father haggled with the king for a decent price, a leprous beggar approached Brigid. With the kindness for which she was to become famous, Brigid surrendered to the beggar the one item of value she could lay her hands on—the sword her father had left in the carriage. Returning to the carriage, the price now settled, Brigid's father and the king soon discover her act of charity. "Why do you steal your father's property and give it away?" The king asked her. Brigid replied without the least hint of intimidation, "If I had the power, I would steal all your royal wealth and give it to Christ's brothers and sisters." Needless to say the deal was off. Brigid remained a prisoner in her father's house until her escape. She later became Abbess of a large double monastery of both men and women.

The fact is that many of the monastic orders were essentially youth movements that gravitated toward ministry among the poor. Given the demands of life among the urban slum dwellers in the 21st century, college-educated youth will likely play a critical role. Some aspects of urban transformation require people who know something about global economies. Dealing with child prostitution and child labor draws upon those who have been through the rigors of law school. Solving some of the sanitation and health issues that plague the urban poor will call for people with formal education in these areas. We need those willing to go and live among the slum-dwellers to understand the intricacies of how change might affect those communities, not simply those who would bring "remote-control" solutions while sitting in comfortable offices. Likely it will require healthy, educated men and women without children willing to take up residence in urban hovels. Ultimately, this kind of devotion is intensely spiritual. Without a sense of holy calling and commissioning, it is unlikely educated young people from the West would last long in a slum community.

This book has attempted to gather into one place a portion of the diverse dialogue that exists in the area of urban transformation. Everything from housing to street children along with a healthy collection of articles around a theology of urban poverty is addressed, albeit briefly. This is the sort of material designed to stimulate the imagination of those exploring the question of how to address with compassion and conviction the stark realities of urban poverty.

Notes

1. United Nations Human Settlements Programme (2003) The Challenge of Slums: Global Report on Human Settlements 2003, United Nations Human Settlements Programme, Earthscan Publications, London.
2. Sider, Ronald, editor (1982) Lifestyle in the Eighties: An Evangelical Commitment to Simple Lifestyle, Philadelphia, PA: Westminster Press, p. 19.
3. Bakke, Ray (1997) A Theology as Big as the City, Downers Grove, IL: InterVarsity Press, p. 93.
4. Mother Teresa (1997) In the Heart of the World: Thoughts, Stories, and Prayers, Novata, CA: New World Library, p. 67.
5. Cahill, Thomas (1996) How the Irish Saved Civilization, New York, NY: Doubleday, p. 172-176.

Part I
Spiritual Hope

SECTION A
THEOLOGY OF POVERTY

I remember with some discomfort the shallow theology of poverty embraced by the North American church as it was waved before delegates at a conference I attended. A gathering of six hundred Christian student workers had assembled in Korea. There were only about forty or fifty North Americans in attendance. Sri Lankan theologian and missiologist Vinoth Ramachandra was addressing the delegates. Taking a popular Bible dictionary produced by an American publisher, he opened to the word *pottery*. "Three pages," he announced, "have been devoted to the entry on pottery." Turning the page, he said, "But under the entry on *poverty*, I find only a column and a half! Does the Bible really say more about pottery than poverty?" The rebuke was stinging only because it was so true. The North American church, perhaps the entire church of the West, is bankrupt when it comes to a theology of poverty. We have waxed eloquent over the archeological shards of the ancient world, discussing them at length in the comfort of our seminaries and universities. All the while we have conveniently ignored Scripture's emphasis that the poor and broken people of the world are vital in the eyes of God. We have not sat long enough at the feet of the church of the poor in Latin America, Asia, and Africa. After all, the church is predominantly made up of the poor in these parts of the world.[1]

Melba Maggay is a Filipina theologian who does not have the luxury of avoiding the poverty so ubiquitous in the developing world. She cannot drive across town without encountering squatter communities or begging children. She says, "Truly, the Gospel is more than a set of things to believe about Christ. It is a radical call to come under the discipline of the Kingdom, bidding a rich young man to sell all that he has to give to the poor, or a corrupt tax collector to go and repay all he had robbed." Yet even in her native Philippines the church battles the tendency to divide the spiritual and physical in an attempt to define a theology of poverty. "We must always remember that we are not talking to disembodied spirits," she states. The first section of her book, *Transforming Society* is wonderfully instructive to a church that has been so quick to relegate social concern to the realm of the temporal and therefore declare it irrelevant to the eternal. The personal piety that for so long has defined Christianity in the

West must recover the social leavening power inherent in the good news about the Kingdom.

While it is important to look into the mirror which brothers and sisters in the developing world would hold up to us, it is also important to listen to the voice of North Americans who have sojourned with the poor and can speak as a Westerner to the church of the West. Bryant Myers, in an excerpt from his book, *Walking with the Poor*, lays out a number of theological frameworks from which we can more adequately hang a theology of poverty. He introduces us to the notion of the kingdom of God and the idea of shalom—two, all-encompassing theological structures that easily handle the weight of the whole gospel. Myers helps us gain a new perspective by which to understand all facets of global transformation, using the light of the person of Christ and the redemptive stories of the Bible.

If our understanding of creation, redemption, and the role of the church does not plant us face to face with the poor, then we have embraced a theology that is not supported by the Scripture. Our first duty is to understand the metanarrative of God and the oppressed which has been woven throughout the Bible before we go on to the question of how to transform a broken and dying world. This section will help us to do just that.

Notes

1.   Philip Jenkins, *The Next Christendom: The Coming of Global Christianity* (Oxford: Oxford University Press, 2002).

CHAPTER 1
THE TASK OF THE CHURCH

Melba Maggay

Introduction
Lazarus at the gate, or the Politics of Discipleship

I do not like politics. Like many of that generation which figured in the First Quarter Storm of the early 1970s, the white heat I used to feel over political issues has been tempered by years of disappointment, or, perhaps, by the tiring and corrosive effect of having worked too hard and too long at social change with only marginal success.

The 1960s, to us, were a time of promise. A whole generation was raised in the hope that things could be done better. And then came the hard reality of power. By a stroke of the pen, the country was turned this way and that, and the dream merchants scattered.

To the many of our people who live on the bottom side of what academics call the "great cultural divide," government is at best a necessary encumbrance. We would rather it remain out of sight, a low-key presence to enable us to buy things fairly cheaply in the marketplace and to walk the streets in relative safety. Centuries of colonial rule have made us wary; used to uncongenial governments, we have learned to carry on without great expectations. Culture and history conspire to make us profoundly uninterested in our daily political fare of scarce bread and unamusing circus. Let the gods have their money and their romp. As for us, we shall take the byways and live as best as we can without incurring the wrath of the powers.

There is a healthy measure of realism in all this. Government, after all, is a sleeping monster that is better left alone. It is too big for us to handle and too stupid to ever dream. There are things in life a lot more interesting: gurgling babies, cookery, dead stars that shine or a line of poetry. The clutter in our lives is enough to distract us for a lifetime.

But then we walk the streets and there are the hungry eyes and the outstretched hands, and the threat of menace from police bursting big and burly with their pot-bellies. Hovels litter the roadside, reeking with slime and refuse, and the smell of putrid air and urine. There are the run-down whores plying their wares, assorted derelicts with big, lonely eyes staring out of dingy halls—the pure, unedited, expurgated text of the seamy side of this nation.

What are we to make of all these? Where is God in all this? Where is he in all the hungering and thirsting and the backbreaking and the angry aching for justice and for some way out of the grinding toil and the never-ending wrong that always seems to thwart our best efforts?

Maybe, if we were a little richer, if we had been born in some place such as the United States where poverty is, at least, not always visible and does not meet you in every corner, maybe it would be possible to keep God out of politics. We can sing songs to Jesus endlessly and not have to bother about Lazarus sitting at the gate. Maybe.

But we are not in the United States or some such place. We are being called to be disciples in a situation where the needs of the many do not take the form of loneliness nor angst, but of empty bellies and uncertain justice. It is here, in this land where the small people cannot hope to find redress, where their anguished cry is lost in the dark, that we are being called to respond to a God who takes the side of the poor—not because he loves them more but because in this life power is usually on the side of the oppressor (Ecclesiastes 4:1).

These are the realities we have to deal with. They jump and rail at us, and it is a wonder we do not notice them. Maybe, as in the story of the rich man and Lazarus (Luke 16:19-31), it is because we have become so used to the sight of poverty that we no longer see it.

The rich man is described as dressed in purple and fine linen, feeding sumptuously and living luxuriously every day; Lazarus is described as sitting at the gate, a beggar covered with sores and longing to be fed from the crumbs that fall from the rich man's table. The dogs come and lick his sores. This is the first scene.

In the second scene, both die. The rich man ends up in hell, while Lazarus ends up in the bosom of Abraham. The rich man, says Abraham, has had his fill of good things while on earth; so now he is in torment. Lazarus, on the other hand, has had only bad things; so now he is in comfort.

From a purely literary point of view, this sounds like poetic justice. But then we ask, Are the rich punished simply for being rich, and the poor rewarded simply for being poor?

The story is curious in that nothing really happens. There is one scene of stark contrast and one scene of startling reversal. We are not told what happened in-between, what the rich man did to Lazarus to merit the radical reversal. But I suppose that this is exactly the point: the rich man was punished, not so much for what he did, but for what he failed to do. It was not so much that he oppressed Lazarus, but that he, in his callousness, failed even to take notice of Lazarus sitting at his gate.

In a study of farmers in the northwest United States, it was found that they classified the world into three categories: people, machines and land. What they considered to be "people" were their own kind: kith and kin, and other farmers who owned land and were white, Protestant and middle-class. The rest, such as Mexican migrant laborers, were seen as "machines," tools for production or farm inputs. The American Indians were seen as "landscape," part of the scenery in that vast expanse of land. This kind of categorizing is not limited to farmers in the northwest United States. It is also found among the more affluent sectors of Manila.

Every day we go blindly in our tinted air-conditioned cars in and out of our subdivisions, taking no notice of Lazarus sitting at the gate. We become so used to the sight of poverty that we no longer see it. It has faded into the scenery, part of the permanent fixtures of our national landscape.

If there is anything that this story tells us, it is the fact that we live in the presence of one another. Human solidarity is such that we all suffer together: we all suffer traffic problems, power cuts, coups, earthquakes, inflation and instability together. Whether we like it or not, one person's deprivation is an indication of the guilt and humiliation of all. It may not be what we have done, but what we have failed to do in the face of someone else's need or degradation.

Part of the reluctance to address the problem of the poor has to do with the general tiredness over political questions in a time when market forces seem to have taken over as an omnicompetent solution even to problems of compassion. On the part of the church, the inertia of indifference springs from the notion that we can live our lives with integrity without having to concern ourselves with the poor. It is as if one can talk about the love of God without in some way relating it to the heartbreaking need that stares us in the face.

I once heard it said with great conviction that it is not the duty of the church to feed the poor; its duty is to evangelize. I had always thought, even as an outsider to the community of the faith, that it was my duty to respond in some way to the misery of the poor. Now that I presume to be in the community of the faith, I am told that this is not really our concern or, at least, not a primary concern. There are others who can address the problem just as well themselves. Leave the dead to bury their dead. Our task is primarily to preach.

I am not a theologian and I have no intention of becoming one. It may be that I do not appreciate the subtleties of this argument. But I certainly do not see how I can operate as a witness to the transforming power of the gospel without having to spell out what it must mean to those who cannot and do not hope to break the cycle of poverty that has been their lot for centuries.

It was Martin Luther who once said that if our speaking fails to address the precise point at which the world of our time aches, we are not really preaching the Word. In the Philippines, at least, it does not seem possible to speak without hearing the cry that rises from the poor.

This is the difficulty posed by the realities of our situation to those of us who belong to "purely evangelistic" institutions. Is it really possible to speak with integrity without addressing socio-political issues? Admittedly, the thrust of such institutions is not political. And it is possible that focusing on political issues can cost us the liberty of preaching the Word. This, at least, was evangelicalism's common justification for acquiescence to the Marcos regime in the days when dissent seemed a dangerous option.

I suspect that much of the church's apolitical tendency springs from a sense of threat to the survival of its institutions and evangelistic enterprises. It is fair to ask: in our willingness to bypass large social issues so as to secure our freedom to preach, are we not acting like any other vested interest, willing to stick its neck out on matters of principle only as long as its own interests are not being threatened? In the light of our social realities, can we remain unmoved and still be faithful to all that we are being called to bear as disciples in this country?

The story of the rich man and Lazarus tells us that there is no immunity, no escape, from the general misery and contamination that afflicts our nation. We cannot make a separate peace, retreating into our own little islands of precarious peace and dubious plenty. We are not allowed to find rest until the sight of Lazarus sitting at the gate ceases to be ever before us.

Some will say that we are trying to dig up with our nails again the bones of issues long buried for most people. It may well be that most of us cannot help surrendering to the forces of the market and going through the rites of passage leading to the comfortable, vegetable life of the bourgeoisie, with middling hopes both for ourselves and for society. We wake up in the morning worrying about bills to pay and the onset of midlife desperation.

But those of us who bear the name of Christ are called to respond to a finer, higher tune and dance to a different drummer.

We cannot help but rage and dream again when the kingdom calls and the cry of the poor rises from the earth like a miserere.

―――――

The Church in the World

The church as an agent of change may sound like news to people who see it largely as a moribund institution on the side of the gilded and privileged elements of society. Historically, it conjures images of the dark age of the Inquisition, the violent militance of the Crusades, the colonial expansionism of Spain and of Western Protestant empires.

There is another story, however, an undercurrent which occasionally breaks into the arena of history now and again: a small community of believers gets fed to the lions for charges of being subversive of Caesar; a band of beggars spreads like a wild romance among the poor and brings freshness to the dissipated foppery of medieval Christendom; a handful of legislators propose to overturn a class-ridden society by introducing a bill abolishing the institution of slavery.

The church in the world, while historically ambiguous, at its best has, through the centuries, served as leaven, permeating and transforming the social order. If, today, we recognize the limits of authority, solidarity with the poor, or structural protection for the weak and dispossessed, much of it is to be owed to the quiet influence of the Christian faith. In this section we turn ourselves afresh to whatever it is about this faith which now and again turns the world upside down.

Evangelism and Social Action

After more than two decades of debate, social concern is now entrenched as a part of the church's agenda. However, there are at least two errors which surface when attempts are made to define the relationship between the two.

The first error is to confuse evangelism for social action, and social action for evangelism.

Evangelism is social action. This mistake is made by those who argue that the surest way to change society is to change the people in it through the transforming power of the gospel. Sinful structures are made *by* sinful men; therefore, our task is to strike at the root of social problems, which is sin. Hence, the slogan, "Change people, change society." Although a case could be made for the liberative power of authentic Christianity in people who live out the faith, experience shows that having more Christians does not necessarily ensure a just society. For the past decade and a half, for instance, there has been tremendous growth in "born-againism" in this country, but so far this has not issued in justice and righteousness in this society.

There are at least two possible reasons for this failure. One is that people may experience saving faith, but may not necessarily move towards the far-reaching

17

social implications of that faith, either for lack of understanding or failure to obey. One's Christianity may be so undeveloped that it has little influence in the places where it should matter and where it should bear witness sociologically.

Another reason is that society is complex and does not lend itself easily to facile generalizations on how to change it. Would that the doing of justice were merely a matter of personal obedience. Unfortunately, there are entrenched powers and monstrous structures we need to address and contend with. There is such a thing as organized injustice, which calls for thoughtful social analysis and complex solutions. You may have an army of bleeding hearts tending the sorrowful and the hungry, and yet not see an end to the causes of the hunger and the thirst. Unjust social structures require more than the presence of changed individuals. Evangelism is not a cure-all, and cannot substitute for concrete redemptive action in our political and social life.

Social action is evangelism. This mistake is made by those who say that the struggle for justice and human dignity is evangelism in itself. To denounce all that hinders human wholeness is to proclaim the work of Christ, which is the liberation of people and the world from every force, power or structure that oppresses and dehumanizes. This rightly recovers for us the cosmic dimensions of what we mean by witness and salvation; things that, for so long, have been understood in subjectivist and pietistic terms. It tends, however, to lose sight of the *proclamation* aspect of *the* Gospel, the fact that it is *News*, a thing you shout from the housetops or send a towncrier for. It also tends to gloss over the equally important demand for personal repentance and righteousness.

The second error is to dichotomize, that is, to make unbiblical distinctions between what is "secular" and what is "holy'" or between what belongs to the realm of "nature" and what belongs to the realm of "grace."

Social action, for instance, is said to belong to the realm of the temporal and the physical, and evangelism to the realm of the spiritual and the eternal. Understood in this way, evangelism naturally takes priority over social action in the minds of many Christians. Helping the poor, while part of our duty, is secondary to the task of discipling the nations. Meeting temporal needs is something that all people can do. Evangelism is something that only Christians can do. The one is good for this world only, the other is significant even for the world to come.

In this there is, clearly, an inability to see life whole, to see all of life as subject to the lordship and the redeeming power of Jesus. The work of Christ is seen either in purely political terms as in some variants of liberation theologies, or in purely personal terms, as in mostly evangelical church communities. There is no longer any sense that all of life, when lived in the presence of God, is sacred: the very ordinary and prosiac act of giving a cup of water can become a sacrament, a touching deed that shall always be remembered, on par with obviously supernatural acts such as the casting out of demons (Mark 9:38-41).

In this work we shall try to steer clear of the tendency either to polarize or to wed in an unholy synthesis evangelism and social action. At the same time, we would like to push further the often repeated thesis that while the two are distinct, both are parts of our Christian duty. We would like to go so far as to say that the gospel not only has "social implications;" its very substance has a social character. Social action is not just an implication, an addendum to the Gospel; it is an intrinsic part of the Gospel. The preaching of the Gospel is more than a verbal exercise; it is an engagement, a living among men and women that serves notice of the Kingdom that has come.

The Gospel of the Kingdom

What is the relationship between evangelism and social action? Our answer to this question depends largely on our answer to the question, What is the Gospel? If evangelism is telling the Good News, what is the news? What was the new thing Jesus sent his disciples to tell?

The answer is clear enough: "Preach as you go, saying, 'The Kingdom of heaven is at hand.' Heal the sick, raise the dead, cleanse lepers, cast out demons" (Matthew 10:7-8). The news is that the long-awaited Kingdom, its reign of peace, justice and righteousness, has finally come. The Messiah, He who is to come, dwells among us. Kingdom is a political term, and Jesus' messiahship was understood by himself and by his hearers as having to do with more than just the "soul." When Mary heard of the good and joyful tidings that the Lord himself was to grow big in her womb, she immediately rejoiced that here was one who would bring down the mighty from their thrones, who would fill the hungry with good things and send the rich empty away (Luke 1:45-55). When Jesus announced his messianic career, he put it in unmistakably social terms: it shall be "good news" to the poor, release to the captives, sight to the blind, and liberty to those who are oppressed (Luke 4:16-21). His coming marked "the year of the Lord," to the Jews of his day a reference to the Jubilee Year when debts are cancelled and property is redistributed according to the old tribal allotments.

There is an obvious political and social element in Jesus' personality and work. The idea that he is king is a provocative one. It is natural that it should serve as an occasion for suspicion as his political intentions.[2] Contrary to the notion that his is a purely spiritual kingdom, Scripture is clear that he is not just king over the human heart; he is "King of the Jews," a nation seething restlessly under the yoke of Roman rule.[3] He never said that his kingship was not in the world. It was simply not of the world (John 18:36).

This social element, quite strangely, has been lost in present-day preaching.

Jesus' lordship has been subjectivized, confined to the narrow boundaries of one's personal life. It is rarely understood that because he is king over all of life, we may have confidence to make every human institution subject to his will and purposes. The powers have been defeated. When we say "Jesus is Lord," it is not just a confession, it is a cosmic and social fact.[4]

The process of conversion has likewise been unduly spiritualized. Repentance is described as merely a turning from one's personal sins, and occurring mostly in the individual's subjective consciousness. A dichotomy has been made between faith and works, such that it is now possible to speak of becoming a Christian without becoming a disciple, or of justification as merely an abstract legal status.

This split is alien to the thought of Scripture. As has been pointed out, justification is not just a legal abstraction; it is a social reality. To be "justified" is to be "set right" in one's relationship it is a "making peace," a breaking down of the wall of hostility between Jew and Gentile: ". . . the relationship between divine justification and the reconciliation of men to one another is not a sequential relationship. It is not that 'faith' occurs first as an inner existential leap of the individual . . . and then God operates a change in him which enables hint to love his brethren. . . . These two cannot be distinguished in Paul."[5] As someone else puts it, conversion does not take place in two moves—first, a conversion to Christ, and then a "second conversion" from Christ to the world.[6] Both occur in one single act.

Clearly, it is inaccurate to speak of social concern as a "product" of the new birth, an indirect "result" of Gospel proclamation. It is part and parcel of the Christian message. The Gospel is intrinsically prophetic. T.S. Eliot is right when he argues that "The church's message to the world must be expanded to mean 'the church's business to interfere with the world.'"[7] The gospel when faithfully preached always turns the world upside down.

To speak of Jesus as lord is to demand subjection of personal and social life under his kingly rule. To call for repentance is to ask people to turn away, not simply from their individual vices, but from participation in the collective guilt of organized injustice. To invite people to come in faith is to challenge them to walk in trusting obedience, to know God in the agony of commitment and concrete engagement in the life of the world.

Truly, the Gospel is more than a set of things to believe about Christ. It is a radical call to come under the discipline of the Kingdom, bidding a rich young man to sell all that he has to give to the poor, or a corrupt tax collector to go and repay all he had robbed. After all, Jesus tells us, what will separate the sheep from the goats is not their ability to spout pious doctrine. It is their constant readiness to visit the sick, clothe the naked, feed the hungry and give drink to the thirsty (Matthew 25:35-36.).

It will be noticed that when Jesus sent out the disciples, his instructions had two components. One was prepositional: "Repent, for the Kingdom of heaven is at hand." The other was experiential: "Heal the sick, raise the dead, cleanse lepers, cast out demons." There is a verbal as well as a visual aspect to this kind of witness. The proposition does not stand alone; it is backed up by realities. It is not enough to say that the kingdom has come; such things as the healing of the sick must stand as proof (cf. Luke 11:20).

It seems clear from this that evangelism is more than something we say; it is also something we do. To speak of Jesus is not only to say things about him. We also need to show what his character and his power must be like.

Evangelism as "show and tell" clears up much of the fog in heated debates over the subject. Some who see it as a purely verbal activity tend to isolate it into a sideshow by itself, simply a matter of preaching and listening. Some who see it from its purely social aspect tend to reduce it into mere social work. In contrast, there is a fullness, a wholistic quality to the growing awareness that "evangelism is not just a testimony to God's acts in Christ, but a participation in those acts."[8]

That we need to see it this way springs from the recognition that evangelism needs a context, a setting in which the things we say about Jesus become truly incarnate. The Word must take flesh; it does not and was not meant to stand above the world and its need. The saving power of God needs to be made visible; otherwise it is only empty words.

Context is something the preacher alone cannot provide. For the Word to have a body, the Church and its entire gamut of gifts is needed. The whole Body of Christ is to stand as a Sign, a visual aid to the Kingdom that has come. It is important to grasp that this Body which makes the Word visible is not limited to the local church. The *ecclesia visibilis* is God's people making the presence of the Kingdom felt in all areas of life, the leaven which permeates all of human activity. It is the Church in academia, the Church in politics, the Church in the marketplace.

It is precisely because the Church has retreated from the world that the Gospel now lacks a context. We have allowed the world to become secularized, and the Church's influence to be narrowed within the four paltry walls of the local church. In the process, the Word has become ghostly, a pale shadow of the Logos who, as John describes, has been seen with the eye, has been looked upon and touched with the hands.

The lack of a caring community that incarnates the Word makes us more and more incapable of being heard. The world no longer sees the big, strong hands that once healed, broke bread, and touched wounds and aches lodging in the human heart.

This is not to say that we must do social action to make the faith more credible. It is simply to recognize that we are, as C.S. Lewis puts it, "impure spirts"—people whose appreciation of things spiritual has to be mediated through things material: a sign, a sacrament, a body that needs to be fed before it can begin to focus on things that are above. We must always remember that we are not talking to disembodied spirits. We are talking to human beings who cannot hear us with a rumbling stomach. That is why we must take care to put people in a situation where they can respond in a responsible way to the preaching of the gospel. It is our duty to locate people in an economic setting that makes the hearing of the gospel possible. Otherwise, Ellul warns us, we might simply be throwing pearls to the pigs.[10]

It is clear from all this that social action is not an option; it does not simply follow the proclamation of the gospel. It is a thing that needs to be done if the gospel is to be heard at all, especially in Third World settings. It is part of the process we call "evangelism."

It may be claimed that the term evangelism has a specifically "heralding" aspect which becomes obscured if we say that every thing that the Church does is evangelism. For this reason we prefer to use the term witness to denote all that the Church does to make itself shine like a city upon a hill. The word carries with it the need to have "presence" as well as "proclamation" in our preaching of the Kingdom.

Social action would correspond to the "presence" aspect, and evangelism to the "proclamation" aspect in its narrower sense of "chattering" or "announcing" the gospel. The relationship could be illustrated this way:

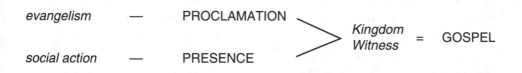

In summary, while evangelism and social action are distinct, both are essential parts of our witness to the fact that the Kingdom has come; The proclamation of the Kingdom has a verbal as well as a visual aspect. For this reason the Church must be both a *herald* as well as a *sign*. It must serve as a context in which the saving power of God is made visible. Witness to the Kingdom requires more than preachers; it demands the whole Body of Christ to be visibly present in all areas of human life. In doing so, the Gospel is wholly preached, and men and women are enabled to adequately respond to the prophetic demands of the Gospel.

Notes

1. See John Howard Yoder, *The Politics of Jesus,* William B. Eerdmans Publishing Company, Grand Rapids, Michigan, 1972, p. 37ff.
2. Yoder makes a case to the effect that Jesus could not have been subject to suspicion if it were not that the claims of the Kingdom clearly overlapped with the claims of Caesar. The Caesar question simply pushed to the forefront the conflict of loyalty implicit in the two claims.
3. When actually charged to confirm if he really was King of the Jews or not, Jesus' answer was "You have said so" (Matthew 27:1.1).
4. "The proclamation 'Jesus is Lord' is a social and structural fact; and constitutes a challenge to the Powers . . . it follows that its claims are not limited to the individuals who accept it, nor is its significance limited to those who listen to it." Yoder, op.cit..
5. See Yoder, op.cit.. the chapter on "Justification by Faith."
6. Emilio Castro, as quoted by SCAN, Partnership in Mission.
7. T.S. Eliot, *The Idea of a Christian Society.*
8. Alfred Krass, as quoted by SCAN, Partnership in Mission.
9. Taylor, *The Christian Philosophy of Law, Politics and the State,* Free University Press.
10. Jacques Ellul, *The Presence of the Kingdom,* Seabury, New York, 1967, p. 141.

CHAPTER 2

WALKING WITH THE POOR

BRYANT L. MYERS

Three Important Theological Ideas

There are three theological ideas that seem useful for Christians working for transformational development.

Incarnation

One of the most incredible parts of this biblical account is the idea that the triune God would stoop to becoming flesh and make his dwelling place among us (Jn 1:14). For many inside and outside the faith, this is a stumbling block of major proportions. The Incarnation is a powerful theological metaphor for those who practice transformational development for several reasons.

First, the Incarnation is the best evidence we have for how seriously God takes the material world. The Incarnation smashes any argument that God is only concerned for the spiritual realm and that the material is somehow evil or unworthy of the church's attention. God embodied himself. God became concrete and real. It was possible to touch God's wounds and hear God's voice. Real people were healed; a dead man lived again.

This suggests that doing transformational development is what God does. We are only following after God. This is the bottom line of the biblical story. This is why "Christians cannot, indeed they must not, simply believe the gospel; they must practice it so that by God's grace they might embody its reality—what the Christian scripture calls the down payment of God's future glory" (Dyrness 1997, 3). To declare that the mission of the church is solely about spiritual things ignores the Incarnation.

Second, the Incarnation provides a highly instructive model for how we must be willing to practice transformational development. God emptied himself of his prerogatives. Are we willing to empty ourselves of ours? Jesus did not come as a conquering, problem-solving Christ. Jesus is not the quick-answer god Koyama warned us against (1985, 241). Jesus was the God who was not able to save himself, and so he was able to save others. There are lessons here for development professionals, full of technical skill and confident of their "good news" for the poor. Any practice of transformational development must be framed by the cross and the broken Christ.

Finally, we must always remember that Jesus chose freely to empty himself of his prerogatives as God, making himself nothing (Phil 2:7), so that every tongue might confess that "Jesus Christ is Lord" (Phil 2:11). The entire purpose of the exercise was to invite people to redirect their lives and to provide the means by which they could do so. Transformational development must have the same end in mind.

Redemption

The point of the biblical story is to redeem and thus redirect the trajectory of the human story after the fall. This was made possible by the finished work of Jesus Christ. We need to remember, however, that this act took place in the concrete world of Israel, at a particular point in real human history with the real death of a real man. Redemption is material as well as spiritual. Both our bodies and our souls are redeemed. The new heaven comes down to earth. The glory of all nations will enter the city at the end of the day. Our cultures, our science, our poetry, our art, even our transformational development—all are redeemed and part of the end of the story.

For this reason we must remind ourselves constantly that the work of transformational development is part of God's redemptive work (Bradshaw 1993, 43). Don't misunderstand me. Transformational development, by itself, will not save. The charitable and transforming acts of Christians will never mediate salvation. But, having said this, it is also wrong to act as if God's redemptive work takes place only inside one's spirit or in heaven in the sweet by-and-by. This disembodied, wholly spiritualized view of redemption is not biblical. God is working to redeem and restore the whole of creation, human beings, all living things, and the creation itself. "For the creation was subjected to frustration, not by its own choice, but by the will of the one who subjected it, in hope that creation itself will be liberated from its bondage to decay and brought into the glorious freedom of the children of God" (Rom 8:20-21). It is in this sense that transformational development is part of God's redemptive work in the world.

Finally, because God is working out God's redemptive purposes in spiritual, physical, and social realms, this also means that we are God's agents of redemption, however flawed and unsatisfactory we may be in this incredible role. When we work for transformational development, we are working as God's hands and feet.

The Kingdom of God

Finally, a word about Jesus and the kingdom of God. The kingdom of God is something Jesus talked about a great deal. It has been recovered as an important biblical concept, beginning with the social gospel movement in the United States early in the twentieth century. The kingdom of God was the subject of Christ's first sermon (Mk 1:14), was the only thing he called the gospel (Mt 4:23), and was the topic on which he focused his teaching to the disciples during his last forty days on earth (Acts 1:3). Jesus said that the kingdom is the key to understanding his teaching (Lk 8:10). In the Sermon on the Mount, Jesus said that the kingdom of God was the first thing we should seek and that everything else will follow (Mt 6:33). The coming of the kingdom is the first petition in the prayer Jesus taught us to pray (Mt 6:10). Luke closes the book of Acts by telling us that Paul "boldly and without hindrance preached the kingdom of God and taught about the Lord Jesus Christ" (Acts 28:31). Jesus even said that "the gospel of the kingdom will be preached to the whole world as a testimony to all nations, and then the end will come" (Mt 24:14). The idea of the kingdom of God is an important idea for those who work for human transformation.

Recalling the importance of the interrelationship of people and the social systems within which they live, E. Stanley Jones, long-time missionary to India, makes an important contribution to kingdom theology when he presents the biblical metaphors of the "unshakable kingdom" and the "unchanging person" (Jones 1972). The kingdom of God is unshakable (Heb 12:28) because it is the true reality, the way things really are. Christ is the unchanging person (Heb 13:8), the reality of the kingdom in human form, the only way to enter God's kingdom.

The kingdom of God, Jones says, is both radical and conservative at the same time. It is radical in that no one or anything is beyond the claim of God's kingdom. It is conservative in the sense that it "gathers up everything that is good [God's good creation peeking through the results of the fall] and fulfills the good, cleanses the evil and goes beyond anything ever thought of or dreamed anywhere. This is the desire of the ages—if men only knew it" (1972, 27). Jones continues, the kingdom of God simply "is and you must come to terms with it" (ibid., 46).

Jones also rejects the reduction that limits the gospel to the individual alone. People and social systems are interrelated. While people create the political, religious, and economic institutions of their society, at the same time these institutions shape (create) the people who live in them. The impact of sin, and hence the scope of the gospel, includes both the personal and the social.

Figure 2.1 The Inseparability of the Person and the Social Order

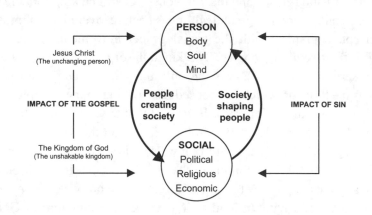

If we reduce the gospel solely to naming the name of Christ, persons are saved but the social order is ignored. This is a "crippled Christianity with a crippled result" (Jones 1972, 30). If we act as if individuals are saved now and the kingdom is only in heaven when Jesus comes, then we in effect leave the social order to the devil. "Vast areas of human life are left out, unredeemed—the economic, the social and the political" (ibid., 31). Into this vacuum other ideologies and kingdoms move with their seductive and deceptive claims of a new humanity and a better tomorrow—socialism, capitalism, nationalism, ethnic identity, and denominationalism—shakable kingdoms all.

Therefore, the scope of the gospel of the unshakable kingdom and the unchanging person is the individual, the social systems in which we live, and the earth on which we depend for life. Jones's argument anticipates Wink's analysis to a remarkable degree. The impact of the fall is on both the individual and the social system, and so the impact of the gospel of the kingdom must be on both. Wink makes this provocative claim, "The gospel is not a message of personal salvation *from* the world, but a message of *a world transfigured, right down to its basic structures*" (Wink 1992, 83). Even the creation itself has "been groaning as in the pains of childbirth" waiting "in eager expectations for the sons of God to be revealed" (Rom 8:22, 19). To work for human transformation as a Christian means working for the redemption of people, their social systems, and the environment that sustains their life—a whole gospel for all of life. This is the kingdom of God.

We must never separate the person and the kingdom, Jones warns us (1972, 37). Jesus, the unchanging person, is the embodiment of God's kingdom. The best news is that God's kingdom is not a theological phrase, but "is now a name with a human face" (Newbigin 1981, 32-33). Better yet, this person came and dwelt among us, "tempted in every way just as we are" (Heb 4:15). The kingdom of God has indeed drawn near in the form of the unchanging person. "Jesus is the kingdom of God taking sandals and walking" (Jones 1972, 34). Any Christian understanding of transformational development must keep the person of Jesus and the claims and promise of the kingdom central to the defining of what better future we are working for and for choosing the means of getting there.

Like the cross, there is something paradoxical about the kingdom that is worth noting. Jayakumar Christian, a development practitioner and colleague in India, has explored the reversal of power in Revelation (1994,11-12). The lamb of God that was slain is the one worthy to open the scroll. The lamb, convicted by Pilate and sentenced to death as a criminal, sits on the only throne that matters at the end of time. The slain lamb, not the British lion, the Indian tiger, or the American eagle, is the symbol of power when history ends. In the kingdom of God, what we believe to be the natural order of things is reversed (Kraybill 1978). Further, because Jesus promised it, this kingdom is peopled by those we think of today as powerless: the poor (Lk 6:20), the meek and the persecuted (Mt 5:5,10). Finally, all expressions of human power, every tribe and language and people and nation, will stand in front of the lamb and acknowledge who he is and what he has done (Rv 7:9-10). The kingdom of the broken and humiliated Christ is the only kingdom standing at the end of time.

This creates some challenging questions for development practitioners. Where do we believe the power is that can help the poor? In whom or in what do we trust? What does the image of the slain lamb say to the development practitioner? Or, even more provocatively, to the development agency?

The Biblical Story and Transformational Development

Evangelistic Intent

This biblical story, of which the Jesus story is the center, is a transformative story. The story of Jesus can heal our story and can heal the story of any community or society by giving it hope and life, if we will accept God's offer of redemption. Failure to share this story is to withhold the only story that

Christians believe brings real hope. No other story leads to life. This is the only story that has good news, transformative news, for human sin and for dominating human systems. There can be no better human future apart from this story. For this reason, transformational development done by Christians must include sharing the biblical story in a way that people can understand and that calls for a response.

Restoring Relationships

The point of the biblical story is ultimately about relationships, restored relationships. "Living as persons in communion, in right relationship, is the meaning of salvation and the ideal of Christian faith" (LaCugna 1991, 292). Relationships must be restored in all their dimensions. First and foremost, in an intimate and serving relationship with God, through Jesus Christ. Second, in healthy, righteous, and just relationships with ourselves and our communities. Third, in loving, respectful, "neighboring" relationships with all who are "other" to us. Finally, in an earth-keeping, making-fruitful relationship with the earth.

The integrating and focusing importance of relationships in the kingdom is a consistent biblical theme. The creation account, including the fall, is a relational account. The Ten Commandments are about relationships with God and each other, with a bias in favor of the well-being of the community. The covenant with Israel was about a relationship between God and God's people. Melba Maggay, a Filipina theologian and practitioner, reminds us that "Israel was sent into exile because of idolatry and oppression, prophetic themes resulting from the laws of love of God and love of neighbor" (Maggay 1994, 69). Loving God and loving neighbor must be the foundational theme for a Christian understanding of transformational development.

Jesus made a radical extension to loving neighbor when he told us to love our enemies (Mt 5:44). This is not like us, but it is like God. God has no enemies who lie beyond the love of God, even the most vicious, grasping, greedy landlord. Therefore, we must love the poor and non-poor alike. This is not, however, a call to a smarmy, uncritical, "I'm OK you're OK" kind of love. God's love is often a very tough love. Egypt suffered greatly so that Pharaoh might know "that I am God" (Ex 7:5, 14:4). God sent his beloved Israel into exile, even to Babylon, and then did not speak to her for almost six hundred years. God's love of us and our neighbor can be a tough, truth-telling, there-are-consequences, your-soul-is-in-danger kind of love. But, there is never hate; the enemy is never demonized or declared hopeless. The offer of grace is always there.

We need to spend a moment exploring the nature of these relationships. What do we mean? How should such relationships be assessed? The biblical image of shalom is particularly helpful here. Nicholas Wolterstorff points out that *shalom* is usually translated by the word "peace," but that it means more than the absence of strife. First, shalom is a relational concept, "dwelling at peace with God, with self, with fellows, with nature." Then, Wolterstorff suggests, we must add the ideas of justice, harmony, and enjoyment to capture the full biblical meaning of the word. Shalom means just relationships (living justly and experiencing justice), harmonious relationships and enjoyable relationships. Shalom means belonging to an authentic and nurturing community in which one can be one's true self and give one's self away without becoming poor. Justice, harmony, and enjoyment of God, self, others, and nature; this is the shalom that Jesus brings, the peace that passes all understanding (Wolterstorff 1983, 69-72).

The idea of shalom is related to one of the interesting ways Jesus described his mission: "I have come that they may have life, and have it in the full" (Jn 10: 10). Life in its fullness is the purpose; this is what we are for and what Christ has come to make possible. To live fully in the present in relationships that are just, harmonious, and enjoyable, that allow everyone to contribute. And to live fully for all time. A life of joy in being that goes beyond having. While shalom and abundant life are ideals that we will not see this side of the second coming, the vision of a shalom that leads to life in its fullness is a powerful image that must inform and shape our understanding of any better human future.

A Holistic Story

Holism is an important word for Christian thinking about development. There are a variety of ways in which we must think holistically.

First, we need to remember the whole story from beginning to end. Sometimes we are tempted to shorten the biblical story and limit it to the birth, death, and resurrection of Jesus. While this is the center of the story, it is not the whole story. To think properly about human transformation, we must see the world of the poor and the non-poor in light of the whole story. We must be clear on what was intended, how things got as they are, what God is offering to do to change them, and what we can and cannot do as participants in the story. We must have a holistic view of time, of biblical time.

The whole story is also important because it helps those who have not heard the story to understand the gospel. It is hard to make sense out of any story if the storyteller insists on starting in the middle. For example, telling people that Christ died to forgive their sins can be hard to understand if people do not know which God you are talking about or understand the idea of sin. We need a holistic view of the narrative to create a complete framework of meaning for all the gospels have for us.

Second, we need a holistic view of persons. This brings us back to an earlier theme: God's redeeming work does not separate individuals from social systems of which they are a part. People come first, of course. Changed people, transformed by the gospel and reconciled to God, are the beginning of any transformation. Transforming social systems cannot accomplish this: "No arrangement of social cooperation, in which power controls power and anarchy is tamed, will produce human beings free from the lust for power" (Wink 1992, 77). Therefore, transformational development that is Christian cannot avoid giving the invitation to say Yes to the person of Jesus and the invitation to enter the kingdom. At the same time, however, this individual response does not fully express the scope of God's redemptive work.

Social systems are made up of persons, but they are also more than the sum of the persons involved in them. Corporations, government ministries, and even church structures have a character or ethos that is greater than the sum of the individuals who work in them. Wink explains this ethos or spirit in terms of the biblical concepts of principalities and powers: "The principalities and powers of the Bible refer to the inner and outer manifestations of the political, economic, religious and cultural institutions" (Wink 1992, 78). As I have said, this social dimension of human life is also fallen and is thus a target of God's redemptive work.

The Great Commission calls for making the nations into disciples, not just people. This commission of the living Christ instructs us to baptize the nations in the name of the triune God, "teaching them to obey everything I have commanded you" (Mt 28:20). What did Jesus command? To love God and your neighbor as yourself. Kwame Bediako, the Ghanaian theologian, articulates the full meaning of the Great Commission nicely:

> The Great Commission, therefore, is about the discipline of the nations, the conversion of the things that make people into nations—the shared and common processes of thinking; attitudes; world views; perspectives; languages; and the cultural, social and economic habits of thought, behavior and practice. These things and the lives of the people in whom such things find expression—all of this is meant to be within the call of discipleship (Bediako 1996b, 184).

Recalling Hiebert's three-tiered worldview scheme in Figure 1-2 in Chapter 1[1], God's redemptive work addresses all three levels. God is the only true God, the God of power and the God who loves and works in the real world of sight, sound, and touch. His redemptive agenda works in truth (upper level), in power (the excluded middle of the West) and in love (the concrete world of science and the earth). A whole gospel for all levels of our worldview.

Finally, one other aspect of holism needs mentioning. The gospel of Jesus and his kingdom is a message of life, deed, word, and sign, an inseparable whole, all expressions of a single gospel message. Mark's account of the calling of the disciples says that Christ "appointed twelve—designating them apostles—that they might be with him and that he might send them out to preach and to have authority to drive out demons" (Mk 3:14-15). When the apostles are sent on their first solo ministry outing, Mark reports that "they went out and preached that people should repent. They drove out many demons and anointed many sick people with oil and healed them" (Mk 6:12-13).

Activists are quick to pick up on the preaching, the healing, and the casting out stuff. They too often overlook that Christ's call was first and foremost "to be with" Christ. Being must precede doing.

I find it helpful to picture the gospel message in the form of a pyramid (Figure 2.2). The top of the pyramid is being with Jesus, life in and with the living Lord. This relationship frames all that lies below it. Each of the corners of the pyramid are one aspect or dimension of the gospel: preaching—the gospel-as-word; healing—the gospel-as-deed; casting out—the gospel-as-sign.

Each of these can be developed in turn. Gospel-as-word includes teaching, preaching, and the doing of theology. Gospel-as-deed means working for the physical, social, and psychological well-being of the world that belongs to God. This is the sole location of transformation for too many Christians. Gospel-as-sign means signs and wonders, those things that only God can do, as well as the things the church does as a living sign of a kingdom that is and has not yet fully come.

The metaphor of a pyramid is helpful because one cannot break off a corner and still claim to have a pyramid. This reminds us that for the gospel to be the gospel all four aspects—life, deed, word, and sign—have to be present. They are inseparable, and so is the holism of the Christian gospel.

Technology and Science have a Place in the Story

One of the increasingly clear features of the modern era is that science has lost its story (Postman 1997, 29-32). Science and technology do not, indeed cannot, provide the answers we need. Science helps us figure out how things work, but not why they work or what they are for.

> Science cannot create. Because science is assumed to be value free, it did not operate within a vision of what ought to be. It could relentlessly and efficiently disassemble; it could not construct an alternative whole (Shenk 1993, 67).

Figure 2.2 The Gospel of the Kingdom:
Being, Preaching, Healing, and Casting Out

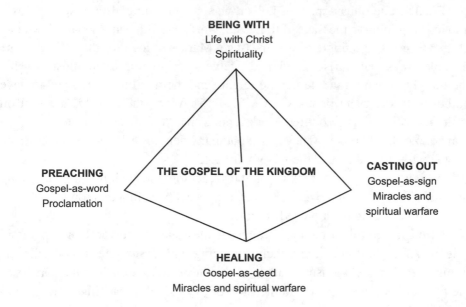

It was not always this way; science was once part of a larger story. Postman reminds us that the "first science storytellers, Descartes, Bacon, Galileo, Kepler and Newton for example—did not think of their story as a replacement for the great Judeo-Christian narrative, but as an extension of it" (1997, 31). Yet in the intervening centuries science and technology increasingly seemed to be able to explain themselves without need to include God as part of the explanation. God became increasingly marginal to their story and was ultimately dismissed as no longer needed. Today science and technology explain themselves: "We work, don't we? Nothing else matters." Relationships, ethics, and justice are pushed to the sidelines.

Yet technology and science are an inseparable part of working for human transformation. Immunizations, water drilling, improved agricultural practices, indigenous or folk science make positive impact in the lives of the poor. Any Christian understanding of transformational development must have space for the good that science and technology offer. Yet, to be Christian, this science and technology cannot be its own story, cannot stand apart from the biblical story that is the real story. We need a modern account of divine action in the natural order (Murphy 1995, 325). If we fail to recover a fully Christian narrative for science and technology, one that recognizes God at work through science in the natural order, and one that places science at the service of life and enhancing relationships, we will bring the poor the same story-less science that is impoverishing the West. This would not be good news. I will develop this more fully in the chapter on Christian witness[2].

The Biblical Story is for Everyone

In our eagerness to be with and for the poor, we must not forget the biblical story is everyone's story, poor and non-poor alike. Both are made in the image of God, both experienced the consequences of the fall, and both are the focus of God's redemptive work. The hope of the gospel and the transformative promise of the kingdom are for both. The only difference is social location. The poor are on the periphery of the social system while the non-poor, even when living in poor communities, occupy places of preference, prestige, and power.

While God's story is for everyone, there are two ways in which human response to the story creates a bias that favors the poor. First, it is apparently very hard for the non-poor to accept the biblical story as their story (Lk 18:18-30). Wealth and power seem to make people hard of hearing and poor at understanding (Lk 8:14). Even Christians who are not poor have a problem living out the story. There is a strong temptation to domesticate the story in a way that uses it to validate their wealth or position. For the Christian non-poor, there is a need to appropriate the whole biblical story as stewards, not owners. The church has lost its way in this regard from time to time.

Second, it is the poor who most consistently seem to recognize God's story as their story. The church has a long history of growing on its margins and declining at its center (Walls 1987). Furthermore, God has always insisted that caring for the widow, orphan, and alien is a measure of the fidelity with which we live out our faith. No story in which the poor are forgotten, ignored, or left to their own devices is consistent with the biblical story. If the poor are forgotten, God will be forgotten too. Loving God and loving neighbor are twin injunctions of a single command.

If the biblical story is for both poor and non-poor, then we must work to understand the poverties of both as seen from God's perspective. Furthermore, we must see how the poverty of both interact, reinforcing each other. Any theory or practice of transformational development must be predicated on an understanding of the whole of the social systems and those—both poor and non-poor—who inhabit them.

This leads us to explore the meaning and expression of poverty. We need to understand who the poor are and why they are poor, as well as who the non-poor are and how their poverty contributes to the poverty of the poor.

Notes

1. Refers to an earlier chapter in the work from which this reading was excerpted, *Walking with the Poor,* by Bryant Myers.
2. Refers to a subsequent chapter in the work from which this reading was excerpted, *Walking with the Poor,* by Bryant Myers.

SECTION B
INCARNATIONAL MINISTRY

Allison Miguel was helping to lead a group of university students through one of Cairo, Egypt's garbage-collecting communities. This team lived at the Coptic monastery located inside the garbage community. Every day the men of the community would return from the city with large mounds of garbage heaped on their carts and trucks. After the raw trash was dumped onto the dirt streets of the community, women and children would mount the rotting heaps and begin picking through the piles, sorting what could be reused or recycled from what could be fed to their animals. As Allison picked her way through the garbage-strewn streets, she saw a young girl on top of a pile of trash. Stopping to watch and pray, Allison was deeply moved. She prayed, "Oh God, how can I show my love and compassion for this girl?" Suddenly she remembered the stories of Jesus reaching his hand out to touch unclean lepers. Inspired by Jesus, Allison decided to climb the pile of stinking garbage to join the girl. As she began sorting, Allison was overwhelmed with nausea and repulsion, as the Cairo heat beat down on her. She prayed for strength to continue working for a few hours under the conditions in which this child worked every day.

God spoke powerfully to Allison that day. He assured her that he was in the garbage-picking business himself, sorting through the rubbish of our sins, looking for the things that could be redeemed. Rubbish does not repel him. One thing I find in Scripture that does repel God is arrogance. Association with the bottom rung of society is something for which God is famous. In one of the garbage communities of Manila, Philippines, is a statue of Jesus holding the type of garbage-collecting bag and sorting stick used by the people there. To these dumpsite scavengers, Jesus took on the identity of a fellow scavenger.

In Scripture Jesus said, "As the Father has sent me, I am sending you" (John 20:21). The fact that Jesus took on our reality has not escaped the attention of theologians. They refer to God's act of becoming human and planting himself into a first-century Palestinian peasant world as the incarnation. He not only draws near to us, he became one of us. That is how the Father sent the Son, and that is how the Son sends his followers. The relationships Allison developed over the course of the summer with this child and her family were monumental as she was knit into this family in ways that no missionary living on the outside could have been. To that young girl and her garbage-collecting family, Allison became a picture of Jesus that looked like them.

In his book *Companion to the Poor*, Viv Grigg describes his life as a missionary living in a squatter settlement in Manila, Philippines. It was in that slum community that his journey toward a theology of incarnation took on new dimensions. With one foot remaining in the more affluent, academic, and expatriate-missionary world and one foot in his scrap-wood squatter home, Grigg wrestles with questions of incarnation among the urban poor. Does God call us to live lives of destitution in order to reach the destitute? In this chapter Grigg explores what it means for the rich to have an economically just lifestyle and what identification with the poor might look like.

Ken Baker, a missionary with SIM in Africa, wonders in his article "The Incarnational Model: Perception of Deception" just how far rich, Western missionaries can identify with the poor. Does living in a squatter settlement really engender solidarity and trust or does it raise questions and suspicions? Does voluntary poverty really open doors with those who are involuntarily poor? Baker raises some valid concerns about the incarnational model.

But if incarnation is simply the process of becoming real to those whom God has called us, then economics must remain part of the equation of becoming real to people who live in slum communities. The following readings are meant to engage us in the tricky process of standing alongside the poor without deceiving ourselves into thinking we have fully become as they are.

CHAPTER 3

NEVER THE SAME AGAIN
FACE TO FACE WITH POVERTY

VIV GRIGG

The people of Tatalon had good reason to wonder why a white New Zealander would move into Aling Nena's home. Many of my friends were also wondering why I had left a ministry among Manila's middle class to live with the poor. However, the decision to move to the slum was not made on a whim. It was one step in a journey of carrying the cross. In this cross are meaning, reality, and destiny. Only in this cross are there ultimate answers to the deep questions that are the wellspring of human life and experience.

I first learned of the impact of that cross as a ten-year-old. While hunting for books in the uppermost garret of Dunedin, New Zealand's oak-paneled public library, I discovered a treasure trove of biographies of famous Christians. One was to set the direction of my life. It was the story of a sickly, bespectacled man—Toyohiko Kagawa of Japan.[1]

As a student, Kagawa realized that if the slum people of neighboring Shinkawa were to be saved, he must move there and preach the gospel. The poor would never accept something offered by the wealthy and respectable who came from across the river, dispensed their charitable gospel, and then returned home. A church planted in the slums must be tended day and night.

On Christmas Day 1909, Kagawa, twenty-one years old, frustrated after efforts to persuade his superiors of the needs of the poor, packed his belongings into a little handcart, crossed the bridge, and walked into the slums of Shinkawa to serve his Lord. For the next fourteen years and eight months, he lived there, teaching, preaching the gospel, and ministering to the poor.

He became a strategic figure in the development of the labor unions of Japan, brought widespread reforms to stem the flow of the poor to the cities, was a key man in the reconstruction of Tokyo after it was devastated by the 1923 earthquake, helped fashion a law that abolished slums, and was a leader in the reconstruction of Japan after World War II.

In all these activities, he constantly proclaimed the cross. He inspired nationwide evangelistic campaigns, preached to the country's political leaders and to the Emperor himself, and established many churches and Bible schools among the poor. Thousands entered the kingdom through his life.

It was the truth I learned as a child, an unquestioned assumption learned from Kagawa—living among the poor is the only possible way to plant the Christian faith among them.

Kagawa chose the rugged, rough-hewn cross of his pauper Master. He chose the suffering of the cross. With the wisdom gained from a good education, he could have been rich. But the poverty he chose shows his true wisdom.

We, too, must reach the poor. The cross is our method, the cross is our message, and the cross is our life.

Kagawa once wrote:

In the blood-drops dripping
Along the sorrowful road to the Via Dolorosa
Will be written the story of man's regeneration.
Tracing the blood-stained and staggering footprints
Let me go forward!
This day also must my blood flow, following
In that blood-stained pattern.[2]

Rugged Cross or Jeweled Replica?

After training and preparation, I was sent from New Zealand to Manila as a missionary. During my first year in Manila, I lived with a missionary and his family, serving and learning from him, and assisting in his ministry of teaching discipleship in a Bible school. I taught two classes of 60 students.

I recruited nine of these students to join me, under the leadership of an experienced missionary, in establishing a predominantly middle-class church.[3]

Theologians and church-growth specialists would say that we were on the forefront of missions, the cutting edge of the great commission, the thick of the battle to establish new beachheads for the gospel.

But my life was unfulfilled. The philosopher within me found no answers to the search for meaning; the artist found no fulfillment in the search for perfection and ultimate truth; the leader had not found the center of destiny and purpose towards which to lead others. All three voices told me I still was far from the place of God's call.

I became relatively proficient at passing on skills and programs, reproducing laborers who could pass on skills and programs to other believers. But was this the discipleship of Jesus? My students came from poor families. For many, Bible college became the stepping-stone to economic security as a paid "professional" pastor. My own wealth, and our deliberate focus on a middle-class target group, precluded me from passing on the disciplines of the Beatitudes: poverty of spirit, meekness, peacemaking (bringing justice with love)—qualities at the heart of discipleship.

The cross I was carrying and handing on was only a half-size one. I realized my life must portray a dramatically different picture of ministry if I wanted to lead these men and women into the way of the cross. Discipleship had to be taught in the context of a Jesus-style ministry to the poor—in the context of rejecting pride and status seeking, power, and economic security.

A Thief in the Slums

Cross-centered discipleship came into sharp focus the week I visited the home of one of my students. He lived in the slums of a pineapple factory in Mindanao, the large southern island of the Philippines.

We traveled by jeepney. Four people sat in the front seat, seven sat along the sides, and another four hung precariously along the back in various ways—all laughing and talking in unknown dialects. A load of vegetables sat on my feet, and chickens squawked under the seat.

We stopped at a military outpost. A soldier cautiously inspected each passenger, and then climbed aboard the front seat to provide protection from rebels, bandits, or guerillas. Villagers stared at us from small nipa huts huddled along the road.

Finally, we arrived at Lario's home on a pineapple plantation, stretching for mile after mile on land confiscated or bought from hundreds of peasant farmers.

For the first time, I saw the effects of Western consumerism in the Two-Thirds World. Accumulated profits are taken to America, juggled between three different companies. Meanwhile, 7000 workers, many of them former owners of the land on which they now work, live on a pitiful wage in one square mile of squatter homes. The transnational company argues that at least these workers have some income. But they deliberately keep this below subsistence level in order to circumvent union troubles. We Westerners eat the canned pineapple produced, with little thought for the social and economic process behind it.

Lario's house consisted of bamboo posts and pieces of wood he had scrounged from the dump and elsewhere. As I stooped through the door, the first thing I did was put my foot through the floorboards.

They called in all their *utang* (the debts of old friends) to feed me, and gave me their blanket, a mosquito net, and a sleeping mat.

Lario's mother and father both work. During my visit, his father was ill with a skin disease on his legs. Their income could not provide enough money for medicine.

The toilet had blown over in a typhoon, so Lario and I began to dig a deep hole. The neighbors came to see this Americano. They had never seen a white person work with his hands before.

"Hey. Joe, what are you doing?" I had learned that Filipinos call white men "Joe" because of the many American soldiers who had lived there over the last century.

"I'm digging a toilet," I answered. "Why don't you come over this evening? We will preach the gospel and explain why!"

In the afternoon, I talked with Lario's mother. As she ironed with a charcoal iron, she told the story of their poverty, of the personal tragedy that had caused it and the oppression that had perpetuated it. Tears fell. She told of how the Lord had sustained her, how in him alone was her comfort.

As evening came, smoke from the wood fire wafted through the house, driving away the mosquitoes. Estella, Lario's twelve-year-old sister, picked up a homemade wooden guitar and began to sing of the Lord who understands the pain and sorrow of his children, who is building a mansion "just over the hilltop."

"*Mahirap*," she said to me sadly at the end of her song. "Life is so hard, so poor."

In the light of the kerosene lamp, we ate our rice and fish for supper. Then we placed a lantern outside and set up some bamboo for seats. It was Easter Friday, and I began to speak about the cross.

The lantern cast its eerie light on the tattered clothes of the men sitting on the bamboo seats we had made. It was quiet. One could sense the listening ears of neighbors in the surrounding houses as they sat in their windows. They listened to the story of those nails that shattered his wrists, the jolting of that wooden post as they dropped it into the ground, the blood flowing from his crown of thorns.

I spoke of the thief beside Jesus who cried, "Jesus, remember me," and of Jesus' reply, "This day you will be with me in paradise." Samson, a big denim-clad youth sitting at the front, began to weep quietly. He, too, had been a thief. He repented, and the Spirit of God entered his life.

In the midst of this twentieth-century scene—surrounded by the poor, in the presence of the Spirit of God, declaring the cross—I was aware that I was standing in the central stream of history. Two thousand years earlier, with a similar pair of dusty sandals on his feet, my Lord had declared his destiny with these words: "The Spirit of the Lord is upon me because he has anointed me to preach the gospel to the poor" (Luke 4:18).

Here also the pauper apostles of history had stood through the centuries. Here was meaning, destiny, and truth, enough to satisfy the deepest searchings of the human heart.

The proclamation of the cross stands at the center of all meaning. In it justice and truth, mercy and compassion meet. But it is framed by suffering, poverty, and the pain of humanity. It is framed by the poor.

The dignity, the human quality of the leadership of Jesus, had captivated me as a child and brought me into his kingdom. Like the disciples who had walked before me throughout history, God had overwhelmed me with his love.

But once we know him, we continue to seek him. "I count everything as loss because of the surpassing worth of knowing Christ Jesus my Lord" (Philippians 3:8).

Where can Jesus be found and known today? To find him, we must go where he is. Did he not say, "Where I am, there shall my servant be also"?

Such a search invariably leads us into the heart of poverty. For Jesus always goes to the point of deepest need. Where there is suffering, he will be there binding wounds. His compassion eternally drives him to human need. Where there is injustice, he is there. His justice demands it. He does not dwell on the edge of the issues. He is involved, always doing battle with the fiercest of the forces of evil and powers of darkness.

That night, in a squatter settlement on a pineapple plantation, my heart found rest. There could be no turning back from God's call. I must preach the gospel to the poor.

In a Heap of Ruins

After the week with Lario and his family, I returned to Manila, asking myself, *Where would Jesus be involved if he were in Manila?*

One day I climbed to the top of a one-hundred-foot-high mountainous pile of rotting, decaying food and rubbish. I looked at the shacks of 10,000 of Manila's poorest and at their emaciated figures scavenging paper, bottles, and cans to resell them to middlemen who would then recycle them.

The people had work—they were happy in that. I watched as little children, older women, and comparatively healthy workers picked their way through the pile. They carried their goods in sacks on their shoulders back to their homes, where the goods were sorted and classified.

I walked through the squatter community. The smell was indescribable. Sickness was rife. The houses were constructed from old sacks, metal, and other old garbage. Children reached out their hands in laughter to touch me, but pulled back when they saw my tears. As I wept, my heart cried out in anger. *Lord, how long can you permit the degradation and destruction of your people? Why don't you do something?*

Suddenly, I knew his answer: "I have done something. Two thousand years ago I stepped into poverty in the person of my Son. And I have dwelt there ever since in the person of my sons and daughters. Today I am calling for other sons and daughters to enter into the poverty of the poor in order to bring my kingdom to them."

Jesus would dwell today wherever there is need. Here, in the slums of Manila, the Prince would become one of the paupers: "For you know the grace of our Lord Jesus Christ, that though he was rich, yet for your sake he became poor that by his poverty you might become rich" (2 Corinthians 8:9).

Here, among the poorest of the poor, he would preach, heal, and bring justice.

Job described these poor: "Yet does not one in a heap of ruins stretch out his hand, and in his disaster, cry for help? Did not I weep for him whose day was hard? Was not my soul grieved for the poor?" (Job 30:24–25).

It would be in a "heap of ruins" such as this smoldering rubbish heap, a modern-day urban Gehenna, that Jesus himself would minister.

Four Hundred Communities

In 1978 the National Housing Authority of the Philippines identified 415 squatter communities in Metro-Manila. Of these, they identified 253 as communities that could be upgraded on site. In the remaining 162 communities, the demolition and relocation of unwanted squatter settlements by truckloads of armed men would proceed.

Yet Jesus would have ministered to these very people. Surely we too must live among them, bringing them the tangible blessing of his kingdom. His compassion compels. The cross compels. The search for meaning and reality compels.

We must call men to that task and place the cross where the battle is hardest fought. The church must not only be planted; it must be planted where the gospel has never been known. And where but among the poor of these cities is a harder place to plant the church?

Our ideals, however, are constantly limited by the realities of our humanity and its incipient sinfulness, both personal and collective. Identification with or among the poor cannot be accomplished in a day, a week, or even a month. A missionary must always limit his own idealism.

I needed to move in this new direction harmoniously with the body of co-workers in which God had placed me. I needed to build a ministry to the poor on the solid foundation of Scripture. My idea of disciplemaking had to be refined. The attainment of my calling to Manila's poor would take time.

TO HAVE OR NOT TO HAVE? ECONOMICALLY JUST LIFESTYLES

Disciplemaking is a commitment of one life to another through thick and thin. But since I was not called to these professionals, I could not give my heart to them. I could not be a true pastor, and true disciplemaking could not really occur. All I could do was to set a framework, a structure, and handle the problems as they occurred.

The office Bible studies continued to multiply; the university groups began to come together; a graduate group began at the University of the Philippines; several pastors were asking for help. The ministry grew from seventy to a hundred professionals and college students. And God was giving freedom in my preaching after five years of hard discipline developing story-telling skills and crafting sermons.

But the call of the poor still beat relentlessly in my mind. I was compelled by an inner drive. I must take the gospel to the poor. All my creative energy must be directed towards the poor, the needy, and the broken.

But there would be a cost. What would happen to the relationships with my middle-class co-laborers as I sought to involve them among the poor? How could I involve the middle-class and rich in the needs of the poor? What lifestyle is appropriate for them to live? What models could I use from the past?

Substance and Simplicity

Job and Abraham are interesting examples of rich men with a deep commitment to the poor. Both were patriarchs, men of great social standing and influence, living at a time when society was built around a clan structure. Abraham was a man committed to simplicity of lifestyle. Though he had great wealth, he employed it wisely to support his hundreds of dependents (a model for factory owners!). Though he knew how to build cities, having grown up in Ur of the Chaldees, he chose to live simply in a tent. Hebrews tells us: "By faith, he sojourned in the land of promise, as in a foreign land, living in tents with Isaac and Jacob, heirs with him of the same promise. For he looked forward to the city which has foundations whose builder and maker is God" (Hebrews 11:9–10).

Such men can be used to minister to the poor. Abraham established a pattern that is consistent throughout the Scriptures: "The blessing of the Lord makes rich and he adds no sorrow with it" (Proverbs 10:22). Yet those who have wealth are not to live luxuriously but simply, "to be rich in good deeds, liberal and generous" because "the love of money is the root of all evils" (1 Timothy 6:6–8, 10, 18).

In the Scriptures, greed (or covetousness) and excessive luxury are sins as bad as immorality or adultery (Ephesians 5:3–5). Indeed we are not even to have lunch with a brother who is greedy (1 Corinthians 5:11).

If we want to live out a gospel of justice and grace, we must see that living a life of luxury is collaborating with injustice. Piety and luxury cannot co-exist. Living luxuriously in the midst of poverty is a denial of justice: "If anyone has the world's goods and sees his brother in need, yet closes his heart against him, how does God's love abide in him?" (1 John 3:17).

To be obedient to this command surely means that nobody should have excessively more than others. The poor should be uplifted, the rich brought low, and equality should result. (Though clearly we don't keep giving till we too become destitute, for then we only add ourselves to the problem.)

And clearly there is a need for some men to have capital, as Abraham had capital. But we must use it to benefit the workers, as Abraham used it to benefit his people.

Job, the greatest of all patriarchs of the East, also had great capital. He too used it to benefit his people. In his justifications, Job describes how to be a godly rich man:

> I delivered the poor (ani) who cried,
>   and the fatherless who had none to help him . . .
> I caused the widow's heart to sing for joy.
> I put on righteousness, and it clothed me;
>   my justice was like a robe and turban.
> I was eyes to the blind, and feet to the lame.
> I was a father to the poor (ebyon),
>   and I searched out the cause of him
>   whom I did not know.
> I broke the fangs of the unrighteous,
>   and made him drop his prey from his teeth.
> (Job 29:12–17)

Rich people are to live simply and use their capital to benefit the poor. This is justice. For a Western missionary or a Christian businessman to live otherwise is a great evil.

The poor have an intuitive knowledge about such issues. They know it is unjust that I am a rich man and they are poor. Of course everyone, rich and poor, knows that riches are a gift from God and that sin is a cause of poverty. But the poor man of understanding knows more than a rich man who is wise in his own eyes. He knows it is often the sins of oppression, exploitation, and injustice committed in the name of "fair profit" that have made him poor.

But justice is not to live in equal *destitution* with the destitute. Justice for Jesus was to live humbly, simply, without excess, and share whatever he had with those around—to share with the destitute. Justice was not to have more than that required by our daily needs—"Give us this day our daily bread"—and yet, at the same time, it was to enjoy all the good things God has made.

In seeking a just society, to live as poor among the poor, we cannot live a life of destitution—the destitute poor have no respect for this themselves. They are trying to move upwards, at least to a level of sufficiency for their own needs.

Paul describes a balanced personal justice: "There is great gain in godliness with contentment; for we brought nothing into the world, and we cannot take anything out of the world; but if we have food and clothing, with these we shall be content" (1 Timothy 6:6–8).

Other rich men like St. Francis of Assisi, for the salvation of their own souls, have decided to follow another command—one Jesus gives to the rich young ruler: "If you would be perfect, go, sell what you possess and give to the poor, and you will have treasure in heaven; and come, follow me" (Matthew 19:21).

My observation is that most converted rich are encouraged to do as Abraham and Job—remain rich, but use their wealth wisely, turn their income into capital which can create work for the poor, and live simply yet not be destitute. Unfortunately, despite the number of testimonies we hear from the wealthy and the popularity of "prosperity theology," it is extremely difficult to hang on to our wealth and on to Jesus at the same time. In the house church movement among the rich of Djakarta, Indonesia, believers sagely use the phrase, "Repent of your sins, then repent of your wealth!"

Prosperity theology teaches a "be saved and get rich" Christianity, using the teaching of the Pentateuch, Job and Proverbs about the righteous rich, but ignoring the Psalms, prophets, and teaching of Jesus about the godly poor. Prosperity theology works against genuine spirituality.

Commitment Without Identification

People often ask, "Were you called to minister to the poor?" We are all called to minister to the poor. Such a ministry is the logical obedience of any disciple imitating the attitudes, character, and teaching of Jesus. He commands everyone to renounce all (Luke 14:33), give to the poor, and live simply. But we would need a special call to minister primarily to the rich or middle-class, for the focus of Christian ministry is "good news to the poor."

Not all, however, are called to a life of *identification* with the poor by living among them!

Is there a reasonable lifestyle for middle-class Filipinos who desire to minister to the poor?

Lazarus, Mary, and Martha are examples of the middle-class of Israel. They had a large home, kept it, and used it for the Lord and his disciples as a retreat center.

I have not discerned God calling many of my middle-class friends to lives of identification with the poor. Some heard and refused his call, but in general, the Lord seemed to be calling them to a ministry among their middle-class peers. To expect them to choose identification with the poor was to expect them to become apostles and missionaries across a great social, economic, and cultural barrier.

Just as the expatriate missionary community is trapped by structures, expectations, and affluence into middle- and upper-class ministries, so the average middle-class Filipino is driven by materialism and the intense demands of upward mobility (through education and post-graduate degrees). Many of the *nouveau riche* in the Philippines come from genuine poverty. They are compelled by family responsibilities to keep moving up to take their family safely out of the danger of poverty. The poor who are still poor constitute a danger to this class. Any relationship to poor people outside of their own clan would drain hard-won finances.

To expect people from this class to jump the class barrier and live among the poor was expecting more than I myself had sacrificed. Never having experienced *involuntary* poverty it was much easier for me, as a "rich Westerner" and a member of the "upper class," to choose *voluntary* poverty. I still had resources, security and friends. But for a person waging personal and family warfare with poverty, there is no romance in returning to a life of frugality.

Nevertheless, like Lazarus, Mary, and Martha, the middle-class can have a significant commitment to the poor. Some fifteen of these middle-class co-laborers have spent extensive time helping in the slums, some making attempts to help economically, some with a Bible study group with a poor family. Others come and stay overnight, some for two or three weeks, to provide companionship.

I couldn't call such people to live among the poor. The best I could do was to set the pace, trusting God to inspire some others by my example. And I could speak of Jesus who tells us: "As thou didst send me into the world, so I have sent them into the world" (John 17:18).

The Carpenter's Justice

He had been born as a little babe in a dairy shed; he grew up as a refugee child. His parents were so poor, they could not afford a sheep at his dedication and so had to offer two turtledoves. Tradition tells us that as a teenager he worked to support his mother and family. He chose to be a rabbi, men renowned for their poverty, rather than a rich high priest. He had no place to lay his head. He had calloused hands, wore wooden sandals, and died a poor man's death.

He was Jesus, the just one! Nobody could fault him for economic injustice in his standard of living. Justice demanded equality between the sent one and people. Justice demanded identification or "solidarity" with the poor. He lived at the level of the people, identifying himself with them in voluntary simplicity.

Jesus, the just one, asked more from his middle-class companions than acceptance of the status quo. He demanded renunciation of possessions: "So therefore, whoever of you does not renounce all that he has cannot be my disciple" (Luke 14:33).

He told his team: "Fear not, little flock . . . Sell your possessions, and give alms; provide yourself with purses that do not grow old, with a treasure in the heavens that does not fail" (Luke 12:32–33).

Jesus here used the word "forsake" or "renounce." It is an action word; it is not just an attitude.

Many of us would like it to focus purely on attitude: "Whoever has many possessions, but uses them wisely will be my disciple." But Jesus was very blunt. It is junk *or* Jesus. Just junk or just Jesus—not junk *and* Jesus. Forsake first an attitude, but let the attitude result in action.

You cannot serve God and affluence, says Jesus elsewhere (Matthew 6:24). Not "may not," but *cannot!* There is no choice.

But what does Jesus mean by renouncing *all?* Our Lord did not live in destitution. He grew up in a good home, possessed carpenter's tools, probably played with toys as a child and had a common purse (bank account) with the disciples. He wore clothes. He had breakfast each morning.

He was not a beggar; he was not unemployed. He provided for his twelve followers through the ministry of women (Luke 8:3). They always had enough. He told them (in Matthew 6) that the Father would provide their food and clothing.

"Food and clothing" is a phrase for basic necessities. It may include shelter, work tools, books, children's toys, decorations, and provision for celebration. In most situations today, it involves buying a home—just as the Levites were to own no possessions in Israel, but were to have their own home and enough garden to provide for themselves. But the same phrase excludes a life of ease, luxury, and wealth. It is not a call to destitute poverty, but it *is* a call to simplicity. Just as involuntary and destitute poverty has no intrinsic virtue, so wealth often destroys spirituality.

The attitudes involved are important. But at issue is whether we will eliminate external, glittering possessions and follow him, developing an internal concentration on him—unfettered and unhindered by excess material baggage.

One way to apply this, a symbolic start, is to sit down with our families and go through each of our possessions and the use of our money to get rid of all excess—whatever detracts in time, money, and energy from Christ.

Celebration!

But Jesus was no ascetic. He came eating, drinking, and enjoying life, and was much criticized by the "Bible-believers" of his day for his lack of frugality.

Job, too, enjoyed feasting and drinking. The Old Testament is full of commands for festivals and celebration. We need to live out a "celebrating lifestyle of renunciation."

Ironically, the conflict between the biblical concepts of celebration and renunciation was resolved in my mind one day as I was sitting relaxing with some middle-class friends eating ice cream. The Lord brought to mind the passage immediately preceding his call to renunciation: "When you give a dinner or a banquet, do not invite your . . . rich neighbors . . . But when you give a feast, invite the poor, the maimed, the lame, the blind, and you will be blessed, because they cannot repay you" (Luke 14:12–14).

We are to enjoy life, but *with* and *for* the poor and needy. We are to die to our economic selves, but we are to live glorious economic resurrection lives for others.

My message to the middle-class could be summed up by the following five slogans:

Earn much
Consume little
Hoard nothing
Give generously
Celebrate life.

Notes

1. Comments on Kagawa are taken from Cyril J. Davey, *Kagawa of Japan* (Epworth Press, 1960).
2. Toyohiko Kagawa. "The Cross of the Whole Christ," in *Meditations on the Cross* (SCM, 1936), 16.
3. For a study of this church-planting venture see Cary Perdue, "The Case of the Kamu Bible Christian Fellowship," *Asia Pulse* (Evangelical Missions Information Service, Box 794, Wheaton, Illinois 60187, July 1982), Vol. 15, No. 3.

CHAPTER 4

THE INCARNATIONAL MODEL: PERCEPTION OF DECEPTION?

KEN BAKER

I have always struggled with wealth. Raised in a home of very moderate income, I knew the chronic tension of "making ends meet." Yet, I never really considered myself a "have not." Though I had never seen abject poverty, I knew it did not mean me. Even so, I matured in an environment where I always considered "wealthy" as something I was not. Then I went to Africa. . . .

Suddenly, I was one of the "haves," and I did not like it. As a single newcomer to the inner city of Monrovia, Liberia, I descended into the trenches where every Western missionary to the Third World battles with identity and response. This is not to imply that I was on the top of the pile. There were numerous expatriates and Africans who were far wealthier than I, but it was the stark, inescapable contrast which wore on me day after day. Gradually, I attempted to negotiate a private truce, a coping policy, but it hardly seemed adequate; the guilt was constantly knocking.

Although at times familiarity seems to mute the emotional intensity, the daily ache of economic disparity continues in West Africa. For my family, this disparity is not theoretical. We live in a remote, bush region of subsistence farmers and nomads in eastern Niger. We are the lone Westerners in the area. It is one of the poorest, most precarious corners of the world. Church-planting here is a deep privilege, but we live the vast economic contrast every hour of the day. As ambassadors of the King, how then should we live? What should our lifestyle be? This dilemma impacts our choices in a myriad of ways, such as, how much should we help the local believers as they construct a new church building? Our tithe for 14 months could fund the entire project. . . should we? If not, how much should we give as participants in this community of believers?

The relative affluence of traditional missionaries and their methods is a reality. That is, the missionary may not be "wealthy" in his/her home culture, but,

51

cross-culturally, the difference is more apparent. While there is a broad spectrum of practice in this regard, the Western missions movement displays considerable wealth in comparison to host cultures and churches. No doubt almost every Western missionary to the developing world can attest to the awkwardness money brings.

First, there is the discomfort missionaries feel when they face living in a vastly different economic climate. Secondly, there is the natural separation that Western lifestyle introduces to a Third World context. These are the varied, contrasting habits which are universal in Western living (personal vehicle, privacy, time scheduling, indoor bathrooms and kitchens, etc.). Thirdly, there is the perception of our affluence through the eyes of our cultural hosts in the Third World.

Living in the midst of these tensions we sense the need to do more than just cope. Instead, we want to live and give the whole gospel. For believers, there is always this deeper, personal level. The poor and destitute are not a nameless block of humanity. They are suffering, hurting persons, each living an individual drama. They need love, justice, compassion and Christ, individually. We recognize these realities, but the economic contrast still hammers away daily.

Likewise, the evolution of development in the world is increasing the awareness of disparity. The rising economic tide which makes parting with our material comforts ever more difficult also creates a more enticing climate of expectation within the developing world. These factors indicate that we cannot focus upon economics alone. Rather, we need to engage our character as disciples of Christ. Here is where the real rub comes. The material aspect is not easy, but it is not the hardest part.

In recent years various ideas have surfaced while addressing the dilemma of living an affluent lifestyle in the midst of poverty. One particular perspective has gained a wide hearing within the missions community, the "incarnational lifestyle." This approach invokes the example of our Lord Jesus who "became poor" in order to become flesh in this world. Thus, this act of identification with the poor, by eliminating the distractions of affluence, creates a climate of acceptance of the gospel otherwise blocked by Western wealth.

The incarnational approach has made several contributions to the discussion of our response to world economic disparity and missions practice. First, it points to the impact our affluence has had upon the evangelistic outreach and the growth of the Church. For the most part, we have had our head in the sand when it comes to personal and organizational awareness of the situation. Secondly, the incarnational model emphasizes the importance of personal sacrifice. The Scriptures clearly demonstrate the cost involved in mission, but this discipline has not been the primary characteristic in the history of missions. Likewise, Christ's incarnation is a powerful, but mostly ignored, motif in Christian living. Instead, we have grown accustomed to "sanctified materialism," especially in evangelical America.

In my opinion, there are many Western missionaries who are increasingly disillusioned with the current climate of superficial, activity-oriented mission commitments. Too often it appears that mission organizations have succumbed to a marketplace mentality, focusing upon personal fulfillment as the driver in recruitment, training, deployment, ministry and evaluation. Even so, as much as I would like to embrace the incarnational perspective, I believe the categorical tone of particular writers on this subject loses many in the process. The incarnational model is built upon three foundational assumptions: (1) Identification with the poor is possible; (2) The incarnational approach is the biblically intended model for mission; and (3) Relative affluence is always an "unbridgeable" gap.

Identification with the Poor is Possible. The dominating theme in this argument is the insistence upon the example of Christ's incarnation. Presented in economic terms, this model holds that our message to the world should follow exactly the pattern of Jesus' message, to incarnate ourselves among the poor. However, when it comes to the practical applications of incarnational theory in real life, the complicating details are often avoided. Take, for example, Jonathan Bonk's criteria, delineated in a 1989 article for Missiology: "needs must not be defined by Western standards, but by local conditions. Real renunciation [of affluence]—not just the appearance of renunciation—must be practiced" (1989, 442).

This assertion is consistent with the writer's interpretive approach, but has he fully considered the implications in real life, year after year? Perhaps, but Bonk appears to avoid the issue four years later when he says, "Little needs to be said here concerning family and personal obstacles to simpler missionary living" (Phillips and Coote 1993, 123). On the contrary, I immediately relate it to my wife, three children and the lifestyle choices we make each day. On the field it is not theory. Much needs to be said about health concerns, MK education, social differences, etc.

Are "needs" of the locals around me truly the standard of measurement? If so, where does it stop? As a husband and father in a very poor country, what does this mean for my family? What about a bed? a toilet? mosquito netting? diapers? extra clothes? books? toothpaste? The locals do not need these; so, in order to properly apply the incarnational principle, we must not use them.

The Incarnational Approach is the Biblically Intended Model for Mission. Central to this second assumption is the idea that missionary affluence is a personal distraction which once removed would allow the message of Christ to flow freely. According to Bonk, "He [the missionary] would not only seem to want to identify, he really would identify" (Phillips and Coote 1993). Thus, identification is the goal. If we identify with the poor, true identification with all that implies, then the message of Christ will be communicated. Furthermore, this assumption implies that the more "incarnate" (economically) the greater the spiritual power. Yet, the continual emphasis on measuring spirituality and obedience through economic criteria seems to avoid the holistic approach of Jesus' teaching. Zaccheus did not become poor, but Jesus found great delight in his new faith and the generosity it produced (Blomberg 141).

In my opinion, we must be very careful not to assume Christ's incarnational model is possible for us. The differences are legion. Jesus could do and say what he did because he really was a part of that culture. Our Lord's incarnation was total. We cannot duplicate that, not even remotely. He was born into a culture which was his own. To me, it seems reckless to imply that we can replicate this ultimate act of "emptying ourselves."

I know a missionary couple in West Africa who was approached by a delegation of village elders after they had lived there several months. The elders explained that the couple was the object of ridicule from other villages because the foreigners lived in a hut like the rest of the villagers. Rather than bring more shame on the village they were asked to please build a "city" house. This creates a dilemma for those seeking to follow the incarnational model. Do the missionaries assume they know better and ignore the request because they believe that someday the people will come to understand and appreciate their identification and believe in Christ? Presuming that "we know better," and that what we think we are communicating is actually received as such, not only projects a false confidence, but it risks compromising any love we seek to communicate. This presumption pertains to living style, dress, behavior or any form of contextualization.

Here in eastern Niger any Westerner who would choose to live like the farmers or nomads would be seen as someone who loved money! Why? Because it is assumed that he is stashing his money "back home" rather than using it here. All denials would be taken as lies, because the people here know that Westerners have money or access to it. If one would choose to renounce Western citizenship and foreign support to live here, it would not be perceived as love, but as something to suspect. Perhaps the police in his home country were chasing him and he is hiding here! Again, what we think we are communicating is often not what the people among whom we minister are receiving.

Relative Affluence is Always an "Unbridgeable" Gap. Jeff Hahn's statement, "Choosing to live poor can never duplicate the psychosocial dynamics of unchosen poverty" exemplifies the vast difference between "voluntary poverty" and the real thing (Hahn 2001). Harriet Hill realized this illusion as she described the unrealistic aspirations of an incarnational model; in the end, aren't we pretending to be something we are not (1990, 199)? The incarnational theory leads us to believe that our affluence is the only barrier to communicating the true Gospel, or at least the only barrier that matters. Yet removing the issue of wealth, assuming it is really possible, eliminates only one supposed barrier . . . Many others remain. What about education, culture, expectation, worldly exposure, health, worldview, etc.? These are all integral parts of who we are; we cannot excise them from our lives, yet they are representative of the gulf which separates regions and peoples.

While it is certainly true that God has a special compassion for poor people, nowhere does he honor poverty. There is no virtue in poverty, as an economic situation. All people have dignity and worth; rich or poor, all are created in the image of God. Poverty is a consequence of the Fall, as are selfishness and greed. Idolizing poverty is no different than idolizing wealth.

The "incarnational" model is an attempt to cultivate a particular and, perhaps, artificial social image. Furthermore, this approach implies that true relationship only develops where there is equality. In other words, for there to be "connectedness" between members of two cultures there must be economic parity. However, this fixation with material status overlooks an entire spectrum of realities which impact intercultural relationships. Likewise, we must be very careful that the pursuit of an incarnational lifestyle does not become an idol. All of us have room to grow and adapt in the face of economic disparity, but it is unwise to make identification the goal. A decade ago a pioneering church-planting effort almost imploded because of the incarnational model. By pushing it so insistently, some on the team alienated the others, giving the impression that they were the elite in missionary efforts. Interestingly, no members of the "elite" group remain on the mission field. When we place too much emphasis on the method we bypass the crucial element, the gracious work of the Holy Spirit. Our Lord is a master at using imperfect people.

As Western missionaries, affluence is an integral characteristic of our heritage. As much as we would like to deny this reality, its influence is unavoidable. Even Bonk would agree that affluence encompasses much more than economics. Often to our deep chagrin, affluence also represents a "First-Worldness" which we cannot fully shed. But, by God's grace, we can transcend the baggage of wealth . . . and if we do, it is only by grace.

The core of the affluence issue pertains to the idolatry of individualism, believing we have the right to do/have what we want—the service of self.

Francis Schaeffer was right, "personal peace and affluence" define our culture. Why? Because individualism is based on the first sin, independence (people craving to be independent from God, longing to be in control). This pursuit defines Western culture, the pervasive quest to manage our environment, control our world through technology, eliminate surprises and predict every eventuality. The Y2K scare was so menacing because it exposed our great fear that we really did not have everything under control. Of course, the irony shouts from every corner of the world. We obviously do not have control but, at least in the West, we surround ourselves with every convenience to help us deny this reality.

We Western missionaries are products of this perspective, though we tend to present a sanctified version. Even so, we still create islands of comfort and security where we can feel safe and make our cross-cultural lives more manageable, such as our transplanted Western homes and family/social life. In turn, we resist anything that threatens our controlled, managed existence, especially the uncertainty of cross-cultural relationships. Everyone brings to any given context a varied combination of numerous factors—age, sex, marital status, education, nationality, family heritage, gifting, experience, skills, church background (to name a few)—which influence one's perspective and choices. But in spite of this spectrum, we all face the need to move away from self and towards Christ.

As disciples, no matter what our setting or calling, we must constantly and deliberately move beyond the edge of our comfort zones by actively pursuing contexts (particularly relationships) which stretch us to respond in dependence upon God. It is at this point where we begin to rethink and reorient our lifestyle choices, because we are forced out of comfort, out of our independence and control.

As missionaries I believe that we can sometimes view our movement toward cross-cultural ministry as the ultimate jump over the comfort boundary; then, having made this leap, we are justified in recreating a new security zone. Our home constituencies see us as way over the edge; but, in reality, we know that we have only carved out a new hideaway. The Lord knows where we all are in the pilgrimage; but, if we are not continually and daily, moving to the "edge," then we are stagnating.

Having identified our "baggage" we recognize our need for personal transformation in order to face the challenge of living in the midst of economic disparity. The incarnational model supposes that the biblical mandate for disciples is to comply with the challenge given to the "rich young ruler," to divest of all possessions and follow Christ. This may well be the calling for a select few, but to make it universal is to go beyond the inference of Scripture. In my personal experience and exposure, I have found that only single Western missionaries are really capable of enduring a full "incarnational" motif, as often is the case with

Peace Corps volunteers. Even for them, though, it is rarely to the degree that Bonk proposes, and only for the short term. For couples and families the model is essentially impossible for the long-term commitment. Instead, the New Testament directs us toward a relational lifestyle characterized by personal self-sacrifice.

As ambassadors of the King we are called to sacrifice ourselves through the role of a bondslave to Christ. Why then do we recoil from the costliness of that life (cf. 1 Thess. 2:8)? Giving of ourselves to people usually means committing our time when it is not convenient, sharing our material blessings, accepting lesser roles than our education and ambition could demand, considering other's interests more important than our own, involving our families in people ministry, learning to communicate in another's language and giving up personal agendas and careers for the sake of the King.

The parable of the Good Samaritan demonstrates this dynamic. In defining ministry to our "neighbor" Jesus described a man who gave self-sacrificially for a needy individual, one who was of another heritage and culture. He gave up his time, money, privacy, fear and plans in order to demonstrate loving compassion, particularly to someone with whom there was traditional animosity.

A genuine give-and-take relationship diffuses fear. The whole body of choices that we bring to a relationship builds toward or away from trust. The way we conduct every aspect of our lives, beginning with love and acceptance, defines our personal and ministry character, regardless of our economic environment.

Conclusion. Through this article I have sought to encourage a balanced perspective toward the challenge Western missionaries face living in the midst of poverty. Being more than just economics, our affluence creates many obstacles toward truly effective cross-cultural ministry. We cannot deny these realities, nor can we shed them. We have a choice: remain in our protective comfort zones or give ourselves to a renewed passion for people, rich or poor. I believe the way forward in the dilemma of relative affluence is through giving of ourselves in cross-cultural relationships. This does not solve the complexities, but it creates a living network of resources for navigating through them. Self-sacrifice for the King is not a strategy, rather, it is who we seek to become. By faith, we can transcend the bonds of affluence, not through pursuing a new model or approach, but by listening to the voice of our Shepherd.

A pastor friend once told of a lifelong desire to visit Scotland, the land of his ancestors. Having read and imagined the Scottish countryside throughout his lifetime, he finally had the opportunity to make that journey. One day after driving back roads through the Scottish glens he stopped for some tea. Engaging a local man in conversation he expressed a disconcerting feeling, "Where are the shepherds and sheepdogs I've heard about?" Amused at the stereotype, the Scot said, "We don't need shepherds; we have fences." Let us take care that we do not abandon our Shepherd for fences.

References

Blomberg, Craig L. 1999. Neither Poverty Nor Riches: A Biblical Theology of Material Possessions. Grand Rapids: Eerdmans.

Bonk, Jonathan. 1985. "Affluence: The Achilles Heel of Mission," EMQ 21 (October): 382-390.

————. 1989. "Doing Mission out of Affluence: Reflections on Recruiting 'End of Procession' Churches (1 Cor. 4: 1-13)." Missiology 17 (October): 427-452.

————. 1991. Missions and Money: Affluence as a Western Missionary Problem. Maryknoll, NY: Orbis

————. 1993. "Mission and the Problem of Affluence." Toward the Twenty-First Century in Christian Mission. Edited by James M. Phillips and Robert T. Coote. Grand Rapids: Eerdmans: 295-309.

Hahn, Jeff. 2001. Personal e-mail message. 2 January.

Hill, Harriet. 1990. "Incarnational Ministry: A Critical Examination." EMQ 26 (April): 196-201.

SECTION C
MISSION

I remember a story related to me by my mentor, Bill McConnell. Bill and his wife, Beth, raised their family in Brazil, where for fifteen years they served Alianca Biblica Universitaria, an evangelical, Brazilian university student movement. Bill loved growing flowers and vegetables and had great affection for his garden. One day during planting season, his five-year-old daughter came bounding outside as Bill was working in the garden. "Daddy, can I help you?" she asked him. He paused and thought for a moment. He knew that if he invited her to join him in planting the garden, the rows would be crooked, the seeds might get planted too deeply, and besides, she would certainly get dirty and tired! At this point in telling the story, Bill's eyes filled with emotion as he confided, "But oh, what fellowship we had planting that garden!"

God certainly doesn't need us in his mission. If he chose, he could implant the message of forgiveness of sins through Christ's death and resurrection into our genetic code, along with exactly how to right all the wrongs that exist in the world. He could use dreams and visions to communicate, quite apart from any human agent. Better yet, he could come personally in the skies and shout the message so all could hear at once. In fact, there is something in our genetic code that causes us to reach out for God. Humans do have some innate knowledge of right and wrong. Some people do have supernatural experiences that encourage, guide, and inform them. And make no mistake, Christ will come again to set things right. But Scripture is clear that the central vehicle for establishing God's dawning kingdom is his church—weak, fallible, and self-centered though it may be.

It's a little like the way in which salvation comes to Middle Earth in the epic book *The Lord of the Rings*. The future of Middle Earth hangs in the balance as evil grows in power, consuming more and more of the world. Salvation lies in the destruction of a single ring. It is not to the fair elves or the brave dwarves or the valiant men of Middle Earth to whom this dangerous task falls but to the child-like, comfort-seeking race known as Hobbits.

As unlikely as it seems, God has entrusted the greater part of his mission to his people. Like my mentor Bill, God is delighted for the fellowship of joy and suffering that comes as he works together with his people in the garden of his kingdom, despite the frailty and fallibility of his followers. Leslie Newbigin defines *mission* as simply God's people wanting to be where he is, and he dwells in the lonely places where his kingdom has yet to be established.[1]

The following readings explore the role of the church in working to accomplish the mission of God. The reading excerpted from *Mission as Transformation* is an attempt on the part of Christian men and women from all parts of the world to describe Christian mission. It is a cry of repentance for our failures and a call to renewal in our quest to love God and neighbor as we pray, "Thy kingdom come."

In "Planting Covenant Communities of Faith in the City," Richard Gollings looks at the communal aspects of the church's mission. Part of our mission is expressed in covenant relationship with one another and with God. Our covenant is a calling to worship God and to serve the world with justice and compassion. As individualistic North Americans, too often we view mission with a program-centered, task-oriented mentality. Gollings urges us to move from a contract view of mission to a covenant view of mission that includes our responsibilities to one another.

The mission of the church must be seen in its internal, transformative power to change the missionary and to mature the church as well as its external quest to confront evil and bring a knowledge of the glory of God to the whole earth in both word and deed.

Notes

1. Leslie Newbigin, *The Gospel in a Pluralistic Society* (Grand Rapids: Eerdmans Publishing, 1989).

CHAPTER 5

KINGDOM AFFIRMATIONS AND COMMITMENTS

VINAY SAMUEL AND CHRIS SUGDEN, EDITORS

Preamble

From March 1–5, 1994, 85 Christians from six continents gathered in Malaysia to seek the Spirit's guidance on how an understanding of the Kingdom could help integrate the three streams of world evangelisation, social action, and renewal in the Spirit. After prayer, dialogue, and searching of the Scriptures, we offer these Kingdom affirmations and commitments to the church worldwide because we believe that focusing on the Gospel Jesus himself announced can unite and empower the church today for costly obedience and holistic mission.

After John was put into prison, Jesus went into Galilee, proclaiming the good news of God. "The time has come," he said. "The Kingdom of God is near. Repent and believe the good news."[1] Our Lord Jesus commanded His disciples to pray daily, "Your Kingdom come, Your will be done on earth,"[2] and to "seek first the Kingdom of God"[3] in the totality of their lives. By word and action, in Galilee, Golgotha and the empty tomb, Jesus powerfully and visibly demonstrated God's reign over all of life. That reign is now powerfully present among us and will reach its fulfillment at Christ's return.

Around the world, in many different places and traditions, the theme of the Kingdom has become central in a new way in our time. It has inspired charismatics, pentecostals, evangelical social activists, ecumenical leaders, and people devoted to world evangelisation. Unfortunately, many Christians have yet to discover the full importance of Jesus' good news of the Kingdom. But we believe that developing our theology and mission with particular attention to the way Jesus himself defined his person and work will help to unite the church to offer God's healing to a lost and broken world.

We Confess That All Too Often

We have obscured our witness to the Kingdom by tearing apart the inter-related tasks of proclamation of the Word and social transformation, and tried to do both without total dependence on the power of the Holy Spirit.

We have ignored the centrality of the Good News of the Kingdom of God in the teaching of Jesus, failing to present the Gospel the way Jesus did.

We have distorted Jesus' Gospel by failing to preach and demonstrate that it always includes Good News for the poor.

We have failed to recognize that love is the definite mark of the Kingdom of God—neglecting to love the Lord with all our heart, soul, strength and mind, and our neighbors as ourselves.

We have diluted Jesus' Gospel by neglecting to proclaim and live its radical challenge to the evil in every culture, society and socioeconomic system.

We have disgraced the Gospel by failing to live what Jesus taught.

We have mocked by our proud divisions Jesus' prayer that our visible love for each other would convince the world he came from the Father.

Some have one-sidedly emphasised the individual and personal aspects of the Kingdom of God to the neglect of the corporate and communal, and others have done the reverse.

We have failed to serve our neighbors and witness to the Kingdom in the affairs of government, education, business, economics, trade unions, science, welfare, medicine, the media and the arts.

We have prayed Your Kingdom come and ignored the command to seek it first in our personal and societal lifestyles.

Therefore we repent of our failure to let Christ be King in these areas. We will redress these failures with biblical teaching, small group accountability, robust theological debate and wholistic congregations and ministries that integrate proclamation, social transformation and renewal in the power of the Holy Spirit.

Biblical Foundations

The Lord is a great God and King above all gods.[4] As the Creator, Sustainer, Owner and Ruler of the whole universe God has never given up, nor will God ever give up, his rule over this universe.

God placed the world under the stewardship of women and men made in God's own image.[5] Tragically they rebelled against their Creator, bringing devastation, disorder and evil into the entire created order.[6] Yet God still desired to establish his authority and rule in the lives of persons and societies. Through

Israel, his chosen people, God began to reveal the plan of salvation and restoration of creation. The prophets promised that some day the Messiah would come to bring God's actual rule on earth in a new, powerful way. In that day, there would be salvation, justice, and peace—wholeness in all areas of life—for men, women and children.[7]

Jesus the carpenter, son of David and eternal Son of God, fulfilled the prophetic promise and inaugurated the Messianic age by proclaiming and demonstrating the Kingdom of God.[8] As he healed the sick, cast out demons and announced the Good News of the Kingdom, he demonstrated and taught that the reign of God had broken decisively into history in his person and work.[9]

The character of this dawning Kingdom became clear through Jesus' astonishing words and works which followed his anointing by the Holy Spirit. He taught that God freely welcomes all who repent of their sins and seek God's forgiveness. He identified the enemies of God's Kingdom as Satan with his evil forces and all people who join him in opposing God.

Jesus challenged the evils of his society and showed special concern for the poor, weak and marginalized. To those denied human power and dignity, Jesus offered full access to the love and power of God and a dignified place in the human community. He taught that his Kingdom was not a political kingdom of this world that one could install through military power.[10] But he also showed that his Kingdom was becoming visible in this world both in miraculous signs and wonders and in the new community of forgiven sinners—women and men, prostitutes and tax collectors, young and old, rich and poor, educated and uneducated—who were beginning to live the Kingdom principles he taught. In fact, Jesus insisted that the love and unity of his disciples would be so powerfully visible that it would demonstrate that he had come from the Father.

So sweeping was his challenge to the established social order and so unacceptable his claims to be Messiah and only begotten Son of the Father, that the authorities crucified him to prove that his claims were false. On the cross, Jesus atoned for our sins and reconciled us to God so that we could freely enter his new Kingdom as forgiven sinners. His resurrection on the third day confirmed that the Kingdom of God had broken decisively into history. It also showed that Jesus' example of suffering love, self-denial and suffering for righteousness' sake is normative for believers and a central way in which the kingdom brings life in this world.

After his resurrection and return to the Father, Jesus sent the Holy Spirit to equip and empower men and women to live, proclaim and demonstrate the Good News of the Kingdom to the ends of the earth.[11] In different settings and contexts, the first Christians described the Gospel as the Good News of Christ,[12] of God,[13] of salvation,[14] of grace,[15] and of peace.[16] They were not preaching new, divergent Gospels but rather retelling with different words the one story about Jesus, the Galilean teacher who is the expected Messiah, risen Lord and only Savior, who now offers salvation freely to all who repent, believe, and join his Messianic community. The Risen Lord called the members of that new community to submit their total lives to his Lordship.[17] As the early church did that, society's sinful walls dividing men and women, Jews and Greeks, rich and poor came crashing down. So different was this new community of the King that Paul dared to teach that the very existence of this multi-ethnic, multi-class body of men and women was a central part of the Gospel he proclaimed and a major demonstration of the power of the cross.[18]

The early church's failure and sin underlines the truth that the Kingdom will not be present in its fullness until Christ returns.[19] Meanwhile the battle with Satan and the kingdom of darkness continues to rage. But the resurrection demonstrates that the Risen One will ultimately prevail.[20] At His return, Christ will complete God's plan of restoring the entire created order to wholeness. That ultimate salvation includes not only the resurrection of persons, but the restoration of the groaning creation,[21] and the inauguration of the new Jerusalem filled with the honor and glory of the nations.[22] Then the kingdoms of this world will truly be the Kingdom of our Lord.

The King and His Kingdom

1. We believe that the Kingdom of God and Jesus Christ the King are inseparable.[23]

    Therefore we make the Lord Jesus Christ our central focus. We refuse either to substitute human program for the King and his kingdom or to divorce the naming of the King from the doing of his will.

2. We believe that the Kingdom of God becomes evident where people confess the King and do his will.

    Therefore by word and deed we seek to share the Gospel with men, women and children everywhere, inviting them to accept Christ as Savior and Lord, join his new community, and submit their total lives to his rule.[24]

3. We believe that wherever people do God's will, signs of the kingdom emerge in human society.

    Therefore we will co-operate with all who do God's will in their searching for peace, justice, life and freedom. In so doing we will always witness that the foundation and fulfillment of God's will are found in Jesus the King of the Kingdom.

4. We believe that God, through the Spirit, enabled Jesus to proclaim and demonstrate the Kingdom of God while he was on earth.[25]

Therefore we encourage women and men to seek the gifts of the Holy Spirit and know the Holy Spirit's empowering as they seek first the Kingdom of God.

5. We believe churches are called to be the visible expressions of Christ's dawning Kingdom.

Therefore we seek to be transformed communities whose loving unity convinces the world that Jesus came from the Father; we seek to be caring communities that demonstrate to our confused world that the divisions of race, gender and class can be overcome in Christ; and we seek, like Jesus, to challenge all that is evil in society, showing special concern for the weak, poor and marginalized.

6. We believe the Bible is the basis for our understanding of God's Kingdom.[26]

Therefore we fully acknowledge the trustworthiness of the Scriptures of the Old and New Testament, confess that Christ is their center, and seek to interpret all matters of faith and conduct in the light of its teaching under the guidance of the Holy Spirit.

Signs of the Kingdom of God

We believe that the following are significant signs of the presence of the Kingdom of God:

1. The presence of Jesus in the midst of his gathered people.[27]

Therefore we look to the Church to be both a sign of, and a signpost to, the Kingdom of God as we experience the joy, peace and sense of celebration which Christ's presence brings.

2. The proclamation of the Gospel.[28]

Therefore we will seek to communicate the Gospel as Jesus did by all means, in all places, at all times and encourage all followers of Jesus to do likewise.

3. Conversion and the new birth.[29]

Therefore we will expect to see the Holy Spirit bringing people out of the kingdom of darkness and into the Kingdom of God.

4. The existence of the church, Jesus' new Messianic community, which unites in love young and old, rich and poor and people from all ethnic groups.

Therefore we pray and expect the church to be a faithful, although imperfect picture of Christ's coming Kingdom—a strikingly different community where the world's brokenness and sinful dividing walls are being overcome.

5. Deliverance from the forces of evil.[30]

We take seriously the power of evil in human affairs: in people's personal behavior, in the godlessness, injustice and inhumanity seen in every culture, and in occult practices.

Therefore we will minister in the name of Jesus to all who are under the influence of the devil, challenging the faulty teachings, world views, unjust social structures, and cultural and cultic practices that oppress men, women and children today.

6. The Holy Spirit working in power.[31]

We expect to see God transforming people, performing miracles and healings today, and sustaining people in their suffering.

Therefore we will seek to be willing vessels through whom the Holy Spirit can demonstrate that the Kingdom of God is amongst us.

7. The fruit of the Holy Spirit in the lives of people.[32]

Therefore we pray earnestly that all who confess and follow Christ be transformed from day to day into His image and likeness from one degree of glory to another.[33]

8. A courageous, joyous bearing of suffering for righteousness' sake.[34]

Therefore, as Jesus suffered, we will not be surprised if suffering comes to us.

Entering the Kingdom of God

1. We believe that persons enter the kingdom of God not by works and human effort but by the unmerited grace of divine forgiveness as they repent of their sins, trust in God's forgiveness accomplished at the cross, believe in Jesus Christ the crucified and risen Lord, and are born again by the Spirit.[35]

Therefore we do all in our power to urge women and men of all races to accept Christ, join his new community and submit every part of their lives to his Lordship.

2. We believe that faithful communication of the Good News of the Kingdom requires costly, incarnational identification with people whatever their need.[36]

    Therefore we commit ourselves to forms of kingdom witness that minister to the whole person in his or her context and refuse to isolate proclamation from social involvement.

3. We believe that Jesus both joyfully welcomed all people into the Kingdom and also taught a particular concern for the poor, weak, and oppressed, even warning that it would be hard for the powerful, the wealthy or the influential of this world to enter it.[37]

    Therefore we resolve to practice a costly incarnational witness that demonstrates to the poor as clearly as Jesus did that the Gospel is for them and makes clear to the rich and powerful that they cannot accept Jesus' full Gospel without identifying with the poor the way that Jesus did.

The Kingdom of God and the Church

1. We believe that the Church is the community of the King, the Body of Christ, a visible evidence of his presence and God's chosen people to demonstrate the Kingdom in this world.[38]

    Therefore we will resist the constant temptation to conform to the brokenness of surrounding society, seek to renew the Church so that it is a convincing picture of Christ's dawning Kingdom, and mobilize all Christians to be salt and light in their local communities and around the world.

2. We believe that the local congregation has many interrelated tasks—worship, fellowship, nurture, education, proclamation and social engagement.[39]

    Therefore we will seek to develop biblically balanced, Spirit-filled congregations whose inward communal life and outward mission in the world faithfully reflect all that our Lord summoned the church to be and do.

3. We believe the Church transcends all denominational differences, and is

made up of women and men from all nations, cultures, ages and walks of life who are being transformed by the power of the Spirit of God.[40]

Therefore we will seek to demonstrate visibly love and unity in the worldwide body of Christ so that the world may believe that Jesus came from the Father.[41] Furthermore, the worship and life of each local congregation should affirm the heritage of each culture represented in its midst, allowing this diversity to enrich and enhance our service of God. In addition, since no local congregation can embrace all the diversity of the global body of Christ, we will express in our international relationships a partnership that demonstrates our equality in Christ.

4. We believe that Church growth is a normal outcome of seeking first the Kingdom of God.[42]

    Therefore where Christians do this, local congregations will grow and new congregations will be planted and established.

5. We believe that a loving, servant heart towards God and other people is the prime characteristic of being Kingdom people.[43]

    Therefore we seek to demonstrate this in our congregations, communities and all other areas of life.

6. We believe that the Church does not exist for itself but was established by Christ as a witness to the Kingdom of God.[44] Therefore in every area of Church life, we will make decisions not in terms of ecclesiastical self-preservation but rather in terms of what promotes the Kingdom.

7. We believe that God delegates authority to women and men in the Church, raises up men and women as leaders at all levels and expects those in such positions to act responsibly and with humility.[45]

    Therefore we encourage those in authority in the Church to model servant leadership, act with integrity, seek accountability, encourage teamwork, and nurture the spiritual gifts of everyone.

Opposition to the Kingdom of God

1. We believe that Satan is opposed to the Kingdom of God and that there is continual and hostile conflict between the Kingdom of God and the kingdom of darkness.[46]

    Therefore, expecting opposition to the establishment of the Kingdom of God in our own lives, in our families, in our local communities and in our world, we will boldly engage in the kind of spiritual warfare taught in the Scriptures.

2. We believe that the apostle Paul's teaching on the fallen principalities and powers refers to supernatural rebellious beings and the distorted social systems and unjust structures of society.[47]

   When Christians name the unrighteousness of social structures, they become a target of these powers which attack through human or demonic means.

   Therefore we combat the fallen powers by prayer, spiritual warfare, careful socio-economic analysis and political engagement. We reject onesided views that claim that we must either pray or do social analysis, either engage in spiritual warfare or political action. We will do all this in the power of the Spirit.

3. We believe that in the cross, Jesus disarmed the principalities and powers and broke down the dividing walls between groups that they create and reinforce.[48]

   Therefore we will seek to ensure that the church is a community which admits no division of race, class or gender, thus becoming a central witness to the principalities and powers that their dominion is over.[49]

4. We believe that Satan regularly seeks to seduce God's people to substitute false gospels for the truth Jesus revealed.

   Therefore we reject one-sided gospels of wealth, health, self-esteem and salvation through politics. We refuse to replace divine revelation with subjective experience, to substitute personal preferences for divine commandments, and to exchange management skills and marketing techniques for intercessory prayer and dependence on the Holy Spirit.

The Kingdom of God and Society

1. We believe that God now reigns, though often unacknowledged, over every area of life, that God restrains evil and promotes good in society, and that God desires his will to be done on earth as in heaven..

   Therefore we seek not only to live as Jesus' new redeemed community in the church, but also to work as responsible citizens influencing social institutions and systems toward the wholeness God intends.

2. We believe that the Kingdom of God transcends, judges and seeks to trans-

form all cultures. It is radically different from, and challenges the fallenness of the status quo in every society.[50]

Therefore, we will, using the standards of the Kingdom of God, affirm the unique strengths and continuing good of each culture, judge every society, and seek to transform distorted cultural values and evil social structures.

3. We believe that God wills human community to be based on stable family life and life-long fidelity between husband and wife. The Kingdom of God calls into being family-like relationships of brother and sister and mother and father and provides a model for church life which assists in building healthy families. The rule of Christ thus brings dignity and sanctity to both the single and married states.[51]

Therefore we will model and support fidelity within a permanent marriage covenant between one man and one woman, and chastity outside of marriage.

4. We believe that God has ordained a variety of institutions in society and that God wills that political rulers recognize their significant but limited role.

Therefore as we pray for all in authority, we will emphasise the importance of non-governmental institutions including church and family and seek the good of the social order by examining carefully what things are best done by government and what things are best done by intermediate institutions. We reject the political fallacy that the government should or can solve all problems, remembering that divine grace and personal conversion are needed to produce the transformed persons, and wholesome families that are so essential for a good society. We also reject the view that dismisses government's responsibility to promote the good and seek justice.

5. We believe that the Kingdom of God affects the whole of every person's being.[52]

Therefore we are concerned about physical, cultural, social, spiritual, intellectual and emotional wholeness in human lives.

6. We believe that God is the rightful owner and ruler of this universe, but he has given the care of the earth to men and women.[53]

Therefore we are committed to a wise and responsible stewardship of all creation and we are opposed to all forms of greed and abuse.

7. We believe that an understanding of the Kingdom of God will bring men and

women to a deeper appreciation of the peace and justice of God.[54]

Therefore we determine to act justly, search diligently for nonviolent approaches, and promote freedom, peace and justice in society.

8. We believe reconciliation is at the heart of the message of the good news of the kingdom and is God's ultimate intention for humanity[55]

Therefore, while recognizing that complete reconciliation among persons is impossible without reconciliation with God and thus that violence and hatred will continue until Christ returns, we nevertheless work for that partial reconciliation between hostile cultures, nations, races and ethnic groups that is possible now, knowing that God's will is peace on earth.

9. We believe the Kingdom of God encourages caring and sharing lifestyles as opposed to materialism and individualism.[56]

Therefore we urge cooperation rather than excessive competition, and oppose the consumerism and materialism of much of society. We are personally committed to living a sacrificial and simpler lifestyle.

The Kingdom of God and the Future

1. We believe that Jesus Christ will return and that it is God's intention to reconcile all things through Christ.[57]

Therefore we wait expectantly for the time when the full reign of the Kingdom of God will be seen and the whole creation will be healed and restored.

2. We believe that the Kingdom of God is both a present reality and a future expectation. It is both already and not yet fully. We live in the period between the inauguration and consummation of the Kingdom. At that consummation all the kingdoms of this world will come under the reign of Christ.[58]

Therefore we seek its demonstration here on earth while awaiting its full revelation in the future.

3. We believe that there is an important role for this earth in the future under the rule and reign of Jesus Christ the King.[59]

Therefore we will value not only the spiritual but also the material and care for the creation as a sign of Christ's coming restoration of all things.

Commitment to the Kingdom of God

1. We believe that commitment to the cause of the Kingdom of God will mean costly discipleship for people in terms of time, possessions, money and abilities.[60]

   Therefore we urge prayerful evaluation of priorities, mutual accountability, and sacrificial obedience and call Christians to evaluate everything they possess in relation to the Kingdom.

2. We believe that people were created to live within the kingdom of God and that they thrive under its rule.[61]

   Therefore, it is living by the principles of the Kingdom of God in the community of the King, that people reach their maximum potential and experience life in all its fullness. Thus the Kingdom of God is not a threat to humanity, but God's wonderful gift.

3. We believe that the Kingdom of God confers a new identity on everyone who enters it whatever their standing in life. It affirms their ability to contribute to their neighbors.

   Therefore we will encourage all members of the Church to see their work as service to God and to discover and exercise the gifts with which God has endowed them.

4. We believe that the Kingdom of God calls people to devote their talents to the service of the hungry, the stranger, the naked, the sick, the prisoners whom Jesus identified as his brothers and sisters.

   Therefore we encourage people to develop their God-given talents in order that they may risk them in the service of the poor, weak and marginalized.

Final Summation

As Christians gathered together from six continents, we affirm that Jesus' Good News of the Kingdom requires that we observe his Kingly rule:
in all things.
Therefore there is no human activity, no region of human endeavor which is beyond God's reign.
at all times.
Therefore we repudiate any distinction between the sacred and the secular which obscures that biblical truth that God is King of all times and places.

in all situations.

Therefore we urge all Christians to seek first the Kingdom of God in the home, in the Church, at work, in study, in their local community, during recreation and in all other activities of their lives as our highest priority in our lives.

as our highest priority in our lives.

Therefore we will not permit anything to distract or deter us from seeking first the Kingdom of God and His righteousness.

It is therefore our consensus and determined resolve, with prayer and the Holy Spirit's enabling, to commit ourselves to the outworking of these affirmations and commitments. It is also our prayer that all who read them will join us in this commitment.

Notes

1. Mark 1:14-15.
2. Matthew 6:10.
3. Luke 12:31; Matthew 6:33.
4. Psalm 95:3.
5. Genesis 1:27-28; Psalm 8:6-8.
6. Genesis 3.
7. Isaiah 9:6-7; Isaiah 65:17-25.
8. Matthew 9:35; Matthew 4:17-24.
9. Matthew 12:27-28.
10. John 18:36.
11. John 14:16-18: Acts 1:8; 1 Corinthians 14:1-5.
12. Phillipians 1:27.
13. Romans 1:1; Romans 15:16.
14. Ephesians 1:13.
15. Acts 20:24-25.
16. Acts 10:36; Ephesians 6:15.
17. Phillipians 3:7-8.
18. Galatians 3:26-28; Ephesians 2:11-3:6.
19. Revelation 11:15; 1 Corinthians 15:20-28.
20. Hebrews 2:14-15; 1 Corinthians 15:20-28.
21. Romans 8:19-21.
22. Revelation 21:22-22:2.
23. John 3:3-18; Mark 10:17-21; Philippians 2:9-11.
24. Matthew 28:18-20.
25. Luke 4:18-19.
26. 2 Timothy 3:16.
27. Matthew 18:28.
28. Mark 1:15.
29. John 3:3,5.
30. Matthew 12:28; Ephesians 6:10-18.
31. Luke 11:20; 1 Corinthians 12:4-11.
32. Galatians 5:19-26.
33. 2 Corinthians 3:18.

34. Matthew 15:1-12; 1 Peter 4:12-16.
35. John 3:3,5; Acts 2:38; Romans 1:17.
36. Matthew 25:31-46.
37. Mark 10:25.
38. Ephesians 1:22-23; Ephesians 3:10.
39. Acts 2:42-47; 1 Corinthians 12; Ephesians 4:7-11; Romans 12:4-8.
40. Galatians 3:28.
41. John 17:21.
42. Acts 2:42-47.
43. Luke 10:25-37; Matthew 20:25-28.
44. John 13:34-35; Ephesians 3:8-10.
45. Hebrews 13:17; 1 Timothy 3; Acts 18:24-26; Romans 16:1,7.
46. Matthew 12:28; Colossians 1:12-13.
47. Colossians 2:8; Ephesians 6:12.
48. Colossians 2:15.
49. Ephesians 3:8-10.
50. Galatians 3:28.
51. Matthew 19:4-6; 1 Corinthians 7.
52. 1 Thessalonians 5:23; Matthew 25:31-40.
53. Psalm 24:1; Genesis 1:28, 2:15; Psalm 8:6-8.
54. Micah 6:8; Romans 14:17.
55. Colossians 1:20; 2 Corinthians 5:18-21.
56. Acts 4:32-35.
57. John 14:3; Colossians 1:19-20.
58. Luke 17:21, 19:11; Revelation 11:15.
59. Romans 8:19-22; Revelation 21:24, 22:2; Zechariah 14:9; Psalm 2:8; Colossians 1:18-20.
60. Mark 8:34-38; Luke 18:22-20; Luke 14:25-33, Philippians 3:7-11.
61. Matthew 6:25-34.

CHAPTER 6

PLANTING COVENANT COMMUNITIES OF FAITH IN THE CITY

RICHARD GOLLINGS

With what shall I come before the Lord
*   and bow down before the exalted God?*
Shall I come before him with burnt offerings,
*   with calves a year old?*
Will the Lord be pleased with thousands of rams,
*   with ten thousand rivers of oil?*
Shall I offer my firstborn for my transgression,
*   the fruit of my body for the sin of my soul?*
He has showed you, O man, what is good.
*   And what does the Lord require of you?*
To act justly and to love mercy
*   and to walk humbly with your God. Listen!*
The Lord is calling to the city . . .

Micah 6:6-9a

The Story

It was the last year of my family's missionary term in Mexico City, after which we would move to Tijuana to plant a new church there.

Our mission church, Nuevo Nacitniento, had bought a house to use as a templo (church). We needed an alhañil (a brick and concrete worker) to direct the job of enlarging the templo's sturdy concrete roof. We had arranged for a maestro alhañil to help us, a man whose house we had helped to rebuild after the 1985 earthquake.

One day, two men appeared at the templo door saying that Don Jesus, the maestro alhañil had sent them. One look told us much about these men. They were small, with Indian features, rough, dirty clothing, and submissive demeanors. They came from an ejido, a government-organized communal farming village.

The Mexican government bought unproductive farmland and gave it to the peasants to farm as cooperative ejidos. Until recently, no one in Mexico could buy or sell ejido land. Because parents divide the land and give it to their children, each succeeding generation possesses less and less land. The typical ejido's crop fulfills only about forty percent of what its family needs. The peasant men migrate either to do underpaid farm labor on big Mexican or American agribusiness concerns, or serve as underpaid unskilled construction workers in the cities. With the ejido system, the Mexican government subsidizes Mexico's private agribusiness and urban development by maintaining a docile population of underpaid laborers.

The two men at our church door were yearly migrants to the urban construction industry. The maestro had sent them because they were good workers, were evangelicals, and had not eaten recently. Pastor Ruben immediately invited them in to share dinner. He gave them a free room in the templo, where his family also lived. He invited them to participate in church activities. When we were able to enlarge the concrete roof, they assisted the maestro albañil in directing the job, with church members (and one gringo missionary) functioning as the unskilled labor.

As we got to know each other better, they told us a sad story. They were Pentecostal Christians. There was a small church in their village, but the members could not support a pastor. Whenever these two men came to Mexico City for work, they would go to Pentecostal churches requesting preachers to come to their village to hold meetings. But city-dwelling preachers of their own denomination—the stream of Christianity that is supposedly the most effective in contextualizing the gospel for the poor of Latin America—would not go out to the "interior" to minister to their village. Unlike Pastor Ruben, no pastor had ever invited them in for a meal, let alone have them live in his home rent-free.

Reading the Context

This story illustrates an aspect of the church's idea of community for both members and non-members of the "household of God."[1] When people seek an experience of true community, will they find it in the church?

In every society, humans crave fellowship in some form. In the Old Testament, the search for a sense of community took on a particular social and ethnic form in the people of Israel. In the New Testament—especially in the Book of Acts—the church takes shape as a unique type of community, based on Jesus' words, "All men will know that you are my disciples if you love one another" (John 13:35).

Evangelizing and transforming a city requires enlightened church structures—local congregations—more than dedicated, hardworking mission structures. Mission structures will minister to people, but church structures must be present for personal growth, community fellowship, and the incarnation of Christ's love.

The question before us is not, "Is Christian ministry directed to the formation of community?" Instead, it is "To what kind of community is Christian ministry directed?" I believe that to address in a practical way issues of ministry in the city such as those examined in this book, the local church must recognize that it is a community formed by the covenants of God.[2]

Rereading the Scriptures

God called and formed his people by his covenants. In Genesis 15:7-21, we see his covenant with Abraham, an unconditional covenant. In Exodus 20, we have the first statement of the conditional Sinai covenant. The rest of the Pentateuch explains what the covenant means and what God expects of his human partners. The entire Old Testament shows the people of Israel struggling with the implications of their unique covenant. The prophets rephrase the covenant and its stipulations in contemporary terms, fearlessly identifying and condemning the people's rebellion. In Matthew 26:26-28 and its parallel gospel passages, God extends the new covenant in Jesus Christ to all humanity. This new covenant is unconditional to those who would join in it, but informed by the detailed Old Testament definition of God's covenants.

We are more familiar with contractual relationships than with covenantal ones in contemporary Western society. A contract is a legal document. Its major purpose is to limit the responsibilities of the partners to one another. Whether it is between humans or between a human and God, a covenant enlarges the mutual responsibilities of the partners because it invokes and identifies a supportive and loving kinship between them. Trust is the basis for this relationship, not competing self-interest. Mutual trust and faithfulness to their promises determine and shape the actions of the covenanting partners.

In the act of the Exodus and in the Sinai covenant God assumed the role of the go'el—the "kinsman redeemer"—to Israel. Through his own initiative, God bound himself to Israel as his relatives and kin, assuming obligations to them and requiring corresponding attitudes and behavior from them. As God's kin, reflecting his nature was Israel's obligation. In its separateness for God, Israel would incarnate God's justice and compassion, and worship him alone.

The Pentateuch exhaustively explains how this would work in practice, and the rest of the Old Testament shows how both parties act through Israel's history to make mid-course corrections. Micah 6:8 succinctly expresses the requirements God places on those who would be in covenant with him. Israel's relationship with God brought about the people's relationship with each other—their community.

The united worship of God and the mutual demonstration of justice and compassion would cement the people to one another and to God. But the covenant relationship God made with his people also included and enabled community obligations to strangers and outsiders. Israel had to treat strangers with compassion and justice "for you were aliens in Egypt" (Exod. 22:21). It would be the gravest of contradictions for people whom God had redeemed and adopted to become themselves oppressors of the poor.

As Israel developed over the centuries and interacted with the surrounding nations and cultures, it increasingly mimicked its neighbors in the development of oppressive and unjust social and economic practices. Israel also divided its spiritual loyalties. In the Sinai Covenant, God made Israel's rulers responsible for maintaining the nation's ethical standards. Instead, it appears that they led in the nation's spiritual degeneration. Even Solomon built the temple with Israelite forced labor.

This drift and degeneration called forth the office and anointing of the prophets. The prophets strongly directed their messages at Israel's sins against their covenant with God and with their neighbors. One can see a "theology-on-the-way" recorded in the Old Testament. It shows a struggle over the centuries between those who sought to concentrate power in the hands of a ruling class while turning the faith increasingly into ritual, and those led by the prophets, calling the nation back to its original covenant obligations.

Even through Israel's rebellion, degeneration, and punishment, God further clarified the ramifications of his covenant. The Israelite nationalists saw the Babylonian conquest as their final punishment and humiliation. Yet Jeremiah 29:1-13 tells them that Israel's covenant relationship with God calls and enables them to undertake covenant responsibilities (those of community) with the Babylonians, the outsider pagans who were their conquerors.

Through the sacrifice and blood of Jesus, the new covenant is unconditional, as Paul explains in Galatians 5. But, again, it echoes the demands of the prophets in setting the expectations for those in covenant with God, as in Matthew 5-7.

In Matthew 18:21-22, Peter asks Jesus, "Lord, how many times shall I forgive my brother when he sins against me? Up to seven times [and then I'm off the hook]?" This expresses a contract mentality, limiting one's responsibility Jesus responds, "I tell you, not seven times, but seventy-seven times [as many times as necessary]," expressing the true covenantal attitude.

In John 21:15-17, Jesus twice asks Peter, "Do you agape me?" Jesus was asking for covenantal love. But Peter responds, "You know, Lord, that I phileo you," promising a contractual love. Finally Jesus says, in effect, "Even if you only phileo me, still, feed my sheep," calling Peter to a covenantal understanding of their relationship.

Beginning with the image of a vine and its branches (John 15 and 16), Jesus gives perhaps the clearest New Testament explanation of what it means to be in covenant with God. He also explains that the covenanted human can live up to this covenant only because the Holy Spirit now lives in him or her.

Reading the Context

The most basic contextual fact is that power corrupts. As religions and churches become established by the power structures, the system tends to co-opt them. They end up either actively supporting the government and the powerful, like the Roman Catholic Church in Latin America, or passively supporting or permitting the status quo, like American Protestantism.

People have quickly watered down the concept of a covenant, especially in the religious realm. We bargain with the supernatural. This happened in Israel and now occurs in modern societies. We bargain for current and future benefits from God in return for minimal ritual acts on our part. It may mean doing certain good deeds or fulfilling religious obligations.

The following acts are valid transactions in Mexico: Getting drunk at the annual religious fiesta for your village or for the neighborhood's patron saint. Paying for a new paint job or for clothing for the community's idols. Paying the priest to do a ritual that placates the Virgin in heaven who then pays off God for you. Based on a medieval theology, this system justifies the old contractual arrangements and destroys the possibility of covenantal communities of trusting and loving faith.

In contrast to medieval (and Iberian) Roman Catholicism, the Reformation called Christianity back to its biblical and covenantal norms. These norms included personal faith, loving behavior, and a covenantal understanding of the church as a community of believers. This effort continued in the settlement of North America.

New England Puritans sought to extend the covenant to include the civil community. Baptists pulled away from the Puritans partly because of this issue, arguing that the biblical covenant community could only include those who joined it voluntarily. There was less concern in both communities with following a minutely defined body of doctrine. The sense of community with God and within the congregation as demonstrated by godly living and loving behavior was more important.

Although surprisingly few people joined in these covenant communities, many lasting social blessings came to the general population from the Puritans and Baptists as part of their covenantal sense of responsibility. As commerce strengthened the appeal of individualism, however, the church and the larger society weakened their focus on covenantal responsibilities and moved toward more contractual-style limited obligations.

Throughout the nineteenth century, Baptist churches—particularly on the expanding American frontier—used written covenants to guide their people in living up to their Christian calling. Some communities turned inward to focus on maintaining covenant purity, as others looked outward and led much community social action.

The twentieth century produced a frontal assault on the concept of the church as a covenantal community. The American cultural value of individualism-above-all has crippled the Christian's willingness to submit to the discipline of a covenantal community. The fundamentalist-modernist wars in the U.S. left evangelicals afraid to involve themselves in "social gospel" ministries.

Mexico has its own radical individualism and "insider-outsider" separation. Also, American missionaries of an-earlier age founded and continue to inform the attitudes of Mexican Baptist churches. After moving to Tijuana, I discovered that ministry in Tijuana involves living in the midst of divisive forces representing all the above perspectives. Whether from the U.S. or from Mexico, whether Protestant or Catholic, each viewpoint seems to militate against the search for covenantal community in Tijuana.

What are some contemporary models of church community and ministry that will help us develop the local church and its ministries in the desired direction? We can see the thinking and action of a contemporary urban Christian ministry being laid out along a continuum, as in Figure 6.1.

For a church living and working within its own context, "A" would include liberation theology, incarnated in the Roman Catholic base ecclesial communities that have grown in some parts of Central and South America. These communities exist because of their common struggle against the political, social, and economic powers that oppress the people. The members of these communities support one another morally, and struggle together to attain political, social, and economic goals.[3]

These communities demonstrate that Latin Americans, even the poor who are accustomed to being severely limited by authoritarian structures and culture, can find in Scripture and in committed communities the motivation and strength to address the needs of their society. This church model, however, too easily becomes a virtual mission structure (a sodality), existing primarily because of its sociopolitical and economic usefulness for change. While true spiritual transformation can result, the group's mission focuses mostly on the sociopolitical and economic realms.

In Tijuana, we can observe an instantaneous, easy, uninvolved version of purely socioeconomic action ("A" in the continuum—see Figure 6.1) in the many U.S.-based churches that come down briefly to build houses, distribute food and clothing, maybe hold a quick evangelistic meeting, and then immediately return to the U.S. These U.S.-based churches do not think in terms of follow-up for seekers and converts, or of forming partnerships with Mexican churches for mutual strengthening, much less of long-term covenantal relationships that foster solid community

Figure 6.1: Doing and being in urban ministry

A		B
To do		To be
Outward		Inward
Materialism		Evangelism
Political struggle		Spiritual struggle

Position B (see Figure 6.1) is "body life." This is not simply old-fashioned evangelical church as usual, focused only on evangelism and worship, preaching against personal sin, and avoiding political entanglements. Ray Stedman (1972) and later Peter Wagner (1974) developed the body life concept some time ago. The focus is on the spiritual end of the continuum, but with the members exercising their gifts to reach out in evangelism and active ministry to the physical and spiritual needs of community members.

A danger in the body life focus is the development of what Peter Wagner has called "koinonitis." Wagner describes it this way:

Koinonitis is a [church pathology] caused by too much of a good thing . . . Fellowship, by definition, involves interpersonal relationships. It happens when Christian believers get to know one another, to enjoy one another, and to care for one another. But as the disease develops, and koinonia becomes koinonitis, these interpersonal relationships become so deep and so mutually absorbing, they can provide the focal point for almost all church activity and involvement. Church activities and relationships become [introverted and self-seeking, rather than oriented toward mission in the community] (1979: 77, 78).

So "koinonitis" (or the inflammation of the koinonia) involves an overemphasis on internalized fellowship to the point of a loss of interest in, and compassion for, those outside the group. The openness about personal things and the egalitarianism of Stedman's body life ministry go against the grain of self-protection and competition evident in Mexican Protestantism. Yet we have seen committed caring, deep sharing, and powerful ministries of intercession develop in congregations in Mexico City and Tijuana that modeled covenantal community.[4]

Mexican evangelical churches generally demonstrate an introverted exclusivism that approximates a fortress mentality. Historically, this can partly be explained by Mexican cultural factors, the anticlerical Mexican government prohibiting social ministries by the church, the militant hostility of the Catholic church (Mexicans who consider it their Catholic duty still persecute, beat, and occasionally murder Mexican evangelicals out of love for the Virgin), and the competitive and divisive attitudes of U.S. and Protestant missionaries of an earlier generation. Rather than excusing the lack of covenantal community, this history should make more urgent the call to the development of covenantal community in our urban churches today.

A True Covenantal Vision

A truly covenantal vision and lifestyle in a church would combine the best of both of the continuum's poles (see Figure 6.1), yet would transcend the contractual level. Concerning "doing," the covenantal community would understand its calling and commitment to action for holistic blessing of the nations who do not yet know Jesus Christ. Concerning "being," the people of God would profoundly know that God calls them to be in covenant with him and with each other as a community with a God-given purpose, as shown in Figure 6.2.

Greenway and Monsma (1989) can help us with this. They point out four key aspects of urban ministry modeled by Paul and his coworkers. First, they taught a clear, concise doctrine of Jesus Christ, of judgment and salvation. Second, they described a moral system of behavior for the discipline of new Christians. Third, in organizing local churches, they promoted a high level of cohesion and group identity centered in a common confession. Fourth, the church experienced active fellowship—even amid persecution—giving it an atmosphere of growth, witness, and ministry.

Without a thorough teaching ministry, the Antiochan believers would not have matured into the kind of people their critics dubbed "Christians," and no urban strategy today can be expected to produce great fruits unless it includes in-depth instruction in the Scriptures, Christian life, and discipleship (Greenway and Monsma 1989:37).

An example of this is John Perkins of Voice of Calvary Ministries. Perkins returned to his hometown of Mendenhall, Mississippi, with the purpose of evangelism and church planting. Yet contrary to much urban ministry (including ours in Tijuana), evangelism preceded and empowered social action. Perkins did not start with outside funds or workers. Those whom God raised up as converts in Mendenhall became the backbone of Voice of Calvary ministries.

Evangelism creates the committed people, the concern for the needs of people and the broad community base from which to launch social action. Social action, in turn, fleshes out the Lordship of Christ, reaching people's spiritual needs through their felt needs and developing an indigenous economic base for the work (Perkins 1976:221).

Evangelism and church planting remained the priority. But as the church developed as a community covenanted together under Christ, the Christians also recognized their covenantal responsibility to address the problems of their neighbors.

Mission Action

If a local church were more convinced of its identity as a special community formed by its biblical covenant with God, how would it minister more effectively to members and the larger community?

Figure 6.2: Being and doing in covenant in urban ministry

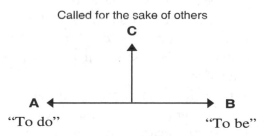

Called for the sake of others
C

A ← → B

"To do"   "To be"

"Being" and "doing" in covenant (covenantal community):
  • "Full covenant"
    • Community with outsider
    • Holistic
      • Evangelistic and cultural mandates

Scripture uses signs, story, and teaching to express, explain and model the concept of the covenant between God and his people. For a group or individual to exist in covenant with God, there are privileges (adoption, salvation, and empowering) and obligations (personal and group sanctification and ministry), particularly in the areas of justice, compassion and the worship of God alone.

God commissions a church to be salt and light to its population. It must demonstrate sanctification but also reach out into the community, to call people to the worship of the true God in Jesus Christ and serve with justice and compassion.

Charles Deweese calls for modern churches to write and adhere to covenants in the tradition of the Puritans and Baptists in America. Such a covenant would define behavior instead of doctrine and be informed by God's covenants in the Bible. Covenanting and the regular study of the meaning of God's covenants would militate against the individualism of today's Christians.

Clearly, we should not allow this covenantal relationship to become a new legalism. Instead, as in the case of the prophet Hosea, churches must base covenant on intimate, self-giving love that calls for the radical transformation of the entire covenant community (Deweese 1990).

Whether written or implicit, church covenants tend to become self-centered, anachronistic, and overly-specific boundary-setters. Just as Deuteronomy commands the king and people of Israel to read periodically, study and recommit themselves to God's covenant in its full meaning (including the people's covenant responsibilities toward the stranger), so the local church must repeatedly study the biblical covenants to understand and fulfill its covenant duties.

Christians would have to teach and model this vision of covenant community in evangelism, discipleship, and church teaching. They would have to teach and preach about it regularly in church and Sunday school. A curriculum like that of Shenk and Stutzman (1988) would help achieve this goal. The pastor must be convinced of its importance for the idea to take hold.

Traditionally, in Mexico a congregation looks for its pastor to be an autocratic leader. Part of the challenge would be for the pastor and the people to submit to a covenantal form of relationship, with pastor and people accountable to Jesus Christ, the Head of the church.

For now, it may be easier to inculcate the covenant community vision in newly planted churches than to cause such a radical change in established churches. This has been our experience in Mexico.

Retelling the Story

The Lord called us to leave Mexico City and go to Tijuana. Because of those two humble brothers who appeared at our church door in Mexico City, the church there eventually developed a powerful ministry of intercession and action for the physical and spiritual needs of its city and neighborhood.

What we had learned in Mexico City helped us start fresh in Tijuana. Once there, we discovered that the situation in Tijuana had interesting similarities and relationships with the situation in Mexico City—in spite of the geographic and cultural distance. At least it did not seem so in the case of Paco. His story resembles the "Andrew connection" of John 1:35-51.

We knew Paco in Mexico City when we had helped his older brother plant a church there. He was a Christian, but rather lazy and shiftless, with no passions beyond soccer. Soon after we settled in Tijuana, we received a letter from Paco asking if he could stay with us while he learned English, got a visa and moved to the U.S. We were not eager to reply.

One night, I returned to our house to find Paco on the doorstep! He lived in our home, got a factory job, and studied English. He also worked with me building houses in the El Florido area of Tijuana, holding evangelistic worship meetings, and doing pastoral visitation.

After living with us for a year, Paco returned to Mexico City and began to infect the youth of his home church with the idea that they could and should serve others. Before long, the youth group of that lower middle class church started work parties in their own neighborhood. Then they began to travel to small mountain villages to assist Baptist churches in construction, evangelism, and teaching. When the youth of a number of related churches from around Mexico met at this church for their annual retreat, they too spent the retreat ministering in social and spiritual ways to another poor church. This has become a tradition among these churches.

Paco's example served to energize his pastor brother to an enlarged vision. Later, that pastor, Miguel Altamirano, left a good position in Mexico City to move to the ugly outskirts of Tijuana and help us plant a church there. Paco accompanied his brother when they came from Mexico City, and now leads the youth of the Monte Horeb church in evangelism, discipleship, and ministry in the community.

In Tijuana, we planted a church in a migrant settlement by helping impoverished families build houses. The church that grew out of that ministry, Monte Horeb, and its pastor, Miguel Altamirano, carry out a number of servant ministries to their neighborhood, including house-building, relief distribution, and a Christian school. Experiencing ministry and seeing the Holy Spirit working in power through the congregation motivates the Monte Horeb church to lean more on Jesus and fulfill its part of the covenant.

Like the church in Mexico City, Monte Horeb is also learning that the church is a moral community, not just a voluntary association. A moral community's goals and gifts to its members are wrapped up in belonging, identity, transcendence, intentionality, and reciprocity. This is a covenant community of faith where people may hear the following confession:

I belong. I am recognized as an integral part of a distinct community, and I make a difference.

I am somebody. Those inside the community recognize me as someone special, someone important. To those outside, I have an identity in part because I belong to this group.

My church is bigger than you or me. God formed it. It focuses on him and he empowers it. It has a long history, stretching around the world and back through history.

My church was formed and exists for a purpose—to glorify God. God gave us our reasons for existing and they include caring for each other and for the world in his name.

We have responsibilities to each other and for each other. I have received freely and I must give freely. My brother and sister and I are responsible to live up to the terms of our covenant with God and with one another. I will help my brothers and sisters and they will help me. My church will nurture me so I can grow through receiving and giving.

We can reach the goal of building churches as true covenant communities. As a part of its covenant relationship with God, the congregation can develop a commitment to the city. We have seen halting steps in this direction in both Mexico City and Tijuana. When people came into the shanty town of El Florido, Tijuana, asking for the Monte Horeb church, they reported that people on the street tell them, "Monte Horeb? Oh, yes! It is the church up on the hill—the church that helps its neighbors."

Notes

1. See Lesslie Newbigin, The Household of God; Lectures on the Nature of the Church (New York: Friendship, 1954).
2. Cf. Paul D. Hanson, The People Called: The Growth of Community in the Bible (New York: Harper & Row, 1986).
3. Guillermo Cook (1985) describes the thought and work of base ecclesial communities in Brazil.
4. Jacques Ellul (1970) offers some interesting perspectives on the church in the city about this end of the spectrum. To Ellul, the modem city is antithetical to God. and his kingdom. We cannot live without the city, but it taints all of us. Although the church must exist and work in the city, nothing of lasting good will come until Christ breaks in and remakes and redeems the city himself.

Part II
Physical Hope

SECTION D:
HISTORY

It might have been the packs of stray dogs that made me think of it. Living for a month in the garbage village, I could not avoid them. There must have been hundreds, traveling in packs of ten or so, mangy, snarling, and fighting with other dogs. Although this was twenty-first-century Egypt, it was the dogs that made me feel that I was living in some sort of medieval time warp. Dogs were the first domesticated animal and have only recently been spayed or neutered by the rich. Packs of wild dogs have long been part of human settlements. Scenes like the ones I experienced above were part of the seventh circle of hell in Dante's fourteenth-century *Divine Comedy*. So watching that pack of skinny dogs scampering along crowded, dirt streets was like watching pieces of the history of human settlements.

In the garbage village—this little corner of the so-called modern world—dead rats line the streets. The smell of animal and human waste mixes with smells of baking pita bread, cooked lamb, and rotting garbage. Donkeys haul carts of trash or goods for sale. Pigs, goats, and chickens bustle about as if on a mission. Half-naked children run laughing through muddy streets. These sights and smells have been experienced time and again throughout history. I imagine the streets of any town of medieval Europe, Africa, or Asia to be nearly identical to this twenty-first-century garbage village, complete with the teeming packs of dogs. These scenes seem strange to me only because I have lived such an infinitesimally short time on a tiny, economically affluent island.

We are chained to a window that looks out on a tiny speck of humanity for only a moment in history. We can read a little about people and times that have passed into obscurity, but any available information could only have been recorded by the handful of literate people who have populated history. Of that handful of literate people who have ever lived, only a fraction of them chose to write something about their world. Of all that has ever been written, next to nothing has survived that is more than two hundred years old. Still less has been written or translated into the only language I can read: English. And yet without some basic understanding of history, we are doomed to effect little real, lasting change.

"History is more than entertainment, more than instruction, more than an enjoyable avocation. It is also a compass for voyagers in a storm-tossed sea."[1] Even though the story of slums has just begun to be written, we must learn what we can about how they have evolved and how cities and towns have operated before the advent of the modern slum community. Winston Churchill said that the farther back we look, the farther ahead we can see. If we are trying to look into the future of urban poor communities, then we need to take time to look back at their development.

After World War II a number of things happened in a short period of time throughout the developing world. First, over one hundred countries gained independence from colonial powers. Second, the medical revolution put a serious dent in global mortality rates. Third, the industrialization process went into full swing. And fourth, agricultural productivity increased dramatically. The results were wonderful and horrific. The following excerpt from *A History of World Societies* chronicles the head-spinning changes of the past one hundred years that have given rise to our impoverished urban reality today.

In his book *The Urban Transformation of the Developing World*, Josef Gugler briefly scans the urban centers in the Asian, Latin American, and African landscapes, noting the similarities and differences in how urban issues have played themselves out. Both of these readings survey the evolution of the urban world and give us important building blocks as we seek to understand how to pursue renewal and restoration for the millions who live in the global slum community.

Notes

1. Michael Bauman, *Historians of the Christian Tradition: Their Methodology and Influence on Western Thought* (Nashville: Broadman & Holman Publishers, 1995), p. 5.

CHAPTER 7

CHANGING LIVES
IN THE DEVELOPING COUNTRIES

JOHN P. MCKAY, BENNETT D. HILL, JOHN BUCKLER,
AND PATRICIA BUCKLEY EBREY

After the Second World War everyday life in the emerging nations of Asia and Africa changed dramatically as many peoples struggled to overcome the legacy of imperialism and build effective nation-states. Some of the changes paralleled the experiences of Europe and North America, but most observers stressed the enormous differences in development between the emerging nations and the industrialized nations. The new nations—along with the older states of Latin America—suffered widespread poverty, shared a heritage of foreign domination, and discerned a widening economic gap between themselves and the industrialized nations of Europe and North America. Thus many leaders and intellectuals in Asia, Africa, and Latin America felt that they were all joined together in an underlying unity, which was generally known as the Third World.

From the mid-1970s onward this sense of shared experience and Third World solidarity gradually broke down. Different countries and whole regions went their separate ways. Above all, some countries in East Asia experienced remarkable economic progress and emerged as middle- and lower-middle-income nations. Countries elsewhere were less fortunate. Much of sub-Saharan Africa in particular experienced economic retreat and great hardship. Thus the Third World fragmented increasingly into a wide range of so-called developing countries, and the global class structure became more complicated and diverse.

- How have the emerging nations of the Third World sought to escape from poverty, and what have been the results of their efforts?

- What has caused the prodigious growth of cities in Africa, Asia, and Latin America, and what does this growth mean for their inhabitants?

- How have thinkers and artists in the developing countries interpreted the modern world and the experiences of their peoples before, during, and after foreign domination?

These are the questions we will explore in this chapter.

The Emergence of the Third World

Beginning in the late 1950s many thinkers, journalists, and politicians viewed Africa, Asia, and Latin America as a single entity—the "Third World." Or, as some scholars would say today, they imagined and "constructed" Africa, Asia, and Latin America as a unity for effective analysis and action. For a long generation, in spite of all these countries' differences in history and culture, they did share some common characteristics. These characteristics linked them together and encouraged a Third World consciousness and ideology. There are several reasons for this important development.

First, many writers and politicians argued that virtually all the countries of Africa, Asia, and even Latin-America had experienced political or economic domination, nationalist reaction, and a struggle for genuine independence. This shared past gave rise to a common consciousness and a widespread feeling of having been oppressed and victimized in dealings with the West. A variety of nationalists, Marxists, and anti-imperialist intellectuals nurtured this outlook, arguing forcibly that the Third World's problems were the result of past and present exploitation by the wealthy capitalist nations. Precisely because of their shared sense of past injustice, many influential Latin Americans identified with the Third World, despite their countries' greater affluence. The term also came into global use in the cold war era as a handy way of distinguishing Africa, Asia, and Latin-America from the "First World" and the "Second World"—the capitalist and communist industrialized nations, respectively.

Second, in the 1950s and 1960s a large majority of men and women in most Third World countries lived in the countryside and depended on agriculture for a living. Agricultural goods and raw materials were the primary exports of many Third World countries. By contrast, in Europe, Canada, the United States, and Japan, most people lived in cities and depended mainly on industry and urban services for employment.

Finally, the agricultural countries of Asia, Africa, and most of Latin America were united by a growing awareness of their common poverty. By no means was everyone in the Third World poor; some people were quite wealthy. The average standard of living, however, was low, especially compared with that of people in the wealthy industrialized nations, and massive poverty was ever present.

Economic and Social Challenges

As postindependence leaders confronted the tough task of preserving political unity and building cohesive nation-states, the enormous challenges of poverty, malnutrition, and disease weighed especially heavily on rural people. In the 1950s and 1960s most Third World leaders and their advisers believed that rapid industrialization and "modernization" were the answers to rural poverty and disease. Industrialization and modernization would also kindle popular enthusiasm and thus serve nation building, which in turn promised economic self-sufficiency and cultural renewal. Moreover, having raised people's hopes in the struggle for freedom, these leaders had to start delivering on their promises if they were to maintain trust and stay in power. For all these reasons the leaders and peoples of the Third World set themselves the massive task of building modern factories, roads, and public health services like those in Europe and North America. Their considerable success fueled rapid economic progress.

Yet social problems, complicated by surging population growth, almost dwarfed the accomplishment. Disappointments multiplied. By and large, the poorest rural people in the poorest countries gained the least from industrialization, and industrial expansion provided jobs for only a small segment even of the urban population. By the late 1960s widespread dissatisfaction with policies of all-out industrialization prompted a greater emphasis on rural development.

Poverty

After World War II the gap in real income—income adjusted for differences in prices—between the industrialized world and the former colonies and dependencies of Africa, Asia, and Latin America was enormous. According to a leading historian, in 1950, when war-scarred Europe was in the early phase of postwar reconstruction, the real income per capita of the Third World was five or six times lower than that of the developed countries. . . . In the developed countries, a century and a half of Industrial Revolution had resulted in a multiplication by more than five of the average standard of living in 1950. . . . For the average Third World countries the 1950s level was practically that of 1800 or, at best, only 10-20 percent above.[1]

The people of these poor Third World countries were overwhelmingly concentrated in the countryside as small farmers and landless laborers.

Poverty meant, above all, not having enough to eat. For millions hunger and malnutrition were harsh facts of life. In India, Ethiopia, Bolivia, and other extremely poor countries, the average adult ate fewer than two thousand calories a day—only 85 percent of the minimal requirement. Although many poor countries fared better, in the 1960s none but Argentina could match the three thousand or more calories consumed in the more fortunate industrialized world. Even Third World people who consumed enough calories often suffered from the effects of unbalanced high-starch diets and inadequate protein. Severe protein deficiency stunts the brain as well as the body, and many of the poorest children grew up mentally retarded.

Poor housing—crowded, often damp, and exposed to the elements—also contributed significantly to the less-developed world's high incidence of chronic ill health. So too did scanty education and lack of the fundamentals of modern public health: adequate and safe water, sewage disposal, immunizations, prenatal care, and control of communicable diseases. Village women around the world spent much of each day carrying water and searching for firewood or dung to use as fuel, as they must still do in many countries. Infant mortality was savage, and chronic illness weakened and demoralized many adults, making them unfit for the hard labor their lives required. Generally speaking, people's health was better in Asia and Latin America than in the new states of sub-Saharan Africa.

The Medical Revolution and the Population Explosion

The most thoroughgoing success achieved by the Third World after the Second World War was a spectacular medical revolution. Immediately after winning independence, the governments of emerging nations began adopting modern methods of immunology and public health. These methods were often simple and inexpensive but extremely effective. One famous measure was spraying DDT in Southeast Asia to control mosquitoes bearing malaria, one of the deadliest and most debilitating tropical diseases. In Sri Lanka (formerly Ceylon), DDT spraying halved the yearly death toll in the first postwar decade—at a modest cost of $2 per person. According to the United Nations' World Health Organization, which helped provide medical expertise to the new states, deaths from smallpox, cholera, and plague declined by more than 95 percent worldwide between 1951 and 1966.

Asian and African countries increased the small numbers of hospitals, doctors, and nurses that they had inherited from the colonial past. Sophisticated medical facilities became symbols of the commitment to a better life. Some critics, however, maintained that expensive medical technology was an indulgence that Third World countries could not afford, for it was ill suited to the pressing health problems of most of the population. Such criticism eventually prompted greater emphasis on delivering medical services to the countryside. Local people were successfully trained as paramedics to staff rural outpatient clinics that offered medical treatment, health education, and prenatal and postnatal care.

Many paramedics were women, as many health problems involved childbirth and infancy, and villagers the world over considered it improper for a male to examine a woman's body.

The medical revolution significantly lowered death rates and lengthened life expectancies. In particular, children became increasingly likely to survive their early years, although infant and juvenile mortality remained far higher in the Third World than in rich countries. By 1980 the average inhabitant of the Third World could expect to live about fifty-four years; life expectancy at birth varied from forty to sixty-four years depending on the country. In developed countries life expectancy at birth averaged seventy-one years.

A less favorable consequence of the medical revolution was the acceleration of population growth. As in Europe during the nineteenth century, a rapid decline in death rates was not immediately accompanied by a similar decline in birthrates. Third World women continued to bear five to seven children each, as their mothers and grandmothers had done. The combined populations of Asia, Africa, and Latin America, which had grown relatively modestly from 1925 to 1950, increased between 1950 and 1975 from 1,750 million to 3,000 million. It was an unprecedented explosion, which promised to continue for many years.

The population explosion aroused fears of approaching famine and starvation. Thomas Malthus's gloomy late-eighteenth-century conclusion that population always tends to grow faster than the food supply was revived and updated by "neo-Malthusian" social scientists. Such fears were exaggerated, but they did produce uneasiness in the Third World, where leaders saw that their countries had to run fast just to maintain already low standards of living.

Some governments began pushing family planning and birth control to slow population growth. These measures were not very successful in the 1950s and 1960s. In many countries Islamic and Catholic religious teachings were hostile to birth control. Moreover, widespread cultural attitudes dictated that a "real" man keep his wife pregnant. There were also economic reasons for preferring large families. Farmers needed the help of plenty of children at planting and harvest times, and sons and daughters were a sort of social security system for their elders. Thus a prudent couple wanted several children because some would surely die young.

The Race to Industrialize (1950-1970)

Throughout the 1950s and most of the 1960s many key Third World leaders, pressed on by their European, American, and Soviet advisers, were convinced that all-out industrialization was the only answer to poverty and population growth. The masses, they concluded, were poor because they were imprisoned in a primitive, inefficient agricultural economy. Only modern factory industry appeared capable of creating wealth quickly enough to outrace the increasing number of people.

The two-century experience of the West, Japan, and the Soviet Union seemed to validate this faith in industrialization. To Third World elites economic history taught the encouraging lesson that the wealthy countries had also been agricultural and "underdeveloped" until the Industrial Revolution had lifted them out of poverty, one by one. According to this view, the uneven progress of industrialization was primarily responsible for the great income gap that existed between the rich countries and the poor countries of the postindependence Third World.

Theories of modernization, which were particularly popular in the 1960s, also assumed that all countries were following the path already taken by the industrialized nations and that the task of the elites was to speed the trip. Marxism, with its industrial and urban bias, preached a similar gospel. These ideas reinforced the Third World's desire to industrialize.

Nationalist leaders believed that successful industrialization required state action and enterprise. Many were impressed by socialism in general and by Stalin's forced industrialization in particular, which they saw as having won the Soviet Union international power and prominence, whatever its social costs. In Asia and Africa capitalists and private enterprise were often equated with the old rulers and colonial servitude. The reasoning was practical as well as ideological: socialism meant an expansion of steady government jobs for political and ethnic allies, and modern industry meant ports, roads, schools, and hospitals, as well as factories. Only the state could afford such expensive investments.

The degree of state involvement varied considerably. A few governments, such as communist China, tried to control all aspects of economic life. A few one-party states in Africa, notably Zambia, Ghana, and Ethiopia, mixed Marxist-Leninist ideology and peasant communes in an attempt to construct a special "African socialism." At the other extreme only the British colony of Hong Kong downgraded government control of the economy and emphasized private enterprise and the export of manufactured goods. A large majority of governments assigned the state an important, even leading, role, but they also recognized private property and tolerated native (and foreign) business people. The "mixed economy"—part socialist, part capitalist—became the general rule in the Third World.

Political leaders concentrated state investment in big, highly visible projects that proclaimed the country's independence and stimulated national pride. Enormous dams for irrigation and hydroelectric power were favored undertakings. Nasser's stupendous Aswan Dam harnessed the Nile, demonstrating that modern Egyptians could surpass even the pyramids of their ancient ancestors. The gigantic state-owned steel mill was another favorite project. These big projects testified to the prevailing faith in expensive advanced technology and modernization along European lines.

Nationalist leaders and their economic experts measured overall success by how fast national income grew, and they tended to assume that social problems and income distribution would take care of themselves. India, the world's most populous noncommunist country, exemplified the general trends. After India achieved independence in 1947, Mahatma Gandhi's special brand of nationalism was redirected toward economic and social rebirth through state enterprise and planning. Jawaharlal Nehru and many Congress party leaders believed that unregulated capitalism and free trade under British rule had deepened Indian poverty. Considering themselves democratic socialists, they introduced five-year plans, built state-owned factories and steel mills, and raised tariffs to protect Indian manufacturers. Quite typically, they neglected agriculture, land reform, and village life.

The Third World's first great industrialization drive was in many ways a success. Industry grew faster than ever before, though from an admittedly low base in Africa and most of Asia. According to the United Nations, industry in the noncommunist developing nations grew at more than 7 percent per year between 1950 and 1970, which meant a per capita rate of about 4.5 percent per year. This was very solid industrial growth by historical standards. It matched the fastest rates of industrialization in the United States before 1914 and was double the rates of Britain and France in the same years.

Industrial expansion stimulated the other sectors of Third World economies. National income per capita grew about 2.5 percent per year in the booming world economy of the 1950s and 1960s. This pace was far superior to the very modest increases that had occurred under colonial domination between 1900 and 1950. Future historians may well see the era after political emancipation as the era of industrial revolution in Asia and Africa.

Nevertheless, by the late 1960s disillusionment with the Third World's relatively rapid industrialization was spreading. The countries of Asia, Africa, and Latin America did not as a whole match the "miraculous" concurrent advances of western Europe and Japan, and the great economic gap between the rich and the poor nations continued to widen.

Also, most Third World leaders had genuinely believed that rapid industrial development would help the rural masses. Yet careful studies showed increasingly that the main beneficiaries of industrialization were business people, bureaucrats, skilled workers, and urban professionals. Peasants and agricultural laborers gained little or nothing. It was estimated that about 40 percent of the population in fast-growing, dynamic Mexico, for instance, was completely excluded from the benefits of industrialization. Moreover, the poorest countries—such as India and Indonesia in Asia, and Ethiopia and the Sudan in Africa—were growing most slowly in per capita terms. The industrialization prescription appeared least effective where poverty was most intense. Economic dislocations in the global economy after the 1973 oil crisis accentuated this trend, visiting particularly devastating effects on the poorest countries.

Perhaps most serious, industrialization failed to provide the sheer number of jobs needed for the sons and daughters of the population explosion. Statisticians estimated that the growth of Third World manufacturing between 1950 and 1970 provided jobs for only about one-fifth of the 200 million young men and women who entered the exploding labor force in the same period. For the foreseeable future, most Third World people would have to remain on the farm or work in traditional handicrafts and service occupations. All-out modern industrialization had failed as a panacea.

Agriculture and the Green Revolution (1960-1980)

From the late 1960s onward the limitations of industrial development forced Third World governments to take a renewed interest in rural people and village life. At best this attention meant giving agriculture its due and coordinating rural development with industrialization and urbanization. At worst, especially in the very-poorest countries, it deflated the optimistic vision of living standards approaching those of the wealthy industrialized nations and led to the pessimistic conclusion that it was possible to ease only modestly the great hardships.

Nationalist elites had neglected agriculture in the 1950s and 1960s for various reasons. They regarded an agricultural economy as a mark of colonial servitude, which they were symbolically repudiating by embracing industrialization. They wanted to squeeze agriculture and peasant producers in order to provide capital for industry. Thus governments often established artificially low food prices, which also subsidized their volatile urban supporters at the expense of the farmers.

In addition, the obstacles to more productive farming seemed overwhelming to unsympathetic urban elites and condescending foreign experts: farms were too small and fragmented for mechanization, peasants were too stubborn and ignorant to change their ways, and so on. Little wonder that only big farmers and some plantations received much government support. Wherever large estates and absentee landlords predominated—in large parts of Asia and in most of

Latin America, excluding Mexico, though not in sub-Saharan Africa—landless laborers and poor peasants who had no choice other than to rent land simply lacked the incentive to work harder. Any increased profits from larger crops went mainly to the absentee landowners.

Most honest observers were convinced that improved farm performance required land reform. Yet ever since the French Revolution, genuine land reform has been a profoundly radical measure, frequently bringing violence and civil war. Powerful landowners and their allies generally succeeded in blocking or subverting redistribution of land to benefit the poor. Land reform, unlike industrialization, was generally too hot for most politicians to handle.

Third World governments also neglected agriculture because feeding the masses was deceptively easy in the 1950s and early 1960s. Before 1939 the countries of Asia, Africa, and Latin America had collectively produced more grain than they consumed. But after 1945, as their populations soared, they began importing ever-increasing quantities. Very poor countries received food from the United States at giveaway prices as part of a U.S. effort to dispose of enormous grain surpluses and help American farmers.

Crops might fail in poor countries, but starvation seemed a thing of the past. In 1965, when India was urged to build up its food reserves, one top Indian official expressed a widespread attitude: "Why should we bother? Our reserves are the wheat fields of Kansas."[2] In the short run, the Indian official was right. In 1966 and again in 1967, when the monsoon failed to deliver its life-giving rains to the Indo-Pakistan subcontinent and famine gripped the land, the United States gave India one-fifth of the U.S. wheat crop. More than 60 million Indians lived exclusively on American grain. The effort required a food armada of six hundred ships, the largest fleet assembled since the Normandy invasion of 1944. The famine was ultimately contained, and instead of millions of deaths, there were only a few thousand.

That close brush with mass starvation sent a shiver down the world's spine. Complacency dissolved in the Third World, and prophecies of disaster multiplied in wealthy nations. Paul Ehrlich, an American scientist, envisioned a grisly future in his polemical 1968 bestseller The Population Bomb:

> The battle to feed all of humanity is over. In the 1970s the world will undergo famines—hundreds of millions of people are going to starve to death in spite of any crash programs embarked upon now. At this stage nothing can prevent a substantial increase in the world death rate.[3]

Countering such nightmarish visions was the hope of technological improvements. Plant scientists and agricultural research stations had already set out to develop new hybrid seeds genetically engineered to suit the growing conditions of tropical agriculture. Their model was the extraordinarily productive hybrid corn developed for the American Midwest in the 1940s. The first breakthrough came in Mexico in the 1950s, when an American-led team developed new high-yielding dwarf wheats. These varieties enabled farmers to double their yields, though they demanded greater amounts of fertilizer and water for irrigation. Mexican wheat production soared. Thus began the transformation of Third World agriculture—the so-called Green Revolution.

In the 1960s an American-backed team of scientists in the Philippines turned their attention to rice, the Asian staff of life; they quickly developed a "miracle rice." The new hybrid required more fertilizer and water but yielded more and grew much faster. It permitted the revolutionary advent of year-round farming on irrigated land, making possible two, three, or even four crops a year. The brutal tropical sun of the hot dry season became an agricultural blessing for the first time. Asian scientists, financed by their governments, developed similar hybrids to meet local conditions.

Increases in grain production were rapid and dramatic in some Asian countries. In gigantic India, for example, farmers upped production more than 60 percent in fifteen years. By 1980 thousands of new grain bins dotted the countryside, symbols of the agricultural revolution in India and the country's newfound ability to feed all its people. China followed with its own highly successful version of the Green Revolution under Deng Xiaoping.

The Green Revolution offered new hope to the Third World but was no cure-all. At first most of its benefits seemed to flow to large landowners and substantial peasant farmers who could afford the necessary investments in irrigation and fertilizer. Subsequent experience in China and other Asian countries showed, however, that even peasant families with tiny farms could gain substantially. Indeed, the Green Revolution's greatest successes occurred in Asian countries with broad-based peasant ownership of land.

The technological revolution shared relatively few of its benefits with the poorest villagers, who gained only slightly more regular employment from the Green Revolution's demand for more labor. Pakistan, the Philippines, and other countries with large numbers of landless peasants and insecure tenant farmers experienced less improvement than did countries such as South Korea and Taiwan, where land was generally owned by peasants. This helps explain why the Green Revolution failed to spread from Mexico throughout Latin America: as long as 3 to 4 percent of the rural population owned 60 to 80 percent of the land, as was still the case in many Latin American countries, the Green Revolution usually remained stillborn.

In the early years of the transformation sub-Saharan Africa benefited little from the new agricultural techniques, even though land reform was a serious challenge only in white-ruled South Africa. Poor transportation, inadequate storage facilities, and low government-imposed agricultural prices must bear much of the blame. More generally, the climatic conditions of black Africa encouraged continued adherence to dry farming and root crops, whereas the Green Revolution was almost synonymous with intensive irrigation and grain production.

The Green Revolution, like the medical revolution and first industrialization drive, represented a large but uneven step forward for the Third World. East Asian countries in particular were increasingly able to feed themselves and could support growing urban populations and more diversified economies. Yet even in the best of circumstances, relatively few of its benefits flowed to the poorest groups. These poor, who lacked political influence and had no clear idea about what needed to be done, increasingly longed to escape from ill-paid, irregular work in somebody else's fields. For many of the strongest and most enterprising, life in a nearby town or city seemed a way out.

The Growth of Cities, 1945 to the Present

The changing lives of Third World people were marked by violent contrasts, which were most striking in urban areas. Shiny airports, international hotels, and massive government buildings were constructed next to tar-paper slums. Like their counterparts in the industrialized world, these rapidly growing cities were monuments to political independence and ongoing industrial development. They were also testimonials to increasing population, limited opportunities in the countryside, and neocolonial influence. Runaway urban growth became a distinctive feature of the developing countries.

Rapid Urbanization

The cities of the Third World expanded at an astonishing pace after the Second World War. Many doubled and some even tripled in size in a single decade. The Algerian city of Algiers jumped from 300,000 to 900,000 between 1950 and 1960; Accra in Ghana, Lima in Peru, and Nairobi in Kenya grew just as fast. Moreover, rapid urban growth continued. The less-developed countries became far more urbanized in recent times than most people realized. In Latin America three out of five people lived in towns and cities by 1975; in Asia and Africa one in four people lived in an urban area by the same year.

The urban explosion continued in the 1980s, so that by 1990 fully 60 percent of the planet's city dwellers lived in the cities of Africa, Asia, and Latin America, according to United Nations estimates. Rapid urbanization in the developing countries represented a tremendous historical change. As recently as 1920, three out of every four of the world's urban inhabitants were concentrated in Europe and North America.

In most of the developing world the largest cities grew fastest. Gigantic "supercities" of 2 million to 10 million persons arose. It was expected that in the year 2000 about one-half of the urban population of Africa and Latin America would live in thirty-four very large agglomerations containing more than 5 million people. The capital city often emerged as the all-powerful urban center, encompassing all the important elite groups and dwarfing smaller cities as well as villages. Mexico City, for example, grew from 3 million to 12 million people between 1950 and 1975, and it was expected to have about 22 million people in 2000. The pattern of a dominant megalopolis has continued to spread from Latin America to Africa and Asia (though not to Asia's giants, China and India).

In the poorest countries of Africa and Asia the process of urbanization is still in the early stages, and the countryside still holds the majority of the people. Thus if United Nations projections hold true, the urban population will triple from 1.4 billion persons in 1990 to 4.4 billion in 2025. Such rapid urbanization has posed enormous ongoing challenges for peoples and governments.

What caused this urban explosion? First, the general growth of population in the Third World was critical. Urban residents gained substantially from the medical revolution but only gradually began to reduce the size of their families. At the same time, the pressure of numbers in the countryside encouraged millions to set out for the nearest city. More than half of all urban growth has been due to rural migration.

Another factor was the desire to find jobs. Manufacturing jobs in Third World nations were concentrated in cities. In 1980 half of all the industrial jobs in Mexico were located in Mexico City, and the same kind of extreme concentration of industry occurred in many Third World countries. Yet careful study shows that this accounts for only part of the urban explosion. In the words of a leading authority, "After about 1930, a new-phenomenon which might be termed 'urbanization without industrialization' began to appear in the Third World. This phenomenon very rapidly acquired an inflationary character and in the early 1960s began to present most serious problems of urban employment and underemployment."[54] In short, urban population grew much faster than industrial employment.

Thus many newcomers streamed to the cities for nonindustrial employment. Many were pushed: they simply lacked enough land to survive. Large landowners found it more profitable to produce export crops, such as sugar or coffee, for wealthy industrialized countries, and their increasingly mechanized operations provided few jobs for agricultural laborers. The push factor was particularly strong in Latin America, with its neocolonial pattern of large landowners and foreign companies exporting food and raw materials. More generally, much migration was seasonal or temporary. Many young people left home for the city to work in construction or serve as maids, expecting higher wages and steadier work and planning to return shortly with a modest nest egg.

Finally, the magnetic attraction of Third World cities was more than economic. Their attraction rested on the services and opportunities they offered, as well as on changing attitudes and the urge to escape from the traditional restraints of village life. Most of the modern hospitals, secondary schools, and transportation systems in less-developed countries were in the cities. So were most banks, libraries, movie houses, and basic conveniences. Safe piped water and processed food, for instance, were rare in rural areas, and village women by necessity spent much of their time carrying water and grinding grain.

The city held a special appeal for rural people who had been exposed to the seductive influence of modern education. One survey from the 1960s in the Ivory Coast found two out of three rural high school graduates planning to move to the city; only one in ten illiterate persons expressed the same intention. Africa was not unique in this. For the young and the ambitious, the allure of the city was the excitement and opportunity of modern life. The village took on the curse of boredom and failure.

Overcrowding and Shantytowns

Rapid population growth placed great pressure on existing urban social services, and in many Third World cities the local authorities could not keep up with the demand. New neighborhoods often lacked running water, paved streets, electricity, and police and fire protection. As in the early days of Europe's industrialization, sanitation was minimal in poor sections of town. Outdoor toilets were shared by many. Raw sewage often ran in streets and streams.

Faced with a rising human tide, government officials and their well-to-do urban allies sometimes tried to restrict internal migration to preserve the cities. Particularly in Africa, politicians talked of sending newcomers "back to the land" to reduce urban unemployment, crime rates, congestion, and environmental decline. In Africa as elsewhere, these antimigration efforts proved unsuccessful, and frustrated officials often threw up their hands in despair.

Surging population growth had particularly severe consequences for housing. As in Western Europe in the early nineteenth century, overcrowding reached staggering proportions in a great many Third World cities. Old buildings were often divided and redivided until population density reached the absolute saturation point.

Makeshift squatter settlements were another striking manifestation of the urban housing problem. These shantytowns sprang up continuously, almost overnight, on the worst possible urban land—dismal mud flats, garbage dumps, railroad sidings, steep hills on the outskirts, even polluted waterfronts. Typically, a group of urban poor "invaded" unoccupied land and quickly threw up tents or huts. Often beaten off by the police, they invaded again and again until the authorities gave up and a new squatter beachhead had been secured.

Squatter shantytowns, also known more positively as self-help housing, grew much faster than more conventional urban areas in most Third World cities. In the giant Brazilian city of Rio de Janeiro, for example, the population of the shantytowns grew four times faster than the population of the rest of the city in the 1950s and 1960s. As a result, the Third World's self-help settlements came to house up to two-fifths of the urban population. The proportion was particularly high in Asia. Such settlements had occasionally grown up in American mining towns and in Europe, but never to the extent they did in Latin America, Asia, and Africa. The Third World created a new urban form. The meaning of spontaneous self-help housing has been hotly debated. For a long time most observers stressed the miseries of squatter settlements—the lack of the most basic services, the pitiful one-room shacks, the hopelessness of disoriented migrants in a strange environment, the revolutionary discontent. However, by the 1970s some excellent studies stressed the vitality of what were seen as real neighborhoods, whose resourceful residents often shared common ethnic origins and kinship ties.

Moreover, the shantytowns themselves evolved. Poor but enterprising inhabitants relied on their own efforts to improve their living conditions. With much sweat labor and a little hard-earned cash, a family replaced its mud walls with concrete blocks and gradually built a real home. Or the community pressured the city to install a central water pump or build a school. Low-paid office workers in search of cheap housing sometimes moved in and continued the upgrading process. Nor were people who lived in squatter communities particularly attracted to revolutionary doctrines. In short, when self-help settlers were not threatened by eviction, they showed themselves capable of improving their housing.

Better understanding of spontaneous settlements led most governments to re-evaluate their hostility toward, them. Efforts to bulldoze them out of existence in the 1960s and 1970s were generally abandoned. Under pressure from these still primitive neighborhoods and their activists, some governments, particularly in Asia, turned to supporting improvements—gradually installing piped water, public toilets, lighting, and some paved streets. New self-help settlements continued to spring up on the urban fringes, but in the largest cities they became less desirable because poor transportation made getting to and from work a nightmare. As a result, more centrally located slums and old shantytowns became more congested and densely populated. They also became more attractive to government planners and capitalists, who sometimes combined to banish the poor and build new housing for the middle and upper classes.

Rich and Poor

After the developing countries achieved political independence, massive inequality continued, with few exceptions, to be the reality of life. A monumental gap separated rich and poor. In about 1975 in most developing countries, the top 20 percent of the people took more than 50 percent of all national income. At the other end of the scale, the poorest 60 percent received on average less than 30 percent of all income, and the poorest 20 percent got about 5 percent of the income. Thus the average household in the top fifth of the population received about ten times as much monetary income as the average household in the bottom fifth in the 1970s. This situation did not change significantly thereafter.

Such differences have been the rule in human history. The distribution of income in the Third World strongly resembled that of Europe prior to the First World War, before the movement toward greater equality accelerated sharply. It is noteworthy that types of economy—rightist or leftist, capitalist or socialist—have had a limited effect on shares of income. For example, in the 1970s income inequality was almost as pronounced in Mexico, with its progressive, even revolutionary, tradition, as in Brazil, with its rightist military rule.

Differences in wealth and well-being were most pronounced in the exploding towns and cities of the Third World. Few rich or even middle-class people lived in the countryside. Urban squatters may have been better off than landless rural laborers, but they were light-years away from the luxury of the urban elite. In Asia and Africa the rich often moved into the luxurious sections previously reserved for colonial administrators and white business people. Particularly in Latin America, upper-class and upper-middle-class people built fine mansions in exclusive suburbs, where they lived behind high walls, with many servants and protected from intruders by armed guards and fierce dogs.

A lifestyle in the "modern" mold was almost the byword of the Third World's urban elite. From French perfume and Scotch whisky to electronic gadgets and the latest rock music, imported luxuries, especially automobiles, became the unmistakable signs of wealth and privilege. In Swahili-speaking East Africa, the common folk called the elite wa Benzi, "those who ride in a Mercedes-Benz." Even in Mao Zedong's relatively egalitarian China, the urban masses saved to buy bicycles, while government officials rode in chauffeur-driven, state-owned limousines.

Education also distinguished the wealthy from the masses. The children of the elite often attended expensive private schools, where classes were taught in English or French and had little in common with the overcrowded public school classes taught in the national language. Subsequently, they often studied abroad at leading European and North American universities, or they monopolized openings at local universities. While absorbing the latest knowledge in a prestigious field such as civil engineering or economics, they also absorbed foreign customs and values. They mastered the fluent English or French that is indispensable for many top-paying jobs, especially with international agencies and giant multinational corporations. Thus elites in the developing countries often had more in common with the power brokers of the industrialized nations than with their own people, and they seemed willing tools of neocolonial penetration and globalization.

The middle classes of the Third World generally remained small relative to the total population in most countries, although some notable exceptions emerged in Asia in the 1980s and 1990s. White-collar workers and government bureaucrats joined the traditional ranks of merchants and professionals in the urban middle class. Their salaries, though modest, were secure and usually carried valuable fringe benefits. Unlike recent migrants and the rural poor, white-collar workers often received ration cards entitling them to cheap subsidized food.

An unexpected component of the urban middle classes until quite recently was the modern factory proletariat, a privileged segment of the population in many poor countries. Few in number because sophisticated machines require few workers relative to agriculture or traditional crafts, they were often well organized and received high wages for their skilled work. On the Caribbean island of Jamaica in the late 1960s, for example, aluminum workers in big, modern American-owned plants earned $60 to $65 a week. Meanwhile, cane cutters on sugar plantations earned $3 a week, and many laborers on small farms earned only $1 a week. Thus modern factory workers in the Third World tended to be self-satisfied.

In the 1980s and 1990s the growth of economic liberalism and global competition tended to undermine the factory worker's relatively privileged position. Many of the plants of the first industrialization drive, like those In Latin America in the 1930s, had grown up with strong unions behind tariff walls that protected them from more sophisticated producers in the wealthy industrialized countries. As barriers to trade came down, these factories had to cut costs in an attempt to survive. Factory workers often encountered lower wages, permanent layoffs, and plant closings.

More generally, the majority of the exploding population of urban poor earned precarious livings in a modern yet traditional "bazaar economy" of petty trades and unskilled labor. Here regular salaried jobs were rare and highly prized, and a complex world of tiny, unregulated businesses and service occupations predominated.

As in industrializing countries a century ago, irregular armies of peddlers and pushcart operators hawked their wares and squeezed a living from commerce. West African market women, with their colorful dresses and overflowing baskets, provided a classic example of this pattern. Sweatshops and home-based workers manufactured cheap goods for popular consumption. Maids, prostitutes, small-time crooks, and unemployed former students sold all kinds of services. This old-yet-new bazaar economy continued to grow prodigiously as migrants streamed to the cities, as modern industry provided too few jobs, and as the wide gap between rich and poor persisted.

Migration and the Family

Large-scale urban migration had a massive impact on traditional family patterns in the Third World. Particularly in Africa and Asia, the great majority of migrants to the city were young men, married and unmarried; women tended to stay in the villages. The result was a sexual imbalance in both places. There were several reasons for this pattern. Much of the movement to cities (and mines) remained temporary or seasonal. At least at first, young men left home to earn hard cash to bring back to their villages. Moreover, the cities were expensive, and prospects there were uncertain. Only after a man secured a genuine foothold did he marry or send for his wife and children.

Kinship and village ties helped ease the rigors of temporary migration. Often a young man could go to the city rather easily because his family had close ties with friends and relatives there. Many city neighborhoods were urban versions of their residents' original villages. Networks of friendship and mutual aid helped young men (and some women, especially brides) move back and forth without being overwhelmed.

For rural women the consequences of male out-migration were mixed. Asian and African women had long been treated as subordinates, if not inferiors, by their fathers and husbands. Rather suddenly, such women found themselves heads of households, faced with managing the farm, feeding the children, and running

107

their own lives. In the East African country of Kenya, for instance, one-third of all rural households were headed by women in the late 1970s. African and Asian village women had to become unprecedentedly self-reliant and independent. As a result, the real beginnings of more equal rights and opportunities, of "women's liberation," became readily visible in Africa and Asia.

In Latin America the pattern of migration was different. Whole families migrated, very often to squatter settlements, much more commonly than in Asia and Africa. These families frequently belonged to the class of landless laborers, which was generally larger in Latin America than in Africa and Asia. Migration was also more likely to be once and for all. Another difference was that single women were as likely as single men to move to the cities, in part because there was a high demand for women as domestic servants. The situation in Mexico in the late 1970s was typical:

> They [women] leave the village seeking employment, often as domestic servants. When they do not find work in the cities, they have few alternatives. If they are young, they frequently turn to prostitution; if not, they often resort to begging in the streets. Homeless peasant women, often carrying small children, roam every quarter of Mexico City.[5]

Some women also left to escape the narrow, male-dominated villages. Even so, in Latin America urban migration seemed to have less impact on traditional family patterns and on women's attitudes than it did in Asia and Africa. This helps explain why the women's movement lagged in Latin America.

Growing Diversity Since 1980

The ongoing urban explosion was one of several factors promoting growing diversity in the developing world. First, the transformation of modest cities into gigantic agglomerations sharpened the contrast between life in urban areas and life in rural areas. This difference in experiences made individual countries and their citizens less homogeneous. Second, continuing urban expansion diversified further the class structure, expanding especially the middle classes and thereby strengthening the forces of democratic reform. Third, the growth of middle-income people was very uneven. It depended primarily on economic performance, which varied substantially by country and region beginning with the world recession of the early 1980s.

Momentous economic changes occurred in East Asia. The rapid industrial progress that characterized first Japan and then the "Four Dragons"—Taiwan, Hong Kong, Singapore, and South Korea—was replicated in China in the 1980s and most of the 1990s. After Deng Xiaoping took over in 1978 and launched economic reforms, the Chinese economy grew through 1993 at an average annual rate of about 9 percent. Average per capita income in China was doubling every ten years, three to five times faster than in successfully industrializing countries such as the United States and Britain before 1914. According to the World Bank, the number of very poor people in China declined by 60 percent after 1978. The spectacular economic surge of almost one-fourth of the human race helped to vitalize all of East Asia. Starting from low levels, first Indonesia and then India did fairly well among big countries; Malaysia and Thailand led the smaller newly industrializing countries. A vibrant, independent East Asia emerged as the world's economic pacesetter, an event of enormous significance in long-term historical perspective.

One key to China's success was the example of South Korea and Taiwan, which with Hong Kong and Singapore showed the way in East Asia. Both South Korea and Taiwan were typical underdeveloped countries in the early postwar years—poor, small, agricultural, densely populated, and lacking in natural resources. They also had suffered from Japanese imperialism and from destructive civil wars with communist foes. Yet they managed to make good. How was this possible?

Radical land reform expropriated large landowners, who were mainly Japanese or pro-Japanese, and drew the mass of small farmers into a competitive market economy, which proved an excellent school of self-reliance and initiative. As in Japan, economic development became a national mission in South Korea and Taiwan. Probusiness governments cooperated with capitalists, opposed strikes, and did nothing to improve the long hours and low wages of self-sacrificing workers. These governments protected their own farmers and industrialists from foreign competition, while also securing almost free access to the large American market. And like Japan, both countries succeeded in preserving many fundamentals of their interrelated Korean and Chinese cultures even as they accepted and mastered Western technology. Tough nationalist leaders maintained political stability at the expense of genuine political democracy

When China turned toward the market in 1979, it could build on the national unity and radical land distribution inherited from Mao. Introducing economic reforms gradually and maintaining many tools of economic regulation, China's Communist party leaders encouraged native entrepreneurs and also drew on the business talent of wealthy "overseas" Chinese in Hong Kong and Taiwan. They knew the world market, needed new sources of cheap labor, and played a key role in the emerging "Greater China." Harsh authoritarian political rule encouraged China's people to focus on "daring to be rich," as Deng advised them.

No other region of the Third World (or Europe or North America) came close to matching East Asia after 1980. Latin America had some bright spots, most notably Brazil and Argentina. But West Asia and North Africa, wracked by war, political instability, and low oil prices, experienced spiraling urbanization without much new industrialization or economic development. The situation in sub-Saharan Africa was particularly grave. Severe famines, bitter ethnic conflicts, and low prices for African exports of raw materials weighed heavily on the vast region, vivid testimony to the growing diversity in the developing world.

In the late 1990s lingering visions of underlying Third World unity appeared less fanciful once again. In 1997 the great boom in East Asia came to an end. Indonesia, South Korea, Malaysia, and Thailand experienced financial crashes and industrial decline that undermined China and worsened conditions in stagnating Japan. In August 1998 the financial crisis spread to Russia, threatened Latin America, and caused uneasiness in markets in Western Europe and North America. Frantic efforts to limit the global impact of the Asian economic crisis highlighted again the world's interdependency.

Mass Culture and Contemporary Thought

Ideas and beliefs continued to change dramatically in the Third World after independence. Education fostered new attitudes, and mass communications relentlessly spread the sounds and viewpoints of modern life. Intellectuals and writers, in their search for the meanings of their countries' experiences, articulated a wide spectrum of independent opinions in keeping with growing regional and national diversity.

Education and Mass Communications

In their efforts to modernize and better their societies after securing independence, political leaders became increasingly convinced of the critical importance of education. They realized that "human capital"—skilled and educated workers, managers, and citizens—played a critical role in the development process. Faith in education and "book learning" then spread surprisingly rapidly to the Third World's masses, for whom education principally meant jobs. Thus young people in the developing countries headed for schools and universities in unprecedented numbers. There still remained, however, a wide education gap between them and the rich countries, where more than 90 percent of both sexes attended school through age seventeen.

Moreover, the quality of education in the developing countries was often mediocre. African and Asian universities tended to retain the old colonial values, stressing law and liberal arts at the expense of technical and vocational training. As a result, many poor countries found themselves with large numbers of unemployed or underemployed liberal arts graduates. These "generalists" competed for scarce jobs in the already bloated government bureaucracies, while less prestigious technical jobs went begging.

A related problem was the "brain drain" in the developing nations: many gifted students in vital fields such as engineering and medicine ended up pursuing their careers in the rich countries of the developed world. For example, in the early 1980s as many Indian-trained doctors practiced abroad, mainly in advanced countries, as served India's entire rural population of 480 million. The threat represented by the brain drain helped explain why the Third World's professional elite received high salaries even in very poor countries.

In recent years many observers have concluded that the education drive, like its forerunner the industrialization drive, served the rural masses poorly. It sometimes seemed that its greatest beneficiaries were schoolteachers, who profited from the elite status provided by a permanent government job. Instruction was often impractical and mind numbing. The children of farmers generally learned little about agriculture, raising animals, or practical mechanics. Instead, students often memorized passages from ancient literary works and religious texts and spewed back cut-and-dried answers. No wonder children stayed away from schools in droves. Village schools succeeded best at identifying the exceptional pupils, who were then shipped off to the city for further study and were lost forever to the village.

Whatever its shortcomings, formal education spread with another influential agent of popular instruction: mass communications. The transistor radio penetrated the most isolated hamlets of the developing world. Governments universally embraced radio broadcasting as a means of power, propaganda, and education. Relentlessly, the transistor radio propagated the outlooks and attitudes of urban elites and in the process challenged old values.

The second communications revolution—the visual one—is now in the process of reaching rural people everywhere. Television is bringing the whole planet into the bars and meetinghouses of the world's villages. Experience elsewhere—in remote French villages, in Eskimo communities above the Arctic Circle—shows that television is having a profound, even revolutionary, impact. At the very least the lure of the city continues to grow.

Interpreting the Experiences of the Emerging World

Popular education and mass communications compounded the influence of the developing world's writers and thinkers—its purveyors of explanations. Some intellectuals meekly obeyed their employers, whether the ministry of information or a large newspaper. Others simply embellished or reiterated some received ideology, such as Marxism or free-market capitalism. But some intellectuals led in the search for meaning and direction that has accompanied rapid social change and economic struggle.

Having come of age during and after the struggle for political emancipation, numerous intellectuals embraced Third World solidarity, and some argued that genuine independence and freedom from outside control required a total break with the former colonial powers and a total rejection of Western values. This was the message of Frantz Fanon (1925-1961) in his powerful study of colonial peoples, The Wretched of the Earth (1961).

Fanon, a French-trained black psychiatrist from the Caribbean island of Martinique, was assigned to a hospital in Algeria during the bloody war for Algerian independence. He quickly came to sympathize with the guerrillas and probed deeply into the psychology of colonial revolt. According to Fanon, decolonization is always a violent and totally consuming process whereby one "species" of men, the colonizers, is completely replaced by an absolutely different species—the colonized, the wretched of the earth. During decolonization the colonized masses mock colonial values, "insult them, and vomit them up," in a psychic purge.

Fanon believed that the battle for formal independence was only the first step. Throughout the Third World the former imperialists and their local collaborators—the "white men with black faces"—remained the enemy:

> During the colonial period the people are called upon to fight against oppression; after national liberation, they are called upon to fight against poverty, illiteracy, and underdevelopment. The struggle, they say, goes on . . . We are not blinded by the moral reparation of national independence; nor are we fed by it. The wealth of the imperial countries is our wealth too. . . . Europe is literally the creation of the Third World. The wealth which smothers her is that which was stolen from the underdeveloped peoples.[6]

For Fanon national independence and Third World solidarity went hand in hand with outrage at the misdeeds and moral posturings of the former colonial powers. Fanon's passionate, angry work became a sacred text for radicals attacking imperialism and struggling for liberation.

As countries gained independence and self-rule, some writers looked beyond wholesale rejection of the industrialized powers. They too were "anti-imperialist," but they saw colonial domination as only one chapter In the life of their peoples. They were often activists and cultural nationalists who applied their talents to celebrating the rich histories and cultures of their peoples. And many did not hesitate to criticize their leaders or fight against oppression and corruption.

The Nigerian writer Chinua Achebe (b. 1930) rendered these themes with acute insight and vivid specificity In his short, moving novels. Achebe wrote In English rather than his native Ibo tongue, but he wrote primarily for Africans, seeking to restore his people's self-confidence by reinterpreting the past. For Achebe the "writer in a new nation" had first to embrace the "fundamental theme":

This theme—quite simply—is that the African people did not hear of culture for the first time from Europeans; that their societies were not mindless but frequently had a philosophy of great depth and volume and beauty; that they had poetry and above all, they had dignity. It is this dignity that many African peoples all but lost in the colonial period, and it is this that they must now regain. The worst thing that can happen to any people is the loss of their dignity and self-respect. The writer's duty is to help them regain it by showing what happened to them, what they lost.[7]

In Things Fall Apart (1958) Achebe achieved his goal by vividly bringing to life the men and women of an Ibo village at the beginning of the twentieth century, with all their virtues and frailties. The hero, Okonkwo, is a mighty wrestler and a hard-working, prosperous farmer, but he is stern and easily angered. Enraged at the failure of his people to reject newcomers, and especially at the white missionaries who convert his son to Christianity and provoke the slaying of the sacred python, Okonkwo kills a colonial messenger. When his act fails to spark a tribal revolt, he commits suicide. Okonkwo is destroyed by the general breakdown of tribal authority and his own intransigent recklessness.

Summary

As Third World leaders and peoples threw off foreign domination after 1945 and reasserted themselves in new or revitalized states, they turned increasingly inward to attack poverty and limited economic development. The collective response was an unparalleled medical revolution and the Third World's first great industrialization drive. Long-neglected agriculture also made progress, and some countries experienced a veritable Green Revolution. Moreover, rapid urbanization, expanding educational opportunities, and greater rights for women were striking evidence of modernization and fundamental human progress. The achievement was great.

But so was the challenge, and results fell far short of aspirations. Deep and enduring rural poverty, overcrowded cities, enormous class differences, and the sharp criticisms of leading Third World writers mocked early hopes of quick solutions. From the late 1960s onward there was growing dissatisfaction and frustration in developing nations, lessened only slightly by the emergence of China and East Asia as economic powerhouses. Thus, as Chapter 36 will show, in recent times many observers came to believe that the developing nations can meet their challenges only by reordering the global system and dissolving the unequal ties that bind them to the rich nations.

Notes

1. P. Bairoch, Economics and World History: Myths and Paradoxes (Chicago: University of Chicago Press, 1993), p. 95.
2. Quoted in L. R. Brown, Seeds of Change: The Green Revolution and Development in the 1970s (New York: Praeger, 1970), p. 16.
3. P. Ehrlich, The Population Bomb (New York: Ballantine, 1968), p. 11.
4. P. Bairoch, The Economic Development of the Third World Since 1900 (London: Methuen, 1975), p. 144.
5. P. Huston, Third World Women Speak Out: Interviews in Six Countries on Change, Development, and Basic Needs (New York: Praeger, 1979), p. 11.
6. F. Fanon, The Wretched of the Earth (New York: Grove Press, 1968), pp. 43, 93-94, 97, 102.
7. C. Achebe, Morning Yet on Creation Day (London: Heinemann, 1975), p. 81.
8. C. Achebe, A Man of the People (London: Heinemann, 1966), p. 161.
9. V. S. Naipaul, The Mimic Men (New York: Macmillan, 1967), p. 38.

CHAPTER 8

REGIONAL TRAJECTORIES IN THE URBAN TRANSFORMATION: CONVERGENCES AND DIVERGENCES

JOSEF GUGLER

The last phase of the urban transformation is now unfolding in the less developed countries of the world. We used to lump most of them together as the "Third World," a term born in the 1950s from the desire of leaders from countries newly independent or soon to become independent, to establish a third force in world affairs, aligned with neither the capitalist "First World" nor the socialist "Second World." Only a handful managed to remain non-aligned. Third World" continued to be used, its original intent largely forgotten, to designate the less developed countries of "the South," outside the Eastern Bloc. With the dissolution of the "Second World" the term has become obsolete altogether.

"Third World" is a designation with clearer historical than current applicability. Yet, the tradition of scholarship that focuses on the less developed countries in the "Third World," to the exclusion of others, retains some unity and momentum. This collection remains within this tradition in delineating its purview. It covers much of Asia, Africa, and Latin America, but leaves aside not only highly industrialized Japan but also those Asian countries that were once part of the Soviet Union. Nor does it include in its purview those European countries that may be considered less developed. More than four billion people, more than three-quarters of the world's population live in the South thus defined. More than a third of them, more than one and a half billion people, live in urban areas.[1]

The less developed countries of Asia, Africa, and Latin America share, by definition, one characteristic: they are poor compared to most of the rest of the world. In many other respects there are significant differences. Here we intend to show that some of these differences can be delineated as distinct regional patterns.[2] We will focus on the urban dimension of these regional patterns and relate them to major differences in level of economic development, political economy, and cultural heritage.

Table 8.1 Demographic, Economic, and Human Development Indicators for Major Developing Countries and Regions, about 1990

Country/region	Total population (m)	Annual population growth-rates (%)		Total fertility[a] rate (%)	Urban population (% of total population)		Urban population annual growth-rates (%)		Percent of urban population in largest city	Urban sex ratio (males per 1000 females)	GNP per capita (US$)	GNP per capita annual growth (%)		Real GDP[b] per capita (US$)	Infant mortality (per 1000 live births)
	1992	1960-92	1992-2000	1992	1960	1992	1960-92	1992-2000	1990	1990-1	1992	1965-80	1980-92	1992	1992
China	1184	1.9	1.0	2.0	19	28	3.1	3.8	4	1083	480	4.1	7.6	1950	44
India	884	2.2	1.8	3.8	18	26	3.4	3.0	6	1119	310	1.5	3.1	1230	82
Indonesia	189	2.1	1.5	2.9	15	33	4.7	4.3	17	999	680	5.2	4.0	2950	58
Arab states[c]	230	2.6	2.9	4.8	30	50	4.5	3.5	31	—	—	—	—	4452	67
Africa South of the Sahara[c]	510	2.8	2.9	6.3	15	30	5.0	4.5	—	—	559	1.4	-1.8	1346	97
Latin America and the Caribbean[c]	450	2.4	1.8	3.1	50	73	3.6	2.4	24	—	2791	2.7	1.0	5730	45
Developing countries	4220	2.3	1.8	3.5	22	36	3.8	3.2	—	—	982	4.6	4.0	2595	70
WORLD[c]	5420	1.9	1.5	3.1	34	44	2.7	2.6	—	—	4534	—	—	5430	—

[a] The total fertility rate is the average number of children born to a woman during her lifetime.
[b] Real GDP is based on conversion in terms of purchasing power parity.
[c] The values for regions, developing countries, and the world are appropriately weighted, except for total population.

Sources: United Nations Development Programme (1995), tables 2, 4, 15, 16, 20, 39 (corrected by UNDP); urban sex ratios from United Nations (1994), table 6.

The distinct patterns of urbanization in different regions are shaped by the legacy of their urban history as well. This history differs markedly across the South. The roots of urbanization reach farther back in Asia than anywhere else. Subsequent urban developments in Africa and the Americas remained more limited until well after the imposition of colonial rule. The impact of colonialism varied with different imperial powers. To take only the most visible legacy: the distinct approaches of the Spanish, Portuguese, British, French, and Dutch affect the morphology and architecture of many cities in their former colonies to this day.

The Urban Transition

The South is urbanizing rapidly, but its various regions differ markedly in the level of urbanization they have attained at this time (Table 8.1). At one extreme, nearly three-quarters of the population of Latin America and the Caribbean live in urban areas, just about the same level of urbanization as in developed countries. At the other extreme, two-thirds or more of the population remain rural in China, India, Indonesia, and Africa South of the Sahara. The Arab states fall in between. Of course, these averages hide major variations among countries, e.g. between the highly urbanized Southern Cone of South America and Central America, and within countries, e.g. between the coastal provinces of China and inland regions.

The differences in level of urbanization among the regions correspond roughly to the differences in per capita income.[3] This is the case whether the conventional measure of GNP per capita is used or real GDP per capita, i.e. domestic product figures converted into US dollars in terms of purchasing power parity.[4] The causality in the relationship between levels of urbanization and of income is easily assumed to go from a larger, more productive urban population to higher incomes. The opposite causal relationship is, however, more plausible in a world where industrialization no longer provides the major thrust to urbanization. Higher incomes allow the concentration of resources in urban areas in terms of public bureaucracies, of elite and middle-class standards of living that support a large service sector, and of public works. To take the most dramatic example, the high levels of urbanization of oil-rich countries are a function not of the requirements of producing these riches but of the urban consumption they finance.

The very same distribution in terms of level of urbanization—China, India, Indonesia, and Africa South of the Sahara low; the Arab states intermediate; Latin America and the Caribbean high—obtained three decades ago. However, the differences in the rate of urban growth among the regions over the last three

117

decades are quite striking (Table 8.1). China, India, and Latin America and the Caribbean report less than 4 percent annual growth in their urban populations, Indonesia and the Arab states 4.7 and 4.5 percent annual growth respectively, and Africa South of the Sahara 5 percent, i.e. the population of African cities and towns doubled every fourteen years.

Natural population growth is a major element in urban growth, but rural–urban migration makes an even larger contribution in many less developed countries.[5] Thus the populations of India and Indonesia grew at about the same rate over the last three decades, but the cities and towns of Indonesia grew substantially faster than those of India.[6] And the Arab states and Africa South of the Sahara had similar population growth-rates, but urban growth was faster in Africa. Noteworthy are the small differences between China and India because they ran counter to the common assumption that China effectively restricted rural–urban migration.

A consideration of economic growth can serve to explain some of these differences. Thus GNP per capita in India grew at a markedly slower pace than in Indonesia between 1960 and 1992. The case of Africa South of the Sahara, however, calls for another explanation. The region experienced urban growth much faster than any other, while its economic performance was the worst among the regions. This peculiar constellation may be accounted for by two factors: the fastest rate of natural population growth and particularly pronounced urban bias.

Current urban-growth trends indicate distinct changes from the patterns of the last three decades (Table 8.1). In China, urban growth has accelerated even while population growth has declined. A booming economy has stimulated large-scale rural–urban migration that is no longer fettered by migration controls. Elsewhere urban growth is slowing down along with population growth. Africa South of the Sahara continues to have the most rapid urban growth: its urban population is expected to increase by more than half in the 1990s.

Urban concentration may be measured in terms of the proportion of a country's population living in its largest city (Table 8.1). China and India show a pattern typical of very large countries where several large urban centers dominate different regions. Thus Shanghai has only 4 percent of China's, Bombay only 6 percent of India's population, while Beijing and Tianjin, Calcutta and Delhi, with populations around ten million, are not much smaller. The Arab states, Africa South of the Sahara, and Latin America and the Caribbean present a sharp contrast. In each region a quarter or more of the average country's population lives in its largest city. The similarity among these three regions is all the more striking as their level of urbanization varies so widely.

Urban sex ratios vary considerably across the Third World (Table 8.1). In

China and India men outnumber women by a substantial margin. In Indonesia the urban sex ratio is balanced. Male-dominated urban populations are characteristic of most countries in the Arab World and Africa South of the Sahara. In Latin America, however, women outnumber men in every country, frequently by a substantial margin that cannot be explained by sex differentials in mortality.[7]

Rural–Urban Migration

Distinct patterns of rural–urban migration account for most of the differences in urban sex ratios across the Third World. Where men outnumber women in the urban population this is a function of men predominating in net rural–urban migration.[8] Some of these men are young and single, some stay in the city only for a short while. However, given widespread urban unemployment, the more common pattern is for these men to become long-term urban workers while leaving wives and children in their rural area of origin. As Weisner (1972) put it, they have "one family, two households."

The Industrial Revolution engendered the distinction of workplace and home, but the separation of men from their wives and children has been drastically magnified in less developed countries. Many men spend long years, commonly their entire working life, in the city and visit their village-based families as employment conditions and transport costs permit. But they are not the only ones to visit their rural homes. Many urban families maintain strong ties with a rural community which they continue to consider their home and where they anticipate retiring eventually. Such a pattern of "life in a dual system" can be quite enduring (Gugler, 1996).

In India, Indonesia, the Arab states, and Africa South of the Sahara large numbers of people pursue such temporary migration strategies: short-term migration, single long-term migration, or family long-term migration. In China, recent reforms have brought a large "floating population" of temporary migrants to the major cities. Large numbers of urban dwellers in these regions are not permanent residents but temporary sojourners who remain deeply involved in a rural community. Latin America presents a distinct contrast: temporary migration is very much the exception, characteristic of some Indian communities.[9]

Temporary migration is predicated on maintaining a rural base. The "dual-household" migrant leaves wife and children on the farm to grow their own food, perhaps to raise cash crops as well. The strategy is a function of high fertility and limited educational and earning opportunities for women. An added factor in some areas is the lack of compensation for those who leave land that is communally controlled. This is the case in much of Africa South of the

Sahara. The "dual-system" strategy entails social and economic investments that allow the family to return to the village. Either strategy assures the migrant of a measure of security, meager but more reliable than what the city offers most of its citizenry.[10]

Where women outnumber men in the urban population by a substantial margin, this reflects a pattern of permanent rural–urban migration in which women predominate. The distribution of this pattern—it has been long-established throughout Latin America and the Philippines—invites a cultural explanation for the "Latin" pattern. However, recent data indicate that this pattern is appearing elsewhere. This suggests a historical transition from a preponderance of men to a preponderance of women in net rural–urban migration: a "gender transition in rural–urban migration." It would appear that later marriage, reduced fertility, and greater independence are modifying cultural definitions of women's roles as wives and mothers and set them free to move. Never-married, separated, divorced, and widowed women usually are faced with limited rural opportunities and are attracted by cities that offer the better opportunities in terms of work as well as (re-)marriage (Gugler, 1994). Thus the contrast between India and most Arab and African countries where men predominate in urban populations, and Indonesia and Latin America where they do not, corresponds roughly to their different fertility rates (Table 8.1). The notable exception is China where fertility has been dramatically reduced by drastic government policies.

Major variations in the participation of women in manufacturing may also be related to the regional differences in fertility rates. In India, women hold only 9 percent of the jobs in manufacturing. And in the few Arab and African countries for which data are available, women usually hold only about 10 percent of the jobs in manufacturing.[11] In sharp contrast, between one-quarter and close to half of the labor-force in manufacturing is female in China and in the Latin American countries that provide information (International Labour Office, 1994).

Urban Social Organization

The history of urbanization and current patterns of migration have a major impact on urban social organization. In the cities and towns of Africa South of the Sahara that have grown so rapidly over the last three decades, and where there has been substantial return migration to rural areas, the great majority of residents have been born and raised in rural areas. In stark contrast, most urban residents are urban-born in Latin America where urban growth has been considerably slower and where there is little return migration. India had a similarly low rate of urban growth but substantial return migration. In Indonesia return migration continues to be common, while urban growth was faster. The Arab states had similar fast urban growth, and return migration was probably significant, at least in several of the larger countries. China had urban growth as slow as that of India and Latin America, but an assessment of the proportion of migrants in the urban population is wrought with pitfalls because there are at least three specific factors that make the Chinese experience distinct: low population growth implies a larger share of migrants in urban growth; the same implication follows from the campaigns that forced school-leavers to move to rural areas—to the extent that they have not returned since; on the other hand, there was probably very little voluntary return migration because it meant the loss of the privileged status of urban resident, a status exceedingly difficult to obtain under a regime of stringent migration controls.

First generation migrants tend to have significant ties with kin and "home people." Most were received by relatives or friends from home when they first arrived in town, some settled amongst them. Ties among first generation migrants of common origin are reinforced where they remain involved in their community of origin. Regional distinctions, in particular the different languages spoken by migrants from various parts of a country such as India—and nearly all African countries are similarly multilingual—foster social networks delineated in terms of region of origin. Such social relationships are reinforced by a common cultural idiom, typically quite distinct from any traditional legacy, to establish an ethnic identity. Such ethnic identities usually cut across divisions of class.

Religion affects urban social organization. Religious practice fashions social relationships and cultural identities. Fundamentalist movements, such as are found in most Arab states, tend to be particularly effective in this respect. A religious identity may coincide or cut across ethnic identities. In either case it becomes more salient if it articulates itself in opposition to other religious identities.

Kinship patterns vary across the Third World and differentially affect urban social organization. The rather independent nuclear family imported by the European colonizers in Latin America and the Caribbean provides only narrowly circumscribed support. When the family comes under stress, severe hardship for some of its members is common. Mothers who have been deserted, divorced, or widowed can expect little support from kin, children may be left to their own devices. In Africa and in India, in contrast, kinship support beyond the nuclear family is more readily available.

The Chinese experience has demonstrated the strong impact state policies can have on urban social organization. Job security and the public allocation of housing, in particular, entailed an unusually high stability in social relations within the neighborhood and in the work setting. There have been major reforms since

121

the 1970s, but job security has been maintained in state enterprises, and movement amongst the tenants of existing housing remains limited (Davis, 1996).

The Political Arena

Only a decade ago, most Third World countries were ruled by dictators. While their popularity varied, their power was usually solidly based on the support of the armed forces. Only in exceptional cases did revolutionary movements succeed in challenging them effectively.[12] The two revolutions that were successful in the late 1970s demonstrated the heavy sacrifices such victory required. In Iran, demonstrators took to city streets again and again to confront troops who were shooting to kill. And in Nicaragua, poorly equipped youngsters, led by Sandanista units, battled with the National Guard in one city after another.

Since the 1980s, major political transformations have taken place in a large number of countries. Again, as in Iran and Nicaragua, urban actors, more precisely actors in key cities, particularly capital cities, played the central role. But there was a remarkable break with earlier revolutions: street demonstrations and strikes sufficed time and again to persuade rulers to compose with the opposition, and casualties usually remained quite low. Many strong-men regimes were suddenly found to be quite fragile.

The urban character of these opposition movements, the pivotal importance of the capital city, and the political significance of physical control over symbolic urban space were dramatically demonstrated in China. The dissidents were urban-based, their activities focused on Beijing, and they occupied Tiananmen Square, the capital's most prestigious location, for a month and a half in 1989. However, unlike many other regimes in recent years, the Chinese leadership was not prepared to compose with the opposition, and opted for brutal repression.

There thus remain distinct regional contrasts. Indonesia, like China, is characterized by authoritarian rale, but India has maintained democratic practices since it became independent in 1948. All of the Arab states continue to be ruled by authoritarian regimes—isolated efforts at democratization foundered on the increasingly bitter conflict between secularizing and fundamentalist orientations. In Africa South of the Sahara, the democratization wave brought civilian governments and competitive elections to a number of countries, but some of the most repressive and exploitative regimes are found in this region as well. All of Latin America could pride itself on civilian rule by 1994.

Religious, caste, and ethnic conflicts are articulated in the urban arena. Opposing identities may draw on "tradition,", but they are fashioned in urban confrontations. Religious fundamentalisms are proclaimed by urban intellectuals and attract followings among the urban impoverished. Castes are redefined in changing urban labor markets. And while ethnic identities may refer to rural societies and draw on rural traditions, they are delineated, in some cases invented, in the urban encounter with other groups.

Distinct regional patterns may be discerned. India has known all three types of conflict. The salience of caste, and the conflicts it can engender, is specific to the country. There have been recurrent ethnic conflicts, typically between "sons of the soil," i.e. people from a city's hinterland, and "outsiders," i.e. migrants from more distant lands. And recurrent confrontations between Hindus and Muslims have claimed all too many victims since the country was partitioned in 1948.

In China, authoritarian rule has suppressed the expression of communal antagonisms. Liberalization, when it comes, may well set free the articulation of ethnic conflicts. Indonesia has seen murderous confrontations between Javanese and Chinese as well as conflicts between people indigenous to the islands. And there is a distinct prospect of a fundamentalist challenge to the political order.

In the Arab states, much conflict focuses on religion. In some countries secularizing and fundamentalist orientations are locked in bitter opposition. Elsewhere the adherents of different Muslim sects, who may also represent different regions, confront each other.

The great majority of urban residents in Africa are rural-born and most maintain ties with the village. Identities of origin thus are salient. Political conflict and competition over economic opportunities time and again take on ethnic connotations. Today, nearly every African country is deeply divided on ethnic lines. These divisions are exacerbated to the extent that regimes take on ethnic identities and major economic opportunities are seen to be monopolized by members of particular ethnic groups. In a few countries different ethnic groups are identified with Islam and Christianity respectively, and conflicts are increasingly cast in terms of religious belief and practice.

Latin America appears to be remarkably free of communal conflicts, with the important exception of the few countries where significant Amerindian populations have survived. In the absence of cross-cutting communal identities, stratification is all the more salient in the region. The substantial urban working class has organized for many decades in trade unions sufficiently strong to secure major benefits and to play at times a major role in national politics (Alves, 1996; Bergquist, 1986; Drake, 1988). The strength of squatter movements which have secured free land for a large proportion of the urban population in a number of Latin American countries is also specific to the region (Castells, 1983). These movements assemble people who are permanently committed to the city and seek both to improve their accommodations and to gain a measure of security for their old age.

In recent years a wide variety of urban social movements organized and demanded civil and political rights throughout much of the South. They derived strength from increasingly sophisticated media and the growing presence of non-governmental organizations. And the authoritarian regimes they challenged could no longer count on the Cold War reflexes of the major powers to support client regimes irrespective of their internal politics. A multitude of social movements appeared, disappeared, and emerged afresh in new forms—and increased the awareness and participation of the citizenry.[13]

The democratization process was particularly successful in Latin America. According to the Freedom House Survey (1994), every country in South America and Central America was "free" or "partly free" in 1993, while more than half of the countries in Africa South of the Sahara were "not free" in 1993. Relatedly, the urban protests sparked by the austerity measures adopted by many debt-ridden countries, typically under pressure from the International Monetary Fund, were most successful in Latin America. Stunned governments frequently rescinded or ameliorated their austerity measures, or provided compensations. In addition, protests sometimes initiated a successful movement to depose a government, or added a push to a teetering regime. Particularly notable, the protests contributed to persuade external actors—foreign governments, the International Monetary Fund, private bankers—to retreat from austerity policies, at least for large-debt countries (Walton and Shefner, 1994).

Quite different urban transitions are taking place in the various regions we here distinguish, and they are different again from the urban transitions the industrialized countries experienced a century ago. But the world keeps shrinking: ideas, people, and goods travel ever faster; the exchange of goods and services keeps increasing; and the political pressures of foreign states and international organizations are quickly felt across the globe. "Third World" ghettos have emerged in the industrialized countries, and ballot boxes are spreading in poor countries.

Notes

1. Kasarda and Crenshaw (1991) provide a comprehensive review of the burgeoning literature on what is still commonly referred to as Third World urbanization. Stren (1994-5) presents the findings of a large international project surveying past urban research and proposing an agenda for future research in Asia, Africa, and Latin America. For accounts of urbanization in some of the less developed countries not covered here, see Gugler (1980) on Cuba, Levine and Levine (1979) on Papua New Guinea, McGee (1988) on Malaysia, and Portes et al. (1994) on Costa Rica, the Dominican Republic, Guatemala, Haiti, and Jamaica.
2. Less developed countries can be usefully categorized in other ways. One obvious difference is in terms of levels of income, e.g. the countries here lumped together as Arab states range all the way from the Sudan with a real GDP of $1620 per capita to Qatar with an estimated

$22,380 in 1992. Another approach distinguished less developed countries committed to a socialist paradigm from the rest. Some of the work in this tradition had the merit of including Eastern Europe in its purview. Abu-Lughod, in Chapter 6, uses income criteria as well as political orientation to distinguish five types of Arab states.

3. Bradshaw and Noonan (1996) found Africa South of the Sahara and Latin America to be highly urbanized relative to GNP per capita in a cross-national analysis of the effect of investment dependency and pressures from the International Monetary Fund on the level of urbanization in less developed countries.

4. Even real GDP per capita fails to reflect welfare adequately. It is an average figure that hides more or less severe inequality in income distribution. Infant mortality, on the other hand, is quite sensitive to inequalities. Thus the infant mortality rate reported for China is remarkably low for such a poor country, even allowing for the effect of low fertility (Table 8.1).

5. Between 1975 and 1990, the contribution of rural–urban migration to urban growth amounted to 50 percent in nine Asian, 75 percent in four African, and 49 percent in eleven Latin American countries (Findley, 1993).

6. Mohan and Hugo, in Chapters 4 and 5, provide detailed discussions of urban growth in India and Indonesia.

7. For a discussion of differences in urban sex ratios among African countries, see Chapter 7; for more comprehensive data and a detailed discussion of the role of gender in rural–urban migration, Gilbert and Gugler (1992: 74-9).

8. I emphasize net migration, because women more commonly migrate at marriage than men and hence frequently predominate in gross migration.

9. For a detailed analysis of contrasting migration strategies among Amerindians in Peru and Mexico, see Moßbrucker (1996). For a more detailed discussion of these migration strategies, see Chapter 7.

10. Women hold about a third of manufacturing jobs in Botswana and Swaziland, countries where men prefer to find work across the border in South Africa.

11. The contrast with national wars of liberation is striking: they succeeded everywhere in throwing off colonial oppression eventually.

12. On the "new social movements" in Latin America, see Roberts (1996) who observes that new groups found an effective voice: Indian communities, the young and the old, and women.

References

Alves, Maria Helena Moreira (1996), "The New Labour Movement in Brazil," in Josef Gugler (ed.), Cities in Asia, Africa, and Latin America: Multiple Perspectives (Oxford University Press), repr. from Susan Eckstein (1989) (ed.), Power and Political Protest: Latin American Social Movements (Berkeley: University of California Press), 278-98.

Bergquist, Charles (1986), Labor in Latin America: Comparative Essays on Chile, Argentina, Venezuela, and Colombia (Stanford, Calif.: Stanford University Press).

Bradshaw, York W. and Noonan, Rita (1996), "Urbanization, Economic Growth, and Women's Labour Force Participation: A Theoretical and Empirical Reassessment," in Gugler (ed.), Cities in Asia, Africa, and Latin America.

Castells, Manuel (1983), The City and the Grassroots: A Cross-Cultural Theory of Urban Social Movements (Berkeley: University of California Press).

Davis, Deborah (1996), "Social Transformations of Metropolitan China, 1949-1993," in Gugler (ed.), Cities in Asia, Africa, and Latin America.

Drake, Paul W. (1988), "Urban Labour Movements under Authoritarian Capitalism in the Southern Cone and Brazil, 1964-83," in Josef Gugler (ed.), The Urbanization of the Third World (Oxford University Press), 367-98.

Findley, Sally E. (1993), "The Third World City: Development Policy and Issues," in John D. Kasarda and Allan M. Parnell (eds.), Third World Cities: Problems, Policies, and Prospects (Newbury Park, Calif.: Sage), 1-31.

Freedom House Survey Team (1994), Freedom in the World: The Annual Survey of Political Rights and Civil Liberties 1993-1994 (New York: Freedom House).

Gilbert, Alan and Gugler, Josef (1992 [1982]), Cities, Poverty and Development: Urbanization in the Third World, 2nd edn. (Oxford University Press).

Gugler, Josef (1980), "'A Minimum of Urbanism and a Maximum of Ruralism': The Cuban Experience," International Journal of Urban and Regional Research, 4: 516-34.

——— (1994), 'The Gender Transition in Rural–Urban Migration," paper presented at the World Congress of Sociology, Bielefeld, July.

——— (1996), 'Life in a Dual System Revisited: Urban–Rural Ties in Enugu, Nigeria, 1961-1987," in Josef Gugler (ed.), Cities in Asia, Africa, and Latin America: Multiple Perspectives (Oxford University Press); repr. rev. from (1991) World Development, 19: 399-409.

International Labour Office (1994), 1994 Yearbook of Labour Statistics (Geneva: International Labour Office).

Kasarda, John D. and Crenshaw, Edward M. (1991), 'Third World Urbanization: Dimensions, Theories, and Determinants," Annual Review of Sociology, 17: 467-501.

Levine, Hal B. and Levine, Marlene Wolfzahn (1979), Urbanization in Papua New Guinea: A Study of Ambivalent Townsmen, Urbanization in Developing Countries (Cambridge University Press).

McGee, T. G. (1988), 'Industrial Capital, Labour Force Formation and the Urbanization Process in Malaysia," International Journal of Urban and Regional Research, 12: 356-74.

Moßbrucker, Harald (1996), 'Amerindian Migration in Peru and Mexico," in Gugler (ed.), Cities in Asia, Africa, and Latin America.

Portes, Alejandro, Itzigsohn, José and Dore-Cabral, Carlos (1994), 'Urbanization in the Caribbean Basin: Social Change During the Years of the Crisis," Latin American Research Review, 29: 3-37.

Roberts, Bryan (1996), 'The Social Context of Citizenship in Latin America," in Gugler (ed.), Cities in Asia, Africa, and Latin America.

Stren, Richard (1994-5) (ed.), Urban Research in the Developing World, 4 vols. (Toronto: Centre for Urban and Community Studies, University of Toronto).

United Nations (1994), 1992 Demographic Yearbook (New York: United Nations).

United Nations Development Program (1995), Human Development Report 1995 (New York: Oxford University Press).

Walton, John and Shefner, Jonathan (1994) 'Latin America: Popular Protest and the State," in John Walton and David Seddon (eds.), Free Markets and Food Riots: The Politics of Global Adjustment (Oxford: Blackwell), 97-134.

Weisner, Thomas Steven (1972), 'One Family, Two Households: Rural–Urban Ties in Kenya," Ph.D. dissertation (Harvard University).

SECTION E
HEALTH

We first met Oma Romany and three of her little daughters at the orphanage run by the Sisters of Charity inside the garbage community. Oma Romany was dressed in the flowing garments of a rural woman from Upper Egypt. The Romany family was visiting the youngest child of the family, Demiana, who lived with the Sisters. So many of the children at the Sisters' orphanage were not orphaned but rather, were given to the Sisters because their parents could not afford to care for them. Oma Romany and her husband, Josef, had moved to Cairo with the hopes of finding work and escaping the harassment suffered by Coptic Christians in rural Egypt. What they found instead was poverty and sickness.

The Romany family had six children. One child was given to a home for the handicapped because of a birth defect or disability, which we did not fully understand, even with the help of Egyptian friends who spoke English. Demiana had been given to the Sisters of Charity shortly after birth, until the family could become more financially stable. The remaining four children (aged twelve and under) were reasonably cared for in their cinder-block and corrugated-tin, two-room home.

When we met Josef, he was suffering from some kind of kidney disease that regularly kept him home from work. As a tailor's assistant, Josef only made one or two dollars per day and could not afford to miss work. Nearly his entire wage was needed to pay the rent, so the family didn't eat very well and could not afford the medication he needed to get well. The sicker Josef got, the less he worked, the less he made, the less he ate, the sicker he got. To compound matters, Oma Romany had tuberculosis and also had trouble working steadily. Within a year of our meeting, Josef was dead and the family plunged deeper into poverty. It is doubtful now that this family will ever establish enough financial independence to care for the remaining children, let alone welcome Demiana back into the home.

In the developing world, people are fifteen times more likely to die of infectious diseases than people living in higher-income countries and thirty-three times more likely to die from childhood diseases like diphtheria or polio. The problem is exacerbated when living in substandard housing with poor water quality, infestations of vermin, no waste management, and high population density, as is often the case in slum areas. Where there is poverty and poor housing, there is often sickness and disease. Any attempt to address the quagmire of urban poverty must have a basic appreciation for the health issues that wrap themselves around the poor like a python.

The AIDS pandemic especially wreaks havoc in poor communities. Wherever there is despair, there seems also to be drug use and sexual promiscuity—breeding grounds for AIDS. Peter Okaalet lays out with clarity the interrelationship between poverty and AIDS. He suggests that addressing either part positively impacts the other. For a variety of reasons, the church (especially the church in the West) has been very slow to take a leading role in solutions to the pandemic. The poor do not have the luxury of ignoring AIDS. So it is with Jesus, who died on their behalf and counts himself among them. He walks among the AIDS-ridden communities of our world.

Bringing physical health was central to the earthly life of Christ. There is hardly a page in the Gospels where Jesus is not addressing serious health issues of his day. The blind, the lame, the lepers, the sick, the dying, and even the dead were restored to health by him. Something so fundamental to his ministry cannot be ignored by those who would claim to follow him. Stan Rowland reminds us in his chapter from *Transforming Health* that good health arises from harmony with God, self, others, and nature. He identifies the need for what he calls *community health evangelists*: people who will engage health issues at multiple levels. The transformation of slum communities cannot be achieved without significant attention to the health of those in these communities.

Notes

1. United Nations Habitat, *The Challenge of Slums: Global Report on Human Settlements 2003* (London: Earthscan).

CHAPTER 9

REDUCING POVERTY BY COMBATING AIDS

PETER OKAALET

It has been stated that an estimated 9 out of 10 people with HIV/AIDS live in situations marked by poverty, discrimination, and a subordinate status for women and children. Moreover, according to the World Health Organization and other authorities, poverty increases the vulnerability of human communities to HIV/AIDS. If we are to seriously address HIV/AIDS, then, we need to seriously address poverty and other related issues. In other words, by combating poverty we shall automatically be combating HIV/AIDS.

The World Council of Churches states that AIDS has become an issue affecting development. The pandemic imposes a heavy burden on the health care systems of communities, and the cost of treatment is often completely disproportionate to the incomes of the affected families. Therefore, HIV/AIDS needs to be addressed on its own merit.

I agree with this view. Indeed, we need a multipronged approach to fight both HIV/AIDS and poverty. To start with, poverty has always been a development issue. It has always been felt that if we address the development issues like the economy and education, other areas will automatically fall in place. This view may have to change. Now, health in general and HIV/AIDS in particular must be seen as development issues in their own right.

Every community on earth is feeling the effects of HIV/AIDS. I would argue that HIV/AIDS is actually leading to greater poverty than existed before the infection. In other words, a stable case of poverty is made worse by the onset of HIV/AIDS and its associated ill effects on individuals, families, communities, and nations.

Consider, for example, a case where a bank manager who is the breadwinner for his family suffers from HIV/AIDS-related diseases. By the time he dies he has spent most of the family's resources on medical care. His survivors now face a lower standard of living than they are used to. To cope with their lower status in the society and to relieve anxiety and depression associated with poverty, some family members may turn to using mind-altering drugs. They may inject drugs intravenously, thus predisposing and exposing themselves to HIV/AIDS infection. And they may resort to other high-risk behavior, such as prostitution, in order to make money to fill the void left by the breadwinner.

Poverty creates living conditions that promote disease. Without decent protection, many of the poor are exposed to severe weather, as well as to bacteria and viruses carried by other people, hence the high rates of infectious diseases among them. The chances are that the bank manager's family may slide from affluence to relative poverty to absolute poverty or destitution within a very short time, because HIV/AIDS and poverty form a vicious circle. Each stage of both poverty and HIV/AIDS is worse than the previous one.

By addressing HIV/AIDS now, therefore; we shall also be addressing a severe form of poverty that is exacerbated by the pandemic.

Understanding Poverty

Diverse Concepts of Poverty

When a person is reduced to poverty, he or she cannot afford the basics of life. As a result, poor people may be denied literacy, good nourishment, and good health. We need to distinguish the different types of poverty:

Relative poverty. Having fewer resources or less income than most others within a society or country.

Food poverty. Food consumption below a normative minimum level of nutrition that the human body needs for healthy growth and maintenance.

Income poverty. Lack of adequate income or expenditure to meet minimum basic needs. It is always measured in terms of income or expenditure.

Absolute poverty. Defined in monetary terms by a fixed standard such as the international one-dollar-a-day poverty line, which compares poverty levels across different countries. Someone in absolute poverty lacks basic human facilities such as adequate and nutritious food, clothing, housing, shelter, and health services. This is the most pervasive form of poverty, and it is what we need to guard against even as we fight the HIV/AIDS pandemic.

Vulnerability. A condition of risk. People not currently considered poor can become poor, while those at some milder level of poverty can move into extreme and/or absolute poverty. People who are not poor may become poor due to a number of factors; at present, one of the major factors is HIV/AIDS infection.

Indicators of Poverty and Well-Being

According to the UNICEF document "Challenges for Children and Women in the 1990s," there are two standard indicators of absolute poverty (UNICEF 1991). The head count index shows the percentage of a country's people living below the poverty line. It does not, however, show how far below. The poverty gap gives the percentage increase in total consumption that would be necessary to lift all the poor in a given country above the poverty line.

The World Bank distinguishes between "the poorest" and "the poor." Extremely poor people have annual incomes below US$275 per person. Poor people have annual incomes below US$370 per person. The World Bank estimates that there are 120 million extremely poor people and 185 million poor people in the world. The rest of the world's population is in the vulnerable category.

Another tool sometimes used is the Human Development Index, an attempt by the United Nations Development Programme to consider life in more than a single dimension. It measures human development as a composite of three basic variables: life expectancy at birth; educational attainment (measured as a function of both adult literacy and average mean years of schooling); and real GDP per capita (in purchasing power parity).

The State of the Poor

Whether we are talking of relative poverty, food poverty, or absolute poverty, we need to remember that poor people face many constraints in life. They include:

- Low status in society
- Poor infrastructure
- Declining government services
- Lack of income-earning opportunities
- Insecurity
- Political unrest
- Inability to access resources
- Lack of political power
- Illiteracy

Illiteracy means that the poor cannot obtain information that might help them to better their lot. They are deprived, as well, of good nutrition and a clean living environment, vaccinations and curative drugs, and testing and counseling services for HIV/AIDS.

Dignified living can be viewed as a basic human right. Dignity is the ability to meet socially perceived minimum basic needs. These needs are:

- Reliable food security

- Land holding/ownership
- Ownership of basic household items
- Peace
- Decent housing
- Adequate disposable income
- Access to knowledge and health

HIV/AIDS in Kenya

Poverty in Kenya

Kenya is ranked the eighth-poorest country in Africa. Most of the land is arid or semi-arid, and crop failure is common.

Income inequality is pronounced in Kenya. The richest 10 percent of Kenya's population received 47.7 percent of national income in 1998 (a rate of inequality nearly as high as Brazil's, where the richest 10 percent had 51.3 percent of income). According to a 1998 Kenyan government survey, more than 50 percent of the poor are located in 17 of the country's 60 districts. Around 15 percent of the poor live in four districts: Makueni, Siaya, Kitui, and Bungoma.

Women from poor households had a total fertility rate of 6.6 children per woman, compared to 6.1 children for their nonpoor counterparts. Only 14 percent of youth from poor households had completed secondary school, compared to 27.3 percent of nonpoor youth (Kenya 1998).

Incidence and Pervasiveness

The first reported case of HIV/AIDS in Kenya was in 1983 or 1984. Within the last 15 years or so, HIV prevalence has been increasing by leaps and bounds. Kenya's National AIDS/STD Control Programme estimates that in 1998, adult HIV prevalence stood at 13.9 percent (NASCOP 1999).

Last year the president of Kenya declared HIV/AIDS a national disaster. The situation is so bad that in some areas AIDS patients occupy 50 percent of hospital beds. The disease has not spared our schools. Some statistics indicate that almost 20 percent of schoolchildren in Kenya are HIV-positive. The death toll in the uniformed forces is alarming. This disease is not only destroying our past; it is also destroying our future.

A recent workshop on HIV/AIDS curriculum development organized by MAP International, a nongovernmental relief organization, was attended by tutors drawn from theological and pastoral training institutions in Kenya. I asked the participants: What makes us believe that HIV/AIDS is "real"? Here are some of the responses I received:

- "I have lost a relative to this disease—my cousin, in fact."
- "We lost a student to HIV/AIDS in our school two weeks ago."
- "I have buried several people who are said to have died of this disease."
- "The fact that we are here, attending a workshop on developing a curriculum on HIV/AIDS, means that this disease is for real!"
- "I understand from reliable sources that about 50 percent of the bedspace in the hospitals in the western part of Kenya is now occupied by HIV/AIDS patients."
- "There is already an escalation of the number of orphans in Kenya—as is true in other nations of Sub-Saharan Africa."

These responses point to one fact: AIDS is real. Its effects are already being felt in our midst, even infecting and affecting the church and the theological institutions in our society.

The Impacts of HIV/AIDS

The HIV/AIDS pandemic can no longer be ignored. It is a threat to humanity with wide-ranging and devastating demographic and economic impacts.

The *demographic impact* is marked by lives lost, especially of young people between the ages of 15 and 49. There are increasing childhood deaths, and a growing number of orphans. AIDS will have a significant impact on population size.

The *economic impact* of AIDS includes, on the one hand, losses to firms. In 1995 AIDS-related expenses came to US$45 per employee per year. By 2000 these expenses are expected to increase to US$120 per employee per year.

AIDS also has a severe impact on agriculture and the rural economy. Eighty to 90 percent of all Kenyans live in rural areas and make their living from agriculture. AIDS has affected commercial agriculture by decreasing the supply of both skilled and unskilled labor and by driving down the productivity of those who are working.

Equally dire has been the impact on smallholder farmers. The ravages of the disease have meant a decrease in the acreage under cultivation (for example, on sugarcane and vegetable farms) and corresponding loss of income.

The macroeconomic impact of AIDS results in part from the medical expenses associated with HIV/AIDS treatment. These include palliative care, which can run US$20 per patient per year, and the cost of dealing with opportunistic infections, ranging from US$30 to $200 per patient annually. Antiretroviral therapy costs between US$10,000 and $20,000.

Going beyond medical expenses, the macroeconomic impacts of the disease also include absenteeism, declining labor productivity, increasing training costs for new recruits, increasing labor turnover costs, and the cost of mortality.

Combating HIV/AIDS

Root Causes: What Drives the Pandemic?

Transience and loneliness are factors in spreading HIV over large populations and geographic areas. People on the move include migrant workers, refugees, and long-distance drivers. Prisons are another setting in which HIV can spread rapidly.

Violence contributes to the spread of HIV. Cases of rape and abduction are common in conflict situations.

Poverty fuels a sex industry in which commercial sex workers spread HIV, and is also associated with alcoholism and drug abuse.

Cultural and traditional practices that can foster the spread of HIV include wife inheritance, sharing of wives, "widow cleansing," rituals such as circumcision, and superstitious practices such as adult men having sex with virgins.

Finally, the stigma of HIV/AIDS leads to fear, shame, silence, and denial, all of which stand as obstacles to prevention and treatment of the disease.

Preventing Transmission

HIV/AIDS infection can be prevented in various ways.

1. Interventions to prevent transmission through heterosexual contact:

   - Promoting abstinence before marriage
   - Promoting faithfulness to one partner
   - Promoting the availability and use of condoms in special circumstances
   - Controlling other sexually transmitted diseases

2. Interventions to limit mother-to-child transmission:

   - Preventing infection in women
   - Reducing transmission during childbirth
   - Reducing transmission through breastfeeding
   - Reducing number of pregnancies
   - Antiretroviral therapy

3. Promotion of a safe blood supply.

4. Combined interventions.

5. The role of individuals. Individuals must undergo behavior change, thus:

    • The HEAD: "Don't be like the people of this world, but let God change the way you think" (Romans 12:2, CEV).
    • The HEART: "Trust in the Lord with all your heart and lean not on your own understanding." (Proverbs 3:5, NIV).
    • The HANDS: "Who may ascend the hill of the Lord? . . . He who has clean hands and a pure heart" (Psalm 24:3, 4).

6. Challenge of community mobilization efforts:

    • Keep land ownership alive at the community level
    • Achieve long-term sustainability
    • Strengthen household economic resources
    • Respond to village-driven needs
    • Implement relevant monitoring and evaluation systems at the community level
    • Support changes in sexual behavior

Resources and Institutions to Fight the Pandemic

When faced with a problem of the magnitude of HIV/AIDS, we sometimes forget that we have resources available for the fight. These include:

• Government
• Nongovernmental organizations
• Community-based organizations
• U.N. agencies, including UNAIDS, WHO, UNICEF, UNFPA, UNDP, and the World Bank
• The churches and other religious bodies
• Universities, colleges, schools, and other institutions of learning
• Workplaces, e.g., insurance companies, banks, and industries
• People living with HIV/AIDS

All these need to be unified as a common front to fight the scourge. However, this has not been the case in the past.

Why Have Past Approaches Too Often Failed?

According to UNAIDS, the Joint United Nations Programme on HIV/AIDS, past approaches have often failed because of:

- Lack of political commitment
- Failure to involve communities and churches/religious bodies, which have been given limited roles in policy and planning
- Reliance on short-term quick fixes that are not sustained
- Focus on single-shot interventions
- Top-down approaches
- Donors' many contradicting agendas
- Conspiracy of silence (mainly cultural and traditional beliefs), due to the stigma attached to HIV/AIDS
- Denial of the problem

For the fight against HIV/AIDS to succeed, we need some minimum common actions in each country. These actions must unfold at three levels: the political level, the institutional level, and the community level, involving the mobilization of all for the health of all.

The Church's Involvement In Combating HIV/AIDS

Edward Dobson, a U.S. pastor quoted in "Facing AIDS: The Challenge and the Churches' Response," captures the feelings of most church people when he asks: "Given the inadequate knowledge and even ignorance about HIV/AIDS in our churches, how many people will die in the next two years? What are we going to do to help our people?" (World Council of Churches 1997).

In fact, the Church can do a great deal, and should be in the forefront of the fight against HIV/AIDS, because:

- It has a long history of presence, proclamation, and persuasion
- It has well-developed structures
- It is self-sustaining
- It has a captive loyal audience that meets every week
- It has predictable leadership
- It cuts across geographical, ethnic, national, gender, and other barriers
- It has grassroots support and understands the language at the grassroots level
- It gives hope beyond the grave
- It has the Bible, a manual with tested and proven effectiveness in changing behavior and morals

Giving Hope: The Christian Response

The whole message of the Bible is about HOPE, LOVE, and the FUTURE. This what humankind is looking for. The Church is the custodian of this message.

Psalm 31:24: Be strong and take heart, all you who hope in the Lord.

Psalm 33:22: May your unfailing love rest upon us, O LORD, even as we put our hope in you.

The Church can lead by:

Understanding hope by knowing facts about HIV/AIDS:

Proverbs 23:18: There is surely a future hope for you, and your hope will not be cut off.

Discovering hope in the HIV/AIDS epidemic through our biblical foundations:

Romans 15:4: For everything that was written in the past was written to teach us, so that through endurance and the encouragement of the scriptures we might have hope.

Psalm 119:114: You are my refuge and my shield; I have put my hope in your word.

Psalm 130:5: I wait for the LORD, my soul waits, and in his word I put my hope.

Spreading hope by mobilizing the church to perform HIV/AIDS ministries:

Psalm 9:18: But the needy will not always be forgotten, nor the hope of the afflicted ever perish.

Developing hope by changing feelings and attitudes about HIV/AIDS:

2 Timothy 2:25: Those who oppose him he must gently instruct, in the hope that God will grant them repentance leading them to a knowledge of the truth.

Sharing hope through pastoral care to families and communities affected by HIV/AIDS:

2 Corinthians 1:7: And our hope for you is firm, because we know that just as you share in our sufferings, so also you share in our comfort.

Offering hope through HIV/AIDS pastoral counseling:

Psalm 62:5: Find rest, O my soul, in God alone; my hope comes from him.

Giving hope to parents and youth for AIDS-free living:

Psalm 71:5: For you have been my hope, O Sovereign Lord, my confidence since my youth.

Ministering hope through home-based care to people with AIDS:

Romans 12:12-13: Be joyful in hope, patient in affliction, faithful in prayer. Share with God's people in need. Practice hospitality.

Romans 15:13: May the God of hope fill you with all joy and peace as you trust in him, so that you may overflow with hope by the power of the Holy Spirit.

Conclusion

In September 1999, representatives of Christian development organizations and UNAIDS gathered in Gaborone, Botswana, to discuss collaboration around HIV/AIDS issues. The gathering adopted an "Affirmation of Presence and Continuity" that states in part:

> We are in an evolving epidemic of HIV/AIDS. Loss and death are real for all of us. Through the strength of fellowship we must face our fear of death. Only then can we celebrate life fully—now, and after death.

> We have a vision of the Church as a servant with the courage to truly participate in communities so as to realize shalom. We look forward to rethinking and reworking of the relationships and ethos of participating in community, care and change. We also look forward to a movement beyond ourselves and beyond our boundaries. We together are on a "JOURNEY INTO HOPE" . . . !

May this be our commitment, too, as we seek ways and means of reducing poverty through combating HIV/AIDS.

Bibliography
Kenya. 1998. "Economic Survey." Nairobi.
NASCOP (Kenya National AIDS/STD Control Programme). 1999. "AIDS in Kenya." 5th ed. Nairobi.
UNICEF 1991. "Challenges for Children and Women in the 1990s: Eastern and Southern Africa in Profile." UNICEF Eastern and Southern Africa Regional Office, Nairobi.
World Council of Churches. 1997. "Facing AIDS: The Challenge and the Churches' Response." WCC Study Document. Geneva.

CHAPTER 10

CHRISTIAN WITNESS THROUGH COMMUNITY HEALTH

STAN ROWLAND

Without Christ, we are only treating the symptoms of our separation from God, not the disease of sin. Our role in healing is to show how people can receive Christ and appropriate his healing wholeness.

Community health evangelism (CHE) is a strategy to restore harmony or wholeness in individuals. The purpose of CHE[1] is to transform individual lives physically and spiritually in local communities by meeting people at their point of need. These transformed individuals are then involved in transforming their neighbors, thereby transforming the community from the inside out. This is multiplied to other areas, eventually transforming an entire country for Jesus Christ

The CHE strategy combines three essentials: first, the integration of physical and spiritual ministry; second, multiplication through the training of national leadership; and third, community ownership of a program directed by villagers themselves with a minimum of outside resources.

Many community health projects aim to change the whole community. If the community as a whole does not participate or implement projects, then people are dissatisfied. Our emphasis is on transformed *individual lives*. We do not focus on the community as a whole but rather rely on the multiplication effect of neighbor influencing neighbor.

"My passport to heaven"

Early in a Uganda CHE project, we met a 92-year-old man named Samwell. Samwell greeted us outside his house and warmly welcomed us inside.

One of our staff trainers started sharing the gospel with Samwell using "The Four Spiritual Laws Picture Book." Samwell listened intently. By the end of our conversation, he was sitting on the edge of his chair with tears running down his cheeks.

When Samwell was asked if he would like to invite Christ into his life, he said, "Yes, yes." After his prayer, he held up the booklet, turned to us and said in English, "My passport to heaven. My passport to heaven."

Samwell then explained to us that normally by that time of day (11:00 A.M.) he was drunk and fighting with his neighbors. Now he understood why he had not started drinking that day. God had ordained this meeting.

More than a year later, Samwell remains strong in his walk with the Lord. He has not had another drink of alcohol since the day he received Christ. He has others read to him daily from the Bible and has memorized many Scripture passages. He cannot walk long distances and so is unable to attend church services. But he has built a small shelter outside his home under which he "preaches" to family members and friends.

Samwell was trained as a community health evangelist (also "CHE"), learning to tell his neighbors how they could live a healthy life, both spiritually and physically. He regularly visits his neighbors to share what he has learned. Because of the tremendous changes that have taken place in Samwell's life, especially the joy he shows, he has become a strong witness that Jesus Christ changes lives, both physically and spiritually.

Samwell exemplifies the reason spiritual values must be integrated with any village health program. The need for transformed lives is as necessary as the need for improved health care.

Biblical Basis

Christian community health care should be based on the Bible. We are commanded in Luke 10:27 to love God totally and to love our neighbors as ourselves. If we love our neighbors as ourselves, we will truly be concerned with their physical and spiritual welfare. We will want to help them live a more abundant, meaningful life here on earth and to share how they can have eternal life. Because of God's love for us, we desire to share that love with others.

From the very beginning of his ministry, Jesus was concerned about the whole person. In Luke 4:16-21, just after he returns home to Nazareth, Jesus reveals why he came: to fulfill the prophesy found in Isaiah 61:1-2 concerning the coming Messiah. The Messiah came to preach good news to the poor, bind up the brokenhearted, release the prisoners and proclaim the year of the Lord's favor. Jesus said that the Scripture was fulfilled that day. As the Scripture foretold, he came to deal with the whole person.

Jesus made a startling statement in Matthew 25:34-40. He asserted that as we give food and drink to those in need, take in strangers, clothe the naked, visit the sick and those in prisons, we are doing these things to him. Most of us would find it easy to do these things for Christ and even for our own family, but Jesus says we must do them for the lowliest of people, including those we don't know or who may even despise us. We are called to serve all people!

Jesus commands us in Matthew 28:19-20 to go and make disciples of all nations. We do this in the name of God and under his authority. This is not an option for the Christian; it is a command. In addition, Jesus says he will be with us now and always. We should do these things in God's strength made available through the Holy Spirit, not in our own power. The emphasis of Christ's Great Commission is on spiritual needs.

We are told in II Timothy 2:2 to find faithful men we can teach to teach others and who, in turn, will teach still others. This verse speaks of multiplication. This should apply both spiritually and physically, because we want to see the world physically improved as it is reached for Christ. As we pour our lives into faithful men, they will catch the vision for teaching others who in turn help others.

When Jesus walked this earth, he was concerned about the whole person. He healed the sick as he preached and taught. As Christians, we too must be concerned for the well-being of the whole person. This involves meeting both physical and spiritual needs. When Jesus sent out his twelve disciples to minister to others in Luke 9:1-2, he commanded them to heal the sick and to be concerned for the physical needs of others as they preached the Good News.

Good Health is Wholeness.

What is good health? God's Word uses the word *shalom* to mean peace, wholeness, soundness, well-being and good health. In the Old Testament, *shalom* is used when there is harmony between people and between people and things. To be in harmony means to live in peace with someone or something. To be in good health, a person must live in harmony.

But with whom must we live in harmony? First God, then oneself, then others, then nature. But what does it mean to live in harmony with God, oneself, others, nature?

Living in harmony with God begins by establishing a relationship with God through Jesus Christ. That relationship is nurtured by reading his Word, as we speak to God regularly in prayer, and as we praise God and give him the glory. We try to live righteously as we seek God's will and obey it. We look to him to meet our needs as we submit ourselves to God and desire to please him.

Living in harmony with ourselves means to be happy and at peace, to see ourselves as God sees us. It means to understand ourselves as we accept the reality of sin in our lives and realizing our need to ask forgiveness. Also, we know that good health is physical, spiritual, emotional and social well-being. Not to say disease will never attack us, but we will still be at peace no matter what the situation. We must know that many times our behavior and attitudes negatively affect our health, giving us ulcers, depression, headaches, and other ailments.

Living in harmony with others means to live the commandment to "love your neighbor as yourself" (Luke 10:27b). Our love of God should result in our loving others as we minister to their physical, spiritual, emotional and social needs. This means being helpful in every way possible. We have to realize, though, that others affect our health by what they do to us. They can give us diseases; we can give them diseases.

Living in harmony with nature means to know that God created the natural realm with its laws. Winds, earthquakes, and storms are part of the natural order. Viruses, bacteria, and parasites affect us. To have good health, we must live in harmony with the natural things around us. Also, we need to know that most of our physical ill health is caused by living in disharmony with nature, such as stripping our land of trees and causing drought and starvation. Pollution of our air and water causes many health problems. We must respect God's land and animals and not destroy nature around us.

If good health is living in harmony with God, ourself, others and nature, then what is illness? Illness is being out of harmony with God, others, self or nature. A break in fellowship with one of these causes illness.

Healing, then, is bringing restoration or wholeness to the person as we restore our relationship with God, ourselves, others and nature. Remember that Christ came to bring healing. The Old Testament deals with laws for being pure so we can worship God. Also remember that Christ died to make us whole.

In the case of Samwell, for much of his 92 years he was living in disharmony with God, himself, others and maybe even nature because of his drunkenness. He was continually harming his physical and mental health with alcohol. He harmed his social health because of his fighting with his neighbors. He did not know God, so he could not live in harmony with God. But Jesus changed him.

Without Christ, we are only treating the symptoms of our separation from God, not the disease of sin. Our role in healing is to show how people can receive Christ and appropriate his healing wholeness.

Does CHE Work Toward Wholeness?

The preventive side of health care is development. Christian development is helping people become all that God intends them to be. It brings lasting benefit and freedom when people develop themselves under God's direction. CHE is God's love in action.

The CHE strategy is one way that Christian development can take place in local villages. It begins by training nationals who are mature Christians and capable of teaching. A team of trainers, one of whom usually has a medical background, enter a cluster of villages where the CHE program is introduced. The villages then elect their own committee, which becomes the administrator of the program. The people also choose their own community health evangelists (again, "CHEs"—see note 1), who will be the front-line workers.

Training Community Health Evangelists

Both the local committee and the CHEs are trained over the ensuing six months by the training team. The CHEs are taught the following:

- To recognize the signs and symptoms of key diseases found in their area.
- To use simple, locally available methods for cure.
- To prevent disease in the first place involves protecting their water sources, building pit latrines, and growing and using the right crops.
- To put what they learn into practice in their home.
- To take what they learn and teach their neighbors.
- To trust Jesus Christ as their personal Savior and grow in their faith.
- To share this Good News with their neighbors.
- To follow-up and disciple new believers.

During this training, nearly all who are not already believers come to faith in Jesus Christ. Then a fascinating thing occurs. Since all committee members and CHEs are volunteer workers, those who do not come to Christ lose their motivation to go on with the program. Non-Christians drop out of the program, leaving an inherently Christian organization, which at the same time has the essential quality of being truly representative of the community. Thus the program is both community-owned and Christian.

Each CHE regularly visits up to 50 neighboring families, impacting more than 400 people. When CHEs share Christ with their neighbors, up to 40 percent accept Christ as their Savior. Since CHEs are sharing with their neighbors, it is easy for them to help others begin and mature in their walk with Christ.

CHEs use 17 picture books on physical and spiritual topics when they teach in homes; this helps to make all their learning transferable. A Bible study is used to deepen CHEs' walk with the Lord as they learn ministry skills that they put into practice in a chosen target area. The CHEs then lead their own Bible studies using the same materials.

Once CHEs graduate from the six-months' training program, they begin to share what they have learned with neighbors in their villages. For instance, they organize the people in their communities to protect local springs. This brings the people good water and greatly reduces sickness and death. Vaccination programs are begun in the villages. The villagers are encouraged to start vegetable gardens and improve the nutrition of their children. The same process is then begun in surrounding areas. Teaching success is not measured by the projects in and of themselves, nor by people putting into practice what they have learned. Again, the CHE process is concerned with multiplication. Success is measured in terms of people using what they have learned and then teaching others to do the same.

CHEs and the Community

Many Christian development organizations are excited to teach people to do something that changes their lifestyle. They see success when the people are using what they have learned in their daily lives. If they are planting gardens and eating the vegetables, this is success. But many times this focus becomes project-oriented. CHEs teach the people to plant a garden, eat the vegetables, teach their neighbors what they have learned, and then see their neighbors put the teaching into practice and teach their neighbors in turn. Simply putting into practice what a person has learned is good, but not good enough. Multiplication takes place through the use of transferable materials such as "The Four Spiritual Laws Picture Book" and 17 other picture books.

When people talk about health care, they are usually talking about curing a disease after someone has gotten it. But it is also important to talk about preventing the disease in the first place. The concept of cure versus prevention applies in spiritual truths as well. When people sin, they need to be cured of their sin, which is done by confessing to God and accepting his forgiveness. Sin can be prevented from entering our lives by reading and memorizing God's Word, breathing spiritually[2] and praying.

Available curative care is critical to the success of a CHE program. But such clinics do not need to be run by the same organization doing CHE. We are more concerned with prevention than cure, although the CHEs know how to deal with a problem when it affects others. Many of our projects have a clinic that acts as a training and referral center for nearby CHE projects.

A foundational principle for a CHE program is that the community sees the project as their own, not as started by outsiders. Too many times organizations have come from the outside to do something for the people, but when the outsiders leave, their accomplishments disintegrate; there is no sustainability. The people expect the outsiders to provide the funds, parts or labor to maintain or repair the project.

When outsiders do things for people in a community, the people always see what has been done as belonging to the outsiders. From the beginning, the emphasis must be on the community saying, This is ours and we will make it happen. We need to enable people to take more responsibility for their health, under God's direction.

If the program is to continue after the training team leaves, it is critical to involve a cross-section of the community, the broader the better. Otherwise, one small group within the community may be seen as controlling the project, and the rest of the community sees the project as belonging to that group. If the community as a whole never takes responsibility for the project, the likelihood of its sustainability decreases.

To easily implement CHE, there need to be training materials to train the three groups of people involved in a project: the trainers, committee members and CHEs. One hundred lesson plans equip the trainers during the training of trainers (TOTs) in our learner-centered approach. The trainers then choose from more than 250 lesson plans on physical and spiritual topics to equip the CHEs and committee members.

Not one action but many enable community ownership to take place. We work alongside the people, never doing for them what they can do themselves. The people must be actively involved from the beginning and at all times in planning, budgeting, implementing and evaluating the program. They must see themselves as responsible for their success or failure.

Churches and CHE

A program may begin from a church base in areas where the community is fragmented. The community may have so little sense of unity that the churches may be used to initiate a CHE program. Such a case might be in an urban slum area. Or in like manner, Christians may be in a small minority in a community dominated by anti-Christian groups.

The committee members and CHEs will probably be made up of church members. If there is more than one evangelical church in the community, there should be equal representation from all churches regarding the committee and CHEs.

The churches must view this strategy as a means to reach out to their non-Christian neighbors in a holistic way, rather than exclusively using it for their own church members. For a successful program to be started, the local congregation must have a missionary vision for evangelism and a desire to minister physically in the community. The Christians must be concerned with man as a whole and not just his spirit. They must see CHE as a way to win people to Christ and to help them grow as whole persons.

Churches must view development as being important for the community. They must be willing to give up control in order to see community involvement and commitment. Initially, the change agents may be church members who multiply themselves physically and spiritually in the community. The church must minister with, not to, the community.

Multiple churches in the community should work together in the program as a cohesive unit. Working with one small congregation generally dooms the program to slow growth and little impact, as there are not enough resources, manpower or money for the program to spread.

The church-based model is especially useful in an urban slum setting. In general, slum dwellers do not have a sense of belonging but feel they are just there temporarily. They also hold very few things in common since they are from all over the country. So the community is very fragmented. A church can be a community within a community: it has recognized leadership, some sense of unity, and members hold their Christian faith in common.

We are developing such models in the slums of Guatemala City, Manila, and Kampala, Uganda. From these experiences we have found that we must follow the above guidelines or we will never gain community acceptance and ownership.

To God be the Glory

This Christian ministry to the whole person is having results beyond our wildest dreams. The Lord calls each of us ministering in his name to deal with people as whole persons. The starting point and center of good health is our Lord Jesus Christ.

Community health evangelism is a strategy that works. To God be the glory!

Notes

1. According to the context, the acronym CHE may stand for community health *evangelism,* community health *evangelist,* community health *education,* or community health *educator.*
2. One approach to the spiritual discipline of confession is breathing out sins and breathing in God's forgiveness. This is known as spiritual breathing.

SECTION F
PROPERTY

Michael Duncan, in his fascinating book *Costly Mission: Following Christ into the Slums*, recounts the evolution of the Damayan Lagi slum community in Manila into which he and his family moved as agents of change and purveyors of hope. The story of Damayan Lagi's existence is followed through the life of Mary, an early resident in the area. Mary was inducted into poverty the way that most poor are: by inheriting destitution from her parents. Born-poor and married-poor, Mary and her husband took up residence illegally on a wide and vacant area outside of Manila in the 1940s. The original owner of the property needed quick cash and sold the land to a bank. Mary's presence was hardly noticed.

It is not clear from the story how Mary attained the privilege of charging rent to the other squatters, but that's just what happened. Mary occupied her property before the migratory flood of humanity began to dot the landscape. Some of these people were friends and relatives Mary had invited from the countryside. It is estimated that the number of Manila squatters, like Mary, increased in the 1960s more than tenfold to a population of about one hundred thousand.[1] The fresh water running behind Mary's makeshift home soon became putrid sewerage, and makeshift housing of cardboard and scrap metal started filling in the empty spots on the land. People multiplied but city services remained nonexistent. Military coups and dictatorships came and went with their broken promises, as the Damayan Lagi community began to burst at the seams. Natural disasters and economic crises drove even more people into these informal housing conglomerates. But who has rights to this property and can poor squatters eventually obtain rights to the land on which they are living? What rights should the wealthy banks and landowners have to the land? Should they be allowed to drive squatters away with a bulldozer or arson?

In Manila a handful of Spanish families bought up the majority of the land some time ago, effectively locking out millions who have come looking for a small piece of property and willing to work hard to pay for it. Land rights, or land tenure as it is often referred to in development circles, is an important piece to the puzzle of slums. Hernando De Soto, in his book *The Mystery of Capital*, claims it is the single most critical piece. De Soto has documented in several countries the many hundreds of steps required to obtain a piece of property. Even then, in some countries it was questionable whether the deed people held really gave them the rights to the property. Fair land laws, says De Soto, are what give the poor power to climb out of poverty. Even if it takes an entire generation to work up the money to buy a piece of property, a poor family then has a capital asset giving them power to borrow money and to build wealth—wealth that might keep their grandchildren from begging bread.

The reading provided from *The Challenge of Slums: Global Report on Human Settlements 2003* is relatively technical but interesting. The UN Habitat authors take some issue with De Soto, feeling he argues too strongly in favor of the benefits of formal ownership. Sometimes the informal way is best and those who live outside of informal settlements do not always appreciate the systems that emerge within slum communities. This report also looks at the question of infrastructure and services needed within the informal housing sector.

Whether by formal ownership or through a good informal system, the question of housing security is prominent. How can families living in slum communities be protected from the powerful landowners, banks, or developers who have no intent to leave room for them? How can slum dwellers establish a sense of permanence with regard to their residence? If we cannot answer these questions, we cannot effectively assist those living in squalor to improve their state.

Notes

1. Michael Duncan, *Costly Mission: Following Christ into the Slums* (Monrovia, CA: MARC, 1996), 12.

CHAPTER 11

THE MYSTERY OF MISSING INFORMATION

Hernando De Soto

Economics, over the years, has become more and more abstract and divorced from events in the real world. Economists, by and large, do not study the workings of the actual economic system. They theorize about it. As Ely Devons, an English economist, once said at a meeting, "If economists wished to study the horse, they wouldn't go and look at horses. They'd sit in their studies and say to themselves, 'What would I do if I were a horse?'"

—Ronald H. Coase, *The Task of the Society*

Imagine a country where nobody can identify who owns what, addresses cannot be easily verified, people cannot be made to pay their debts, resources cannot conveniently be turned into money, ownership cannot be divided into shares, descriptions of assets are not standardized and cannot be easily compared, and the rules that govern property vary from neighborhood to neighborhood or even from street to street. You have just put yourself into the life of a developing country or former communist nation; more precisely, you have imagined life for 80 percent of its population, which is marked off as sharply from its Westernized elite as black and white South Africans were once separated by apartheid.

This 80 percent majority is not, as Westerners often imagine, desperately impoverished. In spite of their obvious poverty, even those who live under the most grossly unequal regimes possess far more than anybody has ever understood. What they possess, however, is not represented in such a way as to produce additional value. When you step out the door of the Nile Hilton, what you are leaving behind is not the high-technology world of fax machines and ice makers, television and antibiotics. The people of Cairo have access to all those things.

What you are really leaving behind is the world of legally enforceable transactions on property rights. Mortgages and accountable addresses to generate additional wealth are unavailable even to those people in Cairo who would probably strike you as quite rich. Outside Cairo, some of the poorest of the poor live in a district of old tombs called "the city of the dead." But almost all of Cairo is a city of the dead—of dead capital, of assets that cannot be used to their fullest. The institutions that give life to capital—that allow one to secure the interests of third parties with work and assets—do not exist here.

To understand how this is possible, one must look to the nineteenth century, when the United States was carving a society out of its own wilderness. The United States had inherited from Britain not only its fantastically complex land law but also a vast system of overlapping land grants. The same acre might belong to one man who had received it as part of a vast land grant from the British Crown, to another who claimed to have bought it from an Indian tribe, and to a third who had accepted it in place of salary from a state legislature—and none of the three might ever have actually laid eyes on it. Meanwhile, the country was filling up with immigrants, who settled boundaries, ploughed fields, built homes, transferred land, and established credit long before governments conferred on them any right to engage in these acts. Those were the days of the pioneers and the "Wild West." One of the reasons it was so wild was that those pioneers, most of them nothing but squatters, "insisted that their labor, not formal paper titles or arbitrary boundary lines, gave land value and established ownership."[1]

They believed that if they occupied the land and improved it with houses and farms, it was theirs. State and federal governments believed otherwise. Officials sent in troops to burn farms and destroy buildings. Settlers fought back. When the soldiers left, the settlers rebuilt and returned to scratching out a living. That past is the Third World's present.

A Surprise Revolution

Before 1950, most Third World countries were agricultural societies organized in ways that would have made an eighteenth-century European feel right at home. Most people worked on the land, which was owned by a very few big landlords, some of them indigenous oligarchs, others colonial planters. Cities were small and functioned as markets and ports rather than industrial centers; they were dominated by tiny mercantile elites who protected their interests with thick wrappings of rules and regulations.

After 1950, there began in the Third World an economic revolution similar to the social and economic disruptions in Europe in 1800. New machines were reducing the demand for rural labor just as new medicines and public-health methods were cutting the rate of infant mortality and extending life spans. Soon hundreds of thousands of people were trundling down the newly built highways to the cities so alluringly described in the new radio programs.

150

The population of the cities began to rise rapidly. In China alone, more than 100 million people have moved from the countryside to the cities since 1979. Between 1950 and 1988, the population of metropolitan Port-au-Prince rose from 140,000 to 1,550,000. By 1998, it was approaching 2 million. Almost two-thirds of these people live in shantytowns. Experts were already in despair over this surge of new city dwellers as early as 1973, long before the largest influx had taken place. "Everything happens as if the city were falling apart," wrote one urbanist. "Uncontrolled construction, anywhere anyhow. The sewage system is incapable of helping drain rainwater and stuffs up every day. The population concentrates in defined areas where no sanitation infrastructure is provided. . . . The sidewalks of the Avenue Dessalines are literally occupied by small vendors. . . . This town has become unlivable."[2]

Few had anticipated this enormous transformation in the way people lived and worked. The fashionable theories of the day about "development" sought to bring modernity to the countryside. Peasants were not supposed to come to the cities looking for the twentieth century. But tens of millions came anyway, despite a backlash of mounting hostility. They faced an impenetrable wall of rules that barred them from legally established social and economic activities. It was tremendously difficult for these new city people to acquire legal housing, enter formal business, or find a legal job.

The Obstacles to Legality

To get an idea of just how difficult the migrant's life was, my research team and I opened a small garment workshop on the outskirts of Lima, Peru. Our goal was to create a new and perfectly legal business. The team then began filling out the forms, standing in the lines, and making the bus trips into central Lima to get all the certifications required to operate, according to the letter of the law, a small business in Peru. They spent six hours a day at it and finally registered the business—289 days later. Although the garment workshop was geared to operating with only one worker, the cost of legal registration was $1,231—thirty-one times the monthly minimum wage. To obtain legal authorization to build a house on state-owned land took six years and eleven months, requiring 207 administrative steps in fifty-two government offices. To obtain a legal title for that piece of land took 728 steps. We also found that a private bus, jitney, or taxi driver who wanted to obtain official recognition of his route faced twenty-six months of red tape.

My research team, with the help of local associates, has repeated similar experiments in other countries. The obstacles were no less formidable than in Peru; often they were even more daunting. In the Philippines, if a person has built a dwelling in a settlement on either state-owned or privately owned urban land, to purchase it legally he would have to form an association with his neighbors in order to qualify for a state housing finance program. The entire process could necessitate 168 steps, involving fifty-three public and private agencies and taking thirteen to twenty-five years. And that assumes the state housing finance program has sufficient funds. If the dwelling happens to be in an area still considered "agricultural," the settler will have to clear additional hurdles for converting that land to urban use—45 additional bureaucratic procedures before thirteen entities, adding another two years to his quest.

In Egypt, the person who wants to acquire and legally register a lot on state-owned desert land must wend his way through at least 77 bureaucratic procedures at thirty-one public and private agencies. This can take anywhere from five to fourteen years. To build a legal dwelling on former agricultural land would require six to eleven years of bureaucratic wrangling, maybe longer. This explains why 4.7 million Egyptians have chosen to build their dwellings illegally. If after building his home, a settler decides he would now like to be a law-abiding citizen and purchase the rights to his dwelling, he risks having it demolished, paying a steep fine, and serving up to ten years in prison.

In Haiti, one way an ordinary citizen can settle legally on government land is first to lease it from the government for five years and then buy it. Working with associates in Haiti, our researchers found that to obtain such a lease took 65 bureaucratic steps—requiring, on average, a little more than two years—all for the privilege of merely leasing the land for five years. To buy the land required another 111 bureaucratic hurdles—and twelve more years. Total time to gain lawful land in Haiti: nineteen years. Yet even this long ordeal will not ensure that the property remains legal.

In fact, in every country we investigated, we found that it is very nearly as difficult to *stay* legal as it is to *become* legal. Inevitably, migrants do not so much break the law as the law breaks them—and they opt out of the system. In 1976, two-thirds of those who worked in Venezuela were employed in legally established enterprises; today the proportion is less than half. Thirty years ago, more than two-thirds of the new housing erected in Brazil was intended for rent. Today, only about 3 percent of new construction is officially listed as rental housing. To where did that market vanish? To the extralegal areas of Brazilian cities called *favelas,* which operate outside the highly regulated formal economy and function according to supply and demand. There are no rent controls in the *favelas*, rents are paid in U.S. dollars, and renters who do not pay are rapidly evacuated.

Once these newcomers to the city quit the system, they become "extralegal." Their only alternative is to live and work outside the official law, using their own informally binding arrangements to protect and mobilize their assets. These arrangements result from a combination of rules selectively borrowed from the official legal system, ad hoc improvisations, and customs brought from their places of origin or locally devised. They are held together by a social contract that is upheld by a community as a whole and enforced by authorities the community has selected. These extralegal social contracts have created a vibrant but undercapitalized sector, the center of the world of the poor.

The Undercapitalized Sector

Although the migrants are refugees from the law, they have hardly retreated into idleness. Undercapitalized sectors throughout the Third World and in former communist countries buzz with hard work and ingenuity. Street-side cottage industries have sprung up everywhere, manufacturing anything from clothing and footwear to imitation Cartier watches and Vuitton bags. There are workshops that build and rebuild machinery, cars, even buses. The new urban poor have created entire industries and neighborhoods that have to operate on clandestine connections to electricity and water. There are even dentists who fill cavities without a license.

Unauthorized buses, jitneys, and taxis account for most of the public transportation in many developing countries. In other parts of the Third World, vendors from the shantytowns supply most of the food available in the market, whether from carts on the street or from stalls in buildings they construct.

In 1993, the Mexican Chamber of Commerce estimated the number of street-vendor stands in the Federal District of Mexico City at 150,000, with an additional 293,000 in forty-three other Mexican centers. These tiny booths average just 1.5 meters wide. If the Mexico City vendors lined up their stands on a single street with no gaps at intersections, they would form a continuous row more than 210 kilometers long. Thousands upon thousands of people work in the extralegal sector—on the streets, from their homes, and in the city's unregistered shops, offices, and factories. An attempt by the Mexican National Statistics Institute in 1994 to measure the number of informal "microbusinesses" in the entire country came up with a total of 2.65 million.

These are all real-life examples of economic life in the undercapitalized sector of society. In the former communist nations, you may see even more sophisticated activities off the books, from the production of computer hardware and software to the manufacture of jet fighters for sale abroad.

Russia, of course, has quite a different history from Third World countries such as Haiti and the Philippines. Nevertheless, since the fall of communism, the former Soviet states have been slipping into the same patterns of informal ownership. In 1995, *Business Week* reported that four years after the end of communism, only "some 280,000 farmers out of 10 million own their land" in Russia. Another report paints a familiar Third World picture: "[In the former Soviet Union], rights of private possession, use, and alienation of land are inadequately defined and not clearly protected by law. . . . Mechanisms used in market economies to protect land rights are still in their infancy. . . . The State itself continues to restrict use rights on land that it does not own."[3] Estimates based on electricity consumption indicate that between 1989 and 1994, unofficial activity in former Soviet states increased from 12 percent to 37 percent of total production. Some put the proportion even higher.

None of this will come as news to those who live outside the West. You need only open a window or take a taxi from the airport to your hotel to see city perimeters crowded with homes, armies of vendors hawking wares in the streets, glimpses of bustling workshops behind garage doors, and battered busses crisscrossing the grimy streets. Extralegality is often perceived as a "marginal" issue similar to black markets in advanced nations, or poverty, or unemployment. The extralegal world is typically viewed as a place where gangsters roam, sinister characters of interest only to the police, anthropologists, and missionaries.

In fact it is legality that is marginal; extralegality has become the norm. The poor have already taken control of vast quantities of real estate and production. Those international agencies that jet their consultants to the gleaming glass towers of the elegant quadrants of town to meet with the local "private sector" are talking to only a fraction of the entrepreneurial world. The emerging economic powers of the Third World and former communist nations are the garbage collectors, the appliance manufacturers, and the illegal construction companies in the streets far below. The only real choice for the governments of these nations is whether they are going to integrate those resources into an orderly and coherent legal framework or continue to live in anarchy.

How Much Dead Capital?

Over the past decade my researchers, assisted by knowledgeable local professionals, have made surveys of five Third World cities—Cairo, Lima, Manila, Mexico City, and Port-au-Prince—in an effort to gauge the value of the possessions of those people who have been locked out of the capitalized economy by discriminatory laws. To be more confident of our results, we focused our attention on the most tangible and detectable of assets: real estate.

Unlike the sale of food or shoes, auto repair, or the manufacture of phony Cartier watches—activities that are difficult to count and even more difficult to value—buildings cannot be hidden. You can ascertain their value simply by surveying the cost of the building materials and observing the selling prices of comparable buildings. We spent many thousands of days counting buildings block by block. Wherever authorized to do so, we published our results obtained in each country, so that they could be openly discussed and criticized. In collaboration with people on the spot, we tested and retested our methods and results.

We discovered that the way the people build in the undercapitalized sector takes as many forms as there are legal obstacles to circumvent. The most obvious form is the shanty built on government-owned land. But our researchers discovered far more creative ways of getting around the real estate laws. In Peru, for instance, people formed agricultural cooperatives to buy estates from their old owners and to convert them into housing and industrial settlements. Because there are no easy legal ways to change land tenure, farmers in state-owned cooperatives illegally subdivided the land into smaller, privately held parcels. As a result, few if any have valid title to their ground. In Port-au-Prince, even quite expensive properties change hands without anybody bothering to inform the registry office, which is hopelessly backlogged anyway. In Manila, housing springs up on land zoned solely for industrial use. In Cairo, residents of older four-story public housing projects build three illegal stories on top of their buildings and sell the apartments to relatives and other clients. Also in Cairo, the legal tenants of apartments whose rents were frozen in the early 1950s at sums now worth less than a dollar a year subdivide these properties into smaller apartments and lease them out at market prices.

Some of this housing was extralegal from day one, constructed in violation of all kinds of laws. Other buildings—the Port-au-Prince houses, the Cairo rent-controlled apartments—originated in the legal system but then dropped out as complying with the law became too costly and complicated. By one route or another, almost every dwelling place in the cities we surveyed exited the legal framework—and the very laws that could have hypothetically provided owners with the representations and institutions to create capital. There still may be deeds or some kind of record in someone's hands, but the real ownership status of these assets has slipped out of the official registry system, leaving records and maps outdated.

The result is that most people's resources are commercially and financially invisible. Nobody really knows who owns what or where, who is accountable for the performance of obligations, who is responsible for losses and fraud, or what mechanisms are available to enforce payment for services and goods delivered. Consequently, most potential assets in these countries have not been identified or realized; there is little accessible capital, and the exchange economy is constrained and sluggish.

This picture of the undercapitalized sector is strikingly different from the conventional wisdom of the developing world. But this is where most people live. It is a world where ownership of assets is difficult to trace and validate and is governed by no legally recognizable set of rules; where the assets' potentially useful economic attributes have not been described or organized; where they cannot be used to obtain surplus value through multiple transactions because their unfixed nature and uncertainty leave too much room for misunderstanding, faulty recollection, and reversal of agreement—where most assets, in short, are dead capital.

How Much Is This Dead Capital Worth?

Dead capital, virtual mountains of it, lines the streets of every developing and former communist country. In the Philippines, by our calculation, 57 percent of city dwellers and 67 percent of people in the countryside live in housing that is dead capital. In Peru, 53 percent of city dwellers and 81 percent of people in the countryside live in extralegal dwellings.

The figures are even more dramatic in Haiti and Egypt. In Haiti, also according to our surveys, 68 percent of city dwellers and 97 percent of people in the countryside live in housing to which nobody has clear legal title. In Egypt, dead-capital housing is home for 92 percent of city dwellers and 85 percent of people in the countryside.

Many of these dwellings are not worth much by Western standards. A shanty in Port-au-Prince may fetch as little as $500, a cabin by a polluted waterway in Manila only $2,700, a fairly substantial house in a village outside Cairo only about $5,000, and in the hills around Lima, a respectable bungalow with a garage and picture windows is valued at only $20,000. But there are a great many such dwellings, and collectively their value dramatically outweighs the total wealth of the rich.

In Haiti, untitled rural and urban real estate holdings are together worth some $5.2 billion. To put that sum in context, it is four times the total of all the assets of all the legally operating companies in Haiti, nine times the value of all assets owned by the government, and 158 times the value of all foreign direct investment in Haiti's recorded history to 1995. Is Haiti an exception, a part of Francophone Africa mistakenly put into the American hemisphere, where the Duvalier regime delayed the emergence of a systematized legal system? Perhaps.

Then let's consider Peru, a Hispanic and Indo-American country with a very different tradition and ethnic makeup. The value of extralegally held rural and urban real estate in Peru amounts to some $74 billion. This is five times the total valuation of the Lima Stock Exchange before the slump of 1998, eleven times greater than the value of potentially privatizable government enterprises and facilities, and fourteen times the value of all foreign direct investment in the country through its documented history. Would you counter that Peru's formal economy has also been stunted by the traditions of the ancient Inca Empire, the corrupting influence of colonial Spain, and the recent war with the Maoist Sendero Luminoso?

Very well, then consider the Philippines, a former Asian protectorate of the United States. The value of untitled real estate there is $133 billion, four times the capitalization of the 216 domestic companies listed on the Philippines Stock Exchange, seven times the total deposits in the country's commercial banks, nine times the total capital of state-owned enterprises, and fourteen times the value of all foreign direct investment.

Perhaps the Philippines, too, is an anomaly—something to do with how Christianity developed in former Spanish colonies. If so, let's consider Egypt. The value of Egypt's dead capital in real estate is, by the tally we made with our Egyptian colleagues, some $240 billion. That is thirty times the value of all the shares on the Cairo Stock Exchange and, as I mentioned previously, fifty-five times the value of all foreign investment in Egypt.

In every country we have examined, the entrepreneurial ingenuity of the poor has created wealth on a vast scale—wealth that also constitutes by far the largest source of potential capital for development. These assets not only far exceed the holdings of the government, the local stock exchanges, and foreign direct investment; they are many times greater than all the aid from advanced nations and all the loans extended by the World Bank.

The results are even more astonishing when we take the data from the four countries we have studied and project it over the Third World and former communist nations as a whole. We estimate that about 85 percent of urban parcels in these nations, and between 40 percent and 53 percent of rural parcels, are held in such a way that they cannot be used to create capital. Putting a value on all these assets is inevitably going to come up with a rough number. But we believe that our estimates are as accurate as they can be and quite conservative.

By our calculations, the total value of the real estate held but not legally owned by the poor of the Third World and former communist nations is at least $9.3 trillion.

This is a number worth pondering: $9.3 trillion is about twice as much as the total circulating U.S. money supply. It is very nearly as much as the total value of all the companies listed on the main stock exchanges of the world's twenty most developed countries: New York, Tokyo, London, Frankfurt, Toronto, Paris, Milan, the NASDAQ, and a dozen others. It is more than twenty times the total direct foreign investment into all Third World and former communist countries in the ten years after 1989, forty-six times as much as all the World Bank loans of the past three decades, and ninety-three times as much as all development assistance from all advanced countries to the Third World in the same period.

Acres of Diamonds

The words "international poverty" too easily bring to mind images of destitute beggars sleeping on the curbs of Calcutta and hungry African children starving on the sand. These scenes are of course real, and millions of our fellow human beings demand and deserve our help. Nevertheless, the grimmest picture of the Third World is not the most accurate. Worse, it draws attention away from the arduous achievements of those small entrepreneurs who have triumphed over every imaginable obstacle to create the greater part of the wealth of their society. A truer image would depict a man and woman who have painstakingly saved to construct a house for themselves and their children and who are creating enterprises where nobody imagined they could be built. I resent the characterization of such heroic entrepreneurs as contributors to the problem of global poverty.

They are not the problem. They are the solution.

In the years after the American Civil War, a lecturer named Russell Conwell crisscrossed America delivering a message that stirred millions of people. He told the story of an Indian merchant who had been promised by a prophet that he would surely become rich beyond all imagining if only he would seek his treasure. The merchant traveled the world only to return home old, sad, and defeated. As he re-entered his abandoned house, he needed a drink of water. But the well on his property had silted up. Wearily, he took out his spade and dug a new one—and instantly struck the Golconda, the world's greatest diamond mine.

Conwell's message is a useful one. Leaders of the Third World and former communist nations need not wander the world's foreign ministries and international financial institutions seeking their fortune. In the midst of their own poorest neighborhoods and shantytowns, there are—if not acres of diamonds—trillions of dollars, all ready to be put to use if only the mystery of how assets are transformed into live capital can be unraveled.

Notes

1. Donald J. Pisani, *Water, Land, and Law in the West: The Limits of Public Policy, 1850-1920* (Lawrence: University Press of Kansas, 1996), p. 51.
2. Comments by the architect and urbanist Albert Mangonese in *Conjonction*, No. 119, February-March 1973, p. 11.
3. Leonard J. Rolfes, Jr., "The Struggle for Private Land Rights in Russia," *Economic Reform Today*, No. 1, 1996, p. 12

CHAPTER 12

SLUMS IN THE HOUSING SECTOR

UN HABITAT

The commonly accepted idea of a slum relates particularly to poor quality housing and residential infrastructure. The slum conjures up either a Dickensian vision of urban tenements, dire poverty and disease; a Chicago Southside of empty buildings and decay, suburban flight, roaming gangs and crack dealers; or a Calcutta or Jakarta, with endless vistas of makeshift shacks on the edge of town, filled with people in despair. In each case, the image suggests that the deprived urban environment has caused the poverty, when the reverse is mostly the case; people in poverty have sought out the accessible housing that they can best afford.

The misconception of some planning systems of the modernist tradition is that inadequate housing somehow breeds inadequate incomes, and middle-class distaste for poor housing has led quite frequently to dangerously inept policies. Housing is, in fact, possibly the trickiest market in which to interfere, since well-intentioned measures can have the opposite effects from what was intended. Comprehensive slum clearances have often eliminated better communities than they have created, at huge cost. Squatter evictions have created more misery than they have prevented. "Indeed, it is now generally agreed that forced eviction represents a dimension of urban violence," and in 1996, all governments agreed to end illegal evictions when they adopted *The Habitat Agenda* in Istanbul.[1] Measures designed to limit costs in housing markets have, instead, ham-strung new investment in housing supply and maintenance, and caused residential investment to fall to nothing.

The distaste of more affluent urban citizens for slums impacts on every level—through slum clearance, harassment of informal-sector workers, and the unavailability of urban public and private services, finance or affordable housing. The largest problem is the lack of recognition of slum dwellers as being urban citizens at all. When services are not provided, the poor provide for themselves. The poor are currently the largest producers of shelter and builders of cities in the world—in many cases, women are taking the lead in devising survival strategies that are, effectively, the governance structures of the developing world, when formal structures have failed them.[2]

Housing issues almost inevitably refer to appropriateness (or adequacy), availability and affordability. These three issues take different forms in varied environments where standards are very different. They also interact with each other: sometimes in a trade-off, as affordability and adequacy usually do, and sometimes in concert, as availability and affordability mostly do.[3]

Tenure and Security:
The Formal-informal Housing Continuum

The two most obvious problems facing people occupying informal-sector housing are related: tenure security and the provision of services. Obviously, providers of main services are less willing to invest in pipes and other engineering works if dwellings in an area are likely to be removed. Furthermore, public authorities may use the availability of services as a weapon in the campaign against informal development. However, the old contrast between formal and informal is now much more clouded, resembling a continuum with many intermediary positions rather than a dichotomy:

> The removal of tenure-insecurity related obstacles that prevent or constrain households from using their housing effectively as a productive asset is possibly the single most critical poverty reduction intervention.[4]

The United Nations Millennium Goals have specifically articulated, as Indicator 31, the "proportion of people with access to secure tenure." The Global Campaign for Secure Tenure (GCST), a major international initiative since 1999, identifies the provision of secure tenure as essential for a sustainable shelter strategy, and as a vital element in the promotion of housing rights. It promotes the rights and interests of the poor, "recognizing that the urban poor themselves provide the vast majority of their shelter."[5] At its heart, the campaign addresses the outcomes of unstable tenure, including the inability to mobilize household capital, social exclusion and poor access to basic facilities. Lack of housing security makes it very difficult for people to participate in society, to establish firm roots and to build upon their networks and assets in order to obtain regular access to income-earning opportunities. People living in poverty are extremely vulnerable to changes in circumstances, and having safe, secure housing represents a substantial improvement in the quality of life for most. Without a fixed address it is almost impossible to have a formal-sector job, to receive any benefits that may be on offer, or to participate in political processes that might make a difference to local fund allocations for neighborhood improvement.

Insecure tenure is one of the hallmarks of the informal sector, and gaining security can be the most important improvement for residents. Tenure can be complex, involving different bundles of rights over land or structure; but the main forms of tenure are discussed below.

Formal Home-ownership

Formal home-ownership generally means that the owner of the structure has freehold or long leasehold title over the land, with the ability to sell or mortgage the improvements (in the present context, usually a dwelling), to leave it to descendants and to make any changes to the structure that are desired. However, there are other forms of titling for ownership, such as "qualified titles" (Malaysia), "provisional titles" (South Africa) and "use right titles" (Indonesia). These may have different implications on inheritance and sale.

Home-ownership is undeniably the most secure tenure in that it provides the maximum control over dwelling and land within the confines of local planning and building regulations. While support for home-ownership has had an almost religious character in some countries, such as the US and Australia, its benefits are often exaggerated, and many affluent European countries have preferred a mix of social and private rental as their primary housing solution. As a pension scheme, home-ownership has considerable advantages in providing housing and assets for the aged, although it is often argued that a maldistribution of housing resources then occurs as an elderly couple or single person lives on in their family home.[6] Home-ownership is also alleged to contribute to participation and social activism,[7] although it often takes the form of not in my backyard (NIMBY)[8] action in order to exclude diversity of land use and of residents who do not fit the exclusive local profile.

Formal Private Rental

Formal private rental usually involves a lease or equivalent entitling the lessee to quiet enjoyment of the property for a fixed time, or until certain conditions are fulfilled, as long as the rent is paid and the property is maintained. There are no property rights inherent in most forms of lease, changes to the property cannot usually be made and, unless specifically legislated, most leases heavily favor the landlord in any dispute. In some cities, rental may also be more expensive in the long run than ownership.[9]

Private rental is dominant in cities in a diverse group of countries, including Germany, France, Denmark, many cities in Canada and the US; the Republic of Korea, Indonesia, Bangladesh and parts of India in Asia; Belize, Colombia and Jamaica in Latin America and the Caribbean (LAC); and in most African countries. However, in some it is discouraged or even illegal.

Informal Home-ownership: Squatting

Squatters are people who occupy land or buildings without the permission of the owner. Squatting occurs when an occupant has no claim to the land she or he occupies that can be upheld in law. In some countries, most squatting takes place in unused buildings, in which case the squatter has no legal claim to occupy the structure. In some countries and periods, squatting has been a legitimate way of occupying unused land. Examples include the settler periods in the US West and in parts of Australia, and, currently, desert land on the edges of Lima in Peru. Particularly in longstanding settlements, squatters, in many countries, have gained some form of informal title that is recognized by the community and can be traded in the housing market.[10] Squatters in self-built housing have been the primary focus of urban housing development programs in the developing world over the last four decades.

Squatter housing generally divides into housing of poor quality or impermanent materials, and more established housing that may have been in place for a long period but has no official title to the land. In some countries such as Indonesia, Bangladesh, Kenya and parts of India, most squatter housing is rented from informal-sector landlords; in other places, such as Latin America, it is typically occupied without cost.

Informal Home-ownership: Illegal Subdivisions

Illegal subdivisions refer to settlements where the land has been subdivided, resold, rented or leased by its legal owner to people who build their houses upon the plots that they buy. These settlements are also illegal owing to the following additional factors: low standard of the services or infrastructure provided, breaches of land zoning, lack of planning and building permits, or the irregular nature of the land subdivision. Purchasers of land on illegal subdivisions often feel more secure than squatters because they have been through a process of buying the land from its owner and therefore do not fear that the owner will reclaim the land. This is a very common circumstance in rapidly developing cities.

Public Rental

Public rental housing generally grants unlimited tenure, even to the next generation, at a subsidized rental; but it grants no property rights. Public rental was the social solution to housing during the inter-war and post-war periods in Europe and elsewhere, and very large housing estates were built—such as the Karl Marx Platz in Vienna, a housing block that is 5 kilometers long and includes many small businesses within its walls. In developing countries, the heyday of public rental housing was in the immediate post-World War II period when 'homes for heroes' and accommodation for the new urban workers were needed.

Along with other aspects of the state, public housing was originally available for everyone; but in many countries it is now increasingly targeted towards low-income earners and those with social problems. Large estates have, therefore, become major zones of exclusion, and the low incomes of the residents have damaged their financial viability so that increasing levels of subsidy have been required to meet basic costs such as maintenance. These residualized areas have become recognized as the "new slums" in some countries, with residents sometimes being ashamed to admit their addresses to outsiders.[11]

As one writer points out:

> The British example demonstrates that the state, under certain conditions, can plan, produce and deliver high quality housing. It also demonstrates that, under other conditions, the state can become a slum landlord and can provide housing which is directly or indirectly a source of social exclusion and disadvantage.[12]

On ideological grounds, the stock of public housing in many countries has either been sold off at a large discount to existing tenants (in the UK and many of its former colonies, and in some transitional countries where it was transferred outright) or semi-privatized into housing associations (in The Netherlands and the UK).[13] The results of this exercise are still not clear; but lack of coordination and the ability to place tenants across the stock has become an issue.

Informal Rental

Informal renting can take many forms, from occupying backyard shacks in public housing in South Africa, to subtenants in squatter housing in the *favelas* of Brazil, to pavement dwellers in India who make regular payments to someone in authority in order to keep their position. This group, along with new squatters, have the most fragile housing situation, short of having no shelter. They are able to live where they do until someone moves them along.

The subtenant category continues to be significant largely in sub-Saharan Africa. Backyard shacks and other forms of subletting are commonplace throughout much of sub-Saharan Africa. Some German and Venezuelan cities, as well as Trinidad and Kuwait, also have significant proportions of subtenants.

Subletting appears also to be on the increase in those transitional countries where new housing investment has virtually been discontinued.

Private renting, both formal and informal, is the main alternative to home-ownership throughout much of the world. It is capable of providing accommodation not only to those with transient lifestyles, but also to those with limited resources who would not otherwise be able to afford the capital required for owner-occupied housing. However, most of the households who pay high proportions of their incomes on housing are private renters. While some countries make providing housing for rent difficult through rent controls, higher rates of tax on rental incomes, and legislation that makes recovering rented property from tenants very difficult, the importance of rental housing is likely to increase during the next few decades as incomes continue to fall behind the cost of providing formal-sector housing.

Customary Tenure

Parts of many cities, particularly in Africa, have no state-formalized ownership of land and the land is not marketable. Instead, it is held by traditional leadership entities, such as chiefs, in trust for the community and its use is controlled through leases that allow rights of surface use for a fixed period (or in perpetuity to members of the local community). Some customary systems have central administrations in which documents are kept and can be consulted in case of dispute (as in the Asantehene's Lands Office in Kumasi, Ghana), while others do not. In the latter case, clouded titles (where the real owner or user is difficult to trace and there may be many conflicting claims) are a frequent problem. Customary and formal title can co-exist although this can cause much confusion.

Tenure Distribution

Estimates of the incidence of different tenures worldwide are presented in Table 12.1 and Figure 12.1.[14] These estimates include all housing: slums and non-slums. It shows that about 19 percent of households worldwide are in squatter housing (including those paying rent), about 42 percent are in formal ownership and about 34 percent are formal renters. On a regional basis, ownership levels are now highest in the transitional countries because of the substantial privatization programs that have taken place during the 1990s, and rental is highest in the developed countries. There is a small residual group of customary tenures, family houses, homeless people, etc, which is most significant in Africa.[15]

Squatter housing is most prevalent in Africa and South Asia and is now only a small proportion of the stock in South America, following substantial regularization programs. Formal rental, both public and private, is most common in the high-income areas.

Slums and Tenure Insecurity

The relationship between slums and tenure insecurity is not immediately obvious, particularly in the Western world where slums actually developed within a context of defined tenure rights. However, the situation in the rapidly urbanizing developing world is rather different. Large visible tracts of squatter or informal housing have become intimately connected with perceptions of poverty, the negative effects of globalization, and lack of access to basic services and insecurity.

Many people living in informal settlements have been subject to continual harassment by authorities in their endeavors to provide themselves with appropriate and affordable housing. The unsatisfactory tenure of the majority of the urban poor has long been recognized, as access to secure tenure has often been a prerequisite for access to other opportunities, including credit, public services and livelihood. The ownership of land is a major area of gender discrimination. It is estimated that one out of every four countries in the developing world has a constitution or national laws that contain impediments to women owning land and taking mortgages in their own names. These are highest in Africa (41 percent of cities), the Middle East and Northern Africa (29 percent) and Asia and Latin America 44 percent).[16]

Work in informal settlements in Peru and elsewhere was influential in encouraging international agencies to engage in large-scale formalization

Table 12.1 Broad Tenure Categories, 1998 (Percentages)

Region	Formal owner	Formal rental	Squatter (including informal rent-paying)	Other
Africa	25	23	38	15
Asia (without China)	29	19	45	7
China	35	50	9	6
Eastern Europe and Central Asia	65	34	1	3
Latin America and the Caribbean	48	21	25	6
Western Europe and other HICs	40	57	2	1
World	42	34	19	5

Source: Estimated from UNCHS (Habitat), 1996c and UN-Habitat, 2002f by Flood, 2001.

Figure 12.1 Housing Tenure, 1998

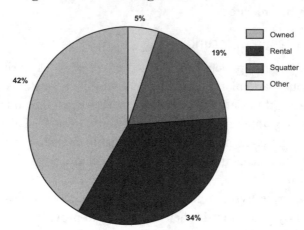

programs.[17] For example, security of tenure issues received high priority in the housing sector policy development, emphasizing that its lack led to underinvestment in housing and reduced housing quality. *The Habitat Agenda* stated unequivocally:

> Access to land and security of tenure are strategic prerequisites for the provision of adequate shelter for all and the development of sustainable human settlements. It is also one way of breaking the vicious circle of poverty.

One study identifies bureaucracy and elaborate red tape as major mechanisms that exclude the poor from participating in legal enterprises and legal ownership of dwellings.[19/20] These requirements mean that the poor do not have the resources to register enterprises or dwellings; therefore, they simply do not bother and stay outside of the legal system—thereby restricting legality only to the privileged few. An "impenetrable bureaucracy bounds the formal economy" that is not interested in increasing wealth, just its redistribution.

A more recent study has taken the argument a stage further, stating that the granting of secure tenure is the single most important catalyst in mobilizing individual investment and economic development, since it is the foundation upon which capitalism has been established.[21] It argues that the substantial increase of capital in the West over the past two centuries is the consequence of gradually improving property systems. This has not happened in the developing world, where eight out of ten people hold their assets outside of the formal system, resulting in an estimated US$9.3 trillion of "extra-legal" real estate assets in the form of "dead capital," which is not transferable or fungible.[22] It cannot be accessed for other purposes, such as businesses, since it is held in a defective form without title.

A number of authors have been quick to refute the above arguments, saying that they misrepresent the situation in irregular settlements and underestimate the ability of informal systems to deliver, as follows: [23]

- Within most informal settlements, property is regularly traded according to some form of *de facto* titling system, which is based heavily on official systems. Formal titling is expensive, slow and subject to dispute where the land is privately owned in the formal system, and establishing formal title does not make much difference to the turnover of capital.[24] Housing turnover may not increase following legalization.[25] The importance and value of being able to transfer ownership rights increases with development, as skills become more hetero-geneous.[26]

- Access to informal credit is also a feature of most informal settlements. Formal finance is not forthcoming after legalization in the places where it has occurred.[27] The poor are, often for good reasons, suspicious about borrowing from banks in many countries.[28]

- Formal titling draws housing within the ambit of the land tax system, which the poor may not wish to pay.[29]

- While a minimum level of security is necessary before households will upgrade or undertake repairs, the literature showing the relationship between tenure and property maintenance is complex.[30]

The pro-tenure improvement arguments outlined above have also been said to misrepresent the situation in developed countries:

- Property and tenure rights in Europe grew from feudal and bourgeois concerns and not from any desire to tap the capital controlled by the poor. There have been healthy self-build and cooperative sectors in many developed countries; but most urban housing policy has concentrated on mobilizing the surplus income and capital of the middle class, either by building or subsidizing social housing with tax receipts, or by encouraging private landlords to invest in low-cost housing.[31]

- Home-ownership tends to be a preoccupation of formerly frontier societies such as the US and Australia, and of agricultural societies. Home-ownership is actually at lower levels in Europe than in most of the developing world. There is a well-known inverse relationship between levels of home ownership and GDP in Europe, with the richest countries tending to have the lowest levels of ownership.[32]

- Until the liberalization of mortgage markets during the 1980s, it was not an easy matter in most countries to borrow against owner-occupied housing for other purposes. This required high levels of equity and attracted penalty interest rates and other costs. Property rights and economic growth have tended to advance hand in hand. If anything, economic growth has acted as a precondition for distributing capital more widely, to the point, recently, where financial institutions have felt safe in providing universal instruments with low transaction costs, allowing households to access the capital in their homes for other purposes.[33]

Excessively complex, restrictive or inefficient systems of housing and land provision have a deleterious effect on both housing supply and housing prices and rents that, while appearing to improve conditions for existing occupants actually reduce housing security for prospective and existing occupants.

Security of tenure and security of supply are, therefore, not necessarily complementary, since:

- There appears to be an upper limit beyond which increasing security of tenure may be counterproductive. In countries with formal supply systems, the poor have relatively few resources to invest in housing, and only the middle classes tend to supply housing capital. Many developed countries have, therefore, chosen to limit security of tenure in order to maximize housing supply, thereby encouraging the middle class to invest in housing for private tenants.

- As a particular example, the experience with draconian forms of rent control has been poor in all countries, resulting in poor supply, little or no housing maintenance or investment and overcrowding.[34]

- The practical experience with formal titling in irregular settlements has not been encouraging. As already discussed, some writers suggest that formal titling is of doubtful benefit to the poor, slowing and formalizing supply, and in some cases dramatically reducing affordability.[35] Better targeted partial changes to tenure rights can often avoid the undesirable effects of full-scale titling.

- There is no doubt that formal titling increases the value of properties; but there are cases where formal markets do not appear following regularization, and it is difficult for owners to realize the improved value.[36] There are too many areas where housing is not routinely marketable, especially in sub-Saharan Africa, for markets to be an assumed norm. Even where there are markets, regularization may simply raise the price of housing and reduce affordability across the board.

Legality is not particularly valuable to the poor; many of the outcomes of legality are desirable, but can be achieved in different ways.[37] There are differences between legitimacy and legality, and a number of tenure arrangements stop well short of formal titling while providing the desired benefits. Others discern a trend in interventions from tenure regularization towards security of tenure, recounting other strategies that achieve similar benefits to formal titling but without the costs:[38]

> Secure de facto tenure is what matters to their inhabitants first and foremost—with or without documents. It is the security from eviction that gives the house its main source of value.[39]

Not only is it unclear under what conditions improving formal security of tenure will improve the conditions of the majority of slum dwellers: but there are also very many people who do not live in slums and still have insecure tenure. Conversely, there are many individuals who live in slums who have legal tenure and/or are not poor. In addition, customary forms of tenure, which exist throughout sub-Saharan Africa and elsewhere, provide reasonably secure tenure even though these rights may not be recognized explicitly by the state.[40]

What is generally agreed is that secure tenure represents a bundle of different rights and is related to a number of other important issues. The specific legal rights to which tenure refers include the right to occupy/use/enjoy; to restrict who develops or uses the property; to dispose/buy/inherit; to cultivate/produce/sublet/sublet with fixed rent; to benefit from change in value; to access services; and to access formal credit. The tenure types that carry with them combinations of some or, ultimately, all of these are pavement dweller, squatter tenant, squatter "owner," tenant in unauthorized subdivision, owner in an unauthorized subdivision, legal owner of an unauthorized building, tenant with a contract, leaseholder, and freeholder. These have progressively more rights.

The tenure figures in Table 12.1 have been used to obtain broad measures of insecure tenure, as in Table 12.2. These estimates are bound to be approximate; but they are probably fairly indicative of the relative magnitude of the tenure types. About 28 percent of households live in insecure tenure worldwide. Some 17 percent of these are renters (7 percent in informal tenure), while another 7 percent are squatters who pay no rent.

In the light of the figures presented in Table 12.2, it may seem strange that so much attention has been lavished, over the past decade, on self-help for non-rent paying squatters. As there are so many more renters than squatters, it is strange that there are so few programs that assist tenants with their rights and/or assist informal landlords to mobilize capital and participate in housing supply or estate

Table 12.2 Insecure Tenure by Region (Percentages)

	Squatters, No Rent	Renters	Other	Total
Southern Africa	8	16	6	29
Rest of Africa	13	30	7	50
China	5	2	8	15
East Asia and Pacific, excluding Australasia	7	26	9	41
South and South-eastern Asia	14	31	5	50
Middle East	8	28	6	42
Western Europe	2	19	4	25
Northern America and Australasia	1	10	4	16
Latin America and Caribbean	11	17	6	34
World	7	17	4	28

Source: Flood, 2001

improvement in various ways. It has been pointed out that helping someone to build their own dwelling is rather inefficient as it only results in one dwelling. Contrarily, if a successful self-builder decides to build dwellings for a business, the same agencies cannot help, and many official obstacles are put in the way of such small businesses.[41] There is a great need to assist small-scale enterprises in the construction sector—which probably provide the majority of all new dwellings—so that their methods of supply are as efficient as possible. At the same time, consumers need advice and knowledge on what represents good workmanship and value for money. The single householder-house interface represented by assisting self-help builders should be replaced by the twin interfaces of contractor-house and householder-contractor.[42]

While the importance of informal capital has been exaggerated, self-help has had the merit of producing innovative solutions to improve tenure conditions. The tenure data do not necessarily invalidate arguments regarding informal capital, although they clearly weaken them.[43] The few studies that have attempted to find out just where all of this informal capital for rental housing is coming from demonstrate that owners who build rental rooms are often little better off than the renters, especially where traditional or shack housing is constructed. Most also continue to live in part of the house with their tenants, or close by.[44] Recent studies describe the considerable enterprise of slum dwellers; one major livelihood opportunity for women, in particular, is in providing rental housing.[45]

Aid programs for rental tenure remain a neglected element of international assistance, and knowledge about informal landlords and tenants and the kinds of programs that might benefit them are rare. Data relating to secure tenure are, overall, quite poor, even in those countries with established statistical systems, and the Millennium Goals program offers a good opportunity to improve knowledge regarding housing tenure and the kinds of programs that will improve the situation of those in insecure tenure.

Notes

1. Agbola and Jinadu, 1997.
2. UN-Habitat, 200lb.
3. Higher quality housing is inevitably more expensive; as a result, improving adequacy reduces affordability. Furthermore, if housing is more widely available it is usually cheaper from the functioning of supply and demand.
4. Moser, 1996.
5. See www.unhabitatorg/tenure/tenure.htm.
6. Flood and Yates (1989) note that, in Australia, home-owners aged over 65 have considerably more valuable housing than the general population, while renters aged over 65 occupy considerably less valuable housing than the average, although their average cash incomes are similar. However, the very large dwellings occupied by many owners after their children leave home could be regarded as a maldistribution of the stock. In developing country contexts, many elderly people actually extend their dwellings in their old age to house their grown-up children or to use the now vacant rooms as rented rooms to supplement their income; see Tipple, 2000.
7. UNCHS (Habitat), 1996a.
8. NIMBY suggests a desire for necessary urban externalities, or other activities that potentially reflect negatively on house prices, to be located elsewhere in the city. This is often complemented by the more obstructive BANANA: build absolutely nothing anywhere near anyone.
9. Private renters eventually end up paying the full capital cost of dwellings through their rent, as well as all of the other costs of ownership. They also have to meet the management costs and risk/vacancy premium of the landlord, which an owner does not have to pay. Most significantly, they do not receive any direct benefit from capital gains and pay higher rents as property values inflate. In some cases, however, landlords do not make a good return from their rooms and sometimes voluntarily charge less than market prices for rooms out of social concern for renters. They may also allow family members to live rent-free. See Tipple and Willis, 1991; Willis and Tipple, 1991.
10. Payne, 2002.
11. Hall, 1997.
12. Murie, 1997.
13. Priemus and Dielemann, 1997, 1999.
14. It is clear that these estimates are not perfect, especially given the many intermediary positions in the formal-informal continuum; but they are the only ones available. Furthermore, housing tenure varies a great deal between otherwise similar or neighboring countries, depending upon social attitudes and the policies that have been followed, so diversity is very considerable within each region. For example, home-ownership is around 70 percent in North America and Australia, and is even higher in some countries where

most people still live in rural areas; but it is under 50 percent throughout Europe.

15. Amole et al, 1993.
16. UN-Habitat, 2002f.
17. Especially Turner, 1976; de Soto, 1989.
18. For example, World Bank, 1993.
19. de Soto, 1989.
20. In Egypt, acquiring and legally registering a lot on a state-owned desert land involves at least 77 bureaucratic procedures at 31 public and private agencies. In Peru, building a home on state-owned land requires 207 procedural steps at 52 government offices, says de Soto (1989). In The Philippines, establishing legal ownership takes 168 steps, and between 13 and 25 years. In Haiti, obtaining a lease on government land—a preliminary requirement to buying—takes 65 steps. Similar numbers of procedures surround the registering of legal business enterprises. In Mozambique, for example, registering a new business requires 19 steps and five months, and costs more than the average annual income per capita (World Bank, 2001a).
21. de Soto, 2000.
22. This value was stated by de Soto (2000) without demonstrating the method, and has been criticized by Woodruff (2001), Gilbert (2001) and Payne (2002) as a considerable overestimate. However, the number is widely quoted in UNCHS (Habitat) (2001b): www.un.org/ga/lstanbul+5/32.pdf.
23. Including, Payne, 1998, 2002; Gilbert, 2001; Angel, 2001.
24. Payne, 2002. In fact, self-help housing is only rarely traded in Columbia, according to Gough (1998), and is not well suited to commodification.
25. Gilbert, 2001.
26. Deininger and Binswanger, 1998.
27. Gilbert, 2001.
28. Payne, 2002.
29. Angel, 2001.
30. Angel, 1983, 2001; Deninger and Binswanger, 1998.
31. The cooperative movements and assisted self-build initiatives have been widely encouraged in a number of countries in a situation of housing shortages.
32. For example, UNCHS (Habitat), 1996a.
33. It remains to be seen exactly what the effects of this relaxed lending regime will be; but the current high stock market valuations can be partly attributed to liberalized mortgage and finance markets.
34. Malpezzi and Ball, 1991.
35. Angel, 2001; Fernandez, 1998; Payne, 1997, 2001, 2002.
36. Gilbert, 2001.
37. Payne, 2002.
38. Durand-Lasserve and Royston, 2002.
39. Angel, 2001.
40. Durand-Lasserve and Royston, 2002.
41. Usually on the grounds that public money would be helping a few entrepreneurs to make profits.
42. Tipple, 1994.
43. de Soto, 2000.
44. Kumar, 1996; Tipple and Willis, 1990.
45. de Soto, 2000; Gilbert, 2000.

Part III
Emotional Hope

SECTION G
PROSTITUTION

On the Burmese border of northern Thailand, edging the Golden Triangle, money means opium and heroin, and every spring the thatched bamboo huts of the villages are roofed with poppy heads drying in the sun. The only other commodity here is young girls. In Mae Sai town, the flashing red and yellow fairy lights outside a local brothel cast a surreal glow over Kok, 11, as she sits quietly with ten other frilly-dressed girls waiting for her customers. At first it seems unbelievable that this small child is working as a prostitute, but she is available for sex at $38 a night. . . .

Her eyes are made up heavily with black kohl, lips reddened, and fingernails lacquered pink. But no amount of make-up can disguise the child-sized feet in tiny red flip-flops, the pre-pubescent figure hidden under a sailor-collared shirt or the high-pitched voice. "My father sold me for 200 baht [$5] two months ago," she says. "He comes to the brothel every month to collect 3000 baht ($190) from Big Ma. I clean Big Ma's house in the day and then work as a prostitute at night. I don't get money at all—just food. I get one man a night but most of the girls go with six or seven men a night." Kok says she has never used a condom.[1]

Prostitution is an integral part of the poverty landscape that cannot be ignored, though it would be far more comforting if we could just turn our heads away from the reality of eleven-year-old prostitutes. We'd like to imagine prostitution in a sanitized form: willing and eager call girls dispatched to lonely, rich men. We'd rather not imagine what goes on in the lives of girls as young as six years old being sold as sex slaves to entertain as many as ten men a day. But there are untold numbers of these girls (and boys) on the streets of every major and many smaller cities.

The prostitution industry is not primarily nurtured and driven by women who choose prostitution as a career, although that does happen. Prostitution is perpetuated by brothel owners and pimps who prey on women and children forced into this life by dire poverty and by despairing men who seek sexual highs to satisfy an addiction or relieve their own depression. Prostitutes must develop an emotional distance from their work. Some view their work with the kind of detachment with which a janitor cleans a public toilet. Nonetheless, prostitution is not benign. It is destructive to the prostitute, to the nuclear family structure so vital to a healthy society, and ultimately to the men who visit prostitutes. Those with a variety of gifts are needed to befriend prostitutes and help them move out of this industry. Those with law degrees are needed to aid the process of shutting down brothels. Counselors are needed to help prostitutes deal with the emotional damage that inevitably comes with such a lifestyle. People with business skills are required to create healthy employment opportunities for former prostitutes. And I am convinced there is a demonic element to prostitution that requires addressing by someone with spiritual discernment. In addition, hardly anyone seems to be dealing with the unique problems of male prostitutes, and fewer still seem to be dealing with the demand side of prostitution: the millions and millions of users, many of whom also have deep issues and needs.

The two readings selected below tell the ugly truth about prostitution. The first reading from El Universal, an online Mexican newspaper, reports on the sad reality of sex trafficking between San Diego and Mexico. In part, this is the story of an investigators challenge to get governments on both sides to acknowledge the problem. The second reading is a seminal investigative report from Human Rights Watch Asia allowing the prostitutes themselves to tell their stories. These readings give voice to prostitutes and help to build an understanding of the sex industry from the perspective of the women who have found themselves in a situation nearly impossible to climb out of without help.

Notes

1. Jocasta Shakespeare. "Saving the Child Sex Slaves," http://www.burmalibrary.org/reg.burma/archives/199406/msg00057

CHAPTER 13

THE SEX TRAFFICKING OF CHILDREN IN SAN DIEGO

ANABEL HERNANDEZ GARCIA
TRANSLATED BY CHUCK GOOLSBY

When Rick Castro, a deputy sheriff for San Diego County burst into the house in Vista, a lower middle class neighborhood to the north of San Diego, the first thing that he saw was the destitute brown eyes of a slight girl no older than fourteen, whose hair hung to the middle of her back, dressed in a short black miniskirt and a white tee shirt with the red and blue letters "USA" on it.

The officer was moved by her beauty, but was moved even more by the look of terror in her eyes. Paola had just arrived a few weeks ago at this house of prostitution, dragged there from Morelos, Mexico by the Salazar brothers. Julio, Tomas and Luciano Salazar-Juárez are the dons of the largest local network trafficking and sexual exploiting Mexican girls and adolescents, who have operated for over ten years in the agricultural camps and suburbs of San Diego.

The three men from the Mexican state of Oaxaca had found in the land of opportunity the perfect place to build their empire, trafficking from southern Mexico to the U.S. border with their human merchandise. In their path, they kidnap, extort, corrupt and violate our national laws and those of the United States, with nobody to stop them.

This is part of an investigation conducted by El Universal, during which we received testimonies, data, documents and physical evidence showing the methods used by this criminal organization, that according to our information has extended its reach to Fresno, Nevada and New York.

Christopher Tenorio, U.S. Department of Justice prosecutor for the Southern District of California, and San Diego deputy sheriff Rick Castro revealed for our newspaper the details of how this gang operates. At the end of 2001 the FBI began a formal investigation against the Salazar brothers, who were also presumed to be involved in drug trafficking.

Hundreds of girls, from 12 to 18 years old, originating in Oaxaca, Michoacan, Morelos and Veracruz, have been kidnapped or duped into being stripped of all of their human rights and converted into sexual slaves in local farm labor camps. The locations in San Diego where this network operates are: Vista; Las Casitas de Escondido; Las Antenas, Carlsbad; Carrizales, Oceanside; Del Mar, and Los Gatos, in Valley Center.

Paola, the "USA" girl, having been filed away in the gang's "system" was handled by Tomas Salazar. During her few days in the American union she had been passed through all of the exploitation camps. Because of her beauty, she became preferred merchandise, and day and night had to service long lines of men, indoors and out. Of the 20 dollars that each "client" paid, she never saw one dollar. Tomas kept all of the money.

The Houses of Prostitution

This is the largest prostitution outfit in all of San Diego, deputy sheriff Castro assures us. Since 1996, Castro, of Mexican ancestry born in the U.S., has followed the tracks of the Salazar brothers. "When I came to work with the sheriff, I was the only one who spoke Spanish, so at that time they gave me the task of investigating cases of child prostitution. The case had been open for two years, but no movement was made because none of the officers spoke Spanish," recalls Castro, 39, who today is the primary source of information for the FBI. He spent months tracking Tomas and Luciano Salazar. He photographed the houses in Vista where minors were prostituted; he patrolled the highways, tracking trucks full of clients going to the exploitation camps, and he received testimony from neighbors.

Three years later, working with the INS and armed with a court's search warrant, Castro entered the prostitution houses located near Kelly's Bar on North Santa Fe Avenue. He found dozens of women, among them girls between 12 and 16 years old, victims of commercial sexual exploitation.

"When we went in we found record books tracking the number of clients served by each woman and stopwatches to limit their service to clients to ten minutes. We confiscated dozens of empty boxes of condoms, each box having held a thousand condoms. We were able to calculate how many clients the house had and how much money it generated. We also found refrigerators full of beer, shelves full of alcoholic beverages and handguns."

Deputy Castro recalls that when they interrogated the minors, the girls stated that they were older, 19 or 20 years old, "but their bodies and their eyes reflected a much lower age." That's how deputy Castro met Paola. The older women refused to testify in court, but in exchange they did supply officers with the addresses of other houses held by the Salazars, and police were able to shut down 25 such locations.

How They Get Their Victims

Nobody knows how many people are in the Salazar organization, but investigations by the authorities reveal that this is an organized crime gang made up of various components: the procurers, who locate victims; the traffickers, who take them to the U.S.; and the "big daddy's" (pimps) who conduct the sex trade with their victims.

The adolescent girls trafficked by the Salazar brothers are poor in every sense of the word. They don't have money, they don't have a future and they don't know how to read or write.

The Salazar brothers have various ways of procuring their victims: they build an emotional relationship with them; they convince the minor girl and her family to let her be taken to the U.S. to work; or they kidnap them. Many of the girls have children, either by one of the three brothers or by other men. These children are snatched from their mothers and are kept as hostages. When a girl tries to escape, she is told that her child will be killed.

To transport these minor girls to the U.S., the exploiters pay coyotes up to $1,500 each, deputy Castro tells us. Usually, they are taken across the U.S. border at Tijuana and Tecate. The main members of the gang are: Miguel Hernandez or "Tonatiuh," Edmundo Zitlapopoca, and Arturo and Pedro Lopez, both from Atlixco, in Puebla [state].

The Three Salazars

The Salazar brothers came to San Diego without a penny. They began a "business" prostituting their wives. Now their legacy is one of tales of the cruel exploitation of children, the wads of dollars that they take from the exploitation camps, and the hellish punishment that anyone who tries to escape them awaits.

Once, in one of the Salazar brother's houses in Vista, Julia, 17 years old, refused to work. Tomas, who exploited her, closed the business and in front of everyone else beat her with a hook until he ripped flesh from her arms, legs and back. Tomas was imprisoned for domestic violence and is serving a 20-year sentence, made easier by the thousands of dollars that he continues to make every week from exploiting women, even while behind bars.

Luciano was detained at the end of last December [2002] when he came to a wake with three of the prostituted women. So far, he has only been jailed for being undocumented, but according to prosecutor Tenorio and deputy Castro, authorities have successfully obtained evidence allowing Luciano to be charged with exploiting minors, thus unmasking the network.

Julio who is 37 years old, is the oldest brother and the leader of the organization. He is the only legal [U.S.] immigrant and has his own tow truck business, which, it is rumored is used to transport drugs. Deputy Castro notes that Julio is still free, and that he is the worst one of them all.

TRAFFICKING AND SEXUAL EXPLOITATION

The first time that Marissa Ugarte saw Reyna was at the end of 2001, at the San Diego Police Department. The 15-year-old girl, who looked 30, with her split lip and an eye swollen shut from the beating that she had just received, remained strong, in the pose of a fatalistic woman. It was then that she began to reveal the past that had worn her down, allowing a wounded child to shine again.

Marissa, the granddaughter of Salvador Ugarte, founder and former owner of the commercial bank Bancomer, never imagined when she came to live in this city five years ago that she would be a witness to such a criminal tale, without a happy ending, and would spend hours listening to the most profound grief that she had ever heard.

Who would imagine that San Diego, a paradise for thousands of children who year after year visit Sea World, Wild Animal Park and the San Diego Zoo can, for some children, turn into hell. This is the dirty secret of this city, as the non-governmental organizations call it, a secret that Reyna lived through during seven months. Reyna was one of the victims of the child sex trafficking and exploitation gang that operates in San Diego, lead by three Mexican men: Julio, Tomas and Luciano Salazar-Juarez.

Marissa began to hear rumors about the trafficking of children, fake adoptions and the sale of children when she worked in the DIF (Desarrollo Integral de la Familia—The State System for the Full Development of the Family) in Tijuana in 1997. She heard that these children where being taken to San Diego to be exploited to make pornography.

That was until 2000, when she began her work as a sociologist with EYE, an agency aiding children in crisis in San Diego, where she began to be certain about what was happening here. In this county, from Escondido to Point Loma to Balboa Park, in the heart of the city, all forms of illegal sexual exploitation exist: child pornography; trafficking in mostly underage male and female sex workers; and high risk homeless children who prostitute themselves to survive. This is due, says Marissa, to the fact that this is one of the most important military communities in the United States, in addition to the fact that there is a strong market for sexual services from farm laborers.

We began to hear that an American "corridor" for the trafficking of children utilized for commercial sexual exploitation existed, and, together with the University of San Diego, Children's Hospital and the legal counsel's office for San Diego County, we created the Bilateral Safety Corridor Coalition for the Prevention of the Commercial Sexual Exploitation of Minors, which is now composed of 35 Mexican and American organizations. Marissa is the organization's Executive Director.

In 2001 the commission informed the Mexican consulate about what was occurring in the farm labor camps. Mexican girls and adolescents were being sexually exploited by their own fellow countrymen. "They ignored me, believing that the story wasn't true, and that it was exaggerated. I decided to go to UNICEF in Mexico to denounce the abuses that were occurring. I was later called by the Mexican consulate and they asked me for a formal complaint supported by concrete evidence." The consular official contacted Rick Castro of the San Diego Sheriff's Department, who had been investigating the Salazar brothers' gang during the past three years. The Mexican Consulate made its formal complaint directly to the U.S. Government, and demanded an investigation.

"Three weeks later, we got our first case," recalls Marissa.

We were called by a child protection network in San Diego. We were informed that the network had a girl who did not fit within the criteria used by the Polinsky Children's Center, because the case involved a girl who was a sex trafficking victim, and they didn't know where to send her.

Marissa contacted deputy sheriff Castro because the case was from the neighborhood of Vista. The local police department had received an emergency call reporting that a young girl had escaped from prostitution in the farm labor camps and had been beaten by her pimp, Arturo Lopez, who worked for the Salazar brothers.

When the police found her she had a split lip, and she was bruised and scared. "She wore a tiny miniskirt and a jacket, and was so over-painted that you almost couldn't recognize her real face. She looked to be between ten and fifteen years older than her real age. Her hair was short and dyed brown, her mouth was small, she had the eyes of a dreamer and a very seductive attitude.

"When we began to interview her she broke down and out came an agonized human being drowning in pain." She was sent to a shelter for battered women.

The Mexican consulate contacted the local U.S. federal prosecutor and Reyna agreed to make a formal criminal complaint. Starting at that point, little by little, Reyna began revealing her story. She was from Puebla, Mexico. She had barely finished second grade. Her mother died when she was seven years old. Reyna was then supported by her grandmother, who also died. After that, her father was left in charge of her. One day, when she was 11, her own father gave her as a gift to a local police chief who raped her without end. After having been so neglected, and with a baby now in her arms, Reyna met Arturo Lopez, from the town of Atlixco in the state of Puebla. Arturo, after pretending to fall in love with her, convinced Reyna to work as a servant in the United States, for which Arturo recommended that she leave her baby with some of his relatives. Reyna had no other options, so she accepted the offer.

Reyna was taken to Tijuana, and while she waited to be crossed over the border, she was threatened that her baby would be killed, to prostitute herself in the red zone known as "la Coahuila." She was finally transported across the U.S. border by a coyote, Alonso Sapien, also known as "El Chivero."

In San Diego, Reyna came to live in a neighborhood in Vista where she found other girls like her. A week later she found herself in the sexual exploitation camps for farm workers.

"The real horror is in the sheer number of men that, at the age of 15, Reyna was forced to serve as a prostitute. In one hour she had to serve 20 men, and they made her work from 8 AM until 2 in the afternoon. We are not talking about just prostitution, but also about slavery, about the violation of all of Reyna's human rights," noted Marissa.

Reyna began to become physically sick. One should understand that for any person who is forced to submit themselves to being a victim of sexual exploitation, the physical, emotional and spiritual deterioration is profound. Reyna, to cope and survive in that world, began to use drugs and alcohol.

One day, during the judicial process, Reyna became tired of telling her story again and again to the authorities, because each time she had to relate the story she was forced to relive what had happened to her.

"It was a terrible re-victimization. What I did was to stay with her two or three hours at a time, but that wasn't enough. When she came to the shelter she was drowning in her own pain, and then the post-trauma began, as she recalled the tragedy of her life from the time of her young childhood," noted Marissa, who accompanied the girl throughout the entire process. She still remembers Reyna banging her head against the wall.

"One day she came and asked me 'how is my makeup.' She didn't have a drop of makeup on. That's when she stopped being Reyna and returned to being the little girl that she was. It took over nine months for her to accept her real name. The child could not take any more. The judicial process stopped and the only thing that Reyna asked for was that her child be returned to her. During the middle of 2002, the Mexican consulate began to search for her child.

In Oceanside Arturo Lopez's brother Pedro was detained, and he convinced his brother to turn Reyna's son over to the Mexican DIF in Puebla. After passing through numerous legal hurdles, the DIF returned the child to Reyna.

At the beginning of May, 2002, Adrian Martinez, a Mexican consular official in charge of human rights protection, traveled with Reyna to Tlaxcala to recover her child.

"The baby was now three months old, and actually didn't recognize his mother. His first reaction was to cry, but thirty minutes later he didn't want to leave his mother."

While Reyna was recovering her child, Marissa lost her own child to a fatal cerebral tumor.

Today, Reyna has obtained a "T" visa for victims of trafficking, and she participates in a special program for child victims of exploitation in Phoenix, Arizona. Arturo Lopez Rojas, the man who exploited Reyna, escaped to Puebla. It was said that he would be charged but to this day nothing has happened. The PGR (Attorney General of the Republic) is investigating the case in Mexico.

MINORS ARE PROSTITUTED IN FARM LABOR CAMPS IN SAN DIEGO

Thirty five minutes outside of San Diego is the suburb of Oceanside, which is popular for its splendid residential zone and its commercial fields of strawberries bordered by fields of golden reeds. This is where the nickname of "the reed beds" (Los Carrizales) came from. Here is where the "fields of love" are located. That is what the Mexican criminal gang of Julio, Tomas and Luciano Salazar-Juarez, traffickers and exploiters of Mexican girls and teens, called the exploitation camps where their victims where taken to provide sexual services for between 100 to 300 farm workers at a time. For all of these "clients" there is service every day, at every hour. We're talking about prostitution in the open, without walls, nor windows, nor beds nor sheets. There, on the ground in "caves" made of reeds, is where the only taste left in the mouths of these girls is dirt, alcohol and the sweat of their "clients."

"The first time I went to the camps I didn't vomit only because I had an empty stomach. It was truly grotesque and unimaginable," recalls Patricia, our fictitious name for a medical doctor who works with government supplied resources, and who for the last five years has been in contact with the Salazar brothers, working to prevent HIV/AIDS and other venereal diseases in these exploited minor girls.

"If I wanted to help these girls I had to develop a relationship with the pimps. I learned that in the city of Guadalajara, where I worked for many years. I had to convert myself into someone who doesn't judge, who doesn't express opinions, but only listens. At one point one of the Salazar brothers took me to the girls in Los Carrizales because the girls didn't come out of the fields to meet me that time."

If ones travels along North River Avenue, at first there are only enormous houses valued at around $300,000 dollars each. California-style houses. Red tile roofs, painted from cream to orange, with flowers in their gardens. Just behind these houses are the fields of Japanese farmer Victor Sang.

"To get to the "fields of love" one has to pass by the Super 7 and the CIT 60 gas station on North River Avenue, at the corner of College Boulevard.

A few meters from the gas station, by the sidewalk of a Baptist church, you find a sign marking the location of an oil pipeline, which has a towel wrapped around it. Beyond that are the fields and a passageway.

It is an area of fields of reeds so thick that you can't see who is next to you. Once you enter these fields, a kilometer from the street, the reeds become thicker and you have to bend over to walk.

In these dense reeds you will find around eight "caves" made within the reed thickets, one right next to the other. Pieces of plastic bags are tied to the reeds. These are used by the minors to throw condoms and the toilet paper that they use to clean up with after each encounter with a "client." After the bags are filled they are disposed of so as not to leave any evidence behind.

Within the caves, on the ground, you find empty beer bottles, boxes of liquor bottles, shreds of cloth, pieces of blankets, plastic junk, hats, tee-shirts. All deaf witnesses to hours of horror.

All of this junk is mixed in with open condom packets and dozens of used condoms that leak semen into the ground. The musky smell floods the air, making your stomach turn. This is hell . . . virtual fields on fire. "When I came here, in one hour I counted that one little girl had been with 35 men, one after the other. She just lifted her skirt. It is just vaginal masturbation," notes Patricia. "Generally they do this to the girls who are no longer virgins. They spend six months being transported back and forth through the various camps."

"The girls that I saw that time [in the fields] were very young, they were not over 14 years old, they had been sold a lot to 'los gringos' (American men)." "This area is full of red necks, they are far right-wing white American men to whom they sell the virginity of little girls" notes Patricia.

I was present many times when these gringos called Julio [Salazar] asking to be sent a "cherry girl" (a virgin).

It is here, in one of the five corners of San Diego, where the Salazar brothers have extended their network.

This is where Paola, Reyna and dozens of other young girls were brought. All of them innocent "Erendiras," [a character in a novel by Nobel laureate author Gabriel Garcia Marquez, whose deflowering was motivated by greed.]

The ages of the girls that are brought here become younger as time goes on, now starting at nine and ten years old. "I once saw a seven year old girl. What was a seven year old girl doing in a place of prostitution? She wasn't anyone's daughter, they were using her," recalls the doctor in her desperation.

We are talking about defenseless persons, who have tragic life histories behind them. They live in a condition of post-traumatic stress syndrome, and in that condition they cede all authority to their victimizers.

The Escape of Julio Salazar

It was exactly here, in Los Carrizales, where one year ago the gang of the Salazar brothers was almost detained.

In December of 2001, in an operation coordinated by the U.S. Immigration and Naturalization Service (INS), more than 100 INS and FBI agents and sheriffs officers conducted a raid.

The agents didn't dare to enter the reed fields for fear of being ambushed, so they waited for the subjects to come out of the fields.

More than 50 people were apprehended. They included five minor girls who were prostituted in the fields, clients, and Julio Salazar, leader of the gang, who during the confusion managed to evade the officers and escape.

"A lot of money is involved in this business, thousands and thousands of dollars. I have seen myself how U.S. INS agents have sex with these minor girls for free, in exchange for protection. These agents even enter the houses of prostitution in uniform. May a lightning-bolt split me in half if I am lying!" exclaimed the social worker [Patricia].

The minor girls were placed in U.S. INS detention, where they were interrogated without the assistance of psychiatrists who could have intervened in the crisis. What the agents wanted was a formal complaint against the Salazar brothers, allowing them to be charged, but the girls declined to cooperate. The girls were deported, and all of the persons detained were freed.

"I fought a lot with the U.S. government and they told me that I shouldn't do anything, that I had signed a federal agreement of confidentiality and that I could not form a complaint from anything that I had been told [in this case]."

I understood that I could not stand up in face-to-face confrontation like Samson, concluded Patricia.

The Deaths in Carlsbad

At another location similar to Los Carrizales, in [the San Diego neighborhood of] Carlsbad, the last two years the bodies of minor Mexican girls, with signs of torture and abuse, have begun to appear, San Diego deputy sheriff Rick Castro tells us.

Nobody knows who these murder victims are. Nobody even claims their bodies because it is presumed that they are undocumented. They could be girls trafficked by the Salazar brothers. Castro assures us that he knows nothing about the case of the murder of [hundreds of] women and girls in Cuidad Juarez [Juarez City], Mexico, but given the common pattern of the abuse of victims in both cases, the modus operandi appear to be similar.

CHAPTER 14

RAPE FOR PROFIT: PATTERNS OF ABUSE

HUMAN RIGHTS WATCH/ASIA

There are two distinct patterns to the trafficking of girls and women from Nepal. The best known and oldest involves the enticement of mainly Tamang girls from hill districts where the flesh trade has become an almost traditional source of income. But the incidence of forced trafficking from other parts of Nepal is also on the rise.[1] Poor migrant women and children whose families have moved to Nepal's urban areas in search of employment are the principal victims. These girls and women come from all castes and ethnic groups. Human Rights Watch/Asia visited Nepal and interviewed women from several areas of Nepal who had been trafficked to India and had returned. In all cases, families, neighbors and friends play an active role in forced trafficking by concocting fictitious marriage and job offers, contacting recruiters and brokers, or simply luring girls away from home on outings or errands, kidnapping and selling them. Regardless of the victims' origins, their reports of abuse in Indian brothels are remarkably consistent.

The average age of the thousands of Nepali girls recruited every year for prostitution in brothels in India has reportedly dropped in the past decade from fourteen to sixteen years in the 1980s, to ten to fourteen in 1991, despite new laws promulgated in both countries in 1986 designed to stem trafficking and child prostitution.[2] Police in areas with a high incidence of trafficking state that the average age of new trafficking victims is about thirteen. However, trafficking victims are frequently coached by captors to conceal their true ages. Girls forced into prostitution in Bombay's brothels may remain trapped in the brothel system for more than ten years, during which time they may be sold from one brothel to another many times.

CASE HISTORIES

The following cases, based on interviews conducted by Human Rights Watch/Asia in March 1994 with young women in Nepal who had returned from Bombay, and in July 1994 with women still employed in Bombay's brothels, describe some of the patterns typical of trafficking between Nepal and India. The first, "Maya" represents a case of simple abduction. Although she filed a complaint against her traffickers, no one was ever prosecuted.

"Maya"

"Maya" is from a small village in Nuwakot district. She is twenty-three, but looks much older. She has dark circles under her eyes; her skin is dry and lined. A local health worker thinks she was ejected from a brothel in Bombay after testing positive for HIV, a story Maya denies. Maya said she first left her village when she was eighteen and returned to her village in July 1993, after spending three years in an Indian brothel.

Maya was married to a man from a nearby village when she was around thirteen. Soon after, her husband began seeing someone else. He moved out when Maya was sixteen, married a second wife and took her to Kathmandu. Maya had lived alone for two years when her father-in-law told her she should follow her husband to Kathmandu. He took her there. At her husband's house she was beaten and treated very badly.

In 1990 a fellow villager began visiting the house. The second time he came to visit, he brought another man along. They invited Maya and her husband to come out to see a movie. Maya's husband told her to go ahead without him. The three of them boarded a bus, which Maya said kept going farther and farther from Kathmandu. Eventually, they went through the border at Kakarbhitta. They were never stopped or questioned by the police.

After two days traveling by bus, they reached Bombay and the men left Maya at a house and told her they would pick her up the next day. They never came back. Maya realized she was in a brothel when she saw that the house was occupied by about twenty-five women, all but three of whom were from Nepal. Two or three were girls she had known from her own village. The brothel where Maya worked was called a "pillow house," lowest in the brothel hierarchy where most new girls start out. It was a large building, with several rooms where the women lived, slept and worked. There were eight beds in each room and curtains dividing the beds. All of the girls' and women's earnings were turned over to the brothel owner, a woman named Renu Tamang from Urleni in Nuwakot district. The women worked from noon to 1:00 a.m. They were given no days off.

After a year, the owner told Maya that the broker had been paid for her and that she was responsible for paying back her purchase price, but she was never told how much she owed. The owner told her she could go home only after she paid off her debt. Maya noted that another brothel inmate, a woman from Trisuli, had worked there for thirteen years and had never managed to pay off her debt.

Maya was beaten severely for the first four or five days she was held in the brothel because she refused to have sex with customers. They continued to beat her until she submitted. Later on, she was beaten with bottles and thick sticks because she was not earning enough. She said that all the brothel inmates were beaten if they did not earn enough. Her customers included Indians and foreigners—Germans, Singaporeans, Filipinos and Saudi Arabians. The customers would select the women they wanted, and the women could not refuse, or they would be beaten.

In the three years Maya was held in the brothel, she never received any form of contraception. Girls who became pregnant would be given abortions. The brothel did not provide condoms, but occasionally customers brought their own. Maya said that she never asked clients to use condoms because she did not know they could prevent AIDS. She said she had heard about AIDS, but did not know anything about it. Because she stayed in the brothel only a short time, she did not know the symptoms.

After one year in Bombay, Maya began to get sick. She developed a high fever and was taken to the doctor who gave her an injection, but she did not know what it was. She then returned to work. Maya told Human Rights Watch/Asia that she and two other girls, one from Sindhupalchok who was sick, and one from Gorkha, decided to escape from the brothel. All of them had been beaten often and thought they should flee to save their lives. Maya said that while some police officers often came as clients to the brothel, one branch of the police force frequently raided the brothel looking for child prostitutes. The three women appealed to these police to help them escape, and the police took them to the border and handed them over to the Hanuman Dhoka police station in Kathmandu. Maya was sent on to the police in Ranipowa and then Trisuli, where she was held in detention for ten days. From there it took her six days to reach Nuwakot. As Maya understood the police policy on returnees, the police inform the girl's family by letter and then hold her until relatives come to collect her.

Maya and the two other women filed complaints at the Hanuman Dhoka police station in Kathmandu, and the police told them that they would be informed once the traffickers were found, but as far as she knows, no one was ever arrested.

Maya's health deteriorated after her return. She lost weight and suffered from diarrhea, high fevers and stomach aches. Since returning to the village, her health has improved slightly. In January 1994, she was treated with traditional medicine and feels that she has been cured, although she remains very tired and weak and cannot work. Local health workers suspect Maya may not have escaped but was ejected from the brothel in India because she had contracted HIV.

"Tara"

At thirty-four or thirty-five years old, "Tara" is a senior woman in a brothel in Bombay. She was described as the "in-charge" of the younger brothel inmates by a local activist. Senior women like Tara are frequently used by gharwalis to keep track of newer inmates. They watch for escape attempts, listen for forbidden conversations with customers, and accompany younger girls when they leave the premises for medical treatment. The interview with Tara was instructive because it reflected both her experiences as a young trafficking victim, and her attitudes now which are closer to those of brothel management.

Tara arrived in Bombay eighteen or nineteen years ago when she was sixteen years old. She told Human Rights Watch/Asia that she grew up in Nuwakot jilla [district] and got trapped into prostitution when she went with two girlfriends to see the cigarette factories at Janakpur, on the Nepal/India border.

We fell into the clutches of a dalali [procuress]—a Nepali dalali at that. We were three girls together, in the beginning. We spent two years together, but then we were separated. I don't know what happened to the other two girls. I often wonder what happened to them. When I was captured, I could not escape or return to my home: they would have caught me for sure. If I had known what was to happen to me, I would have killed myself halfway. [But] leaving this life is not an option for me, I simply cannot think about it. My purity was violated, so I thought: why go back, go back to what? I may as well just stay here. If I ever catch that damn dalali, I don't know what I would do to her. If I ever catch her, you have simply no idea what I will do to her.

Tara described her bewilderment upon arrival in Bombay:

When they brought me here, it was in a taxi. I kept looking around, wondering what kind of work was going on in this area of this big city. Everywhere I looked, I saw curtained doorways and rooms in this area. Men would go and come through these curtained entrances. People on the street would be calling out, "Two rupees, two rupees." I asked the other Nepali women if these were offices; it seemed the logical explanation. In two days I knew everything. I cried.

The building in Bombay where Tara lives and works has two floors, and probably houses about fifty women. There are two "maliks" [bosses] for the building. Tara said there were four rooms on her floor, and four Nepali girls and two Indian in her room. She said that when she first came, there were mostly Nepali girls working there, and a Nepali gharwali. Now both Indian and Nepalis work together. She said that like her, these younger Nepali girls came from the mountain areas of Nepal.

Despite the fact that Tara was herself an unwilling victim of the industry, she remained caught in the system for nearly twenty years and is now a senior inmate with management responsibilities. Her testimony, bitter when referring to the past or to women who have managed to escape, was generally sympathetic to her gharwali—with whom she probably shares a similar history. The fact that she has not attempted to return to Nepal or to open her own establishment suggests that she has not escaped the cycle of debt.

Many girls return to their home area, build houses. Money is everything. It gets you acceptance in the village. There is no one in Nepal who does not know about Bombay, and this business, not one person in Nepal. The gharwali is good to the girls and does not harm them. She makes the food arrangements, takes care of their needs. It is when a girl falls into the clutches of bad men, thugs, *goondas* [thugs], that she is defiled by them, and ill-treated in many ways.

Tara's testimony reflects some of the most persistent myths of the trafficking industry—that all prostitution is voluntary and driven by economic hardship, and that many prostitutes become rich and return home. Brothel inmates report being coached to give stock answers to questions from investigators and curious customers, and oft-repeated success stories help keep inmates striving to earn. "Santhi," a woman whose case is described below, told Human Rights Watch/ Asia "In the brothels we were told by the owner to tell the police we came by ourselves because we didn't have food. We were told to say we were twenty-five years old. If we didn't say that we would be beaten." A relief worker who had done research in Bombay and knows Santhi says brothel inmates she interviewed gave her similar answers when she questioned them about their past.

THE PATH TO BOMBAY

The Nepali girls and women who were interviewed by Human Rights Watch/Asia were forcibly trafficked into India. They did not work as prostitutes voluntarily but were held in conditions tantamount to slavery. Promises of jobs and marriage are common techniques by which recruiters entice their victims to leave home. But other, more overtly coercive tactics such as kidnapping are also reported. Girls who are already in debt bondage in other industries, particularly carpet factories, are particularly vulnerable.

The Traffickers

Traffickers are most typically men in their twenties or thirties or women in their thirties and forties who have traveled the route to the city several times and know the hotels to stay in and the brokers to contact. Traffickers frequently work in groups of two or more. Male and female traffickers are sometimes referred to as *dalals and dalalis,* (commission agents) who are either employed by a brothel owner directly, or operate more or less independently. Professional agents who recruit for the bigger brothels reportedly may be paid up to Rs.6,000 [$200] per girl. But most traffickers are small-time, local recruiters who earn considerably less. In either case, to stay in business they need the patronage of local bosses and the protection afforded by bribes to the police.

Female traffickers are referred to as *didi* or *phupu didi* (literally, paternal aunt). In Nuwakot district, according to local activists, the majority of *didis* are returned prostitutes from five or six Village Development Committees (VDCs) in eastern Nuwakot.[3] The peak trafficking months in Nuwakot and Sindhupalchowk are between June and late August or early September when the *didis* return to the villages to participate in local festivals and to recruit girls to bring back to the cities. These months precede the harvest, when poverty is felt most acutely, making it easy to recruit.

People become especially vulnerable every year from June to August, which are known as the "hungry months." At this time, every mountain village of Nepal suffers from more than the usual level of poverty, while they wait for the new harvests. Villagers have depleted their store of grains, and their hunger drives them to the local moneylender and feudal lord. This impossible situation has forced many young people from the mountain villages to urban centers, where they search for employment and a better future. Most young men work in factories, transportation, and construction, whereas the young girls and women work in garment and carpet factories, and in domestic service. A proportion of the young women will disappear to India.[4]

Family members—uncles, cousins, stepfathers—also act as trafficking agents. Of seven trafficking victims interviewed by Human Rights Watch/Asia in March 1994, six were trafficked to India with the help of close family friends or relatives. In each case, the victim complained of deception.

Girls are recruited in a number of ways. Village girls and their families are often deceived by smartly dressed young men who arrive in the village claiming to have come from Kathmandu and offering marriage and all the comforts of modern urban life. They go through a local ceremony and leave the village never to be seen again. The girls end up in Indian brothels.

Sometimes older men promise the girls employment in the city. Another avenue is through distant relatives or friends who pretend to arrange a marriage with relatives or friends in another village, but instead abduct the girl and send her to India. Sometimes a trusted individual abducts the girl on the pretext of educating her in India.[5]

Trafficking appears to be on the increase throughout Nepal and to be growing most rapidly in areas where it has so far received the least attention—towns and villages along the east-west highway, border towns, tourist centers and, according to some reports, the camps that house Bhutanese refugees in Jhapa district in eastern Nepal.[6]

Local women who have returned from India are also employed as recruiters. These women are exceptionally well-placed to identify potential trafficking victims because they already know the local girls and their families.

Women who are already in the sex trade and have graduated to the level of brothel keepers, managers or even owners travel through the villages of their own and neighboring districts in search of young girls. Though not very typical, the following story encapsulates the essence of the dream of success and glamour that these women symbolize to the simple village girls.

Only a short time before my visit, a madam had alighted upon this remote hill village in Sindhupalchowk in a helicopter rented from Kathmandu, for which she must have had to pay a sum of about $1,000. She descended like a celestial fairy mother in the midst of these poor village folk, in all her resplendent finery, and doled out little gifts of baubles and cosmetics to the starry-eyed adolescent girls. . . . When this madam left the village, seven young girls disappeared with her.[7]

The typical agent is far less glamorous, and the number of Nepali prostitutes who manage to become wealthy in India is minuscule. Most recruiters are women desperately trying to escape the abuse and debt bondage of the brothel system themselves.

Perhaps the most pernicious and lamentable examples in this category are those women who are themselves forced into prostitution and who have been told by their brothel keepers that the only way they can procure their release is by furnishing a substitute. At any given time, several of these women travel to their villages in the hope of cajoling a younger female relative, a friend or just another village woman to accompany them. Most often they are successful . . . and return with another victim, in lieu of themselves. However, once free they do not make an exit from the prostitution market, they merely end up working as . . . [independent] prostitutes and finally hope to set up their own little shop with five women working under them.[8]

These local agents buy girls from their families, sometimes for as little as Nepali Rs.200 [$4], or tempt them with promises of future earnings, and take them to the Indian border where they are sold to a broker for anything from Indian Rs.1,000-Rs.8,000 [$22-$266]. These middlemen then sell them to brothel owners in Bombay and elsewhere for Rs.15,000-Rs.50,000 [$500–$1,666], depending on the girl's age and beauty. Virgins command higher prices.

"Padma"

"Padma" is the *gharwali* of a small brothel in Bombay. She told Human Rights Watch/Asia that like many others, she came to India as a young girl, from a remote village in the mountains of Nepal. After twenty years in the profession she now runs a brothel which employs between three and six girls.

It took us six days of trekking to get to Kathmandu. Nowadays there is a bus service, so it is not so bad. Can you imagine: Six days! That was really bad. I don't know anyone else in the profession from my own village, but I know others, a couple of others, from neighboring villages. In my house ['ghar'], there are usually three or four girls. Sometimes there are six, but that is the maximum. There is no fixed number. In fact, there really is no telling from moment to moment. Just last month, two new girls arrived.

Notes

1. Trafficked Nepali women sometimes conceal their villages or towns of origin. For example, all the Nepalis in activist Preeti Pai Patkar's study said they came from one of three major areas: Chitwan, Narayanghat, or Nuwakot District. The activist noted that this was a suspiciously narrow range of answers. Not one girl said she came from a more remote region, despite evidence to the contrary. None reported coming from villages in Sindhupalchowk, where an enormous amount of trafficking occurs. There might be several reasons for this. While it is possible that these answers were an attempt at deliberate obfuscation, research by Human Rights Watch/Asia found that many *kothas*, or brothel compounds, are operated by and employ women from one specific area. Girls from Nuwakot and Sindhupalchowk work for madams from their own communities, madams from eastern Nepal recruit girls from eastern Nepal. It is possible that activists might have more contact with women from one region's kothas rather than from others.

2. Sanghera, Federation Internationale Terre des Hommes, Presentation to the U.N. Working Group on Contemporary Forms of Slavery, Geneva, July 29 to August 2, 1991.

3. Nepal is divided into five development regions, fourteen zones and seventy-five districts. Under the panchayat system these zones were administered by "zonal panchayats," which fed into the Rastriya Panchayat, but since 1990, zones no longer function as administrative units. Districts are broken down into subsectors called "village development committees" (VDCs), and "municipalities." There are 3,995 VDCs in Nepal and thirty-six municipalities. VDCs are the smallest local administrative unit. The Villager Development Committees of Betini, Bal Kumari, Sikharbeshi, Gyanphedi, Samundratar and Gaunkharka are noted as centers for trafficking. Urleni VDC is also the alleged home village for several brothel owners.

4. Gauri Pradan, "The Road to Bombay: Forgotten Women; Maya and Parvati: The End of a Dream," *Red Light Traffic, the Trade in Nepali Girls* (Nepal: ABC Nepal, 1992), p.33.

5. Omar Sattur, Anti-Slavery International and Child Workers of Nepal Concerned Centre, *Child Labor in Nepal,* No. 13 (Kathmandu: ASI's Child Labour Series, 1993), p.60.

6. Dr. Aruna Upreti of the Women's Rehabilitation Centre, a relief organization in Calcutta, told a journalist with *The Telegraph* in December 1993 that the number of Nepalis in Calcutta's brothels had doubled in the past year. She said that besides a large number of Tamang girls from Nepal's hill districts, Bhutanese girls from the refugee camps in eastern Nepal were arriving in India, and that girls from the southern town of Butwal had been found in places as far away as Hong Kong. *The Telegraph*,"Nepal Girl-runners Turn to City," (Calcutta, India) December 1, 1993.

7. Sanghera, Federation Internationale Terre des Hommes. This story is frequently repeated in Nepal to illustrate the enormous wealth accumulated by some Bombay brothel owners. Some newspaper reports identify the madam as Simla Tamang, who was convicted of trafficking in 1993 . According to press reports, Simla Tamang admitted in court to owning brothels in Bombay which employed some five hundred prostitutes. The Simla Tamang case is discussed at length in this section.

8. Sanghera, p.7.

SECTION H
CHILDREN

I remember rushing from one end of Mexico City to another, which is quite a challenge even with an efficient metro. Appointments with several development agencies on this particular day meant speeding through the labyrinth of multi-level subway tunnels and squeezing through what I call the Hildago Press. One million people a day pass through this junction of several metro lines. You don't step onto the metro in Hildago, you are carried along, sometimes against your will, by a moving mass of humanity. We needed to get to the north bus terminal in order to catch a bus to a remote area of Mexico City where Compassion International had a children's program. As we ran down one metro passage, my attention was drawn to a boy about ten years old. He was squatting with his back against a wall and his arms wrapped around his legs. His face was buried in his knees and he was sobbing uncontrollably. Mexico City is home to more than four hundred thousand street children. I had a split second to make a decision: was I going to stop or pass by? I pass many desperate people in my travels. But my heart and my spirit told me to stop and sit down next to the boy. Even with broken Spanish, I could sit with him for a moment and ask to help. I had money and connections with a ministry for street children. Perhaps I could do something. At least I could offer an arm around the shoulder and a smile. The two people I was following to the appointment were already quite a bit in front of me. A moment's delay and I could lose them. I made my choice as I rushed past the boy, without even pausing. The image of him huddled and crying in the metro has haunted me to this day.

The World Health Organization (WHO) estimates that there are between ten million and one hundred million street children worldwide, which is a number so large as to be meaningless to most of us.[1] The fact remains that there are way too many ten-year-olds crying in metro stations. In every large city in the world, a person can see them: children under fifteen years of age on the streets after 10:00 PM with a five-year-old brother or sister in tow. The problems are difficult to unravel and the solutions even more complex. Add to that the horrific statistic that about two hundred and fifty million children between five and fourteen years of age are working for a living.[2] Many of them work with hazardous materials, fight wars, or live in bonded slavery. Anyone attempting to affect urban transformation cannot ignore the plight of children. We may eradicate slums, create jobs, and open affordable housing for the current generation and be immediately inundated by the unfathomable army of children who live in an earthly hell waiting to take their place. They will bring with them into adulthood all the abuse which has been heaped on them. How will they know what it is to devote themselves to a spouse and to children, or to extend trust and acceptance to others, or to live in a way that does not take advantage of those who are weaker, if they themselves have never experienced such things? If you think one hundred million street kids or two hundred and fifty million working children create an intimidating problem, just wait. From the time I write these words until they are published, another great throng of street children will graduate into adulthood and begin having children, filling in the ranks that they left vacant.

United Nations Children's Fund (UNICEF) has published a report that looks at three factors that affect urban poor children: physical infrastructure, housing, and the social environment. Looking at the plight of children from these three angles helps to build a more comprehensive understanding of all that might go into delivering children from the harsh realities of urban poverty. The second reading was produced by Jeff Anderson, who works with children on the streets of Manila with Action International. His voice is one of a practitioner who has invested his heart with children on the streets and grants us a profile of the kind of children he works with everyday. Improving the lot of one urban poor child has a disproportionate effect on dozens of lives that child will impact in the future. Ignoring the plight of even one urban poor child can have the opposite disproportionate effect.

Notes

1. WHO, "Working with Street Children," WHO/MSD/MDP 00.14 (Geneva: WHO, 2000), iii.
2. UNICEF, "Worst Forms of Child Labor Data," The Progress of Nations (New York: UNICEF, 2000), http://www.globalmarch.org/worstformsreport/global.html.

CHAPTER 15
CONDITIONS FOR CHILDREN IN URBAN AREAS
UNICEF

Urban areas present some very specific challenges for those in poverty, and these challenges, in turn, have significant and often disproportionate impacts on children and adolescents, undermining their rights and their well being in ways that require particular responses. This section considers the implications for children of a poor urban environment. The environment in urban settlements is extremely complex and is made up of a wide range of intricately linked elements. This Digest focuses on three of these elements—physical infrastructure, housing and the social context—while recognizing, of course, that these categories are intimately connected.

Physical Infrastructure

Environmental conditions are generally particularly poor (and risky) in low income urban districts. Wherever there are high concentrations of people and of waste, the potential for contamination, contagion and disease is great. When this potential is not countered by effective provision, health costs are very high and infants and young children are disproportionately affected. Millions of urban infants and children die each year, and many more suffer from illnesses or injuries that can and should be prevented.[1] Age-related risk factors include immature immune systems, higher exposure to pathogens, greater susceptibility to particular chemicals and inadequate understanding of how to avoid hazards.[2]

In cities served by piped water, sanitation, drainage, waste removal and a good health care system, child mortality rates are generally around 10 per 1000 live births, and few deaths are the result of environmental hazards. In contrast, in cities or neighborhoods with inadequate provision, it is common for child mortality rates to be 10 or 20 times this, and for environmental hazards to be major causes. And aggregate figures can disguise significant intra-urban variations; for example, surveys in seven settlements in Karachi found that infant mortality rates varied from 33 to as many as 209 per 1000 live births.[3] Differentials are also evident in cities in high income nations, although mortality rates are much lower and are not as closely related to environmental factors. In Glasgow, United Kingdom, in 1990, the infant mortality rate in a poor area was 47 per thousand live births, compared to 10 per thousand for a more affluent suburb.[4] Similarly, in Washington DC in 1997, infant mortality rates, broken down by ward, show considerable variation—from a rate of 2.8 per thousand in a high income area to a rate of 16 per thousand in one of the poorer wards.[5]

The information base for a precise identification of the relative importance of different causes or risk factors is limited: there is a clear need for better data if the dynamics and effects of urban poverty are to be understood and effective action is to be taken. For example, there are few city-level data on child morbidity in low and middle income nations, and even fewer on children's or caregivers' perceptions of their needs and priorities. There are, however, many detailed studies within particular urban neighborhoods which provide strong evidence of the impacts that urban conditions can have.

Water and Sanitation

Diarrheal diseases are still a primary cause of infant and child death for large sections of the worlds urban population. Human excreta are the primary source of diarrheal disease pathogens.[6] When provision for water and sanitation is poor, diarrheal diseases and other diseases linked to contaminated water (such as typhoid) or contaminated food and water (such as cholera and hepatitis A) are among the most serious health problems within urban neighborhoods—or whole cities. The impact of diarrheal diseases can be considerably underestimated since, when combined with malnutrition (as they often are), they can so weaken the body's defenses that diseases such as measles and pneumonia become major causes of child death.[7] Long-term impacts for children are not restricted to health: a city study in Brazil has related early diarrheal disease in children to impaired cognitive functioning several years later.[8]

An essential factor in ensuring children's health is the availability of safe, sufficient water supplies and provision for sanitation—something frequently absent in poor urban settlements in low and middle income countries (Box 15.1). Too little water is a critical problem, making it impossible to maintain the sanitary conditions essential for preventing endemic disease that contributes so heavily to the death and repeated illness of many children.[9] When water has to be carried or bought by the bottle, many households make do with far less than they need to ensure children's health. In urban Brazil, infants were five times as likely to die in households using public standpipes as in those with water piped to the house.[10] In the absence of adequate supplies of clean water, the maintenance of hygiene during food preparation becomes especially difficult, and this, together with inadequate storage for food, contributes to the likelihood of contamination. Bottle-fed babies and young children being weaned are at particularly high risk.[11]

The impact of inadequate water provision is compounded by the effects of poor sanitation. Only a small proportion of poor urban residents have adequate provision for sanitation, and here too, the problems are not confined to informal settlements. In Azerbaijan, 33 percent of the urban population still use traditional pit latrines, and another 9.7 percent use open pits.[12] Most urban centers in Africa and Asia and many in Latin America have no sewers.[13] Although non-sewered sanitation can work well, the sheer volume and concentration of human waste and waste waters in cities usually make these ineffective. Where sewers do exist, these are often open, presenting a serious risk to public health. Tens of millions

---

Box 15.1: Water and Sanitation: Examples of Conditions in Cities and Smaller Urban Centers

BANGALORE (India): More than half of the 6 million inhabitants depend for water on public fountains, often with broken taps or pipes and damaged platforms.[85] Almost a third have little or no access to piped water. 113,000 have no access to a latrine, and defecation in the open in common.[86]

FAISALABAD (Pakistan): Two thirds of the 2 million inhabitants live in areas with little or no official provision for services; and most new housing and land development occurs without official approval. Less than half the population has piped water and less than a third is connected to the sewer system.[87]

LUANDA (Angola): In this city of some 4 million inhabitants, 75 percent live in informal settlements with little or no infrastructure and services.[88]

IBADAN (Nigeria): Only 22 percent of the population are served by the municipal water supply system, and the city has no sewer system. Inhabitants rely on pit latrines and latrines connected to septic tanks.[89]

NAIROBI (Kenya): More than half the population live in informal settlements squeezed onto less than 6 percent of the city's land. Most plots in these settlements have no toilet or water connection.[90]

MBANDJOCK (Cameroon): Only about 20 percent of the population (estimated at 20,000 in 1996) have access to piped water; the rest rely on wells and springs which test positive for fecal contamination. The city has no sewer system.[91]

FRONTIER TOWNS IN BRAZIL: In two small town in Rondonia and three in Southern Para, between 44 and 95 percent of households rely on 'informal' water supplies (local wells without pumps or water collected from rivers); between 67 and 95 percent rely on "informal" sanitation (defecation pit latrines or in the open).[92]

of households in informal settlements only have access to overused and poorly maintained communal or public toilets—one settlement in Kumasi, Ghana, had 320 persons per latrine and long queues were inevitable.[14] Provision for sanitation is so poor in many cities that significant proportions of the population resort to open defecation.[15]

The use of public latrines is particularly problematic for young children. Taking a small child any distance to a toilet is impractical, and the darkness, smell and large pit openings in most latrines make their use unpleasant or even frightening for young children. Evidence from a number of urban settlements indicates that hardly any children under six use these latrines and that in most cases their excrement ends up being thrown into yards, drains or streets, creating a potent source of contamination. Women and adolescent girls may also be reluctant to use public latrines because these facilities afford little or no privacy, and the lack of security increases the risk of these women falling victim to sexual abuse or violence. They face similar problems of privacy and safety when the absence of sanitary facilities forces them to use open land. The absence of drainage and garbage collection contributes further to the likelihood of contamination and disease. Most informal settlements have no service to collect solid waste. In many African cities, only 10-30 percent of all urban households' solid wastes are collected, and services are inevitably most deficient for informal settlements.[16] Uncollected garbage, along with excreta, is often dumped in drainage ditches—which can quickly become clogged. When wastewater and storm water cannot be easily drained, flooding spreads waste and excreta widely through the surrounding area. Drainage is an especially serious concern for the many urban communities on steep or swampy land.[17] Children can be at particular risk, since they play wherever there is open land, and may be drawn to wade or play in standing water or to scavenge in piles of garbage. Furthermore, housing built over water-logged sites and linked by poorly constructed wooden walkways in informal settlements is a clear source of danger for small children.

Conditions may improve over time in many illegal or informal settlements through a combination of self-help, mutual cooperation and negotiation with government agencies for some public services. But at best this is a slow and haphazard process. Residents have to negotiate for every kind of infrastructure or service separately. In parts of cities where poorer groups are not living in illegal settlements—for instance in tenement districts—there is generally more provision for infrastructure, but conditions may be as bad as in most informal settlements because maintenance is generally poor and levels of overcrowding extreme.

The impacts of inadequate water, sanitation, drainage and waste removal are not limited to diarrheal diseases. Many case studies in low-income settlements have shown the high proportion of children who have debilitating intestinal worm infestations.[18] The prevalence among children of various skin and eye infections such as scabies and trachoma that are associated with a lack of water supplies for washing is also particularly high among those living in poor quality homes and neighborhoods.[19] Moreover, malaria, which is often considered a rural disease, is now among the main causes of illness and death among children (and adults) in many urban areas. The occurrence of malaria is often related to poorly drained locations as the *Anopheles* mosquitoes breed on standing water.[20] Similarly, the diseases spread by *Aedes* mosquitoes (including dengue fever, dengue hemorrhagic fever and yellow fever) are related to poor drainage and to inadequate or intermittent water supplies, since these mosquitoes breed in standing water and water containers.[21] Many other disease vectors, including houseflies, fleas, lice and cockroaches, thrive where there is poor drainage and inadequate provision for rubbish collection, sanitation and piped water.[22]

Chemical Pollutants

Although they do not present the same health burden as biological pathogens, toxins and pollutants in water supplies and food, in the air and in unprotected dumps, are a world-wide concern. This is especially the case in urban areas and, disproportionately, in areas inhabited by the poor. Children are particularly vulnerable to harm from exposure because of their rapid growth and immaturity, both physiologically and metabolically.[23]

Lead ingestion is a particular problem for urban children, especially in countries where leaded fuel and paint are still used. In Kaduna, Nigeria, for instance, 92 percent of children examined had blood lead levels above acceptable limits.[24] In high income nations, exposure occurs predominantly through the ingestion of dust in households containing lead-based paint, a problem particularly in lower income areas with deteriorating housing stock; in the USA, this remains the most common environmental health problem affecting children.[25] Children are also at risk due to exposure to harmful chemicals, indeed, pesticides are increasingly becoming a source of concern in some inner city areas, where they are used to control roaches, rats and other vermin.[26]

The single most significant form of chemical pollutant in terms of children's health in low and middle income countries is indoor air pollution resulting from the use of coal or biomass fuels, poor quality stoves and inadequate ventilation. This is a problem in both rural and urban areas, but one from which children are less likely to have relief outdoors in towns and cities, given the poor quality of the outside air. All the same, indoor concentrations of pollutants can be many times higher than even the most polluted outdoor air, and infants and young children are often heavily exposed because they remain with their mothers as they cook or undertake other tasks within the home. The effect of these pollutants, combined with malnutrition, may retard growth and increase the incidence of acute respiratory infections.[27]

In many cities, the concentration and mix of ambient air pollutants is already high enough to cause illness and premature death for more susceptible individuals. Worldwide, 1.5 billion urban dwellers are exposed to ambient air pollution levels that exceed WHO standards—and in many cities, the concentration of pollutants is far above these standards.[28] Some groups are particularly vulnerable: the poorest "scavenging" families who live and work in city refuse dumps regularly inhale toxic fumes from burning plastic and other dangerous substances. Generally, the prevalence and severity of asthma, along with other respiratory ailments, have increased alarmingly in recent years among urban children. Reasons are complex and include exposure to urban pollutants, together with allergens and the psychosocial stresses of urban life. Although this phenomenon has been documented chiefly in the high income countries, it is beginning to receive attention in other urban areas.[29]

Accidental poisonings are common, especially for one to three year olds, most often from kerosene, household products (for instance bleach) and medications. The risk of poisoning is greater in poor quality, overcrowded dwellings where there is no storage space to keep these substances out of reach of children, and where the demands on parents mean that children are not always supervised. Unborn children are also at risk through their mother's expose to chemical pollutants, some of which can cause cancer or birth defects in the fetus or even kill it. Chemicals that are known to harm the fetus by transfer through the placenta include lead, methyl mercury, certain pesticides, PCBs and carbon monoxide.[30] In most low income settlements, however, the developing fetus is more at risk from the mothers nutritional deficiencies or from the impact of parasites and malaria on her health.

Physical Hazards

Millions of urban children around the world are killed every year as a result of preventable injuries that occur within their homes and neighborhoods, and tens of millions more are seriously injured. Heavy traffic, unprotected stairways and heights, unfinished houses, dangerous house sites, piles of debris and a scarcity of safe play space all expose children to high levels of risk.[31] The danger of injury increases when tired, over-worked caregivers are unable to provide adequate supervision. In countries where infectious and parasitic diseases are well controlled, unintentional injury ranks as the leading cause of death for children, accounting for almost 40 percent of deaths in the one to 14 age group.[32] In countries where disease and nutritional problems still kill many children, the percentage of injury-related deaths is lower but the number of injuries per person is considerably higher, especially in the poorest urban communities.[33] Most documentation of children's injuries is based on hospital records, but there are good reasons to believe that these provide a very incomplete picture, since most children's injuries are not treated in hospitals, in part because of the expense and the lack of emergency transport. A community-based study in Ibadan, Nigeria, documented 1,236 injuries involving 436 children over three months: these included puncture wounds, lacerations, sprains and dislocations: less than 1 percent were treated in formal health facilities.[34]

In urban and rural areas alike, falls are the single most common cause of injury, especially for younger children. Burns are common for children under four—from hot water or other hot fluids, and from accidents with open fires, stoves or kerosene appliances. High levels of overcrowding increase the likelihood of these events. A study in a Brazilian squatter settlement focused on 600 children under five, drawing on interviews with mothers. The mothers reported that in the two weeks prior to the interview, 30 percent of the children had had at least one accident and 12 percent of these were serious enough to have required care in a clinic or hospital. Falls accounted for 53 percent of these accidents, followed by cuts (17 percent) and burns (10 percent). Many of the falls were linked to the rough terrain of the settlement. The age of the child was an important determinant of accidents, and peaks in accidents were in the second or fifth years of life.[35]

Road accidents are among the most common causes of serious injury in cities in both high and low income countries. But the rapid growth of road traffic in many low income and most middle income nations, along with poorly maintained roads, multiple use of roadways and an absence of sidewalks and safe crossings has contributed to death and injury rates that are much higher than those in Europe or the USA, per road vehicle or passenger-mile.[36]

Access to Play

Urban safety hazards and health risks have a significant effect on the play opportunities available to children. The availability of stimulating, diverse environments that allow them to pretend, experiment and learn are central to optimal development,[37] and have been related to resilience and improved outcomes in high-risk children.[38] Where homes are overcrowded, children may have little choice but to pass much of the day outside, and they can be extraordinarily resourceful in finding opportunities for play within even the most deprived environments—indeed many poor environments are rich in challenge and diversity. But they can also expose children to serious risk, and caregivers often respond by restricting play.

As children become more mobile, safety becomes an increasing concern. In conditions of urban poverty, excreta, broken glass, plastic bags, rotted food and burning materials are common hazards.

As children begin to move further from home their range of action and the number of risk factors that they face also increase—traffic in particular, but also stray dogs, standing water, open drains and debris-filled lots. Older children are more capable of identifying hazards, but the drive to play and explore and an enjoyment of risk-taking can override the need for caution. As a result, injury rates remain fairly constant throughout childhood, while the kinds of injuries tend to change with age.[39] Girls are generally at lower risk—a function of the greater restrictions imposed upon them.[40]

Opportunities for play are also restricted in high-income nations countries, where spaces for recreation in urban areas are often limited or, increasingly, involve a financial cost, while motor vehicles make streets hazardous for play and open areas are used for parking. Moreover, parents' working patterns, the distance between home and school and the growing use of the car mean that, outside school hours, many children are isolated in their homes and separated from their peers. This isolation may be heightened by parents' concern for the safety of their children in urban areas.

Housing

Many children's rights are rooted in the fundamental human right to decent, secure, affordable housing. Survival, health and optimal development are related to the quality of housing and its surroundings; access to livelihoods, schooling and other services are determined by its location; emotional security, family stability and even the quality of community relations are tied to security of tenure. But the urban poor struggle with housing—getting it, keeping it and coping with its inadequacies.

In most cities in low and middle income nations, between 25 and 50 percent of the population live in illegally built settlements.[41] The quality of housing in these settlements is generally poor and often wretched, made of wood and plastic scavenged from dumps. This is a result not only of low incomes, but also of the reluctance of households to invest because of the uncertainty that they will be permitted to stay.

The location of informal settlements has a logic—they are concentrated in dangerous areas because the more dangerous the site, the greater the chance the residents can avoid eviction. The illegal settlements in a city often coincide with the areas most at risk from flooding or tidal inundation (this is the case for Accra, Bangkok, Buenos Aires, Delhi, Guayaquil, Jakarta, Monrovia, Lagos, Port Harcourt, Port Moresby and Recife) or landslides (Caracas, La Paz, Rio de Janeiro). Similarly, the most poorly constructed housing is also the most prone to severe earthquake damage, as testified by recent devastating quakes in the Colombian town of Armenia (January 1999), the Turkish towns of Adapazari, Golcuk, Istanbul and Izmit (August 1999), and Ahmedabad and Bhuj in the Indian state of Gujurat (January 2001). In many cities, poor groups also live in large concentrations in dilapidated, over-crowded inner city tenements and boarding houses: in these cases there is a trade-off between the far higher costs that households incur, for example with regard to rent and overcrowding, and the advantages provided by the location in terms of access to services and jobs. Furthermore, such problems are by no means restricted to low-income countries. Most poor people in urban areas in the USA, for instance, face serious housing problems, including rents that can exceed 50 percent of their incomes.[42]

An unknown number—but certainly tens of millions—of the world's urban children and adults are actually homeless and sleep in public places (pavements, stations, parks, graveyards) or construction sites and work places. In central Mumbai (formerly Bombay), India, more than a hundred thousand people live on pavements, half of them children, because incomes are insufficient to allow them to live even in cheap peripheral areas.[43]

Homelessness is predominantly an urban phenomenon, in part because of the commercialization of land and housing markets in the world's cities. Even in high income countries, research confirms that homelessness among families with children is increasing despite the recent years of affluence. The experience results in anxiety and depression for both children and parents, and can lead to the break up of families, as children are placed in foster care. In New York City, 60 percent of residents in shelters for adults had children who could not be with them.[44]

Evictions

Millions of urban dwellers around the world live in fear of eviction (see Box 15.2 on demolitions and evictions in Manila). In the case of illegal settlements, even those on undesirable land are at risk. A household survey in six wards of Dar-es-Salaam, Tanzania, in 1998 found that between 10 and 20 percent of households had been evicted in the previous year.[45] A review of 40 eviction cases from around the world between 1980 and 1993 found that eight involved more than 100,000 persons; the largest involved 720,000 people evicted in

Seoul, South Korea in preparation for the Olympic Games.[46] This was not a one time event; between 1960 and 1990, 5 million people were evicted from their homes in Seoul, many of them several times, often from sites provided after previous evictions.[47]

Of course, housing security is not just an economic and political issue. Box 15.3 describes the human impact of evictions in Mumbai, a successful city whose real estate market nevertheless fails to provide for the millions of low-income people that are essential to its economy.

The impact of eviction upon children can be particularly devastating. Evictions usually lead to homelessness and almost always to major economic upheaval. Possessions may be destroyed, family stability jeopardized, livelihoods and schooling threatened and social networks undermined. Children involved describe the violence, panic and confusion of the evictions and the experience of sleeping rough afterwards and being separated from friends. They also face the difficulties in re-establishing a stable life and frequent breakdowns in family relations as a consequence of the stress and economic difficulties.[48]

Evictions or displacement also arise from armed conflict, political violence,

---

Box 15.2: Demolitions and evictions in Metro Manila[125]

Evicting the urban poor, from either private or government land, and demolishing their housing is a long-standing practice in the Philippines' capital city. Between 1997 and 2000, some 26,000 families are believed to have been affected by demolition. In 2001, the number of demolitions fell substantially, but nonetheless, at the end of that year a total of 152,000 families were thought to be living under the threat of demolition, some as part of initiatives to remove squatter settlements and other to make way for government infrastructure projects, including the construction of a high-speed train line. Still others are victims of illegal demolitions, where either official procedures are not fully followed, or no court order is issued.

Sometimes evictions are violent, involving police and even military personnel. Often violence erupts when procedures of notice of demolition are not observed or eviction takes place without offer of compensation or relocation. While the number of demolitions in 2001 decreased, the share of violent evictions increased. In December 2001, two international housing rights non-governmental organizations—the Center for Housing Rights and Evictions and the Asian Coalition for Housing Rights—expressed serious concern over the situation, considering that it contravened ratified international human rights treaties, including the International Convention on Economic, Social, and Cultural Rights, the Convention on the Elimination of All Forms of Discrimination Against Women, and the Convention on the Rights of the Child.

natural disasters and other emergencies that affect millions of adults and children each year, and often result in children being separated from their family. This can mean streams of refugees or displaced rural dwellers flooding into cities where housing is already at a premium. These displaced people are often resented by other urban dwellers. This is especially so if they are undocumented immigrants who often live in constant fear of discovery and forced repatriation. Children from "illegal" or "unwelcome" communities are highly vulnerable to prejudice, harassment, attack and incarceration, especially when they are forced to work for survival.

Housing Quality and Conditions

Even when poor urban families are securely housed, their housing is seldom adequate to support their children's survival, development and the highest attainable standard of health. Numerous hazards are posed by flimsy shelters on disaster-prone land. Accidental fires are common in areas with highly inflammable building materials, and are rendered still more serious by the lack or inadequacy of emergency services. In other cases, fires can be deliberately set to drive households off the land they have occupied. In high-income countries, fires are also related to poor housing conditions, but more often to faulty wiring, defective heating equipment and the absence of smoke alarms. There are also numerous health risks associated with poor quality housing construction and materials. Lack of screens exposes children to flies and mosquitoes, and porous walls and roofing harbor rodents and insect pests. Hard to clean floors increase contact with pathogens—the agents that cause disease—especially for babies and young children.[49]

Poor living environments, including noise and crowding, have long been recognized to generate stress, to undermine coping strategies, interfere with social relationships and contribute to physical and mental illness.[50] In high-income nations, overcrowding is measured by rooms per person; in low-income nations by persons per room. Three or more persons per room is common among poor urban populations, amounting to one or two square meters of space per person.[51] There are particular effects for children. In several countries, including India and the USA, noise and overcrowding have been related to poor cognitive development, behavioral problems, lower motivation, delayed psychomotor development, and difficulties with parents, including child abuse. Many of these outcomes have been related more generally to poor housing quality.[52]

Poor quality, overcrowded housing also favors the transmission of acute respiratory infections, which are the single largest cause of infant and child death in most low and middle income nations. Although these infections are by

---

Box 15.3: Evictions in Mumbai

In Mumbai, which has a population of some 12 million, there has been a systematic program of "slum" clearance. In 1998 alone, the Brihanmumbai Municipal Corporation evicted 167,000 people from their homes. Ambedkar Nagar was a community of 5,000 people living on a reclaimed tidal mangrove swamp at the southern tip of Mumbai. Most of these people had been brought to the city for construction work, and had stayed on, turning this swamp land into valuable real estate through their labor. Over the past ten years, residents of this community have faced eviction 45 times. Each time, the demolition squad has destroyed some or all of the huts, and community members have repeatedly rebuilt them. In May 1998, despite promises made to lawyers, demolition workers and police moved in again and cleared the site. A resettlement site next to the old slum had been allocated to the community, but less than one third of the original households were given plots. Water, sanitation, and drainage were not provided. Most of the residents had no choice but to rebuild their bamboo and plastic shelters once again on the swamp land.

Two months after this eviction, a research team undertook a study of women and children in the community, looking at their health status. Of a sample of 70 children between one and five years of age, 46 were found to be stunted and 12 to be wasted. There was widespread diarrhea, respiratory infections including pneumonia and skin infections.

Even one eviction can upset the stability of a household. Repeated eviction wears away the capacity to recover. Each time their huts were demolished, women explained, money had to be found to rebuild. At first, they used their wages to buy materials, then began to turn to their savings, selling their limited supplies of jewelry and brass vessels. By the time of the 1998 eviction, most households had exhausted these avenues and had turned to moneylenders. Loans with interest rates of over 100 percent were rarely repaid before another loan was needed for another shelter.

---

no means an urban phenomenon, they tend to be more prevalent in urban areas, as the frequency of contact, the density of the population and the concentration and proximity of both infectious and susceptible people promote disease transmission.[53] And, with limited health and financial resources, a child who contracts bronchitis or pneumonia in low and middle income nations is 50 times more likely to die than a child in Europe or North America.[54] Overcrowding is also a risk factor for the transmission of many other diseases that affect children, including diarrhea and tuberculosis.[55]

Social Dimensions

In deprived urban areas where local governance is ineffective, resources are scarce and poorly distributed, communities empowerment is undeveloped, participatory channels are inexistent and support structures are weak, the impact of poverty on the child, the family and the fabric of society can be devastating. These outcomes are further compounded by difficulties associated with the physical environment in poor urban areas.

The Quality of Care

Inevitably, challenging living conditions undermine the capacity to provide optimal care for children. Overburdened caregivers are far more likely to have to leave children unsupervised or to cut corners in the many procedures that are necessary for healthy living—managing water supplies, keeping children clean, preparing and storing food hygienically and dealing with waste and excreta in the absence of adequate services. For example, reduced cooking times are thought to be connected with the retention of toxicity in boiled cassava meal, a staple food in many parts of Africa, especially when combined with a protein-deficient diet.[56]

Even high levels of parental knowledge about health, hygiene and safety cannot guarantee that children will be well provided for in very poor conditions. Heavy demands on caregivers in combination with long distances to work and the absence of viable alternatives can mean that there is no good source of care for many young children for long hours every day. Often the burden of care in households falls upon girls, who are left to look after their siblings while parents work. The psychological stresses imposed by living in poor urban conditions also take their toll. Caregivers in crowded and chaotic conditions have been found to be less responsive to their children, and more restrictive, controlling and punitive.[57] Under the many pressures of poverty this can escalate to abuse and neglect.[58]

When resources are scarce and mothers or child carers are faced with a heavy domestic workload or are forced to work long hours outside the home, one result can be malnutrition. This condition contributes to more than half of all child deaths, to chronic illness and to a slowing of development on all fronts. It also undermines children's immune defenses and increases their vulnerability to disease.[59] Young children during breastfeeding or weaning are particularly vulnerable, but there is also a risk for older children who are often given cheap food or sweets sold by street vendors or local shops. Urban price differentials may also mean that poor families have difficulty finding or affording fresh products, another contributory factor to poor diets. The problem can be compounded by unsanitary environments:[60] sanitation-related diseases cause decreased food intake, impaired nutrient absorption and direct nutrient losses through vomiting and diarrhea, while parasitic infestations can absorb a significant percentage of a child's nutrient intake, as well as interfering with digestion and absorption. Data from 84 countries indicate that the best predictor of nutritional status, next to financial access to food, is the level of access to water.[61] Recent figures demonstrate that, even without disaggregating for income, urban children in low and middle income nations are between one and two standard deviations below the international median in terms of height for age.[62]

The difficulty of providing adequate care for children in poor households can be exacerbated in urban areas by the breakdown of family units and the frequent lack of social support. Many observers have pointed to the relatively high numbers of urban households headed by single mothers around the world as a factor explaining poor outcomes for children. There is no question that female-headed households are disproportionately poor, or that it takes more effort on the part of a single adult to provide high quality care for children. However, there is also evidence that women are more likely to invest their limited resources in children's well-being and long-term success, and that many children do better in female-headed households.[63]

Urban Neighborhoods

Many poor urban children live in rundown inner cities, peripheral squatter communities or barren suburbs where their social, cultural and recreational needs receive little attention. In four Johannesburg neighborhoods, children described settings almost completely lacking in appealing possibilities. There were no recreational facilities, nor any safe places to play or see friends. Parks and empty lots were taken over by drunk, abusive adults and filled with refuse. Swimming pools were too far away and too expensive to use. Mobility was limited by heavy traffic, crumbling sidewalks and broken traffic lights. The bus service was patchy and unaffordable, and streets were so poorly lit that children were afraid to go out at night.[64] Aside from the lack of opportunity, children find the stigma of living in such rundown and marginal communities to be a serious issue. Far from taking their physical environments for granted, children are extremely sensitive to their surroundings, finding them a source of satisfaction but also a cause for humiliation and distress.

Neighborhood quality, accessibility and opportunity for children and adolescents are determined to some degree by the level of formal municipal provision. But local community institutions like churches, cultural centers and recreational clubs also play a significant role, and they depend on the level of social organization and commitment within a community. Many African-American churches in major cities of the US have taken initiatives to mobilize community members to plan and manage their own neighborhoods, but research in the USA has also indicated that this kind of neighborhood resource base tends to be weaker where there are high concentrations of poverty, joblessness and residential mobility.[65]

These same factors have also been related to higher levels of violence and insecurity.[66] In cities around the world community violence has become an increasingly commonplace part of children's experience. Exposure to violence has repeatedly been linked to higher rates of depression, anxiety, distress, aggression and behavioral disturbances for children and adolescents.[67] There seems to be little doubt, moreover, that poverty and the inadequate living conditions, insecurity and marginalization experienced by many poor communities can feed frustration and aggresssion. In one high poverty neighborhood in Chicago, 47 percent of girls and 55 percent of boys between 7 and 13 had reportedly seen someone being shot or stabbed, and over 20 percent lived with someone who had been shot.[68] In Washington DC, 75 percent of a sample of African American elementary school children had witnessed violence in their communities, ranging from physical assaults and gang violence to rape and homicide. Almost half their parents were unaware that they had been exposed to any violence.[69]

Children and adolescents may not only be victims of violence, but also contribute to it. Bullying by peers is a problem for many children, and vandalism, drug use and gang-related crime by young people are the cause of fear and concern in communities around the world. These activities may, in turn, bring children into contact with law enforcement officials. In certain cases where the juvenile justice system is weak or non-existent, children become subject to arbitrary treatment by the police or to other rights abuses. In part at least, phenomena such as vandalism can be related to boredom and the lack of opportunity and hope. In many communities the provision of recreational facilities, job training and options for constructive involvement have resulted in dramatic reductions in crime and gang violence.[70]

Schooling and Work

Schooling, like most other basic services, tends to be more readily available to urban children than their rural counterparts. But school remains either inaccessible or unaffordable for many poor urban children. Moreover, the general quality of schools in poor urban areas can be extremely low, and this constitutes yet another disincentive for parents and children. Especially in illegal settlements, governments may overlook their obligation to provide education or, indeed, any other service. When the large Basic Education for Hard to Reach Urban Children project was developed for children in hazardous labor in Bangladesh, it was quickly discovered that more than half the children attending these small learning centers in slum areas were not "working children," indicating that there was a more general problem with access to schooling.[71] But even when government schools are within walking distance, many urban children do not attend. Of those that do enroll, many drop out in the first few years. Door-to-door surveys in poor neighborhoods in Hyderabad and Secunderabad indicate that the quality of schools and of teaching is a major factor. Overcrowded and rundown classrooms, disinterested teachers, physical punishment, social discrimination and humiliation are some of the reasons cited by parents and children for their lack of motivation over time.[72] In the case of particularly vulnerable groups, such as children with disabilities, the social and physical barriers to attending school in poor urban areas can be insurmountable without special support and provisions.

Many children are denied their right to education in order to undertake household or domestic chores, or to care for younger siblings. This is as true for rural areas as it is for urban ones, but the lack of public utilities and services in many poor urban communities contributes to inappropriate burdens for millions of children, especially girls.

Other children may be withdrawn from school to contribute to household income. A survey in a Kolkata (Calcutta) "slum" revealed that 84 percent of school age children were not attending school, and that of these, 49 percent were working outside the home—as rag pickers, domestic helpers, leather workers or battery breakers.[73] Child labor not only impacts upon educational opportunities, it can also take dangerous and degrading forms. There is probably no city in the world where there are not some children exposed to hazardous work, but the proportion of children in this position is particularly high in many low and middle income nations where, for instance, they make a living picking through waste[74] or working with dangerous machinery, heat, toxic chemicals and dust.[75] Domestic labor in the homes of others is especially prevalent in urban areas, often involving children sent from rural areas, and entailing long hours, little or no pay, little relief from isolation and, frequently, abusive treatment and sexual violence.[76]

An especially serious violation of children's rights is child prostitution, a phenomenon that is particularly associated with major cities with high levels of poverty. A recent estimate from UNICEF in India indicates that there are more than 100,000 child prostitutes in that country's five major cities.[77] In Mexico, a study of the cities of Acapulco, Cancún, Cuidad Juarez, Guadalajara, Tapachula and Tijuana estimated that a total of 4,600 children are sexually exploited in these cities, while some 16,000 are believed to be exploited at the national level.[78] This, in turn, exposes these children to violence, exploitation and sexually transmitted diseases, including HIV/AIDS. The fact that in Thailand close to

$300 million is estimated to be transferred annually from urban to rural areas by women working in the sex trade in urban areas helps to illustrate the direct link between poverty and prostitution in a rural–urban context.[79]

Children on the Street

The phenomenon of children living on the street is a peculiarly urban one, although many of the children involved may originate from rural areas. The demands of work for some urban children push them onto city streets for many hours a day, and in some of these cases links with home can become tenuous. In other cases, work may be secondary, and children may have left home because of abuse, a desire for excitement or relief from oppressive home conditions. At night, these children become particularly vulnerable to all forms of abuse. During winter, cold can be a deadly enemy: in Moscow, where there are estimated to be 50,000 homeless children, many sleep on air vents for the metro system to escape the freezing temperatures, or even risk disease in the city's sewers in order to find relative warmth.[80] A large proportion of children on the street engage in hazardous work—dodging traffic as they sell goods to passing motorists for instance. Many are involved in legitimate work; others choose or are pushed into illegal activity, engaging in petty crime and theft, working in the commercial sex or drug trade or becoming drawn into organized begging or rag-picking rackets. Whether or not they are breaking the law, these children are among the most stigmatized urban dwellers, constantly facing abuse from other citizens and harassment by the police. Often children are arrested for crimes or simply for vagrancy, and can be trapped for long months in the slow moving bureaucracy of the justice system, detained in conditions that violate their basic rights.

Notes

1. WHO (1999) op. cit.
2. For further information on the effects of the physical environment on children, a useful starting point is Bartlett, Sheridan (2002), *Children's Rights and the Physical Environment*, Save the Children Sweden, Stockholm.
3. Surveys undertaken by the Community Health Department of the Aga Khan University quoted in Hasan, Arif (1999), *Understanding Karachi: Planning and Reform for the Future*, City Press, Karachi.
4. Pacione, Michael (1990), "The Tale of Two Cities: The Mitigation of the Urban Crisis in Glasgow," *Cities*, Vol. 7, No. 4, pp. 304-314.
5. District of Columbia Department of Health, State Center for Health Statistics (1997), *A Vital Statistics Data Sheet—1997*, Department of Health, Government of the District of Colombia.
6. Cairncross, Sandy and Richard G. Feachem (1993), *Environmental Health Engineering in the Tropics: an Introductory Text*, 2nd ed., John Wiley and Sons, Chichester.

7. WHO (1992), op. cit.; UNICEF (1997), *The State of the World's Children 1998*, Oxford University Press, Oxford & New York.
8. Guerrant D.I. et al. (1999), "Association of early childhood diarrhea and cryptosporidiosis with impaired physical fitness and cognitive function four-seven years later in a poor urban community in northeast Brazil," *American Journal of Tropical Medicine and Hygiene* 61(5) pp. 707-13.
9. Cairncross, S. (1990), "Water Supply and the Urban Poor" in J. Hardoy, S. Cairncross and D. Satterthwaite, *The Poor Die Young: Housing and Health in Third World Cities*, Earthscan, London.
10. Victoria, C. G. et al. (1988), "Water supply, sanitation and housing in relation to the risk of infant mortality from diarrhea." *International Journal of Epidemiology* 17(3) pp. 651- 654.
11. Rossi-Espagnet, A., G.B. Goldstein, and I. Tabibzadeh, (1991), "Urbanization and health in developing countries; a challenge for health for all," *World Health Statistical Quarterly*, Vol. 44, No. 4, pp. 186-244.
12. UNICEF, Azerbaijan Multiple Indicator Cluster Survey December 2000, Baku. http://www.childinfo.org/mics2/newreports/azerbaijan/Azerbaijan1.pdf.
13. Hardoy et al. (2001), op. cit.
14. Devas, Nick and David Korboe (2000), "City Governance and Poverty: the Case of Kumasi," *Environment and Urbanization*, Vol. 12, No. 1, pp. 123-135.
15. Hardoy et al. (2001), op. cit.
16. Ibid.
17. Cairncross, S. and E. A. R. Ouano (1990), *Surface Water Drainage in Low-Income Communities*, World Health Organization, Geneva.
18. Bradley, David, Carolyn Stephens, Sandy Cairncross and Trudy Harpham (1991), "A Review of Environmental Health Impacts in Developing Country Cities," *Urban Management Program Discussion Paper No. 6*, The World Bank, UNDP and UNCHS (Habitat), Washington DC.
19. See for instance, Landwehr, D., S.M. Keita, J.M. Ponnighaus and C. Tounkara (1998), "Epidemiological Aspects of Scabies in Mali, Malawi, and Cambodia," *International Journal of Dermatology*, Vol. 37, No. 8, pp. 588-590.
20. WHO (1999), World Health Report: 1999 Database. World Health Organization, Geneva.
21. Cairncross and Feachem (1993), op. cit.
22. Satterthwaite, David, Rodger Hart, Caren Levy, Diana Mitlin, David Ross, Jac Smit and Carolyn Stephens (1996), *The Environment for Children*, Earthscan and UNICEF, London.
23. Chance, G.W. and E. Harmsen (1998), "Children are Different: Environmental Contaminants and Children's Health." *Canadian Journal of Public Health* 89 (Supplement 1): S9-13.
24. Nriagu, J., N.T. Oleru, et al. (1997), "Lead Poisoning of Children in Africa: Kaduna, Nigeria," *The Science of the Total Environment* 197(1-3), pp. 9-13. 94
25. Campbell, C. and K. C. Osterhoudt (2000), "Prevention of Childhood Lead Poisoning." *Current Opinion in Pediatrics* 12(5) pp. 428-437.
26. Landrigan P.J., Claudio L, Markowitz S.B. et al. (1999), "Pesticides and Inner-City Children: Exposures, Risks and Prevention," *Environmental Health Perspectives* 107(3) pp. 431-7.
27. Hardoy et al. (2001), op. cit.
28. WHO (1999), op. cit.
29. MacIntyre U.E., de Villiers F.P., Owange-Iraka J.W., (2001), "Increase in Childhood Asthma in an Urbanizing Population," *South African Medical Journal* 91(8) pp. 667- 672; Schwela, D. (2000), "Air Pollution and Health in Urban Areas," *Review of Environmental Health* 15(1-2), pp. 13-42.

30. UNEP and WHO (1990), *Children and the Environment, The State of the Environment 1990*, United Nations Environment Programme and United Nations Children's Fund, Geneva.
31. Bartlett, Sheridan N. (2002), "The Problem of Children's Injuries in Low-Income Countries: a Review," *Health, Policy and Planning*, vol. 17, no. 1, pp.1-13.
32. UNICEF (2001), "A League Table of Child Deaths by Injury in Rich Nations," I*nnocenti Report Card* Issue No 2, Innocenti Research Centre, Florence.
33. Berger, L.R. and D. Mohan (1996), *Injury Control: A Global View*, Oxford University Press, Delhi; Murray, C.J. and A.D. Lopez (1996), *The Global Burden of Disease: A Comprehensive Assessment of Mortality and Disability From Diseases, Injuries, and Risk Factors in 1990 and Projected to 2020*, Harvard School of Public Health on behalf of the World Health Organization and the World Bank, Cambridge, MA.
34. Edet, E.E. (1996), "Agent and Nature of Childhood Injury and Initial Care Provided at the Community Level in Ibadan, Nigeria," *Central African Journal of Medicine*, Vol 42, No 12, pp. 347-349.
35. Reichenheim, M. and Trudy Harpham (1989), "Child Accidents and Associated Risk Factors in a Brazilian Squatter Settlement," *Health Policy and Planning*, Vol. 4, No. 2, pp. 162-167.
36. Manciaux, M. and C.J. Romer (1986), "Accidents in Children, Adolescents and Young Adults: a Major Public Health Problem," *World Health Statistical Quarterly*, Vol. 39, No. 3, pp. 227-231.
37. Wohlwill, J. and H. Heft (1987), "The Physical Environment and the Development of the Child," in D. Stokols and I. Altman, *Handbook of Environmental Psychology*, Wiley, New York.
38. Bradley, R. H., L. Whiteside, et al. (1994), " Early indications of resilience and their relation to experiences in the home environments of low birthweight, premature children living in poverty." *Child Development* 65 pp. 346-360.
39. Jordán, J.R. and F. Valdes-Lazo (1991), "Education on Safety and Risk" in M. Manciaux and C.Romer (eds) *Accidents in Childhood and Adolescence: The Role of Research*, World Health Organization, Geneva.
40. Berger, L. R. and D. Mohan (1996), *Injury Control: A Global View*, Oxford University Press, Delhi.
41. In most cities, there is a "range" of illegality from settlements where all aspects are illegal (buildings, land use, land occupation) to those which have aspects of legality (e.g. illegal subdivisions in which the land is not occupied illegally).
42. Twombly, J. G., S. Crowley, N. Ferris, C. N. Dolbeare (2001*), Out of Reach 2001: America's Growing Wage-Rent Disparity*. National Low Income Housing Coalition, Washington DC.
43. Patel, Sheela and Diana Mitlin (2001), "The Work of SPARC and its Partners Mahila Milan and the National Slum Dwellers Federation in India," *IIED Working Paper 5 on Urban Poverty Reduction*, IIED, London.
44. National Coalition for the Homeless (1999), "Homeless Families with Children," *NCH Fact Sheet No. 7*, NCH.
45. CARE/Tanzania, (1998), *Dar-es-Salaam Urban Livelihood Security Assessment*, Summary Report, CARE/Tanzania, Dar-es-Salaam.
46. Audefroy, Joël (1994), "Eviction trends worldwide—and the role of local authorities in implementing the right to housing," *Environment and Urbanization*, Vol. 6, No. 1, April, pp. 8-24.
47. ACHR/Asian Coalition for Housing Rights (1989), "Evictions in Seoul, South Korea," *Environment and Urbanization*, Vol. 1, No. 1, April, pp. 89-94.

48. Rahmatullah, T. (1997), *The Impact of Evictions on Children: Case Studies from Phnom Penh, Manila and Mumbai*, United Nations ESCAP and The Asian Coalition for Housing Rights, New York.
49. Bartlett, Sheridan, Roger Hart, David Satterthwaite, Ximena de la Barra and Alfredo Missair (1999), *Cities for Children: Children's Rights, Poverty and Urban Management*, Earthscan, London.
50. Harpham, Trudy and Ilona Blue (1995), *Urbanization and Mental Health in Developing Countries*. Avebury, Aldershot; Evans, G. W. (2001), "Environmental Stress and Health" in A. Baum, T. A. Revenson and J. E. Singer. Mahwah, *Handbook of Health Psychology*. New Jersey, Lawrence Erlbaum Associates.
51. UNCHS (1996), Hardoy et al. (2001), op. cit.
52. Evans, G. W., S. J. Lepore, et al. (1998). "Chronic residential crowding and children's well-being: an ecological perspective." *Child Development* 69(5): pp. 1514-1523; Evans, G. W., H. Saltzman, et al. (2001), "Housing quality and children's socio-emotional health." *Environment and Behavior* 33(3) pp. 389-399.
53. WHO (1992), *Our Planet, Our Health*, Report of the WHO Commission on Health and Environment, World Health Organization, Geneva.
54. Pio, A. (1986), "Acute respiratory infections in children in developing countries: an international point of view," *Pediatric Infectious Disease Journal*, Vol. 5, No. 2, pp. 179-183.
55. WHO (1992); WHO (1999) op. cit.
56. Cassava is a natural source of cyanide. It has been suggested that insufficiently processed bitter cassava may have harmful effects, although this link has not been fully established. Other studies associate these effects with other elements in cassava that cannot be removed by processing. See "Toxicological Profile for Cyanide," a report prepared by Research Triangle Institute for the US Department of Health and Human Services, Public Health Service, Agency for Toxic Substances and Disease Registry, September 1998.
57. Wachs, T.D. and F. Corapci (forthcoming), "Environmental Chaos, Development and Parenting across Cultures" in C.Raeff and J. Benson (eds), *Social and Cognitive Development in the Context of Individual, Social and Cultural Processes*, Routledge, New York.
58. McLoyd, V.C. (1990), "The impact of economic hardship on black families and children: psychological distress, parenting and socioeconomic development," *Child Development* 61(2) pp. 311-346.
59. Stephenson, C. B. (1999), "Burden of Infection on Growth Failure." *The Journal of Nutrition,* 129 (2S Supplement) pp. 534S-538S.
60. Rice, A. L., L. Sacco, et al. (2000), "Malnutrition as an underlying cause of childhood deaths associated with infectious diseases in developing countries." *Bulletin of the World Health Organanization* 78 (10) pp.1207-21.
61. Lechtig, A. and B. Doyle (1996), "The impact of water and sanitation on malnutrition and under 5 mortality rates." *WATERfront* 1996(8) pp. 5-19.
62. Montgomery (2002), op. cit.
63. O'Connell, H. (1994), *Women and the Family*, Zed Books, London and New Jersey; UNDP (1995), *Living Arrangements of Women and their Children in Developing Countries*, Department of Economic and Social Information and Policy Analysis, Population Division, United Nations.
64. Swart-Kruger, J. (2001). *"We know something someone doesn't know . . .": Children speak out on local conditions.* Johannesburg, City Council of Johannesburg
65. Wilson, W. J. (1998), "When work disappears: new implications for race and urban poverty in the global economy." *CASEpaper, CASE/17*, Centre for Anbalysis of Social Exclusion,

London School of Economics.

66. Sampson, R.J., S.W. Raudenbush and F.J. Earls (1997), "Neighborhoods and violent crime: a multilevel study of collective action," *Science* 277, pp. 918-919.

67. Buka SL, T.L. Stichick, I. Birdthistle and F.J. Earle (2001), "Youth exposure to violence: prevalence, risks and consequences," *American Journal of Orthopsychiatry* 71(3) pp. 298-310; Veenema T.G. (2001), "Children's exposure to community violence," *Journal of Nursing Scholarship* 33(2) pp. 167-73.

68. Sheehan, K; DiCara, J.A, LeBailly, S, Christoffel, K.K (1997), "Children's exposure to violence in an urban setting," *Archives of Pediatric and Adolescent Medicine* 151(5) pp. 502-4.

69. Hill, H.M. and L.P., Jones (1997), "Children's and parent's perceptions of children's exposure to violence in urban neighborhoods," *Journal of the National Medical Association* 89(4) pp. 270-276.

70. Trust for Public Land (1994), *Healing America's Cities: HowUrban Parks Can Make Cities Safe and Healthy*, The Trust for Public Land, San Francisco, CA.; Vanderschueren, F. (1998), "Towards Safer Cities." *Habitat Update* 4(1), pp. 1-6.

71. Cameron, Sara (2001), *Bangladesh: Basic Education for Hard to Reach Urban Children*, Reaching the Unreached Case Studies, UNICEF, New York.

72. Ramachandran, Vimla (2001), "Getting urban out-of-school children to school," *The Times of India*, 7 June 2001.

73. Ibid.

74. Furedy, Christine (1992), "Garbage: exploring non-conventional options in Asian cities," *Environment and Urbanization*, Vol. 4, No 2, October, pp. 42-61; Hunt, Caroline (1996), "Child waste pickers in India: the occupation and its health risks," *Environment and Urbanization*, Vol.8, No.2, October, pp. 111- 118; Huysman, Marijk (1994), "The position of women-waste pickers in Bangalore," in Ida Baud and Hans Schenk (eds), *Solid Waste Management: Bangalore*, Manohar, Delhi.

75. Lee-Wright, Peter (1990), *Child Slaves*, Earthscan Publications, London.

76. UNICEF (1998), Child Domestic Work, *Innocenti Digest* No. 5, UNICEF Innocenti Research Centre, Florence.

77. UNICEF India (2001), op. cit.

78. UNICEF (2001), *Profiting from Abuse. An Investigation into the Sexual Exploitation of our Children*, UNICEF, New York.

79. Ibid.

80. The Electronic Telegraph (UK), "50,000 children spend Russian winter on streets of Moscow," 20 January 2002.

CHAPTER 16

THE STREET CHILDREN SCENE

160,000,000 Street Children Worldwide

Jeff Anderson

When Jesus said "let the children come" to His impatient disciples, He made it clear how important the world's innocents were to Him. Yet in God's world today, life is tough for children. Around the globe there is perhaps no group more oppressed than children. It's a hard-knock life and death for children. Look at these startling facts:

Children Suffering Worldwide

- Thirty two percent of India's 960 million population—or more than 326 million people—are below the age of 15. (*Bread for the World Institute*) as reported in *WORLD PULSE* July 23, 1999 Vol 34 No. 14.

- In 1998, the global starvation rate among children reached its 600 year peak. (*UNICEF, StaU of the World's Children, 1998*) as reported in *WORLD PULSE* July 23, 1999, Vol 34 No. 14.

- 200 million children under the age of 5 are malnourished, and 50% of the deaths among children under 5 are due to malnutrition. (*World Bank, World Development Indicators*) *WHO World Health Report*, 1998, as reported in *Hesperian Foundation News* Spring/ Summer 1999.

- Every year throughout the world more than 12 million children under the age of 5 die. To understand the magnitude of this tragedy, this number is equivalent to ALL of the children living in the 31 eastern states of the USA dying in a single year. (*USAID 1999*) http://www.info.usaid.gov/pop_health/ cs/cschallenge.htm.

- The global death toll from AIDS was 2.6 million last year alone. Roughly 85 percent of those deaths occurred in Africa. Even as the corpses were buried, some 5.6 million more people—mostly African— became infected with HIV during 1999. (*Newsweek Magazine* January 17, 2000)

The Philippine Street Children

"I am a child of the streets
Seeking justice from abuses in the streets
Like being beaten up, being hurt,

Merciless beatings from parents
Change in my parents is my dearest wish
So that we can be given a brighter future,
I will be taught good manners
So I will become a respectful child
Work is what our parents need
To meet our needs . . .
Getting an education, food and a peaceful home
We also need enough love and care
So we do not have to sweat it out on the streets."
(A poem written by street children during the First
Metro Manila Street Children's Conference, May 1990)

The street children phenomenon in the Philippines and worldwide is a silent scream that societies are ill. Children should not be out on the streets working, begging and involved in prostitution.

A study done by the Philippine Cultural Communications Services Corporation for UNICEF reported that the Philippine scenario reveals an alarming situation for Filipino children and youth. Close to 20 million or 60% of the 33.1 million children and youth population are "in specially difficult circumstances" such as the threat of exploitation. This group includes 1.5 million or 30% of the total child and youth population which is made up of working children, street children and sexually exploited children. There are an estimated 2.8 million urban working children and youth. Figures from 1983 show that of the 2.4 million Filipino children with special needs, only 8000 are being reached.

The National Conference on the Filipino Child in Crisis in January 1986 reported that there is an estimated 3.5 million Filipino child workers in the manufacturing, agriculture, and service sectors of the economy. In Metro Manila estimates show that there are about 50-75,000 street children and youth (Moselina, 1986). More than 5000 children and youth are being cared for in institutions. This means only about 6.6 percent of the larger figure of 75,000 street children were being cared for at that time.

Also, according to statistics, only about 6000 (or less than 10 percent) of the 75,000 street children in Metro Manila are being served by one or more of the 110 non-government organizations (NGOs) that implement projects to provide assistance to street children. The commonly used strategies used by these NGOs are community-based programs, drop-in centers and temporary shelters.

Most assistance from NGOs and GOs provide assistance only until the age of 15 years or so, at which time assistance stops and the child is once again left to fend for him or herself. Frequently, these children either go back to selling and begging on the streets or find work under exploitive conditions.

Summary Baseline Information

Street children account for about 3% of the child and youth population of Metro Manila. In most cases, the families of the street children migrated to Metro Manila from poor provinces in order to look for work. Lacking in urban skills and with a tremendous competition for employment opportunities, these family members find themselves unemployed or underemployed. But in all cases, incapable of supporting their families from their efforts alone.

According to our study of street children in Cubao and Kaloocan, most children earned their income from vending, begging or prostitution. The average weekly income was between $4 to $8 USD. Three girls from Cubao reported that they were earning $20, $40 and $120 USD-per week.

Age-wise, there were more older boys in our study and more younger girls. The age brackets for the boys were 11-12 years of age and 14-15. In Cubao, a number of boys belonged to the age bracket of 16-23. On the other hand, most of the girls were in the age category of 10-11.

Most of the girls said their reason for being on the streets was to work. The boys said that they either ran away or were driven away by their parents. Half of our respondents indicated that they slept at home. The rest said they sleep under the Light Rail Transit station, in parking lots, on the streets, or other outside places. Those who slept outside of the home used cardboard boxes for mats or bedding. During bad weather, they simply took shelter in nearby buildings.

Socio-economic Roots Perpetuating the Problem of Street Children

In her article, "Children of the Streets: Some Bothering Questions" (1985), Roselle Leah Rivera commented that the roots of the problem of street children came from the structures of underdevelopment. Dr. Lugviminda Valencia claimed that child labor is a "complex phenomenon that is rooted in the country's underdevelopment sustained by cultural factors and thus, becomes acceptable." The Fookien Times Philippine Yearbook 1984-85 carried Estefonia Aldaba-Lim's articles explaining that the causes of the street children's problems are the "deep economic roots, inequitable distribution of wealth, economic crisis, poor social planning and the lack of political will to give the child and family the priority they deserve."

She emphatically reiterated that the real problem is "not abandonment, but poverty . . .

- poverty of the land laid to waste by annual typhoons which send families running to the city;
- poverty of education and relevant training which brings humiliating unemployment to those who were once dignified farmers;

- a poverty of potential which leads fathers to despair and give up hope;
- a poverty of esteem and opportunity which prevents mothers from being able to defend their youngsters;
- a poverty of the body which, in the name of hunger, forces children into the streets to work and to be exploited
- a poverty of the spirit which destroys the will of the family to stay together; and,
- a poverty of role models in our society today."

Characteristics of Street Children

During October 1990, ACTION Philippines conducted a survey of both street children and agencies and churches that are working with street children and their families. There are four definitions of street children which emerged from doing the study. They are:

The real street children. These are the children who live and survive in the streets. They are out of school with an average educational attainment of 3rd Grade. They are orphaned, abandoned, runaways or have been driven from their homes.

The working children in the street. They either work to support themselves and their school needs or to help their parents. Most of these children are in school with an average educational level of 6th Grade. A study sponsored by the International Labor Organization on child labor in the Philippines came up with a profile of working children: they belong to households with 4-5 members composed of parents and children and still attend school despite their poverty situation. Most of the children have parents who are seasonally employed result-ing in irregular incomes for their family. This in turn results in more family members seeking employment even in informal sectors to add a little income to meet their families' needs. In urban areas, children work in a variety of street trades, scavenge garbage and fall into the flesh trade. The girls do housekeeping and family-orientated income generating projects such as roadside variety stores or eateries.

The children of the slums & squatter families. They have nothing to do in their homes so they frequently roam the streets but return home at night or during mealtimes.

The children of poor families. These families work in the streets, begging or selling snacks, cigarettes, flowers and other items from their mobile stalls or push carts. The young children of these families must hang out on the streets so their parents can watch them. Some parents send their children to work on the streets in order to earn money for the family. Some street families are involved in earning money for organized crime syndicates.

A Profile of Children and Youth at Risk

The Philippines Mental Health Association conducted a study and came up with this profile on children and youth at risk: The majority of them are minors (below 16 years of age), mostly male, single, out-of-school but have reached elementary school and are literate. Most of them come from large families. Their parents have no regular job and very little education. The youth left home mostly due to poverty, family problems and an adventuresome spirit which leads them to street activities with their friends. Their source of income in the streets does not allow them to save for future needs. Their work is primarily done in the streets, with friends and with leaders who could be policemen or pimps. Healthwise, they are not sick, but malnourished. Their ambition in life is not only to improve their situation, but their families' condition as well.

UNICEF-supported programs have the following data on street children and their characteristics: the great majority stay in the streets to earn money for themselves and their families. They may work long hours but earn very little. The working arrangements are usually performed on an individual basis and in informal activities such as vendors, pickpockets, beggars, and the like. Generally, by the nature of their work, they are defenseless, unorganized and without basic services.

Rivera described them as having an adventurous spirit, restless disposition and extraordinary resourcefulness and independence. Aldaba-Lim (1985) characterized them as "children who find themselves in a state of material helplessness, deprived of their personal integrity and subject to abuse, exploitation and other material and moral danger. The children live in extreme degrees of deprivation, having lost the basic support mechanisms of their families as they come face-to-face with the daily need to survive."

Push Factors: Pushing a child to the streets

Forces that drive children from their homes and communities to the streets:

- Broken homes
- Political forces or organized crime syndicates
- Generational poverty
- Natural calamities: earthquakes, typhoons, volcanoes
- Economic downfall
- Moral and spiritual failure on the part of parents and other family members
- Exploitation and abuse

Pull Factors: Pulling a child to the streets
- Gangs
- Entertainment and attractions
- Prospect of income on the streets
- "Freedom" from authorities
- Demonic forces

The push/pull factors lead to antisocial behavior such as:
- Drug use
- Conception of children out of wedlock
- Petty crime
- Cult or occult practices

This leads to these community responses and perceptions:
- Eyesore to the community
- Threat to business, public safety and life
- Rebellious
- Manipulative
- Wasted life because of unfulfilled potential
- Asset to various businesses such as vending newspapers, food, flowers and trinkets
- Value to organized crime syndicates
- Lost without Christ
- Criminals

Perceptions of Street Children About Their Own Lives[1]

Street children have both positive and negative characteristics. Usually they have a poor self-image even before they leave home but even more so after being on the streets. They leave home for various reasons such as: family break-up, parental abuse and beatings, lack of space, food and money. But basically street children are like any other child in the world. They like to play, help with household chores and learn new things. They value education and good family relationships.

On Family
Even though the children are on the streets, many still communicate with their parents. Also, most of the children still prefer a home atmosphere to the streets. This home needs to be clean, orderly, loving, safe and providing their basic physical needs. Some still desire to go home to their parents, brothers, sisters and other relatives.

On the Streets

Most children have not been lured to the streets by someone. They have come to like the streets because of certain things they find there such as money, freedom, leisure, friends and vices. However, they also have problems on the streets which they may not have had at home such as: hunger, need to beg, beatings by older street people or police, imprisonment, sexual molestation, lack of sanitation, no place to sleep and no one to care for them when they are sick. But to meet these needs they develop friendships with other street people and do have the option of going to social welfare agencies for assistance.

On Aspirations in Life

Usually the children hope that someday they will be able to finish their studies, have a profession and then eventually be employed in a stable, reputable job so they can provide for themselves and their families. They hope to prevent their brothers and sisters from becoming street children. They long for the day when they have a good family where love is felt, where they understand one another, and where there is no more fighting, shouting, cursing and beatings. They also look forward to raising families of their own.

On Agencies, Programs and Services

Generally Positive: Children perceive agencies positively except for the fact that they still ask for more basic and recreational facilities which are in short supply. Some of their other needs are not being met like education and employment. Some staff do not meet their expectations. But due to shortcomings in their homes, and even more so in the streets, they feel good about what is provided in the centers.

There are many reasons for running away from the centers. Despite the fact that most of the children's perceptions are positive, a lot of children run away. This could be due to the fact that even though the children have a sense of gratitude they still have some unmet needs. Various reasons cited for their leaving the centers are: a lack of play space, the manner of discipline used by staff, boredom and unmet needs for employment or education. Also since they are able to earn money on the streets and handle money, they have a sense of security. Other reasons for running away are peer-related like fighting and so-called freedom on the streets to do whatever they desire. At their age, peer influence is very strong.

On Reconciliation with Their Families

If the street child has family, then his or her family needs to be counseled and assisted also. Ultimately the family is responsible for its children. Various reasons for children desiring to be reconciled with family include the following: wanting to be reconciled, wanting to see if their parents have improved since they left home, tiring of street life, missing their family, and desiring a better future.

Reasons for children not desiring to return home are: the family has not changed, fear of having family clashes again, parents cannot afford to send them to school, and a sense that if they return home they will just go back to their old ways again like fighting and gambling.

Reasons for children returning to the streets after being reconciled with their families are: not being ready, parents had not yet changed or improved their ways after they left home, and influence of friends to return to the streets.

Agencies and families meet different needs for the child. Agencies can provide education, job skills or a job, love and understanding through counseling, friendship and family assistance. The family offers basic family stability and security. Families also have a part in changing the child's values and attitudes. They also need to work hard to improve the economic situation of the family so their children are provided for. The children themselves also have a responsibility to do what is needed to remain in school. They also need instruction on how to assist their family develop for the better rather than running away from their problems.

A Story of Injustice

Ron Homenuke

One rainy morning in Cubao, 16-year-old Jojo was hanging out with his friends. Jojo had left home due to family problems and poverty—five sleeping in a 10-foot-by-15-foot shack. His parents had separated and Jojo's mom was living with another man. Jojo had just spent the previous night in jail, where some police officers had caused a good portion of Rugby glue to get stuck in his hair. Rugby is an inexpensive glue used to repair shoes, linoleum and plastics. It is prevalent in the Philippines—especially with street kids. They can be seen carrying it in small plastic bags for inhaling. Being somewhat similar to solvent or paint thinner, the end result is a cheap high.

While speculating on how the Rugby could be removed, Jojo and his friends were approached by a traffic aid who was under the influence of liquor. This man was known to some street workers for being antagonistic towards street kids. Carrying a container of kerosene, he walked up to Jojo, poured it on his head and lit it with a match. Screams of anguish tore down the street as his head exploded with fire. Realizing what he had done, the traffic aid quickly smothered the flames—but not before Jojo had suffered serious burns on his head, ear and neck.

He was rushed to a nearby hospital. A street worker from a nearby church arrived soon after the incident and followed up on the case. After medical treatment, Jojo was released to his care. The situation was discussed with us and other street workers and an attorney was contacted. Jojo was returned home along with some legal papers. The traffic aid was imprisoned, but when his wife pleaded with the street workers to drop the charges, they refused.

We suspect that when Jojo returned to the streets, he may have been given some money by the traffic aid's family because the charges were dropped. The traffic aid was released from jail and temporarily suspended.

The following week, when Jeff Anderson and I were ministering in Cubao, Jojo staggered past us, passing out on the sidewalk. Recognizing him by the ugly open wounds on the back of his head, we attempted to administer first aid. It was not easy as he was vomiting all over himself and the sidewalk. He had been sniffing Rugby and drinking gin to kill his pain.

Since that time, we saw Jojo once more and he was still in bad shape. When I mentioned to Jojo that I wanted to take him to a hospital, he took off. Apparently, he's deathly afraid of doctors.

Before I left, he came back and let me administer first aid on his ear, which was becoming badly infected.

My question is this. What is Jojo's future? Will he become just another statistic on the growing list of mistreated and malnourished street kids in Manila?

This terrifying incident may have given him a permanent phobia, especially against officials. Agreeably, Jojo's daily lifestyle would not earn him any "5-star award," but this kind of treatment is never appropriate. Please pray for Jojo's physical, emotional and spiritual healing. Pray also that justice will be done for all street children.

Something Beautiful

Director, Retorno—Latin America Association
for Girls, Bogotá, Colombia

"The day I was going to move to my new home my old friends tried to talk me out of it, but I told them that I needed to change, because I was very dirty. . . ." Paola, 15, was a long time in coming to this point. From the age of nine her life had been that of a Bogota street girl. Mistreated by her mother and feeling no sense of love in her home, she began to wander the streets. Soon it seemed there was no turning back. The streets were her home and her life.

Paola is but one of thousands. Bogota, Colombia, has a growing street children population and is reputed to have more than 70,000 prostitutes.

Yet Paola longed for something better. It seemed she was always searching for something, a place to call home, someone to love her. She attempted to enter various institutions, but usually found she was not welcome. In the few places where she was invited to stay, she was very uncomfortable and unhappy.

One day a friend invited Paola to a Christian day care center called The Other Way. The friendly people in charge welcomed her with open arms. She felt their love and began to feel at home. It was there, as she began to learn the truths of God's Word, that Paola's life began to change. One day she confided in the leader that she was ready for a change. She wanted to leave the streets, find someplace where she could settle down, go to school, and get on with her life. There was a place for her, said the leader, but she would need to promise to stay. (NOTE: Street kids, used to the unstructured lifestyle and comparative "freedom" of the streets often find it most difficult to adjust to normal life. Many return to the streets.) Paola was ready to make a commitment.

As the day approached for Paola to enter her new home, her friends did their best to dissuade her. "Paola, stay with us. Come with us, let's go out and steal. . . ." It was a difficult decision for Paola. These were her friends and it was hard to say good-bye. They had been through so much together. But she had made up her mind. Says Paola, "I told them, 'NO!' I told them I needed to change, because I was very dirty. . . . I wanted to go to my new home!"

Today Paola is part of a "family" of 15 girls who are receiving a stable home, love and spiritual guidance at Retorno.

Not of this World

Mark Stuckey, Ipatinga, Brazil

"I don't know if I believe in your God but I can't deny the love you folks have and it isn't anything I have ever seen here on earth. It doesn't seem to be of this world."

The words came from one who only a short time ago was a sullen, rage-filled young man who became angry at the mere mention of God.

Tomas came to the Rescue Mission out of desperation.

"I came here in a last-ditch effort to try to change my life and take it from the hell it had become with drugs, fights with my mother, no friends, and death threats from drug dealers. Before coming here I put a bullet in my revolver and spun the chamber, put the gun in my mouth and said if there is a God and if He wants me to live then He won't let me die. When I pulled the trigger the gun didn't go off. . . . If I don't recuperate at the Rescue Mission, with all the love, care and experience you folks have, then it is over for me. I plan on going home, fully loading my revolver and finishing what I started."

Drugs had so destroyed Tomas that he saw no hope, and life had lost all meaning. Society and family had also given up on him and discarded him as hopeless. An atheist, astrologer, drug dealer and addict, Tomas used to be aloof and independent—but now he was scared.

Caught with drugs in his possession a few weeks earlier, Tomas had resisted giving police the name of his drug dealer. They took him out to a secluded place, and when he realized he would be tortured or killed, he gave them the information they wanted. The drug dealers then put a price on his head. His stealing, lying and conniving had already alienated Tomas from his family, and his arrest was just another affront to them. They isolated him even more. Where did he turn?

Shaken by the death threat and scared by his attempt at Russian Roulette, Tomas recognized his need for help. At that point he showed up at AMR (Rescue Mission Association) in Ipatinga, Brazil, where ACTION missionary Mark Stuckey works with troubled youth.

At first Tomas challenged every mention of God, prayer, or spiritual matters, but little by little he began to warm to the workers. They noticed he no longer seemed hostile to the Bible—just disinterested. Soon he stopped challenging everything, and his depression started to dissipate. Then he began to verbalize things he was thinking.

One day he told Mark he wasn't sure he believed in God, but he could feel the workers' powerful love for him. It was unlike any he had known before.

Tomas now asks to go to church, participates gladly in the devotions, prays, and sees that God is working in his life. He still needs much help as he bears the burden of constant rejection in his life and carries a deep-seated hatred toward his father. This writer is not sure if he has yet committed his life to Christ, but it appears he is not far from it!

Ernesto's Story

Heidi Baker, Maputo, Mozambique

Ernesto was afraid all the time as he lived on the street for nearly three years in cardboard boxes. Since he was very small for his age, the bigger boys were always beating him up at night. Nighttime was the best time for stealing the money that the smaller boys got from begging. Ernesto was always afraid of hunger. The gnawing pain of an empty tummy was a feeling he experienced often.

Rain was also a very fearful thing because it inevitably meant malaria fevers. As he shivered in his cardboard hut hoping morning would come soon one of his worst fears of all would haunt him. Would one of the bigger boys come and rape him again tonight? Life for Ernesto was a living hell.

One day one of his best friends told him that he would take him to Casa Elephant for soup and medicine. He did not tell him about the singing and praying that went on in this gathering of street children. When I met Ernesto I was immediately struck by his beautiful gentle face and his intelligent eyes.

After we shared about how Jesus came to preach good news to the poor and set the captives free, he was up in front of the crowd on knees asking Jesus to come into his broken heart. That very night I brought him home to our children's center to live. He loved the warm shower and the clean clothes, but the best part was the bed with a blanket. He felt safe at last.

One day while he was praying he had a vivid vision. He told me that angels came and took him up to heaven. He said it was a beautiful place full of light. No one there was afraid. The angels took him to Jesus and as he sat on his lap Jesus told him to stay in the children's center where he would be safe. Jesus also told him to live a pure and holy life. He said he was coming back to earth very soon so Ernesto had to leave heaven and tell others about Jesus.

Soon after the vision the third most powerful man in Mozambique came to our center. His name was Mr. Komichi. He was a minister in President Chicano's office. After Mr. Komichi gave his speech he asked if any of the children wanted to tell him about what they did in the center. There were over 500 children in the meeting. Up went Ernesto's hand. He was the first one to respond. He ran up to Minister Komichi, looked straight up into his eyes, and said, "We worship Jesus here, and He is all that matters. Jesus takes away our fears and changes everything." Ernesto continued to preach one of the most powerfully anointed Gospel messages I have ever heard. With absolutely no fear at the end of his message he pointed at the minister who was twice his size and said, "You need to know Jesus too." By then many of us including the minister had tears in our eyes.

Ernesto had seen the Lord's face. He was no longer afraid of anything or anyone. He loves preaching on the streets with me even with the threat of prison. One of his favorite things is praying with the children who live on the streets.

Notes

1. *Perception of Street Children on Themselves, Their Families, Their Street Life and on Agency Programs and Services* by Persida D. Evio, University of the Philippines, July 1991.

SECTION I
JUSTICE

The heat of Cairo in the summer can be unforgiving. When that heat is added to the smells in the garbage village, zeal melts into lethargy. I remember climbing the hill to the monastery where we lived with a team of students from the USA inside this garbage-collecting community. Next to me a team of donkeys suffered under an impossible load of garbage, struggling to reach the crest of the hill. Atop the garbage, the donkey-cart driver urged the beasts forward under the motivation of a whip. My daughter Hannah, who has a huge heart for animals, looked at me with pleading eyes as the tormented donkeys struggled up the hill. As much as I felt sorry for myself, panting up the hill in 110-degree heat, I began to have compassion for the donkeys. Why? I wondered. These weren't soul-bearing creatures. They lived to serve. What could *I* do anyway? I couldn't relieve their plight any more than I could relieve my own misery, climbing that insufferable hill.

Step by sweaty step we pressed on. My conscience and my daughter continued to trouble me. Finally, I gave in. Without a glance backward from the donkey-cart driver (nor, do I guess, much noticeable relief for the donkeys), I shouldered the back of the garbage cart and began to push. What good is it, I wondered, to add to my suffering only to give some inconsequential relief to these beasts, without even the benefit of the owner's thanks? Still I kept pushing.

At the top of the hill, I turned right toward the monastery and the donkeys turned left. Immediately, I came upon Romany who was sitting in his usual spot outside his butcher shop. He was waiting for enough business to justify another pig slaughter. Every day we stepped through the blood and entrails that flowed down in little rivers from the hill outside Romany's butcher shop. Romany was a Coptic Christian: one of the ancient Middle Eastern Christian traditions. He had been a good friend to our team and me since our arrival in the garbage village.

As I passed, Romany said three words to me that have changed my life. He said, "God saw that." I had not been aware of Romany's watchful eye from his perch atop the hill. He wanted to remind me that to serve the suffering counts for something in God's eyes. Acts of justice and mercy do not go unnoticed by everyone—God sees. How much more is that true when we seek the justice of people made in God's image, in the midst of their suffering.

For many evangelicals in the West, personal holiness has been the focus of our spirituality. Sin becomes a highly personalized issue to be addressed only by the sinner. Righteousness is considered in individualistic terms. Worship is centered on *my* actions or responses: Have I read my Bible? Did I hurt anyone in my thoughts, words, or deeds? But in Scripture, personal and social righteousness and justice are inextricably linked: "Away with the noise of your songs! I will not listen to the music of your harps. But let justice roll on like a river, righteousness like a never-failing stream!" (Amos 5:24). Leaving concern for justice out of our lives invalidates our worship. To focus on the personal to the exclusion of the social is not biblical.

In his book *Good News About Injustice*, Gary Haugen effectively substantiates the fact that confronting social evil is the thoroughly biblical calling of those who follow Christ. In the selection provided below, "Champions of Justice," Haugen supplies examples of everyday Christians who stood up for the oppressed and changed social systems.

Likewise, in Grigg's chapter "With Justice for All" from his seminal book *Companion to the Poor*, a convincing case is built for Christians to confront power holders, as they stand alongside those whose rights are being trampled.

God gives power, not for personal aggrandizement, but as a trust to utilize on behalf of those who have none.

CHAPTER 17

CHAMPIONS OF JUSTICE

GARY A. HAUGEN

In *The Screwtape Letters,* an ingenious reflection on the forces that drain the lifeblood from Christian faith, C. S. Lewis makes a startling statement. He writes that "Despair is a greater sin than any of the sins that provoke it."[1] And surely for Christians looking at our incredibly evil world of injustice and oppression, despair can always be found lurking at the door of our hearts, waiting to hobble us the moment we begin to take our first steps forward. After all, what can *we* do? How can *we* make a difference in a world of such massive and brutal injustice?

Strongholds of Injustice

Sister K.L, Brother E. and Sister J. know about the temptations of despair.

In Sister K.'s country there is a booming business in forced prostitution. The local police protect it and even hunt down girls who try to run away, often returning them to the stockades where they are held. Sister K. is personally aware of almost sixty brothels where she has found hundreds of young girls kept in subjection by "whip, fist, boot and bulldog"—some girls only thirteen and fourteen years old.

A state-appointed investigator assigned to look into the issue visited a single brothel and concluded that there was "no necessity for state interference in the matter." But Sister K. knows differently, and the brutal reality is beyond comprehension. She learned that one of the women held in prostitution was actually murdered by being soaked in oil and burned alive. The coroner's report of her death even named the perpetrator. It read: "Burned to death by W. H. Griffin." But the man was never charged with a crime. Local politicians prevent any legal action from being taken against the forced prostitution rings because they owe their position and influence to the wealthy business interests behind the brothels.

In the face of such injustice what can Sister K. do?

In Brother E.'s country abusive child labor is a plague on the land. Where he lives, about two million children between the ages of ten and fifteen years old work in textile mills, tobacco-processing plants, mines and other factories. Children work twelve hours a day, six days a week, sometimes on dangerous night shifts. Some must endure working eighty-two hours per week in a factory during peak weeks of the year. Many of the girls work in silk mills just as the boys work as "breakers" in the coal mines. Every day the breaker boys breathe in the heavy soot that covers them as they pick the debris out of the coal by hand. According to one person, the children of the breakers and the mills are "stooped and skinny, often missing thumbs and fingers and always giving the impression of being older than they were. Only when they were maimed so seriously that they can no longer work did such children attend school." As a prominent national lawyer commented, "You sell your boys to be slaves of the breakers and your girls to be slaves in the mills."

In the face of such oppression what can Brother E. do?

In Sister J.'s country summary execution by mobs is a way of life. The majority ethnic group maintains its dominance over the minority ethnic group through the intimidation of extrajudicial murder. Every year fifty, sixty or a hundred people are burned alive or hanged after being accused of committing some offense against the majority ethnic group. These brutal events are gruesome public affairs, often performed in the presence of local officials on the basis of a simple denunciation by a member of the majority group. Without any opportunity to defend themselves, the accused are hustled off to a terrifying death. Local law-enforcement officials simply refuse to intervene and occasionally carry out the executions themselves.

In the face of such brutal human-rights violations what can Sister J. do?

Sister K., Brother E. and Sister J. are very real people. The circumstances described are documented beyond any dispute. They are, in fact, part of history. Kate, Edgar and Jessie are actually devout Christians of another era, and the country in which they encountered such staggering injustice is the United States of America. But today, although Americans have certainly not purged injustice from their society, these conditions simply no longer exist, in large part because of the courageous obedience of Christians to the call of God. In the face of brutal injustice and oppression that rivals anything anywhere on our globe today, courageous Christians simply refused to despair. Thankfully, America has never been the same.

Kate Bushnell: Abolishing Forced Prostitution

A hundred years ago Dr. Kate Bushnell served as a national evangelist for the Women's Christian Temperance Union (WCTU) in the United States. A devout evangelical Christian, Dr. Kate Bushnell was heartbroken by the plight of girls victimized by white slavery in America. Hard as it may be to imagine today, the dens of forced prostitution described earlier were rampant in the logging camps and mining communities of northern Wisconsin and Michigan in the 1880s. It was in Ashland, Wisconsin, that Dr. Bushnell encountered the murder of the woman who was burned alive with impunity.

While in some cases police responded to the pleas of women who were seeking to escape their bondage, other times they didn't listen and even returned runaways to their brothels. The existence of these dens and dance halls of rape was largely supported by the local community. The owners and patrons of such establishments exercised enough political power to prevent legal action against the brothels. Local doctors supported their existence because their frequent examination of the women provided a source of additional income. And local businessmen found that brothels provided a boost to the local economy.

Dr. Bushnell looked in vain for someone to properly investigate these conditions. Finding no one willing to take the risks, she did it herself. Facing tremendous personal danger, she infiltrated scores of brothels and interviewed hundreds of women held in bondage. "She would search for reliable witnesses having personal knowledge of an involvement in the case under investigation. She insisted on talking to inmates, viewing the situation herself. One side of the story, from one witness, was not enough. . . . Having penetrated the brothel by one excuse or another, she was able by various pretexts to obtain proof of the conditions that existed there."[2]

Dr. Bushnell reported her findings at a Chicago convention of the WCTU The state of Wisconsin vehemently denied her findings, and the state inspector even attempted to discredit her by accusing Dr. Bushnell herself of "unchastity." When she appeared before the Wisconsin state legislature, she had to be escorted by police because of threats of violence against her. Standing before the hostile assembly, she initially felt overwhelmed as the only woman in the room. But being a woman of prayer, she lifted her heart to God, "whereupon the door opened quietly, and about fifty ladies of the highest social position at the State Capitol filed in, and stood all about me. There were no seats for them; they stood all the time I talked—and I had plenty of courage as I realized how good God was to send them."[3]

Despite the attacks on Dr. Bushnell and her study, "the whole country was agitated on the white slave question by the disclosures" she had made.[4] Her findings were substantiated by subsequent studies conducted by both public officials and private researchers. The result of her work was the passage of a bill in the Wisconsin legislature that finally dealt with the scourge of forced prostitution in a serious way. The bill was appropriately labeled "the Kate Bushnell Bill" Later

Dr. Bushnell took her Christian witness to India and China, where she and other Christians challenged the complicity of British colonial officials in the rampant trafficking of woman and girls in forced prostitution.

Edgar Murphy: Transforming the Destiny of Child Laborers

Today we look with horror and despair at reports of the millions of young children who toil under abusive labor conditions around the world. And yet at the turn of the century similar conditions were not uncommon in North America. Edgar Gardner Murphy, a minister of the gospel from Alabama, was certainly familiar with them. The Reverend Murphy was particularly burdened by the oppression suffered by the tens of thousands of children under age fourteen who toiled in the textile mills of his native American South. I found myself thinking of my sister's own six-year-old daughter as I encountered the comments of an observer from 1902 who described the fate of just one of these children.

> Mattie . . . is six years old. She is a spinner. Inside a cotton mill for 12 hours a day she stands in a 4-foot passage-way between the spinning frames where the cotton is spun from coarser into fine threads. From daylight to dark she is in the midst of the ceaseless throb and racket of machinery. When I first met her it was Christmas Eve. The eve of the children's festival when the whole of Christendom celebrates the birth of the Child whose coming was to bring freedom to children. She was crying, and when I asked the reason, she said between her sobs, that she wanted a doll that would open and shut its eyes. "When would you play with it?" I asked the little toiler, whose weary eyelids were ready to close over her tired eyes directly after the long day's work was over. "I should have time aplenty on Sunday," replied the little slave whose daily wage of ten cents helped to swell the family income.[5]

As a disciple of Jesus Christ, Rev. Murphy chose not to surrender to despair in the face of such a tragedy. In 1901 in response to his expanding knowledge of the atrocities of child labor in the mills, Murphy founded the Alabama Child Labor Committee. Rev. Murphy began to write to inform the public of the horrors he witnessed. He authored nine pamphlets on the subject and distributed twenty-eight thousand copies throughout the United States, often at his own personal expense. His writing effort has been called "the first body of printed material of any considerable extent or value" in favor of legislation restricting child labor in the American South.[6]

Rev. Murphy believed that children belonged in "God's outdoors, in the home, or in the schoolroom."[7] On one occasion Rev. Murphy examined a seven-year-old's hand that had had three fingers torn from it during dangerous mill work. When the mill owner explained that the child had been careless, Rev. Murphy replied, "Hasn't a child seven years of age got a right to be careless?"

In 1904 Murphy joined with other advocates of reform to found the National Child Labor Committee (NCLC). The NCLC came to be regarded as the most effective voice in bringing about the abolition of child labor in America, and Rev. Murphy is referred to by contemporaries and historians alike as its father and founder. Perhaps Murphy's greatest personal victory came, however, when his home state of Alabama finally issued legislative restrictions on child labor in 1907. Even more substantial, though probably unrecognized by Murphy himself, was the fact that he had "pricked the conscience of the country alive to the existence of child labor as a shame and a curse to America."[8] One man's faithful devotion to his Master's call to care for "the least of these" helped transform the destiny of millions of American children.

Enough Is Enough: Church Women and Lynching

In recent years summary executions by vigilante groups and "disappearances" by secret death squads have been among the uglier human-rights violations that have struck terror in the hearts of millions of people living in communities of social and political conflict around the world. Such state-sanctioned horror may seem distant, but there was a time not long ago, a time within the memory of many living Americans, when millions of their compatriots lived under such a threat.

In the first two decades of this century, thousands of African-American citizens were publicly lynched—including almost a hundred women. In four years, from 1918 to 1921, twenty-eight African-Americans were burned at the stake by mob action.[9] As late as the 1940s lynching was still a common method of social control and intimidation in the Southern states. But again it was the courageous faith of devout Christian women who helped bring this scourge to an end.

In the segregated South the practice of lynching was largely defended as a means to protect the honor of white women. It was often perpetrated against African-American men who were accused of raping a white woman or of simply addressing a white woman in a socially inappropriate fashion. Jessie Daniel Ames, a Southern white woman, believed that the most effective voice against lynching could come from those it was intended to benefit. In 1930 with only twelve compatriots, she created the Association of Southern Women for the Prevention of Lynching (ASWPL). These twelve women simply "went home and began to work and to talk and to retell the facts as they learned them."[10]

Ames and the other charter members were all officers in various Protestant denominations. Apart from the brutal injustice of the practice, they were deeply concerned that the lynching of African-Americans by white "Christians" tended to "discredit Christianity, and impede the work of missionaries among non-white peoples." As Ames later stated, "That was one of the strongest appeals we could make."[11]

Although Ames was its only salaried worker, the ASWPL had councils in all eleven former Confederate states and more than forty thousand active members. The key to her success seemed to be her reliance on volunteers and a preexisting network of religious and secular women's organizations, which provided cohesiveness for the ASWPL. By the early 1940s, 109 women's associations, representing 4 million women, supported the ASWPL's work. Not only did the women's organizations of the southern Protestant churches endorse ASWPL, but they also included antilynching literature in their respective educational materials.

Through literature, speeches and word of mouth within its vast network, ASWPL undermined the chivalric notions that fueled lynching and revealed the truth of the barbaric practice. They circulated petitions to show elected officials that there was widespread support for antilynching laws. They persuaded law-enforcement officials to sign a pledge expressing opposition to lynching. By 1941, 1,355 police officers had signed the pledge. Also in that year police officers in forty documented cases had successfully opposed lynch mobs. Furthermore, ASWPL exposed by name officers who failed to uphold the law. In some instances ASWPL women physically confronted the mobs. ASWPL members were credited with "preventing the lynching of scores of blacks, because of their timely phone calls to a sheriff or visits to a local jail."[12]

While Southern senators blocked federal antilynching legislation and thwarted any nationwide remedy, the ASWPL was able to fundamentally change the cultural mores and beliefs that undergirded the practice. And the impact was dramatic. As the distinguished Yale historian Dr. C. Vann Woodward has observed, "Efforts of civil rights groups to secure passage of federal anti-lynching laws failed repeatedly, but effective work by white and Negro groups, *many of them Southern church organizations,* virtually eliminated lynching for a time. The NAACP conceded the 'virtual disappearance of this form of oppression' in the early 1950s."[13] Of course the women of the ASWPL were not perfect and manifested many of the narrow attitudes common to many Southern white women of the day. Nevertheless, as one historian has commented on the era,

"From its inception, the anti-lynching campaign was rooted firmly in a tradition of evangelical reform."[14]

Ordinary People, Extraordinary Faith

To me these stories are part of the great encouragement of a Christian heritage. Sometimes when I am utterly overwhelmed by the injustice in our world, recalling or reading about the faithful heroes of the past allows me to find my courage. When I raise my eyes, even for a moment, to the history of God's courage expressed in his people, I find hope and steadiness of heart.

Without the encouragement of stories like these, I can easily get buried in the intimidations of today. I can easily lose all perspective and hope. It makes me think of days as a small boy playing at the ocean and experiencing the terrific intimidation and disorientation of the waves as I waded farther and farther from the beach and other people. I vividly remember one occasion when, having been lulled to inattention by the temporary calm, a swelling wave blind-sided me without warning. It picked me up and rolled me over and over underwater. With something close to terror, I kicked and flailed my arms trying to swim to safety. Then just as wild panic began to grip my heart, my head was shoved above the surface just long enough to steal a glance down the shoreline. There, very near me, were my two brothers, standing sturdily—in the same three feet of water in which I was flailing. Letting my feet float down, I quickly found the hard, sandy bottom and stood up—embarrassed a bit but greatly relieved.

Alone in the waves, I had lost perspective. Things were not as they appeared. The water felt infinitely deeper than it was. I had no idea of the sturdy ground that was actually well within reach. I felt helpless, lost and overwhelmed. And as long as I felt that way, I possessed neither the power nor the presence of mind to stand amid the waves.

Likewise, when I see the great forces of injustice that crash upon our world, I find myself going from moments of easy obliviousness to moments of total disorientation and despair. But it is in these moments that I need to look down the shoreline of history and see my brothers and sisters of the faith—Dr. Bushnell, Rev. Murphy, the Christian women of the ASWPL and so many others—standing amid the crashing waves. The injustice and oppression in the world is powerful, relentless and pervasive, but as these three faithful witnesses attest, we are neither without a foothold to withstand its blows nor powerless to rescue those pulled under by its force.

There is a testimony of great hope in seeing how God has used ordinary people—from all nations—extraordinary in their Christian faith, to bring rescue to those who were hurting.

What Can We Learn from Faithful Christians?

These champions of justice teach us a couple of truths which at times we may question: bringing about justice can be within our reach, and it is also an integral part of our faith.

First, we learn that *we can change things.* Our despair, cynicism and laziness may insist to us that nothing ever really changes and that we can never really make a difference. But on high we see a great cloud of witnesses stand to their feet with a different testimony. Rank upon rank of vulnerable and voiceless girls tell us that for them Dr. Bushnell's faithfulness to God made a difference. Legions of children, each with a name, stand to bless Rev. Murphy for his obedience to Christ. Likewise, in honor of the faithful Christians who took a stand, countless African-American families can testify to the difference it makes to live in an American South without lynching. Still more give thanks to God for Dr. Martin Luther King Jr. for the opportunity to live in a South without apartheid. Like the blind man healed by Jesus, these witnesses show little interest in quibbling over historical or theological complexities. They only offer simple stories about the difference faith can make: "One thing I do know. I was blind but now I see" (John 9:25).

We are not caught up in a Pollyanna-like dream of bringing heaven to earth and abolishing injustice. On the contrary, we know that an ocean of oppression will pound humanity until he whom "even the wind and waves obey" shall command the storm to cease (Matthew 8:27). Moreover, we know that there are waves of injustice in this world against which even the most faithful will not be saved. But still we do not despair. As Dr. Martin Luther King Jr. said at his commencement address at Springfield College, "The moral arc of the universe is long, but it bends toward justice."[15] Calling us to "action in hope" the great missiologist David Bosch declares that "like its Lord, the church-in-mission must take sides, *for* life and against death, for justice and against oppression."[16]

> Precisely the vision of God's triumph makes it impossible to look for sanctuary in quietism, neutrality, or withdrawal from the field of action. We may never overrate our own capabilities; and yet, we may have confidence about the direction into which history moves, for we are not, like Sartre, peering into the abyss of nothingness, nauseated by the emptiness of our freedom, leaping into a future which only confirms the meaninglessness of the present moment.[17]

In the words of the apostle Paul, "Let us not become weary in doing good, for at the proper time we will reap a harvest if we do not give up" (Galatians 6:9). This is not a vague affirmation about the happy ending of history, the evolving goodness of man, the triumph of the scientific mind or the promise of a civilized world.

It is a bedrock conviction about the nature of God and what it means to serve him in faithfulness. As he gives us eyes to see those in need, we will simply respond in love. As Bosch declared, "We hope because of what we have already experienced. Christian hope is both possession and yearning, repose and activity, arrival and being on the way. Since God's victory is certain, believers can work both patiently and enthusiastically, blending careful planning with urgent obedience, motivated by the patient impatience of the Christian hope."[18]

Second, we learn from Dr. Bushnell, Rev. Murphy and the Christian ladies of the ASWPL that *the biblical mandate to seek justice and rescue the oppressed is an integral and magnificent theme of the Christian heritage* (Isaiah 1:17). They may be unfamiliar to us now, but many of the greatest heroes of biblical Christianity in history were fully engaged in the work of seeking justice.

It would never have occurred to the great evangelicals of the nineteenth-century who battled so bravely to abolish slavery—William Wilberforce, Charles Finney, William Lloyd Garrison, Edward Beecher, Elijah Lovejoy, Theodore Dwight Weld—that Jesus could be honored by a life of Christian devotion that did not include a response of Christian love to those who are oppressed. For some it was precisely their conversion to Christ that moved them to take up the slavery cause. For John Gregg Fee, the evangelical founder of Berea College in Kentucky, it was while on his knees in anguished prayer that he confronted the costs of discipleship. "I saw that to embrace the principle of abolition and wear the name was to cut myself off from relatives and former friends." But he prayed, "Lord, if needs be, make me an Abolitionist." Later he said that he rose from prayer that day "with the consciousness that I had died to the world and accepted Christ in all the fullness of his character as I then understood him."[19]

In fact, historians have long recognized that the great achievements in humanitarian reform and social justice in the West during the nineteenth century—the abolition of slavery, prison reform, the establishment of hospitals and schools for the poor, women's rights, opposition to forced prostitution, the fight against child labor—were largely built on the faithful zeal of evangelical Christians. As American historian Sydney Ahlstrom of Yale University explained about that great humanitarian movement, "If the collective conscience of evangelical America is left out, the movement as a whole is incomprehensible." It was built, he said, on "the Puritan's basic confidence that the world could be constrained and re-formed in accordance with God's revealed will," and fueled by the revivalists' "demand for holiness, [and their] calling for socially relevant Christian commitment as the proper sequel to conversion."[20]

Recovering Our Ministry of Justice

In a detour away from biblical faith many Christians in the twentieth century neglected this heritage of service to a hurting world. As Bosch observed,

> It was a stupendous victory of the evil one to have made us believe that structures and conditions in this world will not or need not really change, to have considered political and societal powers and other vested interests inviolable, to have acquiesced in conditions of injustice and oppression, to have tempered our expectation to the point of compromise, to have given up the hope for a wholesale transformation of the status quo, to have been blind to our own responsibility for and involvement in a world en route to its fulfillment.[21]

But Christ has not neglected us, and now he calls us to recover the ministry of justice that once was ours. As the great evangelical theologian Carl F. H. Henry has said of evangelicals of the eighteenth and nineteenth centuries, their

> evangelical movement was spiritually and morally vital because it strove for justice and also invited humanity to regeneration, forgiveness, and power for righteousness. If the church preaches only divine forgiveness and does not affirm justice, she implies that God treats immorality and sin lightly. If the church proclaims only justice, we shall all die in unforgiven sin and without the spirit's empowerment for righteousness. We should be equally troubled that we lag in championing justice and in fulfilling our evangelistic mandate.[22]

As we peer down the halls of Christian history, we give thanks for those great champions of justice and evangelism who give us hope. For God intends that we remember his ancient work in equipping his people "to act justly and to love mercy and to walk humbly" (Micah 6:8). As the psalmist urges us, "Look to the LORD and his strength; seek his face always. Remember the wonders he has done, his miracles, and the judgments he pronounced" (Psalm 105:4-5).

And even as we remember, we lift our eyes to the horizon and ask, What great work of justice might God perform through us, in our time, to the glory of Christ? How might God renew through us the witness for biblical justice in the world? What child in bonded labor in India, what girl held in prostitution in Manila, what innocent man rotting in a Kenyan jail might yet stand and testify that the hand of a faithful God touched them and loved them through the obedience of Christians who refused to despair?

CHAPTER 18
WITH JUSTICE FOR ALL
Viv Grigg

One day as I was walking down the road to my house, the leader of the women's group called out her greetings. I stopped, and we talked. She invited me in and began to tell me about an event that had taken place some years ago.

The landowner had ordered the squatters to be evicted many times. This time he brought both the court order and the local police chief. The squatters had been warned! Behind him came a bulldozer to push down the squatter homes.

The protest began. The people, screaming, lay down and kneeled in front of the bulldozer. Thugs hired by the landowner dragged them away.

A local priest arrived and tried to calm the people. He asked the bulldozer driver to be patient. The driver was angry, too, but quieted down. Police re-inforcements arrived. The priest organized the people to lie down in front of the bulldozer. He spoke about non-violence. He talked with the police chief, informing him that the mayor had been called and would be arriving soon.

As a Christian called to work in the slums, what would you do when your people's homes are about to be destroyed? What would you do in response to violence, murder, oppression, and injustice? Does your heart burn with anger and reaction, with the desire to fight back and defend?

God feels the same way. He is a God of justice. He defends the poor and needy. In this case, the mayor defended the squatters' rights. Years later, they obtained legal rights to the land.

Just Lifestyles

I stumbled across a small passage in Jeremiah 22:13–17. For years I had taught that the knowledge of God comes through Bible reading and prayer. These activities are certainly basic to all else. However, the logical outcome of such a doctrine was to spend more and more time in prayer and Bible reading and less and less in the activities of life. Ultimately, one becomes a hermit.

The verses in Jeremiah challenged me: "to know God" is "to do justice and righteousness . . . [to judge] the cause of the poor and needy."

A hunger for God throws us not into pietism, but into the thick of injustice on this earth.[1]

"Justice and righteousness" is a phrase similar to our concept of social justice. Perhaps, since the phrase "social justice" may have radical overtones, we might talk about living "just lifestyles." In whatever work or area of social responsibility we are involved, a just lifestyle requires bringing just dealings, creating just programs, reforming unjust practices, and standing against unjust actions.

A Call for Missionary Servants

God is a God of justice. From these devastated masses of destitute humanity that are Manila's slums, three million cries for help and mercy reverberate around the throne room and entry halls of his court.

God hears! And he rises in indignation and anger!

He looks for one who will stand before him for the poor of this city. Two thousand years ago, finding none, he sent his own Son, declaring:

Behold, my servant, whom I uphold.
My chosen, in whom my soul delights;
I have put my Spirit upon him,
He will bring forth justice to the nations.
(Isaiah 42:1)

Notice his choosing. Note his empowering. And note his purpose: a missionary call to bring forth justice to the ends of the earth. Jesus repeated these thoughts in Luke 4:18, when he said the Spirit of the Lord was upon him to preach the gospel to the poor. Jesus' gospel was good news to the oppressed, good news of a kingdom where justice will reign. Note also the servant's methodology, his manner of bringing justice:

He will not cry or lift up his voice,
or make it heard in the street. (Isaiah 42:2)

God does not send high-flying diplomats on shuttle diplomacy. God's servant is not an articulate demonstrator, megaphone in hand. Or a flashy, traveling evangelist with glossy promotional materials.

He comes humbly, riding on an ass, washing others' feet, healing sword-cut ears. Isaiah tells of the Messiah's gentleness:

A bruised reed he will not break,
and a dimly burning wick he will not quench. (42:3)

He doesn't snap off those of us who are broken reeds, but gently binds us up. He does not snuff out, like a candlewick between his fingers, those who are almost burned out. Instead, he fans us back until we become a blazing light.

Such is God's method of bringing justice. And this justice is sure:

He will not fail or be discouraged till he has established justice in the earth. (42:4)

We are his body, called to the same role as our Master. We are servants of the Servant.

"If anyone serves me," he says, "he must follow me; and where I am, there shall my servant be also" (John 12:26). How high a calling!

As the basis of his lifestyle, Paul claimed a passage from another one of these servant songs. It defined the task of the servant as follows: "My servant . . . I will give you as a light to the nations, that my salvation may reach to the end of the earth" (Isaiah 49:6).

We, too, are called to declare this salvation to the ends of the earth as God's servants. Incarnating God is to incarnate justice and righteousness in a servant lifestyle:

For he delivers the needy when he calls,
the poor and him who has no helper.
He has pity on the weak and needy,
and saves the lives of the needy.
From oppression and violence he redeems their life;
and precious is their blood in his sight.
(Psalm 72:12–14)

Personal Justice

There are four levels of doing justice: first, in personal dealings; second, in peacemaking, bringing reconciliation between parties; third, in establishing movements of people who live justly; and fourth, in causing change at the upper levels of society.

The first level of justice begins with the fear of the Lord—the Lord who hears the poor and acts on their behalf. This gives us a deep fear of offending or humiliating a poor man. Personal justice begins in small things. Once, I forgot to pay the girl from the squatter home next door. She typed for me two or three days each week. I had almost reached my destination in another province when I remembered: "Oh no, I forgot to pay my typist!" I felt a sinking feeling in my stomach as this verse flashed into my mind: "You shall not oppress a hired servant who is poor and needy . . . You shall give him his hire on the day he earns it, before the sun goes down (for he is poor, and sets his heart upon it); lest he cry against you to the LORD, and it be sin in you" (Deuteronomy 24:14–15).

In addition to justice in small things, personal uprightness in its biblical context includes social justice. Ezekiel describes the righteous person as one who: "does not oppress any one, but restores to the debtor his pledge, commits no robbery, gives his bread to the hungry and covers the naked with a garment, does not lend at interest or take any increase, withholds his hand from iniquity, executes true justice between man and man, walks in my statutes, and is careful to observe my ordinances—he is righteous" (Ezekiel 18:7–9).

Justice as Peacemaking

Being rich among the poor, however, requires more than personal justice with a social component. In a situation of injustice and oppression, discipleship involves a second level of doing justice: peacemaking, bringing reconciliation between parties, seeking justice for those unjustly treated.

"Open your mouth, judge righteously, maintain the rights of the poor and needy," commands the King of Massa in Proverbs 31:9. Speaking out is danger-ous. The disciple in the slums will alternately be labeled "CIA" or "Marxist," depending on who is against him. Neither label is correct, for we work not for the communist nor the capitalist cause. We work only to do the righteousness of the kingdom.

Consider the sad letter I received from my Filipina *kumadre,* my "blood sister":

Eli has now no employer, so we are not earning even a single penny. We are just making a living through borrowing and debts. With regard to our kids, they are often contaminated by common illnesses successively. You know, Viv, we do not know how to solve our problems. Incidentally, the government agency that owns our land is asking us to vacate the place where we are in for the reason of not remitting our payment since we have lived here.

I responded by helping them make their payment. Her next letter was even more troubling, and explained how the cost of 3,825 pesos for their house had now become 9,460 pesos over two-and-a-half years.

Doing justice in that case meant finding out whether this 300 percent increase in the price of a house was due to unjust policies written by the govern-ment or whether a corrupt official was behind it. Justice meant trying to rectify the situation. It meant giving to my brother and sister in need, never expecting it back. It meant finding work for my *kumpadre*. And where my lack of resources and time made all of this impossible immediately, it meant looking to God to bring his judgment on those who perpetuate such legal crimes. For God: "will not revoke the punishment . . . because they sell the righteous for silver, and the needy for a pair of shoes—they that trample the head of the poor into the dust of the earth, and turn aside the way of the afflicted" (Amos 2:6–7).

Injustice Cries Out from the Land!

The servant missionary seeking to bring justice and righteousness to the people in the slum must understand the history of exploitation that forced the people there.

In the rural Philippines, the provinces' leading families, Spanish priests, American businessmen, and the Japanese war machine have all contributed to this poverty. Now, feudal barons who own the land farmed by tenants reinvest their profits in industry, land speculation, and multinational companies in Manila. Eventually, the money is shipped out of the economy through the multinationals to the United States, Japan, and elsewhere.[3]

One day as I was out jogging in the Filipino countryside (sometimes I did culturally unacceptable things like jogging alone), I ran past the massive gates of a mansion. I stopped and peered through the gates at the grounds and the building, just visible behind the guards.

I jogged to a basketball court nearby and began talking with some local farmers. I asked them where their landlord had earned the money to build his mansion. They sat around on their haunches, joking back and forth about the question. In between the jokes (a way of covering embarrassment or shame), they told me how most of the local families gave 50 percent of their crop to the landlord. Before the land reform law was implemented, he used to provide them with help if they were sick or in need. Those that obtained ownership rights to the land no longer received such help in time of need. They were forced to go into debt to the money-lender, who charged a much higher rate than the landlord exacted. (For every five pesos, the lender receives six pesos the next day—this system is called "five-six.") Proverbs comments: "The fallow ground of the poor yields much food, but it is swept away through injustice" (13:23). Most poor farmers are constantly confronted with these injustices. But working in a government job does not guarantee fair treatment either.

One of our friends in the slum, Susan, moved into an accountant's position in the local municipal office. She soon discovered that her bosses "fiddled" the books for profit. The auditor was in the know and received his cut. The investigator from the Bureau of Internal Revenue was paid off when he came. How could Susan continue to work and maintain her integrity as a Christian? If she exposed the system or rebelled against it, she would lose her job.

Is God Biased for the Poor?

Does God have a bias for the poor? Is he involved in a class war? The Scriptures do not support a Marxist analysis of class war. In James 5:1–6, God *does* appear to have a bias for the poor, but only an *apparent* bias. God seems to prefer the poor only if we compare his care for them with our own lack of concern.

As a good father will protect his youngest from being beaten by his eldest son *precisely because* he is a good and just father, so God particularly prefers, protects, and identifies with the poor. But let us not call him partial. Although he is a compassionate God, we know that he is an impartial God. He treats *all* as of infinite value and worth.

But his compassion and justice compels his involvement with the less fortunate. He condemns the unconcerned, luxurious lifestyle and oppression of the rich. James says:

> Come now, you rich, weep and howl for the miseries that are coming upon you. Your riches have rotted and your garments are moth-eaten. Your gold and silver have rusted, and their rust will be evidence against you and will eat your flesh like fire. You have laid up treasure for the last days. Behold, the wages of the laborers who mowed your fields, which you kept back by fraud, cry out; and the cries of the harvesters have reached the ears of the Lord of hosts. You have lived on the earth in luxury and in pleasure; you have fattened your hearts in a day of slaughter. You have condemned, you have killed the righteous man; he does not resist you (5:1–6).

Justice in Christian Community

The third level of doing justice in the slums is to establish movements of believers who:

(a) demonstrate justice in their lifestyles with each other

(b) begin to bring justice into the life and leadership of their immediate community.

Communal justice, like personal justice, also begins with small things. And all justice is rooted in prayer.

For example, God filled us with a desire to pray for an end to the unsanitary garbage in one part of the community. Garbage is a small issue, but seeking God's care in the small issues affects the community. An answered prayer gave us the freedom and respect to relate to community leaders and officials on more major issues such as when the landowners brought in bulldozers to push down homes.

Our responsibility was to become recognized spiritual leaders within the community. If we could establish trust and deepen our relationships day by day, the community might look to us and to God when they faced bigger issues.

Just lifestyles must be seen in believers first. The church must be established in justice as a reference point for non-believers. John Perkins describes the growth of a community of believers who demonstrated justice in their relationships to a racially torn community. Their dream was: "to carve out of the heart of Jackson, Mississippi, a community of believers reconciled to God and to each other. To bring together a fellowship of blacks and whites, rich and poor. Such could make a positive difference in the lives of a community enslaved by poverty and racism."[4]

But is it enough to demonstrate justice through holy living? Some see church planting as bringing a small group of believers out of a life of sin into the Kingdom of God. These believers stay in the community but live separate, holy lives.

Others view church planting as empowering believers to establish the Kingdom of God within their community. Instead of believers entering the Kingdom of God and leaving worldliness behind, believers are encouraged to stay "in the world" and actively work to bring the Kingdom of God into their community.

Because of my Anabaptist and fundamentalist heritage, I focused on a separated group of believers during my first years of church planting. Such separated communities have, paradoxically, brought many major political changes into our own society. They can be true lights and bright beacons on a hill. Armed with a strong conviction of rescuing people from damnation, these Christians have often become deeply involved in the problems of their age.

Quakers developed the early mental hospitals; the Salvation Army pioneered the first sheltered workshop schemes; the Mennonites have consistently worked at peacemaking nationally and internationally. Early Anabaptists advocated separation of church and state, religious liberty, and the role of free choice in matters of faith, each of which became major political issues in their time.[5] Modern non-religious social work often imitates activities developed by such groups.

But as I listened to the urgent cries of the poor, and studied the writings of Booth, Kagawa, Calvin, and Wesley and their work among the poor, as well as the history of missions, my separatist missions strategy was challenged.

I pored over the Bible. Passages such as Proverbs 11:10–11, ("When it goes well with the righteous, the city rejoices . . . By the blessing of the upright a city is exalted") indicate an active involvement by the righteous in community leadership. God was leading me to a desire to establish the kingdom within every level of society—and, where the social structure permits (as in Calvin's Geneva or in last century Tonga), over society.[6]

We discovered a vital principle in Jeremiah's prophecy to the exiled Israelites when they were taken to Babylon: "Build houses and live in them; plant gardens and eat their produce. Take wives and have sons and daughters. . . . But seek the welfare of the city where I have sent you into exile, and pray to the LORD on its behalf, for in its welfare you will find your welfare" (Jeremiah 29:5–7).

As aliens and exiles looking towards our heavenly home, we must also seek the welfare of the cities in which we are living. Although our future in the kingdom is secure, we should not sit back and do nothing. We must obey our Master's command to love our neighbor and try to bring kingdom principles to bear on the structures of society around us.

Upper-class Evangelism

To serve the poor, seeking personal justice, peacemaking justice, and communal justice are not enough. We must seek changes at the upper levels of society. But only a few of us are called to this task.

For most of us, God has called us to apprenticeship: to start where we are, take what we have, and do what we can at a community level. To do this, we might first establish communities of believers, alternative economic structures and small businesses, and then motivate local politicians to right decisions and confront local leaders with their wrongs. God may then give us grace for a wider field of ministry, but let us not be arrogant.

On the other hand, the few Christians of the upper class who have been committed to bringing the kingdom of God into or over every aspect of society have brought about fundamental social changes. The rich are the key to unlocking the poverty of the poor.

This is the cry of that famous passage in Isaiah 59:12–16, where the steps of social breakdown are described and the Lord cries for a man of justice:

We know our iniquities . . .
speaking oppression and revolt . . .

Justice is turned back . . .
for truth has fallen in the public squares,
and uprightness cannot enter . . .
The LORD saw it, and it displeased him that
there was no justice.
He saw that there was no man,
and wondered that there was no one to intervene;
[no intercessor].
Then his own arm brought him victory,
and his righteousness upheld him.

The most famous group of upper-class Christians in English history was the Clapham Sect, friends of William Wilberforce. They were influential noblemen, bankers, politicians, and industrialists in the late eighteenth and early nineteenth century.[7] At one time, they infiltrated and took over the entire directorate of the East India Company, using it to champion the rights of the native races! Their persistent advocacy of morality in all dealings with subject nations did much to create notions of trusteeship and responsible imperial government. The relief of debtors, the destruction of slavery, the mitigation of the savage eighteenth century penal code, the ending of discrimination against Jews, Catholics and Protestant dissenters, the provision of charity to the victims of the Industrial Revolution—these reforms and others like them are credited to these evangelists.

Today, God continues to look for leaders committed to such truth and justice.

Effective Social Change

If great social changes that help the poor are brought about by the rich, why work directly with the poor?

First, mass movements from the grassroots eventually produce changes in the top of society. The members of the Clapham Sect were the direct descendants of the Wesleyan revival. McLelland, in a significant study on entrepreneurs, shows that the two great waves of achievement in England were associated with Protestant reform or revival. Christians with a strong concern for perfection in this world tended to produce an achievement orientation in their sons, which turned the boys to business. Fifty years after revival, England reached a peak of achievement as these men entered national and business leadership.[8]

Perhaps our primary political activity, then, is renewal at the grassroots. As we establish movements of men and women converted and passionately committed to holiness, they will act like leaven in bread and ultimately transform society.

Second, the assumption that the center of power is the Prime Minister or the President is based on a non-Christian concept of power. Establishing spiritual "power bases" among the poor may be the key to changing a society. Spiritual power, as opposed to political power, is used by people able to influence the One who rules over politicians.[9] Power to move the hand that moves the world can be tapped by poor Christians who know the scriptural injunction: "I urge that supplications, prayers, intercessions, and thanksgivings be made for all men, for kings and all who are in high positions, that we may lead a quiet and peaceable life, godly and respectful in every way" (1 Timothy 2:1–2).

Such prayers are not intoned set phrases repeated at weekly worship in dead churches. They are the prayers of people who know how to prevail on God to implement political change, who recognize that "The king's heart is a stream of water in the hand of the Lord; he turns it wherever he will" (Proverbs 21:1).

Righteous poor people who possess spiritual power and renounce natural concepts of power are, perhaps, the key to social change. But they must also be wise in the issues of the time. Poor but wise people, unable to be bought by wealth or power, are the key to godly societies.

St. Francis Xavier, the nobleman who renounced social status and opened Asia to the gospel, was one such poor, wise man. He won to Christ tens of thousands in India, the Moluccas, and Japan. He washed the wounds of lepers, prayed for the sick to be healed, and preached the gospel. Xavier sagely commented: "The world is not ruled by principles of politics or economics, but by the mysterious realities of sin and grace."[10]

Third, we work with the poor rather than the rich because of the example of Jesus. He could have come as a rich man—as the great welfare king. Instead, he came as a babe in a Bethlehem manger, surrounded by common shepherds.

He had a reason, though we don't fully understand it, to identify with and minister among the poor. He had a reason for refusing Herod's courts and Satan's offer.

For Jesus, doing justice involved riding not on a centurion's chariot, but on an ass. The heroes of his stories were children and slaves, not generals and politicians. Instead of overthrowing the unjust Romans and their empire (72,000 angels are a match for most Roman legions), he stopped to heal an ear with his touch.

But there will come a day when he will return with sword in hand, when the grapes of wrath will be pressed out and judgment on oppression, evil, and sin will be executed: "He will not fail or be discouraged till he has established justice in the earth" (Isaiah 42:4).

Jesus is a model of a revolutionary who never revolted, a man of power who refused others' concepts of power, a man of justice who refused to be others' judge, a man with his spirit attuned to the heavens who was constantly involved in dust and dirt, pain and people.[11]

Part of Jesus' genius in working with the poor was that the rich came to him as well. Nicodemus searched out Jesus because of Jesus' credentials. It was not Jesus' political power that attracted him. It was his observation of Jesus' spiritual power worked out in signs among the poor.

"Rabbi," he said, "we know that you are a teacher come from God; for no one can do these signs that you do, unless God is with him" (John 3:2).

In the same way, living among the poor of Manila gives credibility and an opening to the upper-class, for many upper-class Filipinos have a highly developed social conscience and are actively involved in helping the poor of their country.

Rothie was such a man: a politician, an academic, a former revolutionary, a man of integrity and compassion. During the Indonesian communist uprising, Rothie and a friend had flown to Indonesia to fight for justice. Later, as the executive assistant of a university, he had worked to clean up its corruption. This resulted in 117 staff being fired by presidential order—only to be reinstated when Libya put "oil" pressure on those in political power! Rothie left quickly after the reinstatement and for a year was afraid to leave his house.

But that didn't stop him. He began to work with local fishermen, seeking to break the cycle of poverty in which they lived. First he provided a punt boat which enabled their canoes to travel further out to sea, reap bigger catches, and extend their fishing season because of greater safety during the monsoon. He then studied how to better market their fish. He established a "cool" store, so the fish could be sold when the price was highest. Next he helped the fishermen's wives to become productive with gardening, goats, and sewing.

I met Rothie after he had come to a personal knowledge of Jesus Christ. From the moment I met him, I loved him. He was a man who sought after justice with all his heart—both in society and in his own life.

When he was an executive in the university, he organized a great feast for visiting Arab dignitaries. Rothie made sure all was in order and everybody adequately fed, and then he and his wife quietly stepped out the back door to their own room and ate canned sardines and rice.

One day, after he flew home from a meeting with government leaders about rights for a minority group, he told me, "I have cleared my calendar. I have three days. I want you to teach me the Scriptures."

This was a deeply humbling experience for a young, insecure, poorly taught missionary. My mind raced. What could *I* teach this brilliant anthropologist-politician? The only basis of rapport I had with such a man was that I cared enough about his people, the poor, to live with them. Suddenly, I thought of the contrast between God's political perspective and society's.

"We will work through the book of Daniel," I told him. "I think it will help you see God's ways of bringing about political change."

The Loyal Reformers

The Lord has opened doors for other upper-class Christians in Manila working to bring justice for the poor within the structures of government. They speak prophetically to the government and speak out against sin at all levels in society—personally and politically, from their positions of respect and honor. They take seriously our mandate to "pay . . . respect to whom respect is due, honor to whom honor is due" (Romans 13:7) and to "honor all men. Love the brotherhood. Fear God. Honor the emperor" (1 Peter 2:17)—even if he has no clothes!

These passages were written in the context of the great exploitation, oppression, and Machiavellian politics of the Roman Empire, so they hold true for us today no matter how evil a leadership rules over us.

Another example of a man with an *entree* to the seat of power was a colonel, an advisor to the President, whose task was to prepare plans for a sugar factory complex. After his conversion, he consumed book after book on the Christian basis for socio-political and economic development. He thought through a Christian framework as a basis for management-labor relations and profit sharing. His proposals were the basis for discussion at the highest level of government, discussion that inevitably included aspects of the gospel.

A host of biblical concepts on work, justice, and love are basic to labor relations. Take one statement to employers: "You shall not oppress a hired servant who is poor and needy, whether he is one of your brethren or one of the sojourners who are in your land within your towns" (Deuteronomy 24:14).

This brief statement would radically reform a large percentage of the factories and close some multinationals in Manila if it were applied today. The Bible is a never-to-be-put-down textbook on such issues as labor, profit making, work, successful management patterns, and many other areas of business and politics. The Bible clearly points out the responsibilities expected of people in high positions towards the poor.

While not in agreement with the major themes of Gustavo Gutierrez, I do appreciate his excellent summary of the biblical perspective:

The Bible speaks of positive and concrete measures to prevent poverty from becoming established among the people of God. In Leviticus and Deuteronomy, there is very detailed legislation designed to prevent the accumulation of wealth and the consequent exploitation.

It is said, for example, that what remains in the fields after the harvest and the gathering of olives and grapes should not be collected; it is for the alien, the orphan, the widow (Deut. 24:19–21; Lev. 19:9, 10). Even more, the fields should not be harvested to the very edge so that something remains for the poor and the aliens (Lev. 23:22).

The Sabbath, the day of the Lord, has a social significance; it is a day of rest for the slave and the alien (Ex. 23:12; Deut. 5:14). The triennial tithe is not to be carried to the temple; rather it is for the alien, the orphan and the widow (Deut. 14:28–29; 26:12). Interest on loans is forbidden (Ex. 22:25; Lev. 25:35–37; Deut. 23:20). Other important measures include the Sabbath year and the jubilee year. Every seven years, the fields will be left to lie fallow "to provide food for the poor of your people" (Ex. 23:11; Lev. 25:2–7), although it is recognized that this duty is not always fulfilled (Lev. 26:34, 35). After seven years, the slaves were to regain their freedom (Ex. 21:2–6), and debts were to be pardoned (Deut. 15:1–18).

This is also the meaning of the jubilee year of Lev. 25:10 ff. It was . . . a general emancipation . . . of all the inhabitants of the land. The fields lay fallow; every man reentered his ancestral property, i.e. the fields and houses which had been alienated returned to their original owners.[12]

It is difficult to function at upper levels of leadership within a corrupt society. The higher up the ladder, the greater the extent of corruption. In an oppressive regime, it is not unusual for a Christian to reach a high level in government or business, only to have to resign because of injustice.

The more corrupt a society's leaders become, the less Christians are free to function. The church then moves more and more into an Anabaptist, separatist lifestyle. Theologies based on those of Calvin and Luther become less effective. Their theologies came out of contexts where Christians had freedom to play a role at the upper levels of society.

It is interesting to see this principle work out in the roles of the prophets. The pre-exilic prophets in the Old Testament (Amos, Hosea, Micah, Isaiah, and Jeremiah) worked from outside the establishment, perhaps because of the extent of its evil, whereas the post-exilic prophets (Joel, Haggai, Zechariah, and Malachi) worked from within the established political and religious leadership.

Emerging Christian leaders in developing countries today face a situation more akin to the pre-exilic one.

Demonic Politics

Like the pre-exilic prophets, upper class Christians can "respect the Emperor" while standing in political opposition. Some, like Daniel, recognize the spiritual powers that function behind governments. One of the chief angels took three weeks to break out of a battle with the "prince of the kingdom of Persia" and reach Daniel. This supernatural being delayed him until finally Michael came to relieve him (Daniel 10:13).

Most politicians are people of the world, people who live outside of the Word of God. But some in power have been overcome not only by sin, but also by demonic principalities and powers. We readily recognize this in Hitler (even a cursory reading of his life shows all the classic symptoms of demonic possession), in Idi Amin, or in Colonel Gadaffi. Structures that such men create are not only corrupted by the world, as are all structures to some degree, but may be demonized.

It is against such "principalities [and] powers, against the world rulers of this present darkness, against the spiritual hosts of wickedness in the heavenly places" that we are to wrestle when entering the political realm. That is why prayer is our most potent political weapon. In Chapter 2 of Colossians, Paul tells us that the elemental spirits of the universe perpetrate both human philosophies and empty religious traditions. He reminds the Colossians that such "principalities and powers" are disarmed (rendered inoperative) by the cross.[13]

As workers in the slums seeking to bring justice, we are in direct confrontation with powerful demonic forces. How do we best confront such demons? Through love and reconciliation. While rejecting the demonic philosophies, we honor and respect all men. We work side by side with people who reject our faith, recognizing the genuine searchings of the social worker and the good intentions of the religious leader.

John Perkins sums up his own experience in a paragraph, which in many ways is the crux of his book, *With Justice for All:*

> Demanding our rights had not softened the white community as we hoped it would. Instead, it had stiffened their opposition. Lying there on my bed, I was able to see that confronting white people with hostility was only going to create war. If there was going to be any healing it would have to take place in an atmosphere of love. I had been trying to demand justice. Now God was opening my eyes to a new and better strategy—seeking reconciliation.

I could not bring justice for other people. As a Christian, my responsibility was to seek to be reconciled. Then out of reconciliation, justice would flow.

Affirmative action integration and so on might be useful, but they alone were not justice. True justice could come only as people's hearts were made right with God and God's love motivated them to be reconciled to each other.[14]

Contention with Authorities

Defending the right and contending for truth are part of our call to righteousness. Jesus was no spineless coward. When slapped on the face and treated unjustly, he demanded, "Why do you strike me?" (John 18:23).

When the Pharisees misused their authority—an authority given by men but not by God—he refused to recognize it.

"You brood of vipers" is not a statement of a politician trying to win votes by compromise. It was the statement of the rightful King who had come to establish his kingdom.

The Old Testament prophets were not weak in their opposition to evil. Time and time again, God's spokesmen in the Scriptures recognized that he had appointed human authorities. They speak forcefully against sin. They do cry out in defense of cultural identity, and frequently call those in authority to repent. But they never call those under authority to rise up in rebellion.[15]

Moses, while leading a minority group out from oppression, went to the Pharaohs to gain permission and ultimately left the outcome to God. David, while outlawed from his society, refused to fight his king, leaving it to God to judge his case. Jude tells us that even when the archangel Michael contended with the devil, he said, "The Lord rebuke you." He did not presume to pronounce a reviling judgment himself.

But submission, gentleness, and obedience to authority are not humble acquiescence to unjust structures and unjust authority. Giving "honor to those whom honor is due" is not in conflict with contending for truth or standing for the rights of the poor. Love, honor, and reconciliation define the context and attitudes behind contention.

Ezekiel 45:9 has two interesting couplets: "Put away *violence and oppression,* and execute *justice and righteousness.*"

Violence and oppression are linked together as the opposite of justice and righteousness. Some encourage violent revolution as a way of overcoming oppression. But righteousness and justice—not violence and bitterness—are the vanquishers of oppression.

Time and Change

Why do we reject revolutionary violence? Those who would advocate it believe that gradual reforms of society are too slow, that political structures are too evil. By escalating the bitterness and bloodletting, the evil will be destroyed by *sudden change.*

Others champion *managed change,* recognizing that violent change unleashes forces into a community that destroy its fabric for generations.[16]

Christians recognize both components of change. Our action is to preach repentance—introducing reform step-by-step into a society to keep it from going rotten. But as we repent, we must recognize that some societies and structures within society (such as white slavery) are so evil that God will violently destroy them.

He does not desire increasing violence, but ends injustice through leaders who bring national repentance and transformation. Failing to find such people, God intervenes by his own arm. Such was the case of Nineveh in Jonah's day. Because the world's greatest city of its time repented, God did not destroy it!

Gradual reforms and revolutions may improve the lot of the poor. But we are not optimistic that they will create lasting "shalom." Christian reforms keep society from rottenness, but we must recognize our inability to make it holy.

Reforms are not reform enough. Revolutions are not revolutionary enough. But God's strategy is a long-term strategy that cannot fail. His kingdom, like a grain of mustard seed, will continue to grow until it has branches in every nation, tribe, and tongue. It advances through suffering servants who by the death of their Master overcome death, and who by the goodness of their lives disarm evil, hatred, and violence.

This is the good news, the hope that we proclaim day after day.

Political Options

There are three main categories of response. The first category is a "spiritual discipleship" model growing from Anabaptist, fundamentalist, or Pentecostal roots. These models encourage us to be "like Jesus."

The second category, the holistic discipleship model, is developed from a desire to see the kingdom rule *over* or be expressed *in* every facet of human life. It recognizes that Jesus chose to limit himself—to a single human body, to a time, to a people, to a geography, to a three-year ministry. The role he chose was and is today the spearhead of establishing the kingdom. But there are many other roles in the body of Christ.

This category considers kingdom *principles* to be eternal, but *applications* to be time and culture-bound. A Christian should not stay out of law as a career because Jesus was not a lawyer. There is a place for the Christian community development worker even though Jesus was not a community development worker. Because he was not a politician does not imply Christians should give up politics.

All of the Scriptures written across 2000 years need to be known and understood if we would know what is right to do in any given time and place. The Bible can help us be a godly lawyer, community developer, or politician. The principles lived out and taught by Jesus were also lived out by Moses the lawyer, Nehemiah the community developer, and Daniel the politician.

One difference between the first two categories is the understanding of power. Category I sees that since we are fighting against demonic forces and philosophies in government, we must rely primarily on spiritual warfare.

For "the weapons of our warfare are not physical [weapons of flesh and blood] but they are mighty before God for the overthrow and destruction of strongholds" (2 Corinthians 10:4, Amplified). Category I sees the power of God to heal the sick and set people free from demons as the spearhead of the kingdom of God.

Category II relates to those already in positions of political or economic power who need to learn the ethical uses of and limitations of such power. Some may demonstrate, others pray, while others believe that proclaiming the Word of God to the politicians is more effective.

Category III includes non-biblical alternatives that advocate political viewpoints which themselves are not submitted to biblical authority.

Squatter Politics

How does a worker in the slums practically pursue justice at the personal level, in peacemaking, in establishing communities of people, and in causing change at the upper levels of society? There are several key points to keep in mind as we seek to see God's justice come into slums and squatter settlements of the Two-Thirds World.

1. Living among the poor is itself seen as a political action. It is interpreted by many as a symbol of siding with the poor against the oppression of the rich (the government consisting of the rich).

2. Establishing churches where people care for each other and treat each other justly is itself a deeply political action. This involves proclamation, bring-

ing reconciliation into families and between gangs, developing social activities and a social structure for new believers, and becoming involved in economic development projects and leadership training. The worker must relate well to community leaders and government agency employees.

3. Public and private prayer for those in authority enables God to bring justice into society. It is a priority.

4. Since the national Intelligence Service may have a dossier on many Christian leaders, the Christian worker must be careful to clear activities with local leaders so that any questions might be answered beforehand, and all is above board. The worker should avoid becoming aligned with any political faction in a community.

5. The Christian worker needs to treat community leaders with respect and become involved with them at a practical level. These relationships provide a basis for rebuke when they act corruptly or consultation when the community is threatened.

6. Healing the sick, casting out demons, and bringing about changes through prayer also pave the way for a prophetic ministry to community leaders.

7. The basic issue for illegal squatters is to gain land rights. The Christian worker can encourage oppressive landlords or government officials to repent. Similar confrontations may take place over housing programs, water rights, and sewerage.

8. Believers must first maintain right relationships at home, school, and the office. The Christian worker tries to bring conciliation between groups within the community, organizes protests against civil authorities through petitions and lobbying for land, employment, sewerage, and so on. The people in the community should be encouraged to see the social responsibilities they share, like policing crime, wiping out corruption, securing garbage disposal, and improving hygiene. They should cooperate with the government upgrading program if it is designed and implemented well.

9. The servant of God is not called to handle all these issues. Let me cite three areas of citywide injustice too big for any one person to handle.

In July 1982, Madame Imelda Marcos began a new anti-squatting drive. The "benevolent society" wished to clean up Manila, "the City of Man." Thousands of people were loaded into trucks and deposited into relocation sites miles from the city—without water, without work, without promised facilities.[16]

"Thus says the Lord GOD: Enough, O princes of Israel! Put away violence and oppression, and execute justice and righteousness; cease your evictions of my people, says the Lord GOD" (Ezekiel 45:9). No one person could stop this oppression alone.

The slave trade can only occur because the uppermost level of government protects it. Who dares take it on alone?[17]

What about the exportation of Filipino laborers to the Middle East? This is a big source of steady income for family left behind in the squatter settlement, but it has led to thousands of situations of exploitation and trickery. Christian models of recruiting agencies need to be set up. Christian legislation needs to be introduced. Again, who can do this alone?

We need to see ourselves as part of the whole body of Christ and work in partnership to address these larger issues of injustice.

Unattached!

I read Malcolm Muggeridge's book *Something Beautiful for God* on the life of Mother Teresa, and found that while not neglecting programs, she had concluded that the greatest gift is loving people, communicating to them their dignity and their worth, even when there is no final way to meet their physical needs. Transferring the personal love and power of God is ultimately of infinite and eternal value.

Involvement with the poor results in different activities and responses in every community, for each community's needs differ. While we may not solve the problems facing squatters, we must do all in our power to alleviate them.

And we can dream. But we hold lightly our dreams for the cities of the world, because our eyes are fixed on an eternal city designed and built by God. Although unattached to this present world, we freely serve it, for love and justice compel us to. We work with all the energy he inspires within us to preach his kingdom and carve it into the structures of society here on earth. When the King returns, that kingdom of justice and righteousness will be fully established. The end of those who oppress others and show contempt for God will come (Isaiah 29:20). This vision of the holy city keeps us going in the midst of suffering and sorrow. Even so, come quickly Lord Jesus.

Coming Full Circle

Milleth had just taught us a Jewish dance. Everybody was rejoicing. The late afternoon shadows rustled back and forth in the wind. Sito announced our special guest—Aling Nena!

CHRISTIAN POLITICAL OPTIONS

1. "Spiritual" discipleship model

Involvement	Historical Expressions	Focus of Energy
Non-involvement in politics	Under oppressive regimes (authorities controlled by demonic forces)	Alternative communities demonstrating kingdom power in non-violence
Involvement with the needy	Early church monastic orders	Ministry to the poor and needy
"Spiritual" power struggles (the suffering Christ)	Fundamentalists Mennonites Anabaptists	Conflict with demonic forces in heavenly places

2. Holistic discipleship model

Involvement	Historical Expressions	Focus of Energy
Alternative A:		
Political involvement, confrontation, and reform of the power structures (Christ the Reformer)	Under democracies Luther's attempts at an ordered society Franciscans	Reforming structures: Establishment of governments "infiltrated" with kingdom ethics
Alternative B:		
Involvement in structures with the ethically-based use of force or power (Christ the King)	The Salvation Army Tonga Calvin's Geneva	Controlling structures: Establishment of governments ruled by kingdom ethics

3. Christian deviations (non-Christian models—Christian language)

Involvement	Historical Expressions	Focus of Energy
Alternative A:		Accept structures
Abuse of power in the name of Christ (the "Byzantine Christ" of purple and scepter)	Christianized and post-Christian societies that have lost the moral base of legitimate power (Cromwell Post-Constantine era)	Establishment of kingdom of God on earth by force Kingdom of God seen as servant of political structures
Alternative B:		Overthrown structures
Use of power against secular authorities	Oppressive regimes	God's kingdom = revolutionary government
Power struggle with oppressive regimes (Christ the Zealot, Christ the humanitarian)	"Pax Marx" Liberation theology	Identification of the "principalities and powers" with corrupt political structures

CHRISTIAN POLITICAL OPTIONS (CONTINUED)

1. "Spiritual" discipleship model (continued)

Involvement	Response to Violence	Political Action
Non-involvement in politics	Quietist approach	Submit to and pray for those in authority;
Involvement with the needy	Non-resistance	Proclaim gospel to the world; separate from evils of State
"Spiritual" power struggles		Overcome violence with pacifism

2. Holistic discipleship model (continued)

Involvement	Response to Violence	Political Action
Alternative A:		Individual participation
Political involvement, confrontation, and reform of the power structures	Activist approach Non-violence	Use godly power (parents, teachers, etc.); rule justly; promote good legislation; be active in public office
Alternative B:		Prophetic proclamation
Involvement in structures with the ethically-based use of force or power	Establishment approach Violence or revolutionary violence	Organize petitions and boycotts; promote "biblical" civil disobedience; protest by using constitutional rights Civil defense

3. Christian deviations (continued)

Involvement	Response to Violence	Political Action
Alternative A:		
Abuse of power in the name of Christ	Just war Suppress dissent for piety and stability	Participation in exercise of amoral power, unjust rule, and institutional evil
Alternative B:		
Use of power against secular authorities	Combat violence with violence	Protest of evil = unrequited bitterness; Gospel of the Kingdom = gospel of revolution;
Power struggle with oppressive regimes		Establish alternative revolutionary structure; rebel against corrupt authorities; God is dead, so man must destroy evil

She stood up in her finest dress. She had just had her teeth removed and smiled in embarrassment. Then, in clear Tagalog, she began her story.

"I used to be a gambler and a drunkard," she told us. "Now my life is changed. It is Jesus who has done this!"

Although most of us knew her story, we listened in silence.

She continued, "What I want to do now is to go to those poor people who live on the rubbish dump and preach to them about Jesus. They are poorer than we are. I want them to know what Jesus can do!" And so the kingdom spreads.

Notes

1. See also Waldron Scott, *Bring Forth Justice* (Authentic Media, 1997), 64–67.
2. Jose Porfirio Miranda, *Marx and the Bible,* trans. John Eagleson (Wipf & Stock Publishers, 2004), 93.
3. In his book *Beyond Manila,* Castillo provides a well-researched analysis of the structural causes and effects of Philippine rural poverty—which is the major cause of urban poverty. Celia T. Castillo. *Beyond Manila, Philippine Rural Problems in Perspective,* International Development Research Center, Box 8500, Ottawa, Canada K1G 3H9, 1980.
4. John Perkins, *With Justice for All* (Regal Books, 1982), 105. Used by permission.
5. Donald Durnbaugh, "Is 'Withdrawal' Involvement?", *The Other Side,* Box 158, Savannah, Ohio 44874, March-April 1974, pp 21–23.
6. Alan R. Tippett. *People Movements in Southern Polynesia* (Moody Press, 1971).
7. Ian Bradley, "Saints against Sin," reprinted from the Observer in *The Other Side,* March-April. 1974, pp 24–27.
8. McLelland, "Business Drive and National Achievement," in *Social Change: Sources, Patterns and Consequences* (Basic Books, 1973), 171 ff.
9. For a theological analysis of the problem of power see Martin Hengel, "Christ and Power," trans. by Everett R. Kalin, *Christian Journals,* (Ireland) Ltd, 1977. The diverse perspectives are analyzed by Tom McAlpine, *Facing the Powers: What are the Options?* (Monrovia: MARC, 1991).
10. Xavier Leon Dujour S.J. *Saint Francis Xavier, The Mystical Progress of the Apostle,* Fr. Henry Pascual Diz, S.J., (Bandra, Bombay: St. Paul Press Training School, 1950).
11. For a broader discussion of Jesus' rejection of revolution see John H. Yoder, *The Original Revolution* (Scottdale, PA: Herald Press, 1971), and Ronald Sider, *Christ and Violence* (Wipf & Stock Publishers, 2001).
12. Gustavo Gutierrez, *A Theology of Liberation,* 15th edition, Sr. Caridad Inda and John Eagleson, trans and eds. Maryknoll, (Orbis Books, 1988).
13. See Henrik Berkhof, *Christ and the Powers,* trans. John H. Yoder, (Herald Press, 1962, 1977), for a theological analysis of the demonic in politics.
14. Perkins, John, ibid, p. 102. Used by permission.
15. Leon Morris, "The Responsible Make Legends Happen," *Christianity Today,* September 7, 1979.
16. *Wretched of the Earth,* Concerned Citizens for the Urban Poor, Series 2, and Danilo-Luis M. Manano, *The Last Campaign,* Observer, Manila, 19 September 1982.
17. Spencer Davidson and David De Voss, *Lust City in the Far East* (Time May 10, 1982), or for fuller analyses Ron O'Grady *Third World Stopover* (WCC, 1981), and F. Landa Jocano, *Slums as a Way of Life* (University of the Philippines Press, 1975), chapter IX.

Part IV
Social Hope

SECTION J
COMMUNITY DEVELOPMENT

The rusted and broken corrugated-tin roof sagged perilously over the bed where the four children slept in the two-room apartment. The parents were afraid of what might happen when it finally gave way. The mother pleaded with me to help. I was leading a team of students to serve the poor. I felt that to ignore her cries would be hardhearted. I asked how much it would cost to repair the roof. Quickly, she summoned the landlord who lived nearby. He estimated the cost to be about $30. It seemed a small price for the safety of this family. I agreed and handed over the money to the family. What I didn't realize is just how quickly Western money can make a mess of things. When I returned four days later, I discovered that the family had used the money to pay off some debts; they earned only $1 a day and had borrowed money just to survive. Now the landlord was upset and the men he had agreed to hire to fix the roof were furious. Within minutes the room was crowded with half a dozen people all yelling at each other, with me and $30 at the epicenter of the controversy. In a number of ways, I mishandled this situation. One of the key problems, however, was using only outside money to solve the dilemma and not involving the family, landlord, and broader community.

By contrast, two students on the team, Justin and Megan, had developed a friendship with another family. This family also had structural problems with their home. Their walls were open in many places, and the rats were coming in and out freely, biting their two-month-old infant whenever the parents laid her on the floor. The students brought in a local carpenter to assess the situation. The cost of repairs was estimated at $70. Justin and Megan decided that they could put up $30. The couple looked at one another. With some scrimping they decided they could come up with $10—quite a chunk of their monthly income. Then came the dilemma: how to come up with the remaining $30? It would have been very easy at this point for Justin and Megan to increase their contribution to cover the rest of the cost of construction, but they restrained their urge to make up the difference. As they faced the real possibility that this family would not be able to receive these needed repairs, the carpenter chimed in. He also lived a life of poverty in the same slum community and was a Christian. Inspired by

Justin, Megan, and the couple's spirit of sacrifice, he said, "I too want to share in this blessing!" With that he offered to donate enough of his time and materials to close the financial gap.

Transformation of slum communities will never happen without a concerted effort on the part of the people who live in the slums. A blessing imposed from the outside is rarely a blessing at all. Outside money and outside help can often create power dynamics that end up doing more harm than good. Those whose lives are most affected need to help identify the problem and play an integral role in the solution.

Robert Linthicum, in his book *Transforming Power*, offers a framework for understanding the anatomy of community organizing. He describes the catalytic potential of someone willing to simply visit individuals, ask questions, and call groups of people from the community together to talk to one another. With a little leadership, a group of individuals recognizing a common struggle can move quickly to formulating plans for action. Soon the person playing the catalyzing role is in the background and the community has taken ownership of the change process.

Bryant Myers, in *Walking with the Poor*, suggests that a poor community has a story and has developed a strategy for survival, whether spoken or unspoken. It includes addressing physical and spiritual powers. The development workers must merge their own stories with the community's story and must be willing to learn from the community about where they think power lies.

Unless you humble yourself to sit at the feet of the community whom you have been sent to serve, you will seek to enact plans in which you are the central figure. And a plan that can't live without you is not a plan destined to serve the community.

CHAPTER 19

ORGANIZING FOR COMMUNITY ACTION

ROBERT LINTHICUM

As I reached the brow of the hill one rainy day in November 1990, I could see the slum of Carton City lying below in the lush river valley of Nairobi, Kenya. Although my eyes could not yet tell the condition of the slum, my nostrils could. I could clearly smell the stench of burned and charred buildings. A great fire had most certainly occurred recently in Carton City.

The Reverend David Ashiko and I began down the winding path, and as we approached Carton City, I could begin to see the extent of the damage. Scores of homes lay before us roofless and with scorched walls, many burnt to the ground. When we arrived in the slum, the people gathered around us, eager to tell their story to anyone who would listen.

Carton City, they told us, was an old slum—one of the first in the city of Nairobi—created soon after Kenya won freedom from the British. Dating back generations, it was constructed on government land in the floodplain of the Nairobi River, close to the military airport. Its inhabitants, primarily poor and uneducated freedom fighters in Kenya's struggle for independence, had simply squatted on that government land, seeking to scratch a living from its rich alluvial soil. It was named Carton City because so many of its people lived in cardboard cartons with sheet-metal roofs.

The government had tolerated the existence of Carton City for decades. But recently it had decided the slum had to go. Only the night before, the police had entered Carton City during an intense tropical storm. They roused all the people from their beds and made the families gather their belongings and stand in the pouring rain. Then, waving batons and firing pistols in the air, the police forced the father of each family to set fire to his own house. The people stood there helplessly in the pouring rain, watching their simple homes burn to the ground. For many it was the bitter end. They were defeated, broken, homeless, the men exposed before their families for the helpless victims they were. The people of Carton City had no place to go and were unwanted where they were.

I returned to Carton City sixteen months later. What now greeted my eyes was a significantly transformed community. Solid two- and three-room mud-brick houses filled the slum. The dirt streets were swept clean, with no litter anywhere except in designated pits some distance from the homes. Behind each home was a pit latrine so that each family had its own toilet, and community showers had been installed throughout the complex. There was both a piggery and a fowl farm in operation, and a large vegetable garden provided food for all in the slum and for sale. Carton City had radically changed. What had happened?

When I asked, I received a very simple answer: "Clement Adongo came to be with us!" Adongo was one of a team of four organizers led by the person who had originally accompanied me into Carton City, David Ashiko. Ashiko led World Vision Kenya's community organizing effort, Urban Advance, which was developing throughout Nairobi. When Ashiko accompanied me into Carton City in November 1990, we both agreed that this was a slum in which we should begin the Urban Advance organizing effort. Ashiko, an accomplished organizer, worked there part time until he employed and trained Adongo. And then Adongo began working in Carton City full time.

Adongo started by entering into the lives of the people of Carton City. He spent innumerable hours conducting individual meetings with them—asking questions, listening to their stories and learning about their lives. He heard that many of the men had fought for freedom from Britain, that there were no jobs after independence and that the people had come to squat in Carton City, hoping for day labor at the nearby military base. He learned that many of the women had resorted to begging, stealing or prostitution to support their families. He listened to their pain and frustration and their sense of abandonment and even betrayal by the government they had helped bring to power. And Adongo allowed his heart to be broken by the things that were breaking the hearts of "his" people.

Once he had built trusting relationships with a majority of the residents of Carton City, Adongo began gathering them together into house meetings. In those small groups, they told their stories, shared each other's pain and then began to talk about how they could make Carton City a better place to live.

Almost immediately the people began to identify what they had to do. Before they could act powerfully in the Kenyan political context, they had to begin building economic power. They started small. They created three income-generating projects, and with the production and selling of clothes, baskets, charcoal and furniture, a stream of income began flowing into the community. The only member of the community who could read and write besides Adongo went into a bank for the first time in her life; there she opened an interest-bearing account for the monies the community was generating. The people decided to build the latrines and community showers and then created the two farms and vegetable garden.

Then a new deputy chief was appointed for the district of Nairobi in which Carton City lay and he visited Carton City. Taking note of the people's improved standard of living, he decided he wanted some of it. Soon he informed the residents of Carton City that they had to pay a new tax. But the people discovered that there was no new tax. This was simply a way for the deputy chief to steal from the people. So the citizens of Carton City refused to pay.

One night the police entered the slum again. Under the orders of the deputy chief, they set fire to selected houses. But this time the people didn't meekly stand by and watch their homes burn. Instead of cowering in fear, the residents of Carton City rose up in anger. The community descended *en masse* upon the government, and there demanded and got an audience with the chief, the immediate superior of the deputy chief. They issued a complaint against the man and demanded retribution. But the chief refused to cooperate. So the community leaders went to the district commissioner, threatening to reveal the whole scandal to the newspapers. Immediately the district commissioner removed the deputy chief from his post and paid for the destroyed homes. And the people tasted significant victory for the first time against Nairobi's "principalities and powers."

But the people didn't leave it there. Adongo got the people to reflect on what they had learned from this incident and on what their next steps in dealing with the government should be. They decided to take two crucial steps. First, they would build permanent homes for each other. By Kenyan law, the building of a permanent home on unclaimed land "stakes a claim" to that land for its owner. Second, they notified the government that the slum would monitor every meeting of the District Development Committee (the local legislative body) to hold the government accountable. A Carton City representative has attended every meeting since. And the people have taken a number of actions to be sure their voice is heard.

The community then created its own construction firm and began building permanent homes for each other. These homes are substantial by Kenyan standards—two and three rooms, constructed of permanent brick and appointed with glass windows and wooden doors. One by one the people replaced their cardboard huts with these new homes.

The story of Carton City is a clear example of what community organizing is meant to do as it teaches people how to use power. The success of the people of

Carton City is a clear manifestation of the Iron Rule of organizing: "Never do for others what they can do for themselves." But God's people can most effectively practice this Iron Rule when we follow the strategy "power precedes program."

Power Precedes Program

Our tendency as Christians is to program absolutely everything. Think how programmed the church is. Committees, boards, task forces—we build our life and ministry on programs.

But organizing operates on an entirely different (and I think a far more biblical) rationale. It works on the premise that the way to bring about significant change is not to build a program but to build power. The way to enable people to "do for themselves" is by enabling them to work together to empower each other, not by developing a program that only strengthens their dependency.

Think of how Jesus built the church. He launched no programs; he created no committees; he developed no projects. Instead he invested himself in twelve men and seven women.[1] He spent time with them, listened to them, affirmed them, challenged them, made them think and taught them. He built relationships with them, both as individuals and as a group. And he motivated—in fact, pushed—them to "do for themselves." He had them preach, heal the sick, cast out demons, raise the dead, walk on water. "You . . . will do greater works than [mine]," he told them (Jn 14:12). And he did this, not just for individuals, but also as a community together. In other words what Jesus was doing was building a community of power. His essential task was to build his disciples into people of power so that once he had ascended to the Father they could build a community of faith throughout the world. What Jesus was about was the building of a permanent organization, and he did that through the building of relationships.

Power is rarely built through a program. It is built through intentional relationships that knit together the fabric of a community—an organization. And once that organization is sufficiently built, *then* that organization can address the issues and concerns of the people in significant ways, because it has built the power base to do so.

How is power built? All we need do is refer back to the way Nehemiah built the power of a particularly powerless Jewish people. Think of all the steps Nehemiah took to build a powerful Jewish community, as we examined them in chapter five. He *built relationships* with key people necessary for rebuilding both the walls and the corporate life of the Jewish people. From his individual meetings with the people, he *identified leaders* with strong leadership capabilities. He *identified the problems and opportunities* the people were facing. He *"rubbed raw" the problem,* getting the community to talk about the problem. He also *conducted a power analysis,* researching which system leaders would be cooperative and which would oppose the rebuilding.

Nehemiah also publicly *turned the problem into the issue,* so the people could act on it. Then the people *developed the implementing strategy* and determined a *clear objective,* identifying specific *targets*[2] for the work, a *desired response* for each target, followed up with particular *actions*[3] needed to achieve *the win*—the rebuilding of the walls.

So the people *organized and implemented the strategy.* As the work continued, they *reflected often* to adapt to changing situations. They *successfully completed each action* and *evaluated* every action and the lessons learned. They *celebrated* their victories and *set the next objectives and actions.* Ultimately, Nehemiah *built a strong organization,* a relational community of people that could act powerfully by acting collectively. In other words, Nehemiah was building a power organization.

Four Pivotal Strategies

The book of Nehemiah magnificently demonstrates how to build a power organization upon intentional relationships. By studying it, we can discern the steps that a pastor, church lay leader or community worker must take to build a people of power (rather than a programmed people). But our discussion is not complete without reflecting on the four pivotal strategies by which we can organize for community action: individual meetings, house meetings, research actions and actions.

Individual meetings. I have dedicated an entire chapter to individual meetings to give you a sense of how important these are. To build relational power, one must build it person by person by person. Individual meetings are the foundation upon which organizing a people of power is built. It is the first thing you do. And it is the continuing thing you do. Every pastor's ministry, every teacher's profession, every worker's job, every student's day would be transformed if we only spent time intentionally visiting, listening to, affirming, challenging and getting people to think through the causes of the pain and the joy in their lives. Biblical relational power cannot be built except upon the foundation of people sharing their deepest concerns.

House meetings. The second major strategy is that of house meetings. By *house meetings,* we mean meetings of a small enough group of people that they can meet comfortably in someone's parlor or family room. A house meeting is seven to fifteen people gathering in a church basement, at a restaurant, in a school classroom or in a house to share their deepest concerns and hopes and to reflect together about what those gathered at that meeting can do about it. A house meeting can be made up of people gathered *geographically* (that is, the people with whom you have held individual meetings in a given neighborhood), *institutionally* (people from the same church), or *by issue* (people who have identified a specific problem as their highest concern).

In essence a house meeting is an expanded individual meeting; it can accomplish in a group setting what is accomplished in a one-on-one meeting. However, the house meeting should not be seen as a substitute for individual meetings. Both types of meetings are necessary for building relational power.

Like an individual meeting, a house meeting provides the opportunity for people to share their pain and their hopes, to tell their stories, to express their convictions and to make commitments. But unlike an individual meeting, a house meeting allows people to share their pain and hopes with many people. This type of meeting moves beyond the one-on-one of the interviewee and the interviewer. And that is the genius of house meetings: they result in people building solidarity and community together.

Conducting a house meeting provides the opportunity for people who might otherwise never talk to each other to share their concerns and hopes and to hear each other's stories. Even for people who meet each other socially every week, the house meeting provides an opportunity to share at a far deeper level about things that really matter (for example, our children's education, the increase in crime in our community, the problems of growing old in this society). Most meetings in church are social or are oriented around the conduct of the business of the church, but few are substantive and focus on issues that really matter to people. By its very nature, the house meeting is designed to move people beyond superficiality, individualism and piety to the intense sharing of issues that really matter—and to do that through the telling of stories.

However, that happens only if the one leading the house meeting asks agitational questions. The chief objective of the pastor, community organizer or community worker leading such a meeting is to agitate people. But agitation is not irritation. It is not seeking to annoy, to attack, to confront or to be sarcastic. Agitation is the effort to "rub raw" the concerns and particularly the *passions* of people by asking those hard questions that will make them think and express their feelings to each other. It is asking questions like, "How does that make you feel when you're treated that way?" "Why do we feel we can't fight City Hall?" "What keeps you awake at night, worrying?" "What makes you angry?" "When you look at the kids in our neighborhood, what breaks your heart?" or "Why are we reluctant to do something about it?" Only agitational questions will cause people to move beyond their comfort zones and begin both to share their anger and to build the resolve to act together regarding the problems articulated at that house meeting.

The genius of house meetings is built on the turning of "hot anger" into "cold anger." Christians have a real problem with accepting anger within themselves or others, feeling it isn't very Christlike. But, along with love and as a natural extension of love, it is the primary emotion attributed to God—and God's anger is almost always directed toward either injustice or spiritual unfaithfulness. Paul, who understood anger very well, commands us, "Be angry but do not sin; do not let the sun go down on your anger, and do not make room for the devil" (Eph 4: 26-27).

Paul is telling us that anger is a part of life, and therefore it is important to be in touch with your anger. What angers you about injustice is triggered by similar injustice you experienced in your past. Sharing your stories with others both grounds your anger (so you understand it better) and connects you with others of similar experience or conviction. "Sinning" in your anger is holding onto your anger as hot anger, letting it seethe inside you but not doing anything about it. To fan the anger within you but to do nothing about it internalizes that anger, turning it inward on yourself, and thus does damage to you. Or the other alternative is to refuse to acknowledge the anger you feel and thus submerge it inside you. To do so allows that anger, particularly if it is recurring, to move into your subconscious and to thus become personally destructive. To handle anger in these ways is to "sin."

Paul continues, "Do not let the sun go down on your anger." By that he means the way to deal with your anger is to share it with others and to find allies who feel the same way. If you let the sun go down on your anger, it will become a festering wound within you and will harm you and those whom you love the most. But if you share that anger and the injustice that caused it, you will begin to move in healthy ways to deal with it by organizing with others to remove the injustice. In other words, Paul is saying that you must turn your hot anger into cold, deliberate anger that works toward a solution.

Finally Paul concludes, "And do not make room for the devil." You make room for the devil to control you when you internalize, deny or suppress your anger. God's way to deal with your anger is to join with others of common anger to work toward change in the situation or in the systems whose injustice caused the anger. The accomplishment of this task is the primary purpose of the house meeting.

Unlike individual meetings that never cease, house meetings are temporary. They are a transitional step between individual meetings and the involvement of people in ongoing issue-based groups within the larger organizing effort. But house meetings are a very necessary step; without them, people would rarely move from an individual complaint to joint action with others.

To build a strong organization of a community and its churches, the organizing effort needs to provide the means by which the people can be involved in hands-on action in the areas of their expressed concerns. The way most community and broad-based organizations do that is by the formation of "action teams," with each team dedicated to one specific area of concern. Thus you could have one action team dealing with crime and gangs, another with public education, another with housing and homelessness and another with jobs and unemployment. The understanding is that each action team does the research and groundwork necessary to prepare for action in that area of concern. But the entire organization and all its member churches and institutions have an obligation to support that action team in any action the organization approves.[4]

The house meeting is a vehicle by which people can move from an individual meeting to an action team by meeting together to share concerns, receive support, build relationships and decide to actually do something about the issue that matters most to them. This in turn leads to the third basic strategy of organizing—the strategy of research actions.

Research actions. Each action team in a community or broad-based organization exists to do the research and groundwork necessary to prepare for action in its area of concern and then to manage and coordinate the efforts of the organization to carry out actions.

A community organization's action team conducts a research action to gather information or to test the will or intention of a public or private official. *Action* is a technical term in the field of organizing that refers to an intentional and deliberate act on the part of the community organization to require a response of an official or leader on the issue the organization has determined needs to be acted upon. A *research action,* therefore, is an intentional and deliberate act that is done in order to provide information to that organization.

For example, the community organization might want to propose particular legislation to bring about a reform in public education. The action might be a public meeting at which those legislators present are asked to support the legislation. A research action, on the other hand, might be an intermediate step to find out if given legislators would attend that public meeting. If the research actions indicated that most legislators could not attend that meeting because of a scheduling conflict, the community organization might heed that research and decide to change the date of the meeting.

The purpose of a research action, therefore, is to gather information or to test the will of an official or leader. With the information gathered from that research, the community organization's action team can then sharpen the issue and make a more informed determination of who should be the "target" (the person targeted by the organization's action who has the authority to make the decision the organization is requesting be made), what the objective of the proposed action should be, what the action should be, what strategy would be most likely to succeed, who will support the proposed action and who will oppose it. In other words, the research action supplies information the organization needs to make the decisions that will most likely meet with success.

There are many kinds of research actions. The first kind is the gathering of statistical and technical data. Having sufficient and relevant data is essential. When the community organization's leaders meet with those who represent the political or economic powers, the community and church leaders must be able to demonstrate that they know as much about the subject matter as the target does. When the target realizes how well informed these leaders are, she will more likely enter into negotiation with them because other alternative responses won't work.

A second kind of research action is to meet with individual officials of unilateral institutions. This would include legislators, administrators of public institutions (for example, the superintendent of a school district) and corporate officials (the vice president of a corporation or the bishop of a diocese). Such meetings would be for the purpose of gaining support for the action, for soliciting information or for building a working relationship.

A third kind of research action is that of meeting with a delegation or an assembled body to seek support. That might include a legislative committee, a board of directors or an elected body. Unlike an action that would demand a particular kind of response, this would be an exploratory meeting to share the problem or issue, ask for support or advice, or request commitment. But the primary purpose of such a research action is to find out how this body would respond to this issue and to initiate a working relationship.

How should a research action be undertaken?

1. The action team needs to determine what the issue and their tentative action would be. The research action would test that tentative action or issue to see if it is indeed workable and winnable.

2. The action team should determine the research needed to test that tentative action. Is it data we need to gather? If so, what? Is it legislators we need to influence? Is it officials with whom we need to build working relationships? If so, who?

3. The research must be undertaken and the results gathered.

4. The gathered information and responses are examined, and from that examination, the actual action, objective, target and campaign is created.

The gathered information might lead to conducting a power analysis. A power analysis is an examination of how power *actually* flows in a given situation, as opposed to how it theoretically flows according to some organizational chart. In light of the information gathered, simply write on a whiteboard or flip chart the names of the people who your research indicates are the key decision makers. Then determine which of these people talk with whom to move toward a decision. Ask questions like, "Who goes to whom to deal with an issue? Who is most pivotal in the making of a strategic decision? Who would we need to get to support us? What would be the most likely strategy to get that person's support?" Draw lines from strategic decision makers to other strategic decision makers. He who gets the most lines wins—that's the key person you need to influence.

Actions. "The action is in the reaction." This statement captures the heart of a public action. An action is an intentional and deliberate act on the part of a community organization to require a response of a target on the issue the organization has determined needs to be acted on. An action is therefore the heart of organizing; it seeks to call a government or business official to accountability.

In essence the objective of an action is to get the target to react to the demand the community organization is making of him. He is being faced with a demand of the people that requires him to make a choice. How the target reacts to the community organization's action determines how the organization will react to the target and that target's institution.

The reaction of the target can take several forms. The first is to agree with the demand. That agreement can take three forms. The target may accept the specific demand placed before her. Or she may propose changes in the demand that are acceptable to the community organization. Or she may propose an alternative that accomplishes what the community organization wants accomplished but goes about it a different way. Of course simply getting agreement from the target doesn't mean the situation is resolved. One can say "yes" but never follow through. (One must be particularly culturally sensitive here because in some cultures it is considered rude to give a direct "no" but is considered appropriate to agree and then do nothing.) To make sure a "yes" is truly a yes, it is incumbent on the action team to set a date for the issue to be resolved, let the target know the people's organization will monitor the situation and then hold her accountable to fulfill her agreement.

The second reaction is to reject the demand. That too can take three forms. First, the target can simply say, "No, I won't do it," and take the consequences (loss of credibility with the electorate, loss of votes, loss of business). The second is to "blow smoke"—that is, to seek to obfuscate the response by saying, "I can't do it because . . ." If the community organization and its action team have done adequate research, they will be able to dismantle that excuse. The third is to say, "I need to study your proposal." That is the trickiest response of all. It can mean one of two things: that the person and his staff really do need to study the proposal to determine its feasibility, or that the target is politely saying "no" (that is, to apparently study it but never intend to make a decision on it). The community organization must immediately decide which study response the target is actually making by pushing for a date for a further meeting and a final answer. If the target genuinely needs to study it, he will gladly set a date. If this is a way to say "no" without saying "no," he will refuse to set a date. In such a case, the organization must proclaim to the gathered body and the media that the official's answer is, in reality, "no."

If the response of the target is no, it now becomes incumbent on the community organization to take the next step. How will the people respond to the reaction of the target? Of course, an effective organization will not quickly reveal its plans; rather it will keep the target on pins and needles by saying, "You will hear from us later." Then the organization and its action team will carefully plan their next move with the ultimate objective being to get the target or the target's superior to accept the demand of the people.

In reality, an action is an exercise of power. It is the ultimate act of power of a relational organization; it uses power in such a way that it declares to the target that relationship with that organization, its constituent institutions, its thousands or tens of thousands of people and all whom that organization influences will be denied the target if she ignores those matters most important to the people. It is calling that official to accountability before the people who elected him to office or who supply the tax dollars to pay his salary, or who purchase that company's services or products. An action is democracy in action, expecting officials to be servants of the people rather than to act as if they are the people's lords and masters.

Organizing in the Local Church

Thus far we have examined the principles and strategies of community organizing for neighborhood and city transformation. However, organizing can also be used to transform the interior life of your congregation. The principles of organizing can be used to build a powerful relational congregation centered on glorifying God through working for the transformation of the world rather than through building programs.

Individual and house meetings throughout an entire congregation can be a central activity of both church elders and pastors, engaging members in conversations about those issues and concerns that really matter to them. Rather than building the church around committees to which members are reluctantly recruited, both the interior work and the mission outreach of the congregation can be built around action teams enabling members to address both community and church issues about which they really care. Hundreds of very successful churches have used organizing principles to recreate their institutions into powerful relational congregations and to make a profound difference in their neighborhoods.[5]

This chapter has explored the process for organizing for community or church action in the public arena. These are principles and strategies that work. But are they truly biblical? Nowhere in Scripture will we find a text that reads, "Thou shalt do community organizing." But the principles of community organizing are woven through the warp and woof of Scripture as it presents a theology of relational power. How else can we understand the intense encounters Jesus had with people like the Samaritan woman than as individual meetings—listening to their hearts, affirming and challenging them, and agitating them to think through their faith, beliefs and convictions? How else can we understand the investment of time Jesus made in his disciples than as an ongoing, traveling house meeting—reflecting with them, teaching them, calling them forth to become all he intended them to be? How else can we understand Nehemiah's meetings with King Artaxerxes, Asaph and Sanballat than as research actions? And how else can we understand Moses' confrontation of Pharaoh than as an action?

The Scriptures are replete with both the wise use of relational power and the abuse of unilateral power. If the church would allow Scripture to speak for itself, we would begin to discern the ministry to which God is calling us as he seeks to use us to work for the transformation of the public life of our communities, cities and nations. God has called us to work for the transformation of the world. But such transformation can occur only as we learn to use the relational power at our disposal.

Notes

1. The male disciples were Simon Peter, Andrew, James and John (both sons of Zebedee), Philip, Bartholomew, Thomas, Matthew, James Alphaeus, Thaddaeus, Simon the Zealot, and Judas Iscariot (Mt 10:1-4). The seven female disciples were Mary Magdalene (Lk 8:3); Mary and Martha, sisters of Lazarus (Lk 10:38-41; Jn 11:1-44); Joanna (Lk 8:3; 24:10); Susanna (Lk 8:3); Salome (Mk 15:40; 16:1); and Mary the mother of James (Lk 24:10). There was also a Mary the wife of Clopas listed (Jn 19:25), but I assume she is also the mother of

James; if not, that means there were eight female disciples.

2. The vocabulary of community and broad-based organizing uses the word *target* for the specific official whom the organization selects to receive the issue and to act upon it. *Target* is intentionally used because he or she is the person "targeted" to respond to the demands of the organization. Normally the target is that person in a government, public organization or business who has the authority to make the decision required by the community organization. Why use the word *target* for that person? Simply because to use the word *enemy* or any other pejorative is to create a condition that could lead to a permanent division between the community organization and that person. One doesn't want to allow such alienation to occur, because the target may become the community organization's supporter on another issue. This nuance is captured in the organizing expression "There are no permanent friends or enemies!"

3. The word *action* is another technical term in the field of organizing. An action is an intentional and deliberate act on the part of the organization to require the response of a target on the issue that the organization has determined necessary to act on.

4. Most community and broad-based organizations operate on the understanding that each member church and institution makes a decision whether or not to participate in each issue. The organization does this out of sensitivity to the potential differences between churches and institutions. The basic assumption is that each member institution participates as much as possible in each issue proposed by each action team, but no institution is expected to participate when this would go against the convictions or priorities of that institution.

5. There is little written on the application of organizing principles to the interior life and institutional development of the local church. However, my book *Building a Church of Power*, scheduled for release late in 2004 or early in 2005, will concentrate on this theme.

CHAPTER 20

DEVELOPMENT PRACTICE: PRINCIPLES AND PRACTITIONERS

BRYANT MYERS

To this point we have developed an understanding of what poverty is and why people are poor. To this we have added an understanding of what transformational development is from a Christian perspective. The next question is, How do we work with the poor and the non-poor in order to help them articulate a vision for transformation and the means by which they can attempt to move toward this vision?

Answering this question takes some care. If we jump too quickly to development methodology, we can make some serious mistakes. There are some underlying assumptions that need clarification. Whose project is being planned? Who does the planning? What way of thinking about planning is best suited for development work? What requirements will we make of development-planning methodologies?

Finally, there are a whole series of considerations relating to the development practitioner. We need to address the mindset and characteristics of the holistic practitioner. What kind of formation and spirituality enables effective development promotion?

The Principles

Respecting the Community's Story

Transformational development takes place in the context of converging stories. The story of the development promoter and the agency of which he or she is a part is joining the story of the community and the individual stories of the people and groups in the community. Thus it is important to be very clear as to whose story the transformational development project belongs to. I also pointed out that everyone is quick to say that the story belongs to the people, and that it is a great deal harder to live this out in practice. Too often development workers unwittingly assume that their story is a better story; after all, they know how to do sustainable agriculture and understand maternal child health. It is a great and humbling challenge to lay down our own story and not pick it up again until the poor ask us to do so.

At the same time, however, this convergence of stories means that the story of the community and the holistic practitioner will never be fully the same. Each story affects all the other stories. The poor will borrow from our story and, if we are not too proud, we will learn from theirs. There is no longer a single narrative in the community. This is why engaged, respectful relationships are so important to transformational development. Each story needs to engage all the other stories, and all need to engage the larger story of which all stories are part.

The History of the Community

The community's story, up to the time the development practitioner arrives, is its history. The community comes from a past, and its memory of that past is the beginning of any new story. The community has been coping, adapting, and surviving. It has tried to innovate, sometimes with success and sometimes with failure. Good things have happened; the community has done things it is proud of. The positive elements of the past can be a source of vision and energy for the future.[1] Leszek Kolakowski has reminded us that we study history, not to find out what happened, but to discover who we are. Thus, helping the community tell its own story is critical to understanding its present and its identity as well as getting a glimpse of a possible future. Listening to its story also tells the community that we think its story is valuable.

There is also a need to help the community and ourselves recognize the activity of God in the story of the community. Whether Christian or not, whether religious or not, there is evidence of God's creative and redemptive work in the life of the community, if only we look for it. Wherever a disaster was averted or a blessing was unexpected, God was at work. Wherever things worked for life and against death, Christ's fingerprints can be seen—"All things were created by him and for him. He is before all things and in him all things hold together" (Col 1:17-18). Recognizing and naming God's part in the story of the community is an act of discernment, a spiritual act. It is also an act of healing. Asking the community to locate God in its history is a way of helping its members to discover that they are not god-forsaken.

However, there is also a dark side to recovering this history. This dark side takes two forms.

First, the history of the community is often told by those in positions of power, and usually they tell the history in a way that either supports their continuing claim to power or disempowers the community in terms of thinking about change (Christian 1998a, 15). Religious leaders sometimes reinforce fatalism by claiming that God wills what is or that the situation today is a just response to bad behavior in the past. Political or economic leaders may justify their positions of power on the basis of having been blessed or righteous or having served as the community's benefactors in the past. History is thereby distorted to serve an end. Illiteracy means the poor never have a chance to write their own history or read alternative views that subvert the stories of the powerful. But the poor do remember their history and can be helped to recover it and reread it. Any journey of transformation needs to begin by helping the community, and its various subgroups, recover their own true stories.

Second, we need to be concerned about who made the community's history. Jayakumar Christian has pointed out that some people are freer to make history than others (1994, 201). Some have argued that if you are not a history maker, you become a tool in the hands of those who do make history. Thus, the very process of history-making can be a source of powerlessness and poverty. Knowing who participated in history-making in the past and why is critical to any effort to create a different kind of history-making in the future.

Listening to the Whole Story

We must also remember to listen to their story in terms of both the seen and the unseen world. Hiebert, Shaw, and Tineou (1998) remind us that each level of worldview answers different questions. The top level of the unseen world is the domain of formal religion. Listening to people talk about this will reveal a community's understanding of the formal side of Islam, Christianity, or whatever belief system it accepts. This is where we will hear stories and propositions that answer questions about ultimate origins, about the purpose and identity of the universe, our community, and ourselves.

The middle level of the worldview, while still spiritual and unseen, is the world of folk religion. There is a folk version of everything—folk Islam, folk Buddhism, and even folk Christianity. This level addresses questions about managing everyday life. Who has to power over this or that area of life? What do they demand of us? How do we live a full life? How can we be prosperous or avoid failure? What do we need to know about our past? How can we make the future more secure? What is the right moral order for us? The answers point to the interdependence of all things, to the sources of power and the management of power.

The lower level of worldview is the natural order, the material world. This is the world of science in both its modern and folk expressions. Nomadic people understand why and when to move their herds. Village healers have extensive knowledge of local herbs, barks, and leaves. The community has rules for how to live and work together. This is the world of hearing, seeing, touching, and feeling things.

The development practitioner is usually most interested, and most comfortable, working in the bottom level of the worldview. After all, this *is* the part of the world in which most development activities take place. This is where we dig wells, immunize children, improve agricultural practices, and carry out micro-enterprise activities. The problem arises when this is the only part of the community's story that we listen to or ask about. Its formal and folk religious views also have important information that we need to hear. Whether we agree or not, these domains of the unseen spiritual world are where the community will tend to locate the cause of its problems and the hope for their solutions. If we are unwilling to view the world from the community's perspective, and begin from there, then we are top-down development practitioners after all.

They Know How to Survive

The community already has a survival strategy. The community has well-established patterns for making sense out of its world and staying alive in it. Only in disaster situations will we find such severe dislocations that its people are unable to cope and survive. This already existing survival strategy is that part of the community's story that we call the present. Understanding this survival strategy is critical to any attempt to create a vision for a better future. There are two reasons why this is true.

First, we need to see the world the way the community sees it. Helping the community describe its survival strategy is also a way for us to see what the community considers important as well as the community's understanding of what causes things to happen or not happen. The community's survival strategy reveals its capabilities, resources, skills, and knowledge as well as its vulnerabilities, those areas of life over which the community feels it has little or no control. Capabilities are assets that can be invested in future development. Vulnerabilities are the things for which alternatives or mitigating strategies are needed.

Second, allowing a community to describe its survival strategy reinforces in the minds of the community members the idea that they have skills, local knowledge, and ways of working that are good and worth building on. Not everything in the community is wrong and ineffective. Enabling people to discover and declare their survival strategy is part of healing the marred identity of the poor.

Ravi Jayakaran has created a framework for reporting the community's description of its survival strategy. The part of the world the community feels it can control represents the seen or material world of nature where material cause and effect hold sway, the inside of the circle (Figure 20.1). They believe they can make things change, for good or ill, as a result of their own actions. This part of their survival strategy does not invoke religious or spiritual cause and effect.

The other part of their survival strategy, the part outside the circle in Figure 20.1, deals with what the community believes is outside its direct control. This is the world of spirits, gods, demons, and ancestors, the inhabitants of Hiebert's excluded middle.[2] Only spiritual explanations work in this part of their world. In search of some measure of influence in these areas of vulnerability, the community will assign gods or shrines or sacred places to these areas. The greater the lack of control, or the greater the perceived efficacy of the god, the larger the shrine.[3] The smaller gods that are invoked as the source of cause and effect in this unseen world represent a map of the community's vulnerability. To gain influence over this part of their life, the community also turns to shamans and diviners as those who have access to the unseen world and who can work for good or ill on behalf of individuals and the community. At this point the religious system and worldview can prove exploitative.

This unseen world is a challenge for the development practitioner from the West. We must be able to accept talk about sacred places, shrines, and temples where people make offerings, doing the best they can to negotiate with the unpredictable and capricious unseen spirits who can change their lives for better or for worse. The map of its divinities is the way the community describes its vulnerabilities.

In Figure 20.1, for example, the health of children lies both within the domain the community can control and outside of it. This represents the uncertainty the community associates with the health of its children. Sometimes the cause of illness is germs or not having enough food. Since this is empirical and certain, people can take action to create change. Therefore, sick children are taken to the health hut or emergency feeding is sought. Other health problems are attributed by the community to the evil eye or an angry ancestor or spirit. For this, divining and sacrifices are the remedy. The survival strategy as the community describes it acknowledges power in both the seen and the unseen world.

This can get confusing. Both elements of the survival strategy are often described in religious language and involve religious institutions. We must be careful to discern the difference between religious language describing a physical process in contrast to religious language describing the unseen world of the spiritual. As an example of the former, the pre-modern water systems of Bali are marked by temples belonging to a large family of gods. The respective

FIGURE 20.1 The Survival Strategy of a Community.

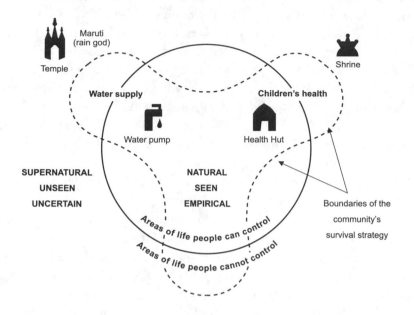

religious rituals associated with each temple serve to link all the temples in a way that results in a system of water management that ensures that even downstream users get their fair share of water (Lansing 1991, 59). This is an example of spiritual language and ritual providing the framework for a material distribution system.

For the part of the world the community cannot explain and control, such as bad weather, the coming of locusts, or failed businesses, the community invokes the unseen world of the spirits as the source of success or failure. The solution is sought in sacred places, shrines, and temples. Being able to untangle these accounts of cause and effect is important to development planning that begins where people are.

Bruce Bradshaw (1997) has developed a framework for describing survival systems. He suggests that any survival strategy must describe the sources the community looks to for provision, peace, justice, healing, guidance, and salvation. The following diagram describes how three tribal groups in Kenya described the sources of these things within the context of their traditional worldview. It is interesting to note that some elements deal with the supernatural, while others connote the recent arrival of Western science and education. The holistic practitioner must work with the community in a way that allows both worlds to be described and understood. This survival strategy is the point of departure for the development journey. To enhance our own understanding of how the community understands cause and effect, we must understand the survival strategy in their categories. The community will work more willingly to participate and take ownership when development interventions resonate with the survival strategy and attempt to enhance it. Then we can ask the transformational questions, What are the barriers to the community growing in its ability to survive? and Whose interests are served by these barriers?

Respecting Indigenous Knowledge

One of the more recent discoveries among development professionals is how much local communities actually know that is true and valuable.[4] With a humility that comes from experience, more and more development practitioners are giving the local view of almost everything a more serious hearing. Traditional medicine is not all superstition and nonsense. In fact, Western pharmaceutical companies are abandoning the random search for drugs in the laboratory in favor of listening to traditional healers and their knowledge of barks, leaves, and grubs.

In Kenya, they still tell the story of Lord Delamare, who "discovered" the rich grasslands north of Nakuru and couldn't understand why the Masai didn't graze their cattle there. He spent a fortune importing English cattle only to discover that the grass in that part of the Rift Valley lacks a key nutrient that results in poor milk production, resulting in the death of most of the calves. This, of course, was something that every Masai boy knew but was never asked.

Olivia Muchena points out that the problem is in the eye of the beholder (Muchena 1996, 179). As long as the facilitator assumes that taboos, myths, and related ethnic values and concepts of the community have no value, they will have nothing to offer the development process. Muchena points out that these "superstitious" ideas are the way communities encode knowledge. If they are taken seriously, important local knowledge can emerge.

In rural India an old man watched a water specialist use a vertical electrical sounding device for seeking the best site for an open well. "You don't need that," the old man announced. "Dig under the highest termite mound,[5] Or dig under those big trees that stay green during the dry season. Everyone knows that is where the water is." And so it was.

Respecting and seeking indigenous knowledge "requires a different way of relating to the local community, for they must become partners in the ministry, helping to educate the 'ministers' to the realities from their perspective" (Muchena 1996, 178). We need to listen with an expectation that there are things we can learn.

There are two reasons that we need to seek and value local knowledge. First, as the foregoing illustrations suggest, local knowledge may add to Western knowledge, providing we have the humility to believe that our knowledge system is not complete. Within the African worldview, illness may be the result of material causes, but it may also be the result of broken relationships. The whole person is sick, not just the material body. This kind of thinking is slowly being taken up in the West and is making our approach to medicine both more humane and more relational.

The second reason for respecting indigenous knowledge is more serious. Koyama calls attention to it in an interesting way when he tells his own story as a missionary in rural Thailand, fresh from a seminary in Japan. He describes the angry response of a Thai woman to his conversation about the gospel:

> She was annoyed at me for looking at her *in my own terms*. She felt that she was only an object of my religious conquest. I had a message for her, but I did not think of the possibility that she might have a message for me (Koyama 1974, 90).

Do we believe that the poor have a message for us? When we fail to listen, to see what we can learn, we are in fact telling them that they are without useful information, without contribution. By dismissing what they know, we further mar the identity of the poor. Our good intentions deepen the poverty we seek to alleviate.

Even when indigenous knowledge seems to be wrong, we need to take care. In a village in Tanzania the local people told a development worker that no motor vehicle was allowed to approach their one-and-only spring. If this should happen, they said, the spirit who lived in the spring would cause the spring to go dry. Wishing to show the villagers that this was not true, the development worker drove his four-wheel-drive vehicle by the spring. The water promptly ceased to flow. While there was a natural explanation for this,[6] it is nonetheless true that the development worker created several barriers to any hope he may have had for change. On the one hand, he had shown no respect for the view of the community, and on the other hand, he had reinforced their traditional worldview, something that may hinder development in the future.

Learning Our Way Toward Transformation

We have to stop and ask, What kind of planning is best suited for transformational development? For a long time, there was only one kind of planning. Processes were assumed to be linear or sequential and, providing we understood them properly, we simply set objectives and created a sequential plan for achieving the objectives. Development planning for a long time was simply an adaptation of this approach. With the exception of purely mechanical tasks, like getting a well dug or building a building, everyone in the development business tells stories of development plans that did not work or that came out very differently than planned. Communities consistently failed to behave or change as planned, but we did not know why.

The problem is that social systems are not linear. There are so many feedback loops in social systems (communities) that the only thing we can safely predict about the future is that it will be counter-intuitive. Something will happen, even good things will happen, but they will seldom be what we originally intended. With the arrival of chaos theory[7] and our growing understanding of complex (or dynamical) systems (Gleick 1987), we now know why.[8] There is underlying order in complex systems (snowflakes always end up looking like snowflakes), but the future of such systems cannot be predicted (no one knows what an individual snowflake will look like until it is formed).

Since social systems are complex, they also contain order, an order that will in time find expression. But social order can be recognized only when one looks at what was and what is. The ordering of the social system cannot be predicted. Such is the nature of complex systems. Said another way, social systems, and this most certainly applies to transformational development,[9] are self-organizing and therefore cannot be programmed with any accuracy over the long term.

What does this mean to development planning? We need to do two things, First, we need to shift our planning framework from the traditional management-by-objectives approach with five- to ten-year plans to a vision-and-values approach (Myers 1992a). Second, we need to make evaluation more frequent. Since the future cannot be predicted, we have to evaluate often enough to "learn our way" into the future.

How does this work? With a vision of where we want to be (the better future), and having identified the values by which we do our work, we set a mark on the horizon. However much off course our short-term work ends up, regular evaluations allow us to know where we are in terms of where we want to go. With a clear vision and values, we can now work on short-term plans, stopping periodically to see if where we ended up is directed toward our vision. If it is, we plan another step and evaluate again. If it is not, then we redirect our plan, take another short-term step, and evaluate again.

This shift has other implications. Chambers has identified what happens when the planning framework changes from making things happen to a more people-centered approach (1997, 37).

From Participation to Empowerment

If the development story belongs to the community, then local participation is demanded as an acknowledgment of this fact. If poverty is in part a reflection of the marred identity of the poor, then participation is essential to any effort to restore their identity. If we agree that there are already resources within the community, then participation is the logical means by which this knowledge can be discovered and can become part of the development process. If we have the humility to know that we do not know enough to do someone else's development for them, then seeking local participation is the only safeguard against our doing unwitting damage. By any measure, local participation is a critical success factor for transformational development.[10]

The Quality of Participation

The quality of participation matters, however. Norman Uphoff, a development practitioner and scholar at Cornell University, claims that "the value of participation depends upon what kind it is, under what circumstances it is taking place and by and for whom" (Uphoff et al. 1979, 281). Uphoff goes on to suggest that we should assess the quality of participation in three ways: Who is participating? What kind of participation? How is the participation occurring?

If participation is limited to local leaders, government personnel, and agency staff, then participation is limited to the non-poor and will necessarily be flawed because of their desire to sustain their privilege. They are easily tempted to play god in the lives of the poor.

These are Chambers's "uppers," people whose place and circumstances of birth, education, and professional training result in an unspoken (sometimes) sense of superiority that greatly interferes with their hearing and seeing (1997, 58-60). Development with them will be "top-down" and will almost always fail to change any social power relationships. Chambers quips (1997,101):

All powerful uppers think they know
What is right and real for those below.
    At least each upper so believes
But all are wrong; all power deceives.

But even if community residents are involved, care needs to be taken that the group includes all social groups, men and women, non-Christian and Christian, young and old. If they do not, those involved tend to act like the non-poor in relation to the others who are not included (D'Abreo 1989, 161). Leaving any group out sows seeds for future injustice and strife.

Figure 20.2: From Things to People.

Point of departure	Things	People
Mode	Blueprint	Process
Key word	Planning	Participation
Goals	Preset	Evolving
Decision-making	Centralized	Decentralized
Analytical assumptions	Reductionist	Whole systems
Professional mindset	Instructing Motivating	Enabling Empowering
Local people as	Beneficiaries	Partners, actors

Participation can also be flawed in terms of the level of participation. Having an opportunity to hear someone else present a plan for you is a very limited form of participation. Participation is meaningful when it means ownership of the process, all the process: research and analysis, planning, implementing, and evaluating.

Finally, we need to be concerned with how participation is occurring. For its impact to be significant, the basis of participation must be as genuine partners, even senior partners. The form of participation must be integral and central, not occasional and formalistic. The extent of participation must be complete and without limit. Finally, the effect of participation must be empowerment. Empowerment is, after all, one of the means of transformation.

Said another way, this kind of full and complete participation is a form of making systematic local autonomy or self-direction real. Communities discover that it is indeed *their* development process that is underway and that they are capable of exercising choice and becoming capable of managing their own development. The following guidelines for effective participation are adapted from a set proposed by Sam Voorhies (1996, 129-35):

- Participation begins at the beginning, with the community's story and analysis.
- Start small, in a manner that the community can manage largely on its own.

293

- Use a process or learning approach, not a blueprint. Help them learn how to learn.

- Encourage the community to mobilize its own resources. Get community members to invest.

- Encourage community members to run the program and experience the joy of their successes and learn from their mistakes.

- Build capacity. Participation that empowers needs to be learned; help them succeed.

- Invest in organizing; help them find new ways of working together.

- Have a bias toward peace. Participation means power, and power tends to divide. Be very inclusive.

- Communicate, communicate, communicate.

Changing People Changes History

There is a more important reason that authentic participation is critical, more important than enhancing dignity or acting out our egalitarian values, as good as these reasons are. It can be argued that empowering participation is the single most critical element of transformation.

James Rosenau, in his analysis of change and continuity in the twentieth century, argues that, of the five basic forces at work at the end of the century, the most powerful one is that people have changed.[11] Ordinary people in the West now have a set of analytical skills that allows them to understand why things are happening to them and an orientation toward authority that is more self-conscious. "Today's persons on the street are no longer as uninvolved, ignorant and manipulable with respect to world affairs as their forebears" (1990, 13). If this kind of change—the ability to understand why things are as they are and the conviction that we can exert some level of influence over what happens to us—is one of the keys to social change in the West, then empowering participation must be at the core of transformational development among the poor. Only changed people can change history. If people do not change, little else changes in the long term.

Building Community

As we bring our story to the story of the community, we face a challenge. How do we merge these stories so that they enhance each other and everyone learns and grows? The key is becoming community to each other. This is one of the reasons we respect all the elements of their story, that we take a social-learning approach to working together, and that we encourage genuine participation. Building community is what good neighbors do.

One of Kosuke Koyama's endearing contributions to missiology is what he calls "neighborology" (1974, 89ff.). Koyama reminds us that people need good neighbors much more than they need good theology or good development theory. Our work is about people before it is about ideas, about relationships before teaching or programs. Development workers who use being good neighbors as their metaphor for working alongside the poor will do better than those who see themselves as problem-solvers or answer-givers.

By listening to the stories of the poor, our new neighbors, and by sharing our stories with them, we become neighbors to each other. To have community we must have good neighboring. This takes time. Loving neighbors is not something that can be rushed. Something gets lost when we hurry.

Taking our neighbor's questions into account is so time consuming that it is better to forget about time. It is better to learn to be patient, We must learn to speak our neighbor's language and understand our neighbor's memberships in overlapping communities. We must come to know what makes our neighbor laugh and cry. Once we come to love our neighbor, we realize that our love is rooted in the pain of God, the pain God feels when our neighbor is not loved (Erickson 1996,154).

If we cannot genuinely love our neighbor, where can development begin?

Notes

1. See the later section on Appreciative Inquiry.
2. We will not find the important gods of formal religion here. Vishnu, Krishna, Allah, Ngai, and the other high gods are not to be bothered with the mundane details of everyday life. The exception is the Christian view of God, which, because of the ongoing work of the Holy Spirit, the prayer of Christ on our behalf, and the Father's commitment to the culmination of history, remains engaged in our world.
3. Ravi Jayakaran reports that each Indian village develops its own, usually unique, constellation of gods. The way a community does this is highly empirical. If community members suspect a god or spirit has some influence over an area of life, they make a small shrine out of stones and make a simple offering. If this god continues to produce, the shrine is upgraded by covering it and the offering is increased. If the god continues to be useful, the covered shrine is replaced by a small temple and walls are built around it. Gods and spirits can also be "demoted" for lack of performance. This is a different kind of empiricism than we are used to in the West (personal interview, 1997).
4. One of the best summaries on indigenous knowledge is Warren et al. 1995. See also a related book on indigenous organizations, Blunt and Warren 1996.
5. To live in a multilevel mound, termites have to have some kind of natural cooling system. Underground water close to the surface provides for this.
6. Small physical disturbances in the soil can cause soil compaction that results in small springs drying up temporarily.
7. In the last twenty years, a great deal has been learned from the study of complexity in nature. Chaos theory offers a way of seeing order and pattern where formerly only the random, erratic, and unpredictable had been observed. For a helpful, nontechnical

introduction, see Gleick 1987.

8. Additional reading on complexity should include Lewin 1992 and Kellert 1993.

9. Uphoff has an intriguing chapter on complex systems theory and development as he found it expressed in an irrigation program in southeastern Sri Lanka (1996, 388). Chambers also mentions complexity theory briefly (1997, 194ff.).

10. One helpful resource on participatory development designed to empower is Save the Children 1982.

11. The other four are (1) changing technology; (2) cross-border threats like AIDS, pollution, and the drug trade; (3) the reduced capability of governments to solve social issues; and (4) sub-groupism, that is, the tendency of people to resist globalism and seek identity in ethnic and religious groupings.

12. I first heard this name for the Christians who promote holistic transformational development from Dr. Sam Kamaleson, formerly vice president for pastor's conferences at World Vision, now retired.

13. Ravi Jayakaran, personal interview, 1997.

14. While it is true that Christians have been struggling for two thousand years to develop a biblical worldview and still have a ways to go, we should not back away from this challenge. The fact that we see things only dimly is not an invitation to sit on the sidelines and withdraw from mission or theological reflection. A Christian worldview, however flawed, is essential to enabling the transformational development this book describes.

15. There is more to a simple lifestyle than simple self-denial. Francis of Assisi understood that "he had to enter into the space of the poor of his day, because only in this space of the poor could he approach the condition God assumed in the Incarnation" (Motte 1996, 71).

16. See the section "Doing no harm" in Chapter 4 herein; see also Anderson 1996b and Slim 1997.

17. There is also an African resource that develops discipleship within the framework of dying to oneself: Bayo Famonure's *Training to Die: A Manual on Discipleship* (1989).

18. We've already determined the importance of the whole biblical story to the task of transformational development. The use of the Bible in transformational development will be further developed in Chapter 8.

19. Four helpful resources are Gutierrez 1984; Galilea 1984; Beltrans 1986; and Green 1979.

20. For some helpful resources, see Mitchell and Everly 1996; Figley 1995; and Parkinson 1997.

SECTION K
ECONOMICS

Credit card companies are built on the premise that we will borrow more money than we can pay back. They want us to be locked into a pattern of forever paying on our debt and never paying it off. When God established the nation of Israel, he required loans to be settled within seven years. "At the end of every seven years you must cancel debts" (Deuteronomy 15:1). Any loan that was not paid off in seven years would be forgiven. This ensured a number of things. Firstly, it made sure that no family would ever become indentured servants to another family. Israelites were commanded to not put one another in a position of unending debt, particularly those who found themselves in the unfortunate situation of a crop failure or a devastating natural disaster or their entire herd of livestock being wiped out by disease. Secondly, this law kept the playing field relatively level. Nobody could get extremely wealthy from another person's desperation, and no child would inherit the poverty of parents who could not pay their debts. This is especially evident in the jubilee law, which required that every fifty years the land reverted to the original distributions laid out in the book of Joshua. Families could not amass land holdings. Thirdly, it held in check the amount of capital that people were willing to loan. Most loans would have been small and manageable. If you wanted to mobilize a lot of resources, you would have to do so gradually, building capital with small amounts slowly over time. Finally, it tied the destiny of the rich lender to that of the poor borrower. If the borrower failed, the rich would lose the loaned money. It is a healthy thing for the rich to be tied to the poor, so that the rich become more intimately concerned with the success of the poor.

So much of the world's prostitution, drug dealing, theft, and terrorism are fueled by poverty. And so much of the world's poverty today is passed down generation to generation by indebtedness, keeping whole family lines trapped in a cycle of destitution. We have yet to devise an economic system that keeps the powerful from making rules that benefit themselves financially. Biblical economic ideas often center on wealth as something that is managed rather than amassed. Wealth is leveraged, not consumed. In the Bible, money is both personal and social.

Microcredit is a great way to live out the biblical principles surrounding money. Small loans circulating through a poor community are leveraged to create wealth for those locked out of the banking system. Makonen Getu enumerates several of the benefits of microcredit. The tangibles of opportunity and self-reliance are described alongside the intangibles of hope and self-esteem. Yet setting up small loans for entrepreneurial poor families to utilize in starting a business does not work well without a good support structure. Getu describes the role of the government, donors, and the church in helping to expand the role of microcredit in moving people out from under the crushing weight of poverty.

Prahalad and Hammond take an entirely different approach. They see the poor as a viable market, not to be exploited but to be served and engaged in creating wealth. Though not arguing from a Christian frame of reference, their insight is revolutionary. Although the poor have few resources, they do have some, and because of their numbers, they have incredible aggregate power. The poor are, by and large, willing to work hard. The poor end up spending more on certain basics like water and food than even the rich do. What's more, the poor do consume many items considered to be luxury items. While I do not advocate encouraging materialism and consumption, the authors make an excellent case that the four billion people of the world making less than two thousand dollars a year represent a market that is willing to work and willing to pay fair prices for a great many goods and services.

Profit is not evil. Making a reasonable profit for a product or a service is healthy for society. The poor are not served well by handouts, subsidies, and below-fair-market interest rates. They are individuals and communities of value and strength who lack the means and opportunities to leverage their gifts and ingenuity for the greater good. Creating wealth among the poor need not be a choice between charity and exploitation.

CHAPTER 21

POVERTY ALLEVIATION AND THE ROLE OF MICROCREDIT IN AFRICA

MAKONEN GETU

Despite its natural wealth and human resources, Africa is the poorest continent in the world. Thirty of the world's 40 poorest countries are in Africa, and more than 50 percent of the continent's 600 million people suffer from absolute poverty. Over the last five decades, the International Monetary Fund and the World Bank, which were set up in the 1940s to help with reconstruction of the war-torn European economies, have been actively involved in the developing world. Since the early 1980s, the World Bank has promoted structural adjustment programs (SAPs) in more than two-thirds of Sub-Saharan African countries. As part of these programs, economies have been liberalized, state-owned economic enterprises privatized, local currencies devalued, subsidies withdrawn, and bureaucracies downsized. Multiparty democratic elections have been held, and anticorruption and anti-inefficiency measures have been taken. The ultimate purpose of implementing SAPs has been to alleviate or reduce Africa's ever-growing poverty.

However, the overall results have been disappointing. Although basic improvements have been made in GDP growth, efficiency, and democratization, most Sub-Saharan African countries have remained socially, economically, and politically poor and weak after 15 to 20 years of implementing SAPs.[1]

This paper provides an overview of microenterprise development, discusses its socioeconomic impact on the poor, and suggests some meaningful and effective ways to enhance the microenterprise development industry.

Essentials of Microenterprise Development

Microenterprise development (MED) involves providing credit and financial services and related training to poor microentrepreneurs to enable them to enhance their businesses and create employment and income for themselves and their communities. MED is, therefore, an intervention aimed at poverty alleviation and development. It is not charity, nor is it a subsidized program.

MED practitioners promote microcredit programs on the premise that the poor are creditworthy. Their problem is not lack of thriftiness and creativity; it is lack of opportunity. Because formal banking and other financial institutions are structured to serve small and large businesses in the formal sector, those who operate in the informal sector are excluded and marginalized. They rely on loans from relatives, or on local moneylenders who often charge exorbitant interest rates. It is thus difficult for them to increase capital and improve technology in order to grow their businesses and create more employment and income. By offering credit, training, and services to poor microentrepreneurs, MED helps them overcome these constraints. The conviction is that the poor will be able to run profitable businesses, repay their loans, become self-sufficient (after some repeated loans), and eventually liberate themselves from poverty (Reed and Morser 1998: 2-4).

Unlike the subsidized, mainly rural, credit schemes run by governments in the 1960s and early 1970s, MED programs run purely on business principles. Loans are given on the basis of systematic appraisal of applications to determine which business proposals are viable. Commercial interest rates as well as administrative and processing fees, including late payment fees, are charged. Loan terms are deliberately designed to take short cycles of 4 to 6 months for the first few loans and then from 12 to 36 months for "mature" loans. The cycles are designed to make repayments easier and circulation of loan funds faster and wider.

Since the mid-1970s, the microcredit/microfinance industry has gone through a process of evolution. Particularly in the 1990s, more diversified and qualified lending products, loan tracking and reporting systems, governance tools, and internationally accepted best-practice standards have been developed. The aim has been to achieve financial excellence and lasting impact (Reed and Morser 1998: 2-4). Some of the major common standards that have evolved over the last 20 to 25 years are described below.

Outreach

Microfinance institutions (MFIs) are expected to reach out to increasing numbers of poor microentrepreneurs. The more clients an MFI serves, the better the coverage. However, outreach is not only about numbers; it is also about depth. It is about reaching poorer areas and poorer people. This, in turn, involves larger programs, larger loan funds, and more complex technology and systems. Many MFIs have committed themselves to the Microcredit Summit goal of reaching out to 100 million poor households, especially female-headed households, by the year 2002.[2]

Quality

Quality implies efficiency in portfolio management and deals with the rates of loan recovery and the cost of lending. At the moment, the best-practice standards include 5 percent arrears rate, 10 percent loan portfolio at-risk rate, and US$0.20 per dollar lent. The greater the number of clients handled by a loan officer, the better, as it is a good indicator of productivity and efficiency. The industry applies a combination of individual, solidarity group, and trust/village banks approaches. The client-loan officer ratio, therefore, varies from product to product.[3]

Impact

All MFIs want to see their programs result in significant and sustainable socioeconomic changes among the poor. The emphasis varies among players. Some emphasize the economic aspect and tend to take a minimalist approach. Others look at the whole person and try to encourage holistic transformation in the people they serve. Opportunity International's goal, for example, is not only to increase the amount of money in the pockets of the poor but also to "enable the poor to become agents of transformation in their communities" (Opportunity International 1998: 4). The aim is to use microcredit as a means of facilitating deeper economic, social, political, and spiritual changes among the poor. This is a view shared, particularly, by all Christian MFIs.

Sustainability

Sustainability has to do with the viability of the MFIs themselves as lending institutions. MFIs need to move toward self-sufficiency in order to continue serving poor people for a longer period of time. Currently, most MFIs depend on donor grants, but the aim is to reduce and ultimately eliminate that dependency. The progress toward achieving this goal is measured by the level of operational and financial sustainability achieved by MFIs. The income generated through interests and fees is meant to cover the repayment of loan funds, operating expenses, administrative expenses, expected loan losses, and return on capital. When interest and fee incomes cover operational and actual financial costs, MFIs reach operational sustainability. When these incomes cover all expenses, including inflation, financial sustainability is achieved.

The higher the ratios and the shorter the time it takes to achieve operational and financial sustainability, the better. MFIs are expected to reach 100 percent operational sustainability during the first three to five years of operation and financial sustainability within five to seven years. The pressure to move toward sustainability has led to the current drive to help nongovernmental MFIs evolve into private financial institutions that obtain commercial loans and take deposits as a means of raising more loan capital other than grants (Campion and White 1999:3).

Although a good number of the leading MFIs now implementing best-practice MED as described above emerged in the early 1970s, most of the MFIs in Africa are relatively new. Most of them entered the industry after the mid-1980s, mainly in the 1990s. Many more are still entering the market. The accumulated experience in the field and hence the overall capacity is therefore very limited. However, as will be seen below, they have achieved much in the limited time they have been in existence.

The Role of MED: What Microcredit Does for Poor People

Positive changes in a number of areas occur in African economies in general and among the poor in particular as a result of MED interventions.[4]

From Having Little or No Access to Having Credit Opportunity

The poor are powerless partly because they lack access to credit and means of production. They are ignored by the formal financial sector on the grounds that they are "not creditworthy."

Microcredit challenges this conventional negative perception of the poor. As described above, best-practice MED takes the view that the poor do not lack ability but only opportunity. The poor are recognized as creditworthy and bankable and are given credit and related services. This positive recognition is empowering in itself.

From Dependency to Self-Reliance

The poor have little or no uncommitted money. They have too little surplus income to improve their businesses or their household economies. Very often they depend on loans or assistance from relatives, friends, and neighbors to meet their business and consumption needs. They borrow and borrow with shame and pain on their faces.

Microcredit enables poor people to expand and grow their businesses, create employment and generate income for themselves and their communities. The increased personal and household incomes enable them to invest in their businesses and household assets. They are freed from the bondage caused by lack of savings, reduce their dependency, and increase their self-reliance.

From Enslavement by Local Moneylenders to Freedom

In the absence of credit opportunities, the poor frequently must resort to borrowing from local usurers at exploitative interest rates that are destructive. Microcredit has helped the poor reduce their dependency on local moneylenders. This is liberating and empowering.

From Bad to Better Education, Health, Housing, Clothing, and Food Security

With microcredit, poor families can send their children to school and pay for the requirements that go with it. They can send not only one or two children, but all their children of school age. They become able to pay for medical care when necessary and can obtain timely care for both prevention and treatment. Housing and clothing conditions are improved. Microcredit also enables the poor to have adequate food, to eat better-quality food, and to store more food for disaster times. Food shortage decreases and the quality of nutrition improves. This is another area of empowerment.

From Low to Higher Self-Esteem and Dignity

The poor frequently have low self-esteem. They may see themselves as having little value to society, and others may also see them this way, causing them to lose social respect and dignity.

Microcredit enables the poor to use their ability and creativity to run businesses, develop innovative products, provide services, and create employment. They may even begin to make financial contributions to community projects, make short-term loans to others, and sell on credit. All these lead to a positive appreciation of the role that poor people play in society, increasing their self-esteem and dignity.

From Silence to Increased Voice

In the absence of freedom of expression, the poor are often silent, and even when they speak, little attention is given to them.

When the poor form groups and receive four to eight weeks of orientation, and when they are exposed to ongoing interaction with one another and with credit officers, the level of their political information and awareness increases. This helps them to know their basic social rights and obligations. They then can begin to exert pressure through lobbying, advocacy, and negotiations with local and national authorities to provide the necessary services. As they act collectively, they begin to be heard and to influence the course of development in their communities.[5]

From Marginalization to Integration

Because of their low economic status, low self-esteem, and limited political awareness, poor people do not tend to take an active part in political affairs. For the most part they participate in electing well-off activists and rarely run for political office themselves. The poor are often excluded by the political system.

As they begin to develop confidence through the material, political, and organizational changes that follow from involvement in MED, they dare to run in elections, winning positions in political institutions at the community level. They then move from the periphery to the center.

From Gender Inequality to Gender Equity

Among the poor, women are the most disadvantaged and powerless. For cultural and other reasons, they have limited control over resources, including land, credit, and other assets. They are often financially dependent on their husbands.

The majority (up to 80-90 percent, and in some cases up to 100 percent) of microfinance clients are women. Microcredit enables them to increase their access to credit and to own increased assets, including housing and land. This in turn allows them to reduce their dependence on their husbands, thereby lessening the "gender gap" at the household level. Although some findings seem to indicate that microcredit results in less family time and an increased workload for women, family relationships have seen general improvement. Some women have also been able to participate in local elections and gain seats on local councils, or have taken leading positions in women's and other local committees.

From Immoral to Moral Values

Some poor people turn to crime, including stealing or prostitution, in order to survive.

By creating productive alternatives, microcredit has helped to reduce such vices and to enhance moral values among the poor. The poor involved in microcredit have been empowered to say no to and give up such humiliating and immoral activities.

From Hopelessness and Fear to Hope and Courage

The poor face many obstacles in their lives. Superstition and witchcraft practices leave some in fear and bondage. The crippling effect of poverty today and the uncertainty about tomorrow often reduce them to hopelessness.

Through direct and indirect witnessing, Christian MFIs have enabled many of their clients to become followers of Christ, thereby liberating them from the bondage of sin and fear. This has helped many poor men and women and their families to become hopeful and courageous. Because of what they have been able to achieve through microcredit, the poor have begun to see their future as bright. The days of daydreaming and "I can't do it" perceptions are gone. The poor have begun to realize their potential and appreciate their opportunities positively. They have begun walking with their heads up as capable people and not as hopeless people.

From Being Easy Victims to Preventing HIV/AIDS

It is estimated that 20-30 percent of the population in most Sub-Saharan African countries are infected with HIV/AIDS. Millions are dying each year, leaving large numbers of orphans. Many studies of HIV/AIDS have found a strong linkage between poverty and AIDS. The main victims of increased poverty are women, youth (especially girls), and unemployed people.

MED has served and is likely to continue serving as a critical intervention in preventing the spread of AIDS in Africa, primarily through employment creation and income generation. MED offers employment opportunities to women who are unemployed and likely to become sex workers. It also offers income to women who otherwise cannot say no to dangerous sex because of their economic vulnerability. Noninfected people are enabled to provide material support to relatives and dependents with AIDS. In other cases AIDS patients themselves are helped to run businesses to generate their own income.

From Micro to Macro

In many cases, MED clients have moved from micro to small and medium businesses. They have moved from informal to formal ventures. The increased number of machines and workers as well as capital that MED clients are investing in their businesses and the rate of diversification indicate that these businesses are moving from micro to macro levels. With the increased effective demand and technology and innovation taking place in the industry, it is likely that MED will serve as the breeding place for homegrown industrialization and national economic development. In the absence of foreign capital, and given the meager domestic private investment, it is likely that the MED industry will be the motor force of Africa's future development.

In summary, it can be said that microenterprise development has enabled the poor to experience radical changes in their lives and in their communities. As a result of the financial gains, they have been able to break the shackles of their poverty. As a result of the improved standard of living they have achieved and the contributions they have made in their communities, they have earned social respect and dignity. As a result of training, organizing, and exposure, they have gained increased political awareness and can participate in affairs that affect their destiny. They have also improved their spiritual and moral values. Without any doubt, it can be said that the poor have been transformed and empowered through their participation in MED programs.

What Governments, Donors, and the Church Should Do

In view of the challenges and constraints faced by microfinance institutions and their clients, governments and donors can take a number of steps to promote the MED industry.

Market Distortions

Although a number of senior government leaders have taken part in the three global microcredit summits where commitments to best-practice MED have been made, the subsidy mentality is still prevalent. Some donors and governments are still bound by the old belief that the poor cannot pay commercial interest rates, and this tends to distort the best-practice principles the microcredit industry is trying to apply in the financial market. This is particularly true in cases where governments are implementing public credit schemes with political motives. Also, in cases where credit activities are undertaken as part of integrated programs funded by donors, the tendency is for clients to be charged uneconomic rates with relaxed repayment requirements, thereby creating market distortions in the areas where this occurs. Local churches and some Christian organizations involved in MED also tend to be uncomfortable with charging commercial interest rates. This practice is rooted in the old "handout" mentality and contradicts best-practice principles that call for charging commercial interest rates with no tolerance for arrears.

The poor are not only able but also happy and proud to repay their loans with commercial interest rates and on time. They want to do business on the basis of equal partnership and not take handouts that undermine their integrity. Any government/donor distortions, regardless of good intentions, are likely to tarnish the image of best-practice MED and thereby make it difficult to maintain quality. Governments, donors, and the Church should therefore refrain from taking measures that will distort the market in the microcredit industry. Rather, they should develop policies that are in line with best-practice principles that promote "hand up," not handout, practices.

Funding

MFIs need larger amounts of loan capital, qualified human resources (staff and boards of directors alike), and improved systems to be able to reach out to more poor people and more remote areas, and to ensure financial excellence (quality portfolio management) and durable impact. This will require putting in place state-of-the-art loan tracking systems and recruiting qualified and experienced board members, managers, and staff with ongoing internal training activities. It will also require lending to more poor people, training them, and spending quality time with clients rather than meeting them only to disburse and collect loans.

Despite their will and commitment to build capacity and expand their programs, most MFIs are constrained by lack of adequate funding. Donors have tended to become more selective and restrictive in their giving.

Donors are seldom willing to spend much money on capacity building, research, and innovation in MFIs. What portion of SAP loans, for example, go toward microenterprise development? Whatever the amount, what are the mechanisms put in place to ensure effective delivery? Although the Consultative Group to Assist the Poorest (CGAP) was established on World Bank initiative in 1995, how much in loan funds has this program brought to Africa, and where? It is good that the Africa Capacity Building Facility has recently been established with the cooperation of CGAP and the British government to provide technical assistance to MFIs in Eastern and Southern Africa. It is hoped that this will make a significant contribution to promotion of the microcredit industry in Africa.

Governments have restrictive regulatory and control systems that do not allow MFIs to mobilize savings and deposits from the public or clients for on-lending. Many mature MFIs are at the stage of converting to or establishing banks and/or financial institutions for this very purpose. This requires committed support by governments and donors to facilitate effective transformations. Donors, governments, and financial institutions could help to enhance the MED industry by creating enabling macroeconomic environments, improving infrastructural facilities, and providing grants and concessionary loans to MFIs.

Measurement

In the microcredit world, where the core business is receiving money (from lenders and donors), disbursing money (to borrowers), and collecting money (repayments from clients), measurement issues occupy a major place. Donors, practitioners, and clients all want to measure their performance, results, and the impacts they are making through their activities. They want to see figures. This is not a bad thing, but good indicators have to be selected to measure progress and impact, and to determine the long-term direction.

Problems arise, however, when the focus is only on numbers. These problems worsen when only quantifiable variables are appreciated and unquantifiable ones are suspect. This practice reduces the meaning of life and hence the issues of poverty to the question of having or not having material possessions. Measuring only those variables that are observable and tangible focuses on things that serve the body. It emanates from the belief that the solution to basic human misery is material, and that when the poor improve their production, health, and education, and increase their income, they have been led to a "superior" life.

The full picture of life, however, goes beyond physical possessions. It is not only to have but also to be and to become that gives life a deeper meaning. *Having* is about externals, while *being* concerns the inner person. We need to be loved and to love. We need to be emotionally healthy and spiritually right. Material prosperity on its own cannot make life meaningful. Without the satisfaction of nonmaterial needs, it is unlikely that we can lead whole-person lives. A great and troubling vacuum will always be with us. The nonmaterial dimension of performance and impact measurement is important for faith-based MFIs.

Donors, governments, researchers, and policymakers should go beyond measuring only the quantifiable when evaluating impact. They should begin to take nonmeasurable factors such as the spiritual, emotional, relational, deliverance, moral, and cultural issues of life into account so as to be able to appreciate the total transformation experienced by the poor. This will help to justify allocating resources to these aspects of MED and to enhance transformational development through microcredit.

Perception

Generally speaking, as we are taught we think and as we think we act. Our perception of MED determines how we treat, facilitate, and implement microcredit programs. Currently, most donors and governments see MED as a "survival" intervention and a short-term solution to poverty. Very rarely is it seen as a long-term development strategy. Very little attention and emphasis is given to it in the multiyear strategic development plans of governments and donors. The limited analysis of MED-related activities and the amount of resources allocated to them are indicative of this.

In Africa—where the informal sector employs 70 percent of the urban labor force on average, where foreign direct investment is difficult to attract, and where domestic private investment is insignificant—the potential contribution of MED to efficiency and equity has been insufficiently recognized.

Historically, industrial economies have grown through businesses that moved from micro to small and from small to large ventures. The microcredit industry has witnessed that the poor are growing their businesses in volume, technology, employment, and diversification from "survival" to developmental levels. Some have moved from employing only one or two workers to employing 50 or more and from engaging a portfolio of US$300 to engaging US$15,000 or more. They have moved from using one or two machines to 20 machines, from operating with one or two outlets to 5 or 10 outlets, and from one or two locations to several. Overall, MED enhances two cardinal aspects of national economic development: purchasing power and national effective demand, on the one hand, and savings and domestic investment, on the other. In other words, in Africa, where indigenous accumulation (investment) is still weak and foreign capitalists generally uninterested, the potential of MED in producing future industrialists, manufacturers, exporters, and traders should not be overlooked. In the long term, the microcredit industry is likely to be the foundation of indigenous or "homegrown" (independent) industrialization and national economic development.

Another important aspect of holistic development that is often ignored by non-Christian players is the spiritual dimension. In view of the critical place that spiritual factors hold in people's lives, it is important that organizations recognize that investment in spiritual transformation is part of national development.

Donors, therefore, should lift the pressure they put on Christian organizations to curtail their spiritual activities under the pretext that religion and development are two separate entities. On the contrary, donors should recognize the dialectical relationship between spiritual and physical aspects of development and even provide support and encouragement to organizations and individuals involved in the promotion of spiritual development. It is time that spiritual considerations are included when designing and evaluating development projects in the same way that gender, environmental, and, lately, AIDS aspects are considered. It is time for spiritual issues to be included on the development agenda, and for donors to engage spiritual specialists in the same way they have done for gender, environment, and AIDS specialists.

Coalitions

We are not only in the era of intensive globalization; we are also in an era of coalitions. Nations are entering into regional and global economic and geopolitical coalitions at an unprecedented rate. Multinational corporations, airlines, and telecommunications companies are doing the same on a continuous basis. MFIs are not an exception to the trend.

Realizing the importance of coordination, knowledge sharing, resource mobilization, and synergizing in strengthening the concerted effort of the industry, MFIs have begun establishing global, regional, and national networks and coalitions. The Microcredit Summit mobilizing all MFIs, the Christian Microenterprise Summit mobilizing Christian development organizations, and the SEEP Network are among the global coalitions that have been formed with the spirit of promoting the MED industry in unity.

The Church can and should play a significant role in enhancing the MED industry as part of its mission to facilitate transformational change in people's lives. As an institution, the Church has a wide constituency and social influence. The more people become obedient to God and apply Christian principles, the better the prospects for best-practice MED. Through its Christian teaching, the Church could create a stronger presence of good stewardship, accountability, reliability, and integrity. These are important ingredients of best-practice MED because they promote financial discipline among clients.

A study carried out by the USAID Best Practice Project in December 1999 found that a good number of MFIs have been affected by the AIDS epidemic, which has claimed the lives of many of their staff and clients. Because they work in deprived communities and mainly serve women, among whom the rate of HIV infection is much higher than among men, MFIs may be more exposed to the effects of HIV/AIDS than society at large (Versluysen 1999: 1).

The HIV/AIDS epidemic is an economic, spiritual, and moral problem. The more spiritual people become, the less sexual immorality there is. Under normal conditions, a spiritually and morally grounded woman or man will not make sexual contact with another partner outside marriage. It is an immoral and hence a sinful act. The spiritual transformation that the Church facilitates in communities is highly likely to contribute to the reduction of the HIV/AIDS epidemic and hence encourage the promotion of MED. The Church can do this not only through its teaching of the gospel but also through credit activities related to MED. When getting involved in MED, it is important that the Church recognize that it is not an MFI, nor should it attempt to become one. It should collaborate with and seek technical assistance from experienced Christian MFIs.

It is important, therefore, that donors and governments properly appreciate the role of the Church in the promotion of MED and poverty alleviation, including spiritual poverty, and try to cooperate with the Church. This includes engaging in dialogue with the Church, and making available financial resources to the Church that will enable it to contribute to policy formulation and poverty alleviation in meaningful ways.

Conclusions

As an antipoverty intervention, MED has played a positive role by creating employment and generating income among the poor, especially women. More broadly, microcredit has proved to be an effective tool for facilitating transformation among the poor and empowering them to influence their own destinies.

It is time, therefore, to stop treating MED as a survival intervention and a short-term solution to poverty, and to view it instead as a long-term development strategy and a potential source of capital accumulation. It is time for MED to be given stronger financial and technical support to ensure that it is implemented in such a way that the poor are holistically transformed and empowered.

Notes

1. Many critics of SAPs have attributed Africa's failure to World Bank policies and conditions "imposed" upon countries implementing SAPs. My view is that Africa's failure is a combined result of many external and internal factors, including SAPs.
2. The declaration of the Microcredit Summit was signed by about 3,000 participants (practitioners, donors, government leaders, private sector representatives) who attended the first Microcredit Summit held in Washington, D.C. in 1997.
3. The various ratios were calculated and published by the SEEP (Small Enterprise Education and Promotion) Network and by Calmeadow, a Canadian NGO specializing in microfinance.
4. The positive changes that have taken place among the poor as a result of their participation in microenterprise programs have been documented by various studies, including impact evaluation reports. See, for example, the impact studies issued by the AIMS project (Assessing the Impact of Microenterprise Services) of the U.S. Agency for International Development's Office of Microenterprise Development.
5. Here is an example. A client who was a member of a loan group in Botswana was rearing and selling chickens, and had a near monopoly in her community. Eventually, the school administration decided to sell chickens they had raised for educational purposes in the market. The prices they charged were lower than the client's, and she lost customers as a result. She reported to her group that she was not making money because the school's participation in the market had depressed the price for chickens. The group leaders went to the school administration to lobby, telling them that they should not distort the market by selling subsidized products. The school administration responded to their request positively (Getu 1995: 15).

Bibliography

Campion, A., and V. White. 1999. "Institutional Metamorphosis: Transformation of Microfinance NGOs into Regulated Financial Institutions." Occasional Paper 4. The MicroFinance Network, Washington, D.C.

Christen, R. C. 1997. "Banking Services for the Poor: Managing for Financial Success." ACCION International, Washington, D.C.

Getu, M. 1995. "Microenterprise Development in Theory and Practice." World Vision Australia, Melbourne.

Microcredit Summit Secretariat. 1997. "Microcredit Summit Declaration." Washington, D.C.

Opportunity International. 1998. "Network Five-Year Vision Statement." Chicago. 1999. *Annual Report 1999*. Chicago.

Reed, L., and S. Cheston. 2000. "Measuring Transformation: Assessing and Improving the Impact of Microcredit." *Journal of Microfinance* 1 (1).

Reed, L., and T. Morser. 1998. "The Market for Funding of Microenterprise Development Trends." Processed. Thurman, E. 1995. "Is Interest Christian?" *Opportunity International Update.*

Versluysen, E. 1999. "East and Southern African Microfinance Institutions and the AIDS Epidemic." U.S. Agency for International Development, Washington, D.C.

CHAPTER 22

SERVING THE WORLD'S POOR, PROFITABLY

C.K. Prahalad and Allen Hammond

Consider this bleak vision of the world 15 years from now: The global economy recovers from its current stagnation but growth remains anemic. Deflation continues to threaten, the gap between rich and poor keeps widening, and incidents of economic chaos, governmental collapse, and civil war plague developing regions. Terrorism remains a constant threat, diverting significant public and private resources to security concerns. Opposition to the global market system intensifies. Multinational companies find it difficult to expand, and many become risk averse, slowing investment and pulling back from emerging markets.

Now consider this much brighter scenario: Driven by private investment and widespread entrepreneurial activity, the economies of developing regions grow vigorously, creating jobs and wealth and bringing hundreds of millions of new consumers into the global marketplace every year. China, India, Brazil, and, gradually, South Africa become new engines of global economic growth, promoting prosperity around the world. The resulting decrease in poverty produces a range of social benefits, helping to stabilize many developing regions and reduce civil and cross-border conflicts. The threat of terrorism and war recedes. Multinational companies expand rapidly in an era of intense innovation and competition.

Both of these scenarios are possible. Which one comes to pass will be determined primarily by one factor: the willingness of big, multinational companies to enter and invest in the world's poorest markets. By stimulating commerce and development at the bottom of the economic pyramid, MNCs could radically improve the lives of billions of people and help bring into being a more stable, less dangerous world. Achieving this goal does not require multinationals to spearhead global social development initiatives for charitable purposes. They need only act in their own self-interest, for there are enormous business benefits to be gained by entering developing markets. In fact, many innovative companies—entrepreneurial outfits and large, established enterprises alike—are already serving the world's poor in ways that generate strong revenues, lead to greater operating efficiencies, and uncover new sources of innovation. For these companies—and those that follow their lead—building businesses aimed at the bottom of the pyramid promises to provide important competitive advantages as the twenty-first century unfolds.

Big companies are not going to solve the economic ills of developing countries by themselves, of course. It will also take targeted financial aid from the developed world and improvements in the governance of the developing nations themselves. But it's clear to us that prosperity can come to the poorest regions only through the direct and sustained involvement of multinational companies. And it's equally clear that the multinationals can enhance their own prosperity in the process.

Untapped Potential

Everyone knows that the world's poor are distressingly plentiful. Fully 65% of the world's population earns less than $2,000 each per year—that's 4 billion people. But despite the vastness of this market, it remains largely untapped by multinational companies. The reluctance to invest is easy to understand. Companies assume that people with such low incomes have little to spend on goods and services and that what they do spend goes to basic needs like food and shelter. They also assume that various barriers to commerce—corruption, illiteracy, inadequate infrastructure, currency fluctuations, bureaucratic red tape—make it impossible to do business profitably in these regions.

But such assumptions reflect a narrow and largely outdated view of the developing world. The fact is, many multinationals already successfully do business in developing countries (although most currently focus on selling to the small upper-middle-class segments of these markets), and their experience shows that the barriers to commerce—although real—are much lower than is typically thought. Moreover, several positive trends in developing countries—from political reform, to a growing openness to investment, to the development of low-cost wireless communication networks—are reducing the barriers further while also providing businesses with greater access to even the poorest city slums and rural areas. Indeed, once the misperceptions are wiped away, the enormous economic potential that lies at the bottom of the pyramid becomes clear.

Take the assumption that the poor have no money. It sounds obvious on the surface, but it's wrong. While individual incomes may be low, the aggregate buying power of poor communities is actually quite large. The average per capita income of villagers in rural Bangladesh, for instance, is less than $200 per year, but as a group they are avid consumers of telecommunications services. Grameen Telecom's village phones, which are owned by a single entrepreneur but used by the entire community, generate an average revenue of roughly $90 a month-and as much as $1,000 a month in some large villages.

Customers of these village phones, who pay cash for each use, spend an average of 7% of their income on phone services—-a far higher percentage than consumers in traditional markets do.

It's also incorrect to assume that the poor are too concerned with fulfilling their basic needs to "waste" money on nonessential goods. In fact, the poor often do buy "luxury" items. In the Mumbai shantytown of Dharavi, for example, 85% of households own a television set, 75% own a pressure cooker and a mixer, 56% own a gas stove, and 21% have telephones. That's because buying a house in Mumbai, for most people at the bottom of the pyramid, is not a realistic option. Neither is getting access to running water. They accept that reality, and rather than saving for a rainy day, they spend their income on things they can get now that improve the quality of their lives.

Another big misperception about developing markets is that the goods sold there are incredibly cheap and, hence, there's no room for a new competitor to come in and turn a profit. In reality, consumers at the bottom of the pyramid pay much higher prices for most things than middle-class consumers do, which means that there's a real opportunity for companies, particularly big corporations with economies of scale and efficient supply chains, to capture market share by offering higher quality goods at lower prices while maintaining attractive margins. In fact, throughout the developing world, urban slum dwellers pay, for instance, between four and 100 times as much for drinking water as middle- and upper-class families. Food also costs 20% to 30% more in the poorest communities since there is no access to bulk discount stores. On the service side of the economy, local moneylenders charge interest of 10% to 15% per day, with annual rates running as high as 2,000%. Even the lucky small-scale entrepreneurs who get loans from nonprofit microfinance institutions pay between 40% and 70% interest per year—rates that are illegal in most developed countries. (For a closer look at how the prices of goods compare in rich and poor areas, see Table 22.1)

It can also be surprisingly cheap to market and deliver products and services to the world's poor. That's because many of them live in cities that are densely populated today and will be even more so in the years to come. Figures from the UN and the World Resources Institute indicate that by 2015, in Africa, 225 cities will each have populations of more than 1 million; in Latin America, another 225; and in Asia, 903. The population of at least 27 cities will reach or exceed 8 million. Collectively, the 1,300 largest cities will account for some 1.5 billion to 2 billion people, roughly half of whom will be bottom-of-the-pyramid (BOP) consumers now served primarily by informal economies. Companies that operate in these areas will have access to millions of potential new customers, who together have billions of dollars to spend. The poor in Rio de Janeiro, for instance, have a total purchasing power of $1.2 billion ($600 per person). Shantytowns in Johannesburg or Mumbai are no different

Table 22.1 The High-Cost Economy of the Poor

When we compare the costs of essentials in Dharavi, a shantytown of more than 1 million people in the heart of Mumbai, India, with those of Warden Road, an upper-class community in a nice Mumbai suburb, a disturbing picture emerges. Clearly, costs could be dramatically reduced if the poor could benefit from the scope, scale, and supply-chain efficiencies of large enterprises, as their middle-class counterparts do. This pattern is common around the world, even in developed countries. For instance, a similar, if less exaggerated, disparity exists between the inner-city poor and the suburban rich in the United States.

Cost	Dharavi	Warden Road	Poverty premium
Credit (annual interest)	600 percent-1,000 percent	12 percent-18 percent	53X
municipal-grade water (per cubic meter)	$1.12	$0.03	>37X
phone call (per minute)	$0.04-$0.05	$0.025	1.8X
diarrhea medication	$20	$2	10X
rice (per kilogram)	$0.28	$0.24	1.2X

The slums of these cities already have distinct ecosystems, with retail shops, small businesses, schools, clinics, and moneylenders. Although there are few reliable estimates of the value of commercial transactions in slums, business activity appears to be thriving. Dharavi—covering an area of just 435 acres—boasts scores of businesses ranging from leather, textiles, plastic recycling, and surgical sutures to gold jewelry, illicit liquor, detergents, and groceries. The scale of the businesses varies from one-person operations to bigger, well-recognized producers of brand-name products. Dharavi generates an estimated $450 million in manufacturing revenues, or about $1 million per acre of land. Established shantytowns in Sao Paulo, Rio, and Mexico City are equally productive. The seeds of a vibrant commercial sector have been sown.

> Markets at the bottom of the economic pyramid are fundamentally new sources of growth for multinationals. And because these markets are in the earliest stages, growth can be extremely rapid.

While the rural poor are naturally harder to reach than the urban poor, they also represent a large untapped opportunity for companies. Indeed, 60% of India's GDP is generated in rural areas. The critical barrier to doing business in rural regions is distribution access, not a lack of buying power. But new information technology and communications infrastructures—especially wireless—promise to become an inexpensive way to establish marketing and distribution channels in these communities.

Conventional wisdom says that people in BOP markets cannot use such advanced technologies, but that's just another misconception. Poor rural women in Bangladesh have had no difficulty using GSM cell phones, despite never before using phones of any type. In Kenya, teenagers from slums are being successfully trained as Web page designers. Poor farmers in El Salvador use telecenters to negotiate the sale of their crops over the Internet. And women in Indian coastal villages have in less than a week learned to use PCs to interpret real-time satellite images showing concentrations of schools of fish in the Arabian Sea so they can direct their husbands to the best fishing areas. Clearly, poor communities are ready to adopt new technologies that improve their economic opportunities or their quality of life. The lesson for multinationals:

Don't hesitate to deploy advanced technologies at the bottom of the pyramid while, or even before, deploying them in advanced countries.

A final misperception concerns the highly charged issue of exploitation of the poor by MNCs. The informal economies that now serve poor communities are full of inefficiencies and exploitive intermediaries. So if a microfinance institution charges 50% annual interest when the alternative is either 1,000% interest or no loan at all, is that exploiting or helping the poor? If a large financial company such as Citigroup were to use its scale to offer microloans at 20%, is that exploiting or helping the poor? The issue is not just cost but also quality—quality in the range and fairness of financial services, quality of food, quality of water. We argue that when MNCs provide basic goods and services that reduce costs to the poor and help improve their standard of living—while generating an acceptable return on investment—the results benefit everyone.

The Business Case

The business opportunities at the bottom of the pyramid have not gone unnoticed. Over the last five years, we have seen nongovernmental organizations (NGOs), entrepreneurial start-ups, and a handful of forward-thinking multinationals conduct vigorous commercial experiments in poor communities. Their experience is a proof of concept: Businesses can gain three important advantages by serving the poor—a new source of revenue growth, greater efficiency, and access to innovation. Let's look at examples of each.

Top-Line Growth

Growth is an important challenge for every company, but today it is especially critical for very large companies, many of which appear to have nearly saturated their existing markets. That's why BOP markets represent such an opportunity for MNCs: They are fundamentally new sources of growth. And because these markets are in the earliest stages of economic development, growth can be extremely rapid.

Latent demand for low-priced, high-quality goods is enormous. Consider the reaction when Hindustan Lever, the Indian subsidiary of Unilever, recently introduced what was for it a new product category—candy—aimed at the bottom of the pyramid. A high-quality confection made with real sugar and fruit, the candy sells for only about a penny a serving. At such a price, it may seem like a marginal business opportunity, but in just six months it became the fastest-growing category in the company's portfolio. Not only is it profitable, but the company estimates it has the potential to generate revenues of $200 million per year in India and comparable markets in five years. Hindustan Lever has had similar successes in India with low-priced detergent and iodized salt. Beyond generating new sales, the company is establishing its business and its brand in a vast new market.

There is equally strong demand for affordable services. TARAhaat, a start-up focused on rural India, has introduced a range of computer-enabled education services ranging from basic IT training to English proficiency to vocational skills. The products are expected to be the largest single revenue generator for the company and its franchisees over the next several years.[1] Credit and financial services are also in high demand among the poor. Citibank's ATM-based banking experiment in India, called Suvidha, for instance, which requires a minimum deposit of just $25, enlisted 150,000 customers in one year in the city of Bangalore alone.

Small-business services are also popular in BOP markets. Centers run in Uganda by the Women's Information Resource Electronic Service (WIRES) provide female entrepreneurs with information on markets and prices, as well as credit and trade support services, packaged in simple, ready-to-use formats in local languages. The centers are planning to offer other small-business services such as printing, faxing, and copying, along with access to accounting, spreadsheet, and other software. In Bolivia, a start-up has partnered with the Bolivian Association of Ecologica Producers Organizations to offer business information and communication: services to more than 25,000 small producers of ecoagricultural products.

It's true that some services simply can not be offered at a low-enough cost to be profitable, at least not with traditional technologies or business models Most mobile telecommunications providers, for example, cannot yet profitably operate their networks at affordable prices in the developing world. One answer is to find alternative technology, A microfinance organization in Bolivia named PRODEM, for example, uses multilingual smart-card ATMs to substantially reduce its marginal cost per customer. Smart cards store a customer's personal details, account numbers, transaction records, and a fingerprint, allowing cash dispensers to operate without permanent network connections—which is key in remote areas. What's more, the machines offer voice commands in Spanish and several local dialects and are equipped with touch screens so that PRODEM's customer base can be extended to illiterate and semiliterate people.

Another answer is to aggregate demand, making the community- not the individual—the network customer. Gyandoot, a start-up in the Dhar district of central India, where 60% of the population falls below the poverty level, illustrates the benefits of a shared access model. The company has a network of 39 Internet-enabled kiosks that provide local entrepreneurs with Internet and telecommunications access, as well as with governmental, educational, and other services. Each kiosk serves 25 to 30 surrounding villages; the entire network reaches more than 600 villages and over half a million people.

Networks like these can be useful channels for marketing and distributing many kinds of low-cost products and services. Aptech's Computer Education division, for example, has built its own network of 1,000 learning centers in India to market and distribute Vidya, a computer-training course specially designed for BOP consumers and available in seven Indian languages. Pioneer HiBred, a DuPont company, uses Internet kiosks in Latin America to deliver agricultural information and to interact with customers. Farmers can report different crop diseases or weather conditions, receive advice over the wire, and order seeds, fertilizers, and pesticides. This network strategy increases both sales and customer loyalty.

Reduced Costs

No less important than top-line growth are cost-saving opportunities. Outsourcing operations to low-cost labor markets has, of course, long been a popular way to contain costs, and it has led to the increasing prominence of China in manufacturing and India in software. Now, thanks to the rapid expansion of high-speed digital networks, companies are realizing even greater savings by locating such labor-intensive service functions as call centers, marketing services, and back-office transaction processing in developing areas. For example, the nearly 20 companies that use OrphanIT.com's affiliate-marketing services, provided via its telecenters in India and the Philippines, pay one-tenth the going rate for similar services in the United States or Australia. Venture capitalist Vinod Khosla describes the remote-services opportunity this way: "I suspect that by 2010, we will be talking about [remote services] as the fastest-growing part of the world economy, with many trillions of dollars of new markets created." Besides keeping costs down, outsourcing jobs to BOP markets can enhance growth, since job creation ultimately increases local consumers' purchasing power.

But tapping into cheap labor pools is not the only way MNCs can enhance their efficiency by operating in developing regions. The competitive necessity of maintaining a low cost structure in these areas can push companies to discover creative ways to configure their products, finances, and supply chains to enhance productivity. And these discoveries can often be incorporated back into their existing operations in developed markets.

For instance, companies targeting the BOP market are finding that the shared access model, which disaggregates access from ownership, not only widens their customer base but increases asset productivity as well. Poor people, rather than buying their own computers, Internet connections, cell phones, refrigerators, and even cars, can use such equipment on a pay-per-use basis. Typically, the providers of such services get considerably more revenue per dollar of investment in the underlying assets. One shared Internet line, for example, can serve as many as 50 people, generating more revenue per day than if it were dedicated to a single customer at a flat fee. Shared access creates the opportunity to gain far greater returns from all sorts of infrastructure investments.

In terms of finances, to operate successfully in BOP markets, managers must also rethink their business metrics—specifically, the traditional focus on high gross margins. In developing markets, the profit margin on individual units will always be low. What really counts is capital efficiency—getting the highest possible returns on capital employed (ROCE). Hindustan Lever, for instance, operates a $2.6 billion business portfolio with zero working capital. The key is constant efforts to reduce capital investments by extensively outsourcing manufacturing, streamlining supply chains, actively managing receivables, and paying close attention to distributors' performance. Very low capital needs, focused distribution and technology investments, and very large volumes at low margins lead to very high ROCE businesses, creating great economic value for shareholders. It's a model that can be equally attractive in developed and developing markets.

Streamlining supply chains often involves replacing assets with information. Consider, for example, the experience of ITC, one of India's largest companies. Its agribusiness division has deployed a total of 970 kiosks serving 600,000 farmers who supply it with soy, coffee, shrimp, and wheat from 5,000 villages spread across India. This kiosk program, called e-Choupal, helps increase the farmers' productivity by disseminating the latest information on weather and best practices in farming, and by supporting other services like soil and water testing, thus facilitating the supply of quality inputs to both the farmers and ITC. The kiosks also serve as an e-procurement system, helping farmers earn higher prices by minimizing transaction costs involved in marketing farm produce. The head of ITC's agribusiness reports that the company's procurement costs have fallen since e-Choupal was implemented. And that's despite paying higher prices to its farmers: The program has enabled the company to eliminate multiple transportation, bagging, and handling steps—from farm to local market, from market to broker, from broker to processor—that did not add value in the chain.

Innovation

BOP markets are hotbeds of commercial and technological experimentation. The Swedish wireless company Ericsson, for instance, has developed a small cellular telephone system, called a MiniGSM, that local operators in BOP markets can use to offer cell phone service to a small area at a radically lower cost than conventional equipment entails. Packaged for easy shipment and deployment, it provides stand-alone or networked voice and data communications for up to 5,000 users within a 35-kilometer radius. Capital costs to the operator can be as low as $4 per user, assuming a shared-use model with individual phones operated by local entrepreneurs. The MIT Media Lab, in collaboration with the Indian government, is developing low-cost devices that allow people to use voice commands to communicate—without keyboards—with various Internet sites in multiple languages. These new access devices promise to be far less complex than traditional computers but would perform many of the same basic functions.[2]

As we have seen, connectivity is a big issue for BOP consumers. Companies that can find ways to dramatically lower connection costs, therefore, will have a very strong market position. And that is exactly what the Indian company n-Logue is trying to do. It connects hundreds of franchised village kiosks containing both a computer and a phone with centralized nodes that are, in turn, connected to the national phone network and the Internet. Each node, also a franchise, can serve between 30,000 and 50,000 customers, providing phone, e-mail, Internet services, and relevant local information at affordable prices to villagers in rural India. Capital costs for the n-Logue system are now about $400 per wireless "line" and are projected to decline to $100—at least ten times lower than conventional telecom costs. On a per-customer basis, the cost may amount to as little as $1.[3] This appears to be a powerful model for ending rural isolation and linking untapped rural markets to the global economy.

New wireless technologies are likely to spur further business model innovations and lower costs even more. Ultrawideband, for example, is currently licensed in the United States only for limited, very low-power applications, in part because it spreads a signal across already-crowded portions of the broadcast spectrum. In many developing countries, however, the spectrum is less congested. In fact, the U.S.-based Dandin Group is already building an ultrawideband communications system for the Kingdom of Tonga, whose population of about 100,000 is spread over dozens of islands, making it a test bed for a next-generation technology that could transform the economics of Internet access.

E-commerce systems that run over the phone or the Internet are enormously important in BOP markets because they eliminate the need for layers of intermediaries. Consider how the U.S. start-up Voxiva has changed the way information is shared and business is transacted in Peru. The company partners with Telefonica, the dominant local carrier, to offer automated business applications over the phone. The inexpensive services include voice mail, data entry, and order placement; customers can check account balances, monitor delivery status, and access prerecorded information directories. According to the Boston Consulting Group, the Peruvian Ministry of Health uses Voxiva to disseminate information, take pharmaceutical orders, and link health care workers spread across 6,000 offices and clinics. Microfinance institutions use Voxiva to process loan applications and communicate with borrowers. Voxiva offers Web-based services, too, but far more of its potential customers in Latin America have access to a phone.

E-commerce companies are not the only ones turning the limitations of BOP markets to strategic advantage. A lack of dependable electric power stimulated the UK-based start-up Freeplay Group to introduce hand-cranked radios in South Africa that subsequently became popular with hikers in the United States. Similar breakthroughs are being pioneered in the use of solar-powered devices such as battery chargers and water pumps. In China where pesticide costs have often limited the use of modern agricultural techniques, there are now 13,000 small farmers—more than in the rest of the world combined—growing cotton that has been genetically engineered to be pest resistant

Strategies for Serving BOP Markets

Certainly, succeeding in BOP markets requires multinationals to think creatively. The biggest change, though, has to come in the attitudes and practices of executives. Unless CEOs and other business leaders confront their own preconceptions, companies are unlikely to master the challenges of BOP markets. The traditional workforce is so rigidly conditioned to operate in higher-margin markets that, without formal training, it is unlikely to see the vast potential of the BOP market. The most pressing need, then, is education. Perhaps MNCs should create the equivalent of the Peace Corps: Having young managers spend a couple of formative years in BOP markets would open their eyes to the promise and the realities of doing business there.

To date, few multinationals have developed a cadre of people who are comfortable with these markets. Hindustan Lever is one of the exceptions. The company expects executive recruits to spend at least eight weeks in the villages of India to get a gut-level experience of Indian BOP markets. The new executives must become involved in some community project—building a road, cleaning up a water catchment area, teaching in a school, improving a health clinic. The goal is to engage with the local population. To buttress this effort, Hindustan Lever is initiating a massive program for managers at all levels—from the CEO down—to reconnect with their poorest customers. They'll talk with the poor in both rural and urban areas, visit the shops these customers frequent, and ask them about their experience with the company's products and those of its competitors.

In addition to expanding managers' understanding of BOP markets, companies will need to make structural changes. To capitalize on the innovation potential of these markets, for example, they might set up R&D units in developing countries that are specifically focused on local opportunities. When Hewlett-Packard launched its e-Incluslon division, which concentrates on rural markets, it established a branch of its famed HP Labs in India charged with developing products and services explicitly for this market. Hindustan Lever maintains a significant R&D effort in India, as well.

Companies might also create venture groups and internal investment funds aimed at seeding entrepreneurial efforts in BOP markets. Such investments reap direct benefits in terms of business experience and market development. They can also play an indirect but vital role in growing the overall BOP market in sectors that will ultimately benefit the multinational. At least one major U.S. corporation is planning to launch such a fund, and the G8's Digital Opportunity Task Force is proposing a similar one focused on digital ventures.

MNCs should also consider creating a business development task force aimed at these markets. Assembling a diverse group of people from across the corporation and empowering it to function as a skunk works team that ignores conventional dogma will likely lead to greater innovation. Companies that have tried this approach have been surprised by the amount of interest such a task force generates. Many employees want to work on projects that have the potential to make a real difference in improving the lives of the poor. When Hewlett-Packard announced its e-Inclusion division, for example, it was overwhelmed by far more volunteers than it could accommodate.

Making internal changes is important, but so is reaching out to external partners. Joining with businesses that are already established in these markets can be an effective entry strategy, since these companies will naturally understand the market dynamics better. In addition to limiting the risks for each player, partnerships also maximize the existing infrastructure—both physical and social MNCs seeking partners should look beyond businesses to NGOs and community groups. They are key sources of knowledge about customers' behavior, and they often experiment the most with new services and new delivery models. In fact, of the social enterprises experimenting with creative uses of digital technology that the Digital Dividend Project Clearinghouse tracked, nearly 80% are NGOs. In Namibia, for instance, an organization called SchoolNet is providing low-cost, alternative technology solutions—such as solar power and wireless approaches—to schools and community-based groups throughout the country. SchoolNet is currently linking as many as 35 new schools every month.

Entrepreneurs also will be critical partners. According to an analysis by McKinsey & Company, the rapid growth of cable TV in India—there are 50 million connections a decade after introduction—is largely due to small entrepreneurs. These individuals have been building the last mile of the network, typically by putting a satellite dish on their own houses and laying cable to connect their neighbors. A note of caution, however. Entrepreneurs in BOP markets lack access to the advice, technical help, seed funding, and business support services available in the industrial world.

So MNCs may need to take on mentoring roles or partner with local business development organizations that can help entrepreneurs create investment and partnering opportunities.

It's worth noting that, contrary to popular opinion, women play a significant role in the economic development of these regions. MNCs, therefore, should pay particular attention to women entrepreneurs. Women are also likely to play the most critical role in product acceptance not only because of their childcare and household management activities but also because of the social capital that they have built up in their communities. Listening to and educating such customers is essential for success.

Regardless of the opportunities, many companies will consider the bottom of the pyramid to be too risky. We've shown how partnerships can limit risk; another option is to enter into consortia. Imagine sharing the costs of building a rural network with the communications company that would operate it, a consumer goods company seeking channels to expand its sales, and a bank that is financing the construction and wants to make loans to and collect deposits from rural customers.

Investing where powerful synergies exist will also mitigate risk. The Global Digital Opportunity Initiative, a partnership of the Markle Foundation and the UN Development Programme, will help a small number of countries implement a strategy to harness the power of information and communications technologies to increase development. The countries will be chosen in part based on their interest and their willingness to make supportive regulatory and market reforms. To concentrate resources and create reinforcing effects, the initiative will encourage international aid agencies and global companies to assist with implementation.

All of the strategies we've outlined here will be of little use, however, unless the external barriers we've touched on—poor infrastructure, inadequate connectivity, corrupt intermediaries, and the like—are removed. Here's where technology holds the most promise. Information and communications technologies can grant access to otherwise isolated communities, provide marketing and distribution channels, bypass intermediaries, drive down transaction costs, and help aggregate demand and buying power. Smart cards and other emerging technologies are inexpensive ways to give poor customers a secure identity, a transaction or credit history, and even a virtual address—prerequisites for interacting with the formal economy. That's why high-tech companies aren't the only ones that should be interested in closing the global digital divide; encouraging the spread of low-cost digital networks at the bottom of the pyramid is a priority for virtually all companies that want to enter and engage with these markets. Improved connectivity is an important catalyst for more effective markets, which are critical to boosting income levels and accelerating economic growth.

Moreover, global companies stand to gain from the effects of network expansion in these markets. According to Metcalfe's Law, the usefulness of a network equals the square of the number of users. By the same logic, the value and vigor of the economic activity that will be generated when hundreds of thousands of previously isolated rural communities can buy and sell from one another and from urban markets will increase dramatically—to the benefit of all participants.

Since BOP markets require significant rethinking of managerial practices, it is legitimate for managers to ask: Is it worth the effort?

We think the answer is yes. For one thing, big corporations should solve big problems—and what is a more pressing concern than alleviating the poverty that 4 billion people are currently mired in? It is hard to argue that the wealth of technology and talent within leading multinationals is better allocated to producing incremental variations of existing products than to addressing the real needs—and real opportunities—at the bottom of the pyramid. Moreover, through competition, multinationals are likely to bring to BOP markets a level of accountability for performance and resources that neither international development agencies nor national governments have demonstrated during the last 50 years. Participation by MNCs could set a new standard, as well as a new market-driven paradigm, for addressing poverty.

But ethical concerns aside, we've shown that the potential for expanding the bottom of the market is just too great to ignore. Big companies need to focus on big market opportunities if they want to generate real growth. It is simply good business strategy to be involved in large, untapped markets that offer new customers, cost-saving opportunities, and access to radical innovation. The business opportunities at the bottom of the pyramid are real, and they are open to any MNC willing to engage and learn.

Notes

1. Andrew Lawlor, Caitlin Peterson, and Vivek Sandell, "Catalyzing Rural Development TARA haat.com" (World Resources Institute, July 2001).
2. Michael Best and Colin M. Maclay, "Community Internet Access in Rural Areas: Solving the Economic Sustainability Puzzle," *The Global Information Technology Report 2001-2002: Readiness for the Networked World,* ed., Geoffrey Kirkman (Oxford University Press, 2002), available on-line at http//www.cid.harvard.edu/cr/gitrr_O3O2O2.html.
3. Joy Howard, Erik Simanis, and Chads Simms, "Sustainable Deployment for Rural Connectivity: The n-Logue Model" (World Resources Institute, July 2001).

SECTION L
ETHNICITY

I always thought that racism in the USA was reserved for uneducated rednecks, that is, until the day I found it lurking in my own *enlightened* heart.

Late again for an appointment one morning, I was driving down Monroe Street in Madison, Wisconsin, hoping for green lights. Hemmed in by parked cars on the right and oncoming traffic on the left, I was stuck behind a slightly dilapidated car, dirty and with the side mirror dangling alongside the driver's door. I saw that the driver was a young, African American kid. I was completely unaware of any sense of internal judgment or bigotry. To me it was just another morning of transportation boredom and mild frustration. The person in front of me was just another young person who didn't take much pride in his car's appearance. When I finally had opportunity to pass this young man, I glanced over at him. It was then that I noticed that he was actually a White kid, wearing a black baseball cap with the bill turned backward. I suddenly became aware of a slight shift in my attitude toward this young man. Instead of viewing him as someone with a callous disregard for property, he quickly became a happy-go-lucky teenager who simply didn't have the time or funds to repair his car. In my mind's eye, he was transformed from a lazy, unambitious adolescent to a kid just too excited about other things in life to be concerned about his car at the moment. The difference in my attitude is embarrassing for me to admit and exposes the deeply engrained racism that coexists with my passion for people who are marginalized and oppressed. A quiet prejudice lives in me, nearly imperceptible to a heart so eager to believe the best about myself and yet so quick to notice and condemn discrimination in others.

Ethnic division is universal. Not all ethnic division is bad. Gathering together in ethnic-specific groupings helps us to celebrate what is good about our culture and lament our cultural downsides. It allows us to cherish family and enjoy a kind of community connection not available when gathered in ethnically diverse settings. But ethnic division can also play itself out in very harmful and insidious ways. It gives fuel to our human tendency to create structures that favor our own ethnicity and make life hard for people of other ethnicities. Ethnic division allows yet one more avenue to exploit some and favor others.

To engage the process of transformation in slum communities without recognizing the reality of ethnic hatred is seriously shortsighted. Mega-cities are collections of ethnic enclaves pressed tightly together. Where you find a slum community, you will often find an ethnic underclass and sometimes violent ethnic tensions that run in multiple directions.

In their book *Ethnic Conflict in World Politics*, Barbara Harff and Robert Gurr survey the ethnic wars of the twentieth and twenty-first centuries and the history behind the hatred. The chapter included here examines how the creation of new states after World War II in the 1950s and 1960s and after the fall of communism in the Soviet Union in the 1990s unleashed suppressed ethnic tensions. For some ethnic groups (like the Chechens) it has meant a quest for political autonomy. For others (like the pan-Arab and pan-Islamic movements) it has meant trying to coalesce ethnicity across geopolitical boundaries. Indigenous peoples and slave descendants in many countries seek simply to be given equal rights and opportunities. Still others (like Croats and Bosnian Muslims in the former Yugoslavia or Tutsis in Rwanda) have faced genocide and created huge refugee crises.

Finally, the chapter "Excluded Neighborhoods" in the book *To Live in Peace* chronicles the fascinating history of Baltimore's African American neighborhood known as Sandtown. Author Mark Gornik describes the social forces at work that have contributed to the hardships suffered by the residents of that community. Together these readings give us an appreciation for the role that ethnicity often plays in creating and perpetuating communities trapped in poverty.

CHAPTER 23

ETHNOPOLITICAL CONFLICT AND THE CHANGING WORLD ORDER

Ted Robert Gurr

Protracted conflicts over the rights and demands of ethnic and religious groups have caused more misery and loss of human life than has any other type of local, regional, and international conflict since the end of World War II. They are also the source of most of the world's refugees. In 2002 about two-thirds of the world's 15 million international refugees were fleeing from ethnopolitical conflict and repression. At least twice as many others have been internally displaced by force and famine. At the beginning of the new millennium millions of people in impoverished countries are in need of assistance, hundreds of thousands of desperate emigrants from conflict-ridden states are knocking at the doors of Western countries, and, to make things worse, donor fatigue among rich states threatens to perpetuate inequalities and misery.

Ethnopolitical conflicts are here to stay. Figure 23.1 shows that the number of countries with major ethnic wars increased steadily from a handful in the early 1950s to thirty-one countries in the early 1990s. We also know that between the mid-1950s and 1990 the magnitude of all ethnopolitical conflicts increased nearly fourfold—an astonishing increase in light of what was hoped for in the aftermath World War II.

The Holocaust should have enlightened us about what ethnic and religious hatred can do when used by unscrupulous leaders armed with exclusionary ideologies. Many people hoped that with the end of colonialism we could look forward to a better world in which nation-states would guarantee and protect the basic freedoms of their peoples. When the United Nations came into existence, were we wrong to believe that a new world order would emerge, one in which minimum standards of global justice would be observed and violators be punished? Is it still possible that a civil society will emerge in which citizens eschew narrow ethnic interests in favor of global issues?

FIGURE 23.1 Numbers and Proportions of Countries with Major Ethnic Wars, 1946–2001

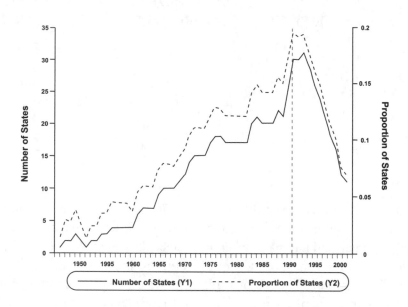

Instead we have witnessed more genocides and mass slaughters, an increase in ethnic consciousness leading to deadly ethnic conflicts, and religious fanaticism justifying the killing of innocent civilians in faraway lands. Some progress has been made to check ethnic wars since the mid-1990s, but we badly need more innovative ideas about how to fight the scourges that plague mankind. To top it off, the international political will to act has been waning in the wake of Somalia, Bosnia, Rwanda, Liberia, Burundi, the Democratic Republic of Congo, and other conflicts that need international attention. There is also the risk that, in the aftermath of the September 11 terrorist attacks on the World Trade Center in New York, the Western "war on terrorism" will divert international attention away from enduring problems.

So why write a book about ethnic conflict? This is what we hope for: If we understand the factors that contribute to the onset of ethnic conflicts, we may be able to suggest ways to stop escalation and find solutions by peaceful political means. We have ample evidence that deadly ethnic conflicts are not inevitable and can be contained or deterred, often without using force or the involvement of major powers. We hope that this book helps to further knowledge about ethnic conflicts and provides some guidelines about how to prevent, deter, or stop escalation.

Defining and Mapping the World of Ethnic Groups

Ethnic groups like the Kurds, Miskitos of Central America, and the Turks in Germany are "psychological communities" whose members share a persisting sense of common interest and identity that is based on some combination of shared historical experience and valued cultural traits—beliefs, language, ways of life, a common homeland. They are often called *identity groups*. A few, like the Koreans and the Icelanders, have their own internationally recognized state or states. Most, however, do not have such recognition, and they must protect their identity and interests within existing states.

Some religious groups resemble ethnic groups insofar as they have a strong sense of identity based on culture, belief, and a shared history of discrimination. Examples are Jews and the various sects of Shi'i Islam. Politically active religious groups, such as offshoots of the Muslim Brotherhood, are motivated by grievances similar to ethnic groups.

Many ethnic groups coexist amicably with others within the boundaries of established states. The Swedish minority in Finland, for example, has its own cultural and local political institutions, which are guaranteed by a 1921 international agreement between Sweden and Finland. For eighty years the Swedish minority has had no serious disputes with the Finnish people or government. Since the 1960s the Netherlands has welcomed many immigrants from the Third World with relatively little of the social tension or *discrimination* aimed at immigrants in Britain, France, and Germany. Even in these tolerant countries the explosive growth of asylum seekers has led to some antiforeign political movements and xenophobic attacks.

If peaceful relations prevail among peoples for a long time, their separate identities may eventually weaken. For example, Irish-Americans were a distinctive minority in mid-nineteenth-century North America because of their immigrant origins, their concentration in poor neighborhoods and low-status occupations, and the deep-rooted prejudice most Anglo-Americans had toward them. After a century of upward mobility and political incorporation, Irish descent has little political or economic significance in Canada or the United States, although many Irish-Americans still honor their cultural origins.

The ethnic groups whose status is of greatest concern in international politics today are those that are the targets of discrimination and that have organized to take political action to promote or defend their interests. A recent study, directed by the second author, surveys politically active national peoples and ethnic minorities throughout the world. As of 2001, the project has identified and profiled 275 sizable groups that have been targets of discrimination or are organized for political assertiveness or both.[1] Most larger countries have at least

FIGURE 23.2 Politically Active Ethnic Groups by Region, 2001

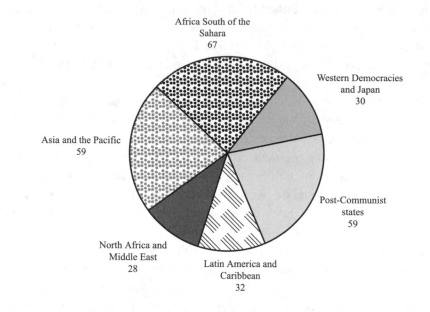

one such ethnic group, and in a few countries like South Africa and Bolivia, they comprise half or more of the population. Taken together the groups involve more than 1 billion people, or a sixth of the world's population. Figure 23.2 shows how these groups were distributed among the regions of the world in 2001. When the Soviet Union dissolved into fifteen independent republics at the end of 1991, the political demands of *ethnonationalists* like the Latvians, Ukrainians, and Armenians were met. Since then, however, at least thirty additional ethnic groups in the new republics have made new political demands.

The Minorities at Risk survey shows that about 80 percent of the politically active ethnic groups in the 1990s were disadvantaged because of historical or contemporary discrimination. Forty percent of these groups (111 out of 275) surveyed face discriminatory policies and practices harmful to their material well-being. For example, almost all indigenous peoples in the Americas have high infant mortality rates due in part to limited pre and post-natal health care; Tamil youth in Sri Lanka have long been discriminated against by university admission policies that favor the majority Sinhalese. The survey also identified 135 minorities subjected to contemporary political discrimination. For example, Turkish governments have repeatedly banned and restricted political parties that sought to represent Kurdish interests; in Brazil people of African descent make up more than 40 percent of the country's population but hold less than 5 percent of seats in the national congress. Cultural restrictions also have been imposed on at least 116 minorities. Muslim girls attending French secondary schools have been expelled for wearing head scarves; principals of Hungarian-language schools in Slovakia have been dismissed for not speaking Slovak at Hungarian teachers' meetings. Such restrictions may seem petty but symbolically their effects can be a painful and enduring reminder that the dominant society disvalues a minority's culture.

Ethnic groups that are treated unequally resent and usually attempt to improve their condition. Three-quarters of the groups in the survey were politically active in the 1990s. They did not necessarily use violence, however. On the contrary, most ethnic groups with a political agenda use the strategies and tactics of interest groups and social movements, especially if they live in democratic states. Figure 23.3 shows the highest level of political action among minorities in 1995. One-quarter were politically inactive (some of them had a history of intense activism), half were mobilizing for or carrying out political action, and only one-quarter used violent strategies of small-scale rebellion (including terrorism) or large-scale rebellion. The latter include the most serious and enduring of all conflicts within states, including ethnic wars between Hutus and Tutsis in Burundi and Rwanda, civil wars by southerners in Sudan and Muslim Kashmiris in India, and wars of independence by Kurds in Turkey and Iraq and by Palestinians in Gaza and the West Bank.

Figure 23.3 also shows the relative frequency of different kinds of political action among world regions. The highest level of mobilization in 1995 was in Latin America mainly among indigenous peoples. Ethnic rebellions were uncommon in Europe and the Americas and when they did occur were mainly terrorist campaigns. Rebellions were much more numerous in Africa, Asia, and the Middle East.

The Changing Global System and Ethnic Conflict

Ethnic conflict is not solely or even mainly a consequence of domestic politics. The potential for ethnic conflict, the issues at stake, and even the lines of *cleavage* between contending groups have been shaped and reshaped by international factors. In this section we introduce three general issues—the tension between the state system and ethnic identities, the impact the end of the Cold War has had on conflicts among nations and peoples, and the changing nature of international responses to ethnic conflict.

333

FIGURE 23.3 Strategies of Political Action Used by Ethnopolitical Minorities in 1995

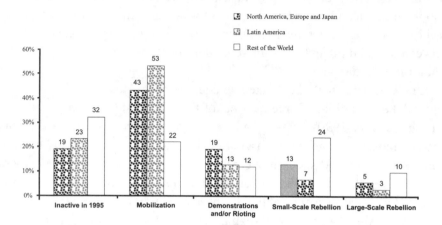

States or Peoples?

Historically, ethnic groups, nations, states, empires, and other forms of large-scale social organization—for example, Islam and Christendom—have coexisted, but since the seventeenth century the dominant form of social organization has been the *state system*—the organization of the world's people into a system of independent and territorial states, some of which controlled overseas colonial empires.

Despite attempts to change the existing world order by insisting that the state was obsolete, as Marxists proclaimed, the state remains the key actor in international relations. Key, because the state at the very minimum controls the principal means of coercion. Ethnic groups rarely are equal in terms of power, legitimacy, or economic resources. But it is wrong to suggest that the state is a single monolithic enterprise. Instead, we may want to think of the state as a recognized territorial entity in flux. It is one thing to think of England as an established state since the Middle Ages, yet Germany in something like its present form has existed only since 1870. The new states that emerged in the Middle East, Asia, and Africa following the demise of empires were often just creations of the former colonizers, endowed with neither historical nor cultural continuity, nor boundaries that recognized the living space of ethnic groups. Thus for example, we have states, such as Burundi and Rwanda in both of which a Tutsi minority rules a Hutu majority, which led to major conflicts and postindependence genocidal killings in both countries.

Some would argue that certain states should have no independent existence, either because the notion of territory was not part of their people's culture or because they would be better off within the boundaries of established states. Indeed, one could ask how viable, necessary, or rational is the division of the Arabian Peninsula into many sheikdoms, some of which have emerged as independent states only since the 1960s. But, what are the alternatives? In tribal communities, local loyalties were very well developed, but rarely extended beyond the narrow boundaries of family or clan, thus leaving local communities at the mercy of would-be conquerors and usurpers. Necessity may have been the force that unified some warring tribes, laws and coercion are the means that have kept them together.

We do not intend to cover in any comprehensive fashion the historical development of the state system but instead offer a brief glimpse into what led to its emergence and what factors may lead to the demise of some existing states.

On the one side, states act independently of their constituent parts, such as peoples and institutions. After all, we talk about the economic viability or capabilities of states, not of the people who reside within the state. Today most states control capital through either public ownership or state-owned enterprises. But some theorists still see the state as passive, reacting mainly to pressures emanating from society. Though scholars disagree on the extent of cooperation and conflict between the state and society, it is still a fact that the state is a legally recognized sovereign entity in international law, endowed with rights and obligations vis-a-vis other states, groups, and its own citizens. Whatever the reasons that gave birth to specific states, the nation-state is today the primary actor in international relations. It is the state that defines, provides, and controls the public good, through regulation and institutions. It is the state that enforces the rules through coercion and punishment.

Let us apply some of these arguments to the historical situation of the Kurds, whose situation is symptomatic of many other *ethnonationalists*. After the demise of the Ottoman Empire following World War I, they were the largest ethnic group within the former empire without a state of their own. Instead, Kurds came to live within five other states, the largest segment of them now citizens of the new Republic of Turkey. Ever since, the Turkish government has tried through incentives, coercion, discrimination, and punishment to undermine Kurdish ethnic consciousness, hoping to deter any attempts to secede. Here the state became omnipotent, using all means at its disposal to subdue Kurdish national aspirations.

An essential question is whether or not a people have rights to a territory on which they resided for many centuries. International law today recognizes that it is inadmissible to acquire territory by waging an aggressive war, but the reality is somewhat different. International law, often invoked but seldom enforced, was used to bolster the legality of the Gulf War in 1990, ostensibly to free Kuwait from Iraqi occupation, as well as U.S. intervention in Panama and Vietnam. Israel, invoking its defensive posture in the 1967 war, holds on to territory inhabited by Palestinians for centuries. The Abkhaz in Georgia have technically won an independence war, but are not recognized by the international community of nation-states. What does this mean for the rights of groups vis-a-vis states? It means that sometimes group rights are recognized by individual states and the international community and sometimes, depending on various power constellations, they are not. However, international law can provide the justification or the means to establish claims to specific territory. Let us look briefly at the state as arbiter, problem-solving agent, or restricter or denier of the rights of collectivities.

Indeed, few states are able to unite a multitude of *ethnies* into a harmonious unit. Although long-established liberal democracies probably are more successful than autocracies in doing so, problems persist. Recall the situation of African-Americans prior to the Civil Rights movement and current issues ranging from outright discrimination to disenfranchisement. Consider that Native Americans are a people organized into a number of self-governing segments or "nations" within the greater American nation yet are economically and politically dependent on the United States.

One of the more heretical thoughts that comes to mind is whether the institutionalized state has a future, given the many ethnic groups that clamor for independence. The answer has to be yes, because what is it that these ethnic groups demand? They seek the right to govern their own territory, which they hope will become a sovereign, internationally recognized state. What this suggests is that the current international system may fragment into hundreds of mini-states unless ethnic demands can be satisfied within existing states. In fact more than a dozen ethnic wars were settled in the 1990s by granting autonomy to ethnonationalists within existing states. Successful settlements like these depend on the political system. Democracies are better able to accommodate ethnic demands than autocracies. But it is also true that in newly emerging democracies, ethnic demands may exceed the capacity of state structures, thus leading to failure of existing states.

The ascendance and expansion of the state system has meant that states are parties to most deadly conflicts: wars between states, civil wars within states, and *genocides* and political mass murders by states. But here we find a different phenomena at work. States wage war, but people decide to make war. Here the collective can triumph over state structures. The collective will as exemplified by prevailing ideologies and political movements within the state system have dramatically influenced ethnic conflict. In the 1920s and 1930s, anti-Semitic doctrines in Germany and other European countries promoted ethnic polarization. They competed with Communist doctrine in the Soviet Union, which emphasized the common interests of all Soviet peoples and minimized the significance of ethnic and nationalist identities. In the 1940s and 1950s anti-colonialism emerged as a major form of resistance against European domination in Asia and Africa. With the help of liberation ideologies, nationalists were able to unite diverse ethnic groups in their efforts to replace colonial rule by European powers with their own independent states. And they succeeded beyond what was expected. By the early 1960s almost all European-ruled colonial territories had gained independence and become members of the state system. But the success came at a cost as tribal and ethnic consciousness soon reemerged in a number of states. Congo immediately after its independence from Belgium in 1970 and Nigeria a decade later experienced major ethnic wars. More recently we have seen a new kind of resistance to the state system that has affected every world region except Latin America: It is an accelerating wave of self-determination movements.

But there are other trends. At times throughout the twentieth century, ethnic peoples have coalesced across boundaries to join in common causes—for example, by joining pan-Islamic, *pan-Arab*, and *indigenous peoples'* movements. In the Arab world such movements have been short-lived and have been characterized by constantly shifting coalitions. Despite paying lip service to equality of economic status, a shared religion, and the brotherhood of a common ancestry, Arabs have continued to fight fellow Arabs.

But rarely has a common ethnic or religious background been sufficient to cause peoples to subordinate the interests of states to a greater transnational identity or cause, even a limited one. This is especially true for peoples of countries with long-established boundaries who have developed identities beyond their immediate tribes and clans.

At present we witness two competing trends in human organization. At one extreme, we see a reemergence of xenophobia in long-established countries—for example, the increase in exclusive ethnic identity that motivates antiforeign excesses in Germany, France, and Great Britain. No less extreme are movements that demand ethnic purity in formerly heterogeneous federations, such as Serbian nationalism in the former Yugoslavia. At the other end of the continuum are oppressive leaders who defend existing boundaries at all costs, despite historically justified claims by national peoples, such as Palestinians in the Middle East and

Kurds in Iraq, for internal autonomy or independence. Ironically, the new elites of former Asian and African colonies share with Saddam Hussein a willingness to fight to maintain existing boundaries and states, despite arbitrarily drawn borders that accommodated European interests but ignored demographic and cultural realities.

The End of the Cold War

The Cold War between the Soviet bloc and the U.S.-led Western alliance created, for better or worse, a sense of stability among most of the world population. Policymakers' calculations concerning conflict outcomes could be made with greater confidence in a more rigidly ordered world. The dissolution of the global system from a loose, bipolar world into an ethnically fragmented multipolar system left in its wake a greater sense of insecurity among the leaders of the established states. This is what U.S. President Bill Clinton alluded to when he told a journalist, "I even made a crack the other day . . . 'Gosh, I miss the Cold War.'" How does one deal with hostile warlords in Somalia and respond to ethnic and nationalist unrest in the Soviet successor states? Finding a workable framework for this new era and defining the role of the United States, Clinton added, "could take years."[2] By the end of the Clinton administration, no clear framework or consistent set of policies had emerged, though the administration had shifted toward more proactive engagement.

But events do not wait for policymakers to devise new frameworks. With the collapse of Soviet hegemony at the end of the Cold War, the citizens of the former Soviet Union and Eastern Europe were freed to act upon communal rivalries with a vengeance. The demise of communism in the former Soviet Union left a political and ideological vacuum that is only gradually being filled. It was ideology that bound historically hostile peoples together; now old rivalries have reemerged, and neighbors have again become antagonists fighting for power, status, and control of adjacent territories. Communist citizens' place in society was predictable, and their economic welfare was guaranteed at a basic level. Communism in its ideal form also instilled a sense of collective responsibility and solidarity that overcame more parochial identities. The transformation of socialist societies into predatory capitalist societies has led to a sense of alienation and isolation and an increased emphasis on narrow group interests and self-interests. This increased sense of isolation has been circumvented by a heightened ethnic awareness and, in some states, a growth in intolerance toward members of other groups.

A decade after the end of the Cold War, the ethnic landscape of post-socialist states is remarkably diverse. The Russian Federation has been widely and justly criticized for fighting a dirty war against rebels in the breakaway republic of Chechnya. But during the 1990s it also successfully negotiated autonomy agreements with Tatarstan, Bashkiria, and some forty other regions in the Russian Federation, thus defusing a number of potentially violent conflicts. A new sense of common interest and identity is being built among most of the peoples of Russia. In East Central Europe, the civil wars that broke up the Yugoslav Federation contrast sharply with Czechoslovakia where ethnic conflict between the Czech and Slovak republics ended peacefully in a "velvet divorce" in 1993. Nationalist governments in Romania and Slovakia cracked down on their restive Hungarian minorities in the early 1990s, but the nationalists were ousted in democratic elections in the late 1990s and Hungarian politicians joined new coalition governments. And the new democratic government of Bulgaria, whose Communist regime had persecuted the country's large Turkish Muslim minority, granted the Turks full cultural, economic, and political rights. The Roma (gypsies) are a worrisome exception to these trends toward ethnic tolerance. They are disliked and discriminated against throughout Europe, East and West.

Contemporary Examples of Ethnopolitical Conflict

Since the 1960s increasing numbers of ethnic groups have begun to demand more rights and recognition, demands that are now recognized as the major source of domestic and international conflict in the post-Cold War world. The protagonists in the most intense ethnic conflicts want to establish their *autonomy* or independence, as is the case with many Kurds. Other ethnic conflicts arise from efforts by subordinate groups to improve their status within the existing boundaries of a state rather than to secede from it. For example, most black South Africans wanted—and gained—majority control of state power. Turkish and other recent immigrants to Germany are worried about their security, seek greater economic opportunities, and hope to become citizens. Native peoples in the Americas want to protect what is left of their traditional lands and cultures from the corrosive influences of modern society. Here we consider some implications of both kinds of ethnic conflict.

The *civil wars* accompanying the dissolution of Yugoslavia into five new states show that subject people's demands for autonomy often escalate into warfare. After Slovenia, Croatia, and Bosnia declared independence in summer 1991, Serbia—the dominant partner in the old Yugoslavian Federation—tried to reestablish its *hegemony* by promoting uprisings by Serbian minorities in the latter two states. These Serbs justified their actions by recounting Croat atrocities against Serbs during World War II. They devised brutal and often deadly policies called *ethnic cleansing*, which involved the murder or forced removal of Croatians, Bosnian Muslims, and other minorities from areas in which Serbs lived and prompted hundreds of thousands of refugees to flee to surrounding countries. In Serbia proper the government and local activists severely restricted the activities of Albanian and Hungarian minorities.

One of the longest modern civil wars was waged by the people of the Ethiopian province of Eritrea, who supported a war of independence that lasted from the early 1960s until 1991. The Eritrean nationalists received some diplomatic and military support from Middle Eastern states such as Egypt, whereas in the first decade of conflict the imperial Ethiopian government relied heavily on military assistance from the United States. Even the military-led *revolution* that overthrew Emperor Haile Selassie in 1974 did not end ethnic conflict. Instead, the new Marxist military leaders of Ethiopia sought and received support from the Soviet Union to enable them to continue the war against Eritrea. By the end of the 1970s many other ethnic groups in Ethiopia were stimulated into rebellion by the Eritrean example. An alliance was eventually formed among Eritreans, Tigreans, Oromo, and others that culminated in the rebels' triumphal capture of the Ethiopian capital, Addis Ababa, in May 1991.

Unlike the situation in Yugoslavia, there was no serious international effort to check the Ethiopian civil war. No major power recognized Eritrea as an independent state; international organizations regarded the conflict as an internal matter, and there was no media-inspired publicity of atrocities that might have prompted greater action. Only when famine threatened the region did the Ethiopian government allow humanitarian assistance but then prevented distribution of the aid in rebel-held areas.

Following thirty years of warfare, the moderate policies of the new revolutionary government allowed for a peaceful reconciliation. The government made and kept a commitment to hold referendums in 1993 to set up autonomous regional governments or, in the case of Eritrea, to allow full independence. The Eritrean referendum in April 1993 resulted in a 99.8 percent vote in favor of independence. Eritrean independence was accepted by the Ethiopian government, and the new state immediately received diplomatic recognition from the United States and many other countries.

But new sources of ethnic tension soon cropped up. Some Eritreans living in the Ethiopian capital were forced to leave the country, with retaliatory threats by Eritreans to expel Ethiopians. Political and economic tensions escalated until May 1998, when the two countries began a deadly two-year war over some scraps of disputed territory. The Eritrea-Ethiopia conflict, like that between Muslims and Hindus in the Indian subcontinent, shows that separation is not a perfect solution for ethnic tensions because it may lead to future conflicts within and between states.

Conflicts over group demands for better treatment within existing states and societies are seldom as deadly as the civil wars in Yugoslavia or Ethiopia; nor are they likely to have serious international repercussions. But they can be just as fateful for the people caught up in them, as the following example suggests. Kara (not her real name) is a woman in her late twenties who works as an assistant manager of a resort hotel on Turkey's Aegean coast. She was born and raised in Germany by parents who had emigrated there as "guest workers." After Kara's graduation from secondary school, her parents accepted money from the West German government to return to Turkey. Kara also had to return, and, like her parents, was prohibited from returning to Germany. Kara does not fear for her life or safety, but she is caught between two cultures: the German society in which she was raised and whose language she speaks fluently, and the Turkish society in which she must live and work. Her desk clerk, a man in his early twenties, has the same story and a similar problem: Turkish girls mock him as "the German" who speaks Turkish badly. Neither likes living in Turkey, and both have doubts about finding marriage partners.[3] Their lives would probably have been more satisfying, and their identities more secure, if they could have gained full citizenship and stayed in the country in which they grew up.

Enduring Conflicts, Changing International Responses

We cannot entirely blame the explosion of ethnic conflict in the early 1990s on the end of the Cold War. Figure 23.1 shows clearly that the extent of conflicts worldwide between ethnic groups and states increased steadily from 1950 to 1989, before the Cold War ended. Thus we need to identify other factors that contributed to that explosion. We begin with three Third World examples, which may offer some clues to why some ethnic conflicts were neither affected by nor indirect by-products of Cold War confrontations.

In the 1970s the newly independent African states of Uganda and Equatorial Guinea experienced intense ethnopolitical conflict that had little relationship to the tensions produced by the Cold War. Dictators Macias Nguma of Equatorial Guinea (1968-1979) and Idi Amin of Uganda (1971-1979) each sought to consolidate power by killing thousands of their ethnic and political rivals. These horrifying events elicited no substantive response from the United Nations and few condemnations from individual states. Amin and Macias were virtually free to kill people they defined as enemies, in part because their countries were of little consequence to either the United States or the Soviet Union.

The third case is Rwanda, in which during a genocide in 1994 800,000 to 1 million Tutsis and moderate Hutus perished. When Tutsi exiles of the Rwandan Patriotic Front launched a major invasion from bases in Uganda in 1993, Hutu armies and militias responded with counterattacks. Intermittent negotiations led to the Arusha Accords, but the mobilization of Hutu militias continued. In neighboring Burundi, massacres following a 1993 coup led to a massive exodus of some 342,000 refugees to Rwanda. Militant Rwandan Hutus sought to undermine the Arusha Accords. They probably arranged the downing of the aircraft that carried the presidents of Rwanda and Burundi, Juvenal Habyarimana and Cyprien Ntaryamira, back from peace talks in Tanzania on April 6, 1994. This signaled the beginning of a killing spree in which Belgian peacekeepers and the moderate Rwandan prime minister, Agathe Uwilingiyimana, were among the first to die. Ethnic Tutsis were the primary targets. In the next 100 days, some 800,000 people were killed by marauding Hutu militias, encouraged by their leadership and hate propaganda. In July 1994, Tutsi rebels seized the capital, declared victory, and named a Hutu president. At the end of July Tanzania recognized the new government and Western powers promised aid. But killings continued in Hutu-dominated refugee camps in Zaire.

What these three cases show is that despite warnings of impending disasters, especially in Rwanda, Western powers had little or no interest in intervening. UN peacekeepers in Rwanda were poorly armed and few in number, and their mandate was to remain impartial.

Could more have been done? We believe the international community has an obligation to protect the rights of minorities, beginning with protecting the most basic rights to life and security For example, and from our point of view, the civil wars and ethnic killings in the breakaway states of the former Yugoslavia could have been preempted by early and active international mediation that would have led to guaranteed independence and security for all newly emerging states in the region and to commitments from all parties to protect the rights of each state's ethnic peoples. But the international community is only gradually acquiring the legal principles, political will, and foresight to respond effectively to such conflicts.

In the three cases described above, the consequences of colonialism were a major impediment to decisive action. Colonial subjects in Africa and Asia had few rights, and many ethnic groups were trapped within artificial boundaries imposed by the departing colonial powers. Faced with challenges from peoples of different cultures and kinships, most leaders of newly independent Third World countries opted to accept existing boundaries, insisting on absolute sovereignty and the inviolability of territorial borders. This insistence on the right to conduct internal affairs without outside interference gave unscrupulous dictators like

Macias and Amin freedom to commit atrocities against their subjects in the name of "nation building." In Rwanda and Burundi, French favoritism, U.S. disinterest, and the UN's self-imposed limited mandate conspired to allow unscrupulous leaders to exploit ethnic tensions.

If the United Nations and the superpowers were indifferent to ethnic conflict and mass murder in peripheral states of the Third World, could regional organizations have responded? Many such deadly episodes occurred in the member states of the Organization of African Unity (OAU, founded in 1963) and the Organization of the Islamic Conference (which represents all states that have significant Muslim populations). But these organizations have usually been politically divided and have had few resources; thus, they have seldom responded to ethnic warfare and severe human rights violations in member states. The OAU, for example, was limited by its charter to mediating conflicts between African states, not within them. In 1981 and 1982, the OAU made its first effort at active peacekeeping when it sent a multinational force to help de-escalate a civil war between communal rivals in Chad; the effort was largely a failure. Partisan support for Rwandan rebels by Uganda did little to defuse the situation. After the Arusha Accords, the OAU verbally condemned international inaction, but had little more to offer than postconflict negotiations.

The impotence of Third World regional organizations combined with the reluctance of the superpowers during the Cold War era to interfere in the internal affairs of states that had little impact on global competition virtually ensured that most ethnic conflicts would remain domestic affairs, even if they led to gross violations of human rights. However, and despite Rwanda, we think that since 1991 the United Nations and the last remaining superpower, the United States, have taken more vigorous action against human rights violators and aggressive states.

No doubt the United Nations, established to create and preserve international peace, has had a mixed record as peacekeeper. A brief review of its record follows.

During the Cold War the UN played a significant peacekeeping role by separating combatants in communal conflicts in Congo, Cyprus, the Middle East, and Kashmir, but this occurred only because the superpowers agreed on the course of action. Since 1991, with encouragement from the U.S. government and other states, it has expanded its role. In Cambodia, for example, the United Nations mounted the biggest and most expensive peacekeeping operation in its history. Under a 1991 peace plan agreed to by warring Cambodian parties, an international force of 22,000 police and military and administrative personnel was stationed in the country to help establish order and oversee the transition to an elected civilian government. The effort was largely completed, and all military forces withdrawn, by October 1993.

The expanded role of the United States is illustrated by the dispatch of U.S. troops returning from the Gulf War to assist flood victims in Bangladesh in April and May 1991 and by the U.S.-led mobilization of reluctant states to intervene militarily in Iraq during the 1991 Gulf War in a renewed spirit of collective responsibility.

Regional organizations also have a mixed record. In the early 1990s the European Union, the world's second most powerful economic entity, was divided about whether and how to respond to escalating ethnic conflict in adjacent East Central Europe. The North Atlantic Treaty Organization (NATO) had the military means to intervene forcefully in European conflict situations, but both its European and North American members were very reluctant to use force to control the Bosnian conflict and ethnic cleansing in 1992-1995. The response in Kosovo in 1998-1999 was a somewhat different story—it was essentially proactive. Although U.S. pressure and promise of participation was probably instrumental in overcoming the lack of political will among the leaders of NATO's European members, international initiatives were not lacking. Some thirteen government and sixteen NGO efforts were made to halt crisis escalation. But the efforts were not sustained until violence occurred, from early 1998 to early 1999, attacks and counterattacks were a daily occurrence. Despite resolutions, mediation attempts, sanctions, and negotiated cease-fires, violence spiraled out of control. Only after NATO bombing in May of 1999 did Serbia under Milosevic withdraw its forces.

Regional organizations in the Third World are also taking a more active role in response to internal conflicts. Their leaders are involved in drafting and arguing for extensions to the human rights conventions that would allow for some exceptions to the rule of nonintervention. In the early 1990s, for example, the OAU established a new mechanism for conflict resolution and prevention that, in effect, redefined the OAU doctrine of noninterference in the affairs of member states. The OAU now monitors elections, makes periodic assessments of emerging conflict situations, and sends envoys to countries in which serious crises are brewing. For example in early 1993 the OAU sent a sixty-man observer mission to Rwanda to monitor a cease-fire between rival Hutu and the Tutsi armies, but it had neither political nor military clout.

Nongovernmental organizations (NGOs) such as Amnesty International, Human Rights Watch, and the International Crisis Group also play a role by calling attention to ethnic conflict and repression. Activists have lobbied their respective governments and the United Nations to take active roles in supporting humanitarian efforts, have denounced various interventions, and have reported human rights violations to international agencies.

Conclusion

We have shown that the "explosion" of ethnopolitical conflicts at the end of the Cold War was, in fact, a continuation of a trend that began as early as the 1960s. It is a manifestation of the enduring tension between states that want to consolidate and expand their power and ethnic groups that want to defend and promote their collective identity and interests. The breakup of the USSR and power shifts elsewhere within the state system have opened up opportunities for ethnic groups to pursue their interests. Coincidentally, the CNN-led explosion of global news coverage has increased public awareness of the human dimension of these conflicts and thus has contributed to pressures on policymakers to take constructive action.

Recent developments send encouraging signals to those who are concerned about checking the rise of ethnopolitical conflict and human rights abuses such as ethnic cleansing. For the first time since World War II, the United Nations has begun to realize the vision of its founders: New leadership in the UN, notably Boutros Boutros-Ghali, past secretary-general, and Kofi Annan, the current secretary-general, have tried to change the role of the UN from reactive to proactive in its role as peacekeeper, intervenor, arbiter, and mediator in communal and regional conflicts. A consensus is emerging that the United Nations should establish minimum standards of global security through collective decision making. Of course, the UN's ability to work for world security is directly dependent upon its ability to influence the outcome of emerging ethnic or nationalistic conflicts. However, the continuing caution apparent among most member states over enhancing UN military capabilities signals those who stir up ethnic hatred that they may face a minor roadblock rather than a major obstacle.

At the beginning of the new millenium we see some resemblance to the period following World War I, in which the collapse of the old order was followed by the birth of many new states, upsurges of ethnic violence and oppression, and the ascendancy of dictators and ideologies of exclusive nationalism. The pattern of conflicts in the Balkans, the Caucasus, the Middle East, and Central Africa fits this scenario and signifies the continuation of challenging times.

THE WORLD OF
ETHNOPOLITICAL GROUPS

Four important types of politically active ethnic groups coexist with modern states: *ethnonationalists, indigenous peoples, ethnoclasses*, and *communal contenders*. The distinctions are important because they summarize a great deal of information about peoples' history, their status in society, and their political agendas. The first two types are peoples who once led a separate political existence and want independence or autonomy from the states that rule them today. Ethnonationalists like Kurds and Palestinians want to (re)establish their own states, while others like Albanians in Macedonia and Russians in Ukraine seek closer ties with their national homelands. Indigenous peoples like Native Americans are mainly concerned with protecting their traditional lands, resources, and culture within existing states. By contrast, ethnoclasses and communal contenders aim to improve their position in existing societies, not to change political boundaries. Ethnoclasses, like African-Americans and Turks in Germany, are descendants of slaves or immigrants who want to break out of the social and economic niches into which they were segregated by the dominant society. Communal contenders like the Druze in Lebanon and Chinese in Malaysia are among a number of culturally distinct groups that compete for a share of political power. The difference is that ethnoclasses live in *stratified societies*, in which ethnic groups are in a hierarchical or ranked relationship to each other. Communal contenders are members of *segmented societies*, in which roughly equal ethnic and religious groups compete for economic and political power.[4]

The numbers of each type of group are shown in Figure 23.4, based on a survey by the Minorities at Risk Project (see note 1). Ethnonationalists are most numerous, with eighty-five. Communal contenders, found mainly in Africa, number sixty-eight. Ethnoclasses, most of which live in advanced industrial societies, number forty-three.

We begin with a sketch of global historical processes that set the stage for political activism by ethnic groups in contemporary states. Some of those processes continue today, including migration from poor to rich countries and the corrosive effects of resource exploitation on traditional peoples. Then we discuss each of the four types in more detail, including the traits that define them, their typical grievances and political strategies, and the international dimensions of their activities. The last section considers some connections between religion and ethnic conflict.

The World Historical Background to Contemporary Ethnic Conflicts

Contemporary conflicts between ethnic groups and states are a part of the heritage of large historical processes: imperial conquest, colonial rule, slavery, frontier settlement, and the international migration of labor. For example, every state that once established an empire did so at the expense of weaker and less fortunate peoples. Typically, European colonial rulers exercised direct influence over the social, cultural, and political lives of their dominions. The same was true of most other peoples who established empires by conquest, including the Han Chinese, the Ottoman Turks, and the Amharas of the Ethiopian highlands.

Local economies were undermined by colonial rule. Through the introduction of new economic systems that favored the dominant group, conquered peoples were forced into servitude, slavery, or dependency. Colonial rule also established hierarchies and rivalries among groups where few or none had previously existed. In colonial Nigeria, the British recruited clerks from the Christian Ibo of the southeast and soldiers from the Muslim northerners, laying the basis for group rivalries that continue to the present. Colonial rule did not create ethnic identities but often led to stratification or segmentation of colonized people along ethnic lines.

The sense of separate identity and grievances that result from imperial conquest and colonial rule can persist for many generations and provide the fuel for contemporary political movements. Burma, a former British colony, has been locked in ethnically based regional conflict since independence in the late 1940s. The conflict began during World War II, when nationalists within the Burman majority attacked the British colonial army, which was recruited largely from ethnic minorities such as the Karens, Chins, and Kachins. Thousands died in the ensuing struggles, laying the basis for enduring conflict between the minority peoples and the independent Burman state.

Societies that were ethnically divided and stratified in this way were fertile ground for conflict when newly formed Asian and African states won independence during the two decades following 1945. The new states were seldom ethnically homogeneous. They inherited borders that had been drawn to fit the political and administrative interests of the colonial powers. In some cases rival ethnic groups were merged into one new state; other groups were divided among several states by European-imposed borders. Nationalists contending for political power in the new states often played communal groups against one another, thus polarizing them. Rivalries in the Indian subcontinent between Muslim and Hindu politicians during the transition to independence led to partition in 1947 and the violent transfer of populations. It laid the foundation for a half-century of rivalry between Pakistan and India that continues today and recurring violence between Hindus and the Muslim minority that remained in India.

Another source of friction in colonial societies resulted from policies that encouraged immigration of outsiders to work newly established plantations or to engage in commercial activities for which the indigenous population lacked social capital. Most immigrants were not incorporated into the indigenous social structure but remained on the political and social margins. The British brought some 60,000 East Indians to their Fiji colony between 1879 and 1916 to work as indentured servants on sugarcane plantations. Native Fijian chiefs and political leaders have fought ever since to maintain control of Fijian politics, especially as East Indians began to outnumber natives. Fiji became an independent democracy in 1970 and rivalries between the two groups are the country's main source of political conflict. When an Indian-led party won elections in 1987 the new prime minister's government was overthrown in a Fijian-led military coup, for example. Similar tensions among immigrants and indigenous peoples have bedeviled the politics of post-colonial Trinidad, Guyana, and Surinam in the Western Hemisphere, and Sri Lanka and Malaysia in Southeast Asia.

The previously mentioned policy of using immigrants and members of favored ethnic groups to staff colonial bureaucracies often gave them privileged status in the host country and also provoked discriminatory measures against their descendants after independence. The Chinese in Malaysia provide an example. They readily adopted Western education, language, and styles and, after independence, were resented by Malays for their privileged status and sometimes were victimized by nationalist movements and state authorities.

In the Americas and Australia, Europeans settled in large numbers, with devastating consequences for indigenous peoples. Some of the latter were agriculturalists; most were hunters. Organized into nations, tribal federations, or bands (particularly in Australia), they were on the losing side of competition with European settlers. The settlers' victories were accomplished through the slaughter, enslavement, forced *assimilation,* or forcible removal of indigenous peoples to reservations in remote and inhospitable areas. Thus, the migration

FIGURE 23.4 Types of Politically Active Ethnic Groups in 2001

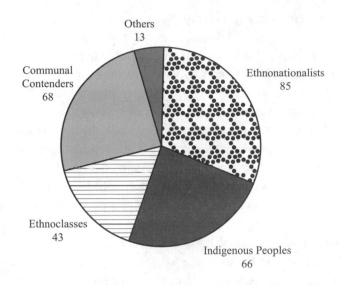

of Europeans throughout the colonial period contributed to ethnic rebellions and mass slaughter and also to the displacement or genocide of indigenous peoples.

Another invidious European practice was to import Africans as slaves to provide labor for plantations in the Americas. In some societies the descendants of slaves were eventually incorporated into the dominant society: Examples are found in Brazil, parts of the Caribbean, and Canada. In the United States, however, slaves liberated by the Emancipation Proclamation of 1863 were rarely given the opportunity to achieve higher status. In the rigid class structure of Southern society following the Civil War, former slaves were free only of their chains.

In summary, each of the major historical processes left legacies of antagonisms and inequalities that fuel contemporary ethnic conflicts. Conquered peoples seek to regain their lost autonomy; indigenous peoples ask for restoration of their traditional lands and protection of their resources from exploitation; immigrant workers and the descendants of slaves demand full equality. Not all ethnic peoples with these kinds of heritages are pursuing political objectives today, yet most have done so in the past or have the potential to do so in the future. It is essential, when one is trying to understand the passion and persistence with which ethnic groups pursue their objectives, to analyze the general historical processes and the particular experiences that have shaped each people's sense of identity and their grievances.

Ethnonationalists

Ethnonationalists are relatively large and regionally concentrated ethnic groups that live within the boundaries of one state or of several adjacent states; their modern political movements are directed toward achieving greater autonomy or independent statehood. Most have historical traditions of autonomy or independence that are used to justify these contemporary demands. In some instances autonomy was lost centuries ago, as was the case of the Corsicans and Bretons in France,[5] but it still motivates modern political movements. More than 100 ethnonational groups—including some indigenous peoples—at some time since the 1950s have supported movements aimed at establishing greater political autonomy. Seventy of these groups have fought armed conflicts for national independence or for unification with kindred groups elsewhere, with twenty-two of these small wars being fought in 2003.[6]

Most people with nationalist aspirations live in the Third World, such as the southern Sudanese, the Kurds in the Middle East, and the Tibetans. They have fought some of the modern world's most persistent wars of self-determination, but only two new internationally recognized states have been born in the Third World in armed ethnonational conflict during the last forty years. They are Bangladesh (1971) and Eritrea (1993). Most other ethnically based wars of self-determination have either failed or ended in negotiated grants of greater autonomy within existing states.

Other ethnonationalists such as the Scots, Basques, Latvians, Albanians, and French-Canadians live in European and North American states. Their campaigns for greater autonomy have usually been pursued by nonviolent political means, although the terrorist campaigns of some Basque nationalists and Albanians in Kosovo and Macedonia suggest that many have the potential for violence. Most ethnonationalists in European societies have gained significant concessions in the past few decades; many won independence in 1991 as a result of the breakup of the USSR and Yugoslavia.

After 1991 two dozen new or revitalized ethnonationalist movements emerged within the boundaries of the Soviet and Yugoslav successor states. For example, 96,000 Muslim Abkhaz in the northwestern corner of the former Soviet republic of Georgia fought successfully, with unofficial Russian assistance, to establish their own state. In October 1993 they decisively defeated the Georgian army and expelled most Georgian civilians from Abkhazia. Since then the Abkhaz are effectively independent of Georgian authority, though no other state recognizes their claim to be a sovereign state. To the east of Abkhazia, 164,000 Ossetians in northern Georgia sought to be united in a new state with 402,000 Ossetians who live in an autonomous region in southern Russia.[7] The term *micronationalism* is sometimes used to describe the independence movements of numerically small groups like these, although there is no minimum size required for statehood. Fifty-six of the UN's 190 member states have populations less than 1.5 million, the smallest being the Pacific island state of Tuvalu with 11,000 inhabitants.

Ethnonationalists usually have some kind of organized leadership and occupy substantial territory. Like the Ossetians, the Basques—who live in adjoining areas of France and Spain—and the Kurds, whose traditional homeland includes parts of five different states, more than half of ethnonationalist peoples straddle recognized international boundaries. Thus, political conflicts over autonomy are likely to have international repercussions. Wars for national independence attract military and political support from nearby states, stimulate similar movements in adjoining countries, and are the main source of international refugees. As a result, major powers and international and regional organizations often try to contain nationalist wars by encouraging negotiations, delivering humanitarian assistance, and sometimes—especially when conflicts threaten regional security—sending peacekeeping forces.

Indigenous Peoples

Indigenous peoples like Native Americans, New Zealand's Maori, and the Naga in India are also concerned about autonomy issues but differ from ethnonationalists in other respects. They are the descendants of the original inhabitants of conquered or colonized regions. Before their conquest, most indigenous peoples lived close to the land as subsistence farmers, herders, fisher folk, or hunters, and many still do. Until recently few had large scale political organizations or a strong sense of collective identity or purpose. Instead, in most countries indigenous peoples were divided among many separate clans or tribes that only gradually developed a larger group identity. Loss of land to settlers, discrimination in daily life, and resource exploitation by more technologically advanced people have been major causes of their growing sense of common identity and purpose.

The best-known indigenous groups are the native peoples of the eighteen countries of mainland North and South America. In the aggregate, the 38 million Native Americans (our 1998 estimate) comprise only 5 percent of the population of the Western Hemisphere, but in Bolivia, Guatemala, and Peru they make up 40 percent or more of the population. In Bolivia, Peru, and Ecuador they have become major political actors, using the electoral process to gain direct representation in governments and to shape decisions about indigenous issues.

There are also many indigenous peoples in Asia. Half a dozen large and politically active indigenous tribes live in northeast India and the borderlands of Bangladesh, among them the Naga, Mizos, and Tripura. In Southeast Asia serious conflicts have developed over the political demands of indigenous peoples like the Cordillerans ("mountain people," a label provided by Europeans) in the Philippines, the Karen and Shan peoples of the Burman uplands, and the native Papuans of the western, Indonesian-controlled half of the island of New Guinea.

Because most of them live in peripheral regions of modern states, these peoples—along with the Scandinavian Saami (who are called Lapps by outsiders), the Australian Aborigines, the cattle-herding Masai of East Africa, and others—have been called "peoples of the frontier." Similar themes are expressed repeatedly by their contemporary leaders: They want to protect what remains of their ways of life from what their advocates call ethnocide—that is, the destruction of their culture—and they seek to regain as much control as possible over their lands and resources.

For centuries, traditional peoples resisted dominant groups through sporadic and uncoordinated uprisings and attempts to migrate to more remote regions. After the League of Nations was established in 1919, a number of North American tribes and the Maori of New Zealand began to petition it and other international bodies for recognition of their rights. Before the 1950s, however only a handful of indigenous peoples secured significant political autonomy from Western-style governments. In New Zealand the Maori gained control of some traditional lands and obtained representation in the English settlers' parliament in 1867. The Miskito Indians of Nicaragua were recognized as constituting an autonomous state from 1860 to 1894. And the Kuna Indians of Panama gained local autonomy as the result of a rebellion in 1920.

By far the most important international development affecting indigenous peoples has been the global indigenous rights movement that took shape in the 1970s. The San Francisco-based International Indian Treaty Council (founded in 1974) and the World Council of Indigenous Peoples (1975) were the first of a growing number of influential nongovernmental bodies that provided a forum for discussions, publicity, and planning of joint action among representatives of indigenous peoples from all parts of the world. UN agencies also have established advisory groups concerned with indigenous issues. The most influential has been the UN Working Group on Indigenous Populations which since 1982 has convened frequent international meetings of indigenous representatives. It has prepared a Universal Declaration of Indigenous Rights, a step in the direction of gaining international legal recognition for groups that are typically not subject of *international law*.[8]

The indigenous people's movement has had great influence, first by encouraging political action by many previously passive local and regional groups, second by making forceful presentations to international bodies, most recently to the World Bank and the World Trade Organization. It has also directly or indirectly affected the policies of many governments toward indigenous peoples. National officials responsible for developing policies toward indigenous peoples meet with their local and international representatives with increasing frequency; their policy goals often change as a result. The indirect impact results from political actions inspired by the global movement, often in collaboration with environmental groups. The main weapons are protest: publicity campaigns directed toward the media and national parliaments, lawsuits against corporations extracting resources from indigenous lands, demonstrations, blockades of access roads, and land occupations. Their cumulative effect has been to soften public, corporate, and official resistance to indigenous demands in the countries in which they take place and to prompt similar protests, and obtain concessions, elsewhere.

Another kind of indirect effect is seen in the work of other international organizations. In the late 1980s, for example, the International Labor Organization (ILO) substantially revised its standards for the treatment of indigenous and tribal peoples. Member states of the ILO were asked to give greater attention to the collective rights and interests of these peoples and to grant them a voice in decision making about development plans that affected their homelands. The ILO is one of the oldest and arguably more progressive organizations within the framework of the United Nations. It has a built-in advantage in dealing with group issues because its membership includes both labor and corporate representatives in addition to governments. The Senate of Brazil, whose treatment of Amazonian peoples and their environment has attracted intense international scrutiny, finally ratified the ILO convention in June 2002, nine years after it was first introduced.[9]

Ethnoclasses

Ethnoclasses are ethnically or culturally distinct minorities who occupy distinct social strata and have specialized economic roles in the societies in which they now live. They are, in other words, ethnic groups who resemble classes. Most ethnoclasses in advanced industrial societies are descended from slaves or immigrants who did the hard and menial work scorned by the dominant groups. Examples include people of African descent in Britain and North America, the Turks in Germany, and Koreans in Japan. Upward mobility and policies of integration have eroded old ethnoclass barriers in Western Europe and North America but members of these and similar groups are still heavily concentrated in occupations at or near the bottom of the economic and social hierarchy.

In Third World societies ethnoclasses also have immigrant origins, but their members are more likely to be economically advantaged merchants and professionals who are subject to political restrictions. Examples include the Chinese minorities in most Southeast Asian countries and the Lebanese communities in postcolonial Africa.[10] There are at least fifty politically active ethnoclasses in the world today, and more are forming as a result of international migration from poor countries to wealthier ones.

Leaders who represent ethnoclasses seek to improve their status within an existing political system: They want greater economic opportunities, equal political rights, better public services. Some, such as the North African Muslims in France, the Koreans in Japan, and many African-Americans, are also concerned about protecting and promoting their peoples' cultural traditions. Unlike ethnonationalists, indigenous peoples, and communal contenders (discussed below), ethnoclasses are usually widely dispersed within a larger population. Even if they live in particular urban neighborhoods or rural villages, they rarely have a single territorial base or traditions of separate nationhood. Therefore, ethnoclasses seldom use the language or demands of nationalists; instead, they are preoccupied with receiving more equitable or favorable treatment from the larger society.

The formation of ethnoclasses continues to be shaped by international factors. The transnational movement of immigrants and refugees fleeing poverty and violence accelerated sharply in the 1990s and continued in the early years of the twenty-first century. Most of these people are visible minorities, which means that they are too easily singled out for special, often discriminatory treatment in their host countries. Few are likely to return to their homelands. In almost any town and village in western Germany, for example one can see—as the authors have on recent trips—people of African and Middle Eastern origin living side by side with native Germans. Host countries often try to smooth their acceptance but, as their numbers increase, the immigrants are the source of political contention and the targets of occasional acts of violence.

Communal Contenders

Communal contenders are ethnic groups whose main political aim is not to gain autonomy or to break through discriminatory barriers but, rather, to share political power. Communal contenders are the most prevalent kind of ethnopolitical group in African states and also in some of the more established states in the Middle East and Asia—like Lebanon, Pakistan, and Malaysia. The most close-to-home example for North Americans is Trinidad, where peoples of African and East Indian descent have jockeyed for political power since independence. In Lebanon, for example, the main contenders historically have been Maronite Christians and the Druze, a distinct Muslim sect. The Sunni Muslim community has been a moderating force in the communal politics of Lebanon; since the 1970s the Shi'i Muslim minority has become a major political actor.

In Lebanon, as in other plural societies, the government's political power has been based on coalitions among the leaders of major ethnic groups. The balance of power between Christians and Muslims in the coalition was spelled out in Lebanon's unwritten "National Pact," agreed to in 1943. In most states, including Lebanon, such arrangements have been informal and vulnerable to manipulation. Multiethnic coalitions are usually dominated by an advantaged group—like the Punjabis in Pakistan and the Malays in Malaysia—that uses a mix of concessions, co-optation, and sometimes repression to maintain its position. Such arrangements become unstable if and when one ethnic group's leader attempts to improve his or her relative position at the expense of others. If constitutional restraints and political guarantees are absent, and if other groups are unwilling to work out a new compromise, such conflicts can escalate into full-scale civil or revolutionary warfare. Recent examples of ethnic wars caused by the failure to establish or maintain multiethnic coalitions in societies have occurred in Lebanon, Sri Lanka, Sierra Leone, and Liberia. In some cases the ethnopolitical group that finds itself losing gives up hope of sharing power and shifts to a strategy of autonomy. This happened in Nigeria in 1967 when the Eastern Region, the home of most Ibos, proclaimed an independent Republic of Biafra and fought an unsuccessful war of secession.

War is not inevitable in such situations. By 1993 the white-dominated South African government had reluctantly but decisively accepted the right of other ethnic groups to participate in governance. The cooperation established between Nelson Mandela, the black nationalist leader, and the white establishment made it possible to establish a new multiracial political order and avoid widely feared civil war along ethnic lines.

Conflicts engaging communal contenders are highly susceptible to international involvement. During the Cold War era, the contenders sometimes became clients of the superpowers, as happened in Angola. The southern Ovimbundu people, represented by an organization called the National Union for the Total Independence of Angola (UNITA), relied on military and political assistance from the United States and South Africa during a fifteen-year war against a coalition of their ethnic rivals, led by the Mbundu people, who held power in the capital of Luanda. The Luanda government, in turn, was strongly supported by the Soviet and Cuban governments. Intense diplomatic efforts by the United Nations, the Organization of African Unity, and the United States throughout the 1980s attempted to defuse the conflict. An internationally brokered agreement among the rivals ended the fighting and led to a national election in 1992, but UNITA leaders rejected the results and were attacked by the government. By 1993 the country was again embroiled in a bitter and deadly civil war that did not wind down until 2002, following the death of UNITA founder Jonas Savimbi.

Dominant Minorities

We also should mention *dominant minorities*, a distinctive type of ethno-class that has historically been more common than it is at present. Dominant minorities are culturally distinct ruling groups like the Afrikaaners of South Africa, before 1993, and the Tutsi overlords who have governed the Hutu peasants of Burundi. Such minorities have used the powers of the state to maintain political and economic advantages over subordinate majorities. Not all members of dominant minorities benefit equally. Some working-class white Afrikaaners, for example, continue to be resentful of blacks' demands for equality. Iraq provides another example. Until the U.S.-led invasion of 2003, its ruling elite was a small clique from the Sunni Muslim minority, most of whom came from Saddam Hussein's hometown of Tikrit.

Conclusion

One of the most widely shared values of the modern world, one that is ratified in numerous international agreements on human rights, is the principle that people of all ethnic and religious backgrounds within each society should enjoy equal economic and political opportunities. This principle has motivated political movements that work for greater equality among disadvantaged peoples throughout the world. It has pushed many governments to reduce discrimination against ethnoclasses and indigenous peoples and has contributed to the toppling of minority-dominated governments throughout the European colonized world, from Algeria to Zanzibar. It also brings international pressures, both political and economic, to bear on dominant groups. Thus, countervailing international factors are at work. On the one hand, migration is creating new ethnoclasses; on the other, advantaged groups are being pressured to incorporate them on an equal basis with other classes and citizens.

The distinctions among the four types of groups are not rigid because the status of ethnic groups and the strategies of their leaders can change over time. An ethnoclass may gain enough power and self-confidence that its leaders shift from seeking equal rights for its members to demanding collective participation in government. Some African-American leaders in the United States have moved in this direction. Or an ethnonational group whose leaders at one time fought a breakaway war of secession may later be persuaded to join a governing coalition with other communal groups. This is the vision many outsiders have for Iraq now that Saddam Hussein's regime is toppled—a democratic coalition or federation of Kurds, the Shi'i community, and the Sunni Arabs. This illustrates the two most promising long-term strategies for accommodating the interests of large ethnopolitical groups. One is to persuade their leaders that it is in their interest to accept a share of power in the governing elite. The other, which can be used in combination with power-sharing, is to grant communal groups regional autonomy within a federal political system.

Religion and Ethnicity

The categories of ethnonationalists, indigenous peoples, communal contenders, and ethnoclasses enable us to compare and contrast most, but not all, politically active communal groups in the contemporary world. Much attention has been given in the past two decades to the resurgence of religious-based conflict, especially conflicts involving Muslims, but not exclusively so. Religion also has been an important identifier in communal conflicts in other world regions. The Protestants and Catholics of Northern Ireland are examples of warring communal groups who define themselves mainly in terms of religious beliefs.

However, there are significant differences in strategies and objectives among religious groups roughly comparable to differences among ethnic groups. Some religious groups work peacefully within existing polities while others are more inclined to use violence. For example, extreme Orthodox Jews in Israel and fundamentalist Christians in the West want to control most or all aspects of civil affairs. Islamists in the Arab world such as the Muslim Brotherhood typically want to achieve a more just order, i.e. government based on Shari'ah, or Islamic law. Jihadists (typically named after martyrs) and movements such as Hammas have revolutionary objectives to eliminate the Israeli state, analogous to the collusion of Jewish Orthodoxy and Zionism that aspires to a Greater Israel purified of Arabs. Al-Qaeda is the most dangerous kind of movement because it calls for cleansing the entire Muslim world of nonbelievers and Western influence. At present it has no counterpart among Christians, Jews, or Hindus.

It is important to recognize that many contemporary religious conflicts in and around the margins of the Islamic world arise not from opposition to the West but from the reassertion of traditional Islamic values in opposition to the values and often corrupt practices of secular governments. Most such conflicts occur between people with the same ethnic background, as, for example, in Jordan, Egypt, and Algeria, So-called fundamentalism is only likely to fuel *ethnic* conflict when the split between traditional Islamic and secular values coincides with ethnic divisions, as is the case in Sudan, where an Arab, traditional Islamic government in the north has attempted to impose an Islamic system of law and government on non-Muslim Africans in the south.[11]

The general principle, exemplified by the situation in Sudan, is that religious differences create a special intensity in conflicts between peoples when a dominant group attempts to impose rules based on its religious beliefs on others. But research done using the Minorities at Risk data (see note 1) show that differences of religion are seldom the only or the most important cause of ethnic conflict. Instead, religious differences usually combine with or reinforce ethnic conflicts that are based on nationality and class differences. For example, the Palestinians' conflict with Israel is first and foremost a nationalist one whose intensity is reinforced by religious differences. Similarly, Northern Ireland's Catholics are motivated in part by their subordinate class status and in part by a nationalistic desire to be united with the Republic of Ireland. A shared religion provides some of the social cement that holds these groups together.

Afghanistan under the rule of the Taliban helps illustrate the complex interplay of religion, ethnicity, and politics in the Islamic world. The Taliban were a Sunni Muslim sect motivated by a vision of a pure Islamic society. The Taliban's local supporters were limited mostly to the Pushtuns, the dominant majority in Afghanistan and a significant minority in western Pakistan, where the sect had its origins. It was opposed by Afghanistan's three other large communal groups: the Harzaris of central Afghanistan—Shi'i Muslims whom the Taliban branded as heretics—and the Tajiks and Uzbeks of northern Afghanistan. The Tajiks and Uzbeks practice a more relaxed form of Sunni Islam and are long-term rivals of the Pushtuns for influence in the central government. In brief, a traditional form of Islam provided the social cement for the Taliban's Pushtun-supported war to establish political control of Afghanistan, which was opposed by the Northern Alliance of three communal groups whose shared objectives were to protect their own territorial bases and thwart the Taliban/Pashtun threat. The U.S.-led campaign in 2001-2002 toppled the Taliban regime and curtailed the influence of militant Islam, but the communal and regional rivalries among the four groups remain. They will continue to drive Afghan politics for generations to come.

A contrasting case is Algeria, where Muslim radicals have indiscriminately attacked civilians in their quest to wrest power from the secular government. Ethnic divisions between Arabs and Berbers are largely irrelevant to this conflict.

Where We Go from Here

We have defined and discussed four major types of politically active ethnic groups in the contemporary world. The claims of ethnonationalists, who want greater autonomy or independence, pose the greatest dilemma for states and the international system; they are the source of some of the most deadly and protracted conflicts of the last half-century. The history of the Kurdish people illustrates both the group type and the issues at stake. Communal contenders who seek a greater share of power in existing states usually pursue their objectives through conventional politics but sometimes become involved in revolutionary wars when their ambitions cannot be met through other means. The Chinese in Malaysia provided the basis for a failed revolutionary movement in the 1950s; they now have a well-defined political and economic role within a multiethnic political system.

The other two important types of politically active ethnic groups are indigenous peoples and ethnoclasses, whose demands and actions are seldom a major threat to regional or international security. Nonetheless, their status is of serious concern to the international community: Most are more disadvantaged and suffer greater discrimination than any other groups in their societies, and domestic conflicts over their status often have important spillover effects that require attention from regional and international organizations.

Notes

1. The study is detailed in Ted Robert Gurr, *Peoples Versus States: Minorities at Risk in the New Century* (Washington, DC: U.S. Institute of Peace Press, 2000). Current information can be accessed on the project's website, www.cidcm.umd.edu/inscr/mar or, alternatively, www.mininoritiesatrisk.com. Five rules were used for identifying groups to be included in the study (1) Only countries with populations greater than 500,000 were analyzed; (2) only groups that numbered 100,000 or exceeded 1 percent of the population of a country were included; (3) ethnic groups that live in several adjoining countries were counted separately within each country; (4) divisions within an ethnic group in a country were not counted separately—for example, Native Americans in the United States were analyzed as one group, not as three hundred plus separate tribes; and (5) twenty-five minorities with political or economic advantages were included.
2. Quoted in "Clinton Seeks Foreign Policy Bearings in Post Cold War Fog," *Washington Post*, October 17, 1993, p. A28.
3. Based on conversations with the authors in Kusadasi, Turkey, June 1990.

4. This is based on Donald L. Horowitz's analysis of differences between ranked and unranked ethnic systems in his classic study, *Ethnic Groups in Conflict* (Berkeley: University of California Press, 1985).

5. In 1730, the Mediterranean island of Corsica rebelled against rule by the Italian Republic of Genoa, which sought assistance from its French allies, which in turn conquered and absorbed Corsica into the kingdom of France in the 1760s. The autonomous dukedom of Brittany was incorporated into revolutionary France in 1759.

6. Most of these "wars" are small-scale terrorist and guerrilla movements. A list of these groups and the status of their conflicts compiled by David Quinn appears in Monty G. Marshall Ted Robert Gurr, *Peace and Conflict 2003: A Global Survey of Armed Conflicts, Self-Determination Movements, and Democracy* (College Park, MD: Center for International Development and Conflict Management, University of Maryland, 2003), pp. 56-64.

7. Population figures are from the 1989 USSR census. The Soviet data on national peoples are approximately accurate, because all citizens were required to carry internal passports that specified their primary nationality. Estimates of the sizes of national and minority peoples in most Western societies are also relatively reliable. In Africa, the Middle East, and most of Asia and Latin America, the data are seldom more than estimates and are sometimes only guesses.

8. Information on developments in the indigenous peoples' movement is available from many websites. Especially useful is Native Web (www.nativeweb.org) and the website of the UN High Commission on Human Rights, with links to groups working on indigenous rights. An analysis of the origins of the movement is Franke Wilmer, T*he Indigenous Voice in World Politics: Since Time Immemorial* (Newbury Park, CA: Sage Publications, 1993). A new study of Amazonian peoples is Pamela L. Martin, *The Globalization of Contentious Politics: The Amazonian Indigenous Rights Movement* (New York: Routledge, 2002).

9. See International Labor Organization (ILO), *Partial Revision of the Indigenous and Tribal Populations Convention,* 1957 (no. 107), Report 6 (1 and 2*),* 75th Session (Geneva: International Labor Office, 1988). The new convention, no. 169, was adopted in 1989 but, like other ILO conventions, is not binding on member states. Rather, it sets a standard against which states labor policies toward indigenous peoples are judged by the international community. This summary is based on a research paper prepared by Jean-Carlos Rivera.

10. The Chinese in Malaysia meet our definition of communal contenders; other Chinese communities in Southeast Asia have been largely assimilated (Thailand, the Philippines). Palestinians are by and large a professional and commercial minority throughout the Middle East and also in Central America; on the latter, see Nancie Gonzalez, *Dollar, Dove and Eagle: 100 Years of Palestinian Emigration to Honduras* (Ann Arbor: University of Michigan Press, 1992).

11. Two comparative studies of ethnoreligious conflict in the Islamic world are Jonathan Fox, "Is Islam More Conflict-Prone Than Other Religions? A Cross-Sectional Study of Ethnoreligious Conflict," *Nationalism and Ethnic Politics* vol. 6 (Summer 2000), pp. 1-24; and Jonathan Fox, "Two Civilizations and Ethnic Conflict: Islam and the West," *Journal of Peace Research* vol. 38 (July 2001), pp. 459-472.

CHAPTER 24

EXCLUDED NEIGHBORHOODS

MARK GORNIK

On the day in 1980 when Baltimore's acclaimed Inner Harbor development opened with speeches and festivities, the *Washington Post* turned west
two miles to the neighborhood of Sandtown for urban contrast. The stalwart and
locally respected community leader Ella Johnson told the paper that Sandtown
"is just an inner city neighborhood . . . It's buried. A good block is where there
are less than five vacant houses."[1] Two decades later, many parts of Sandtown still
look this way. Such differences in a city can be assigned social, economic, and
political meaning. But as Augustine reminds us, ultimately such differences
in a city reflect a struggle between two competing spiritual visions of urban life,
and with it the nature of social arrangements.

Lots of good things are happening in Baltimore. There is a resurgence in
neighborhoods such as Canton, Federal Hill, and Locust Point, a new emphasis
on high-tech development in the Inner Harbor area, a strong and expanding
non-profit sector. And Baltimore has also had a succession of mayors who are
passionate about the city. It is a unique city that is seeking a better future. But we
need to keep things in perspective.

As David Rusk documents in his study *Baltimore Unbound*, the changes in
the city are related to as yet unchanging patterns of flight and abandonment,[2]
Since 1950, the population has dropped from nearly one million to around
630,000, the middle and upper classes having packed up and moved to the
suburbs. About a thousand people a month are still leaving the city. By most
counts, over 40,000 houses are abandoned, with scores of empty lots being
added as demolition crews tear their way across the city's row-house fabric.
Baltimore is the nineteenth largest city in the United States, but in 1999 it had the
second highest per-capita homicide rate. It made sense that the acclaimed television series *Homicide: Life on the Streets* was set in Baltimore. Only recently
has that high rate started (tentatively) to decline.[3] A Johns Hopkins researcher
found that, in terms of psychological damage, the children living in Baltimore's

inner city were more adversely affected than children living in war-torn Bosnia.[4] Observes the geographer David Harvey, "Baltimore is, for the most part, a mess. Not the kind of enchanting mess that makes cities interesting places to explore, but an awful mess."[5] Harvey is substantially right—which I say with great regret because of how much I love the city.

Like other cities, Baltimore is really two cities, and they relate to one another in surreal juxtaposition. The Baltimore most people know is filled with shiny office towers, new sports stadiums, luxury condominiums, and the Inner Harbor development, which is packed with theme restaurants and has a carnival-like atmosphere. The "other Baltimore" is off the tourist maps. It is the Baltimore represented by Sandtown, just two miles west of the Inner Harbor. This Baltimore has substandard houses, lots filled with trash, greasy carry-outs, liquor stores, and corner markets where sheets of cloudy bulletproof glass separate customer and merchant. Its visible economy includes the shopping cart filled with reclaimed cans. Here it is far easier to buy illegal drugs than it is to purchase fresh produce and reasonably priced groceries, far simpler to rent a substandard row house than to obtain a mortgage for a simple and decent one.

Underneath the brick, concrete, and steel skin of these two worlds, the trajectories of social and economic inequalities run even deeper. When it comes to education, health care, employment networks, housing conditions, municipal services, and political influence in Baltimore, Sandtown's distance from the center is far—and growing. Private schools serve the one Baltimore, failing schools the other. World-class hospitals treat one population, a shrinking number of clinics and overworked emergency rooms the other. Connection and opportunity abound in the one Baltimore, disconnection and adversity in the other.[6]

In this chapter I will seek to examine and understand how the 72-square-block community of Winchester, commonly referred to as Sandtown, came into being. I will do this first through a historical analysis. Following the historical analysis, I will propose a theological interpretation of the inner city.[7] I will conclude with a proposal for the inner city that emphasizes the story of salvation and the gracious reign of God.

Sandtown is unique, as is every city and urban community Each individual neighborhood has its own history, cultural identity, geographical relationships, and connections to larger spatial and social forces. Studies of specific neighborhoods are an important way to learn about cities and urban processes. By drawing on a wider body of literature, however, I hope to show that Sandtown is also emblematic of the changing inner city. Moreover, for all the differences between neighborhoods and cities, there are common threads of suffering and shared patterns of development.[8]

Let me also say that I have certain strong reservations about presenting Sandtown as a representative inner-city neighborhood. Sandtown is much more than a neighborhood on the margins—it is a community that people call home, where they form loving relationships, break bread together, create traditions, generate memories, and find shared meaning. It is a community where people share the same dreams as the rest of America—good jobs, decent schools, safe streets, and affordable housing. People not only share these dreams; they work hard to achieve them in both individual and collective ways. Sandtown is a place of life and hope, not just suffering and struggle. As Harold McDougall has pointed out, it is, like other African-American neighborhoods in Baltimore, a place where people are tenaciously building community.[9] Drawing attention to institutional forces that have historically caused oppression and harm to Sandtown (or any distressed urban community) does not take away from the humanity of people for whom it is home; it does not reduce the community to the status of victim. Sandtown is not "the problem," but the site where broader forces are at work constructing exclusion and distance.

How the story of the inner city is seen and told affects everything from a vision for ministry to public policy. The Hebrew prophets began their vocation with seeing the city through the eyes of the poor and the ways of justice. From this viewpoint, and its underlying assumptions about God, the prophets followed with analysis and critique. But accompanying the "tearing down" was also the creative and energizing "building and planting," as we find it in Jeremiah's call (Jer. 1:10).[10] Put another way, there cannot be an appreciation for what God's redemption means for the inner city without understanding what has gone wrong, nor can the gospel be announced with integrity without the identification and denunciation of social sin and injustice. Nor can we study the inner city without being challenged to engage in the reversal of its condition. Because I take it that an analysis of social arrangements influences the shape of faithful social and political activity, I order my reflection accordingly.

The Making of an Inner-city Neighborhood

The pre-history of the African-American inner city can be traced to America's "original sin" of slavery and the violent European quest to create a "New World." Often baptized in Christian ideology, this history set in motion subsequent manifestations of racial injustice and economic oppression that remain codified in various forms to this day.[11] Marking Sandtown's specific struggle is a history of three distinct yet overlapping periods of development. The first period begins at the start of the century and goes through World War II, the second corresponds to the postwar years of de-industrialization and the third follows the inner city into the present era of globalization. Each period retains continuities with the past, especially that of racial and economic inequality, but does so in changing forms.

Period One: The Segregated Inner City

Sandtown has its earliest beginnings in national demographic changes. Given the push of unemployment in the South and the pull of jobs in northern cities, more than "five million blacks . . . moved North during the seven decades starting in 1910."[12] For all that the city would mean negatively, it positively provided blacks with the room to be free in a manner that the South had not. The city was viewed as the "promised land,"[13] though it would not turn out be a city on a hill.

The Sandtown that we know today has its origins in the public decision of this era. According to historian Roderick N. Ryon, whose research on West Baltimore I am indebted to, "Segregationist values, notions that blacks should be separated and subordinate, prevailed throughout the country in these turn-of-the-century years, and Baltimore whites deemed the emerging black community of Old West Baltimore a tolerable, even useful city neighborhood."[14] This is what guided the development of Sandtown, in the heart of Old West Baltimore, as an African-American community. According to Ryon, Sandtown was first developed as a white, middle-class neighborhood, and it functioned that way from 1870 to 1900, when it attracted European immigrants. As the nineteenth century turned to the twentieth, the city's population growth and the mobility afforded whites by the streetcar led to the first in a series of demographic changes on Baltimore's western side.[15] When whites moved socially upward and thus moved to outlying communities, the neighborhoods they left behind became designated for the increasing number of southern blacks migrating to the city. By the end of World War II, Sandtown had become almost exclusively black, Fulton Avenue on the western boundary being perhaps the last major street to undergo a racial transition.

The pattern of residential segregation that created Sandtown was joined to the city's growth and development. With neighborhoods near the industrial jobs in the center of the city reserved for white immigrants only, black Baltimoreans were limited in neighborhood choices, and West Baltimore became a principal place to find housing.[16] This was to the advantage of many urban, affluent whites in nearby neighborhoods such as Bolton Hill, who then had easy access to low-wage black domestic workers.[17] With African Americans cordoned off in one part of the city, they could be, as Ryon points out, "restricted, controlled, watched over,"[18] while still able to contribute to the rise of the privileged and prosperous in other select parts of the city. Sandtown's families lived in overcrowded and substandard rental housing, sharing apartments, while the new white immigrants had more available options. At its peak in the 1940s, the population in Sandtown soared to an estimated 35,000 to 40,000 people.[19]

While poverty was extensive, employment opportunities existed, though they were largely unequal in pay and advancement possibilities when compared to that of their white counterparts. For many, low pay meant long hours, as Ryon points out: "Work, the sheer volume of it, dominated most people's lives."[20] Typically it took a combination of jobs to make ends meet, and blacks were still "last hired and first fired" in the low-paying and menial service sector and in industrial-related work. Local white-owned businesses would hire African Americans only for the most menial tasks.[21] This combination of circumstances usually led to a subsistence existence. However, during the Depression, finding a job was considerably more difficult. Even domestic workers found themselves laid off. Predictably, the effects of an economic downturn became magnified among the most vulnerable.

But racial and social oppression never meant surrender and subordination. West Baltimore's durable black churches were the centerpiece of civic leadership, mutual aid, and political protest.[22] Community pressure led to, for example, the construction of a new building for Frederick Douglass High School. (From 1925 until 1954, the school was located in the heart of Sandtown, serving as the only "colored high school" in the city. Among the prominent alumni of old Douglass are Thurgood Marshall and Cab Calloway.) In the 1930s, Sandtown residents joined together and successfully picketed nearby white businesses in the "Don't Buy Where You Can't Work" campaign, considered a prelude to the civil rights movement.[23] Care and concern for one another, virtues of resistance to the dehumanizing pressures of segregation, were forged in suffering and a common task of building community.[24]

Period Two: The Post-Industrial Inner City

When Martin Luther King Jr. was assassinated in 1968, it marked a social and psychological breaking point for many inner-city neighborhoods, and this was certainly true in Sandtown. Until King's death, there had been a growing sense of optimism in the community—and throughout black America—that the nation would achieve a greater level of justice and inclusion. But with King's death, such hopes seemed to die and be buried. The unrest that ensued in cities like Baltimore reflected a feeling of great loss and bitter frustration, a sense that change would be halted. Indeed, King's death provides a marker for the beginning of the second period of inner-city development, a set of circumstances and forces that had been growing since World War II and that would change life in the city profoundly.

In this period Sandtown entered a new zone of urban wreckage, and the accelerants were multiple in origin. More than ever, poverty was concentrated and opportunities were constricted.

During the decade that followed King's death, Sandtown lost nearly a quarter of its population. Those with more resources headed the trend of evacuation, taking with them social and job networks essential to the health of the community. By 1980, nearly one in every six buildings in Sandtown stood vacant.[25] Businesses closed, and churches became commuter congregations. The once-vibrant and bustling Pennsylvania Avenue, where the great theaters of old like the Royal once proudly stood, became a mix of small businesses, vacant buildings, and empty lots.

By 1990, Sandtown's official population had fallen below 11,000, and the count of vacant row houses hovered near the one-thousand mark, about one in every four houses. At the time, the median income was approximately $10,000.[26] The three elementary schools were in such chronic failure that a state takeover was a regular rumor.[27] The rates for both infant mortality and low birth weight were high enough for the federal government to fund an intensive intervention program. Over half the adult population that could work was unemployed, and perhaps only one in five of the young people between the ages of eighteen and twenty-one had a full-time job. As severe as the problems had been in the 1950s and 1960s, joblessness and struggle in Sandtown seemed to have increased by 1990.

These changes in Sandtown were directly related to wider developments in Baltimore. By the 1970s, the industrial and manufacturing job base of the city, critical to the economic health of neighborhoods such as Sandtown and the city as a whole, was in a free fall. Between 1970 and 1985, manufacturing jobs in Baltimore declined by 45 percent, and entry-level positions not requiring a high-school diploma by 46 percent; knowledge-based jobs requiring at least two years of college increased by 56 percent.[28] The virtual collapse of Baltimore's industrial base hemorrhaged the jobs that had once provided a foundation, no matter how modest and tenuous, for families in Sandtown. People in the neighborhood began giving up on finding formal work, and many left or never entered the formal labor market.

With the enactment of fair and open housing legislation in the 1960s, leaving Sandtown had become a viable option. Many parents, hoping that their children would take the step that they themselves could never have taken, urged them to move out of the neighborhood. It wasn't that the inside of the neighborhood as a community was considered "bad," lifetime resident LaVerne Stokes recalled, but rather that staying "seemed to mean missing out on progress." After all, this was what all citizens of America wanted—the dream of basic rights, opportunities, and responsibilities. Although Sandtown was home, it held bitter memories of the indignities and assaults of segregation.

As the neighborhood's population declined, landlords abandoned their properties. Various forms of redlining (withholding home-loan funds or insurance because the neighborhood was considered an economic risk) increased. Simultaneously, "blockbusting," a real-estate practice that artificially induced the fear of black relocations into white neighborhoods, created panicked selling in nearby areas. The flight of whites opened up adjacent city neighborhoods such as Edmondson Village to the newly mobile black population, quickening the pace of change.[29] Evidence of these population shifts were seen not only in the vacant houses but also in the large churches on Sunday morning. Once neighborhood churches, they became filled with commuter worshipers, the streets packed with their cars.

Along with the economic and demographic changes overtaking Baltimore, Sandtown was significantly impacted by local, regional, and national politics. It is frequently observed that if America had a real urban policy in the postwar years, it was to subsidize the suburbs.[30] Underwritten by government mortgage programs, infrastructure investment, and transportation programs, each wave of suburban sprawl played a heavy role in accelerating the downward turn of conditions in America's cities, Baltimore included. All around the city suburbs grew. New housing demanded new roads. So highway construction was undertaken to ease suburban commuting back to the center of the city for the high-paying jobs. In fact, it cut a hole through West Baltimore. And as the suburbs drained out the urban population, the tax base followed. Political Influence and power shifted to the suburbs as well. Following the population patterns, hospitals and businesses closed in the city to reopen in the suburbs.

One does not have to look hard to see serious shortcomings, failures, and even tragedies in government-driven "urban renewal" and social programs born in the 1960s.[31] But while social policies did not end urban poverty, they hardly caused the crisis facing the inner city, and in many cases they significantly helped people. Head Start, for example, is widely regarded as a positive accomplishment. But such accomplishments were undercut by the war in Vietnam, which drew attention and resources away from inner cities. Later, when support from Washington for cities began to dry up under the "New Federalism" of the 1980s, American cities in general had almost disappeared from the national agenda.[32] What made matters worse in the 1980s was the crack epidemic, with its personal destruction and accompanying violence, which joined the list of crises confronting cities.

The broader story of how Sandtown faced new structural obstacles to the flourishing of life has been well and perhaps best told by William Julius Wilson, a sociologist now at Harvard University. Wilson is perhaps the leading theorist on inner-city dislocations, and his analysis has significantly influenced how scholars and policymakers understand neighborhoods of concentrated poverty. In *The Truly Disadvantaged* (1987)[33] and *When Work Disappears: The World of the New Urban Poor* (1996),[34] Wilson traces the course of major economic and demographic forces that generated the post-industrial inner city, particularly in the "Rust Belt," the northeastern and midwestern regions of the country where heavy industry has declined. Because Wilson's analysis helps illuminate the issues facing Sandtown in very significant ways, I will summarize his main arguments.[35]

As the title *When Work Disappears* suggests, the most substantial factor for Wilson in understanding the inner city is the post-industrial disappearance of work.[36] Drawing on data from Chicago as well as other cities, Wilson identifies a "new urban poverty." He defines the stricken areas as "poor, segregated neighborhoods in which a substantial majority of individual adults are either unemployed or have dropped out of the labor force altogether."[37] Due to post-industrial economic restructuring, scores of factories closed, and many of the remaining manufacturing operations moved overseas. New jobs were being created in suburban neighborhoods, but the potential inner-city worker had few reliable ways to get there. Hence, what labor economists called a "mis-match" developed between the location of workers and the location of employers.[38] The jobs that were being created in cities and that paid well increasingly required advanced degrees and training, leaving out the vast majority of inner-city residents, who had been limited by the failing educational system. Service-sector jobs remained, but actual wages were declining, and the work was typically occasional. Perhaps even more importantly, the informal networks that generate employment leads and placement faded away, creating a growing disconnection from the formal labor market.

Why is the absence of work so destructive to a community? Following Pierre Bourdieu, Wilson concludes that work "is not simply a way to make a living and support one's family. It also constitutes a framework for daily behavior and patterns of interaction because it imposes disciplines and regularities."[39] Employment sets goals and helps give structure to life, family, and community.[40] Especially in our capitalistic society, where identity is measured by economic and individual success, the absence of work brings shame and discouragement. Since our society also defines identity by individual success, the absence of meaningful employment corrodes a sense of self and, by extension, family and community. To feel unable to support a family and the wider community—which is what occurs with the structural absence of work in the inner city—can severely constrain the manner in which one thinks, feels, and acts with respect to the future. The effects of this in Sandtown have been severe.

With the closure of "the opportunity structure," as Wilson calls it, came a cascade of social changes to neighborhoods.[41] As the number of men who were "eligible" to marry—or could even view the future in optimistic terms—declined, the family structure in the inner city was shattered. Welfare rolls expanded, poverty increased, and crime rose. Identifying problems in the inner city as "related" but not "specific" to the context, Wilson assigns them to larger cultural practices, yet with more painful consequences in jobless neighborhoods.[42] As Wilson points out, social and familial breakdown in the inner city "ought not to be analyzed as if it were unrelated to the broader structure of opportunities and constraints that have evolved over time."[43] This does not mean that Wilson grants no place to the role of race.[44] His research in Chicago points to the prevalence of stereotypes in hiring practices, especially related to black males.[45] However, while race played a continuing factor in inner-city poverty, Wilson stresses that it is the macro-economic forces that had become most significant.

Wilson's view on inner-city poverty is not without its difficulties. These arise from implicit assumptions he made, at least in his earlier work, concerning the role of culture and morality in relationship to poverty and the meaning of human behavior. Another issue of dispute, as Brett Williams has pointed out, is Wilson's choice to center his argument on the employment history of men, thus gendering work and family.[46] Additionally, Wilson's focus on the unemployed may have had the unintended effect of relegating to a minor role the working residents of the inner city who have found jobs, although they may be low-paying and tenuous.[47]

While such criticisms need to be taken seriously and modifications made where needed, Wilson's central narration on the process of post-industrial inner-city development is accurate and extraordinarily helpful in comprehending the challenges confronting Sandtown and other communities like it in this period. The post-segregation outflow of residents with resources to less distressed (but no less segregated) urban and suburban neighborhoods, the abandonment of the inner city by all levels of government, the disappearance of meaningful employment for men and women—all combined to send Sandtown into a new spiral of agony. The result was brokenness in family structures and in the world of employment, and serious damage to the fabric of community.

In summary, the inner city in the post-industrial period was not created by the character flaws of the people who live there or by the welfare system, but by the searing dynamics of economy, place, and race.[48] The result was a community in economic depression, isolated and excluded from opportunity. Life in its fullness was more deeply diminished.

Period Three: The Global Inner City

What happens around the world impacts the inner city. Beyond post-industrialism and what Wilson terms "the end of work," Sandtown now has joined every other American inner city and barrio in being drawn into a third phase of development, what can be called the "global inner city."[49] Globalization has come to mean many things. Here I am using it to describe a market economy and cultural forms that move with incredible power and speed throughout the world. On a global scale, this economy produces new winners and losers. Either you are connected to the wired world or you are not. Globalization does not merely impact cities but takes place through them, as Saskia Sassen persuasively argues. Globalization is based in cities, and particularly in the world-class cities such as London, New York, and Tokyo, where the highly specialized tasks of the new economy have become centered.[50] Such cities form the "circuits" of the new economy, Sassen contends, the physical sites that are essential for the complex of its activities.

Globalization has produced not only changes in cities but new differences between cities. Baltimore has not benefitted from the global economy in the way certain other cities have. As a result, Sandtown's present and future increasingly reflect some of the most negative social realities of globalization. In Baltimore, like every other city, most good jobs in the new economy require a highly developed set of knowledge-based skills for which Sandtown residents have not been trained. Current public policies and resources do not suggest this will become a priority. So the jobs being created for the poor are low-wage jobs in areas such as cleaning, food service, and maintenance. The city needs these jobs to keep the sectors producing higher wages operating. A new class division is therefore becoming deeply embedded in the urban landscape. This means a steady stream of low-paying jobs for the "right kind of person" from Sandtown, but usually without health benefits, retirement plans, job security, or potential for long-term advancement. Mixed in with these factors is the reality of the end of welfare and a decreasing social safety net. The new economy has "demanded" this.

Global changes have reinvented the business sector in another way. Major corporations, which had often demanded and received subsidies to stay in the city, have shrunk through mergers and consolidation. In Baltimore, the consequences have been dire: the city has lost almost all of its corporate headquarters in the past few years. Such corporate consolidations are already adding to the tears in the fabric of neighborhoods. Banking provides just one of many examples.

Banking mergers have reduced not only the number of employees in a city but also the presence of "redundant" bank branches. And so scores of area neighborhoods have no local banks or access to their financial services. Sandtown shares one tiny branch with other neighborhoods. Climbing transaction fees have left many in the inner city feeling unwanted by the banks, anyway. Fringe banking institutions such as check-cashing outlets are filling the void, but users face exploitative prices and limited services. More critically, credit for housing and business development is hard to find, and will be nearly nonexistent in a credit crunch. Additionally, since corporations have fewer community roots, corporate giving and civic leadership have declined significantly

As Baltimore becomes faced with its new future, the city is turning to the expansion of an already important tourist trade for economic security.[51] Numerous new hotels are underway or planned for construction along the once-industrial waterfront. The Walt Disney Corporation, Barnes and Noble, ESPN, and Planet Hollywood are among the recent players in downtown development. This is not the first time Baltimore has turned in this direction; the city helped pioneer downtown revitalization in the 1980s.[52] But as with the past spurts of downtown redevelopment, any translation of current projects to living-wage employment for Sandtown residents is modest.[53]

William Julius Wilson identifies three key problem areas for the inner city associated with the global economy: employment, training, and wages.[54] The dictum of "last hired and first fired" will be lethal to the community when the global monetary system convulses, as it did in 1997 and 1998. Low-wage and temporary jobs disappear just as easily as they appear. It is also unlikely that necessary training will take place to give inner-city workers access to a higher level of opportunity and occupation. Nor have wages kept up with the cost of living. Community institutions, hollowed out during the post-industrial transformation between the 1970s and the 1990s, face new vulnerability even as their importance has grown under the architectonic forces of global capitalism. All of this negatively impacts upon family and community stability.

In the end, far too many young men in Sandtown have found the period of the new economy to be only a growth era of incarceration. It is a shattering reality that so many African-American men are caught up in the criminal justice system. Economic redundancy married to globalization has resulted in social control as the dominant urban policy. When "peace" really means order, not public safety, then the global inner city becomes the incarcerating inner city. This is not the final word on the global inner city, on Baltimore or Sandtown. But it returns the neighborhood to where it started—working hard with a constricted horizon and being, in Roderick Ryon's words, "restricted, controlled, watched over."

Notes

1. Saundra Saperstein, "Sandtown Typical of Urban Blight," *Washington Post,* 2 July 1980, pp. Bl, 2. Throughout this chapter, I use the shortened name "Sandtown" rather than its longer official name, Sandtown-Winchester.

2. Rusk, *Baltimore Unbound: A Strategy for Regional Renewal* (Baltimore: The Abell Foundation, 1996).

3. Peter Hermann, "Fewer Than 300 Homicides at Last," *Sun Spot* (on-line *Baltimore Sun*), 1 January 2001.

4. Marego Athans, "Psychological Poverty" *The Sun,* 29 June 1999, E-l, 7.

5. Harvey, *Spaces of Hope* (Berkeley: University of California Press, 2000), p. 133.

6. There are limits, of course, to the helpfulness of the dual-city metaphor; for one thing, it reduces the complexity of the situation. Yet it is helpful in viewing the urban landscape in moral, economic, political, and spatial terms.

7. Nicholas Wolterstorff has stressed the importance of "theologically faithful economics" rather than a "theology of economics" in "Public Theology or Christian Learning?" in A *Passion for God's Reign: Theology, Christian Learning, and the Christian Self,* ed. Miroslav Volf (Grand Rapids: Eerdmans, 1998), pp. 76-77. I am in full agreement with this view of Christian learning, and share Wolterstorff's concern about "theologians" stepping in where others should tread. However, too few economists, Christian or otherwise, have taken up the cause of faithful economics in service of the poor. The poor cannot wait for Christian economists to produce work that will adequately serve them. It is also the case that essential "learning" about the inner city comes only through the experience and the viewpoint of the community. The issue is one of epistemology. The history of the subject in the social sciences, as Alice O'Connor shows in *Poverty Knowledge: Social Science, Social Policy, and the Poor in Twentieth-Century U.S. History* (Princeton: Princeton University Press, 2001), has produced little more than problematic results.

8. Camilo Jose Vergara has spent twenty years examining "ghettos" across the nation, and has gathered his findings in *The New American Ghetto* (New Brunswick: Rutgers University Press, 1995). He identifies three contemporary types of ghettos: "green ghettos," characterized by depopulation, vacant land overgrown by nature, and ruins; "institutional ghettos," which are publicly financed places of confinement designed mainly for the native born; and the "new immigrant ghettos," which derive their character from an influx of immigrants, mainly Latino and West Indian. Vergara finds all three types to be interconnected, "channeling people and land to one another" (pp. 14-20).

9. McDougall, *Black Baltimore: A New Theory of Community* (Philadelphia: Temple University Press, 1993).

10. Brian J. Walsh, *Subversive Christianity: Imaging God in a Dangerous Time* (Bristol: Regius Press, 1992), p. 36; Walter Brueggemann, *The Prophetic Imagination* (Minneapolis: Fortress, 1978).

11. For a history of the African-American experience, see *To Make Our World Anew:History of African Americans,* ed. Robin D. G. Kelley and Earl Lewis (New York: Oxford University Press, 2000).

12. Vergara, *The New American Ghetto,* p. 4.

13. Milton C. Sernett, *Bound for the Promised Land: African American Religion and the Great Migration* (Durham: Duke University Press, 1997).

14. Ryon, "Old West Baltimore," *Maryland Historical Magazine 77,* no. 1 (Sprint 1982): 55.

15. This theme of the streetcar and urban transportation is important for Ryon's history of West Baltimore.

16. Ryon, "Old West Baltimore," p. 55.

17. Ryon, "Old West Baltimore," p. 55.

18. Ryon, "Old West Baltimore," p. 55.
19. Ryon, "Old West Baltimore," p. 62; and Ryon, *West Baltimore Neighborhoods: Sketches of Their History, 1840-1960* (Baltimore: The Institute for Publications Design of the University of Baltimore, 1993), p. 124.
20. Ryon, "Old West Baltimore," p. 61.
21. Ryon, "Old West Baltimore," pp. 60-61.
22. Ryon, "Old West Baltimore," p. 63.
23. Ryon, "Old West Baltimore" p. 63. For a history, see Karen Olson, "Old West Baltimore: Segregation, African-American Culture, and the Struggle for Equality," in *The Baltimore Book: New Views of Local History,* ed. Elizabeth Fee, Linda Shopes, and Linda Zeidman (Philadelphia: Temple University Press, 1991), pp. 57-78.
24. Studies that address the interrelated processes that led to this phase of inner-city development include Gregory D. Squires, *Capital and Communities in Black and White: The Intersections of Race, Class, and Uneven Development* (Albany: State University of New York Press, 1994); Thomas J. Sugrue, "The Structures of Urban Poverty: The Reorganization of Space and Work in Three Periods of American History," in *The Underclass Debate: Views from History,* ed. Michael B. Katz (Princeton: Princeton University Press, 1993), pp. 85-117, and more expansively, *The Origins of the Urban Crisis: Race and Inequality in Postwar Detroit* (Princeton: Princeton University Press, 1996); Michael B. Katz, *Improving the Poor: The Welfare State, The "Underclass" and Urban Schools as History* (Princeton: Princeton University Press, 1993), pp. 77-82; Leonard Wallock, "The Myth of the Master Builder: Robert Mose New York, and the Dynamics of Metropolitan Development Since World War II," *Journal of Urban History* 17, no. 4 (August 1991): 339-62. Perhaps most important has been the work of William Julius Wilson, which I explore below.
25. These statistics come from the report "Sandtown-Winchester," Planning Division: Baltimore City Department of Housing and Community Development, 27 August 1982.
26. "1990 Community Profiles, Baltimore City: Demographic, Housing, Health, Educational, Income, Public Assistance and Crime Data by Census Tracts," Baltimore City Department of Planning, March 1992.
27. This finally came true in 2000, when one of the schools was taken over by a for-profit educational company.
28. Marc E. Levine, "Economic Development to Help the Underclass," *The Sun,* 10 January 1988, pp. E-1, 3.
29. A comprehensive accounting of this can be found in W. Edward Orser, *Blockbusting in Baltimore; The Edmondson Village Story* (Lexington: University Press of Kentucky, 1994).
30. On this wider history, see Kenneth T. Jackson, *Crabgrass Frontier: The Suburbanization of the United States* (New York: Oxford University Press, 1985).
31. Fred Siegel makes this argument in *The Future Once Happened Here: New York, D.C., L.A., and the Fate of America's Big Cities* (New York: The Free Press, 1997). For an important account of the period's dilemmas, see Vincent J. Cannato, *The Ungovernable City: John Lindsay and His Struggle to Save New York* (New York; Basic Books, 2001).
32. For an overview, see Demetrios Caraley, "Washington Abandons the Cities," *Political Science Quarterly* 107 (Spring 1992): 1-30.
33. See Wilson, *The Truly Disadvantaged: The Inner City the Underclass, and Public Policy* (Chicago: University of Chicago Press, 1987), especially chapters 2-4. These themes are also discussed in Loïc J. D. Wacquant and William Julius Wilson, "The Cost of Racial and Class Exclusion in the Inner City," *The Annals of the American Academy of Political and Social Science* 501 (January 1989): 8-25.
34. Wilson, *When Work Disappears: The World of the New Urban Poor* (New York: Alfred A. Knopf, 1996).

35. For developments in Wilson's views, see Wilson, *The Bridge over the Racial Divide: Rising Inequality and Coalition Politics* (Berkeley: University of California Press, 1999); and Teodros Kiros, "Class, Race, and Social Stratification: An Interview with William Julius Wilson" New *Political Science* 21, no. 3 (September 1999): 405-15.
36. Wilson, *When Work Disappears,* pp. 3-50.
37. Wilson, *When Work Disappears,* p. 19.
38. For a review of the literature, see John Kain, "The Spatial Mismatch: Three Decades Later," *Housing Policy Debate* 3, no. 2 (1992): 371-460.
39. Wilson, *When Work Disappears,* p. 73.
40. It seems to me that Wilson is recognizing one interpretive strand of a secularized Puritan view of calling and vocation. At the very least, Wilson suggests how having work that meets certain cultural definitions can become a means of achieving "salvation."
41. Wilson, *When Work Disappears,* pp. 51-110.
42. Wilson, *When Work Disappears,* p. 56.
43. Wilson, *When Work Disappears,* p. 55.
44. Wilson, *When Work Disappears, pp.* 111-46. Some suggested that Wilson was saying this when he published *The Declining Significance of Race: Blacks and Changing American Institutions,* 2d ed. (Chicago: University of Chicago Press, 1980). For his response, see Wilson, *the Truly Disadvantaged.*
45. Wilson, *When Work Disappears,* pp. 111-46. See further Joleen Kirschenman and Kathryn M. Neckerman, "'We'd Love to Hire Them, But . . .': The Meaning of Race for Employer," in *The Urban Underclass,* ed. Christopher Jencks and Paul E. Peterson (Washington, D.C.: The Brookings Institution, 1991), pp. 203-32; and Philip Moss and Chris Tilly, *Stories Employers Tell: Race, Skill, and Hiring in America* (New York: Russell Sage Foundation, 2001).
46. Williams, "Poverty Among African Americans in the Urban United States," *Human Organization* 51, no. 2 (1992): 164-74.
47. See Katherine S. Newman, *No Shame in My Game: The Working Poor in the Inner City* (New York: Alfred A. Knopf, 1999).
48. Wilson's work, especially *The Truly Disadvantaged,* can be understood, in part at least, as a response to Charles Murray's *Losing Ground: American Social Policy, 1950-1980* (New York: Basic Books, 1984). Murray conjured up a picture of inner-city dislocations causally linked to the rise of welfare, a position embraced by then-president Ronald Reagan. Clearly I think that Wilson is right and Murray is very wrong.
49. Carl Husemoller Nightingale, "The Global Inner City: Toward a Historical Analysis," in *W. E. B. DuBois, Race, and the City: The Philadelphia Negro and Its Legacy,* ed. Michael B. Katz and Thomas Sugrue (Philadelphia: University of Pennsylvania Press, 1998), pp. 217-58; Manuel Castells, *The Information Age; Economy, Society, and Culture,* vol. 3: *End of Millennium,* 2d ed. (Oxford: Blackwell, 2000), pp. 128-52.
50. Sassen has provided a powerful accounting of this in *The Global City: New York, London, Tokyo* (Princeton: Princeton University Press, 1991), and *Globalization and Its Discontents; Essays on the New Mobility of People and Money* (New York: The New Press, 1998).
51. *The Tourist City,* ed. Dennis R. Judd and Susan S. Fainstein (New Haven: Yale University Press, 1999).
52. For a view of Baltimore's first downtown renewal through the eyes of one of its primary leaders, see C. Fraser Smith, *William Donald Schaefer: A Political Biography* (Baltimore: The Johns Hopkins University Press, 1999).
53. Marc V. Levine, "Downtown Redevelopment as an Urban Growth Strategy: A Critical Appraisal of the Baltimore Renaissance," *Journal of Urban Affairs* 9, no. 2 (1987): 103-23.
54. Wilson, *When Work Disappears,* pp. 152-55.

Part V
Environmental Hope

PART M
WATER AND SANITATION

Walking along the dirt paths of the garbage community in Cairo, Egypt, my friend Mark and I happened upon Angel, an eleven-year-old friend whom we had gotten to know in the children's program run by our summer mission team. Angel and three of her friends were returning from the local water tap, toting five-gallon buckets of water on their heads. Mark and I were eager to help (and just a little uncomfortable as healthy adult men walking effortlessly alongside these little girls carrying such heavy loads). With a burst of objection from the girls and breaking all the cultural rules that insist guests in the community should not carry the host's load, Mark and I grabbed the buckets and began to lug them to Angel's home. I'm not sure what was more embarrassing: walking next to the girls without assisting them or struggling and grimacing while spilling large amounts of water, carrying the buckets that they so easily balanced on their heads. There was a flurry of angry Egyptian Arabic when we arrived at her home, as Angel's mother seemed to scold her for allowing the foreign guests to do her chore. Angel's mom quickly invited us to sit down in the dark, one-room, concrete hovel while she dipped some of the water out of the bucket and placed it in a pot sitting atop a propane Bunsen burner to prepare the ever-present cup of tea. Angel had a large family and I wondered how often she had to make her barefoot journey through the trash to the community tap, since the average person needs more than a gallon of water a day.

Only one-half of one percent of the water on our planet can be considered available, fresh drinking water. And the consumption of water is increasing at twice the rate of population growth.[1] In densely populated human settlements, there is not only a concentrated need for fresh water but also a correspondingly high concentration of human waste, often introducing contaminants into the available water supply. Ways must be explored to get clean water into slum communities and get the waste out.

A South African company called Roundabout Outdoor has created an innovative solution to increase the clean water supply in poor communities. The company installs merry-go-rounds, or roundabouts, that pump water from a well into a 5,000-liter storage tank. Not only does this provide some recreation for the children in poor communities who rarely see playground equipment but it harnesses their natural energy at play to provide water for them and their families. The costs of installing and maintaining the pumps are covered by the private sector who pay to advertise on the side of the two-story-high tank.

Another innovation tested in the slum community of Kibera in Nairobi, Kenya, is the Vacu-tug. This little, three-by-five-foot device is comprised of a 500-liter tank sitting on a four-wheel frame and powered by a small gas engine. The Vacu-tug will evacuate the solid waste of overflowing pit latrines that characterize many slum communities. It is much smaller than the conventional waste-removal trucks, easy to operate, and requires very little capital to build. An enterprising group of slum dwellers can set up a business that not only generates income but relieves the community of the human-waste problem that so often compromises the health of the poor.

The two readings provided here give an excellent overview to the problems of obtaining clean water and disposing of waste that wreak havoc in so many urban slum communities. The impact of water and sanitation on health and the disproportionate burden borne by women and children are examined.

Unless servants to the urban poor who possess education, creativity, and technical expertise develop a knowledge of the unique water and waste problems in slum communities, those who live in slums and lack the opportunity and resources to obtain an education in water and waste management will be doomed to remain in unlivable conditions.

Notes

1. Maude Barlow, "Water Incorporated," *Earth Island Journal* (San Francisco: Earth Island Institute) 17, no. 1 (Spring 2002).

CHAPTER 25

WATER AND SANITATION

CHRISTOPHE BOSCH, KIRSTEN HOMMANN, GLORIA RUBIO, CLAUDIA SADOFF, AND LEE TRAVERS

Introduction

Approximately 1.3 billion people in the developing world lack access to adequate quantities of clean water, and nearly 3 billion people are without adequate means of disposing of their feces. An estimated 10,000 people die every day from water- and sanitation-related diseases, and thousands more suffer from a range of debilitating illnesses. The impact of inadequate water and sanitation services falls primarily on the poor. Badly served by the formal sector, the poor make their own, often inadequate, arrangements to meet basic survival needs. Many fetch water from long distances or end up paying high prices to water vendors for very small quantities of water.

The clear need for basic water and sanitation services for the poor assumes even greater significance when the linkages with other dimensions of poverty are considered. Water- and sanitation-related sicknesses put severe burdens on health services and keep children out of school. Human waste poses a tremendous social cost through pollution of rivers and groundwater. Figure 25.1 shows how lack of water and sanitation affects poverty through these and other linkages.

Despite significant investments in the sector in recent decades made by governments, nongovernmental organizations (NGOs), bilateral and multilateral agencies, and the private sector, the outlook for access to safe and adequate supplies of water and environmentally sustainable sanitation remains grim. Coverage varies substantially by country, but well over one-third of rural populations in most lower income countries lacks access to safe water or sanitation. This is despite water being consistently identified as a basic need and a top priority by those who lack convenient or affordable access to it. National

Figure 25.1 Linkages between Poverty and Water and Sanitation

	Poverty dimensions	Key effects
Lack of water sanitation and hygiene	Health	• Water- and sanitation-related illnesses • Stunting from diarrhea-caused malnutrition • Reduced life expectancy
	Education	• Reduced school attendance by children (especially girls) resulting from ill health, lack of available sanitation, or water collection duties
	Gender and social inclusion	• Burdens borne disproportionately by women, limiting their entry into the cash economy
	Income / consumption	• High proportion of budget used on water • Reduced income-earning potential because of poor health, time spent collecting water, or lack of opportunity for businesses requiring water inputs • High consumption risk because of seasonal or other factors

indicators on access to safe water and adequate sanitation are compiled by the United Nations.

Lack of access arises both from income shortages and the specific cultural, economic, regulatory, and institutional environment prevailing in the country in question. An urban household located in an informal settlement may not be connected to the piped water system because it does not have the property rights to the land it occupies, preventing the utility from building fixed assets on illegally inhabited land. Among the rural or urban poor, lack of a political voice may prevent their needs from being heard by those in charge of allocating the funds earmarked for water supply and sanitation improvements. In other situations, it may be man-made pollution of water bodies and aquifers that limits easy and less costly access to safe water resources. Without major consumption sacrifices, the poor cannot afford the costs of treatment and the technologies that extract water from deeper aquifers. Although both poorer and higher income segments of the population may face the same polluted resources or inadequate services, higher income households can afford private solutions to these problems—solutions too expensive for the poor population.

This chapter describes possible elements of a contribution by water and sanitation to a national Poverty Reduction Strategy. It highlights the pathways through which water and sanitation services influence poverty status. And it stresses the importance of understanding exactly how the poor use water and sanitation services, and the fact that among the poor such use may vary by region and by rural, town, and urban status, in addition to gender, ethnicity, and depth of poverty. In this complex environment, devising an effective strategy that reaches the target groups will require consultation with those groups. Everyone, no matter what their poverty status, has water and sanitation services. But service levels vary tremendously, even within the broad category of the poor. Some differences in service levels, such as supply pressure, are matters of convenience, but others, such as pathogen loads in drinking water or latrines to isolate feces from human contact, fundamentally affect the health, education, and other attributes that exacerbate or ease poverty. A Poverty Reduction Strategy will focus on the latter aspects of water and sanitation service.

Most rural people and, in most countries, the bulk of the urban poor rely on private provision to meet their water and sanitation needs. Indeed, recent evidence strongly indicates that publicly provided water and sanitation services repeatedly fail to provide efficient service or reach the poorest segments of the population. Any water and sanitation strategy will need to recognize and be built around the centrality of private provision.

Figure 25.2 The Main Pathways of Human Exposure to Pathogens in the Aquatic Environment

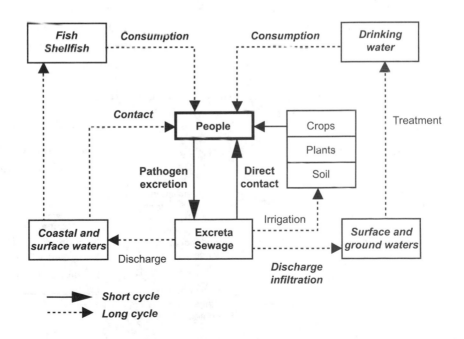

Poverty, Water, and Sanitation: Understanding the Links

Inadequate water and sanitation services to the poor increase their living costs, lower their income earning potential, damage their well-being, and make life riskier. The continuing, nearly universal deterioration of the surface and underground water sources on which people survive means that water and sanitation pressures will simply become worse in the future.

This section seeks to improve understanding of the impact of the lack of water and sanitation on different poverty dimensions. Once the impacts are known and their relevance assessed in a given community or country, priorities for intervention can be decided.

Health effects

The classical mechanisms of transmission of waterborne diseases are poor personal hygiene, described as the "short cycle" (excreta -> hand -> mouth), and environmental pollution, described as the "long cycle." Figure 25.2 highlights these cycles. Typically, physical investments in community sanitation most effectively break the long cycle. Breaking the short cycle requires changes in personal behaviors and practices, which present a more difficult challenge.

Diarrhea accounts for nearly 30 percent of the burden of childhood communicable disease, with an estimated 2.2 million child deaths annually and a much larger number of children (and adults) suffering from illnesses. Repeated bouts of diarrhea contribute to malnutrition. Water and sanitation—and hygiene—are intimately related to diarrheal diseases. The interactions are complex, but adequate quantities of water, even low-quality water, are necessary if people are to adopt the hygienic habits needed to break the disease transmission pathway.

Figure 25.3 Effects of Water and Sanitation Interventions on Health

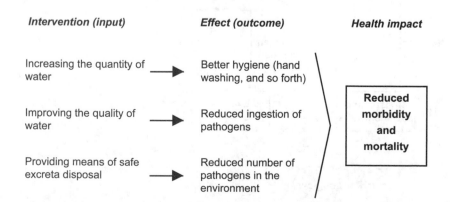

Just as everyone needs water daily, everyone, rich and poor, defecates and urinates daily. But where that takes place has a significant impact on family health. Households with private toilets have measurably lower morbidity rates than households without. Private toilets benefit not only the household but also neighbors who gain protection from the household's feces. The poor and their neighbors often lack private toilets, forcing defecation in public spaces, and leaving them more vulnerable than the nonpoor to communicable diseases.

Figure 25.3 shows the key channels through which physical improvements of water and sanitation services influence health outcomes. The provision of hygiene education, in addition to the physical interventions, helps ensure that feces are safely disposed of, hand washing is done properly, and water is stored safely.

Additionally, inadequate water and sanitation infrastructure slows other health improvements. With regard to sanitation, women often have different privacy requirements than men. When the absence of latrines forces them to use public spaces, they can do so only in the shelter of darkness, during early morning and late evening hours. One response is urine retention, which leads to health problems. From the community perspective, the adequacy of drainage plays a large role in health outcomes. Where drains do not exist, or are blocked, and wastewater stands in the streets, children are particularly vulnerable to disease transmission through direct contact. The standing water may also serve to host other disease vectors, such as mosquitoes transmitting malaria and other diseases.

Effects on Education

In some cultures the lack of toilets in schools serving the poor is known to be a major factor in deterring girls from continuing their education, particularly

---

Box 25.1 Girls, Sanitation, and Education

Reasons for low female school enrollment and attendance related specifically to the water supply and sanitation sector include inappropriate school sanitation or total lack of toilets or latrines, lack of water, and lack of privacy. The following examples illustrate this point:

- In Bangladesh many schools do not have any latrines, although it is recognized that latrines are important not only for health protection but also for the school attendance of girls.

- In the Rohtas district of Bihar State in India, only 59 percent of schools have drinking water facilities and 11 percent have toilets. A study undertaken in this district suggests that to enhance the enrollment of girls it is necessary to motivate the parents and the girls themselves. Key motivating factors include providing midday meals and free learning materials and aids and constructing drinking water and toilet facilities.

Source: Adapted from *Gender in Education and Training for Water Supply and Sanitation: A Literature Review.* International Water and Sanitation Center (IRC). 1997. Unpublished.

after puberty. In these cultures, private toilets (if only latrines) and even the availability of drinking water provide a necessary condition to reach school enrollment goals (see box 25.1).

Children—particularly girls—are often required to help their mothers with the time-consuming task of fetching water, as box 25.2 illustrates by the story of Elma Kassa from Ethiopia. Fetching water has been found in many countries to reduce children's time for schooling or playing.

Gender and Social Inclusion

Groups such as female-headed households, the elderly, and ethnic minorities are disproportionately poor, and among the poor they tend to be most adversely hit by a lack of water and sanitation services. The voices of these vulnerable poor groups may be neglected when such services are established. Even when they are the primary managers of household water, women are often not included in public decision making processes concerning water and sanitation services. Geographically dispersed poor groups (often ethnic minorities) may be excluded in the process of setting up community water and sanitation services. Situations in which marginalized groups are excluded from wider community decision making activities will lead to continued use of unsafe water as well as limited access to existing or future services by these same groups.

Furthermore, a lack of adequate sanitation will endanger girls and women in those cultures where they have to wait until the evening to be able to defecate and urinate. The health consequences have already been mentioned, but security issues also arise as women and girls are more vulnerable to violence, sexual harassment, and other types of crime during the hours of darkness.

Box 25.2 The Lifestyle of a Young Girl in Ethiopia

Elma Kassa is a 13-year-old girl from Addis Ababa, Ethiopia. Her father is a laborer and her mother is a washerwoman. She has one younger sister and a brother.

"I go to collect water four times a day, in a 20-litre clay jar. It's hard work! When I first started collecting water, I was about seven years old. In those days we used to have to walk for over a mile to fetch water. Now there is a tapstand about 10 minutes away from my home, which has made life easier. I've never been to school, as I have to help my mother with her washing work so we can earn enough money. . . . Our house doesn't have a bathroom. I wash myself in the kitchen once a week, on Sunday. At the same time I change my clothes and wash the dirty ones. When I need the toilet, I have to go down to the river in the gully behind my house. I usually go with my friends as we're only supposed to go after dark when people can't see us. In the daytime I use a tin inside the house and empty it out later. If I could alter my life, I would really like to go to school and have more clothes."

Source: DFID (1998).

Effects on Income and Consumption

The lack of water and sanitation infrastructure has complex effects on consumption patterns, which significantly influence people's overall well-being. Figure 25.4 shows these effects, which are discussed in more detail in the subsequent paragraphs.

Figure 25.4 Consumption and Income Effects

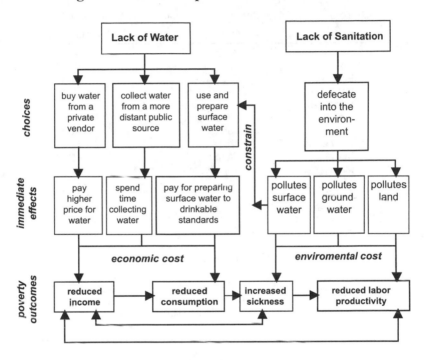

The economic cost of water. Traditional poverty measures focus on income, but the rural and urban poor may face higher costs for water in addition to lower incomes. The lack of network water connections for the urban poor, or of any water service for the rural poor, typically leaves them buying from water vendors at high per liter prices (see box 25.3), waiting in long lines at or walking long distances to public sources, and incurring additional costs for storing and boiling water.

The lack of convenient and affordable access to water reduces a poor household's consumption of other commodities and services, leaves it consuming less than the optimum amount of water for good hygiene, and impacts health and labor productivity of the household members. It may also reduce income-

---

Box 25.3 How Much Do the Poor
in Urban Areas Pay for Water

The problem of lack of water services hits the poor in the slum areas of the large cities in developing countries. Often the only choice for low-income households that cannot afford a house connection is to buy water from private vendors at a relatively high price, sometimes 100 times more than that provided by public authorities. Examples are shown in the following table:

Ratio Between Prices Charged by Vendors and by Public Utilities

Country	City	Ratio
Bangladesh	Dacca	12–25
Colombia	Cali	10
Ecuador	Guayaquil	20
Haiti	Port-au-Prince	17–100
Honduras	Tegucigalpa	16–34
Indonesia	DKI Jakarta	4–60
	Surabaya	20–60
Ivory Coast	Abidjan	5
Kenya	Nairobi	7–11
Mauritania	Nouakchott	100
Nigeria	Lagos	4–10
	Onitsha	6–38
Pakistan	Karachi	28–83
Peru	Lima	17
Togo	Lome	7–10
Turkey	Istanbul	10
Uganda	Kampala	4–9

Source: R. Bathia and M. Falkenmark. 1993. "Water Resource Polices and the Urban Poor: Innovative Approaches and Policy Imperatives." *Water & Sanitation Currents.* United Nations Development Program–World Bank Water and Sanitation Program.

---

generating opportunities of the household, thereby further reducing income and consumption.

The World Health Organization has established a norm of 20 liters per capita per day (lcd) for water use to satisfy basic personal and hygiene requirements. Of that amount, about 10 lcd serve drinking and cooking needs, while the remainder goes to bathing, particularly hand washing. When water is expensive, either in cash terms or in the time and energy needed to collect it, the poor often cut total consumption to 15 lcd or less and cut back on bathing.

A number of studies have shown that the volume of water collected varies little for water sources from about 30 to 1,000 meters from the house. For sources closer than 30 meters, usage increases, and for more than 1,000 meters, usage falls. Figure 25.5 shows this experience in terms of minutes required for a return trip to the water source. Distance matters, but so does queuing time. If users can walk 10 meters to a standpost but then must wait an hour before use, they will collect no more water than someone traveling 200 meters to a standpost who has no wait in line.

The environmental cost. Threats to water sustainability arise in both quality and quantity dimensions, driven by pollution and competing demands from many sectors, including industry, agriculture, and energy. Environmental degradation reduces labor productivity by contributing to the increased burden of diseases and by limiting income potentials (especially in aquaculture).

Nationally, dwindling availability of clean water per capita will increase the economic cost of water and, in a situation of scarcity, limit the potential for economic development. Locally, communities that fail to protect their surface and ground waters from pathogens have fewer options for drinking water and require more expensive technologies for extracting water from deeper aquifers or for treating surface water to drinkable levels. In the urban context, where

Figure 25.5 Water Consumption versus Travel Time

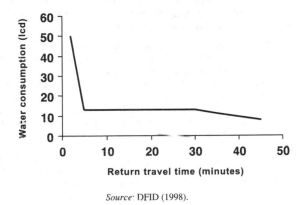

Source: DFID (1998).

water may be supplied from a utility, increasing costs of extraction or treatment are passed on to consumers through higher prices (see box 25.4). The poor have fewer resources; hence, they disproportionately suffer the consequences

Water, sanitation, and risk. Inadequate water and sanitation services can bring with them a particular risk in each of the dimensions already described. And water availability and quality may both be highly seasonal. During the dry season, the urban poor face higher water prices, while the rural poor face longer treks for lower quality water. Moreover, sewage return flows to water bodies, bearing pollutants of various types, make up a bigger proportion of total flows, reducing water quality and making effective treatment more difficult. The risk is faced in household consumption and in the use of water in economic activity such as agriculture. The poor are particularly unequipped to cope with this risk, since coping requires expensive storage or additional treatment. During the wet season, inadequate drainage and other sanitation infrastructure becomes problematic, as overflowing polluted water may stand in the streets for long periods.

Box 25.4 Degredation of Water Quality and Implications for the Cost of Water in Indonesia

In addition to causing environmental damage, water pollution and excessive pumping have effects on the cost of water. To improve water quality, amounts of (often costly) chemicals must be increased. For example, to treat the increasingly polluted raw water entering the Pulogadung water treatment plant in Jakarta, chlorine was increased from an average of 2.6 mg/l in 1982 to about 7 mg/l in 1984. This increase raised treatment costs by Rp 610 million per year (1985 prices) and decreased plant efficiency by 18 percent (Rp 870 million per year). The "finished" drinking water frequently was off-color and exceeded limits for concentration of ammonium, organic matter, and fecal coliform. Another negative long-term effect of high chlorine use is production of chloroform and other carcinogenic residues.

Another large cost of the bacteriological contamination of raw water is that of boiling water to make it potable. The high levels of pollution and the poorly operated treatment and distribution facilities make the public water supply undrinkable unless boiled before use. For the Jakarta special capital province area, this cost has been estimated at Rp 96 billion (1987 prices) or US$52 million per year, equivalent to 1.1 percent of the gross domestic product then generated in Jakarta. A survey conducted in Jakarta showed that a household boils about 4.4 liters of water per capita per day, whatever the water source. Boiling water for between 15 and 20 minutes cost about Rp 7.5 per liter.

Source: R. Bathia and M. Falkenmark. 1993. "Water Resource Policies and the Urban Poor: Innovative Approaches and Policy Imperatives." *Water & Sanitation Currents.* United Nations Development Program–World Bank Water and Sanitation Program.

CHAPTER 26

HEALTH AND THE ENVIRONMENT IN URBAN POOR AREAS: AVOIDING A CRISIS THROUGH PREVENTION

ENVIRONMENTAL HEALTH PROJECT

Unless developing country governments and international donors wake up to it, the coming environmental health crisis of poor urban areas could easily overwhelm health care systems, compromise the health and welfare of an ever-growing number of people—already over a billion—and endanger the productivity and stability of many developing nations. The greatest risk is to children of poor urban families, whose vulnerability is reflected in rapidly rising mortality and morbidity rates from environment-related diseases.

This chapter looks at the factors responsible for this looming crisis and offers some broad-brush suggestions on the role prevention can play in forestalling it. Most of the ideas expressed here originated with the two main presenters at a seminar in January 1995 on urban environmental health, Margaret Catley-Carlson, president of the Population Council and chair of the Water and Sanitation Collaborative Council, and Dr. Diana Silimperi, specialist in integrated child health services and urban health delivery systems with the BASICS Project. The seminar was cosponsored by USAID's Office of Environment and Urban Programs and Office of Health and Nutrition.

The Emerging Health Crisis

An estimated 600 million people in urban areas of the developing world live in life- and health-threatening homes and neighborhoods. In poor urban areas—variously known as informal settlements, squatter settlements, slums, peri-urban areas, shantytowns, *barrios,* and *favelas*—health-threatening environmental conditions are the norm. These make-shift communities, many of which are not legally recognized by the government, are often built on land

Table 26.1 Urban Health in Poor and Nonpoor Areas of the Same City: Infant Morality Rates (per 1,000)

City	Poor	Nonpoor
Porto Alegre, Brazil	43	18
Karachi, Pakistan	152	32
Aggregate urban Guatemala	113	33
Manila, Philippines	210	76
San Paulo, Brazil	175	42
Delhi, India	180	18

Source: Diana Silimperi, based on *Report of the Panel on Urbanization*, 1992 and *World Development Report*, 1993.

that no one else wants: flood plains or steep slopes, near dumps or noxious industrial activities. On these unsafe sites, the poor crowd into shacks made from cast-off materials.

Often there is no water supply, and people are obliged to purchase drinking water from vendors, with no guarantee that it is safe. Sewers are rare; storm drainage is virtually unknown. Greywater is thrown into the streets, adding to standing pools left after rain. Because there is no method for collection or disposal, garbage and trash are thrown into the nearest gully or streambed, endangering children and polluting water. Sanitation facilities are often lacking entirely, so these settlements are awash in human excrement. Vehicular and industrial emissions pollute the air in many urban centers. Unvented heating or cooking stoves using biomass fuels fill indoor air with smoke. All of these conditions—crowding, lack of water, filth, polluted air—threaten the health of millions, especially children. According to WHO, a third of the urban dwellers in developing countries (approximately 565 million persons) live in substandard housing or are homeless. Half of them are children. Table 26.1 gives some examples of environmental health conditions in specific cities.

The dramatic effects that these conditions have on health are only now beginning to be documented. Poverty remains the significant predictor of urban morbidity and mortality, and available studies lead to the recognition that in many countries, the urban poor have the worst health status—even worse than their rural poor counterparts. For example, recent studies have confirmed repeatedly that infant mortality rates are far higher in poorer sections of many cities than in better-off sections—not surprising, given that, according to WHO and UNICEF studies, worldwide, the urban high-income population has 95% coverage for water and sanitation, compared with 64% coverage for water and 45% for sanitation for the poor population. Although comparisons between the urban poor and the vast rural population suggest that urban health in the aggregate is better than rural health, these statistics are highly misleading, for the city numbers are skewed, both by the good health of the more affluent and the common omission of data on the poor. Tables 26.1 and 26.2 summarize the findings of research comparing the health status of persons living in poor versus nonpoor areas of the same city

Impact on Poor Women

As a group, urban poor women sustain unusually high risks for increased morbidity and mortality, the result not only of childbearing but also of adverse exposures through their responsibilities as food gatherers and providers, caretakers of children and the ill, and maintainers of the home shelter. Worst off are the growing numbers of single females heading households; according to U.N. reports, even in Africa, nearly 35% of urban households in poverty are headed by single women, and the proportion is significantly higher in Latin America. Children of single females heading urban households are often the poorest of the poor, with significant morbidity and mortality.

Disease Impacts

Poor environmental conditions give rise to high rates of diarrheal diseases (including cholera), acute respiratory infections (ARI), and vector-borne diseases. In one year alone, over 2 million urban children under the age of five died as a consequence of diarrheal dehydration. Cholera is sweeping Latin America. In the last decade, urban epidemics have erupted as a number of traditionally rural parasitic diseases emerged in cities, due to a combination of rural migration and the proliferation of breeding sites. Malaria and Chagas's disease, both typically rural, are increasingly being seen in urban settings. Dengue is at epidemic levels and spreading in urban centers. In 1995, a state

Table 26.2 Urban Health in Poor and Nonpoor Areas in the Same City: Infectious Disease Morbidity and Mortality Differentials

City	Disease	Difference in Poor vs. Nonpoor
Manila, Philippines	Tuberculosis	9x
	Diarrhea	2x
	Typhoid	4x
Porto Allegre, Brazil	Pneumonia/ influenza mortality	6x
	Septicemia mortality	8x
Sao Paulo, Brazil	Enteritis, diarrhea, pneumonia mortality in infants	2x

Source: Diana Silimperi, based on *Report of the Panel on Urbanization*, 1992 and *World Development Report*, 1993.

of emergency was declared in Guatemala and El Salvador because of the dengue epidemic.

Respiratory diseases are more likely to be prevalent in urban than in rural areas because crowding promotes the transmission of infectious organisms. According to a study published in *World Health Statistics* (I. Romieu, "Urban Air Pollution in Latin America and the Caribbean," Vol. 23, No. 2, 1990), over 2 million city children in Latin America suffer from chronic coughs, and 65 million person-days of workers' time have been lost as a result of urban air pollution.

The toll of morbidity and mortality from accidents and injuries is increasing in urban areas. Motor vehicle accidents lead the list, but fires and home accidents—especially in slums—hit the under-five age group hard. In addition, the makeshift nature of urban slums makes them more susceptible to natural disasters.

In developing countries that have made the transition to industrialization, residents of urban slums are threatened not only by the diseases and hazards associated with development, but also by those more typical of developed countries—cancer, stroke, heart disease, chronic lung disease, accidents, and so on—many of which are also environmentally related.

The Myths: Denial and Defeatism

Only relatively recently have some external support agencies begun to address urban environmental health needs. A rural focus was established in an earlier period as a valid response to urgent rural needs. This rural bias makes less sense today given the substantial demographic shift from rural to urban centers. In addition, in the view of development practitioners with experience in peri-urban areas, three widely accepted myths have blinded health experts to the need for action and to opportunities for effective interventions.

Myth #1: The Growth of Cities Can be Slowed.

Cities are here to stay, and their growth is inexorable. A tidal wave of new inhabitants will inundate the world's cities in the next 30 years, mostly in developing countries. The flood is rising fastest in the poorest countries. In 1950, there were only 285 million urban inhabitants in Third World cities; by 1990, there were 1.5 billion, and by 2025 there will be 4 billion, according to *U.N. World Urbanization Prospects.* Latin America will be the most urbanized region, with almost 85% of its population in urban areas (the same level as the U.S.), compared with 74% at present. In Asia and Africa, the proportion will have jumped 20 percentage points, from around 34% to near 55%. As figure 26.1 shows, a majority of people worldwide will live in urban areas.

Nothing can stop this growth. Efforts to slow city growth by cutting rural-to-urban migration have rarely worked, in part because cities exert a magnetic pull, offering opportunities for jobs, education, and health care. But it is due even more to the fact that 60% of urban growth reflects natural increase, or babies born to people who already live there.

The poor are the victims. Pollution, crime, illness, and crowding tend to affect the urban poor far more severely than the well-off. And it is the poor urban populations that seem to be growing the fastest. For example, in Peru, the overall rate of growth in cities is 3.8%, whereas the growth rate of informal urban settlements is around 6%. Worldwide, the urban population is expected to double in 10 years, while the number of urban poor is expected to double in 5 years. Because the poor are so hard to count, these

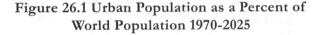

Figure 26.1 Urban Population as a Percent of World Population 1970-2025

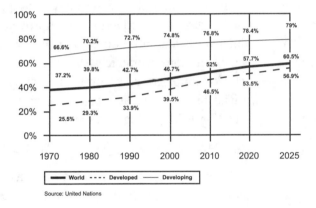

Source: United Nations

numbers may be in dispute. But policymakers should recognize that urbanization is proceeding twice as fast as overall population growth; presently one out of every two people will live in a city; by 2010, one out of every ten people will live in an urban megalopolis.

Myth #2: Investments in Medical Interventions are Sufficient to Address Health Problems in Developing Country Cities.

This premise underlies the majority of developing country health investments. But the proposition that investments in curative and preventive medical interventions can address the health problems of the urban poor is flawed: the truth is that urban health problems are already far beyond the ability of the medical establishment to control, and as they continue to erupt, hospitals and clinics will be overwhelmed.

Resource allocations follow the myth in developing countries. Most countries overtly favor curative health investments. National health budgets are allocated mostly to city hospitals; a smaller percentage of resources has gone to establishing municipal networks of community-based health centers and health posts that provide primary health care. The small number of clinics and hospitals that serve the poor are often overcrowded, understaffed, poorly equipped, and in some cases even culturally inappropriate for their patients.

Redirecting resources to community-based primary health services, including preventive services. A patient-centered medical approach to the advancing health crisis in developing world cities is no longer enough. An approach that focuses instead on community- and family-level preventive activities will begin to root out the causes of illness, in particular the child health risk factors, shown in table 26.3. Such an approach includes protection of water sources; construction of excreta sanitation facilities and safe water supplies; collection and proper disposal of solid wastes; introduction of improved cooking stoves; reducing vector-breeding sites; and promotion of hand washing, safe food handling, and other health-promoting practices. Over the long term these activities are cost-effective. Continuing to count on health-center focused commodity-based programs to withstand the onslaught of growing urban health problems is like depending on the proverbial finger in the dike.

Myth #3: The Urban Poor are Marginal; They Cannot Help Themselves.

The urban poor live on the geographic margin of the city as well as on the economic margin, perpetually in danger of losing their livelihoods, their health, their homes. Yet most of the poor are hard-working individuals who often exhibit considerable entrepreneurial skills. They scrape out an existence in low-paying, unhealthy jobs such as ragpicking, textile piece-work, bicycle rickshaw driving, cooking, or vending and hawking.

The myth that the urban poor cannot help themselves disregards the fact that many of these hard-pressed individuals have both contributed to, and worked in, pilot efforts to improve the environmental conditions in which they live. Successful models are grounded in the opportunities that already exist in urban poor areas, and reach out to include national and local leadership and the private and public sectors in new combinations that bolster local efforts. Above all, the common theme of these urban examples is sustainability. Substituting realism for wishful thinking and optimism for defeatism, these models suggest that practical, pragmatic solutions do exist and that they can help make cities more habitable and healthful.

Table 26.3 Child Health Risk Factors in Urban Slums

Risk Factor	Diseases			Death
	ARI	Diarrhea	Malaria	
poor water quality		X		
poor sanitation		X		
insufficient garbage collection/disposal		X		
poor drainage/free-standing water			X	
crowding	X			
air pollution (indoor and outdoor)	X			
poor/under nutrition	X	X		X
poverty	X	X	X	X
low maternal education				X
lack of nearby primary health care facilities				X

Source: Diana Silimperi

The Opportunities: A Realistic Reassessment of Possibilities

The picture is not totally bleak. Despite the different circumstances in which they live, the urban poor share certain characteristics—not shared by their country cousins—that should enable them to operate as effective partners in affordable solutions to the environmental and health problems in their neighborhoods.

City residents are more tuned-in. City residents are tuned in to modern media and communications, making it easy to reach them with broadcast messages on health and environmental issues. Also, the population density makes it relatively simple to mobilize large groups of poor urban dwellers. The urban poor can join their voices in protest about their environment, and they can combine their energies to develop ways to improve their surroundings. Even in the poorest urban neighborhoods, opportunities exist to address urban health problems in constructive ways. Traditional health and family planning services are not enough. Programs in health and in water and sanitation are necessary if child mortality is to be reduced. Intransigent pockets of urban poverty offer opportunities for innovative integrated attacks—in which population, health, and environmental programs join forces—on the complex of problems that affect the urban poor.

The urban poor live in a cash economy. Cities are the "economic engines" of developing countries. They produce the bulk of GNP. Countries higher on the GNP scale all have higher rates of urbanization than countries lower on the scale. Even the poorest city dwellers can latch onto the commercialism that stimulates urban economic life. These sources of income may not be secure or high paying, but they make it possible for the urban poor to pay for low-cost medical services and environmental improvements such as water supply and sanitation. The urban poor are often quite willing to pay for infrastructure that they see as improving their quality of life.

Cities have more potential woman power. Poor urban women represent a great untapped resource. As guardians of family health and caretakers of children, women have the most at stake in changing hazardous health conditions. And the community has much at stake in enabling women to play such a role. Urban poor women worldwide constitute an immense reservoir of underutilized ability; their capacities must be strengthened and energies mobilized if urban and environmental health objectives are to be attained.

The Solutions

A Workable Paradigm for Prevention

The Network on Services for the Urban Poor of the Water and Sanitation Collaborative Council has developed a program for successful water and sanitation provision in urban poor areas: recognition of *de facto* land holding, user-pay cost-recovery systems, appropriate technology, consumer involvement, and institutional reform. This program can be adopted for broader environmental health efforts in urban poor areas through the addition of four more elements: risk assessment, private sector involvement, intersectoral planning, and integration of service delivery.

Recognition of *de facto* land holding. Granting some measure of legal recognition to urban settlements gives municipalities a basis for extending services or activities to peri-urban communities. Without the security legal recognition provides, the inhabitants themselves are unwilling to make permanent investments in water, sanitation, housing, and so on.

Cost recovery. Through user fees and credit, the poor can and should help shoulder the costs. Full cost recovery promotes conservation and makes it possible to extend service to the unserved. This approach would be welcomed by the poor people without piped water in or near their homes who often pay vendors far more for water than if they were connected to a municipal system.

Some are currently paying as much as 10 times more for a cubic meter of water than residents of New York or Washington.

Appropriate technology. Technologies that work in formal urban areas often fail to work in peri-urban areas because they are not appropriate to the socioeconomic, cultural, and physical setting. Increasingly, technologies such as small-bore condominium sewers are being successfully used in informal settlements.

Involving consumers. The poor should be involved in diagnosing and resolving their local environmental health problems. Consumers should be educated to demand quality services and to pressure municipal leaders and the services they control to respond to community demands.

Institutional reform. Capacity building, or strengthening the institutions responsible for health, population, and the environment, coupled with development of human resources, is essential if the health problems of the urban poor are to be solved. Institutional reform must take place at all levels.

National, provincial, and municipal agencies should all share the burden of health, population, and environmental services. This includes making resources available. Unless a clear, definitive division of authority, responsibility, and resource allocation is made, problems will be deferred and sustainable solutions will not be implemented.

Municipal governmental services should be run more efficiently. At present even fairly large municipalities seldom have adequate health staff, and smaller towns and midsize municipalities may have no trained health professionals except those providing clinical services at provincial or district levels. Local governments should organize public and environmental health departments and hire staff to collect and use available data on health, population, and the environment to advise municipal decision makers. In turn, municipal authorities should be trained in the use of innovative planning and management methods that can be used in complex urban environments.

Urban public health and environmental managers and providers should acquire new skills in communications and marketing. This kind of skill-building is necessary to expand the role of prevention and integrate it whenever possible with essential health services, especially in models which focus on activities outside of clinics and hospitals. Social marketing, including new principles of market segmentation, has particular relevance for heterogenous urban settings and can be used to tailor messages to specific subpopulations. Ethnographic studies can help determine barriers to utilization of services or objections to preventive measures. Public health and environmental managers should also be able to perform and/or understand health care interventions, as well as financial administration and quality assurance monitoring. Although the field of public health will continue to include the control of infectious diseases, professionals must be equipped to deal with emerging chronic diseases and environmental, mental, and lifestyle disorders, including sociological ills such as the current epidemic of violence.

Risk assessment and communication. Plans and choices about urban health should be made on the basis of solid information and on an analysis and prioritization of the environmental health risks a community faces. Critical policymakers—both national and local—must be fully informed regarding urban health and environmental issues. They need urban and intraurban data to make responsible decisions about resource allocations. Many leaders are unaware of the vast differentials in health status, population rates, and environmental conditions among urban groups.

Private sector involvement. New relationships should be formed between the public and private sectors. The role of national and municipal governments is to promote policies that encourage the private sector to participate in efforts to alleviate the environmental health problems of the urban poor. It is important, however, that private sector participants be involved in ways that use their strengths. For example, private nonprofit organizations may be extremely successful at community organization and promoting household preventive behaviors, while for-profit enterprises may be most efficient at developing products or providing large-scale facility services.

Intersectoral planning. Because many health problems are rooted in environmental conditions, different agencies will need to collaborate to successfully address them. Until recently, the norm has been to deliver selected primary health care interventions vertically, that is, through programs (such as diarrhea control, immunization, family planning, health education, income generation, etc.) that are planned and implemented separately. These programs often compete for resources. Urban settings are an ideal testing ground for new, multipronged strategies that can simultaneously attack the various environmental causes of ill health.

Integration of service delivery. Municipal and local authorities should seriously consider integrating services that provide primary health care and primary environmental care, especially at the community and household levels. Both types of services promote basic preventive behaviors that have a synergistic effect on individual health and the environment.

Shift to community-based care. To improve environment-related health conditions for the increasing number of people living in urban poverty, public health must be reinvented, beginning with the development of new institutional roles and responsibilities. Urban demographics and transitional epidemiology require a shift of emphasis from hospital-based care to less expensive community-based care that stresses prevention and health promotion. Without this shift, no city will be able to bear the costs of developing equitable health delivery systems.

A Sense of Urgency

The time has come to pay heed to warnings from the 1990 UNICEF Summit for Children and the June 1992 United Nations Conference on the Environment and Development in Rio de Janeiro, which placed environmental health interventions among the highest priorities for improving the health of the poor in developing countries. Plans for Habitat II: The Second United Nations Conference for Human Settlements (1996) similarly call on the nations of the world "to confront the emerging urban crisis and initiate urgent worldwide action to improve shelter and living environments." The challenge is to convey a sense of urgency to national and municipal governments, to let them see that their national well-being depends on improving their urban environments.

PART N
POPULATION

"Be fruitful and multiply" is the first command given by God in the Bible (Genesis 1:28). In fact, according to Genesis these words are the very first ever uttered by God to humans. Say what you will about the human tendency to ignore God's directives, after surpassing six billion inhabitants on the planet in 2003, it would seem we've done a pretty good job at carrying out this one. At its heart, the command seems to imply that humans were designed to live not in isolation but rather in families, clans, and communities. It may also suggest that the design for humanity bends away from a celibate existence and toward one that involves male-female intimacy. We were meant to create families and communities through sexual intimacy between a man and woman.

Something so profoundly central to God's design seems conspicuously absent from the world of Christian development. Certainly, Christians talk a good deal about the destructiveness of both sex outside of marriage and abortion. Bringing children into the world without the support of a committed nuclear family structure has created untold hardship. And where the nuclear family has disintegrated, so has societal health. In addition, the Scriptures are clear that life in the womb is sacred, soul-bearing, and God crafted. Abortion is the ultimate oppression of a voiceless people. Yet the sensibilities of some believers are offended by introducing the topics of family planning and sex into discussions about how the church can serve the poor.

For some Christians it is God who opens or closes the womb, and to fiddle with birth control is tantamount to playing God. But such a view discounts the fact that God has given humans self-discipline: the ability and freedom to determine when and how often sex should occur, and therefore when and how often potential pregnancy might take place. Natural family planning *is* birth control.[1] This view also ignores the God-given ingenuity of humans to use available resources in order to meet needs. Planes allow us to fly (something we weren't naturally designed to do), and contraceptives are used to influence when we bring children into a family. These issues are profoundly relevant in our quest to bring health and wholeness into densely populated slum communities.

Transformation must address the macro questions of population as well as the micro questions of family planning.

Amartya Sen, winner of the 1998 Nobel Prize for Economics, dispels some common myths in his essay "Population: Delusion and Reality." Sen attacks the notion that food shortage and immigration to the West is linked to overpopulation in the developing world. His main concern is that governments driven by fear are likely to embrace coercive policies of population control: policies like forced sterilization, which take those most affected out of the decision process. In the end, Sen highlights the impact of education for women in Kerala, India, in driving down population in comparison with China's more forceful population policies.

"Birth Spacing: Three to Five Saves Lives," published by the Population Information Program, argues persuasively that helping the poor to space the births of their children more generously will dramatically impact the health of both mother and child. The article looks at some of the factors that affect birth spacing and campaigns that have been effective in helping encourage longer periods between births.

The discussions of birth control, sex, and family planning need to return with candor to people of faith, especially as we seek to bring wholeness and healing to places of brokenness and despair among the urban poor.

Notes

1. Natural family planning is the intentional ordering of when sex occurs in relation to a woman's cycle of ovulation in order to avoid or achieve pregnancy. This method is often encouraged by those who believe birth-control devices are unbiblical.

CHAPTER 27

POPULATION: DELUSION AND REALITY

AMARTYA SEN

Few issues today are as divisive as what is called the "world population problem." During the months leading up to the 1994 International Conference on Population and Development, organized by the United Nations and held in Cairo, these divisions among experts received enormous attention and generated considerable heat. There is a danger that in the confrontation between apocalyptic pessimism, on the one hand, and a dismissive smugness, on the other, a genuine understanding of the nature of the population problem may be lost.[1]

Visions of impending doom have been increasingly aired in recent years, often presenting the population problem as a "bomb" that has been planted and is about to "go off." These catastrophic images have encouraged a tendency to search for emergency solutions that treat the people involved not as reasonable beings, allies facing a common problem, but as impulsive and uncontrolled sources of great social harm, in need of strong discipline.

Such views have received serious attention in public discussions, not just in sensational headlines in the popular press, but also in seriously argued and widely read books. One of the most influential examples was Paul Ehrlich's *The Population Bomb,* the first three sections of which were headed "Too Many People," "Too Little Food," and "A Dying Planet."[2] A more recent example of a chilling diagnosis of imminent calamity is Garrett Hardin's *Living Within Limits.*[3] The arguments on which these pessimistic visions are based deserve serious scrutiny.

If the propensity to foresee impending disaster from overpopulation is strong in some circles, so is the tendency, in others, to dismiss all worries about population size. Just as alarmism builds on the recognition of a real problem and then magnifies it, complacency may also start off from a reasonable belief about the history of population problems and fail to see how they may have changed by now. It is often pointed out, for example, that the world has coped well enough with fast increases in population in the past, even though alarmists had expected otherwise. Malthus anticipated terrible disasters resulting from population growth and a consequent imbalance in "the proportion between the natural increase of population and food."[4] At a time when there were fewer than a billion people, he was quite convinced that "the period when the number of men surpass their means of subsistence has long since arrived." However, since Malthus first published his famous *Essay on Population* in 1798, the world population has grown nearly six times larger, while food output and consumption per person are considerably higher now, and there has been an unprecedented increase both in life expectancies and in general living standards.[5]

The fact that Malthus was mistaken in his diagnosis as well as his prognosis two hundred years ago does not, however, indicate that contemporary fears about population growth must be similarly erroneous. The increase in the world population has vastly accelerated over the last century. It took the world population millions of years to reach the first billion, then 123 years to get to the second, 33 years to the third, 14 years to the fourth, 13 years to the fifth billion, with a sixth billion to come, according to one U.N. projection, in another 11 years.[6] During the last decade, between 1980 and 1990, the number of people on earth grew by about 923 million, an increase nearly the size of the total world population in Malthus's time. Whatever may be the proper response to alarmism about the future, complacency based on past success is *no* response at all.

Immigration and Population

One current worry concerns the regional distribution of the increase in world population, about 90 percent of which is taking place in the developing countries. The percentage rate of population growth is fastest in Africa—3.1 percent per year over the last decade. But most of the large increases in population occur in regions other than Africa. The largest absolute increases in numbers are taking place in Asia, which is where most of the world's poorer people live, even though the rate of increase in population has been slowing significantly there. Of the worldwide increase of 923 million people in the 1980s, well over half occurred in Asia—517 million in fact (including 146 million in China and 166 million in India).

Beyond concerns about the well-being of these poor countries themselves, a more self-regarding worry causes panic in the richer countries of the world and has much to do with the current anxiety in the West about the "world population problem." This is founded on the belief that destitution caused by fast population growth in the Third World is responsible for the severe pressure to emigrate to the developed countries of Europe and North America. In this view, people impoverished by overpopulation in the "South" flee to the "North." Some have claimed to find empirical support for this thesis in the fact that pressure to emigrate from the South has accelerated in recent decades, along with a rapid increase in the population there.

There are two distinct questions here: First, how real a threat of intolerable immigration pressure does the North face from the South, and second, is that pressure closely related to population growth in the South, rather than to other social and economic factors? There are reasons to doubt that population growth is the major force behind migratory pressures, and I shall concentrate here on that question. But I should note in passing that immigration is now severely controlled in Europe and North America, and insofar as Europe is concerned, most of the current immigrants from the Third World are not "primary" immigrants but dependent relatives—mainly spouses and young children—of those who had come and settled earlier. The United States remains relatively more open to fresh immigration, but the requirements of "labor certification" as a necessary part of the immigration procedure tend to guarantee that the new entrants are relatively better educated and more skilled. There are, however, sizable flows of illegal immigrants, especially to the United States and to a lesser extent to southern Europe, though the numbers are hard to estimate.

What causes the current pressures to emigrate? The "job-worthy" people who get through the immigration process are hardly to be seen as impoverished and destitute migrants created by the sheer pressure of population. Even the illegal immigrants who manage to evade the rigors of border control are typically not starving wretches but those who can make use of work prospects in the North.

The explanation for the increased migratory pressure over the decades owes more to the dynamism of international capitalism than to just the growing size of the population of the Third World countries. The immigrants have allies in potential employers, and this applies as much to illegal farm laborers in California as to the legally authorized "guest workers" in automobile factories in Germany. The economic incentive to emigrate to the North from the poorer Southern economies may well depend on differences in real income. But this gap is very large anyway, and even if it is presumed that population growth in the South is increasing the disparity with the North—a thesis I shall presently consider—it seems unlikely that this incentive would significantly change if the Northern income level were, say, twenty times that of the Southern as opposed to twenty-five times.

The growing demand for immigration to the North from the South is related to the "shrinking" of the world (through revolutions in communication and transport), reduction in economic obstacles to labor movements (despite the increase in political barriers), and the growing reach and absorptive power of international capitalism (even as domestic politics in the North has turned more inward-looking and nationalistic). To try to explain the increase in immigration pressure by the growth rate of total population in the Third World is to close one's eyes to the deep changes that have occurred—and are occurring—in the world in which we live, and the rapid internationalization of its cultures and economies that accompanies these changes.

Fears of Being Engulfed

A closely related issue concerns what is perceived as a growing "imbalance" in the division of the world population, with a rapidly rising share belonging to the Third World. That fear translates into worries of various kinds in the North, especially the sense of being overrun by the South. Many Northerners fear being engulfed by people from Asia and Africa, whose share of the world population increased from 63.7 percent in 1950 to 71.2 percent by 1990, and is expected, according to the estimates of the United Nations, to rise to 78.5 percent by 2050.

It is easy to understand the fears of relatively well-off people at the thought of being surrounded by a fast-growing and increasingly impoverished Southern population. As I shall argue, the thesis of growing impoverishment does not stand up to much scrutiny; but it is important to address first the psychologically tense issue of racial balance in the world (even though racial composition as a consideration has only as much importance as we choose to give it). Here it is worth recollecting that the Third World is right now going through the same kind of demographic shift—a rapid expansion of population for a temporary but long stretch—that Europe and North America experienced during their Industrial Revolution. In 1650 the share of Asia and Africa in the world population is estimated to have been 78.4 percent, and it stayed around there even in 1750.[7] With the Industrial Revolution, the share of Asia and Africa diminished because of the rapid rise of population in Europe and North America; for example, during the nineteenth century, while the population of Asia and Africa grew by about 4 percent per decade or less, the population of "the area of European settlement" grew by around 10 percent every decade.

Even now the combined share of Asia and Africa (71.2 percent) is considerably *below* what that share was in 1650 or 1750. If the United Nations'[1] prediction that this share will rise to 78.5 percent by 2050 comes true, then the Asians and the Africans would return to being proportionately almost exactly as numerous as they were before the European industrial revolution. There is, of course, nothing sacrosanct about the distributions of population in the past; but the sense of a growing "imbalance" in the world, based only on recent trends, ignores history and implicitly presumes that the expansion of Europeans earlier on was natural, whereas the same process happening now to other populations unnaturally disturbs the "balance."

Other worries involving the relation of population growth to food supplies, income levels, and the environment reflect more serious matters.[8] Before I take up those questions, a brief comment on the distinction between two rival approaches to dealing with the population problem may be useful. One involves voluntary choice and a collaborative solution, and the other overrides voluntarism through legal or economic coercion.

Alarmist views of impending crises tend to produce a willingness to consider forceful measures for coercing people to have fewer children in the Third World. Imposing birth control on unwilling people is no longer rejected as readily as it was until quite recently, and some activists have pointed to the ambiguities that exist in determining what is or is not "coercion."[9] Those who are willing to consider—or at least not fully reject—programs that would use some measure of force to reduce population growth often point to the success of China's "one child policy" in cutting down the national birth rate. Force can also take an indirect form, as when economic opportunities are changed so radically by government regulations that people are left with very little choice except to behave in ways the government would approve. In China's case, the government may refuse to offer housing to families with too many children—thus penalizing the children as well as the adults.

In India the policy of compulsory birth control that was initiated during the "emergency period" declared by Mrs. Gandhi in the 1970s was decisively rejected by the voters in the general election in which it—along with civil rights—was a major issue. Even so, some public health clinics in the northern states (such as Uttar Pradesh) insist, in practice, on sterilization before providing normal medical attention to women and men beyond a certain age. The pressures to move in that direction seem to be strong, and they are reinforced by the rhetoric of "the population bomb."

I shall call this general approach the "override" view, since the family's personal decisions are overridden by some agency outside the family—typically by the government of the country in question (whether or not it has been pressed to do so by "outside" agencies, such as international organizations and pressure groups). In fact, overriding is not limited to an explicit use of legal coercion or economic compulsion, since people's own choices can also be effectively overridden by simply not offering them the opportunities for jobs or welfare that they can expect to get from a responsible government. Override can take many different forms and can be of varying intensity (with the Chinese "one child policy" being something of an extreme case of a more general approach).

A central issue here is the increasingly vocal demand by some activists concerned with population growth that the highest "priority" should be given in Third World countries to family planning over other public commitments. This demand goes much beyond supporting family planning as a part of development. In fact, proposals for shifting international aid away from development in general to family planning in particular have lately been increasingly frequent. Such policies fit into the general approach of "override" as well, since they try to rely on manipulating people's choices through offering them only some opportunities (the means of family planning) while denying others, no matter what they would have themselves preferred. Insofar as they would have the effect of reducing health care and educational services, such shifts in public commitments will not only add to the misery of human lives but may also have, I shall argue, exactly the opposite effect on family planning than the one intended, since education and health care have a significant part in the *voluntary* reduction of the birth rate.

The "override" approach contrasts with another, the "collaborative" approach, that relies not on legal or economic restrictions but on rational decisions of women and men, based on expanded choices and enhanced security, and encouraged by open dialogue and extensive public discussions. The difference between the two approaches does not lie in government's activism in the first case as opposed to passivity in the second. Even if solutions are sought through the decisions and actions of people themselves, the chance to take reasoned decisions with more knowledge and a greater sense of personal security can be increased by public policies, for example, through expanding educational facilities, health care, and economic well-being, along with providing better access to family planning. The central political and ethical issue concerning the "override" approach does not lie in its insistence on the need for public policy but in the ways it significantly reduces the choices open to parents.

The Malthus-Condorcet Debate

Thomas Robert Malthus forcefully argued for a version of the "override" view. In fact, it was precisely this preference that distinguished Malthus from Condorcet, the eighteenth-century French mathematician and social scientist from whom Malthus had actually derived the analysis of how population could outgrow the means of living. The debate between Condorcet and Malthus in some ways marks the origin of the distinction between the "collaborative" and the "override" approaches, which still compete for attention.[10]

In his *Essay on Population,* published in 1798, Malthus quoted—extensively and with approval—Condorcet's discussion, in 1795, of the possibility of overpopulation. However, true to the Enlightenment tradition, Condorcet was confident that this problem would be solved by reasoned human action: through increases in productivity, through better conservation and prevention of waste, and through education (especially female education), which would contribute to reducing the birth rate.[11] Voluntary family planning would be encouraged, in Condorcet's analysis, by increased understanding that if people "have a duty toward those who are not yet born, that duty is not to give them existence but to give them happiness." They would see the value of limiting family size "rather than foolishly . . . encumber the world with useless and wretched beings."[12]

Even though Malthus borrowed from Condorcet his diagnosis of the possibility of overpopulation, he refused to accept Condorcet's solution. Indeed, Malthus's essay on population was partly a criticism of Condorcet's Enlightenment reasoning, and the full title of Malthus's famous essay specifically mentioned Condorcet. Malthus argued that "there is no reason whatever to suppose anything beside the difficulty of procuring in adequate plenty the necessaries of life should either *indispose* this greater number of persons to marry early; or *disable* them from rearing in health the largest families."[13] Malthus thus opposed public relief of poverty: he saw the "poor laws" in particular as contributing greatly to population growth.[14]

Malthus was not sure that any public policy would work, and whether "overriding" would in fact be possible: "The perpetual tendency in the race of man to increase beyond the means of subsistence is one of the great general laws of animated nature which we can have no reason to expect will change."[15] But insofar as any solution would be possible, it could not come from voluntary decisions of the people involved, acting from a position of strength and economic security. It must come from overriding their preferences through the compulsions of economic necessity, since their poverty was the only thing that could "indispose this greater number of persons to marry early, or disable them from rearing in health the largest families."

Development and Lower Fertility

The distinction between the "collaborative" approach and the "override" approach thus tends to correspond closely to the contrast between, on the one hand, treating economic and social development as the way to solve the population problem and, on the other, expecting little from development and using, instead, legal and economic pressures to reduce birth rates. Among recent writers, those such as Gerard Piel[16] who have persuasively emphasized our ability to solve problems through reasoned decisions and actions have tended—like

Condorcet—to find the solution of the population problem in economic and social conditions favoring slower population growth. In contrast, those who have been thoroughly skeptical of reasoned human action to limit population growth have tended to go in the direction of "override" in one form or another, rather than concentrate on development and voluntarism.

Has development, in fact, done much to reduce population growth? There can be little doubt that economic and social development, in general, has been associated with major reductions in birth rates and the emergence of smaller families as the norm. This is a pattern that was, of course, clearly observed in Europe and North America as they underwent industrialization, but that experience has been repeated in many other parts of the world.

In particular, conditions of economic security and affluence, wider availability of contraceptive methods, expansion of education (particularly female education), and lower mortality rates have had—and are currently having—quite substantial effects in reducing birth rates in different parts of the world.[17] The rate of world population growth is certainly declining, and even over the last two decades its percentage growth rate has fallen from 2.2 percent per year between 1970 and 1980 to 1.7 percent between 1980 and 1992. This rate is expected to go steadily down until the size of the world's population becomes nearly stationary.[18]

There are important regional differences in demographic behavior; for example, the population growth rate in India peaked at 2.2 percent a year (in the 1970s) and has since started to diminish, whereas most Latin American countries peaked at much higher rates before coming down sharply, while many countries in Africa currently have growth rates between 3 and 4 percent, with an average for Sub-Saharan Africa of 3.1 percent. Similarly, the different factors have varied in their respective influence from region to region. But there can be little dispute that economic and social development tends to reduce fertility rates. The regions of the Third World that lag most in achieving economic and social development, such as many countries in Africa, are, in general, also the ones that have failed to reduce birth rates significantly. Malthus's fear that economic and social development could only encourage people to have more children has certainly proved to be radically wrong, and so have all the painful policy implications drawn from it.

This raises the following question: In view of the clear connection between development and lower fertility, why isn't the dispute over how to deal with population growth fully resolved already? Why don't we reinterpret the population problem simply as a problem of underdevelopment (even if we reject the oversimple slogan "development is the most reliable contraceptive")?

In the long run, this may indeed be exactly the right approach. The problem is more complex, however, because a "contraceptive" that is "reliable" in the long run may not act fast enough to meet the present threat. Even though development may dependably work to stabilize population if it is given enough time, there may not be, it is argued, time enough to give. The death rate often falls very fast with more widely available health care, better sanitation, and improved nutrition, while the birth rate may fall rather slowly. Much growth of population may meanwhile occur.

This is exactly the point at which apocalyptic prophecies add force to the "override" view. One claim, then, that needs examination is that the world is facing an imminent crisis, one so urgent that development is just too slow a process to deal with it. We must try right now, the argument goes, to cut down population growth by drastic and forceful means if necessary. The second claim that also needs scrutiny is the actual feasibility of adequately reducing population growth through these drastic means, without fostering social and economic development.

Population and Income

It is sometimes argued that signs of an imminent crisis can be found in the growing impoverishment of the South, with falling income per capita accompanying high population growth. In general, there is little evidence for this. As a matter of fact, the average population of "low income" countries (as defined by the World Bank) has been enjoying not only a rising gross national product (GNP) per capita, but a growth rate of GNP per capita (3.9 percent per year for 1980-92) that is much faster than the rates for the "high income" countries (2.4 percent) and the "middle income" ones (0 percent).[19]

The growth of per capita GNP of the population of low-income countries would have been even higher had it not been for the negative growth rates of many countries in Sub-Saharan Africa, one region in which a number of countries have been experiencing economic decline. But the main culprit causing this state of affairs is the terrible failure of economic production in Sub-Saharan Africa (connected particularly with political disruption, including wars and military rule), rather than population growth, which is only a subsidiary factor. Sub-Saharan Africa does have high population growth, but its economic stagnation has contributed much more to the fall in its per capita income.

With its average population growth rate of 3.1 percent per year, had sub-Saharan Africa suddenly matched China's low population growth of 1.4 percent (the lowest among the low-income countries), it would have gained roughly 1.7

percent in per capita GNP growth. The real income per person would still have fallen, even with that minimal population growth, for many countries in the region. The growth of GNP per capita is *minus* 1.9 percent for Ethiopia, *minus* 1.8 percent for Togo, *minus* 3.6 percent for Mozambique, *minus* 4.3 percent for Niger, *minus* 4.7 percent for Ivory Coast, not to mention Somalia, Sudan, and Angola, where the political disruption has been so serious that no reliable GNP estimates even exist. A lower population growth rate could have reduced the magnitude of the fall in per capita GNP, but the main roots of Africa's economic decline lie elsewhere. The complex political factors underlying the troubles of Africa include, among other things, the subversion of democracy and the rise of combative military rulers, often encouraged by the Cold War (with Africa providing "client states"—from Somalia and Ethiopia to Angola and Zaire—for the superpowers, particularly from the 1960s onward). The explanation of Sub-Saharan Africa's problems has to be sought in these political troubles, which affect economic stability, agricultural and industrial incentives, public health arrangements, and social services—even family planning and population policy.[20]

There is indeed a very powerful case for reducing the rate of growth of population in Africa, but this problem cannot be dissociated from the rest of the continent's woes. Sub-Saharan Africa lags behind other developing regions in economic security, in health care, in life expectancy, in basic education, and in political and economic stability. It should be no great surprise that it lags behind in family planning as well. To dissociate the task of population control from the politics and economics of Africa would be a great mistake and would seriously mislead public policy.

Population and Food Production

Malthus's exact thesis cannot, however, be disputed by quoting statistics of income per capita, for he was concerned specifically with food supply per capita, and he concentrated on "the proportion between the natural increase of population and food." Many modern commentators, including Paul Ehrlich and Garrett Hardin, have said much about this, too. When Ehrlich says, in his *Population Bomb,* "too little food," he does not mean "too little income," but specifically a growing shortage of food.

Is population beginning to outrun food production? Even though such an impression is often given in public discussions, there is, in fact, no serious evidence that this is happening. While there are some year-to-year fluctuations in the growth of food output (typically inducing, whenever things slacken a bit, some excited remarks by those who sense an impending doom), the worldwide trend of food output per person has been firmly upward. Not only over the two centuries since Malthus's time, but also during recent decades, the rise in food output has been significantly and consistently outpacing the expansion of world population.[21]

But the total food supply in the world as a whole is not the only issue. What about the regional distribution of food? If it were to turn out that the rising ratio of food to population is mainly caused by increased production in richer countries (for example, if it appeared that the U.S. wheat output was feeding the Third World, in which much of the population expansion is taking place), then the neo-Malthusian fears about "too many people" and "too little food" may have some plausibility. Is this what is happening?

In fact, with one substantial exception, exactly the opposite is true. The largest increases in the production of food—not just in the aggregate but also per person—are actually taking place in the Third World, particularly in the region that is having the largest absolute increases in the world population, that is, in Asia. The many millions of people who are added to the populations of India and China may be constantly cited by the terrorized—and terrorizing—advocates of the apocalyptic view, but it is precisely in these countries that the most rapid rates of growth in food output per capita are to be observed. For example, between the three-year averages of 1979-81 and 1991-93, food production per capita in the world moved up by 3 percent, while it went up by only 2 percent in Europe and went down by nearly 5 percent in North America. In contrast, per capita food production jumped up by 22 percent in Asia generally, including 23 percent in India and 39 percent in China.[22] (See Table 27.1.)

During the same period, however, food production per capita went down by 6 percent in Africa, and even the absolute size of food output fell in some countries

Table 27.1 Indices of Food Production Per Capita

	1979–81 Base Period	1991–93
World	100	103
Europe	100	102
North America	100	95
Africa	100	94
Asia	100	122
including		
India	100	123
China	100	139

Source: FAO Quarterly Bulletin of Statistics

(such as Malawi and Somalia). Of course, many countries in the world—from Syria, Italy, and Sweden to Botswana in Africa—have had declining food production per capita without experiencing hunger, since their economies have prospered and grown; when the means are available, food can be easily bought in the international market. For many countries in Sub-Saharan Africa, the problem arises from the fact that the decline in food production is an integral part of the story of overall economic decline, which I discussed earlier.

Difficulties of food production in Sub-Saharan Africa, like other problems of the national economy, are not only linked to wars, dictatorships, and political chaos. In addition, there is some evidence that climatic shifts have had unfavorable effects on parts of that continent. While some of the climatic problems may be caused partly by increases in human settlement and environmental neglect, that neglect is not unrelated to the political and economic chaos that has characterized Sub-Saharan Africa during the last few decades. The food problem of Africa must be seen as one part of a wider political and economic problem in the region.[23]

The Declining Price of Food

To return to the balance between food and population: rising food production per capita in the world as a whole, and in the Third World in particular, contradicts some of the pessimism that characterized the gloomy predictions of the past. Prophecies of imminent disaster during the last few decades have not proved any more accurate than Malthus's prognostication nearly two hundred years ago. As for new prophecies of doom, they cannot, of course, be contradicted until the future arrives. There was no way of refuting the theses of W. Paddock and P. Paddock's popular book *Famine—1975!*, published in 1968, which predicted a terrible cataclysm for the world as a whole by 1975 (writing of India, in particular, as a basket case), until 1975 actually arrived. The new prophets have learned not to attach specific dates to the crises they foresee, and past failures do not seem to have reduced the popular appetite for this creative genre.

However after noting the rather dismal forecasting record of doomsayers, we must also accept the general methodological point that present trends in output do not necessarily tell us much about the prospects of further expansion. It could, for example, be argued that maintaining growth in food production may require proportionately increasing investments of capital, drawing them away from other kinds of production. This would tend to make food progressively more expensive if there are "diminishing returns" in shifting resources from other fields into food production. And, ultimately, further expansion of food production may become so expensive that it would be hard to maintain the trend of increasing food production without reducing other outputs drastically.

But is food production really getting more and more expensive? There is, in fact, no evidence for that conclusion either. In fact, quite the contrary. Not only is food generally much cheaper to buy today, in constant dollars, than it was in Malthus's time, but it also has become cheaper during recent decades. As a matter of fact, there have been increasing complaints among food exporters, especially in the Third World, that food prices have fallen in relation to other commodities. For example, in 1992 a United Nations report recorded a 38 percent fall in the relative prices of "basic foods" over the last decade.[24] This is entirely in line with the trend, during the last three decades, toward declining relative prices of particular food items, in relation to the prices of manufactured goods. The World Bank's adjusted estimates of the prices of particular food crops, between 1953-55 and 1983-85, show similarly steep declines for such staples as rice (42 percent), wheat (57 percent), sorghum (39 percent), and maize (37 percent).[25]

Not only is food getting less expensive, but we also have to bear in mind that the current increase in food production (substantial and well ahead of population growth, as it is) is itself being kept in check by the difficulties in selling food profitably as the relative prices of food have fallen. Those neo-Malthusians who concede that food production is now growing faster than population often point out that it is growing "only a little faster than population," and they are inclined to interpret this as evidence that we are reaching the limits of what we can produce to keep pace with population growth.

But surely that is the wrong conclusion to draw in view of the falling relative prices of food, and the current difficulties in selling food, since it ignores the effects of economic incentives that govern production. When we take into account the persistent cheapening of food prices, we have good grounds to suggest that food output is being held back by a lack of effective demand in the market. The imaginary crisis in food production, contradicted as it is by the upward trends of total and regional food output per capita, is thus further debunked by an analysis of the economic incentives to produce more food.

Population and Deprivation

I have examined the alleged "food problem" associated with population growth in some detail because it has received so much attention both in the traditional Malthusian literature and in the recent writings of neo-Malthusians. In concentrating on his claim that growing populations would not have enough food, Malthus differed from Condorcet's broader presentation of the population question. Condorcet's own emphasis was on the possibility of "a continual diminution of happiness" as a result of population growth, a diminution that could occur in many different ways—not just through the deprivation of food, but through a decline in living conditions generally. That more extensive worry can remain even when Malthus's analysis of food supply is rejected.

Indeed, average income and food production per capita can go on increasing even as the wretchedly deprived living conditions of particular sections of the population get worse, as they have in many parts of the Third World. The living conditions of backward regions and deprived classes can decline even when a country's economic growth is very rapid on the average. Brazil during the 1960s and 1970s provided an extreme example of this. The sense that there are just "too many people" around often arises from seeing the desperate lives of people in the large and rapidly growing urban slums—*bidonvilles*—in poor countries, sobering reminders that we should not take too much comfort from aggregate statistics of economic progress.

But in an essay addressed mainly to the population problem, what we have to ask is not whether things are just fine in the Third World (they obviously are not), but whether population growth is the root cause of the deprivation that people suffer. The question is whether the particular instances of deep poverty we observe derive mainly from population growth rather than from other factors that lead to unshared prosperity and persistent and possibly growing inequality. The tendency to see in population growth an explanation for every calamity that afflicts poor people is now fairly well established in some circles, and the message that gets transmitted constantly is the opposite of the old picture postcard: "Wish you weren't here."

To see in population growth the main reason for the growth of overcrowded and very poor slums in large cities, for example, is not empirically convincing. It does not help to explain why the slums of Calcutta and Bombay have grown worse at a faster rate than those of Karachi and Islamabad (India's population growth rate is 2.1 percent per year, Pakistan's 3.1), or why Jakarta has deteriorated faster than Ankara or Istanbul (Indonesian population growth is 1.8 percent, Turkey's 2.3), or why the slums of Mexico City have become worse more rapidly than those of San Jose (Mexico's population growth rate is 2.0, Costa Rica's 2.8), or why Harlem can seem more and more deprived when compared with the poorer districts of Singapore (U.S. population growth rate is 1.0, Singapore's is 1.8). Many causal factors affect the degree of deprivation in particular parts of a country—rural as well as urban—and to try to see them all as resulting from overpopulation is the negation of social analysis.

This is not to deny that population growth may well have an effect on deprivation, but only to insist that any investigation of the effects of population growth must be part of the analysis of economic and political processes, including the effects of other variables. It is the isolationist view of population growth that should be rejected.

Threats to the Environment

In his concern about "a continual diminution of happiness" from population growth, Condorcet was a pioneer in considering the possibility that natural raw materials might be used up, thereby making living conditions worse. In his characteristically rationalist solution, which relied partly on voluntary and reasoned measures to reduce the birth rate, Condorcet also envisaged the development of less improvident technology: "The manufacture of articles will be achieved with less wastage in raw materials and will make better use of them."[26]

The effects of a growing population on the environment could be a good deal more serious than the food problems that have received so much attention in the literature inspired by Malthus. If the environment is damaged by population pressures, this obviously affects the kind of life we lead, and the possibilities of a "diminution in happiness" can be quite considerable.

In dealing with this problem, we have to distinguish once again between the long and the short run. The short-run picture tends to be dominated by the fact that the per capita consumption of food, fuel, and other goods by people in Third World countries is often relatively low; consequently the impact of population growth in these countries is not, in relative terms, so damaging to the global environment. But the problems of the local environment can, of course, be serious in many developing economies. They vary from the "neighborhood pollution" created by unregulated industries to the pressure of denser populations on rural resources such as fields and woods.[27] (The Indian authorities had to close down several factories in and around Agra, since the facade of the Taj Mahal was turning pale as a result of chemical pollution from local factories.) But it remains true that one additional American typically has a larger negative impact on the ozone layer, global warmth, and other elements of the earth's environment than dozens of Indians and Zimbabweans put together. Those who argue for the immediate need for forceful population control in the Third World to preserve the global environment must first recognize this elementary fact.

This does not imply, as is sometimes suggested, that as far as the global environment is concerned, population growth in the Third World is nothing to worry about. The long-run impact on the global environment of population growth in the developing countries can be expected to be large. As the Indians and the Zimbabweans develop economically, they too will consume a great deal more, and they will pose, in the future, a threat to the earth's environment similar to that of people in the rich countries today. The long-run threat of population to the environment is a real one.

Women's Well-Being and Fertility

Since reducing the birth rate can be slow, this and other long-run problems should be addressed right now. Solutions will no doubt have to be found in the two directions to which, as it happens, Condorcet pointed: (1) developing new technology and new behavior patterns that would waste little and pollute less, and (2) fostering social and economic changes that would gradually bring down the growth rate of population.

On reducing birth rates, Condorcet's own solution not only included enhancing economic opportunity and security, but also stressed the importance of education, particularly female education. A better-educated population could have a more informed discussion of the kind of life we have reason to value; in particular it would reject the drudgery of a life of continuous childbearing and child-rearing that is routinely forced on many Third World women. That drudgery, in some ways, is the most immediate consequence of high fertility rates.

Central to reducing birth rates, then, is a close connection between women's well-being and their power to make their own decisions and bring about changes in the fertility pattern. Women in many Third World countries are deprived by high birth frequency of the freedom to do other things in life, not to mention the medical dangers of repeated pregnancy and high maternal mortality, which are both characteristic of many developing countries. It is thus not surprising that reductions in birth rates have typically been associated with improvement of women's status and their ability to make their voices heard—often the result of expanded opportunities for schooling and political activity.[28]

There is nothing particularly exotic about declines in the birth rate occurring through a process of voluntary rational assessment, of which Condorcet spoke. It is what people do when they have some basic education, know about family-planning methods and have access to them, do not readily accept a life of persistent drudgery, and are not deeply anxious about their economic security. It is also what they do when they are not forced by high infant—and child—mortality rates to be so worried that no child will survive to support them in their old age that they try to have many children. In country after country the birth rate has come down with more female education, the reduction of mortality rates, the expansion of economic means and security, and greater public discussion of ways of living.

Is Gradualism Good Enough?

There is little doubt that this process of social and economic change will over time cut down the birth rate. Indeed the growth rate of world population is already firmly declining—it came down from 2.2 percent in the 1970s to 1.7 percent between 1980 and 1992. Had imminent cataclysm been threatening, we might have had good reason to reject such gradual progress and consider more drastic means of population control, as some have advocated. But that apocalyptic view is empirically baseless. There is no imminent emergency that calls for a breathless response. What is called for is systematic support for people's own decisions to reduce family size through expanding education and health care, and through economic and social development.

It is often asked where the money needed for expanding education, health care, and the like would be found. Education, health services, and many other means of improving the quality of life are typically highly labor-intensive in poor countries (because of low wages).[29] While poor countries have less money to spend, they also need less money to provide these services. For this reason many poor countries have indeed been able to expand educational and health services widely without waiting to become prosperous through the process of economic growth. Sri Lanka, Costa Rica, Indonesia, and Thailand are good examples, and there are many others. While the impact of these social services on the quality and length of life has been much studied, they are also major means of reducing the birth rate.

China's Population Policies

By contrast with such open and voluntary developments, coercive methods, such as the "one child policy" in some regions, have been tried in China, particularly since the reforms of 1979. Many commentators have pointed out that by 1992 the Chinese birth rate had fallen to 19 per 1,000, compared with 29 per 1,000 in India, and 37 per 1,000 for the average of other poor countries other than China and India. China's total fertility rate (reflecting the number of children born per woman) is now at "the replacement level" of 2.0, compared with India's 3.6 and the weighted average of 4.9 for low-income countries other than China and India.[30] Hasn't China shown the way to "solve" the population problem in other developing countries as well?

The difficulties with this "solution" are of several kinds. First, if freedom is valued at all, the lack of freedom associated with this approach must be seen to be a social loss in itself. The importance of reproductive freedom has been persuasively emphasized by women's groups throughout the world.[31]

The loss of freedom is often dismissed on grounds that because of cultural differences, authoritarian policies that would not be tolerated in the West are acceptable to Asians. While we often hear references to "despotic" Oriental traditions, such arguments are no more convincing than a claim that compulsion in the West is justified by the traditions of the Spanish Inquisition or of the Nazi concentration camps. Frequent references are also made to the emphasis on discipline in the "Confucian tradition"; but that is not the only tradition for modern Asia (even if we were able to show that discipline is more important for Confucius than it is for, say, Plato or Saint Augustine). Only a democratic expression of opinion could reveal whether citizens would find a compulsory system acceptable. While such a test has not occurred in China, one did in fact take place in India during "the emergency period" in the 1970s, when Indira Gandhi's government imposed compulsory birth control and suspended various legal freedoms. In the general elections that followed, the politicians favoring the policy of coercion were overwhelmingly defeated. Furthermore, family-planning experts in India have observed how the briefly applied programs of compulsory sterilization tended to discredit voluntary birth-control programs generally, since people became deeply suspicious of the entire movement to control fertility.

Second, apart from the fundamental issue of whether people are willing to accept compulsory birth control, its specific consequences must also be considered. Insofar as coercion is effective, it works by making people do things they would not freely do. The social consequences of such compulsion, including the ways in which an unwilling population tends to react when it is coerced, can be appalling. For example, the demands of a "one-child family" can lead to the neglect—or worse—of a second child, thereby increasing the infant-mortality rate. Moreover, in a country with a strong preference for male children—a preference shared by China and many other countries in Asia and North Africa—a policy of allowing only one child per family can easily lead to the fatal neglect of a female child. There is much evidence that this is fairly widespread in China, with very adverse effects on infant-mortality rates. There are reports that female children have been severely neglected as well as suggestions that female infanticide occurs with considerable frequency. Such consequences are hard to tolerate morally, and perhaps politically also, in the long run.

Third, what is also not clear is exactly how much additional reduction in the birth rate has been achieved through these coercive methods. Many of China's longstanding social and economic programs have been valuable in reducing fertility, including those that have expanded education for women as well as men, made health care more generally available, provided more job opportunities for women, and stimulated rapid economic growth. These factors would themselves have reduced the birth rate, and it is not clear how much "extra lowering" of fertility rates has been achieved in China through compulsion.

For example, we can determine whether many of the countries that match (or outmatch) China in life expectancy, female literacy rates, and female participation in the labor force actually have a higher fertility rate than China. Of all the countries in the world for which data are given in the World Development Report 1994, there are only three such countries: Jamaica (2.7), Thailand (2.2), and Sweden (2.1)—and the fertility rates of two of these are close to China's (2.0). Thus the additional contribution of coercion to reducing fertility in China is by no means clear, since compulsion was superimposed on a society that was already reducing its birth rate and in which education and jobs outside the home were available to large numbers of women. In some regions of China the compulsory program needed little enforcement, whereas in other—more backward—regions, it had to be applied with much severity, with terrible consequences in infant mortality and discrimination against female children. While China may get too much credit for its authoritarian measures, it gets far too little credit for the other more collaborative and participatory policies it has followed, which have themselves helped to cut the birth rate.

Comparing China and India

A useful contrast can be drawn between China and India, the two most populous countries in the world. If we look only at the national averages, it is easy to see that China with its low fertility rate of 2.0 has achieved much more than India has with its average fertility rate of 3.6. To what extent this contrast can be attributed to the effectiveness of the coercive policies used in China is not clear, since we would expect the fertility rate to be much lower in China in view of its higher percentage of female literacy (almost twice as high), higher life expectancy (almost ten years more), larger female involvement (by three quarters) in the labor force, and so on.

But India is a country of great diversity, whose different states have very unequal achievements in literacy, health care, and economic and social development. Most states in India are far behind the Chinese provinces in educational achievement (with the exception of Tibet, which has the lowest literacy rate of any Chinese or Indian state), and the same applies to other factors that affect fertility. However, the state of Kerala in southern India provides an interesting comparison with China, since it too has high levels of basic education, health care, and so on. Kerala is a state within a country, but with its 29 million people, it is larger than most countries in the world (including Canada). Kerala's birth rate of 18 per 1,000 is actually lower than China's 19 per 1,000, and its fertility rate is 1.8 for 1991, compared with China's 2.0 for 1992. These low rates have been achieved without any state coercion.[32]

The roots of Kerala's success are to be found in the kinds of social progress Condorcet hoped for, including, among others, a high female literacy rate (86 percent, which is substantially higher than China's 68 percent). The rural literacy rate is in fact higher in Kerala—for women as well as men—than in every single province in China. Male and female life expectancies at birth in China are respectively 67 and 71 years; the provisional 1991 figures for men and women in Kerala are 71 and 74 years. Women have been active in Kerala's economic and political life for a long time. A high proportion do skilled and semiskilled work, and a large number have taken part in educational movements.[33] It is perhaps of symbolic importance that the first public pronouncement of the need for widespread elementary education in any part of India was made in 1817 by Rani Gouri Parvathi Bai, the young queen of the princely state of Travancore, which makes up a substantial part of modern Kerala. For a long time public discussions in Kerala have centered on women's rights and the undesirability of couples' marrying when very young.

This political process has been voluntary and collaborative, rather than coercive, and the adverse reactions that have been observed in China, such as infant mortality, have not occurred in Kerala. Kerala's low fertility rate has been achieved along with an infant-mortality rate of 16.5 per 1,000 live births (17 for boys and 16 for girls), compared with China's 31 (28 for boys and 33 for girls). And as a result of greater gender equality in Kerala, women have not suffered from higher mortality rates than men in Kerala, as they have in the rest of India and in China. Even the ratio of females to males in the total population in Kerala (above 1.03) is quite close to that of the current ratios in Europe and America (reflecting the usual pattern of lower female mortality whenever women and men receive similar care). By contrast, the average female to male ratio in China is 0.94 and in India as a whole 0.93.[34] Anyone drawn to the Chinese experience of compulsory birth control must take note of these facts.

The temptation to use the "override" approach arises at least partly from impatience with the allegedly slow process of fertility reduction through collaborative, rather than coercive, attempts. Yet Kerala's birth rate has fallen from 44 per 1,000 in the 1950s to 18 by 1991—not a sluggish decline. Nor is Kerala unique in this respect. Other societies, such as those of Sri Lanka, South Korea, and Thailand, which have relied on expanding education and reducing mortality rates—instead of on coercion—have also achieved sharp declines in fertility and birth rates.

It is also interesting to compare the time required for reducing fertility in China with that in the two states in India, Kerala and Tamil Nadu, which have done most to encourage voluntary and collaborative reduction in birth rates (even though Tamil Nadu is well behind Kerala in each respect).[35] Table 27.2 shows the fertility rates both in 1979, when the one-child policy and related programs were introduced in China, and in 1991. Despite China's one-child policy and other coercive measures, its fertility rate seems to have fallen much less sharply than those of Kerala and Tamil Nadu. The "override" view is very hard to defend on the basis of the Chinese experience, the only systematic and sustained attempt to impose such a policy that has so far been made.

Priority to Family Planning?

Even those who do not advocate legal or economic coercion sometimes

Table 27.2 Fertility Rates In China and Two Indian States

	1979	1991
China	2.8	2.0
Kerala	3.0	1.8
Tamil Nadu	3.5	2.2

Sources: For China, Xizhe Peng, Demographic Transition in China (Oxford University Press, 1991), Li Chengrui, A Study of China's Population (Beijing: Foreign Language Press, 1992), and World Development Report 1994. For India, Sample Registration System 1979-80 (New Delhi: Ministry of Home Affairs, 1982) and Sample Registration System: Fertility and Mortality Indicators 1991 (New Delhi: Ministry of Home Affairs, 1993).

suggest a variant of the "override" approach—the view, which has been getting increasing support, that the highest priority should be given simply to family planning, even if this means diverting resources from education and health care as well as other activities associated with development. We often hear claims that enormous declines in birth rates have been accomplished through making family-planning services available, without waiting for improvements in education and health care.

The experience of Bangladesh is sometimes cited as an example of such success. Indeed, even though the female literacy rate in Bangladesh is only around 22 percent and life expectancy at birth no higher than 55 years, fertility rates have been substantially reduced there through the greater availability of family-planning services, including counseling.[36] We have to examine carefully what lessons can, in fact, be drawn from this evidence.

First, it is certainly significant that Bangladesh has been able to cut its fertility rate from 7.0 to 4.5 during the short period between 1975 and 1990, an achievement that discredits the view that people will not voluntarily embrace family planning in the poorest countries. But we have to ask further whether family-planning efforts may themselves be sufficient to make fertility come down to really low levels, without providing for female education and the other features of a fuller collaborative approach. The fertility rate of 4.5 in Bangladesh is still quite high—considerably higher than even India's average rate of 3.6. To begin stabilizing the population, the fertility rates would have to come down closer to the "replacement level" of 2.0, as has happened in Kerala and Tamil Nadu and in many other places outside the Indian subcontinent. Female education and the other social developments connected with lowering the birth rate would still be much needed. Contrasts between the records of Indian states offer some substantial lessons here. While Kerala, and to a smaller extent Tamil Nadu, have surged ahead in achieving radically reduced fertility rates, other states in India in the so-called northern heartland (such as Uttar Pradesh, Bihar, Madhya Pradesh, and Rajasthan) have very low levels of education, and of general health care (often combined with pressure on the poor to accept birth-control measures, including sterilization, as a qualifying condition for medical attention and other public services). These states all have high fertility rates—between 4.4 and 5.1. The regional contrasts within India strongly argue for the collaborative approach, including active and educated participation of women.

The threat of an impending population crisis tempts many international observers to suggest that priority be given to family-planning arrangements in the Third World countries over other commitments such as education and health care, a redirection of public efforts that is often recommended by policy-makers and at international conferences. Not only will this shift have negative effects on people's well-being and reduce their freedoms, but it can also be self-defeating if the goal is to stabilize population.

The appeal of such slogans as "family planning first" rests partly on misconceptions about what is needed to reduce fertility rates, but also on mistaken beliefs about the excessive costs of social development, including education and health care. As has been discussed, both these activities are highly labor intensive, and thus relatively inexpensive even in very poor economies. In fact, Kerala, India's star performer in expanding education and reducing both death rates and birth rates, is among the poorer Indian states. Its domestically produced income is quite low—lower indeed in per capita terms than even the Indian average—even if this is somewhat deceptive, for the greatest expansion of Kerala's earnings derives from citizens who work outside the state. Kerala's ability to finance adequately both educational expansion and health coverage depends on both activities being labor-intensive; they can be made available even in a low-income economy where there is the political will to use them. Despite its economic backwardness, an issue that Kerala will undoubtedly have to address before long (perhaps by reducing bureaucratic controls over agriculture and industry, which have stagnated), its level of social development has been remarkable, and that has turned out to be crucial in reducing fertility rates. Kerala's fertility rate of 1.8 compares well not only with China's 2.0 but also with the U.S.'s and Sweden's 2.1, Canada's 1.9, and Britain's and France's 1.8.

The population problem is serious, certainly, but neither because of "the proportion between the natural increase of population and food" nor because of some impending apocalypse. There are reasons for worry about the long-term effects of population growth on the environment; and there are strong reasons for concern about the adverse effects of high birth rates on the quality of life, especially of women. With greater opportunities for education (especially female education), reduction of mortality rates (especially of children), improvement in economic security (especially in old age), and greater participation of women in employment and in political action, fast reductions in birth rates can be expected to result through the decisions and actions of those whose lives depend on them.

This is happening right now in many parts of the world, and the result has been a considerable slowing down of world population growth. The best way of dealing with the population problem is to help speed these processes elsewhere. In contrast, the emergency mentality based on false beliefs in imminent cataclysms leads to breathless responses that are deeply counterproductive, preventing the development of rational and sustainable family planning. Coercive policies of forced birth control involve terrible social sacrifices, and there is little evidence that they are more effective in reducing birth rates than serious programs of collaborative action.

Notes

1. This paper draws on my lecture arranged by the "Eminent Citizens Committee for Cairo '94" at the United Nations in New York on April 18, 1994, and also on research supported by the National Science Foundation.
2. Paul Ehrlich, *The Population Bomb* (Ballantine, 1968). More recently Paul Ehrlich and Anne H. Ehrlich have written *The Population Explosion* (Simon and Schuster, 1990).
3. Garrett Hardin, *Living within Limits* (Oxford University Press, 1993).
4. Thomas Robert Malthus, "Essay on the Principle of Population As It Affects the Future Improvement of Society with Remarks on the Speculation of Mr. Godwin, M. Condorcet,

425

and Other Writers" (London: J. Johnson, 1798), Chapter 8; in the Penguin classics edition, *An Essay on the Principle of Population* (1982), p. 123.

5. See Simon Kuznets, *Modern Economic Growth* (Yale University Press, 1966).

6. Note by the Secretary-General of the United Nations to the Preparatory Committee for the International Conference on Population and Development, Third Session, A/Conf.171/PC/5, February 18, 1994, p. 30.

7. Philip Morris Hauser's estimates are presented in the National Academy of Sciences publication *Rapid Population Growth: Consequences and Policy Implications*, Vol. 1 (Johns Hopkins University Press, 1971). See also Simon Kuznets, *Modern Economic Growth,* Chapter 2.

8. For an important collection of papers on these and related issues see Sir Francis Graham-Smith, F.R.S., editor, *Population—The Complex Reality: A Report of the Population Summit of the World's Scientific Academies,* issued by the Royal Society and published in the US by North American Press, Golden, Colorado. See also D. Gale Johnson and Ronald D. Lee, editors, *Population Growth and Economic Development, Issues and Evidence* (University of Wisconsin Press, 1987).

9. Garrett Hardin, *Living within Limits,* p. 274.

10. Paul Kennedy, who has discussed important problems in the distinctly "social" aspects of population growth, has pointed out that this debate "has, in one form or another, been with us since then," and "it is even more pertinent today than when Malthus composed his Essay," in *Preparing for the Twenty-first Century* (Random House, 1993), pp. 5-6.

11. On the importance of "enlightenment" traditions in Condorcet's thinking, see Emma Rothschild, "Condorcet and the Conflict of Values," forthcoming in *The Historical Journal.*

12. Marie Jean Antoine Nicholas de Caritat Marquis de Condorcet's *Esquisse d'un Tableau Historique des Progrès de l'Esprit Humain, Xe Epoque* (1795). English translation by June Barraclough, *Sketch for a Historical Picture of the Progress of the Human Mind,* with an introduction by Stuart Hampshire (Weidenfeld and Nicolson, 1955), pp. 187-192.

13. T.R. Malthus, *A Summary View of the Principle of Population* (London: John Murray, 1830); in the Penguin classics edition (1982), p. 243; italics added.

14. On practical policies, including criticism of poverty relief and charitable hospitals, advocated for Britain by Malthus and his followers, see William St. Clair, *The Godwins and the Shelleys: A Biography of a Family* (Norton, 1989).

15. Malthus, "Essay on the Principle of Population, Chapter 17"; in the Penguin classics edition, *An Essay on the Principle of Population,* pp. 198-199. Malthus showed some signs of weakening in this belief as he grew older.

16. Gerard Piel, *Only One World: Our Own to Make and to Keep* (Freeman, 1992).

17. For discussions of these empirical connections, see R.A. Easterlin, editor, *Population and Economic Change in Developing Countries* (University of Chicago Press, 1980); T.P. Schultz, *Economics of Population* (Addison-Wesley, 1981); J.C. Caldwell, *Theory of Fertility Decline* (Academic Press, 1982); E. King and M.A. Hill, editors, Women's *Education in Developing Countries* (Johns Hopkins University Press, 1992); Nancy Birdsall, "Economic Approaches to Population Growth" in *The Handbook of Development Economics,* edited by H.B. Chenery and T.N. Srinivasan (Amsterdam: North Holland, 1988); Robert Cassen, et. al., *Population and Development: Old Debates, New Conclusions* (New Brunswick: Overseas Development Council/Transaction Publishers, 1994).

18. World Bank, *World Development Report 1994* (Oxford University Press, 1994), Table 25, pp. 210-211.

19. World Bank, *World Development Report 1994,* Table 2.

20. These issues are discussed in my joint book with Jean Drèze, Hunger and Public Action (Oxford University Press, 1989), and the three volumes edited by us, *The Political*

Economy of Hunger (Oxford University Press, 1990), and also in my paper "Economic Regress: Concepts and Features," *Proceedings of the World Bank Annual Conference on Development Economics 1993* (World Bank, 1994).

21. This is confirmed by, among other statistics, the food production figures regularly presented by the United Nations Food and Agricultural Organization (see the FAO Quarterly Bulletin of Statistics, and also the FAO Monthly Bulletins).

22. For a more detailed picture and references to data sources, see my "Population and Reasoned Agency: Food, Fertility and Economic Development," in *Population, Economic Development, and the Environment*, edited by Kerstin Lindahl-Kiessling and Hans Landberg (Oxford University Press, 1994); see also the other contributions in this volume. The data presented here have been slightly updated from later publications of the FAO.

23. On this see my *Poverty and Famines* (Oxford University Press, 1981).

24. See UNCTAD VIII, Analytical Report by the UNCTAD Secretariat to the Conference (United Nations, 1992), Table V-S, p. 235. The period covered is between 1979-1981 to 1988-1990. These figures and related ones are discussed in greater detail in my paper "Population and Reasoned Agency," cited earlier.

25. World Bank, *Price Prospects for Major Primary Commodities*, Vol. II (World Bank, March 1993), Annex Tables 6, 12, and 18.

26. Condorcet, *Esquisse d'un Tableau Historique des Progrès de l'Esprit Humain*; in the 1968 reprint, p. 187.

27. The importance of "local" environmental issues is stressed and particularly explored by Partha Dasgupta in *An Inquiry into Well-Being and Destitution* (Oxford University Press, 1993).

28. In a forthcoming monograph by Jean Drèze and myself tentatively called "India: Economic Development and Social Opportunities," we discuss the importance of women's political agency in rectifying some of the more serious lapses in Indian economic and social performance—not just pertaining to the deprivation of women themselves.

29. See Jean Drèze and Amartya Sen, *Hunger and Public Action* (Oxford University Press, 1989), which also investigates the remarkable success of some poor countries in providing widespread educational and health services.

30. World Bank, *World Development Report 1994*, p. 212; and *Sample Registration System: Fertility and Mortality Indicators 1991* (New Delhi: Ministry of Home Affairs, 1993).

31. See the discussions, and the literature cited, in Gita Sen, Adrienne German, and Lincoln Chen, editors, *Population Policies Reconsidered: Health, Empowerment, and Rights* (Harvard Center for Population and Development Studies/International Women's Health Coalition, 1994).

32. On the actual processes involved, see T.N. Krishnan, "Demographic Transition in Kerala: Facts and Factors," in *Economic and Political Weekly*, Vol. 11 (1976), and P.N. Mari Bhat and S. I. Rajan, "Demographic Transition in Kerala Revisited," in *Economic and Political Weekly*, Vol. 25 (1990).

33. See, for example, Robin Jeffrey, "Culture and Governments: How Women Made Kerala Literate," in *Pacific Affairs*, Vol. 60 (1987).

34. On this see my "More Than 100 Million Women Are Missing," New York Review of Books, December 20, 1990; Ansley J. Coale, "Excess Female Mortality and the Balance of the Sexes: An Estimate of the Number of 'Missing Females'," *Population and Development Review*, No. 17 (1991); Amartya Sen, "Missing Women," British Medical Journal, No. 304 (March 1992); Stephan Klasen, "'Missing Women' Reconsidered," *World Development*, forthcoming.

35. Tamil Nadu has benefited from an active and efficient voluntary program of family planning, but these efforts have been helped by favorable social conditions as well, such

as a high literacy rate (the second highest among the sixteen major states), a high rate of female participation in work outside the home (the third highest), a relatively low infant mortality rate (the third lowest), and a traditionally higher age of marriage. See also T.V. Antony, "The Family Planning Programme—Lessons from Tamil Nadu's Experience," *Indian Journal of Social Science*, Volume 5 (1992).

36. World Bank and Population Reference Bureau, *Success in a Challenging Environment: Fertility Decline in Bangladesh* (World Bank, 1993).

CHAPTER 28

BIRTH SPACING: THREE TO FIVE SAVES LIVES

V. Setty-Venugopal and U.D. Upadhyay

Couples who space their births 3 to 5 years apart increase their children's chances of survival, and mothers are more likely to survive, too, according to new research. Many women want to space births longer than they currently do. Programs can do more to help them achieve the birth intervals they want.

Over the years research has consistently demonstrated that, when mothers space births at least 2 years apart, their children are more likely to survive and to be healthy. Many programs have recommended 2-year intervals, and the message is widely known: In surveys most women say that a birth interval of 2 years is best.

Now new studies show that longer intervals are even better for infant survival and health and for maternal survival and health as well. Children born 3 to 5 years after a previous birth are about 2.5 times more likely to survive than children born before 2 years.

New Evidence

A 2002 study by researchers at the Demographic and Health Surveys (DHS) program finds that children born 3 years or more after a previous birth are healthier at birth and more likely to survive at all stages of infancy and childhood through age five. The study uses DHS data from 18 countries in four regions and assesses outcomes of more than 430,000 pregnancies.

Among the findings: Compared with children born less than 2 years after a previous birth, children born 3 to 4 years after a previous birth are:

- 1.5 times more likely to survive the first week of life;
- 2.2 times more likely to survive the first 28 days of life;
- 2.3 times more likely to survive the first year of life; and
- 2.4 times more likely to survive to age five.

Mothers Benefit, Too

A 2000 study by the Latin American Center for Perinatology and Human Development reinforces the DHS findings about children, using data for over 450,000 women. It also provides some of the best evidence yet that spacing births further apart improves mothers' health. Among the findings: Compared with women who give birth at 9- to 14-month intervals, women who have their babies at 27- to 32-month birth intervals are:

- 1.3 times more likely to avoid anemia;
- 1.7 times more likely to avoid third-trimester bleeding; and
- 2.5 times more likely to survive childbirth.

While the biological and behavioral mechanisms that make shorter birth intervals riskier for infants and mothers are little understood, researchers suggest such factors as maternal depletion syndrome, premature delivery, milk diminution, and sibling rivalry. For instance, studies suggest that shorter birth intervals may not allow mothers enough time to restore nutritional reserves that provide for adequate fetal nutrition and growth. Fetal growth retardation and premature delivery can result in low birth weight and greater risk of death.

What Programs Can Do

Almost everywhere, women's birth intervals are shorter than they would prefer. If women could achieve their preferred intervals, child mortality would fall. For example, in Kenya under-five mortality would drop by 17%. In most countries substantial unmet need for spacing births remains. In fact, half of the total potential demand for contraception is for spacing. Addressing the unmet need for spacing would help millions of women to achieve their family planning goals.

Communication campaigns in several countries have already begun using a 3-year spacing message. Messages can emphasize that waiting 3 years between births clearly improves child survival, while waiting even longer is even better. Some have suggested a message that a woman should use contraception until her youngest child is two to four years of age. Emphasizing such social benefits as increased savings and time for the couple may be even more appealing than emphasizing the health benefits. Services can focus more on women who want to postpone their next pregnancy. They can ensure that women who want to space have continuity of care, a full range of methods, and a steady source of supply. Family planning and maternal and child health care providers can work together to help women achieve their preferred birth intervals.

Why Are Longer Intervals Better?

Several biological and behavioral mechanisms are often cited to explain how short birth intervals affect infant and maternal mortality. The mechanisms that make longer birth intervals healthier for infants and mothers are difficult to identify. This is because many factors—such as the number of children a mother already has and her age at childbirth—influence birth intervals and affect child and maternal health independently. Also, a birth interval affects more than one child—the preceding child as well as the succeeding child—and either birth interval could be responsible for a child's death (10, 45, 134, 201).

- **Maternal depletion syndrome:** A long-standing hypothesis contends that short birth intervals do not allow a mother enough time to restore her nutritional reserves after childbirth and breastfeeding (80). Although the role—or even the existence—of maternal depletion syndrome is not yet settled (67, 202, 203), recent studies confirm that short intervals affect mothers' energy (107), weight (83, 171), and body mass index (83). A mother's poor nutrition in turn affects fetal nutrition and growth (19, 81, 121) and thus infant survival (32).

- **Premature delivery:** Some studies find that shorter intervals are associated with an increased risk of premature birth (36, 56, 110, 213), but others have found no such association (51, 81, 94, 169). Both premature delivery and fetal growth retardation can result in low-birth weight babies, who are at greater risk of dying in infancy (210).

- **Milk diminution:** If mothers have their next child while they are breastfeeding, they are often less able to produce breast milk for the previous child (2). When children are weaned too soon, their growth suffers, they are more likely to suffer from diarrheal disease and skin infections (26), and they are thus at greater risk of dying (186). Milk diminution is more likely to occur as women have more children and are undernourished (57). The benefits of longer birth spacing do not diminish significantly when the length of breastfeeding is accounted for statistically, suggesting that birth spacing benefits children through other mechanisms in addition to allowing longer breastfeeding (112, 159).

- **Sibling rivalry:** When children are close in age, they compete for resources and for maternal care (128). Mothers may not be able to breastfeed the older sibling properly, either because her milk flow slows or because her time is taken up by the newborn. Mothers also may not be able to breastfeed the newborn properly, placing the newborn at higher risk for nutritional deficiency, infectious diseases contracted from older siblings, and other health problems as immunity declines (23, 165). It is unclear whether siblings' competition for resources is important to explain the effects of short spacing, however. The risk of mortality for the older sibling remains the same when the newborn dies (42, 175), but the risk of mortality for the newborn declines when the older sibling dies (7) or when the older sibling is age five or older (159).

Why intervals longer than 5 years are less healthy. Little is known about why birth intervals longer than five years are less healthy for mothers and their children. The DHS and CLAP researchers suggest that, after five or more years of not having children, mothers may lose the protective benefits of previous childbearing, such as a reduced risk of pre-eclampsia and eclampsia. Thus they may be just as likely to experience the health problems associated with pregnancy as first-time mothers. Their children also could be just as likely to experience health problems or a higher risk of death as first-born children.

Many women in developing countries suffer from reproductive health problems—such as pelvic inflammatory disease and uterine fibroids—and are thus less fertile. These women may become pregnant only at lengthy intervals (95, 140, 193), and their higher risk for pregnancy complications could be due to underlying reproductive health problems, not because of longer intervals (1, 13, 20).

Contraception for Spacing Births

Around the world millions of women use temporary contraceptive methods to achieve their preferred birth intervals. All forms of contraception except for female sterilization and vasectomy are temporary and can be used to space births as well as to limit births—that is, to avoid having any more children.

Many other women, however, are not using contraception even though they would prefer to space their next birth. These women are considered to have an unmet need for family planning. Levels of unmet need for family planning among women who want to space births are even higher than among women who want to limit births, particularly in Sub-Saharan Africa.

The number of women currently using contraception to space births plus the number with unmet need equals the total potential demand for contraception for spacing. While many women with an unmet need for spacing do not intend to use contraception, many others probably would use temporary contraceptive methods if various obstacles were overcome (151). Family planning programs can do more to overcome the obstacles.

Total Potential Demand for Spacing

In developing countries the total potential demand for contraception to space births is large—at about one-third of all women of reproductive age, based on

Population Reports analysis of 54 countries with data from the DHS. Married women with few children account for most of the potential demand for birth spacing. Also, some married women with no children want to delay first births (16, 79).

Almost half of total potential demand for contraception worldwide is among people who want to have more children in the future. In other words, the level of potential demand for spacing births is about the same as for limiting births. In 45 of 54 countries, however, less of the potential demand for spacing is being satisfied. One implication is that family planning programs do not meet the contraceptive needs of younger women and others who want to space as effectively as they meet the needs of women who want to limit births. At the same time, however, women who want to space their next birth may be less motivated to use contraception than women who want no more births (195). The consequences of a wanted, but mistimed, pregnancy may be less than the consequences of an unwanted pregnancy, and thus women who wish to delay their next birth may be less likely to use contraception.

Contraceptive Use for Birth Spacing

Among 54 countries surveyed, fewer than one-third of married women of reproductive age are using contraception to space births. Contraceptive use for spacing births ranges from 2% of women in Pakistan to 29% in Zimbabwe.

In most developing countries aside from Sub-Saharan Africa, contraception is used much more for limiting than for spacing. In Sub-Saharan Africa, however, a majority of contraceptive use is for spacing, because many people want large families, and birth spacing is common in many African traditions (87). Among the 54 countries surveyed, at one extreme, in Niger 84% of the total contraceptive use rate of 8% is among women who want to delay their next birth rather than limit births. In contrast, in India, at the other extreme, contraceptive use for postponing births is just 7% of the total contraceptive use rate of 48%, largely because the national family planning program has traditionally emphasized limiting family size and not spacing (73, 84, 113).

The effect of a country's contraceptive use level on the median birth interval varies among countries but appears to be less influential where contraceptive use is lower. An analysis of DHS data from 1990 to 1995 in 27 countries, largely outside Sub-Saharan Africa, demonstrates a threshold effect in the relation between temporary method use and the length of birth intervals (131). Where fewer than 30% of women use temporary methods, the specific level of contraceptive prevalence for spacing has no major effect on the country's average birth interval. Once use of temporary methods surpasses 30%, however, average birth intervals are longer.

One explanation is that, since women who want to limit births are more motivated to prevent pregnancy, they are usually the first users of temporary contraception in a country. Eventually, use of contraception becomes more acceptable, and women who want to space their births begin to use it as well. As the percentage using contraceptives for spacing grows, birth intervals begin to grow longer (131). This trend is reversed in Sub-Saharan Africa, however, where most contraceptive users have been spacing births (196).

Unmet Need for Spacing

An estimated 17% of married women of reproductive age in developing countries have an unmet need for family planning, a new study has found (156). Among regions, the highest level of unmet need for spacing is found in Sub-Saharan Africa, at 16% of married women. The highest proportion of unmet need for spacing births is also in Sub-Saharan Africa, at 65% of all unmet need for family planning. Worldwide, more than half of the unmet need is for spacing births (156). Ambivalence, lack of information, and personal and family opposition explain the majority of unmet need among women who want to postpone their next birth. Lack of access to family planning services is also a major factor in many countries (151, 195).

The concept of unmet need for spacing births describes women who are not using family planning and say they want more children, but not for at least two or more years, or who are unsure whether they want to have another child, or who want to have another child but are unsure when. Pregnant women whose pregnancies were mistimed and nonmenstruating women whose last births were mistimed also are included in the definition (79, 198).

Young women and postpartum women have substantial unmet need for spacing. More than 23% of married women ages 15-24 have an unmet need for spacing.

Young women account for one-third of all unmet need (156), most of it for spacing (6, 79). In addition, many postpartum women do not use contraception but intend to do so. A study of women within one year after their last birth, among 27 DHS conducted between 1993 and 1996, found that about two-thirds of them had an unmet need for family planning. Almost 40% of the postpartum women intended to use a contraceptive method within the next 12 months (157).

Who Has Shorter Intervals?

Worldwide, women differ widely in their birth spacing practices. A variety of factors influence a woman's birth spacing, including the health status of her previous child as well as her personal characteristics. Also, traditional practices—particularly breastfeeding and postpartum abstinence, as well as cultural norms—affect birth spacing.

Survival and Health of the Previous Child

The health of a woman's previous child often affects the timing of her next birth. If a child dies, particularly within the first year of life, couples tend to have their next child sooner than if the child survives. Similarly, if a newborn is unhealthy in infancy, couples are more likely to have another child without waiting as long as they otherwise would.

Infant survival. Studies around the world, including Bhutan, Egypt, Kenya, Vietnam, and Zimbabwe, show that parents are more likely to have their next child sooner if a newborn dies than if a newborn survives (25, 64, 68, 139, 185, 211, 212). In all 55 countries surveyed by DHS between 1990 and 2001, women are more likely to have their next child within 3 years if the previous child dies.

When a child dies, mothers' subsequent birth intervals are 60% shorter, on average, than when a child survives, according to data from 46 DHS (62). This study also found that the longer the previous child survives, the less the effect on the subsequent birth interval. After age two a child's death appears not to influence the mother's subsequent birth interval at all (62).

Mothers in rural Senegal have their next birth within a median of 15 months if their infant dies in the first month of life. If an infant dies before age one, mothers wait a median of 22 months before their next child. If a child dies between ages one and two, mothers wait a median of 29 months; and when a child survives for two years, mothers wait a median of 33 months to have their next child (153).

Why does a child's death result in more rapid childbearing? Some couples unintentionally have their next child quickly because a child's early death ends breastfeeding, and women return to menses and resume ovulation sooner (62). In Ghana the median duration of postpartum amenorrhea dropped from 12 months to 4 months among women whose child died early (123). Data from the 46 DHS show that, on average, child survival increases the duration of postpartum amenorrhea by 178% (62).

Other couples make a conscious effort to replace the lost child soon. When a child dies, the duration of postpartum sexual abstinence can fall by as much as 47%, according to data from the 46 DHS (62), Some studies have found, however, that resumption of sexual activity is less important than the early cessation of breastfeeding in explaining why the next child is born sooner when a previous child dies (129, 181).

Women whose pregnancies end in miscarriage or abortion are usually more likely to have a next child quickly. Few studies have looked at this relationship, however, because miscarriages, stillbirths, and abortions are rarely recorded. A study by the Latin American Center for Perinatology and Human Development found that half of adolescents age 19 or younger whose pregnancies ended in abortion or miscarriage became pregnant again within 2 years, compared with about one-third of adolescents who had a previous live birth. Among women ages 20 to 24, 28% whose pregnancy ended in abortion or miscarriage became pregnant within 2 years, compared with 21 % of those who had a previous live birth (37).

An African study, however, found that women whose pregnancies end in miscarriage or stillbirths are less likely to have a next child quickly. In The Gambia women who had a miscarriage or stillbirth were more likely than other women to postpone childbearing by using contraception. Some 14% of women who miscarried or had stillbirths used contraception subsequently, far more than the percentage who used contraceptives during breastfeeding or after weaning. When asked why they used contraception after a miscarriage or stillbirth, women reported that they wanted to give their bodies time to rest, recover, and have a better chance of conceiving a healthy baby in the future (21).

Infant health. If a newborn survives but is sickly, women tend to have their next child sooner. One explanation is that sick newborns are less likely to breastfeed (112). If infants cannot breastfeed often and intensely, mothers resume ovulation more quickly and, without contraception or sexual abstinence, may soon become pregnant again (115). Also, if a woman is worried that her sick child will die in infancy, she may try to have a healthy child quickly. For this same reason, mothers whose newborns are low in weight at birth may have their next child quickly, too (18, 112).

Women's Characteristics

A variety of demographic and socioeconomic characteristics influence women's spacing practices. These include a woman's age at the birth of each child, the number of children she already has, and her educational attainment, social status, labor force participation, and place of residence.

Maternal age and number of children. Younger women are more likely than older women to have their next child within 3 years. In all 50 countries with DHS data, 60% or more of women ages 15 to 19 have birth intervals shorter than 3 years. In only 2 of 55 countries do 60% of women ages 40 and older have birth intervals shorter than 3 years. In a few countries, such as Botswana, Brazil, Ethiopia, and Togo, there is little or no difference after age 30.

In most countries women with fewer children have shorter birth intervals than women with more children, but in a few countries the reverse is true. In

21 of 28 countries studied with DHS data, women with one or two children had shorter birth intervals than women with four or five children. In 19 of the 28 countries, their birth intervals were shorter by 2 months or more, and in 4 countries intervals were shorter by 4 months or more. In five countries, however—Brazil, Colombia, Indonesia, Namibia, and Paraguay—women with four or five children had shorter birth intervals (105).

Education. In 38 of 51 countries with DHS data, women with no education were more likely than women with education to space births less than 3 years apart. In seven surveyed countries, however, women with secondary or higher education were more likely to have intervals shorter than 3 years. One explanation is that in these countries women with more education marry at older ages and then have children in quick succession (35, 118, 147). In seven other countries there is little or no difference in birth intervals between women with no education and with secondary or higher education.

Researchers have not explained why women's education levels affect their birth intervals differently from one place to another. Differences in childbearing preferences may account for some birth spacing differences (see box, p. 7). In some countries women with more education are more likely to use contraception to prolong their birth intervals (166, 184). Also, women with more education may work outside the home or live in urban regions, both of which can lead to longer birth spacing.

Social status and employment. Women with lower status, whether within the household or within society, and women who are not employed tend to have shorter birth intervals than women of higher status or who are employed. For example, in Turkey women with less reproductive and economic decision-making power, and who typically do not work outside the home, have birth intervals 5.4 months shorter than women with more decision-making power and who are usually employed (76). In India women of lower social and economic status have median birth intervals of 14 months compared with 21 months among women of higher status (118). In some countries labor force participation has little or no effect on when women have their first child but influences when they have subsequent children (46, 127). Also, women who work outside the home, particularly urban women, may be more educated and more likely to use contraception to space their births (166).

Place of residence. In 51 of 55 countries surveyed by the DHS, women who live in rural areas are more likely than women in urban areas to have birth intervals shorter than 3 years. The greatest differences are in Latin America and the Caribbean, Eastern Europe, and Central Asia. In only three countries—Chad, Mozambique, and Pakistan—are urban women more likely than rural women to have birth intervals shorter than 3 years. In two countries there is little to no difference. These findings are not surprising, as urban women have better access to education and employment opportunities.

Cultural Norms

Cultural norms and customs that influence women's birth spacing practices include social pressure for women to prove their fertility and breastfeeding and postpartum abstinence practices. Preferences for male children can also affect birth intervals.

Pressure to prove fertility. Couples who face pressure for childbearing from their families or society want to have their first child soon after marriage and continue to have children rapidly. In some societies having many children and having them quickly is a sign of male virility and female fertility. In traditional Indian society, for example, childbearing brings prestige to a new wife, and so couples have their first child quickly (118, 148). Social pressure to bear children quickly also is common in Sub-Saharan Africa and the Near East and North Africa (49).

Breastfeeding practices. Whether women breastfeed at all, how frequently, and how long influence their birth spacing practices (54, 72, 119, 208, 209). In nearly all developing countries nearly all women breastfeed their newborn children (65, 93). Breastfeeding differs among cultures both in duration and frequency, however (93, 206). Among developing regions the duration of breastfeeding ranges from an average of 14 months in Latin America and the Caribbean to 21 months in Sub-Saharan Africa (65).

Breastfeeding practices help determine how long women will remain amenorrheic—without menses and thus less likely to get pregnant—after giving birth (207). Women who fully or nearly fully breastfeed their infants remain amenorrheic longer (92). Among 55 countries with DHS data, women in Sub-Saharan Africa have the longest median duration of postpartum amenorrhea, ranging from about 7 months in Comoros to 17 months in Rwanda. Women in the Near East and North Africa have the shortest duration, from 3 months in Turkey to 6 months in Yemen. Having more children and being poorly nourished also lengthen amenorrhea (207).

Postpartum abstinence. Couples who do not practice postpartum sexual abstinence—avoiding sex for several months after a birth—tend to have their next child quickly. Postpartum abstinence is common in many countries, however. When the length of such abstinence exceeds the length of postpartum amenorrhea, this practice can help women delay their next pregnancy.

Traditional beliefs often influence sexual activity after childbirth (149). In

Lesotho, for example, mothers are separated from their husbands for as long as the mothers are breastfeeding because they believe that having sex with a lactating woman would spoil her milk (98).

While taboos against postpartum sexual activity are widespread, particularly in Africa, the duration of postpartum abstinence varies greatly both within and among countries (190). Among 55 countries surveyed by the DHS since 1990, the median duration of postpartum abstinence in Sub-Saharan Africa ranges from 2 months in Uganda to 22 months in Guinea. Elsewhere, with few exceptions the period ranges from 1 month to 3 months. In countries where the period of postpartum abstinence is nearly the same or shorter than the period of amenorrhea—as in Chad, Guatemala, and Nepal—abstinence alone has little effect on birth intervals (62).

In many countries the effects of postpartum abstinence and amenorrhea combined—postpartum insusceptibility—account for birth spacing for up to 2 years (65, 179). In 26 of the 55 surveyed countries, the median duration of postpartum insusceptibility is 1 year or more, and nearly 2 years in Burkina Faso and Guinea. The median duration is less than 6 months in only nine countries surveyed.

Son preference. Couples who prefer sons tend to have their next child soon after the birth of a daughter. In China, for example, among women who had given birth to a girl most had their next child within 37 months. In contrast, among women who had a boy, most had their next child within 46 months (58). Among 55 countries with data, women are more likely to have a next child within 3 years after the birth of a daughter than after a son's birth in all regions except Latin America.

The preference for sons is especially strong in South and East Asia, where people often value male children differently from female children. In Korea, for instance, sons continue the family lineage, perform prayers to ancestors, and can help support parents in their old age (96). Similarly, in India sons tend to have higher economic, social, and religious value to their parents (11), while girls may be considered an economic liability (88).

How Programs Can Help Couples Space Births

Although not always addressed specifically, promoting birth spacing has long been a central goal of family planning programs around the world (150). The new evidence for the benefits of spacing births 3 to 5 years apart argues for renewed emphasis on helping couples space births, especially young women who want to postpone their next pregnancy longer. Expanded access to good-quality family planning services through a variety of avenues will help women achieve their preferred intervals.

Program strategies will be different in communities where preferred birth intervals are shorter than 3 years than in those where preferred intervals are longer than 3 years.

In the former, programs can focus more on developing messages that explain to all family members the benefits of spacing births by 3 to 5 years. Where women and couples already want longer birth intervals, programmatic efforts can focus on increasing access and successful continued use of contraceptive methods to help people achieve their spacing goals.

Developing an Effective Message

The mass media and communication programs could do more to raise awareness of the benefits of birth spacing. A better understanding is needed, however, of what messages elicit the best responses from different audiences. Programs need to test whether people respond to messages that emphasize the health benefits, and also whether they respond to messages that stress the social benefits of longer birth intervals, such as increased savings, time, and attention to the family. In a 1992 survey in Nigeria, for example, at least 85% of women and at least 68% of men agreed with the statements that spacing helps a mother to regain her strength before having her next baby, that child spacing protects the health of mothers, and that child spacing helps the health of children (86). At the same time, in Uganda, interviews in 1992 found that women who viewed birth spacing positively cited other benefits, including having older children to help raise their younger siblings. One woman said that birth spacing helps women look younger. "Delivery every year will make you look unhealthy and ugly," she told the interviewers (50).

Since most women do not make decisions about family planning by themselves, messages for husbands, mothers-in-law, and other family members also are useful. The benefits of spacing can appeal to all members of the household. For example, in a 1996 study in Jordan, one male respondent summarized the variety of benefits of longer birth intervals, saying that births that are spaced "give each child born his rightful level of caring and attention, and they give your wife the time to rest and regain her health. They give the husband the chance to weigh his financial situation and plan his family's future" (52).

Another area needing research is which messages are easiest to understand and remember for all women and couples. Birth to pregnancy intervals may be preferable because they explain when a woman can become pregnant again, rather than when she can have another birth. Some have suggested a message that explains that a woman should use contraception until her youngest child is two to four years of age. Remembering this message, a woman would not need to subtract nine months of pregnancy, as she would using a birth to birth interval, to calculate whether she has spaced sufficiently to receive the health benefits (178). The Nepali slogan, "When the first child goes to school, then only a second child," aired on radio stations across the country, illustrates how long couples should space (104).

Communication campaigns in several countries have already begun using the 3-year message. Posters from the Planned Parenthood Association of Ghana, for example, encourage parents to space their births 2 to 3 years apart (137). Posters from India's State Innovations in Family Planning Services Agency urge couples to wait at least 3 years (176). Nigeria's State Ministry of Health encourages birth spacing of 3 to 4 years (122). In Bangladesh posters suggest that couples wait 5 years between births (158). Most of these communication campaigns point to the social and economic benefits of spacing for their audiences rather than to the health benefits.

Changing the message? Communication programs with the new message of 3 to 5 years may need to address the apparent conflict with the 2-year spacing message of the past. The 2-year message has enjoyed widespread recognition. For example, when asked in surveys what is the best number of months between births, most women in most countries respond that an interval of 2 years or more is best (15). In Malawi 95% of women responded to a survey that an interval of 24 months is desirable and, 59% said that waiting 36 months is even more desirable (189).

Because so many people believe that 2 years is the preferred interval between births, moving away from so well-established a message should be handled carefully. If people start to hear that spacing 3 years is better than 2, they may get confused about why the preferred interval has "changed." The facts themselves have not changed, of course. Messages can communicate that waiting 2 years between births clearly improves child survival, while waiting 3 to 5 years is even better. Above all, messages should convey that the best intervals are those that women choose for themselves based on their individual circumstances.

Finding the right term for birth spacing or longer birth intervals—without confusing the term with family planning in general—is a good starting point for developing messages. In many places where family planning is not yet widely accepted, the phrase "birth spacing" is used as a substitute since it is more acceptable (194). For instance, in Jordan, where many people believe that God alone determines the number and timing of children, a major initiative of the national family planning program was named the Jordan Birth Spacing Project

441

(12, 135, 174). Usually programs with names that include the phrase "birth spacing" focus on increasing contraceptive use rather than specifically on achieving longer birth intervals.

Some languages have no word for birth spacing, and birth spacing advocates may need to develop new terms based on audience research and testing. In Nepal before 1990, the generic Nepali term for family planning, "pariwar niyogen," was commonly used to mean sterilization. Family planning programs were concerned that villagers would interpret a health worker's advice to "use a family planning method" as "have a vasectomy or tubal ligation"—advice that would not be attractive to young couples (204).

In the early 1990s World Education, Inc./Nepal, in collaboration with the Ministry of Education and Culture and the Program for Appropriate Technology in Health, first conducted focus-group discussions to learn how villagers talk about birth spacing. Nepali farmers mentioned that they often leave yams, turmeric, ginger, and sugarcane to grow for 3 years before harvesting and therefore, an analogy to these crops would be meaningful in messages promoting 3- to 5-year birth intervals. A contest elicited several potential terms for birth spacing, and field testing determined that one term ("janma antar"—literally "birth gap") was better understood and more acceptable than other terms among both villagers and family planning administrators. Today, the Ministry of Health, the Nepal Contraceptive Retail Sales Project, and nongovernmental organizations throughout the country use the term "janma antar" in training and client communication materials (168). With more research and use of different birth spacing messages, the best ones will become apparent, making it easier for advocates to raise awareness of the benefits of longer birth intervals.

Expanding Access and Outlets

Many women will be unable to achieve their preferred birth intervals unless they have better access to family planning supplies and services appropriate for spacing. Some technical assistance organizations are focusing on expanding access to enable people to space their births further.

A major focus of the Catalyst Consortium <www.rhcatalyst.org> is to increase awareness of 3 to 5 years as the optimal birth interval (177). By offering technical guidance, holding conferences, and publishing research findings, the Consortium increases awareness among public health agencies and supports governments in developing medical guidelines that recommend intervals of 3 to 5 years, based on the new evidence. EngenderHealth <www.engenderhealth.org> provides technical assistance on birth spacing, particularly in clinic-based settings, so that women have better quality services to achieve their spacing goals.

It assists countries in updating their national service delivery guidelines and protocols to incorporate recommendations of intervals of 3 to 5 years (136).

Continuity of care. People who want to space births have special needs that family planning programs often do not meet adequately. The higher levels of unmet need for spacing than for limiting suggest this. Women who want to space their births need continuity of care to continue using contraception and achieve their preferred birth intervals (30, 77, 192), to stop use to become pregnant and then after delivery to start a method that is appropriate during breastfeeding (82). Many studies have found that such good-quality services enable people to continue using contraception for many years (75, 91).

The PRIME II Project <www.prime2.org> uses Performance Improvement methods to identify how health care providers can improve the quality of family planning services they offer to women who want to space their births. Service providers may need new client-provider interaction skills to respond better to the birth spacing needs of younger, low-parity women. The PRIME II Project emphasizes self-directed learning and interactive instruction so that service providers do not need to leave the service delivery site to learn new skills (78).

Access to sources of supply. Access to good-quality contraceptive services and a range of methods helps people to space births. Sometimes having a nearby source is key to continuation of contraceptive use. Broadening the types of service delivery can provide more choices closer to home, especially for people whom conventional programs have difficulty serving, such as young women, people with low incomes, and women who cannot easily leave their homes (138). Programs can deliver methods through community-based distribution, private-sector sales including social marketing, and private providers, as well as through family planning clinics and hospitals.

A full range of methods. When more contraceptive methods are available, more couples who want to space births can find a method that suits them. All programs should offer at least several temporary methods, such as condoms, pills, injectables, implants, or IUDs, in addition to permanent ones. The options to switch from one method to another and to choose a different method after giving birth are central to continued satisfactory use of family planning (60). Providers should make clear that all clients have the option to switch methods whenever and as often as needed, and that they should return if they experience any problems (188).

Today, some women cannot always get the contraceptive methods that they prefer (157). In many programs stock-outs and other problems in the supply chain prevent women who want longer birth intervals from obtaining a continuous supply of their preferred method (146, 163, 164). Offering a range of methods also helps ensure that at least some methods will always be available even when some shortages do occur (31). Other women do not want to use a supply method of family planning but do not know that they can control their birth intervals by using the Lactational Amenhorrea Method (LAM) or other fertility awareness-based methods (40). Offering a wide variety of contraceptive methods, along with accurate information about the benefits of spacing, will help women space their births longer.

Working with communities. Community norms help shape people's decisions and expectations about their birth intervals. Communication campaigns that speak to the needs of younger couples and new parents can help make 3- to 5-year birth intervals a social norm. Learning more about women's birth spacing practices and their needs can inform effective birth spacing messages. Also, providers can counsel women better if they understand cultural practices and traditional beliefs including taboos on breastfeeding during pregnancy and sexual relations during lactation (187).

The Catalyst Consortium is conducting focus-group discussions in five countries—Bolivia, Egypt, India, Pakistan, and Peru—to learn why women space their births. They hope to understand their ideal interval lengths and, for women who prefer intervals of 3 to 5 years, which benefits motivate them most. The Consortium plans to publish the results in 2002. The results will be used to develop training modules to improve counseling (177).

Prenatal and postpartum care. The prenatal and postpartum periods and up to a year after a woman gives birth are crucial times for information and counseling about birth spacing, since most women see health care providers more often during this period (48). Most of the time these contacts rarely include opportunities for discussion and counseling on birth spacing (157). During a woman's prenatal period, health care providers can discuss the health benefits of spacing pregnancies and can encourage women to continue receiving reproductive health care between pregnancies (89).

As part of postpartum care, providers can tell women about LAM, explaining that during the baby's first six months, fully or almost fully breastfeeding can prevent pregnancy, so long as the woman has not menstruated yet (66, 205). Providers can advise women that IUDs, condoms, and vaginal methods are appropriate methods during breastfeeding. Hormonal methods are not the first choice, but progestin-only pills, injectables, and implants can be used after six weeks postpartum (66, 82). Combined hormonal methods—combined oral contraceptives and monthly injectables—should be avoided because they may reduce production of breast milk.

Child health programs. Because birth spacing helps protect child health, the 3-year message complements efforts of child health programs. Well-baby visits and immunization visits provide opportunities for health staff to counsel parents of young children about the benefits of waiting 3 to 5 years for the next child. Of course, spacing births 3 to 5 years in and of itself will not ensure child survival and good health. Parents can help safeguard their baby's health by ensuring skilled care at delivery, arranging for a clean sterile delivery, keeping the newborn warm, starting exclusive breastfeeding immediately and supplementing with appropriate and nutritious complementary foods after six months, maintaining hygiene during infancy and early childhood, and obtaining all the recommended childhood immunizations (41). Women who are HIV-positive can avoid breastfeeding and use formula instead if they have access to a clean, consistent, and affordable supply (120).

Improving women's status. Over the long term, improving women's status can contribute to longer birth intervals. For example, if parents can feel that their well-being is as secure with female children as with male children, they may want to wait longer before having another child (132). When women have more decision-making power in the household, they tend to have longer birth intervals (see section "Women's Characteristics"). Women's status can be improved by raising age at marriage, increasing education, and expanding employment opportunities. Improving opportunities for women will enable them to make the healthiest choices about birth spacing and about childbearing in general.

Bibliography

An asterisk (*) denotes an item that was particularly useful in the preparation of this issue of Population Reports.

1. Aboyeji, A. and Ijaiya, M. Uterine fibroids: A ten-year clinical review in Ilorin, Nigeria. *Nigerian Journal of Medicine* 11(1): 16-19. Jan./Mar. 2002.

2. Adair, L, Popkin, B., and Guilkey, D. The duration of breastfeeding: How is it affected by biological, socioeconomic, health sector, and food industry factors? Demography 30(1): 63. 1994.

3. Adamchak, D.J. and Mbizvo, M.T. The relationship between fertility and contraceptive prevalence in Zimbabwe. Presented at the Annual Meeting of the Population Association of America, Toronto, Canada, May 3-5, 1990. 8 p. (Unpublished)

4. Adongo, P.B., Phillips, J.F., and Binka, F.N. The influence of traditional religion on fertility regulation among the Kassena-Nankan of Northern Ghana. Studies in Family Planning 29(1): 23-40. Mar. 1998.

5. Agadjanian, V. and Prata, N. War, peace, and fertility in Angola. Demography 39(2): 215-231. May 2002.

6. Ahmed, T. Unmet need for contraception in Pakistan: Pattern and determinants. Demography India 22(1): 31-51. Jan./Jun. 1993.

7. Alam, N. Birth spacing and infant and early childhood mortality in a high fertility area of Bangladesh: Age-dependent and interactive effects. Journal of Biosocial Science 27(4): 393-404. Oct. 1995.

8.   Alan Guttmacher Institute (AGI). Hopes and realities: Closing the gap between women's aspirations and their reproductive experiences. New York, AGI, 1995. 56 p.

9.   Alauddin, M. and Maclaren, L. Reaching newlywed and married adolescents. In Focus, Focus on Young Adults, Jul. 1999. p. 1-4.

10.   Ali, E.D. The proximate determinants of child survival in the northern regions of the Sudan, 1989/90. Proceedings of the Cairo Demographic Centre (CDC) 23rd Annual Seminar on Population and Development Issues in the Middle East, Africa, and Asia, Cairo, Egypt, 1994. CDC, p. 1081-1120.

11.   Arnold, F., Choe, M.K., and Roy, T.K. Son preference, the family-building process and child mortality in India. Population Studies 52(3): 301-315. Nov. 1998.

12.   Bahous, S., Abu Laban, A., Al-Qutob, R., and Mawajdeh, S. Population policies and population communication in Jordan: Shy responses to serious challenges. Presented at the Population Council Symposium on Family, Gender, and Population Policy: International Debates and Middle Eastern Realities, Cairo, Egypt, February 7-9, 1994. 40 p. (Unpublished)

13.   Bajekal, N. and Li, T.C. Fibroids, infertility and pregnancy wastage. Human Reproduction Update 6(6): 614-620. Nov./Dec. 2000.

14.   Bankole, A. Desired fertility and fertility behavior among the Yoruba of Nigeria: A study of couple preferences and subsequent fertility. Population Studies 49(2): 317-328. Jul. 1995.

*15. Bankole, A. and westoff, C.F. Childbearing attitudes and intentions. Calverton, Maryland, Macro International, Dec. 1995. (Demographic and Health Surveys Comparative Studies No. 17) 32 p.

16.   Barkat, A., Houvras, I., Maclaren, L, Begum, S., Chowdhury, E.I., Islam, M., Reza, T., and Sabina, N. The RSDP/Pathfinder Bangladesh newlywed strategy: Results of an assessment. Washington, DC, FOCUS on Young Adults, Aug. 1999.

17.   Barnett, B. and Stein, J. Women's voices, women's lives: The impact of family planning. North Carolina, The Women's Studies Project, Jun. 1998.

18.   Bereczkei, T., Hofer, A., and Ivan, Z. Low birth weight, maternal birth-spacing decisions, and future reproduction. A cost-benefit analysis. Human Nature 11(2): 183- 205. 2000.

19.   Berendes, H.W. Maternal determinants of perinatal mortality and of intrauterine growth retardation and preterm delivery. In: Baum, J.D., ed. Birth Risks. Nestle Nutrition Workshop Series Vol. 31. New York, Raven Press, 1993. p. 47-58.

20.   Bergstrom, S. Genital infections and reproductive health: Infertility and morbidity of mother and child in developing countries. Scandinavian Journal of Infectious Disease 69(Suppl.): 99-105. 1990.

21.   Bledsoe, C, Banja, F., and Hill, A.G. Reproductive mishaps and Western contraception: An African challenge to fertility theory. Population and Development Review 24(1): 15-57. Mar. 1998.

22.   Bledsoe, C.H., Hill, A.G., D'Alessandro, U., and Langerock, P. Constructing natural fertility: The use of Western contraceptive technologies in rural Gambia. Population and Development Review 20(1): 81-113. Mar. 1994.

23.   Boerma, J.T. and Bicego, G.T. Preceding birth intervals and child survival: Searching for pathways of influence. Studies in Family Planning 23(4): 243-256. Jul./Aug. 1992.

24.   Bogue, D.J. Introduction to pregnancy/birth interval analysis. In: Bogue, D.J., Arriaga, E.E., Anderton, D.L., and Rumsey, G.W., eds. Readings in Population Research Methodology. Fertility Research. Vol. 3. Chicago, Illinois, Social Development Center, p. 59-64.

25.   Bohler, E. Has primary health care reduced infant mortality in East Bhutan? The effects of primary health care and birth spacing on infant and child mortality patterns in East Bhutan. Journal of Tropical Pediatrics 40(5): 256-260. Oct. 1994.

26.   Bohler, E. and Bergstrom, S. Subsequent pregnancy affects morbidity of previous child.

Journal of Biosocial Science 27(4): 431-442. Oct. 1995.

27. Bongaarts, J. The measurement of wanted fertility. New York, Population Council, Research Division, (Working Paper No. 10) 35 p.

28. Bongaarts, J. The fertility impact of changes in the timing of childbearing in the developing world. Population Studies 53(3): 277-289. Nov. 1999.

29. Bongaarts, J. and Feeney, G. On the quantum and tempo of fertility. Population and Development Review 24(2): 271-291.

30. Bruce, J. Fundamental elements of the quality of care: A simple framework. Studies in Family Planning 21(2): 61-91. Mar/Apr. 1990.

31. Bruce, J. and Jain, A. Improving the quality of care through operations research. In: Seidman, M. and Horn, M.C., eds. Operations Research: Helping Family Planning Programs Work Better. New York, Wiley-Liss, 1991. p. 259-282.

32. Cabigon, J.V. The effects of birthspacing and breast feeding on childhood mortality in the Philippines. Journal of Population 3(1): 1-18. Jun. 1997.

33. Caldwell, J.C. The population factor in African change. In: Radwan, A.M.A.S., ed. Economic and Demographic Change in Africa. Oxford, England, Clarendon Press, p. 11-35.

34. Chi, P.S. and hsin, P.L. Family structure and fertility behavior in Taiwan. Ithaca, New York, Cornell University, Population and Development Program, (Population and Development Program Working Paper Series 93.05) 13 p.

35. Choe, M.K., Thapa, S., and Achmad, S. Early marriage and childbearing in Indonesia and Nepal. Honolulu, Hawaii, East-West Center, Nov. 2001. 16 p.

*36. Conde-Agudelo, A. Effect of interpregnancy interval on adverse perinatal outcomes in Latin America. Proceedings of the 2nd Champions Meeting on Birth Spacing, Washington, DC, Catalyst Consortium, 20-29 p.

37. Conde-Agudelo, A. Interpregnancy interval among adolescents whose previous pregnancy ended in abortion in Latin America. [Power Point Presentation]. Presented at the Birth Spacing Champions Working Groups Meeting, Washington, D.C., May 2, 2002. Catalyst Consortium. 1 p.

*38. Conde-Agudelo, A. and Belizan, J.M. Maternal morbidity and mortality associated with interpregnancy interval: Cross sectional study. British Medical Journal (Clinical Research Ed.) 321(7271). 1255-1259. Nov. 18, 2000.

39. Conde-Agudelo, A. and Belizan, J.M. Effect of interpregnancy interval on adverse perinatal outcomes in Latin America. Centro Latinoamericano de Perinatologiay Desarrollo Humano, 2002. (forthcoming report)

40. Cooney, K.A., Koniz-Booher, P., and Coly, S. Taking the first steps: The lactational amenorrhea method, a decade of experience. Final report of the Breastfeeding and MCH Division of the Institute for Reproductive Health (IRH). Washington, DC, Georgetown University, IRH, 1997.126 p.

41. Costello, A., Francis, V., Byrne, A., and Claire, P. State of the World's Newborns. Washington, DC, Save the Children, 2001. 50 p.

42. Curtis, S.L., Diamond, I., and Mcdonald, J.W. Birth interval and family effects on postneonatal mortality in Brazil. Dcmography 30(1): 33-43. Feb. 1993.

43. Das, N.P. The effect of birth spacing on current fertility. Journal of Family Welfare 36(4): 36-45. Dec. 1990.

44. De Graft-Johnson, J.E. Maternal morbidity in Ghana. Presented at the Annual Meeting of the Population Association of America, Miami, Florida, May 5-7, 1994. 33 p.

45. Defo, B.K. Effects of infant feeding practices and birth spacing on infant and child survival: A reassessment from retrospective and prospective data. Journal of Biosocial Science 29(1): 303-326. 1997.

46. Derose, L.F. Women's work and birthspacing in Ghana. Presented at the Annual Meeting of the Population Association of America, Cincinnati, Ohio, Apr. 1-3, 1993. 22 p. (Unpublished)

47. Eltigani, E.E. Childbearing in five Arab countries. Studies in Family Planning 32(1): 17-24. Mar. 2001.

48. Engender Health. Postpartum Family Planning. Presented at the FP and Clinical Services Teams Meeting, Jul. 30, 2002.

49. Family Health International Family planning and women's lives. Network 18(4): 35. Summer 1998.

50. Family Planning Association of Uganda and Johns Hopkins School of Public Health. Population Communication Services (JHU/PCS). Family planning: We cannot use what we do not understand. Qualitative research on family planning in Uganda. Baltimore, Maryland, JHU/PCS, Oct. 1992. 43 p.

51. Farahati, M., Bozorgi, N., and Luke, B. Influence of maternal age, birth-to-conception intervals and prior perinatal factors on perinatal outcomes. Journal of Reproductive Medicine 38(10): 751-756. Oct. 1993.

52. Farsoun, M., Khoury, N., and Underwood, C. In their own words: A qualitative study of family planning in Jordan. Baltimore, Johns Hopkins School of Public Health Center for Communication Programs, Oct. 1996. (Field Re port No. 6) 44 p.

53. Forste, R. The effects of breastfeeding and birth spacing on infant and child mortality in Bolivia. Population Studies 48(3): 497-511. Nov. 1994.

54. Forste, R. Effects of lactation and contraceptive use on birth-spacing in Bolivia. Social Biology 42(1-2): 108-123. Spring/Summer 1995.

55. Fortney, J.A. and Zhang, J. Maternal death and birth spacing. Studies in Family Planning 29(4): 436. Dec. 1998.

*56. Fuentes-Afflick, E. and Hessol, N.A. Interpregnancy interval and the risk of premature infants. Obstetrics and Gynecology 95(3): 383-390. Mar. 2000.

57. Garner, P., Smith, T., Baea, M., Lai, D., and Heywood, P. Maternal nutritional depletion in a rural area of Papua New Guinea. Tropical and Geographical Medicine 46(3): 169-171. 1994.

58. Graham, M.J., Larsen, U., and Xu, X. Son preference in Anhui Province, China. International Family Planning Perspectives 24(2): 72-77. Jun. 1998. (Available: <http://www.agi-usa.org/pubs/journals/2407298.html>, Accessed Jul. 4, 2002)

59. Greene, D.L. Contraceptive use for birth spacing in Sub-Saharan Africa. Dissertation Abstracts International 59(8-a): 3221.1999.

60. Greenwell, K.F. Contraceptive method mix menu: Providing healthy choices for women. World Health Statistics Quarterly 49(2): 88-93. 1996.

61. Gribble, J.N. Birth intervals, gestational age, and low birth weight: Are the relationships confounded? Population Studies 47(1): 133-146. Mar. 1993.

*62. Grummer-Strawn, L.M., Stupp, P.W., and Mei, Z. Effect of a child's death on birth spacing: A cross-national analysis. In: Montgomery, M.R. and Cohen, B., eds. From Death to Birth: Mortality Decline and Reproductive Change. Washington, D.C., National Academy Press, 1998. p. 39-73.

63. Gyimah, S.O. The dynamics of spacing and timing of births in Ghana. London, Canada, Population Studies Centre, University of Western Ontario, May 2002. 34 p. (Available: <http://www.ssc.uwo.ca/sociology/popstudies/dp/dp02-02 .pdf>, Accessed Jul. 17, 2002)

64. Gyimah, S.O. Lagged effect of childhood mortality on reproductive behavior in Ghana and Kenya. London, Canada, Population Studies Centre, University of Western Ontario, May 2002. 23 p. (Available: <http://www. ssc.uwo.ca/sociology/popstudies/dp/dp02-03.pdf>, Accessed Jul. 27, 2002)

65. Haggerty, PA. and Rutstein, S.O. Breastfeeding and complementary infant feeding, and the postpartum effects of breastfeeding. Calverton, Maryland, Macro International, Inc., Jun. 1999. (Demographic and Health Surveys Comparative Studies No. 30)281 p.

66. Hatcher, R.A., Rinehart, W., Blackburn, R., Geller, J.S., and Shelton, J.D. The Essentials of Contraceptive Technology. Baltimore, Johns Hopkins School of Public Health, Population Information Program, Jul. 1997. 340 p.

67. Higgins, P.A. and Alderman, H. Labor and women's nutrition: A study of energy expenditure, fertility, and nutritional status in Ghana. Washington, DC, World Bank, Oct 1992. 41 p.

68. Hoa, H.T., Toan, N.V., Johansson, A., Hoa, V.T., Hojer, B., and Persson, L.A. Child spacing and two-child policy in practice in rural Vietnam: Cross sectional survey. British Medical Journal (Clinical Research Ed.) 313(7065): 1113-1116. Nov. 2, 1996.

69. Hobcraft, J. Child spacing and child mortality. Presented at the Demographic and Health Surveys World Conference, Washington, D.C., Aug. 5-7, 1991. Population Investigation Committee, London School of Economics. 14 p.

*70. Hobcraft, J., Mcdonald, J.W., and Rutstein, S. Childspacing effects of infant and early child mortality. Population Index 49(4): 585-618. 1983.

71. Hogan, D.P., Berhanu, B., and Hailemariam, A. Household organization, women's autonomy, and contraceptive behavior in southern Ethiopia. Studies in Family Planning 30(4): 302-314. Dec. 1999.

72. Huffman, S.L. and Labbok, M.H. Breastfeeding in family planning programs: A help or a hindrance? International Journal of Gynecology and Obstetrics 47(Suppl): S23- S32. Dec. 1994.

73. Hutter, I. Reproductive health and child spacing in rural South India: Contribution to a reorientation of population policies in India. Background paper. Groningen, Netherlands, University of Groningen, Faculty of Spatial Sciences, 1998. (Demographic Reports No. 23) 154 p.

74. Ikamari, L. Birth intervals and child survival in Kenya. African journal of Health Sciences 5(1): 15-24. Jan./Mar. 1998.

75. Inaoka, E., Wakai, S., Nakamura, Y., Al Babily, Y., and Saghayroun, A.A. Correlates of visit regularity among family planning clients in urban Yemen. Advances in Contraception 15(4): 257-274.

76. Isvan, N.A. Productive and reproductive decisions in Turkey: The role of domestic bargaining. Journal of Marriage and the Family 53(4): 1057-1070. Nov. 1991.

77. Jain, A. Should eliminating unmet need for contraception continue to be a program priority? International Family Planning Perspectives 25(Suppl.): S39-S43, S49. Jan. 1999.

78. Jansen, W. (Prime II) [Prime II Project Description] Personal communication, Aug. 29, 2002.

79. Jansen, W., Frlck, D., and Mason, R. The "X" factor in birth-spacers: Age and parity in demand and need for birthspacing in 15 developing countries. Presented at the Population Association of America, Atlanta, May 9-11, 2002. University of North Carolina, Chapel Hill.

80. Jeliffe, D. and Maddocks, I. Ecological malnutrition in the New Guinea Highlands. Clinical Pediatrics 3: 423-428. 1964.

81. Kallan, J.E. Effects of interpregnancy intervals on preterm birth, intrauterine growth retardation, and fetal loss. Social Biology 39(3-4): 231-245. Fall/Winter 1992.

82. Kennedy, K.I. Post-partum contraception. Bailliere's Clinical Obstetrics and Gynaecology 10(1): 25-41. Apr. 1996.

83. Khan, K.S., Chien, P.F., and Khan, N.B. Nutritional stress of reproduction. A cohort study over two consecutive pregnancies. Acta Obstetricia et Gynecologica Scandinavica 77(4): 395-401. Apr. 1998.

84. Khan, M.E. and Cernada, G. Promoting spacing: A step towards paradigm shift. In: Khan, M.E. and Cernada, G., eds. Spacing as an Alternative Strategy. India's Family Welfare Programme. Delhi, India, B.R. Publishing Corporation, 1996. p. 1-6.

85. Khanna, H. Present status and future directions for increasing the use of information, education and communication for promoting spacing methods. In: Khan, M.E. and Cernada, G., eds. Spacing as an Alternative Strategy. India's Family Welfare Programme. Delhi, India, B.R. Publishing Corporation, 1996. p. 217-226.

86. Kiragu, K., Krenn, S., Kusemiju, B., Ajiboye, J.K., Chidi, I., and Kalu, O. Promoting family planning through mass media in Nigeria: Campaigns using public service announcements and a national logo. Baltimore, Maryland, Johns Hopkins School of Public Health, Center for Communication Programs, Jul. 1996. (IEC Field Report No. 5) 58 p.

*87. Kirk, D. and Pillet, B. Fertility levels, trends, and differentials in Sub-Saharan Africa in the 1980s and 1990s. Studies in Family Planning 29(1): 1-22. Mar. 1998.

88. Kishor, S. Gender differentials in child mortality: A review of the evidence. In: Das Gupta, M., Chen, L.C., and Krishnan, T.N., eds. Women's Health in India: Risk and Vulnerability. Bombay, Oxford University Press, 1995.

89. Klerman, L.V., Phelan, S.T., Poole, V.L., and Goldenberg, R.L. Family planning: An essential component of prenatal care. Journal of the American Medical Women's Association 50(5): 147-151. Sep./Oct. 1995.

90. Koenig, M.A., Phillips, J.F., Campbell, O.M., and D'Souza, S. Birth intervals and childhood mortality in rural Bangladesh. Demography 27(2): 251-265. May 1990.

91. Kols, A. and Sherman, J.E. Family planning programs: Improving quality. Series J, No. 47. Baltimore, Johns Hopkins School of Public Health, Population Information Program, Nov. 1998. 40 p.

92. Labbok, M.H., Perez, A., Valdes, V., Sevilla, F., Wade, K., Laukaran, V.H., Cooney, K.A., Coly, S., Sanders, C, and Queenan, J.T. The Lactational Amenorrhea Method (LAM): A postpartum introductory family planning method with policy and program implications. Advances in Contraception 10(2): 93-109. Jun. 1994.

*93. Labbok, M.H., Perez-Escamilla, R., Peterson, A.E., and Coly, S. Breastfeeding and child spacing: Country profiles. Washington, DC, Georgetown University, Institute for Reproductive Health, 1997. 97 p.

94. Lang, J., Lieberman, E., Ryan, K., and Monson, R. Interpregnancy interval and risk of preterm labor. American Journal of Epidemiology 132(2): 304-309. Aug. 1, 1990.

95. Larsen, U. Primary and secondary infertility in Sub-Saharan Africa. International Journal of Epidemiology 29: 285-291.2000.

96. Larsen, U., Chung, W., and Das Gupta, M. Fertility and son preference in Korea. Population Studies 52(3): 317- 325. Nov. 1998.

97. Lawoyin, T.O. and Oyediran, A.B. A prospective study on some factors which influence the delivery of low birth weight babies in a developing country. African Journal of Medicine and Medical Sciences 21(1): 33-39. Oct. 1992.

98. Lesotho Ministry Of Health and Social Welfare and World Health Organization. Lesotho Safe Motherhood Initiative women's health survey. Focus group discussions. [Draft]. Lesotho, Apr. 2, 1995. 45 p. (Unpublished)

99. Lindstrom, D.P. and Berhanu, B. The effects of breastfeeding and birth spacing on infant and early childhood mortality in Ethiopia. Social Biology 47(1-2): 1-17. Spring/ Summer 2000.

100. Madise, N.J. and Diamond, I. Determinants of infant mortality in Malawi: An analysis to control for death clustering within families. Journal of Biosocial Science 27(1): 95-106. Jan. 1995.

101. Mahfouz, A.A., El-said, M.M., Alakija, W., Badawi, I.A., Al-erian, R.A., and Abdel

Moneim, M. Anemia among pregnant women in the Asir region, Saudi Arabia: An epidemiologic study. Southeast Asian Journal of Tropical Medicine and Public Health 25(1): 84-87. Mar. 1994.

102. Manda, S.O. Birth intervals, breastfeeding and determinants of childhood mortality in Malawi. Social Science and Medicine 48(3): 301-312. Feb. 1999.

103. Martine, G. Brazil's fertility decline, 1965-1995: A fresh look at key factors. Population and Development Review 22(1): 47-75. Mar. 1996.

104. Mathema, N. (World Education) [Birth Spacing Messages] Personal communication, August 26, 2002.

105. Mboup, G. and Saha, T. Fertility levels, trends and differentials. Calverton, Maryland, Macro International, Demographic and Health Surveys, Aug. 7 1998. (Demographic and Health Surveys Comparative Studies No. 28) 78 p.

106. Mccauley, A., Robey, B., Blanc, A., and Geller, J. Opportunities for women through reproductive choice. Population Reports, Series M, No. 12. Baltimore, Johns Hopkins School of Public Health, Population Information Program, Jul. 1994. 39 p.

107. Merchant, K., Martorell, R., Gonzalez-Cos-Sio, T., Rivera, J., and Haas, J.D. Maternal nutritional depletion: Evidence of responses in women to frequent reproductive cycling. Washington, DC, International Center for Research on Women, Mar. 1990. (Maternal Nutrition and Health Care Program Research Report Series No. 3) 38 p.

108. Mhloyi, M. and Mapfumo, O. Zimbabwe: Impact of family planning on women's participation in the development process. Research Triangle Park, North Carolina, Family Health International and University of Zimbabwe, 1998.

109. Miller, J.E. Birth intervals and perinatal health: An investigation of three hypotheses. Family Planning Perspectives 23(2): 62-70. Mar./Apr. 1991.

110. Miller, J.E. Birth order, interpregnancy interval and birth outcomes among Filipino infants. Journal of Biosocial Science 26(2): 243-259. Apr. 1994.

111. Miller, J.E., Trussell, J., Pebley, A.R., and Vaughan, B. Birth spacing and child mortality in Bangladesh and the Philippines. Demography 29(2): 305-318. May 1992.

112. Millman, S.R. and Cooksey, E.C. Birth weight and the effects of birth spacing and breastfeeding on infant mortality. Studies in Family Planning 18(4): 202-212. Jul./Aug. 1987.

*113. Mishra, S.B. Birth spacing methods in the Indian family welfare program. In: M.E. Khan, G.C., ed. Spacing as an Alternative Strategy. India's Family Welfare Programme. Delhi, India, B.R. Publishing Corporation, 1996.

114. Mozumder, A.B., Barkat E, K., Kanc, T.T., Levin, A., and Ahmed, S. The effect of birth interval on malnutrition in Bangladeshi infants and young children. Journal of Biosocial Science 32(3): 289-300. Jul. 2000.

115. Muhuri, P.K. and Menken, J. Adverse effects of next birth, gender, and family composition on child survival in rural Bangladesh. Population Studies 51(3): 279-294. Nov. 1997.

116. Muhwava, W. and Timaeus, I. Fertility decline in Zimbabwe. London School of Hygiene and Tropical Medicine, 1996. (Center for Population Studies Research Paper No. 96-1) (Available: <http://www.Ishtm.ac.uk/eps/cps/cpsrp961.pdf>, Accessed Sep. 4, 2002)

117. Nath, D.C., Land, K.C. Sex preference and third birth intervals in a traditional Indian society. Journal of Biosocial Science 26(3): 377-388. Jul. 1994.

118. Nath, D.C., Land, K.C, and Goswami, G. Effects of the status of women on the first-birth interval in Indian urban society. Journal of Biosocial Science 31(1): 55-69. Jan. 1999.

119. Nath, D.C., Land, K.C., and Singh, K.K. The role of breast-feeding beyond postpartum amenorrhoea on the return of fertility in India: A life table and hazards model analysis. Journal of Biosocial Science 26(2): 191-206. Apr. 1994.

120. Nduati, R., John, G., Mbori-ngacha, D., Richardson, B., Overbaugh, J., Mwatha, A., Ndinya-achola, J., Bwayo, J., Onyango, F.e., Hughes, J., and Kreiss, J. Effect of

breastfeeding and formula feeding on transmission of HIV-1: A randomized clinical trial. JAMA 283(9): 1167-1174. Mar. 1, 2000.

121. Neel, N.R. and Alvarez, J.O. Maternal risk factors for low birth weight and intrauterine growth retardation in a Guatemalan population. Bulletin of the Pan American Health Organization, Vol. 25 No. 2, 1991. p. 152-165.

122. Nigeria Federal Ministry of Health. Well spaced children are every parent's joy. Lagos, Health Education Division, Poster. 1990.

123. Nyarko, P., Madise, N., and Diamond, I. Infant mortality and the pace of childbearing in Ghana: Some evidence of son preference. Proceedings of the Third African Population Conference: The African Population in the 21st Century, Durban, South Africa, Dec. 6-10, 1999. Department of Welfare, Republic of South Africa, 619-644 p.

124. Obisesan, K.A., Adeyemo, A.A., Ohaeri, J.U., Aramide, F.A., and Okafor, S.I. The family planning aspects of the practice of traditional healers in Ibadan, Nigeria. West African Journal of Medicine 16(3): 184-190. Jul./Sep. 1997.

*125. Ofosu, Y. Breast-feeding and birth spacing: Erosion of West African traditions. In: Adepoju, A. and Oppong, C, eds. Gender, Work, and Population in Sub-Saharan Africa. London, James Currey, 1994. p. 173-190.

126. Oheneba-Sakyi, Y. and Heaton, T.B. Effects of socio-demographic variables on birth intervals in Ghana, journal of Comparative Family Studies 24(1): 113-135. Spring 1993.

*127. Omer, M.M. Factors affecting birth interval in Egypt. In: CDC 23rd Annual Seminar on Population and Development Issues in the Middle East, Africa and Asia, 1993. Research Monograph Series No. 23. Cairo, Cairo Demographic Centre, 1994. p. 633-658.

128. Palloni, A., Pinto Aguirre, G., and Lastiri, S. The effects of breast-feeding and the pace of childbearing on early childhood mortality in Mexico. Bulletin of the Pan American Health Organization 28(2): 93-111. Jun. 1994.

129. Park, C.B., Islam, M.A., Chakraborty, N., and Kantner, A. Partitioning the effect of infant and child death on subsequent fertility: An exploration in Bangladesh. Population Studies 52(3): 345-356. Nov. 1998.

130. Park, C.B., Siasakul, S., and Saengtienchai, C. Effect of birth spacing on infant survival in Thailand: Two-stage logit analysis. Southeast Asian Journal of Tropical Medicine and Public Health 25(1): 50-59. Mar. 1994.

*131. Pathak, K.B., Feeney, G., and Luther, N.Y. Alternative contraceptive methods and fertility decline in India. Mumbai, India, International Institute for Population Sciences, Mar. 28, 1998. 28 p. (Available: <www2.ewc.hawaii.edu/pop/misc/subj-7.pdf>, Accessed Jul. 29, 2002)

132. Pathak, K.B. and Pandey, A. Tempo of fertility in Orissa: A study based on birth intervals. Journal of Family Welfare 39(4): 1-8. Dec. 1993.

133. Pathfinder International. Changing attitudes among newly married couples in Bangladesh. Changing Lives: Highlights of Pathfinder International's Projects Around the World, Spring 1996. p. 1-2.

134. Pebley, A.R. and Millman, S.R. Birthspacing and child survival. International Family Planning Perspectives 12(3): 71-79. Sep. 1986.

135. Petro-Nustas, W. Men's knowledge of and attitudes toward birthspacing and contraceptive use in Jordan. International Family Planning Perspectives 25(4): 181-185. Dec. 1999.

136. Pile, J. (EngenderHealth) [EngenderHealth Birth Spacing Activities] Personal communication, Aug. 26, 2002.

137. Planned Parenthood Association Of Ghana (PPAG). Too close. Accra, Ghana, PPAG, Poster. 1995.

138. Population Action International (PAI). Contraceptive choice: Worldwide access to family planning. 1997 report on progress towards world population stabilization. Washington, DC, PAI, 1997.

139. Prakasam, C.P., Sinha, U.P., Khan, A.G., and Reddy, H. Influence of loss of child on mother's reproduction. Bombay, India, International Institute for Population Sciences, 1993. (IIPS Research Report Series No. 4) 65 p.

140. Program for Appropriate Technology in Health. Infertility in developing countries. Outlook 15(3): 1-6. Nov. 1997. (Available: <www.path.org/outlook/html/15_ 3.htm#infert>, Accessed Aug. 29, 2002)

*141. Rafalimanana, H. and Westoff, C.F. Potential effects on fertility and child health and survival of birth-spacing preferences in sub-Saharan Africa. Studies in Family Planning 31(2): 99-110. Jun. 2000.

*142. Rafalimanana, H. and Westoff, C.F. Gap between preferred and actual birth intervals in Sub-Saharan Africa: Implications for fertility and child health. Calverton, Maryland, Macro International, Mar. 7, 2001. (DHS Analytical Studies No. 2) 21 p.

143. Rahim, A. and Ram, B. Emerging patterns of child-spacing in Canada. Journal of Biosocial Science 25(2): 155- 167. Apr. 1993.

144. Rahman, M. The effect of child mortality on fertility regulation in rural Bangladesh. Studies in Family Planning 29(3): 268-281. Sep. 1998.

145. Rahman, M. and Davanzo, J. Gender preference and birth spacing in Matlab, Bangladesh. Demography 30(3): 315-332. Aug. 1993.

146. Rajaretnam, T. Popularising spacing methods in India: The need and needed efforts. Journal of Family Welfare 40(1): 38-43. Mar. 1994.

147. Rath Nam, P.S. Education as an indicator of women's status and its impact on fertility and contraception in Pakistan. A multivariate analysis. University of Michigan, Ann Arbor, Michigan, 1995. 220 p.

148. Reddy, P.H. A qualitative study of quality of care in rural Karnataka. Population Council, 1994. 44 p. (Available: <http:/www.popcouncil.org/pdfs/aneorta/pdfs/india/sr/isr03. pdf>, Accessed Jul. 22, 2002)

149. Renne, E.P. Changing patterns of child-spacing and abortion in a northern Nigerian town. Princeton, New Jersey, Princeton University, Office of Population Research, 1997. (Office of Population Research Working Paper No. 97-1) 24 p.

150. Rinehart, W., Kols, A., and Moore, S. Healthier mothers and children through family planning. Population Reports, Series J, No. 27. Baltimore, Johns Hopkins School of Public Health, Population Information Program, 1984.

151. Robey, B., Ross, J., and Bhushan, I. Meeting unmet need: New strategies. Population Reports, Series L, No. 8, Baltimore, Johns Hopkins School of Public Health, Population Information Program, September 1996. 35 p.

152. Rodriguez, G. Spacing and limiting components of the fertility transition in Latin America. Notas de Poblacion 20(56): 57-86. Dec. 1992.

153. Ronsmans, C. Birth spacing and child survival in rural Senegal. International Journal of Epidemiology 25(5): 989- 997. Oct. 1996.

154. Ronsmans, C. and Campbell, O. Short birth intervals don't kill women: Evidence from Matlab, Bangladesh. Studies in Family Planning 29(3): 282-290. Sep. 1998.

*155. Rosero-Bixby, L. Assessing and interpreting birth spacing goals in Costa Rica. Journal of Biosocial Science 30(2): 181-91. Apr. 1998.

*156. Ross, J. and Winfrey, W. Unmet need in the developing world and former USSR: An updated estimate. International Family Planning Perspectives (submitted) forthcoming.

157. Ross, J.A. and Winfrey, W. Contraceptive use, intention to use, and unmet need during the extended postpartum period. International Family Planning Perspectives 27(1): 20- 27. Mar. 2001. (Available: <http://www.agi-usa.org/pubs/ journals/2702001.html>, Accessed Jul. 29, 2002)

158. Rural Service Delivery Partnership (RSDP) and Bangladesh Center for Communication

Programs (BCCP). Birth spacing sustains mother's and child's health. Our motto is your satisfaction with improved family health care. Dhaka, Bangladesh, RSDP and BCCP, Poster. 1996.

*159. Rutstein, S. Effect of birth intervals on mortality and health: Multivariate cross-country analyses. [Power Point Presentation]. Presented at the Champions Meeting on Birth Spacing, Washington, DC, Jan. 31, 2002. Catalyst Consortium. 16 p.

160. Rutstein, S. Effect of birth intervals on mortality and health: Multivariate cross-country analyses with data from Egypt and Pakistan. Power Point Presentation. 2002.

161. Rutstein, S. Relationships between pregnancy intervals and perinatal mortality. Proceedings of the 2nd Champions meeting on birth spacing, Washington, DC, May 2, 2002. Catalyst Consortium, 15-22 p.

162. Rutstein, S.O. Effect of birth intervals on mortality and health: Multivariate cross-country analyses with additional information for Nigeria. Power Point Presentation. 2002.

163. Satia, J.K. Strategic perspectives on promoting spacing methods. In: Khan, M.E. and Cernada, G., eds. Spacing as an Alternative Strategy. India's Family Welfare Programme. Delhi, India, B.R. Publishing Corporation, 1996. p. 151-170.

164. Setty-Venugopal, V., Jacoby, R., and Hart, C. Family planning logistics: Strengthening the supply chain. Population Reports, Series J, No. 51, Baltimore, The Johns Hopkins Bloomberg School of Public Health, Winter 2002. 39 p. (Available: <http://www.jhuccp.org/pr/j51edsum.shtml>, Accessed Aug. 2, 2002)

165. Shah, I.H. and Khanna, J. Breast-feeding, infant health and child survival in the Asia-Pacific context. Asia-Pacific Population journal 5(1): 25-44. Mar. 1990. (Available: <www.unescap.org/pop/journal/1990/v05n1a2.pdf>, Accessed Sep. 3, 2002)

166. Shapiro, D. and Tambashe, O. Employment, education, and fertility behavior in Kinshasa: Some preliminary evidence. Population Research and Policy Review 16(3): 259- 287. Jun. 1997.

167. Shipp, T.D., Zelop, C.M., Repke, J.T., Cohen, A., and Lieberman, E. Interdelivery interval and risk of symptomatic uterine rupture. Obstetrics and Gynecology 97(2): 175-177. 2001/2.

168. Shrestha, A., Bimala, M., and Wittet, S. How to Say "Birth Spacing" in Kathmandu. <http://www.path.org/ about/f_birth_spacing.htm> Program for Appropriate Technology, 1991.

169. Shults, R.A., Arndt, V., Olshan, A.F., Martin, C.F., and Royce, R.A. Effects of short interpregnancy intervals on small-for-gestational age and preterm births. Epidemiology 10(3): 250-254. May 1999.

170. Sibanda, A. Reproductive change in Zimbabwe and Kenya: The role of the proximate determinants in recent fertility trends. Social Biology 46(1-2): 82-99.

171. Siega-Riz, A.M. and Adair, L.S. Biological determinants of pregnancy weight gain in a Filipino population. American Journal of Clinical Nutrition 57(3): 365-372. Mar. 1993.

172. Singh, S. and Samara, R. Early marriage among women in developing countries. International Family Planning Perspectives 22(4): 148-157 & 175. Dec. 1996. (Available: <http://www.agi-usa.org/pubs/journals/2214896.pdf>, Accessed Jul. 19, 2002)

173. Skjaerven, R., Wilcox, A.J., and Lie, R.T. The interval between pregnancies and the risk of preeclampsia. New England Journal of Medicine 346(1): 33-8. Jan. 3, 2002.

174. Social Marketing for Change. The Jordan Birth Spacing Project. SOMARC Highlights, No. 2, Washington, DC. The Futures Group International, Apr. 1996. p. 4. (Available: <http://www.tfgi.com/1_4_96.asp>, Accessed Aug. 3, 2002)

175. Srivastava, J.N. Impact of birth spacing on child survival in rural Uttar Pradesh. Demography India 19(1): 141-146. Jan./Jun. 1990.

176. State Innovations in Family Planning Services Agency (SIFPSA). For a healthy family, wait for three years before your second child. You can get these family planning methods

from government health workers, hospitals, and health centers for free. Lucknow, India, SIFPSA, Poster. 1996.

177. Stout, I. (Catalyst Constortium) [Catalyst Consortium Activities] Personal communication, Jul. 9, 2002.

178. Stout, I., Pareja, R., and Richardson, L. Champions meeting on birth spacing. Washington, DC, The Catalyst Consortium, Jan. 2002. 19 p.

179. Stover, J. Revising the proximate determinants of fertility framework: What have we learned in the past 20 years? Studies in Family Planning 29(3): 255-267. Sep. 1998. (Available: <http://www.tfgi.com/reproxdf.asp>, Accessed Aug. 3, 2002)

180. Swenson, I. and Thang, N.M. Determinants of birth intervals in Vietnam: A hazard model analysis. Journal of Tropical Pediatrics 39(3): 163-167. Jun. 1993.

181. Taylor, C.E., Newman, J.S., and Kelly, N.U. The child survival hypothesis. Population Studies 30(2): 263-278. Jul. 1976.

182. Toure, A. Indonesia, an example to consider. Bien-Etre 17(5). Jan./Mar. 1994.

183. Trussel, J. and Menken, J. Early childbearing and subsequent fertility. Family Planning Perspectives 10(4): 209- 218. Jul./Aug. 1978.

184. Tulasidhar, V.B. Maternal education, female labor force participation, and child mortality: Evidence from the Indian census. Health Transition Review 3(2): 177-190.1993.

185. Udjo, E.O. The effect of child survival on fertility in Zimbabwe: A micro-macro level analysis. Journal of Tropical Pediatrics 43(5): 255-266. Oct. 1997.

186. United Nations Children's Fund. The state of The world's children. Oxford, Oxford University Press, 1993.

187. United States Centers For Disease Control and Prevention (CDC). Family planning methods and practice: Africa. 2nd ed. Atlanta, Georgia, National Center for Chronic Disease Prevention and Health Promotion. Division of Reproductive Health, CDC, 1999. 698 p. (Available: <http://www.cdc.gov/nccdphp/drh/africa_fpmp.htm>, Accessed Aug. 3, 2002)

188. Upadhyay, U.D. Informed choice in family planning. Helping people decide. Population Reports, Series J, No. 50, Soring 2001. p. 39. (Available: <http://www.jhuccp.org/pr/j50edsum.stm#top>, Accessed Aug. 3, 2002)

189. Valadez, J., Vargas, W., Seims, L.R., Mljoni, B., Leburg, C, and Johnson, B. Umoyo Network, Malawi: Baseline survey results for six partner organizations. Aug. 2001. 116 p.

190. Van De Walle, E. and Van De Walle, F. Post-partum sexual abstinence in tropical Africa. In: Ronald Gray, H.L., and Alfred Spira, ed. Biomedical and Demographic Determinants of Reproduction. Oxford, England, Clarendon Press, 1993. p. 446-460.

191. Varma, A. Indonesia: Faith and family planning. In: Freeman, J. and Gupte, P. All of Us. Births and a Better Life: Population, Development, and Environment in a Globalized World. New York, Earth Times Books, 1999. p. 96-99.

192. Vernon, R. and Foreit, J. How to help clients obtain more preventive reproductive health care. International Family Planning Perspectives 25(4): 200-202. Dec. 1999.

193. Walraven, G., Scherf, C, West, B., Ekpo, G., Paine K., Coleman, R., Bailey, R., and Morison, L. The burden of reproductive-organ disease in rural women in The Gambia, West Africa. Lancet 357(9263): 1161-1167. Apr. 14, 2001.

194. Ward, V.M., Bertrand, J.T., and Puac, F. Exploring sociocultural barriers to family planning among Mayans in Guatemala. International Family Planning Perspectives 18(2): 59-65. Jun. 1992.

195. Westoff, C.F. and Bankole, A. Unmet need: 1990-1994. Calverton, Maryland, Macro international, June 1995. (DHS Comparative Studies No. 16) 55 p.

196. Westoff, C.F. and Bankole, A. Trends in the demand for family limitation in developing countries. International Family Planning Perspectives 26(2): 56-62, 97. Jun. 2000.

197. Westoff, C.F., Blanc, A.K., and Nyblade, L. Marriage and entry into parenthood.

Calverton, Maryland, Macro International, Mar. 1994. (Demographic and Health Surveys Comparative Studies No. 10) 47 p.

198. Westoff, C.F. and Ochoa, L.H. Unmet need and the demand for family planning. Columbia, Maryland, Institute for Resource Development/Macro International, Jul. 6, 1991. (Demographic and Health Surveys Comparative Studies No. 5)37p.

199. White, M., Djamba, Y., and Dang Nguyen, A. Implications of economic reform and spatial mobility for fertility in Vietnam. Population Research and Policy Review 20(3): 207-228. Jun. 2001.

*200. Whitworth, A. and Stephenson, R. Birth spacing, sibling rivalry, and child mortality in India. Social Science and Medicine In Press, Uncorrected Proof. 2002.

201. Winikoff, B. The effects of birth spacing on child and maternal health. Studies in Family Planning 14(10): 231-245. Oct. 1983.

202. Winikoff, B. And Castle, MA. The maternal depletion syndrome: Clinical diagnosis or eco-demographic condition? Presented at the International Conference on Better Health for Women and Children through Family Planning, Nairobi, Kenya, Oct. 5-9, 1987. 12 p.

203. Winkvist, A., Rasmussen, K.M., and Habicht, J.P. A new definition of maternal depletion syndrome. American journal of Public Health 82(5): 691-694. May 1992.

204. Wittet, S. (Path) [Birth Spacing Terms in Nepal] Personal communication, August 21, 2002.

205. World Health Organization (WHO). Improving access to quality care in family planning: Medical eligibility criteria for contraceptive use. [Draft]. 2nd ed. Geneva, WHO, May 2000.

206. World Health Organization (WHO) Task Force on Methods for the Natural Regulation of Fertility. The World Health Organization multinational study of breast-feeding and lactational amenorrhea. I. Description of infant feeding patterns and of the return of menses. Fertility and Sterility 70(3): 448-460. Sep. 1998.

207. World Health Organization (WHO) Task Force on Methods for the Natural Regulation of Fertility. The World Health Organization multinational study of breast-feeding and lactational amenorrhea. II. Factors associated with the length of amenorrhea. Fertility and Sterility 70(3): 461-471. Sep. 1998.

208. World Health Organization (WHO) Task Force on Methods for the Natural Regulation of Fertility. The World Health Organization multinational study of breast-feeding and lactational amenorrhea. III. Pregnancy during breast-feeding. Fertility and Sterility 72(3): 431-440. Sep. 1999.

209. Worthman, C.M., Jenkins, C.L, Stallings, J.F., and Lai, D. Attenuation of nursing-related ovarian suppression and high fertility in well-nourished, intensively breast feeding Amele women of lowland Papua New Guinea. Journal of Biosocial Science 25(4): 425-443. Oct. 1993.

210. Yasmin, S., Osrin, D., Paul, E., And Costello, A. Neonatal mortality of low-birth-weight infants in Bangladesh. Bulletin of the World Health Organization, Vol. 79 Geneva. World Health Organization, 2001. p. 608-614.

211. Yount, K.M., Langsten, R., and Hill, K. The effect of gender preference on contraceptive use and fertility in rural Egypt. Studies in Family Planning 31(4): 290-300. Dec. 2000.

212. Zenger, E. Siblings' neonatal mortality risks and birth spacing in Bangladesh. Demography 30(3): 477-488. Aug. 1993.

*213. Zhu, B.P., Rolfs, R.T., Nangle, B.E., and Horan, J.M. Effect of the interval between pregnancies on perinatal outcomes. New England journal of Medicine 340(8): 589-594. Feb 25, 1999.

SECTION O
URBAN PLANNING

Our summer ministry team had invited Rebecca Atallah to visit with us at the monastery within the garbage community of Mokattam in Cairo, Egypt, where we lived and ministered. While the monastery grounds were actually quite nice (with a cafeteria, clean running water, toilets, and simply furnished rooms), the sights, smells, and sounds of the garbage community were everywhere. Rebecca had been serving the residents of this community since the late 1980s. On this particular night as she surveyed the village from the top of the great hill on which the monastery stood, she made a startling statement. "This place is like heaven!" she said with a smile. "Heaven?" I thought. "If this is heaven, I'm not sure I want to go there."

We had lived in the garbage community of Mokkatam long enough for many of the things that shocked us at first to begin feeling normal. But the presence of animal waste and human trash coexisting with families who lived atop it all was something I never quite got used to. Young mothers would pick through a pile of raw, stinking trash while their babies ate from the same mound on which their mothers sorted. But Rebecca remembers the garbage community when it was rudimentary. She remembers the lean-tos and shanties where now there are brick buildings. She remembers the chaos and crime where now there is order and relative safety.

Mokattam is as much a community of families and businesses as any North American suburban community—more so in some ways. There are bread shops, bakeries, barber shops, restaurants, churches, and businesses lining the rubbish-strewn streets. The advantage that the residents of Mokattam have in relation to any suburban community in America is a sense of belonging and camaraderie. Many people there look out for one another in ways that would be unheard of in the bedroom communities of the rich. There is a kind of fellowship in suffering not available to the comfortable.

How is it that communities develop? Much of the development of Mokattam happened informally. Can the interplay of home, work, play, and services be arranged in a way to maximize life? Who determines where homes, shops, and bus lines are placed? Most slum communities develop without a master plan in mind; they spring up unpredictably and too fast for government officials to think about zoning or services. Even if they have zoned an area for business, many cities in the developing world lack the resources to stop informal settlements from emerging.

In his book *Clearing the Way: Deconcentrating the Poor in Urban America*, Edward Goetz looks in some depth at the density of poor residents on the north side of Minneapolis, Minnesota. He observes that the urban poor are most often packed into a specific location and that this concentration brings with it a concentration of disadvantages. A concentration of poorly resourced public schools, a concentration of crime and drugs, and a concentration of unwed mothers often accompany these communities. Many efforts to serve the poor have also served to keep the poor crammed together. But attempts to "deconcentrate" these communities and merge them with higher-income neighborhoods bring their own set of challenges. Examining how the city of Minneapolis dealt with one neighborhood gives some clues as to how urban planning can serve cities with dense areas of poor residents.

"Beyond the Third World City: The New Urban Geography of South-east Asia" examines how wealthy developers, American city models, and the minority middle-class have often driven the structure of Asian cities in the developing world. It is a relevant survey of the past two hundred years of urban planning in South-east Asia.

Where are the urban developers who have a heart for the poor and know how to involve them in the decisions that impact their neighborhoods?

CHAPTER 29

BEYOND THE THIRD WORLD CITY: THE NEW URBAN GEOGRAPHY OF SOUTH-EAST ASIA

H. W. DICK AND P. J. RIMMER

Scholars, as area specialists, have typified south-east Asian cities as Third World cities and emphasized their uniquely south-east Asian or even national characteristics. This paper will argue that the early decades of decolonization which gave rise to this perspective were in fact a transitional phase. In the late colonial period south-east Asian cities were already becoming more like Western cities. Since the 1980s, in the era of globalization, this process of convergence has re-emerged. Clearly, there should now be a single urban discourse. This is not to deny that south-east Asian (or Third World) cities have distinctive elements. The problem is the paradigm which shuts out First World elements.

Convergence: Third World City to Global City

By the 1980s, the growth processes in southeast Asian cities were again converging to a remarkable degree with those of the First World and, in particular, those of the US. There is a rich and growing literature that challenges conventional ideas of urban form in the US. Gated communities, shopping malls, edge cities and the decline of public space are issues in the deconstruction of the very notion of "the city" (Christopherson, 1994; Davis, 1990; Garreau, 1991; Gottdiener, 1991, 1994, 1995; Gottdiener and Kephart, 1991; Jacobs, 1984). This vigorous questioning would seem to be in a world remote from south-east Asia. And yet, high-rise offices, gated residential communities, giant shopping malls and freeways have already taken root in south-east Asia and have become key elements in the restructuring of urban space. Although there remain separate debates and literatures for the US and southeast Asia, in reality many issues are the same.

Rising real incomes and the rapidly expanding urban middle class have created a new urban dynamic in south-east Asia. Although there is no reliable way to measure the size of the middle class in Thailand, Malaysia and Indonesia, it is probably at least one-third of the population of Bangkok, Kuala Lumpur and Jakarta (Hewison, 1996; Hughes and Woldekidan, 1994; Robison and Goodman, 1996). Since the 1980s, the swollen middle class has attracted investment in multiple satellite towns surrounding the old central business district (CBD). This is especially true of Jakarta, Manila and Singapore.

As shown in Figure 29.1A, the old relationship between the lower town and the upper town had been a simple one of daily commuting. The proliferation of multiple urban centers in the 1980s diminished the importance of the movement into and out of the CBD in favor of increasing movements between urban centers around the urban fringe (Figure 29.1B). This new pattern was facilitated by rapidly increasing rates of vehicle ownership, which freed the middle class from dependence on public transport. One symptom of this new pattern was the proliferation of suburban centers. However, this second and more complex system of multiple centers proved to be an unstable transitional form.

The logic and momentum which generated activity and movement between satellite towns necessarily generated expansion beyond them into cheaper peri-urban land (Figure 29.1C). In effect, the city is now being turned inside out. The share of movements into and out of the old CBD is now declining. Commuting is occurring over greater distances and along increasingly congested roads. The locational incentives that arise from the urban land market are to locate or relocate workplaces on or beyond the urban fringe. A growing proportion of commuter movements are therefore oriented away from the CBD.

In the extended metropolitan area, settlement has spilled beyond recognized urban boundaries and even beyond contiguous urban areas, especially along main highways (referred to by McGee as *desakota*). Factories are now located where they can draw labor from surrounding villages. There is no sharp rural–urban dichotomy. No longer is it functional to bring labor to the city. It is easier to take work to rural areas to avoid social overhead costs as bulging cities outstrip their modest infrastructure.

Rebundling Urban Elements

A new starting-point may be to recognize that many of the elements of the south-east Asian city are not only familiar, but are also common to the Western city. The elements include, for example, the home, which may be taken as the trip origin, and the destinations of office, shops, restaurants, schools, hospitals, sports center, hotel and cinema (Figure 29.2). These are linked by the same technologies of the motor car and public transport. They may, however, be

Figure 29.1 Turning the City Inside Out

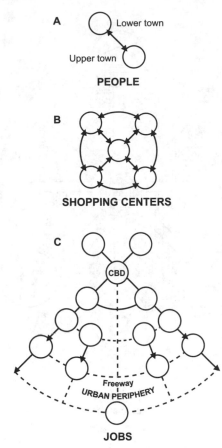

arranged or bundled in different ways. In other words, the city may be viewed in abstract as a set of elements which over time can be bundled, unbundled and reassembled in new urban forms. This process is restructuring, but in a specifically urban context.

In historical perspective, the impulse for restructuring urban space in south-east Asia was the development in the 1960s of the first homogeneous new middle-class communities. These could be observed in Singapore, Kuala Lumpur (Petaling Jaya) and Manila (Makati). In Jakarta, the new town of Kebayoran Baru was under construction in the 1950s, but urban middle-class development slowed down in the 1960s because of the national economic crisis. As these "new towns" acquired a threshold population of mobile consumers with relatively high disposable incomes, there arose market opportunities for entrepreneurs to build

461

Figure 29.2 Unbundled Cities

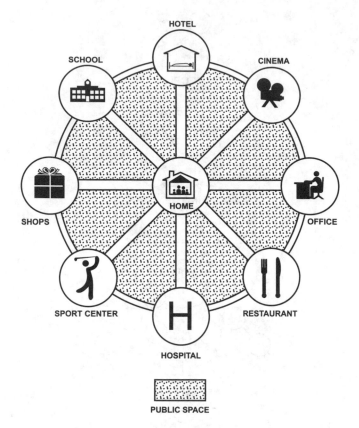

workplaces, and shopping and entertainment facilities in adjacent locations well beyond the old town core. In the 1970s and 1980s, as real incomes grew rapidly because of export-oriented industrialization, new centers proliferated around the urban fringe (Figure 29.2). Foreign aid funds were invested in new freeways and toll roads to link these centers (see Figure 29.1C).

During the 1980s, there were signs that private urban development had reached new thresholds of investment and land area. Hitherto, the process could still have been described as suburbanization. Entrepreneurs for the most part continued to invest in discrete facilities such as hotels and office blocks, each of which generated custom for others. The innovation of the 1980s was the recognition by some of the richest south-east Asian businessmen that enhanced profitability would flow from bundling as many as possible of these discrete facilities into integrated complexes. These complexes comprise hotels, restaurants, shopping malls and office towers (Figure 29.3). Such integrated projects enjoyed enhanced profitability because each facility fed the other, by attracting and circulating custom. The externalities were thereby internalized. These projects required the ability to mobilize huge sums of risk capital to buy up land and finance construction in anticipation of the market.

The problem of these integrated projects was to attract sufficient custom to earn a profit from the huge initial outlays. Because consumers lived in discrete communities, and by virtue of vehicle ownership enjoyed the freedom of choice between competing centers, there was no captive market. As competition drove new developers to open ever more luxurious complexes with hitherto undreamed of facilities (such as bowling alleys and skating rinks), existing developers were at risk either of not recovering their outlay or of failing to enjoy the anticipated return. The solution, which became characteristic of the 1990s, was to buy up even larger tracts of land for integrated residential and commercial complexes (Figure 29.4). The externalities are therefore internalized: facilities help to sell houses and the captive residential clientele sells facilities. A developer owning

Figure 29.3. Semi-bundled Cities

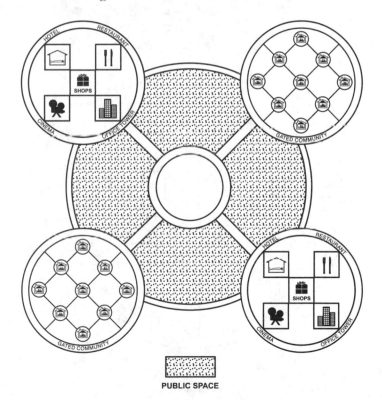

PUBLIC SPACE

10 hectares can build a suburban block, with 100 hectares, an entire suburb; but with 1000 hectares or more, a new town.

The dramatic increase in the scale, range and sophistication of facilities for the urban middle class has been accompanied by the emergence of new institutional forms. Foremost among these is the "gated community." The 20th century phenomenon of suburbanization was a shift in residence from traditional or European two-story dwellings to detached single-story bungalows or mansions; these were set amidst spacious lawns and gardens in quiet shady streets, recognizably the "garden suburb" of Britain or the US (King, 1990).

Such low-density open living is attractive only in a situation of good public security, as in the colonial era. In post-independence south-east Asia, the street is typically perceived as a source of danger. Decorative fences and hedges are no longer a deterrent to thieves. Open suburban living thus becomes very

Figure 29.4 Bundled Cities

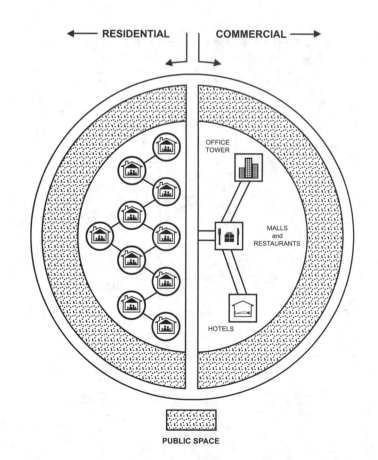

insecure. One solution, especially for expatriates, was the compound—that is to say, a group of dwellings with a single controlled point of entry. An increase in scale allows controlled access and patrolled security to be provided to an entire suburb. By the logic of the market, in which the richest people sought the highest level of personal security, real estate developers were almost obliged to construct gated communities. In the late 1960s, gated communities appeared in Manila; in the late 1970s, in Jakarta; and by the 1980s, in Surabaya. In Singapore, where security was least problematic, the equivalent communities were high-rise condominiums. These have become popular for expatriates in Jakarta and Manila.

The other new institutional feature is the shopping mall. South-east Asian cities had long been familiar with shopping streets, multistory markets and department stores. In the late colonial period, prestige shopping districts became differentiated from low-cost, downtown retailing. Shopping malls or plazas were much larger in scale and integrated many retailing and entertainment functions within a single complex, linked to multistory carparking. They were designed to encourage access by the mobile high-spending middle-class population and to discourage patronage by ordinary people who were for the most part window-shoppers. The step up from shopping-centers-cum-plazas to plaza-cum-malls can be dated to the 1980s in Manila, Bangkok, Jakarta and Kuala Lumpur.

A Jakarta Case Study

This new pattern of urban development is well illustrated by Jakarta. Figure 29.5 shows how "new town" projects and industrial estates have developed ribbon-like along the toll roads feeding into the city's outer ring road. Since the 1980s, Bekasi to the east, and Tangerang to the west, have become the main concentrations for the growth of manufacturing employment and population.

Projects located in the hilly terrain south of Jakarta are more in the nature of resorts and less closely tied to employment centers and toll roads.

The new urban developments are on a huge scale. The entire area of the Capital City Region of Jakarta, roughly equivalent to the area within the outer ring road is 66,000 hectares. By October 1996, over 90,000 hectares outside the Capital City Region had received government approval for urban development (Kompas, 1996). Of this total, only 13,300 hectares had been built upon by 1997.

The balance constitutes a land bank in the hands of developers estimated to meet the supply of suburban residential land until the year 2018. Most of this land bank is controlled by a few large private business groups. Three of the largest projects (between 5,000 and 6,000 hectares) are all currently in progress. However, the largest project of some 30,000 hectares has yet to begin construction and, in view of the recent currency crisis, is likely to be long delayed.

Table 29.1 lists residential projects over 500 hectares by location and size. Until the mid 1980s, 500 hectares was a very large project. Pondok Indah (460 ha), a mainly expatriate gated suburb in south Jakarta, and Citra Garden (480 ha), a middle-class project in several separate blocks near Jakarta International Airport, are good examples from this period. These projects were essentially dormitory suburbs with some associated facilities. For example, Pondok Indah contained a golf course and international school and later a shopping plaza. However, most facilities were being built only when the area had been fully occupied and connected to an outer ring road. In terms of the classification above, they can be regarded as "semibundled."

In 1984 a consortium of leading developers (including participants from the two earlier projects) took the gamble of acquiring 6000 hectares of land to the west of Jakarta and in 1989 they launched the first genuine new town project, Bumi Serpong Damai. The golf course and gated community were developed first; as the density increased, other facilities such as schools, offices and shopping mall were gradually added. Ultimately, this project will include a 300-

Figure 29.5 Jakarta: New Towns and Industrial Estates Approved and Under Construction

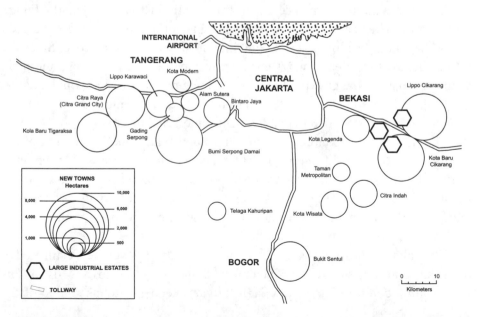

hectare central business district and 200-hectare business park with a projected employment of 140,000 people.

Even more ambitious projects are the new towns of Lippo Karawaci (2,360 ha) and Lippo Cikarang (5,500 ha) in west and east Jakarta respectively (Lippoland, 1996). Since 1991/92, the Lippo Group have sought to build as many facilities as possible at the outset. By 1997, Lippo Karawaci had a central business district with multiple office towers, a 100,000 square meter shopping mall (the largest in Jakarta), two condominium towers (52 and 42 stories), a 328-bed international hospital, a private school and university, the essential golf course and country club and five-star international hotel.

The projected population for 2020 is 1 million people. These projects are unambiguously "bundled" cities which contain all significant elements under the control of a single developer. This is clearly First World not Third World.

The scale of these leading new town developments will make it difficult for the semi-bundled developments of less than 2000 hectares to be viable as genuine new towns. Competition will force some projects launched as integrated towns to be scaled back to residential suburbs that feed adjacent business districts. The biggest rewards will go to those developers who had the foresight to choose the best locations and have the deepest pockets to carry the huge initial outlays on infrastructure.

Jakarta is not an isolated example. Indonesia's second city of Surabaya has a 2,000-hectare new town under construction as well as several adjacent semi-bundled projects of several hundred hectares. In Bangkok, large firms such as Bangkok Land, Tanayong and Land and House have built huge complexes around the city's outskirts. Even Ho Chi Minh has a new town project of 2300 hectares—Saigon South is a joint venture between Taiwanese interests and the Peoples' Committee of Ho Chi Minh City.

The Driving Force

The elements and the patterns that are now observed in new towns and settlements around the main cities of south-east Asia resemble those observed in the US. At first sight, this American architectural "imperialism" seems implausible. If there were to be a convergence between south-east Asian and Western cities, one would surely look for a model towards Europe, with its intensive agriculture and high-density cities. Aside from America's cultural dominance, there seem to be two main reasons why south-east Asia is borrowing institutions more readily from the US. The first is the highly skewed distribution of income in Asia between the expanding middle class and the bulk of the population. The second, and associated reason, is the perceived low level of public security. In the US the respective features are poor minority populations and urban ghettos.

The driving force behind the new urban geography of south-east Asia is the avoidance of social discomfort. In Indonesia and Malaysia, racial antagonism between the Chinese and Indonesians/Malays encouraged wealthy Chinese to

Table 29.1 New Towns Approved or Under Construction Around Jakarta, June 1997

Project	Area (ha)	Launched (year)
North Jakarta		
Jakarta Waterfront City	2700	NA
West Jakarta (Tangerang)		
Teluk Naga	8000	NA
Bumi Serpong Damai	6000	1989
Dkota Baru Tigaraksa	3000	1987
Citra Raya (Citra Grand City)	3000	1994
Lippo Karawaci	2630	1992
Bintaro Jaya	1700	1979
Gading Serpong	1000	1993
Kota Modern	770	1989
Alam Sutera	770	1994
East Jakarta (Bekasi)		
Lippo Cikarang	5500	1991
Kota Baru Cikarang	5400	NA
Kota Legenda	2000	1994
Bukit Indah City	1200	1996
South Jakarta (Bogor)		
Bukit Jonggol Asri	30000	1996
Bukit Sentul	2000–2400	NA
Citra Indah	1200	1996–97
Kota Wisata	1000	1997
Telaga Kahuripan	750	NA
Taman Metropolitan	600	NA

Sources: Various

seek the security of gated communities. In the Philippines, there is also the fear of kidnapping. However, more and more middle-class indigenous Indonesians, Malays and Filipinos are also choosing to live in such secure communities, primarily to protect their property against theft. As people acquire more private possessions, their level of insecurity rises.

The common experience which draws together the separate urban experiences of North America and south-east Asia is the perceived deterioration in personal security. In the US, the fear of public space—in fact, the fear of the city itself—is grounded in racism and drug-related crime. In south-east Asia, the immediate threat is less apparent. However, rising real household incomes and the emergence of an identifiable middle class have been accompanied by a growing differentiation from, and fear of, the rest of the inchoate urban mass. In countries such as Indonesia, Malaysia and the Philippines, where the middle class is disproportionately ethnic Chinese, that fear has a palpable racial edge. Gated residential communities, condominiums, air-conditioned cars, patrolled shopping malls and entertainment complexes, and multi-storied offices are the present and future world of the insecure middle class in south-east Asia.

This preoccupation with comfort and security is reflected in attitudes towards public space. In Europe, despite the popularity of the motor car, public space remains an integral part of social life. In the US, and increasingly in south-east Asia, public space has become an area of uncertainty. Middle-class people, therefore, seek to control their environment by insulating themselves from the uncertainties of casual social interaction with the poor. They live in air-conditioned houses in gated communities, travel in private air-conditioned vehicles to air-conditioned offices and shopping malls. Home, office and mall are increasingly patrolled by private security personnel backed up by overhead video cameras.

The level of insecurity in the street is an important motive for patronizing shopping malls. Other factors are the convenience of park'n'shop and the opportunity to shop, eat or play in a socially comfortable, air-conditioned environment that eliminates the aggravations of pickpockets, jostling, name-calling and the challenge of the crowd. The attitude is reminiscent of 19th-century attitudes towards the threatening London crowd, which was regarded as being uneducated, uncouth and unpredictable. The attitude of the middle class in south-east Asia towards the urban mass is also not so very different from that of the colonial Europeans to their indigenous subjects. A common language does not bridge the cultural gap or the economic divide.

The desire of middle-class south-east Asians for security and social comfort has, therefore, given rise to market opportunities for well-funded entrepreneurs to borrow urban elements from the US. This has occurred because those businessmen have visited or have studied in the US and are familiar with those models.

In fact, the technology transfer has worked through an even more direct mechanism. Most developers of these large projects have hired master planners, design consultants, managers and advisers, property specialists and architects from the US and occasionally also from Australia, Canada, Japan and Singapore.

In Jakarta, for example, Lippo examples are Alam Sutera (SWA Group, California), Bumi Serpong Damai (John Portman and Associates, US, Pacific Consultants International Japan), Bintaro Jaya (Development Design Group, Baltimore, US) and Cikarang Baru (Klages Carter Vail and Partners, US). Even the promotional brochures reveal a style and nomenclature that is characteristically Western. Western retailers such as Wal-Mart, J. C. Penney and TOYS 'R' US and food franchisers such as KFC, McDonalds, Pizza Hut and Wendys are becoming familiar tenants in the large shopping malls.

This heavy reliance on foreign expertise for both master planning and the design of individual elements leads to a social and cultural dissonance with the rest of the city. Although most of these new towns are located close to toll roads, other links with the road network and with the public transport system remain tenuous. Similar problems apply to other infrastructure links. Little attention is given to the housing and welfare of the lower-paid, unskilled workforce that cannot afford to live on these middle-class or luxury housing estates. The consequence is a separating out of two societies. In the US the disintegration of the city is a recent, and to many people, an alarming phenomenon. In south-east Asia, it is familiar to anyone of the older generation. Formerly, it was the situation identified as colonialism; nowadays, the distinction is primarily one of wealth and status.

Nevertheless, the situation is a logical outcome of market forces. Developers make their profit by careful market research and providing people with what they want. Those of higher incomes naturally exercise the greatest influence on the market. Many of these potential buyers do not wish to live in socially mixed and claustrophobic communities like the *kampung*. They can now afford to realize their suburban dream of a happy and independent middle-class family, living in comfort in a secure and green environment beyond the pollution of the inner city.

Conclusion

Rapid urbanization has been a worldwide phenomenon since the industrial and transport and communications revolution of the 19th century. The tempo of trade, investment and technology transfer quickened more than a century ago in the era of high imperialism, long before globalization became the catchword of the 1990s. In the heyday of colonialism, between the late-19th century and the 1930s, south-east Asian cities became much more like Western cities; especially with the separation of central business districts and garden suburbs. There was very little lag in technology or modern design between the colonial mother country and the colony. This period may be considered as one of convergence.

After the 1940s, in the period of decolonization, south-east Asian cities became distinctively Third World cities. Western influence waned (Singapore and Kuala Lumpur) or disappeared (Jakarta). Because the literature on south-east Asian and Third World cities began at this time, there has been a false presumption that their urbanization can be studied as a separate phenomenon. This paper argues that this phase of divergence was an unusual and transitory experience. Consequently, this inward-looking, specialist literature with its echoes of Orientalism, is a misleading guide to understanding the modern development of southeast Asian cities. In a new phase of rapid technology transfer and economic growth, south-east Asian cities are again showing clear evidence of converging with Western patterns of urbanization. South-east Asian cities should now be viewed with a fresh and observant gaze.

All the main trends in Western cities in the 19th and 20th centuries have eventually become formative influences on the development of south-east Asian cities. What has differed over time and between cities is the length of the lag and the extent of the influence. Any attempt to explain either the historical or contemporary urbanization of south-east Asia as a unique phenomenon is therefore doomed to absurdity. The issues and debates in the vigorous literature on cities in the US are highly relevant to what is now happening in south-east Asia. Property developers in south-east Asia have long recognized this; government officials and academics are still grappling with these new realities.

Industrialization and job creation on the urban fringe and in the hinterland of southeast Asian cities reflect the shift of industry from the First to the Third World that has been facilitated by rapid improvements in the speed and cost of transport and communications. International demand has switched from south-east Asia's agricultural products, which required labor and land, to manufactures which are also intensive—intensive but have only a marginal requirement for land. It is this international demand for the manufactures of south-east Asia which is leading footloose industries to locate in the vicinity of main cities and transport hubs in order to exploit abundant cheap labor. The spatial dimension of this process has been portrayed by Ginsburg *et al.* (1991) as *desakotasi*. This helps to draw attention to the phenomenon but confuses as much as it clarifies. It is not a uniquely south-east Asian phenomenon. The emerging urban forms take after North American patterns to a remarkable degree that has yet to be recognized, let alone explained.

The study of south-east Asia's cities must now be informed by knowledge of urban processes, especially those of the US. Scholars need to challenge prejudices which have allowed them to partition the world into separate spheres according to their own particular areas of expertise. Even if the southeast Asian currency crisis of mid 1997 leads to a slowdown in real estate development, with the collapse of some prominent companies and suspension or scaling back of new town projects, the pattern of urban development will not change markedly from that which has been observed in recent years.

References

Abeyasekere, S. (1987) *Jakarta: A History*. Singapore: Oxford University Press.

Allen, C. (Ed.) (1983) *Tales from the South China Seas: Images of the British in South-East Asia in the Twentieth Century*. London: Andre Deutsch and the British Broadcasting Corporation.

AOHD (1981) *The Land Transport of Singapore from Early Times to the Present*. Singapore: Archives and Oral History Department.

Askew, M., and Logan, W. S (Eds) (1994) *Cultural Identity and Urban Change in Southeast Asia: Interpretive Essays*. Geelong: Deakin University Press.

Blusse, L. (1986) *Strange Company: Chinese Settlers, Mestizo Women, and the Dutch in VOC Batavia*. Dordrecht: Foris Publications.

Breese, G. (1966) *Urbanization in Newly Developing Economies*. Englewood Cliffs, NJ: Prentice Hall.

Christopherson, S. (1994) The fortress city: privatized spaces, consumer citizenship, in: A. Ash (Ed.) *Post-Fordism: A Reader*, pp. 409-427. Oxford: Blackwell.

Davis, M. (1990) *City of Quartz: Excavating the Future in Los Angeles*. London and New York: Verso.

Dick. H. and Rimmer, P. J. (1980) Beyond the informal/formal dichotomy: towards an integrated approach, *Pacific Viewpoint*, 21, pp. 26-41.

Dobby, E. H. G., (1950) *Southeast Asia*. London: University of London Press.

Dwyer, D. J. (1962) The problem of in-migration and squatter settlement in Asian cities: two case studies, Manila and Victoria-Kowloon, *Asian Studies*, 2, pp. 145-169.

Fisher, C. A. (1964) *Southeast Asia: A Social, Economic and Political Geography*. London: Methuen.

Forbes, D. K. (1981) Petty commodity production and underdevelopment, *Progress in Planning*, 16, pp. 104-178.

Friedmann, J. and Wolff, G., (1982) World city formation: an agenda for research and action, *International Journal of Urban and Regional Research*, 6, pp. 309-344.

Fryer, D. W. (1953) The million city in Southeast Asia, *Geographical Review*, 43, pp. 474-494.

Garreau, J. (1991) *Edge City: Life on the Frontier*. New York: Doubleday.

Ginsburg, N. S. (1955) The Great City of Southeast Asia, *American Journal of Sociology*, 40, pp. 455-462.

Ginsburg, N. (1991) Preface, in: N. Ginsburg, B. Koppel and T.G. McGee (Eds) *The Extended Metropolis: Settlement in Transition*, pp. xiii-xviii. Honolulu: University of Hawaii Press.

Ginsburg, N., Koppel, B. and McGee, T.G. (Eds) (1991) *The Extended Metropolis: Settlement in Transition in Asia* Honolulu: University of Hawaii Press.

Gottdiener, M. (1991) Space, social theory and the urban metaphor, *Perspectives in Social Theory,* 11, pp. 295-311.

Gottdiener, M. (1994) *The New Urban Sociology.* New York: McGraw Hill.

Gottdiener, M. (1995) *Postmodern Semiotics: Material Culture and the Forms of Post Modern Life.* Cambridge, MA: Blackwell.

Gottdiener, M. and Kephart, G., (1991) The multinucleated metropolitan region: a comparative analysis, in: R. Kling, S. Olin and M. Poster (Eds) *Postsuburban California: the Transformation of Orange County since World War II,* pp. 31-54. Berkeley: University of California Press.

Gourou, P. (1940) *Land Utilization in French Indochina.* New York: Institute of Pacific Relations.

Hewison, K. (1996) Emerging social forces in Thailand, in: R. Robison and D. Goodman (Eds) *The New Rich in Asia,* pp. 137-160. London: Routledge.

Hoselitz, B. F. (1954) Generative and parasitic cities, *Economic Development and Cultural Change,* 3, pp. 278-294.

Hughes, H. and Woldekidan, B. (1994) The emergence of the middle class in ASEAN countries, *ASEAN Economic Bulletin,* 11, pp. 139-149.

Jacobs, J. (1984) *The Mall.* Prospect Heights, IL: Waveland Press.

Keyfitz, N. (1953) Population of Indonesia, *Ekonomi dan Keuangan Indonesia,* 6(1), pp. 640-655.

King, A. D. (1990) *Urbanism, Colonialism, and the World-economy: Cultural and Spatial Foundations of the World Urban System.* London and New York: Routledge.

Knox P.L. (1995) World cities and the organization of global space, in: R. J. Johnston, P. J. Taylor and M. J. Watts (Eds) *Geogrphies of Global Change: Remapping the World in the Late Twentieth Century,* pp. 232-247. Oxford: Blackwell.

Knox, P.L. and Taylor, P, J. (1995) *World Cities in a World System.* Cambridge, Cambridge University Press.

Kompas (1996) [Daily Jakarta Newspaper]. 21 October.

Lippoland (1996) Redefining urban development, Reprinted from *Asia Money* (brochure circulated by the Lippo Company).

Lo, F. C. and Yeung, Y. M. (Eds) (1995) *Emerging Cities in Pacific Asia Tokyo United.*

McGee, T. G. (1967) *The Southeast Asian City. A Social Geography of the Primate Cities of Southeast Asia.* London: G. Bell.

McGee, T. G. (1978) An invitation to the "ball": Dress "formal" or "informal"?, in: P. J. Rimmer, D. W. Drakakis-Smith and. T. G. McGee (Eds) *Food Shelter and Transport in Asia and the Pacific,* pp. 3-28. Department of Human Geography Monograph 12, The Australian National University, Canberra.

McGee, T. G. (1989) *Urbanisasi* or *kotadesasi*? Evolving urban patterns of urbanization in Asia, in: F. J. Costa *et al.(Eds) Urbanization in Asia,* pp. 93-108. Honolulu: University of Hawaii Press.

McGee, T.G. (1991) The emergence of *desakota* regions in Asia: expanding a hypothesis, in: N. Ginsburg, B. Koppel and T. G. McGee (Eds) *The Extended Metropolis: Settlement Transition in Asia,* pp. 3-25. Honolulu: University of Hawaii Press.

McGee, T. G. and Robinson 1. M. (Eds) (1995) *The Mega-urban Regions of Southeast Asia.* Vancouver: UBC Press.

Reid, A. (1993) *Southeast Asia in the Age of Commerce, 1450-1680, Volume II Expansion and Crisis.* New Haven CT: Yale University Press.

Rimmer, P. J. (1986) *Rikisha to Rapid Transit: Urban Public Transport Systems and Policy in Southeast Asia.* Sydney: Pergamon Press.

Rimmer, P. J. (1990) Hackney carriage *syces* and *rikisha* pullers in Singapore: a colonial registrar's perspective on public transport, 1888-1923, in: P. J. Rimmer and L. M. Allen (Eds) *The Underside of Malaysian History: Pullers, Prostitutes, Plantation Workers . . . ,* pp. 129-160. Singapore: Singapore University Press.

Rimmer, P. J. and Forbes, D. K. (1982) Under-development theory: a geographical analysis, *Australian Geographer,* 15(4), pp. 197-211.

Robequain, C. (1944) *The Economic Development of French Indo-China,* trans 1. Ward London: Oxford University Press.

Robequain, C. (1952) *L'Indochine.* Paris: Armand Colin.

Robinson R. And Goodman D. S. G.(1996) *The* York: Routledge.

Roschlau, M. W. (1985) *Public transport in the provinces: A study of innovation, diffusion and conflict in the Philippines.* Unpublished thesis, Department of Human Geography, Research School of Pacific Studies, The Australian National University.

Sassen, S. (1991) *The Global City: New York, London, Tokyo.* Princeton, NJ: Princeton University Press.

Sethuraman, S. V. (1975) Urbanization and employment: a case study of Djakarta, *International Labor Review,* 112, pp. 119-205.

Spate, O. H. K. and Trueblood., L. W. (1942) Rangoon: A study in urban geography, *Geographical Review,* 32, pp. 56-73.

Spencer, J. E. (1952) *Land and People in the Philippines.* Berkeley and Los Angeles: University of California Press.

Spencer, J. E. (1955) *Asia East by South.* Berkeley and Los Angeles: University of California Press.

UN (1995) *World Urbanization Prospects: The 1994 Revision—Estimates and Projections of Urban and Rural Populations and of Urban Agglomerations.* New York: United Nations.

Wernstedt, F. L. and Spencer, J. E. (1967) *The Philippines Island World: A Physical, Cultural and Regional Geography.* Berkeley and Los Angeles: University of California Press.

Wertheim, W. F. (Ed.) (1958) *The Indonesian Town: Studies in Urban Sociology.* The Hague and Bandung: W. van Hoeve Ltd.

CHAPTER 30

CLEARING THE WAY IN URBAN AMERICA

EDWARD GOETZ

We know that poverty by itself doesn't cause urban problems. It's the concentration . . . that eventually strangles those neighborhoods economically, making it impossible for residents to have access to jobs, good schools, health care, transportation. These are living conditions that can, and too often do, foster hopelessness, despair, and antisocial behavior.
—Minneapolis Mayor Sharon Sayles Belton, 1995

If this concentration in Minneapolis continues at the same rate in the next 10 years as it has in the last 10 years, it will be to the proportion that you have today in Detroit and East Saint Louis—overwhelmingly people of color and certainly an over-concentration of drugs and crime.
—Matt Little, president of the Minneapolis NAACP, 1995

By 9 A.M., the protesters who had stood between the bulldozer and the two-story townhomes had already been arrested and taken away. The more than 300 units of low-cost public housing stood largely vacant, virtually in the shadow of downtown Minneapolis—about a mile from the city's financial and cultural heart. More than 600 other public housing units had already been demolished at the site over the previous three years. Some dated back to 1939; all were the product of previous urban revitalization efforts. By the 1990s, however, these homes showed the wear of 50 years, with structural problems made worse by shifting soil underneath. The neighborhood had become the city's most highly concentrated pocket of poverty, with more than 70 percent of the population living below the federal poverty level, and a median income one-third that of the city as a whole. Many residents lived in constant fear of crime and complained about the declining quality of their apartments and the neighborhood. Yet, on a warm June morning in 1999, the remaining protesters stood behind the construction fence, holding their signs and watching as the bulldozer began to tear through the homes. The prevailing question that day was whether the city was indeed clearing the way for the previous residents to have a chance at a better life or merely clearing the way for a new, more affluent class of residents to occupy this prime parcel of real estate.

The United States is in the middle of a large and coordinated effort to "deconcentrate" its urban poor. As the country's most recent antipoverty strategy, deconcentration raises a number of public policy controversies, ranging from the federal government's culpability in prevailing patterns of racial and class-based residential segregation to the proper role of public authority in shaping residential communities for both the poor and nonpoor.

This book examines the premises underlying the deconcentration of poverty, along with its potential effects and political dynamics. While events occurring in cities across the country are discussed to a certain extent, we will focus primarily on a case study of the Minneapolis–Saint Paul metropolitan area.

Concentration of Poverty

The current policy initiative comes from the reality that poverty in America is becoming highly spatially concentrated. The number of neighborhoods in which a majority or near majority of residents live below the federal poverty level has increased dramatically over the past three decades. Unemployment rates in these communities are extremely high. Chances for a productive work life, and even the existence of positive role models in this respect, are relatively rare. Such intense concentration of disadvantage is not restricted, moreover, to our largest and oldest cities, but occurs in cities all over the country.

Various explanations exist for how this growing concentration of poverty came about. Some experts point to a history of racial discrimination and segregation in housing markets, while others point to economic shifts over the past three decades. Evidence shows that the mobility choices of the nonpoor (both black and white) have been a factor. Many have argued that the geographic distribution of subsidized housing in the United States has significantly contributed to concentrated poverty. No one, not even the federal government anymore, contests that in many cities public housing has been systematically placed in the poorest neighborhoods and in neighborhoods with the highest percentage of minority residents. Other publicly subsidized housing developments have also tended to be geographically concentrated in central cities and their more disadvantaged neighborhoods. This concentration of subsidized units has anchored poor and, increasingly, minority residents in these neighborhoods. Home-ownership subsidies, on the other hand, which were targeted to a more affluent and white population, were strictly directed to suburban areas for more than 25 years, facilitating the flow of white middle-class residents out of neighborhoods that were receiving public housing and its housing "cousins."[1]

Further, little argument exists about the results of this extreme concentration of poverty. It produces a range of social problems whose whole is greater than the sum of its parts. For example, school delinquency, school dropout, teenage pregnancy, out-of-wedlock childbirth, violent crime, and drug abuse rates are all greater in these communities than would be predicted by a linear extrapolation of poverty effects. Something about the extreme concentration of disadvantage begets even more community and individual dysfunction. The explanation for such dysfunction is a combination of loosely connected hypotheses that, taken together, can be called the neighborhood-effects arguments. They provide slightly different accounts of the causes behind the effects about which they all agree—that neighborhood environment is critical in determining individuals' opportunities and experiences.

Concerns about the concentration of poverty, therefore, focus on the dysfunctional aspects of poor communities and on the barriers these produce for families trying to make their way out of poverty. However, there are larger fears as well. Concentrated poverty not only affects individual families, but also produces aggregate community effects. Crime rates increase, rates of private investment and economic life (at least legally sanctioned economic activity) decline, and the communities themselves become dysfunctional. Furthermore, residents fear the spread of this blight—its gradual, or not-so-gradual, diffusion throughout larger sections of a city. In Minneapolis, concerned citizens tend to point to the example most geographically proximate—Detroit. Efforts at deconcentrating the poor in Minneapolis stem, to a great extent, from what can be called "the Detroit Scenario." Detroit typifies a city overcome with neighborhoods of high poverty where the middle class has fled to relatively safe and secure havens of racial and class exclusivity. The city is wracked by high property-tax rates on ever-devaluing property, generating insufficient resources to fund essential city services and the elevated level of public and social services necessary to support an impoverished populace. Its schools are underfunded and inadequate, and its streets unsafe as drugs and crime have taken over whole communities. All the while, an affluent ring of suburbs, whose residents benefit from low tax rates because their communities lack a dependent population in need of public and social services, surround the city.

Deconcentration through Dispersal of Subsidized Housing

Given this analysis of urban problems, policymakers have responded with programs designed to deconcentrate the poor through a greater dispersal of subsidized-housing residents. In practice, this has meant five different, though related, policy initiatives. First is the shifting of housing subsidies from project-based assistance (in which the subsidy is tied to a particular unit that is fixed in space—typically in lower-income neighborhoods) to tenant-based subsidies (in the form of vouchers that allow greater locational choice by families). Second is the federal government's attempt to refine tenant-based subsidies to facilitate the greatest possible dispersal of assisted families. Third is an effort, begun in 1990 and made permanent in 1998, to introduce a greater mix of incomes into existing subsidized public housing developments. Fourth is a small-to-modest effort at dispersing project-based subsidies into neighborhoods and communities that previously had little or none. Fifth is the government's largest effort aimed at demolishing or revitalizing extreme concentrations of public housing, scattering the previous residents with household-based subsidies and converting the project sites into mixed-use, mixed-income developments. Each initiative is present in Minneapolis and the Twin Cities region.

The Shift from Project-Based to Tenant-Based Subsidies

Since the mid-1970s, federal housing budgets have shifted away from funding the construction of new housing units or the rehabilitation of existing units to assisting families through vouchers. Furthermore, existing unit-based subsidies have actually been converted to household-based subsidies. This process typically involves either the demolition of housing units and the provision of household-based subsidies to the families in them, or the conversion of subsidized projects to market rate apartments (also accompanied by tenant-based assistance to the families residing there).

At the same time, the tenant-based subsidies themselves have changed. Section 8 certificates, the original form of tenant-based assistance, were gradually replaced by vouchers during the 1980s and 1990s. Finally, in 1998, Congress merged vouchers and certificates into a single form of assistance—the Section 8 Housing Choice Voucher. The current voucher allows families to rent units above the fair market rent (FMR) as long as they pay the difference between the government-established FMR limit and the actual rent. This provision enables Section 8 families to expand their housing search to previously unaffordable neighborhoods.

Refinement of Tenant-Based Assistance

Since the late 1980s, Congress and the U.S. Department of Housing and Urban Development (HUD) have tried to increase the "portability" of Section 8 assistance—that is, the ability of a household given Section 8 in one city to use it in a neighboring community. This policy allows those who receive their assistance from central-city jurisdictions to search suburban areas, thus facilitating a greater spread of assisted households.

Income Mixing in Public Housing

In 1990, Congress authorized a demonstration aimed at exploring the feasibility of introducing a wider mix of incomes into existing public housing projects. Then in 1998, Congress permanently changed the public housing program to require greater income diversity. The experience of the demonstration program is confined to a few cities, while the broader public housing reforms are too recent to have produced any measurable effects. Nevertheless, these initiatives signal a course change in public housing policy based on the deconcentration-of-poverty argument.

Scattered-Site Subsidized Housing

Tenant-based assistance has been instrumental in creating new "mobility" programs in cities around the country. In these programs, families are given vouchers that must be used in neighborhoods of low poverty (or in some cases, with low minority populations). In addition, families are given relocation counseling and assistance, and local agencies aggressively recruit property owners to expand the pool of potential relocation sites.

Not only have Congress and HUD introduced these first four policy initiatives through conventional means (i.e., legislation and the creation of new programs), but HUD has also been able to thread these initiatives into the negotiated settlements of several lawsuits filed against the agency in cities across the country over the past 20 years. In several of these negotiated settlements (consent decrees) in cases alleging discrimination in the planning and operation of the public housing program, HUD has "agreed," as a remedy to the complaints, to various combinations of the four initiatives. In most cases, concentrations of public housing have been demolished, and the subsidies converted to tenant-based Section 8 vouchers. Redevelopment of the sites typically incorporates a mixed-income approach. In some cases, mobility programs have been initiated. In other cities, HUD has agreed to a program of scattered-site public housing to reduce concentrations. Thus, these lawsuits, which HUD was facing as a result of its previous policies, and which had been filed in most cases as discrimination lawsuits independent of deconcentration, were nonetheless used by the agency to accomplish deconcentration-policy objectives. In a few cities, including Minneapolis, the consent decrees incorporated all the elements of the deconcentration strategy.

Redevelopment

The largest single programmatic effort at deconcentrating poverty has been the HOPE VI program. Created in 1992, HOPE VI grew out of a national commission that focused on the worst public housing projects and proposed solutions for improving them. The program funds the re-development of large public housing projects across the country, and for the first few years, HOPE VI grants were restricted to the nation's most "distressed" public housing projects. Over time, however, HOPE VI has moved beyond those projects and now applies to any public housing project for which demolition and redevelopment costs are within 10 percent of rehabilitation costs. Typically, HOPE VI involves demolition of some or all of the units in a particular project and redevelopment of the site as a mixed-use, mixed-income development. The number of public housing units is reduced dramatically, owner-occupied housing is combined with rental housing on the site, and an income mix is achieved. Approximately 100,000 public housing units were scheduled for demolition in the first 10 years of program funding, with the net loss of units projected as high as 60,000 (Keating 2000).

What Is at Stake

Close analysis of a single campaign to deconcentrate the poor, such as the one in Minneapolis, provides us an opportunity to carefully consider the entire edifice of this policy approach. The profile of poverty neighborhoods, as it has emerged in both the social scientific literature and the popular press, is one of a devastated social and economic landscape, with pervasive poverty, an almost complete lack of healthy social and economic characteristics, and prevailing norms of lawlessness and antisocial behavior. The concentration-of-poverty discourse was developed and refined during the height of the nation's war on drugs, when fears of inner-city violent crime, drug-induced criminality, and social breakdown were at their greatest. One issue facing this policy approach, however, is whether or not the concentration-of-poverty scenario exaggerates conditions in poor urban neighborhoods. Are the images of lawlessness and so-cial breakdown, if true even in a limited number of extreme cases, nevertheless a distortion of most poor communities? If so, is deconcentration on a national scale an extreme measure, ill suited to the problems of urban poverty?

A second issue is "choice." Is deconcentration about moving people out of particular neighborhoods because the neighborhoods have been declared dysfunctional, or is it about providing housing choices for a class of people who have not had them in the past? This question may be, in many ways, the most difficult issue for policymakers and planners to address. It repeats a long-standing tension in federal housing policy and case law: In our policy efforts, are we trying to reduce incidences of discrimination that rob people of full choice in the housing market, or are we trying in a more proactive (and interventionist way) to desegregate? The desirability of forced racial desegregation is a matter of contention among both blacks and whites.

The desirability of forced *income* segregation in the housing market, however, is equally contentious. The empirical evidence on the effects of concentrated poverty suggests fairly convincingly that such high levels of income segregation negatively impact disadvantaged neighborhoods. Deconcentration, as the term suggests, is about achieving a greater level of income (and—because of the considerable overlap with race—racial) desegregation. However, when this objective is achieved through anything other than voluntary means, it produces significant political conflict. Do all or most of the residents of concentrated subsidized housing want to move to non-concentrated communities? Experience and even common sense might suggest otherwise. Do all or any of the residents of the "receiving communities"—the neighborhoods into which the poor will relocate—welcome the opportunity to increase the diversity of their neighborhoods? Not typically.

Yet, were we to limit our deconcentration efforts to expanding the mobility "choices" of the poor, what might be the result? Mobility choices are the result of a myriad of considerations by households, and depend on a constellation of market and social factors. Neighborhoods, for instance, provide a package of amenities, including employment access, parks, shopping, public transportation, and other public services. In addition, personal support networks and such market factors as the availability of desired rents and certain types of housing units affect location decisions. The poor relate to many of these amenities in ways fundamentally different from more affluent families. For example, buses are less important to the affluent than to poor families without a car. True choice in the housing market means more than providing a poor household with a rent subsidy. A Section 8 voucher may allow a poor family to afford an apartment that costs an additional $300 per month. However, such a voucher does not put a bus line in front of the building, relocate the community college or affordable day care nearby, and bring along the family's network of friends and relatives for emotional and material support. Housing "choice" is a variable term in any market, highly constrained by factors that deconcentration policy as currently formulated does not begin to address. Thus, whether the objective is desegregation or, more fundamentally, greater choice in the housing market, deconcentration efforts face significant constraints.

Third, efforts to deconcentrate the poor lead inevitably to discussions of the proper role of government in shaping neighborhoods and influencing the housing choice and mobility decisions of all households. This question spans the entire range of housing market interventions, from decisions to forcibly move and relocate poor people on the one hand, to using regulatory power to induce or discourage the development of low-cost housing in suburban areas on the other. What principles should guide such intervention—the desire for specific outcomes (i.e., desegregation) or the concern for equitable processes (i.e., antidiscrimination)? Strongly interventionist efforts such as deconcentration (and urban renewal before it) engage us in fundamental questions of community planning. What is the proper use of public authority when it comes to building communities? What are the public purposes involved in such intervention?

Deconcentration efforts require that communities with little or no low-cost housing make room for subsidized families from high-poverty, central-city neighborhoods. No long and rich history of this exists in the United States, however. Suburban communities have traditionally used their local control over land use to limit low-cost and subsidized housing. To succeed at a significant scale, deconcentration would require a modification of that approach. Modifications of local zoning and development prerogatives have been attempted only through regional governance or state growth management, both extremely rare. Instead, deconcentration policy has been about moving the poor, and only about moving the poor.

While deconcentration was designed to help rectify conditions in America's worst neighborhoods, housing markets since the late 1990s have become very heated, even in or near neighborhoods of concentrated poverty. Efforts at deconcentration must walk a fine line between having enough impact to reverse neighborhood decline and establish a viable multi-income community on the one hand, and triggering gentrification on the other though gentriffccation may represent to some the ultimate success, the ultimate turnaround for a high-poverty neighborhood, it will not appreciably deconcentrate poverty as much as simply moving those concentrations to other places.

Beyond these more macro-level concerns, several notable issues arise at the strategy and policy level. The most overriding is the implicit decision within a deconcentration approach that community development approaches are inadequate at best and outright failures at worst. In his widely read account of a half-century of urban community development policy, Nicholas Lemann (1994) pronounced that these policies had failed. Despite the expenditure of millions of dollars and decades of efforts, America's urban neighborhoods continued to decline. To some extent, this analysis complements the 1980s neoconservative attack on the antipoverty programs of the 1960s. According to Murray (1984), for example, these attempts to end poverty in place not only failed, but also actually exacerbated the problem by creating dependency among people and places on government assistance. Other experts, even those who do not quite share Murray's opinion, nevertheless suggest that community development has come up wanting. Orfield (1997), for example, argues that even community development efforts that are considered successful within the field have failed to turn around their central-city communities. Rusk (1999) argues that the "inside game" (community development) is destined to fail without a complementary strong "outside game" (regional efforts). The debate over addressing poverty in place as opposed to facilitating residents' exit from poor neighborhoods is not new. Nor has the question been resolved in any final sense. Forced deconcentration, however, is an emphatic statement. It stakes out a strong position on one side of the question. Deconcentration says that households should leave their central-city neighborhoods for their own good—that they would be better-off in neighborhoods shared with more affluent families.

Finally, disregarding alternative approaches or questions about the premises of deconcentration itself produces more questions. First, is deconcentration of poverty a step back from a fundamental attempt to eliminate poverty to a less-ambitious attempt to merely spread it around? Have we retreated from our effort to attack those processes, whatever they may be, that produce poverty? Proponents of deconcentration would argue that this is not wholly the case. The concentration-of-poverty argument suggests that living in these environments begets even greater social dysfunction than being poor in a predominantly non-poor community. Thus, there are individual and social benefits to deconcentrating poverty. Troublesome social problems are reduced, and individual families may be better able to work their way out of poverty. They will be closer to jobs, less afraid to venture out to find work. They will benefit from better schools and richer (literally and figuratively) networks of social capital. In addition, their children will be better socialized to succeed. Therefore, according to proponents, deconcentrating poverty will also reduce poverty.

The relative emphasis on forced versus voluntary deconcentration is a central issue. Voluntary mobility avoids many of the more problematic aspects of forced relocation, yet voluntary mobility will probably never achieve the scale necessary to have the impact that proponents desire. The issue of scale is central. The proper and necessary scale for these programs is probably several orders of magnitude higher than what can be achieved purely through voluntary means, and higher, too, than what is politically acceptable to most parties. Political opposition to deconcentration comes from both the right and the left; it comes from both the receiving communities and the communities being deconcentrated. Receiving communities want strict limits to the number of very low income families that are relocated in their midst. The high-poverty communities, too, are quite likely to resist large-scale deconcentration—on several grounds.

A final controversy generated by deconcentration revolves around its impact on the families involved and the communities affected. Proponents point to evidence that deconcentration leads to improvements in employment, education, neighborhood satisfaction, and sense of safety. Opponents point to examples of families in new communities experiencing harassment, higher levels of social isolation, and greater dissatisfaction with public services, such as public transportation, on which the poor rely heavily. Opponents also point to the potential detrimental impacts of subsidized housing units (or families) in receiving communities. Do these families (or units) devalue property, trigger decline in the public schools, or increase incivilities? Proponents suggest that research by and large does not support these claims, and that healthy communities can absorb these families and remain healthy.

The Consent Decree in *Hollman v. Cisneros*

In order to investigate the issues related to deconcentration in a comprehensive manner, this book examines closely one particular case. The city of Minneapolis pursued a deconcentration strategy through most of the 1990s. The initiative's centerpiece, though by no means the only element, was the consent decree in *Hollman v. Cisneros* (originally *Hollman v. Kemp*).

In 1992, attorneys for the Legal Aid Society of Minneapolis filed a lawsuit in U.S. District Court, alleging that the Minneapolis Public Housing Authority (MPHA), HUD, and the city discriminated in siting public housing. The attorneys provided information that they felt showed a clear pattern among Minneapolis and HUD officials of concentrating family public housing projects in the near north neighborhood, the traditional center of the African-American community in the city. The plaintiffs were alleging what had already been demonstrated for Chicago in the *Gautreaux* cases,[2] and what most who were knowledgeable about public housing nationwide knew characterized the program in many cities. When Bill Clinton took office, the law-suit's name was changed to reflect the new HUD secretary and the change of administration. However, settlement negotiations took a new direction, too.

The "new HUD" in 1993 wanted to take a fresh look at its subsidized (and especially public) housing programs. Part of that fresh look was a willingness to admit past mistakes in concentrating housing units and to attempt to correct those mistakes. HUD officials moved to settle a number of other cases against the agency essentially alleging the same thing: discrimination in the siting and placement of public housing in ways that furthered segregation. This approach was part of HUD's new theory about urban problems, based on the concentration-of-poverty argument.

In Minneapolis, what had been initiated as a discrimination lawsuit on behalf of public housing residents whose housing choices were restricted by the concentration of assisted units on the near north side became, during the process of settlement negotiations, an effort to deconcentrate poverty, facilitate a greater geographic spread of assisted units and assisted families, and reduce the number of public housing units on that site. Referring back to the time when the suit was first filed, the lead attorney for the plaintiffs remarked, "I don't think any of us had heard the term 'concentration of poverty'" (Furst 1996a). However, by the time the settlement was reached, deconcentrating poverty was its main objective.

The *Hollman* settlement-negotiation process fit seamlessly with the objectives of both HUD and the city of Minneapolis at the time. Many of the local officials who were ostensibly defendants in the process, from the city council to MPHA and HUD, shared with the plaintiffs the central goals of the agreement: reducing the concentration of public housing units on-site, and dispersing the very low income residents throughout the local housing market. An element of this consensus was a fundamental agreement that the reuse of the site should include a significantly reduced concentration of public housing units.

In January 1995, the agreement between the parties was announced, and HUD promised to allocate $100 million toward settling the case (Diaz 1995). The agreement, ratified by all parties in April, covered four separate public housing projects—the Sumner Field townhomes, the Olson townhomes, and the Glenwood and Lyndale townhome projects. In all, these projects and the public land on which they stood encompassed 73 acres located just one mile from downtown Minneapolis, directly adjacent to Interstate 94 and bisected by Olson Memorial Highway (State Highway 55).

The Near North Side Neighborhood

The near north side site is favorably positioned relative to the city's core and well served by transportation routes. At the same time, however, Interstates 94 and 394 and railroad tracks to the south of the site serve as important physical barriers between the near north side and downtown. In fact, in 1995 the site was virtually surrounded by major transportation routes or industrial properties.

Furthermore, several other subsidized housing developments were also adjacent to the site. The Bryant high-rises (for seniors) were located immediately east of the Sumner Field and Olson projects, while several privately owned but publicly subsidized buildings were located northwest of the site.

There was little question that the city's greatest concentration of poverty was located at this site. As mentioned earlier, median household income was one-third that of the city as a whole, and more than 70 percent of all households functioned below the federal poverty level (the typical threshold in identifying areas of concentrated poverty is 40 percent). The percentage of the population receiving public assistance was six times that of the city as a whole. In addition, the residents of the project site were overwhelmingly (94 percent) nonwhite in a city that was 78 percent European-American at the time. There was little argument that the city over time had concentrated its public housing in that area, and in the near north side more generally. The site was home to four of the five family public housing townhome projects that existed in the city. In fact, the project area contained more than 900 units of public housing, 25 percent of the total non-scattered-site inventory owned by MPHA.

Census data for 1990 showed that concentration of poverty among African Americans was greater in the Minneapolis–Saint Paul region than in most other cities in the United States. In fact, as a whole, minorities in the Twin Cities were more likely to live in poverty than in any other major metropolitan area in the country (Draper 1993). The proportion of African Americans living in high-poverty areas of Minneapolis–Saint Paul had increased from 27 to 47 percent between 1980 and 1990 (Jargowsky 1996). The city's siting pattern had concentrated public housing developments not only on the city's near north side, but also along corridors on either side of Interstate 35W on the city's south side. These same neighborhoods housed the highest concentration of Section 8 participants as well. They were home to just 20 percent of the city's total population, but 51 percent of certificate and voucher holders. Furthermore, these neighborhoods were 57 percent nonwhite in a city that was 78 percent white. At the time the lawsuit was filed, 58 percent of all scattered-site units were located in predominantly minority census tracts (Thompson 1996, 244). Thus, the evidence was clear on a number of dimensions that serious problems of residential segregation characterized the public housing program in Minneapolis, and affected minority populations in particular.

Conditions on the North Side

By 1995, the units in the aging north side project site were suffering from physical decline, neglect, and a host of design problems. Few housing officials or advocates were ready to contest such a characterization. The *Star Tribune,* the city's leading daily newspaper, ran stories of mice and cockroaches overwhelming some residents. According to one of the plaintiffs, "[Cockroaches are] inside my washer, they're in my radio, they're in my telephone, and when I turn on my microwave, they come running out. The roaches even used to get up in the smoke detector and set the thing off" (Morrison 1995).

The projects had been built on a floodplain through which Bassett Creek had run. When the projects were built, the creek was diverted through a storm sewer to connect with the nearby Mississippi River. Over the decades, the unstable soil of the former creek bed had led to shifting and cracking in the Sumner Field project buildings until, in some units, one could allegedly see outside through the cracks. The nature of the soils would later play a prominent role in the decision to demolish all the public housing units on the site (the consent decree only explicitly called for the demolition of the Sumner Field project).

Project building and site designs were also criticized. The HUD HOPE VI program officially adopted the view that much public housing built between 1930 and 1980 in the modernist tradition significantly and negatively affected residents' quality of life. The north side projects were offered as examples. Front doors were indistinguishable from back doors, and, as one Minneapolis reporter put it,

> Garbage carts are as likely to stand by the one that looks most like the front door. Doors open directly to the outside, without a vestibule or any way to personalize the entry. Most of the original canopies have rotted away. Yards belong to everybody and, therefore, no one. And the 5.2 miles of sidewalks that crisscross the six square block project make all spaces open to strangers (Mack 1995).

The site included three square blocks (a so-called superblock) that interrupted the street grid and isolated the projects from the residential neighborhood to its west. All these features had, by the 1990s, come to be seen as destructive of good community life, and obstacles to a safe residential experience. The federal government's official public housing revitalization program, HOPE VI, had officially condemned these design features and adopted the principles of "new urbanism," calling for the return of street grids and personalized spaces, and reintegration of public housing with its surrounding communities.

Deconcentration "Unwrapped"

This book analyzes recent efforts to deconcentrate poverty. In particular, the Minneapolis case is presented within the context of the national effort to disperse poor people throughout metropolitan areas. The argument presented here is based both on the *Hollman* consent decree, and, more generally, on the changes in local revitalization efforts triggered by the concentration-of-poverty argument. Chapter 2[3] lays out the concentration-of-poverty argument. The empirical and theoretical underpinnings of deconcentration are examined, as are the historical contextual conditions that gave rise to it. The strengths and the limits of the neighborhood-effects arguments also are discussed, as are arguments that are corollary to deconcentration, such as the impact of community design on community life.

Chapter 3[4] looks at the policy history—the evolution of public, mainly federal, efforts to provide poor families with housing choice and reduce concentrations of poverty. This history dates to the Johnson administration, although the first meaningful steps in this direction were taken in Nixon's first term. Though poverty deconcentration is a fairly recent initiative, its heritage is rooted in a range of policies that have evolved since the 1960s. The tour through these initiatives will take us from the efforts to produce scattered-site public housing to the regional initiatives of the 1970s and on to the development of the Section 8 program in 1974. This chapter also surveys the importance of the *Gautreaux* cases in Chicago and more recent policy shifts in tenant-based assistance. We will also briefly look at the development of the HOPE VI program. Finally, the chapter examines the impact of dispersal and deconcentration efforts in cities across the country. Studies of Gautreaux in Chicago, HUD's evaluation of Moving To Opportunity (MTO), collected evidence regarding scattered-site housing, and smaller studies of "vouchering out" and lawsuit settlements across the country provide substantial data on the effectiveness of these approaches. We evaluate deconcentration on its own terms: Does it improve the lives of the families deconcentrated, does it have benign effects on the receiving communities, and does it improve conditions in the target communities? Indeed, does deconcentration clear the way for poor families to improve their lot in life?

Chapter 4[5] shifts our analysis to Minneapolis. The Twin Cities region is home to one of the nation's leading advocates of deconcentration, Democratic State Senator Myron Orfield. As a state representative from a south side district during the early 1990s, Orfield successfully shepherded regional fair-share housing legislation through the Minnesota legislature three years in a row. In particular, his efforts were notable for their comprehensiveness. He advocated tax-base sharing; reform of the regional governing body, the Metropolitan Council; and efforts to rationalize regional funding for infrastructure as well. All these initiatives were aimed at a better share of costs, responsibilities, and development support between the center of the region and its fast-growing periphery. Orfield's lasting political contribution was the realization that inner-ring suburbs were facing many of the same issues of decline that central cities had been facing for decades. He molded a winning legislative coalition out of central-city representatives and legislators from the inner-ring suburbs. Though Orfield's legislation was vetoed three years running by a governor whose political base was in the developing suburbs, Orfield has had a profound and lasting impact on the politics of the Twin Cities. In fact, in 1995 the legislature passed and the governor signed a compromise fair-share law (written by two other legislators, but dubbed "Orfield Lite" by locals in tribute to its obvious lineage). The implementation of this law and continuing efforts to get suburban communities to accept low-income housing are the subject of chapter 4.

During Orfield's years of tireless advocacy for regional equity, he spread the word among countless community organizations in the suburbs and the two central cities. The spread of this message, coinciding as it did with an unprecedented rise in violent crime in Minneapolis—much of which the public associated with gangs and drugs—was wide and far. By 1995, few community activists and even fewer local politicians were unfamiliar with the dangers of concentrated poverty. This pervasive concentration-of-poverty argument fundamentally shaped local community development politics in the city for the rest of the decade and beyond.

Chapter 5[6] examines the "new community development" resulting from these changing circumstances and the new awareness of concentrated poverty that shaped local revitalization efforts in the 1990s. Central-city community groups feared more low-cost housing in their neighborhoods, arguing that they had done their fair share already. Minneapolis and Saint Paul council members began to talk about the need for regional approaches to affordable housing, often as a substitute for their own efforts. Officials in the central cities and in some suburban areas began to favor the demolition of some subsidized and low-cost developments in the name of deconcentrating poverty. Affordable-housing advocates found themselves on the defensive, even in communities that had traditionally supported housing rehabilitation efforts.

The main event in deconcentrating the poor in Minneapolis, discussed in chapter 6[7], was the consent decree in *Hollman v. Cisneros*. Settled in 1995, the *Hollman* decree incorporates every form of deconcentration extant: demolition and forced displacement, mixed-income redevelopment, scattered-site subsidized development, and voluntary mobility. Though not the only site in the country to adopt all these approaches, Minneapolis is the one in which implementation has progressed most rapidly. Thus, the north side of Minneapolis provides a perfect opportunity to analyze the effects of these different approaches and the politics of a comprehensive deconcentration strategy.

In 1995 the north side site was home to more than 900 units of public housing, by far the city's largest concentration of poverty. By 2000, every one of those units had been demolished and the families relocated to other homes and apartments throughout the region. Such massive dislocation did not occur without political conflict—considerable political conflict, as it turned out. Three groups, in particular, opposed demolition and redevelopment. Southeast Asian immigrants, who by 1995 made up the largest single ethnic group in the north side public housing, opposed demolition because, for them, spatial concentration was an asset. African-American activists on the north side opposed redevelopment because they feared gentrification and the loss of a historically black community. Affordable-housing activists also opposed demolition because of the loss of 700 units of low-cost housing at a time when the city was experiencing double-digit appreciation in housing values and the vacancy rate in rental units was less than 2 percent. The public debate on deconcentration was, by most measures, well informed and intelligent. The debate illustrated virtually all the potential controversies inherent in the strategy and is the subject of chapter 6[7].

Chapter 7[8] examines the implementation of *Hollman* deconcentration efforts, including relocation of north side families, construction of replacement housing in "non-concentrated" parts of the metropolitan area, and the Special Mobility Program (SMP) that moved families into these non-concentrated neighborhoods. Relocation progressed rapidly to facilitate demolition. Families were not restricted as to where they could move, though relocation counselors tried to facilitate moves to preferred neighborhoods and housing units. Both replacement housing and the SMP, however, involve the placement of housing and families in non-concentrated neighborhoods. In that respect, officials implementing these elements of the decree have faced significant geographical limits. And while replacement housing developments have come about slowly and met with stiff resistance, the Twin Cities' experience does exemplify metrowide cooperation. The progress of this particular element in the decree has been greater in the Twin Cities, in fact, than in most other regions in the country. The Special Mobility Program, however, has fared quite differently. While HUD made more than 900 vouchers and certificates available for SMP candidates, fewer than 100 have been successfully used, even after six years. This chapter examines the difficulties of implementing both replacement housing and the Special Mobility Program.

"*Hollman* families"—those displaced on the north side and those using mobility certificates and living in replacement units—have been scattered throughout the metropolitan area. Some have participated voluntarily; they signed up to participate in the program and used a mobility certificate or moved into one of the replacement units. Others have participated because a bulldozer knocked down their public housing apartment. Chapter 8[9] discusses what has happened to these families and how they feel about it.

The concluding chapter[10] assesses the deconcentration of poverty, not only on its own terms (how well it serves the families and the neighborhoods involved), but also by other criteria. Critics of deconcentration argue that it constitutes a misguided repetition of previous mistakes from urban renewal, when government power cleared the way for reuse of valuable urban land near the core of American cities. Does deconcentration repeat past mistakes? Can deconcentration efforts, as they are currently conceived, ever achieve the scale necessary to make a measurable dent in the country's race- and class-based settlement patterns? What are the political implications? How does the language of deconcentration change neighborhood planning and politics?

Messy Business

After giving a public talk on deconcentration in 1996, I was asked whether it was not simply overwhelmingly self-evident that the problems of America's central-city neighborhoods of poverty should be solved by deconcentration. The empirical evidence had, by then, shown quite convincingly that such concentrations are bad. Other empirical evidence (at that point, primarily the Gautreaux program) had shown that deconcentration benefits families that participate. I agreed then and still do, for that matter, that the logic is compelling.

What the Minneapolis case provides, however, is an understanding of the difference between that rather clean logic of deconcentration on the one hand, and its messy reality on the other. Deconcentration, as it happens to people and communities, is not a clean process. As it plays out on the streets, deconcentration exposes fundamental questions of urban planning and politics. Those in a position to decide whether deconcentration remains a policy option should, at the very least, regard these questions as seriously as they regard the logic behind the strategy.

Notes

1. Other housing programs include subsidy programs for low-income people, such as Section 221 (d)(3) and Section 236.
2. In 1969, a U.S. district court ruled in *Gautreaux v. Chicago Housing Authority* that the Chicago Housing Authority had discriminated in the placement and leasing of public housing in Chicago. In a related case, *Gautreaux v. Harris*, the U.S. Supreme Court ordered

    a regional remedy for the discrimination.
3. Refers to a chapter in the book from which this reading came, Clearing the Way: Deconcentrating the Poor in Urban America, by Edward G. Goetz, (Washington, DC: Urban Institute Press 2003).
4. ibid.
5. ibid.
6. ibid.
7. ibid.
8. ibid.
9. ibid.
10. ibid.

CONCLUSION
Scott Bessenecker

I was confused. Exploring the depths of poverty can do that to a person. We were coming to the end of our time in the Egyptian garbage community in Cairo. Living in this community for over a month had given us new eyes. What at first was repulsive was now quite normal. The hot passionate desperation we felt regarding the conditions in the garbage village during the first few days had cooled to a settled comfortability with life there. Was that OK? Maybe the life of a garbage collector wasn't all that bad. The people there seemed pretty content with life. The conditions were likely no different than life in medieval Europe. Probably better. Should I really be encouraging foreigners to come into such places as agents of change? Especially rich American students?

To be perfectly honest, despite the sights and smells of the garbage village, there were actually multiple classes of people there. There were the rich poor, the middle class poor and the poor poor—people who lived on a dollar or two a day. Some Egyptians even believe that there are fabulously wealthy individuals who hide out in the garbage village, pretending to be poor and hoarding their wealth. While this is probably a lie perpetrated to help salve the conscience of the rich, it was true that some of the flats were somewhat nice inside. You might walk into a garbage strewn, rough brick entry way and ascend a rat infested narrow stairway, passing farm animals on your way up. But when you walked through the doorway of the landlord's flat, you entered a nicely tiled room with a TV and new furniture. Granted, these flats were in the minority, most were quite deplorable. But that such places exist in slum communities can throw ones understanding of poverty into a tailspin.

I began to wrestle with God. This whole thing seemed like a huge mistake. Calling students to long term residency in slum communities with notions of transformation might only amount to bringing Western standards of housing and cleanliness to people who are just fine with how things are with their own culturally defined norms for quality of life. "Oh God," I prayed, "If you want to me to call students to lives of sacrifice and catalyzing change, then you'll have to convince me."

"By the way," I added. "Could you answer me in the next 48 hours before we leave this place?"

Several hours later I had a dream. I dreamed about the dung truck. You smelled the dung truck before you saw it. It was the kind of smell that was more like a taste at the back of your throat, pasty and bitter. The dung truck would pull alongside a building and haul out the animal waste that had accumulated on the ground level of the houses in the community as well as from the make-shift pens inside and outside people's homes. The community was known for their pigs, but goats, chickens, donkeys and dogs were the most abundant creatures in the garbage village.

The men who served in this capacity would shovel dung into large wicker baskets and then carry the baskets on their shoulders or their heads up a plank ramp and dump the contents into the back of a flat bed truck. In the process these men would become caked in dung from head to foot. The 100 plus degree temperatures released the dung's pungent odor with a vengeance, making this task seem even more intense than can be appreciated by someone reading this in comfort.

In my dream I was walking past the dung truck. To my horror I saw my children, Hannah, Philip and Laura, sitting on top of the mountain of dung heaped on the bed of the truck. What struck me most about them was that they appeared perfectly content sitting on the dung, their skin darkened by the animal waste that covered every inch of their bodies. Then I felt the Lord speaking to me. He seemed to be saying, "As their father, are you satisfied? Even if they are satisfied, are you satisfied?"

I am still sifting the impact and meaning of that experience, but the immediate implication was that a child's contentment with a situation does not always reflect a father's heart which yearns for so much more.

I Timothy 6:6–8 says, "But godliness with contentment is great gain. For we brought nothing into the world, and we can take nothing out of it. But if we have food and clothing, we will be content with that." To be sure, many of the poor Coptic[1] Christians in the garbage village combined godliness with contentment. They had found satisfaction in Christ, and as rich Americans we had much to learn from them. But the fullness of the kingdom and the deepest form of shalom had not yet arrived. While many garbage village residents were rich in love, they were also a people with limited opportunities, precarious health, inadequate housing, and the poorest of them battled despair. It was a community doing the best it could while being clobbered by sickness. Out of necessity they employed children who often worked long hours under hazardous conditions. This is not how life is supposed to be. But there is hope that things can change. Indeed things are changing already. Patience and prayer have begun to bear fruit. The garbage village is not what it was 20 years ago. Residents are benefiting from outsiders who care—people who don't think themselves better just because of where they were born; people who are open to learning something from the poor; men and women who are willing to bring their skills and their access to resources into the community; even those who would take up residence there and bind their own destinies to the destiny of the garbage village. The Kingdom of God is drawing near to the poor in the form of the King's servants.

A month after we returned from Cairo my family was going to church. On the way we passed a man sitting by the side of the road with a sign that read, "Out of work. Please help." My daughter, Hannah, moved forward on her seat as we drove past imploring me with her eyes. "Dad," she said. "We've got to stop." I said nothing as my conscience began to affirm her appeal. After dropping the family off at church I turned around and when back. He was still on the corner. "Hey, wanna come to church with me?" I asked. "Why not?" he said and jumped into the van. After church I took him to lunch. His name was Darren.

"You know," Darren confided as we headed off to lunch, "I have a pretty good life. My friends all complain about their wives or their work. But I've got it good. I answer to no one. I can go anywhere I want anytime I want. I may hold up my pitiful sign, but actually, I'm pretty content with life." Darren is one of the few remaining hobos. He hops freight trains and begs his way all over the country. At lunch I asked Darren about the hold alcohol has on him. I can almost always spot an alcoholic even when they seem sober. "Yeah," Darren said, "when I'm dry I like to help people out. I often work for the Salvation Army in whatever town I happen to be in if I'm sober. I'd like to do more . . . but I also like to party." Something about the way he said it seemed to indicate that his love of partying outweighed his love of working for the Salvation Army.

Darren was no stranger to faith issues. He certainly knew how to "talk the talk." So I asked him, "Darren, what if God wants more for you than you even want for yourself? What if you're too easily satisfied?" Darren looked at me as if the thought was new to him. "I don't know." He said tentatively. "Can I pray for you?" I asked, "And then would you ask God yourself if he's got more for you than you are currently experiencing and invite him to show you how to live an even more satisfying life than the one you now live?"

I haven't seen Darren since that day, but I think about him from time to time. I also think about my own life and the lives of those I knew in the garbage village in Cairo. Have I grown content with the fallow places in my life? Places of scarcity and garbage and unwholesome dependence? Does the Father yearn for something greater for me than even I do for myself?

Whenever I encounter the poor the lost or the broken I seem to encounter Christ afresh. It's like the hot-cold game I used to play as a child. Walking around blindfolded you're "getting hotter" the closer you approach the object of desire. When I'm around the marginalized I feel like I'm getting hotter—like Jesus is really nearby. The cocoon of wealth is so often cold when it's not broken open and shared with others. There's not only more of the kingdom to be experienced by the materially poor the spiritually lost and the emotionally broken, but there's more of the kingdom yet to be experienced those of us who live in spiritual ghettos with material abundance. Serving the poor may be a holy quest for change among those who suffer various forms of deprivation. But there is also an intimacy with our Creator and a discovery of self that is unique to standing alongside the poor. The true hope in the slum community is not only a hope for kingdom fullness inside the slum, but it is a hope for a greater fullness of the King inside those who choose to minister on the margins.

Notes

1. Coptic simply means, Egyptian. The Coptic Church is as old as the Catholic Church and is one of the ancient Christian traditions that exist in the Middle East.

DISCUSSION QUESTIONS

Section A: Theology of Poverty

1. What is social about the gospel of the Kingdom?

2. Why is knowing Jesus (i.e. evangelism) so central to transformation?

3. Describe the relationship between Jesus and the poor.

4. Why does God allow poverty to exist?

Section B: Incarnational Ministry

1. List some of the benefits of a voluntary, non-destitute poverty.

2. Describe a righteous rich person.

3. What are some potential drawbacks when a missionary from a wealthy nation like the U.S. goes to live among the poor?

4. Do you believe God has called you to minister among the poor? How might one who is called reduce the tensions their wealth might create?

Section C: Mission

1. What are some signs that God's Kingdom has come to a specific area?

2. What would you say is the one major purpose of the Church and 3-4 objectives which are important to fulfilling that purpose?

3. What's the difference between a covenant and a contract?

4. What are some aspects of covenant that you see in your life? In your church?

Section D: History

1. In your opinion, was the industrial revolution, the medical revolution and the green revolution ultimately good or bad for the poor?

2. List positive and negative effects of colonization.

3. What similarities exist in urban areas across the continents?

4. How does urbanization impact the nuclear family?

Section E: Health

1. How are AIDS and poverty related?

2. What makes the Church a great vehicle for combating AIDS?

3. How does physical health relate to spiritual, emotional or social health?

4. What motivates people to stop unhealthy practices and begin healthy ones whether in relation to body, soul, society or the environment?

Section F: Property

1. List some pros and cons to private home/land ownership.

2. What obstacles exist for the poor in the developing world in gaining ownership of the land they live and work on?

3. What positive things do we learn about the urban poor when we examine slum housing?

4. Is informal ownership bad? Why or why not?

Section G: Prostitution

1. List at least five destructive affects of prostitution.

2. Will we ever see an end to sexual sin this side of heaven? What about child prostitution?

3. How are poverty and prostitution related?

4. What kinds of professions or ministries might be helpful in the process of freeing a prostitute and re-integrating him or her into society?

Section H: Children

1. How do urban poor environments impact the quality of care that moms, dads or caregivers can provide?

2. What kinds of things did you worry about as a child? How might that differ from children living in slum communities?

3. List some of the dangers faced by street children.

4. List all the interactions you can recall between Jesus and children. What can you discern about Jesus' posture toward kids?

Section I: Justice

1. Why should Christians, in particular, care about social justice?

2. What are some things that give you hope that we might see more justice done on earth even within our lifetimes?

3. List a couple of unjust incidents, small or large, of which you are personally aware. Are there things you can do to confirm these injustices and, if true, to confront them?

4. What's the relationship between the Christian and political leaders/the State?

Section J: Community Development

1. How is power built?

2. What role does anger play in community organizing?

3. Every urban ethnic enclave has its own beliefs about the natural and supernatural forces behind bad incidents (e.g. a sick child). Why is it important to respect and understand these beliefs?

4. What things might we learn from the urban poor?

Section K: Economics

1. Why might formal lending institutions be hesitant to loan to the poor? Are those reasons well-founded?

2. Why should spirituality or morality be a consideration in microenterprise development?

3. Is it wrong to make money off of the poor?

4. How can the digital divide—the lack of technological access available to the poor—be reduced and what are the benefits to eliminating this divide to business?

Section L: Ethnicity

1. Should every ethnic group that wants its own state have its own state? Why or why not?

2. Of the four politically active ethnic groups described by Harff and Gurr, which would describe the Hebrew people in Moses' time? Why?

3. What are the forces at work keeping segregated neighborhoods like Baltimore's Sandtown poor?

4. Describe the relationship between ethnicity and economics.

Section M: Water and Sanitation

1. Why are girls and women disproportionately impacted by water and sanitation problems in slum communities?

2. Why is water more expensive for the poor?

3. Why isn't the health crisis among the urban poor simply a matter of providing more health clinics?

4. What makes it hard for municipal authorities to provide water and sanitation services to urban poor households?

Section N: Population

1. What overpopulation fears are realistic and which are not according to Sen?

2. If coercive policies (such as China's one child policy) are morally wrong, what are the alternatives to effectively and quickly curb population growth?

3. Is contraceptive use God's will for humanity? Explain your answer.

4. Why do some women in the developing world have short intervals between children?

Section O: Urban Planning

1. Describe the evolution of "suburbanization" which has occurred in the developing world. Is suburbanization good or bad?

2. The dominant urban plan serves to insulate the middle class from the poor (gated communities, private transportation, malls, etc.). How might the poor have greater voice in urban planning and development?

3. Why are the poor often concentrated in certain areas of a city?

4. What are the pros and what are the cons of rich, middle class and poor families living within the same area?